Microsoft 365 Guide to Success:

Kick-start Your Career Learning the Key Information to Master Your Microsoft Office Files to Optimize Your Tasks & Surprise Your Bosses And Colleagues | Access, Excel, OneDrive, OneNote, Outlook, PowerPoint, Word and Teams | 10 Books in 1

D1296155

TABLE OF CONTENTS

MICROSOFT WORD

Introduction

Are you fed up with Microsoft Word's manual and static formatting? Me too. Microsoft Word 2022 is a new program with a database of formulas, functions, and charts that will help you streamline your tasks in less time. This software has everything from determining how much to charge for a product to calculating the optimal number of hours for a project.

Now with Word 2022, you'll be able to save time by doing the math for yourself, no more struggling to memorize formulas or painstakingly enter numbers by hand! With Word 2022, you can prepare reports and research papers that will astound your superiors and colleagues. Of course, your boss will depend on you for accurate statistics, but you'll have all the time in the world to put on a goldfish bowl.

If you're sick of typing out lengthy lists of numbers and formulas by hand, then Microsoft Word 2022 will make your job a breeze. Simple to use and highly effective, the new program will save you countless hours while making the world a better place.

Have you ever noticed that Word is missing some of the needed features? Have you noticed that Microsoft Word has consistently received complaints about its lack of features and seeming unwillingness to improve? Well, you are in the right place to get help. This book will teach you aspect of using Microsoft Word in ways it never intended and unlock more than 100 new customizations for your computer. In addition, it will teach you many advanced techniques like macros, keyboard shortcuts, and VBA scripts that make using the software easier than ever before.

In this book, you have a chance of learning how to:

- Clean up your Word interface
- Work faster with custom macros
- Create shortcuts for complex tasks
- Set up templates, forms, and letters to perform actions automatically
- Write complex macros for bulk processing of documents and web pages
- And more

Did you know that Microsoft Word has a secret? It's a feature hidden in plain sight that will impact how you use Microsoft Word. We're talking about a new interface that makes writing quickly and efficiently easy without breaking your stride. One that lets you write on any device with work seamlessly across them all. One introduces a new way to capture your thoughts as you think them. One that lets you communicate with others more effectively and efficiently. And one that can help you be more creative for all the writing that inspires you to be creative in the first place.

We're talking about the new Microsoft Word, the application for doing what comes most naturally…writing.

The new Word interface helps readers—yes, that's you—write faster and more comfortably than previous versions of Word. The feature is designed to deliver a writing environment that makes it easier to do what you do best: write. It's a way to help more people get their ideas down on paper and communicate them with others without breaking their stride. One that makes it easier for you to be creative because it talks back. One that brings your ideas to life and then gets out of the way so you can do more great writing.

Writing has always been a challenge for many people. Studies show that experienced writers spend roughly half their time just trying to get started—and twenty-five percent of those hours will be spent on a single page. But research also shows that writing—especially business writing—is critical to success in every field. Since so many people have used Microsoft Office Word for so long, this is an excellent time to step back and ask how it can help writers do their best.

The new Microsoft Word uniquely combines a modern, clean look and feel with powerful tools that are familiar and easy-to-use. In addition, the interface is explicitly built for how people think when they want to move thoughts from their minds to their computers as quickly as possible.

This book is for people who love or are paid to write. It's for people who want to improve their writing and get more done—from students and teachers, journalists and novelists, bloggers and technical writers to corporate professionals. It's for anyone who wants to make powerful changes in their lives that come from being able to create their best work and own their creative process.

Take a step back from how you've always written, and start your journey with a clean slate. Forget about all the distractions that keep you from getting started—such as those smartphones, tablets, and computers in the room with you. Instead, embrace this new way of writing for a more focused approach that is key to accomplishing what matters most to you.

What You Need To Use This Book

The only software you need to use in this book is Microsoft Word. You can still follow along if you're reading this on Kindle. However, if you have an iPhone or iPod touch, now is an excellent time to put it down and pick up the smartphone that isn't going to distract you from writing.

How This Book Is Structured

If you love writing with Microsoft Word, this book is for you. If there are parts of Word that frustrate you or slow you down, don't worry—we'll fix them. You might even discover a new way to work more efficiently and reach more people.

This book takes a book-by-book approach. It starts with the Built for Writers chapter, which provides an overview of the new Word interface, exploring how it's different from previous versions and how it will help you be more productive. Then we'll closely examine the Ribbon interface, showing you where the great features are and how they're accessible.

We'll cover each Word tab and move through the entire Ribbon, discussing how each feature is designed to help you be more productive. Then we'll look at other built-in features that aren't visible in any tab, including those for editing and styles.

We'll also get into Word's new power features, like AutoCorrect and suggested changes.

Finally, we'll provide in-depth coverage of Word's features for working with comments and collaboration, reading documents, and publishing your work.

We'll wrap up the book by taking a quick tour of Word's strategic shortcuts, including those designed to help you be more creative. And we'll recommend some additional resources to help you get the most out of Word.

1 An Overview of the Powerful Writing Tool - Microsoft Word 2022

Microsoft Word 2022 has several new features that make it a powerful writing tool. Among these features are OneNote and integration with other applications like Outlook. The latter offers a great deal of functionality when it comes to business writing. The new version also provides many features to help you organize your information. This will make the entire writing process easier.

Introduction Microsoft Office Suite

Microsoft Office Suite is a package that includes Word, PowerPoint, Excel, OneNote, and Outlook programs. It comes in different versions for different computing environments and includes mobile apps. In addition, there are web-based versions of some of the products. In 2011, Microsoft introduced Office 365, which competes with services such as Google Drive.

Microsoft Office is a popular suite of applications used by most modern-day businesses. The applications are designed to simplify routine office tasks and improve work productivity. They are compatible with operating systems and are available in over 35 languages. Those looking for a business career may want to learn more about the suite.

When comparing Office Suites, make sure to check the compatibility of each piece of software before making a purchase. Software within the same suite integrates better, eliminating the need to copy information. This is especially important for email clients, calendar apps, and scheduling systems. Having all of your tools within the same family of products will reduce the likelihood of any communication issues.

Microsoft PowerPoint is an excellent tool for creating exciting presentations. It offers many features, including the ability to insert images and text. You can also create attractive documents using Microsoft Excel. This program can also create tables and graphs. In addition to PowerPoint, Microsoft Excel offers various tools to assist you organize, store, and sort data.

Microsoft Office also offers an online version. Microsoft 365 is a service that offers access to the office suite. Microsoft offers two software versions: Home & Student and Home & Business. Home & Student users only receive minor updates. Those who want more advanced features and functionalities should upgrade to the Home & Business version.

1.1   What is Microsoft Word?

The new release of Microsoft Word brings a slew of new features. The new feature called Smart Lookup helps you quickly look up a word's definition. It is a feature similar to Google's search bar but works inside Word. It allows you to search the web directly from the document and will even provide a preview of the word.

Another great feature of this product is that it is free for Android and iOS devices. So as long as you possess a Microsoft account, it is possible to use the mobile apps for both iOS and Android. However, if you want to use it on your desktop, you need to buy a subscription to Microsoft 365.

You can download the program's free version online if you don't want to spend money on Word. It works in your web browser and syncs with cloud storage. However, it lacks some features that are available in paid versions. It's possible to edit a document from any computer, and sharing your files is easy.

Word is a document app by Microsoft. It includes OneNote, which is designed for note-keeping. Word is more extensive and includes features like file attachments and sharing options. Word also supports the Grammarly add-in, which helps you improve your writing. A few of its other features are: OneNote supports drawing and audio recording. Microsoft Word can also open PDF files and save them in different formats.

1.2   How Microsoft Word works

Microsoft Word is a word processing program allowing users to create and edit documents easily. It also lets you keep track of changes and write notes in the margins of your documents. This feature helps create personalized documents like newsletters, meeting invitations, or general business correspondence. Microsoft Word also has features that allow you to create lists and spreadsheets.

You can also download the Word app on your smartphone or tablet. You only need an internet connection and a Microsoft account to access it. The app runs inside your web browser and synchronizes with your cloud storage. However, there are some limitations to the free version of Word.

1.3   Where do you buy Microsoft Word?

If you're wondering where you can buy Microsoft Word 2022, we are here to help you. While this popular office suite used to be a one-time purchase, Microsoft has moved to a subscription model that makes more sense if you use multiple computers. The subscription model also includes freebies.

The price for this suite starts at $150 for a single installation. Subscription services to Office 365 start at $69.99 a year and include OneDrive and SharePoint. This package is ideal for students, teachers, and staff working in a school setting. Special offers are also available for students and staff at colleges and universities.

When it comes to word processing, most people and businesses think of Microsoft Word. It's easy to download, requires a Microsoft account, and allows you to edit your documents anywhere. Another great feature of this software is that it syncs with your cloud storage. It can also be used on cell phones, although it has some limitations.

1.   Open your web browser, e.g., Google Chrome.
2.   Go to the office website: www.office.com.

3. Click on **Get office** if you want an office or MS Word on your desktop and buy from the available options:

Office 365 Family and **Office 365 Personal**: You can share Office 365 Family with six people, while Office 365 Personal is limited to only one person. They are both the same in function, and both require continuous subscriptions. Office 365 is the best option for any user who wants access to all the up-to-date office apps and cloud services. It can run on windows 11, 10, 8, 7, and macOS.

Office Home & Student 2021: This is the latest version of office available for a one-time payment and contains only the essential apps (Word, Excel, PowerPoint, Access, Outlook, OneNote, Team, and Publisher). You can only use it on Windows 11, 10, and macOS.

4. Install Microsoft Office, and MS word is available on your desktop for use.

If you are not interested in buying Microsoft office, you can use it freely on the Microsoft official website. The Word online version is new and does not contain all the features in the desktop version. The website version cannot also work without connectivity, making the offline/ desktop version a good choice.

To use MS word freely online;

- visit their website, www.office.com.

- Sign in if you have an existing account or

- create a new one if you do not have one, and MS word will be available for your use.

Microsoft Word vs. Google Docs

Microsoft Word and Google Docs have similarities, but there are many significant differences, too: Microsoft Word is best for writing a long, complex document or a series of related documents. (It has the most powerful tools for working with tables, charts, and images.)

Google Docs is the better choice if you're writing a long blog post or article. Though it doesn't have as many tools as Word, it has some key advantages for small- and mid-sized documents. For example, it's designed to help you write quickly and easily—with a clean, distraction-free interface that gets out of your way. And because Google Docs can be shared with others, it has powerful tools for making your work more collaborative.

Microsoft Word is the best choice for using styles and multiple columns (and for inserting notes and comments). Google Docs is great for quickly capturing ideas in a single long document. However, you won't have much use for styles or columns—unless you want to use them. (Although you can use Google Docs to create a long, single-column document, Word is a better choice for formatting, designing, and editing.)

Microsoft Word has support for many different types of documents, from newsletters to newspapers to instruction manuals. Google Docs is ideal for long—and potentially long-term—writing projects that require collaboration with multiple people. That said, it can display standard documents, too.

Microsoft Word is an excellent choice for people who already use Microsoft software. However, Google Docs is designed for anyone and everyone. (And it's available on any device, making it ideal for collaboration.)

Microsoft Word vs. Apache OpenOffice

Apache OpenOffice is an open-source alternative to Word. Microsoft Word is a proprietary program owned by Microsoft.

Apache OpenOffice is available under the Apache 2.0 License. Microsoft Word is available only with a paid license directly from Microsoft or via a third party.

Apache OpenOffice has almost all the same features as Word but has fewer templates and add-ins. Microsoft Word has more templates and other add-ins

Apache OpenOffice is designed with a different philosophy from Microsoft Word. Microsoft Word has a different philosophy than any other word processing program—emphasizing putting the tools you need in one place and a desire to help you write clearly and efficiently.

Apache OpenOffice has a free, open-source Web-based version that you can use with your computer, smartphone, or tablet. Microsoft Word has a free Web-based word processor called Office Online. But it's designed for people who work on the Web and don't have a Mac or PC, and it lacks some of Word's advanced features like templates and Add-Ins.

Apache OpenOffice has a smaller market share than Microsoft Word, but it's growing quickly. Microsoft Word has a larger market share than OpenOffice. But because it's expensive and proprietary, it has begun to lose market share to open-source programs like LibreOffice, OpenOffice, and Google Docs.

2 Opening a Blank Document or Existing Template

Creating A New Document

Word will present you with a blank document to work on when you launch the application without opening an existing file. Simply type a word to place it on a page. You will eventually want to begin another fresh document, though. You have three options in Word for doing this:

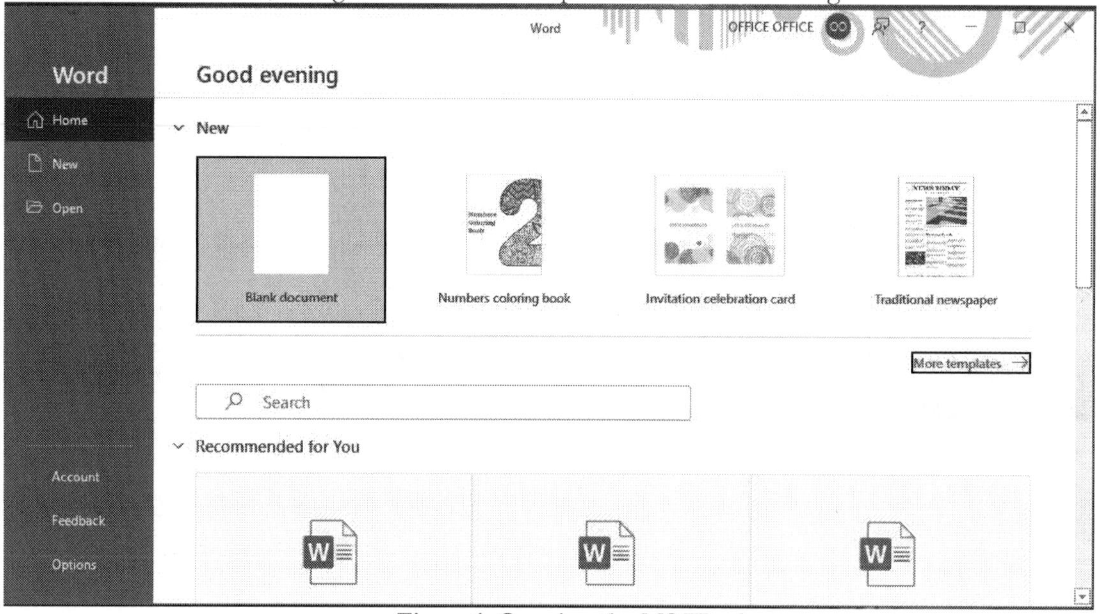

Figure 1: Opening the MS Word

1. Word 2022 may seem a little overdone when you first start it up. This is because the Ribbon will take considerably more space than previous menus & toolbars. This modification might not be significant if you possess a huge screen. However, hiding the ribbon is possible by double-clicking the currently active tab if you intend to use a portion of this space. Then, click the tab whenever you need to view the ribbon elements.

2. Make a new, empty document. A basic, ornamental page is acceptable for creating a straightforward document, such as an essay of 3 pages, babysitting notes, or a news article. Alternatively, if you're just brainstorming and unsure of how your document will look in the end, you might choose to start with a blank table or structure the text using one of the Word templates.

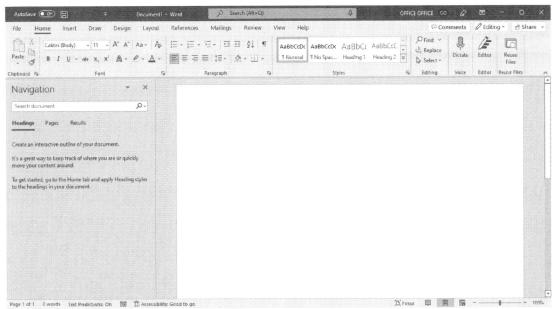

Figure 2: A new word document

3. It is possible to create a new one once you have opened an existing file. Utilizing a current paper as a starting point can help you save time. For example, you can reuse a letter format you like by altering its content repeatedly.

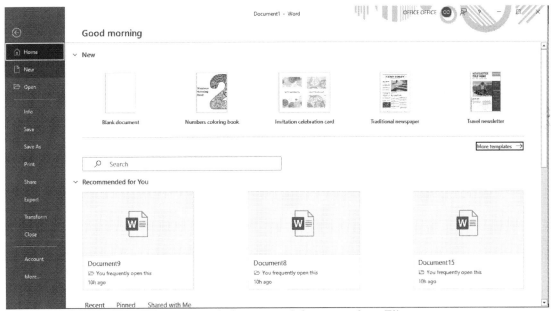

Figure 3: A new word document from File

CREATING A NEW BLANK DOCUMENT

MS Word will always inform you whenever you launch the application, let's say you desire a brand-new blank document. *No issue; here are the steps:*

1. Select File → New.

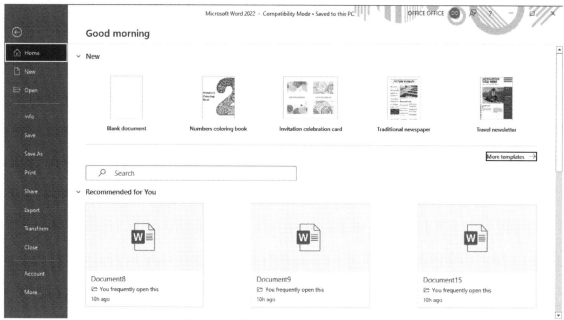

Figure 4: File button for new document

2. Click "Blank Document" in upper left-hand corner.
3. Do not become overwhelmed by the options in the New Document Box. You want to choose "Blank Document," which is in first row to the screen's left.
4. Click Create from the dialog box.

When dialog box vanishes, you see a blank page of a brand-new Word document.

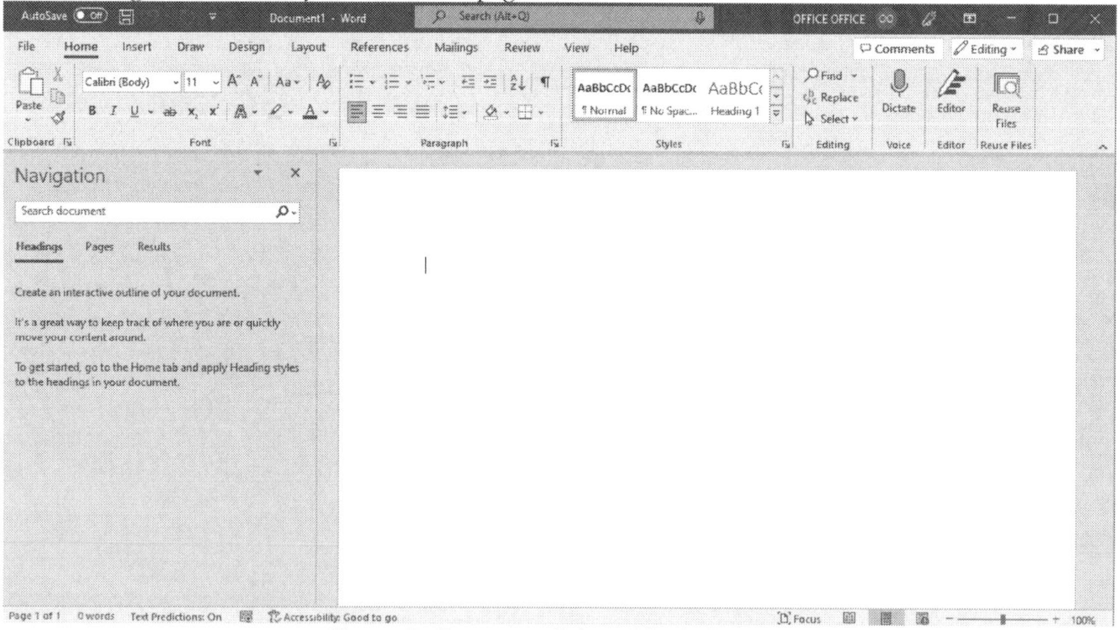

Figure 5: Once you click on blank document

Word provides options once your new document is open (File →New or using the shortcut Alt + F, N). For example, select Blank Document when you wish to open a blank document identical to one that is displayed when first launching the software. The previously produced document can also be opened with a new name through choosing "New from existing" instead.

CREATING YOUR NEW DOCUMENT USING A TEMPLATE

Consider that this is the first time you are recording meeting minutes. You need well-formatted minutes but do not have access to any existing documents to assist you. Word is available to you, complete with templates.

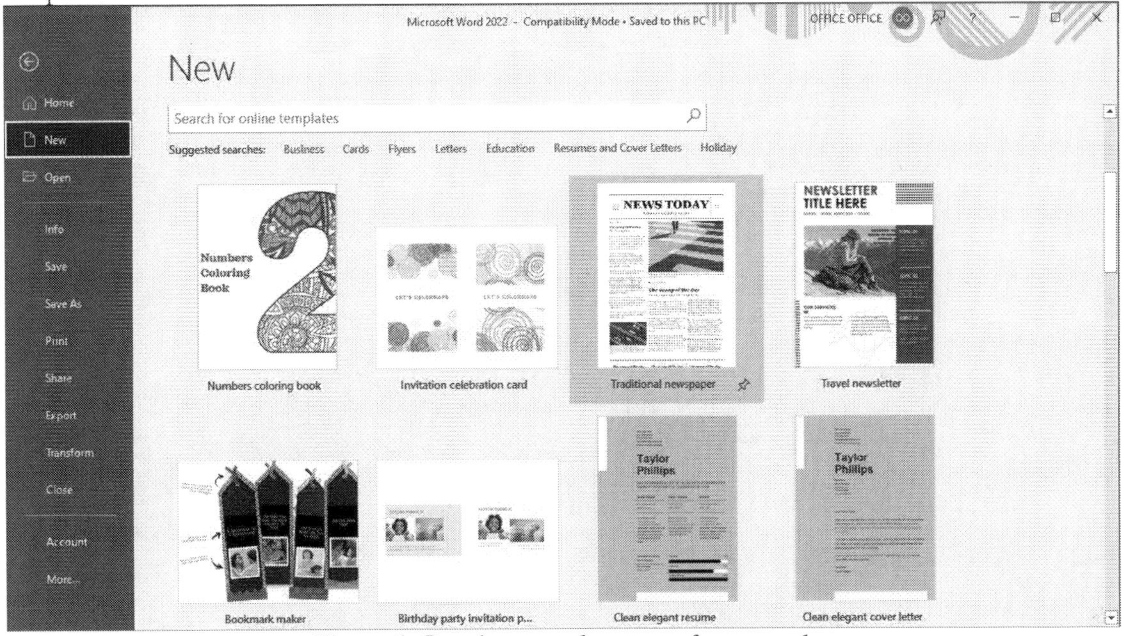

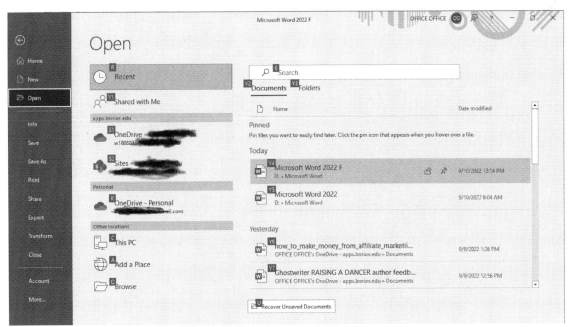

Figure 6: Creating new document from template

You access the previous month's minutes to conduct meetings using existing papers. Enter this month's minutes instead of the previous month's information. Similar principles apply whenever you utilize a template, but a template serves as a general document you may apply to various circumstances. Open and enter your text.

HOW TO OPEN AN EXISTING DOCUMENT

Here are the steps:

1. Select the File → Open button (Alt + F, O). Then, go to folder and choose file you wish to open.

Figure 7: Opening an existing document

2. The My Documents folder, where Word suggests you save your files, first appears in the Open window. Next, click the My Computer icon when your document is at a more remote place, and then go to the relevant folder.

3. Click Open after selecting the file.

Your document will open in Word after the Open box has vanished. You are prepared to begin working. Remember that you are overwriting the previous file whenever you save the opened document (you can use the shortcuts Ctrl + S, or Alt + F, S). Essentially, you are making a better, one-and-only copy of the document you just opened. You achieve this through Save As command (the shortcut is Alt + F, A) and rename if you wouldn't wish to overwrite your existing document.

3   View Options

Microsoft Word has some good layouts you can use to view your documents in different situations. These layouts **are Web Layout, Read Mode, Print Layout, Outline,** and **Draft.**

- To choose a view mode, click **View** tab.

- In **Document Views** group, choose the view mode you desire.

Figure 8: View options

Below is the description of each of the view document groups:

- **Read Mode**: Provides a wonderful way of reading a document.

- **Print Layout**: This allows you to check the appearance of the document once you print.

- **Web layout**: Displays the appearance of a document as a webpage. Also, it helps whenever there are wide tables within the document.

- **Outline**: Displays the outline form where content appears as bulleted points. Comes in handy when creating headings and moving an entire paragraph in your document.

- **Draft**: This Layout switches your view to preview text without pictures (if any). It is helpful for quick editing since you only see the text.

Dark Mode

Do you know you can turn on dark mode on Microsoft Word 2022, especially at night, to give your eye a break? The default background interface is the white mode. The Dark mode is designed explicitly for sight adjustment, mainly for night users and other purposes.

- To turn on dark mode, go to the top left corner and click on the **File** Menu.

- Within the file menu, move to bottom left corner and select Account. This opens up the account screen, and right in the middle is a section called **Office Theme.** By default, it's always on the colorful screen, which tends to be bright.

- Click on the drop-down arrow to see other colors (dark grey, white, black). You can select dark grey or black to make your screen dark

- **Note**: When you change the office theme, not only will it affect word, it affects all other Office apps (excel and PowerPoint).

- When you go back to the word, all the ribbons tabs are dark, but the document still looks bright. To change this; Go to the **Design tab** locate to the right-hand side, and click on the page color. Next, click on theme color, and choose the dark color. Your document color changes to black, and word changes your font color automatically to white.

"Dark Gray" makes your Word background interface a little bit dark. You can select "Black" to get the "Dark mode" if you wish. Note that any change in your themes will also affect other Microsoft Suites such as Excel, PowerPoint, Outlook, and others.

Note: It doesn't affect your document when you want to print. It comes out in its standard color (white).

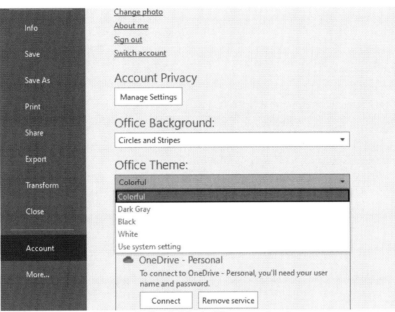

Figure 9: Dark Mode Theme selection

Changing the white document interface

Every of your theme settings or your customized theme settings can only affect the outlook, not the document content itself. To also change your white-board known as your document content area, simply follow these steps below:

- Go to your "Design tab."

- Under "Design," on your right-hand side, locate "Page Color" and click on it

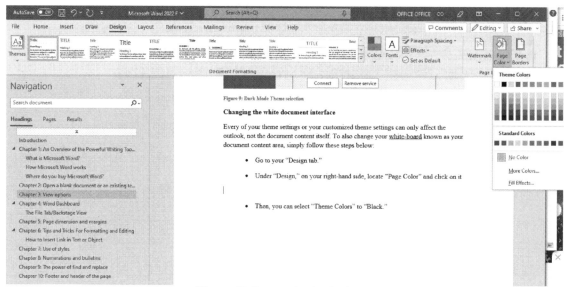

Figure 10: Page color in design tab

- Then, you can select "Theme Colors" to "Black."

- Once you select "Color Black," your document content area will be on Black

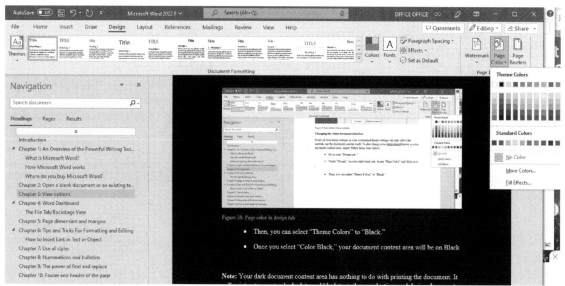

Figure 11: Black document interface

Note: Your dark document content area has nothing to do with printing the document. It will print out your standard white and black text, theme selection, and design document content. It only affects your Word interface, not with the copies to be printed.

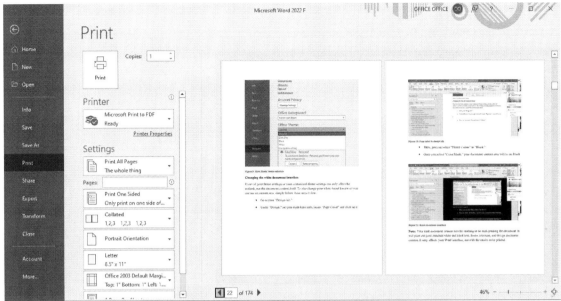

Figure 12: Print option for Black document interface

Changing Views

Make use of these techniques to make adjustments to the views:

- Click **one** of the 4 view options appearing on your status bar right side.

- Navigate to view tab>click **one** of the 5 options in your view group option, identify the immersive group, and click on the focus button.

The Read Mode

Changing to the Read mode helps you concentrate on the actual text and gives you a better view for proofreading. There is no option of entering or editing the text in Read mode. As the name implies, you can only read the text. All the icons are stripped away in this mode, the Ribbon, scroll bars, status bar, etc. All that will be displayed are the text and images (if any) contained in the document. It's a god consideration to use this feature when reading on a tablet.

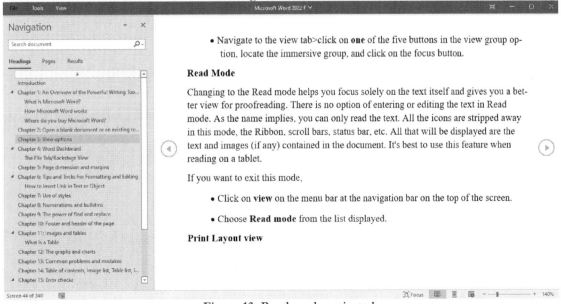

Figure 13: Read mode activated

To exit read mode,

- Click **View** on menu bar at the navigation bar on your screen's top.

- Choose **Edit Document** from the list displayed.

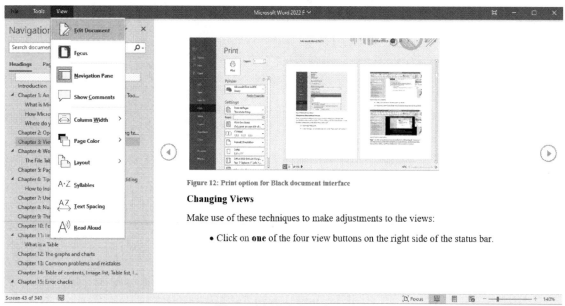

Figure 14: Exit Read mode

Print Layout view

Change the mode to Print Layout view when you anticipate to see or observe the entire document. With this option, you will see clearly how your document may appear on printing. Page borders, headers, footers, and even graphics can be seen clearly. You will also see where there might be a break in the page (marking the end of one page and the start of the next).

In the Print Layout View, there is an option to click on **one page or multiple pages** on view tab to show extended details or less (as the case may be) on the screen.

The Web Layout view

Change to this view when you wish to have a feel of how the document should look like in the form of a web page. The background colors will be displayed (if one has been chosen before). The text will be coined to the window other than around the artwork within your document.

The Outline view

Change to this view when you plan to observe the organization of your work. With this option, we can only see or check headings within a given document. Allows easy movement backward or forward within the sections of your text. This simply means you can have the document rearranged in the Outline view.

The Draft view

Change to Draft view whenever you are writing a document or wish to have more focus on words. Shapes, pictures, and other images will be restricted as opposed to the read mode. You will not be able to see page breaks also. This view is best used when creating drafts.

Focus Mode view

Change to this view if you want reading to be easier and more fun. This view helps with preventing eye strain. All you can do in this view is enter text. All editing commands are taken off the screen. Press the escape key if you want to leave the Focus Mode view.

It's important to state that Word has a provision called Immersive Reader, a special screen for those with poor eyesight and who might need help reading text. This screen provides tools for focusing solely on lines of text, making adjustments to the color page, breaking words into syllables, and hearing the words being read aloud. To activate this mode,

- Go to **the View tab**.

- Select the **Immersive Reader button**, which will open the Immersive Reader Screen.

4 Word Dashboard

Microsoft Word 2022 is a new word processor version allowing users to create and edit documents. In addition, this version includes a new Create PDF feature that will allow you to create and save a presentation in a PDF format. This format will allow you to share your presentation online or send it to others for review. You can also choose the action you want your document to take, such as print or send it as a PDF.

Save

A file has been saved from a computer's memory to a disk. It is usually used to refer to documents, spreadsheets, and other types of electronic files. Save often refers to the action of making an electronic copy of a document on disk so it can be retrieved later.

Microsoft Word is among the famous word processors. It has many features and functions for writing professional documents, such as table of contents, generating indexes, and making on-the-fly grammar corrections. You can also create simple logos and letters. You can also insert graphics or sound in a document, such as a video or audio.

Save AS

The Save As command, located in the File menu of most applications, creates a copy of your document or image. However, unlike the regular Save command, which stores data back in the original folder or file, "Save As" creates a copy in a different location, format, and with a different or new name.

Save-as command has several different uses. The first is for templates, which store text, styles, and keyboard shortcuts. The second is for a new document. When saved in this way, the template will be automatically created from a new document whenever one double-clicks on the file in Windows. Another option is exporting a document to a PDF file. Such will allow one to share the file with other users without sharing the original.

Word has a WYSIWYG (What You See Is What You Print) display, which allows you to keep your screen's content consistent. This feature lets you copy and paste your content into other platforms without worrying about losing formatting.

Zoom In

The Zoom In a feature in Microsoft Word allows you to adjust the magnification of a document. When the magnification is set above the horizontal view limit, a horizontal scroll bar will appear at the bottom of the screen so that you can scroll and examine the document. You can get the Zoom In button on "View" tab of the Ribbon. You can also toggle zoom levels using the + and - commands on the Zoom Control slider.

When you click the Zoom button, a dialog box will appear, allowing you to adjust the zoom level. The default level is 100%. Other settings include 200% and 75%. When you change the zoom level, the percentage displayed on the Zoom slider will change.

COMPONENTS OF THE MS WORD

1. File

File-related options include New (for creating new documents), Open (for opening existing documents), Save, Save As, Print, Share, export, Info, and so on.

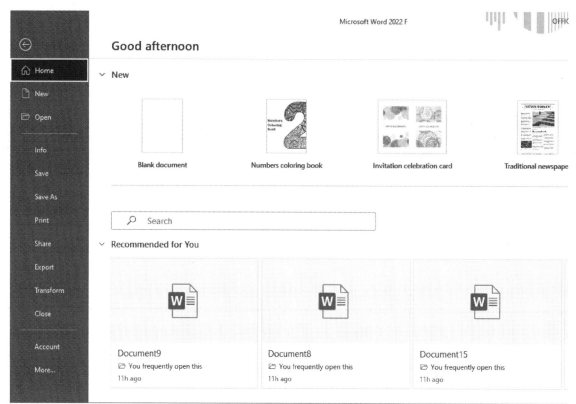

Figure 15: File tab options

2. Home

The default Microsoft Word tab is typically organized into 5 groups: the Clipboard section, Font group, Paragraph elements, Styles section, and Edit package. It gives you the opportunity to customize the text's position, color, emphasis, font, and bullets. In addition, there are options such as font size, font color, font style, alignment, dots, space, etc. Apart from this, all the basic information needed to edit one's document is available in the Home options. It also has functions such as cut, copy, & paste. Once you select Home tab, the following alternatives will on display:

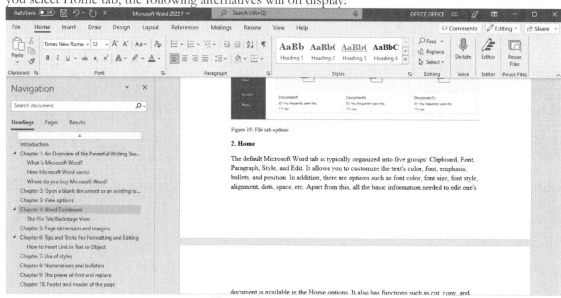

Figure 16: Home tab options

3. Insert

The second tab on the ribbon. It has numerous elements that you might wish to copy and paste into MS Word. For example, tables, word art, linkages, symbols, links, images, header, footer, signature line, shapes, text boxes, graphs, equations, and other options are available, as illustrated in the image below:

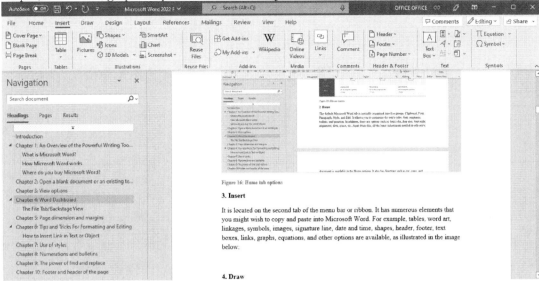

Figure 17: Insert tab options

4. Draw

Stands as third tab on the ribbon. It is used in MS Word for freehand drawing. Provide the following kind of pens for drawing:

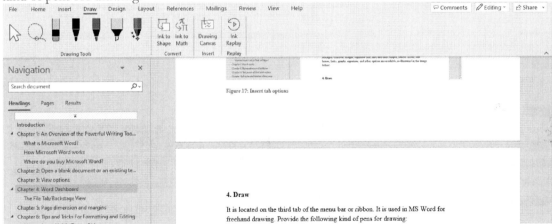

Figure 18: Draw tab options

5. Design

This is the fourth tab of the ribbon. The layout tab provides document layouts that you may choose from, such as left justification of text, page color, watermarks, and so on:

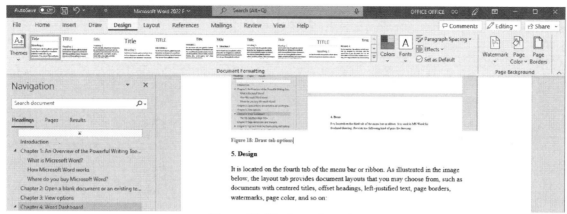

Figure 19: Design tab options

6. Layout

This serves as the fifth tab of the ribbon. It includes all of the choices for organizing the pages of your Microsoft Word document the way you desire. Establish margins, set indentation for paragraphs and lines, display line numbers, apply themes, line breaks, and so on, as seen in the image below:

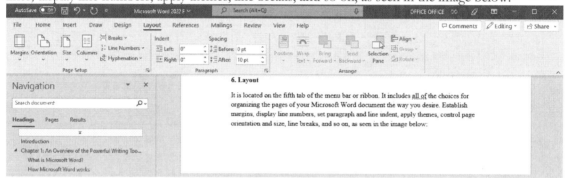

Figure 20: Layout tab options

7. References

It is the sixth tab in the ribbon or menu bar. The References tab allows you to insert references into a document and then generate a bibliography at the end. Typically, references are saved in a master list, which is used to add references to other documents. In addition, table of contents, footnotes, citations and bibliography, subtitles, table of contents, smart look, and other settings are available. You will get the following options after selecting the References tab:

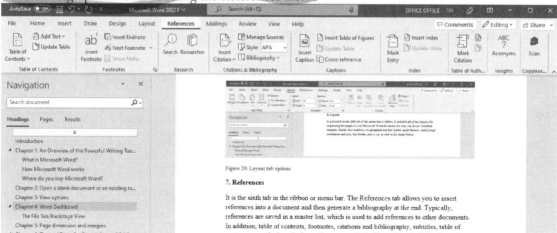

Figure 21: References tab options

8. Mailings

It is the seventh tab in the ribbon or menu bar. It is a less frequently used menu bar tab. This page allows you to design labels, print them on envelopes, merge mail, and so on. Following your selection of mail delivery, you will be presented with the following options:

Figure 22: Mailings tab options

9. Review

It is the eighth tab in the ribbon or menu bar. The Review tab includes comments, language, translation, spell check, and word count options. It's handy for rapidly finding and editing comments. Following the selection of a review tab, you will be presented with the following alternatives:

Figure 23: Review tab options

10. View

It is the ninth tab in the ribbon or menu bar. The View tab allows you to choose between facing and double pages and manipulate the layout tools. Print layout, outline, web layout, task pane, toolbars, ruler, header and footer, footnote, full-screen view, zoom, and other features are included, as shown in the image below:

Figure 24: View tab options

QUICK ACCESS TOOLBAR

No matter which tab is selected, you may access common instructions using the Quick Access Toolbar, located directly above the Ribbon. You can add other actions as necessary, but it shows the Save, Undo, and Redo commands by default.

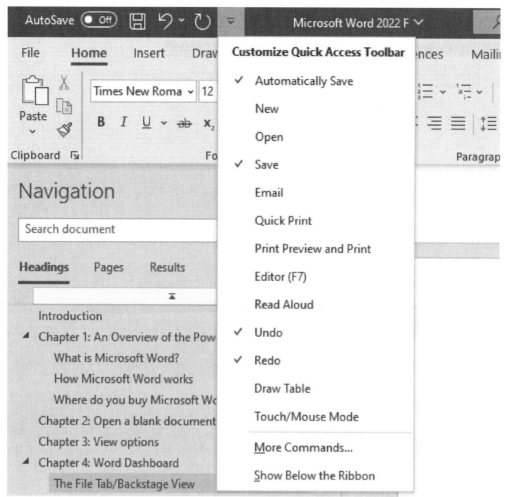

Figure 25: QAT

- Click the drop-down arrow to the right of the Quick Access Toolbar to add a command to the toolbar.
- Choose the desired command from the menu.

The Quick Access Toolbar will now include the command.

4.1 The File Tab/Backstage View

If you are familiar with versions of Word earlier than 2007, you will likely be happy to once again see the File Tab in Word versions 2013 and later. In the 2007 version, Microsoft replaced the File menu with the "Backstage" area or "Office Button." This caused a lot of confusion among users. Microsoft had spent decades teaching us to use the File menu with previous versions – then it was suddenly gone. The File Tab leverages our original training by putting many of the same options under the File Tab as we were used to seeing under the File menu. Let's take a look at each of the links on the File Tab.

(Note that to exit the File Tab and return to the actual document (e.g., for additional writing or editing), click the arrow at the top.)

Figure 26: Backstage view

The Backstage View is the central managing place for all Word documents. To go to the backstage of the Word document, click on the **File** tab in the **Ribbon** Tabs bar.

You can create, save, open, print, or share your document from backstage. Starting from the top, the:

- **New** allows you to open a new Word document.
- **Open** allows you to open the document you created earlier from different locations.
- **Info** gives information about the Word document, allowing you to protect, inspect and manage your document.
- **Save** saves the current document with the same name and location.
- **Save as** will enable you to rename, select the desired location and save the recent document.
- **Print** allows you to print your document in the desired format.

- **Share** lets you share your document through email or online.
- **Export** allows you to create the PDF or XPS document of your Word document.
- **Account** contains all the document holder's details. You can change the look of your Office applications and do some other settings here.
- **Close** allows you to exit the current document. The Top-left-corner **arrow** will enable you to go back to the document area.
- **Options** opens the **Word Options** dialog box

Info
Document Properties

Take a look at the following image. The Info link on the File Tab shows us several of the document's properties, including Size, Pages, Number of Words, Create/Modify Times, etc. Also, notice the "Show All Properties" link at the bottom.

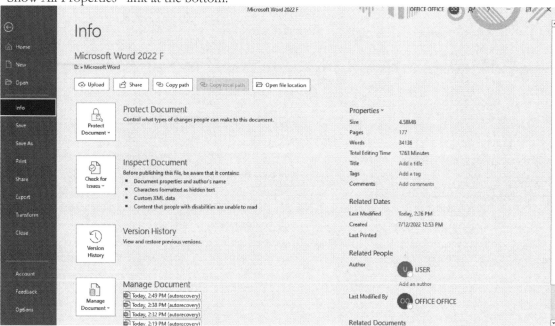

Figure 27: Info Backstage

Document properties, as you may suspect, contain information about the document. These properties have gained significant attention in recent years due to privacy concerns. Some of these properties are editable, while others are automatically calculated. Some are accessible via the "File" Tab (see the previous image), while others are embedded in the document and only accessible via special editing techniques or software tools. In any case, be aware of their existence, usefulness, and potential privacy implications.

New

This link displays a gallery of available document templates. When you click on a template, a new document is created using that template.

Save / Save As

As the names imply, these links save the document, with "Save As" prompting you for a new document name or type first. We recommend creating QAT buttons for these instead. That's faster and easier than using the File Tab for a simple save operation.

Compatibility: Saving As

Windows, MAC, Android, iPads, OpenOffice, LibreOffice…

There are so many more document editing platforms than there used to be – or, at least, it seems like there are. Unfortunately, more platforms mean more compatibility issues. Let's look at how we can address some of those issues by saving our document as an alternate file type.

File Types

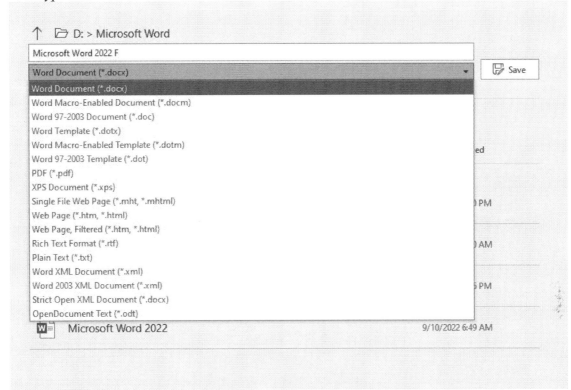

Figure 28: Save file extension types

-DOCX: Word's native file type.

-DOC: Save in this format if you intend to share this file with someone with a pre-2007 version of MS Office. This format is also helpful for some non-Microsoft-based document editors. Be careful, though. You could lose some of your data or formatting when saving in this format.

Note: Don't forget to recommend the Compatibility Pack to those who use MS Office 2003.

-RTF: Many non-Microsoft document editors can read this format. The downside of this format is that its resulting file sizes can become much larger. DOC files with the same content. Thus, sharing these files can become more complex.

-TXT: Use this format if you want Word to strip out all of the formatting from the document leaving only the text. Caution, your document will not look the same.

-PDF: The .PDF format is native to the Adobe Acrobat software application. It's generally considered a good format for sharing your document with others as long as they will not need to edit it. However, once in PDF format, you will be very limited in your ability to edit the document.

-HTML file: The HTML format is read by Internet browsers such as Internet Explorer or Safari. Almost all modern computers will be able to read this format (via an installed browser application), but the editing capabilities are much more limited than the .DOCX format.

Print

This link does two things for us:

-Provides options for printing

-Provides a Print Preview.

As with the Save link, we recommend just creating a QAT button for this.

Share

The "Share" option has been around for many years, but previously, it was focused primarily on sharing via email. Word gives us a few additional options.

Export

Honestly, we are not quite sure why there is a need for the Export link. You can accomplish the same thing with the Save As link.

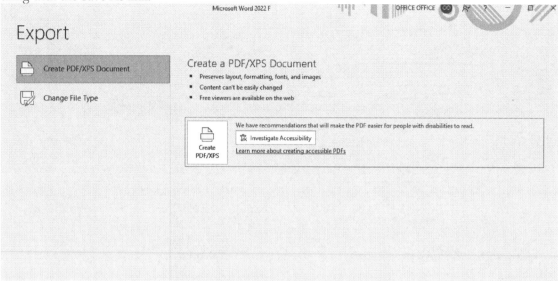

Figure 29: Export option on backstage

Close

Easy explanation here: This link closes your current document. It also prompts you to save the document if any changes have been made since you opened it.

Account

You probably won't spend much time with this link if you are not using OneDrive or any other Microsoft online services. However, if you use any Microsoft services, they will be listed, and any configurable options will be presented.

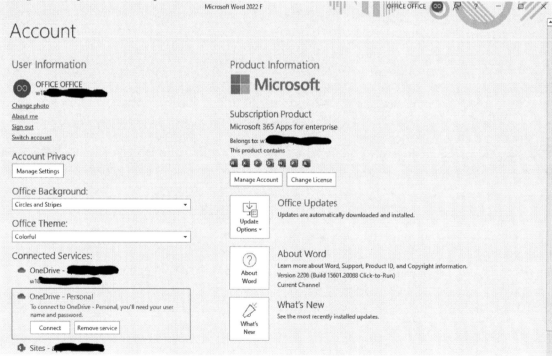

Figure 30: Account option on backstage

Options

Remember the Good ol' Days when you could click on "Tools" in the menu and select "Options?" Well, those days are gone, but the Options live on. The image below shows the Options window with its many, well, options.

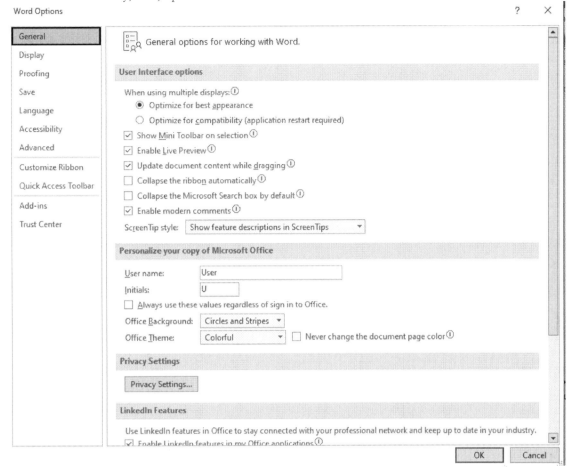

Figure 31: Options on backstage

General
The only thing we ever change on this Tab is the Office Theme. To us, the White option looks too washed out and makes the Word window too difficult to distinguish from any other windows you may have open. We use the "Colorful."
Display
Nothing much of interest for us there.

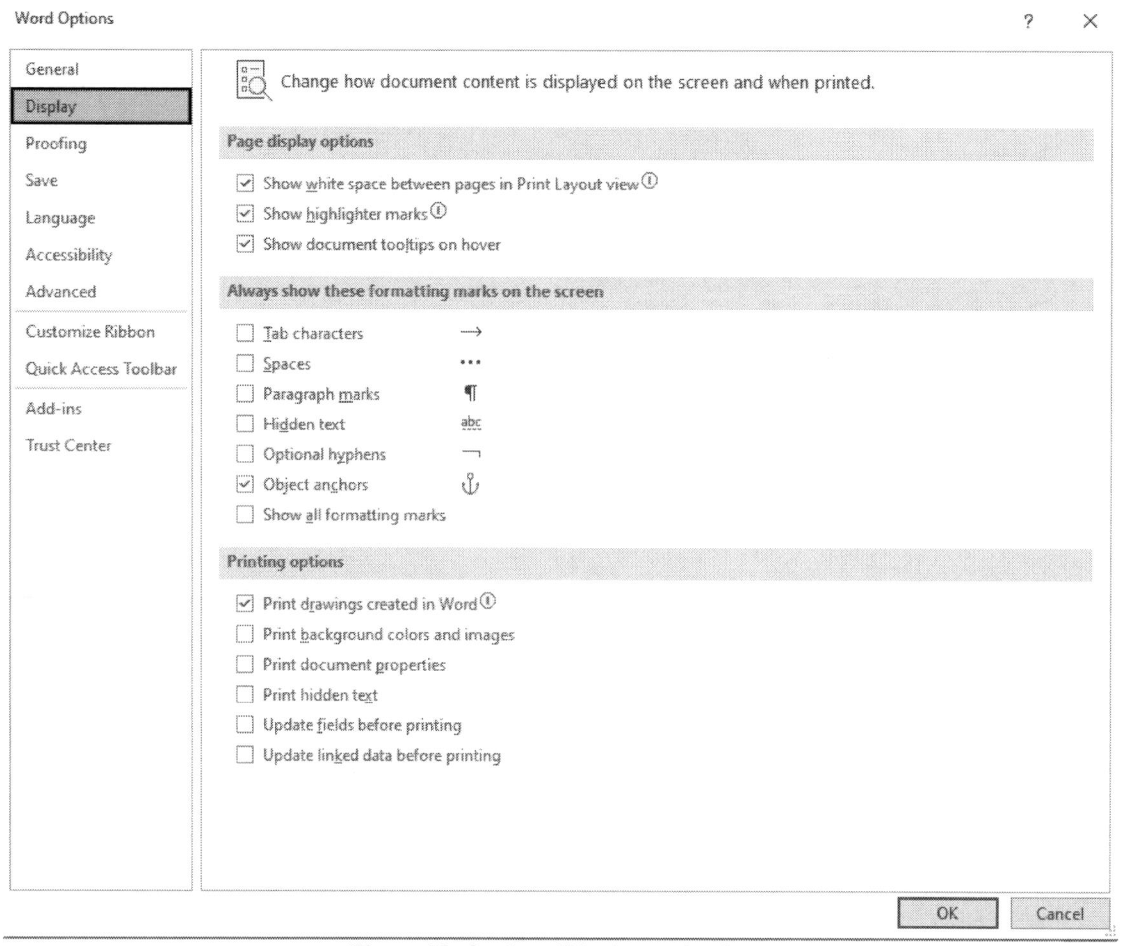

Figure 32: Options Display on backstage

Proofing

Here is where you can tweak your Spellcheck and Grammar options. The following image shows our typical settings; your preferences may vary.

Notice the "Show Readability Statistics" option. More about that feature later.

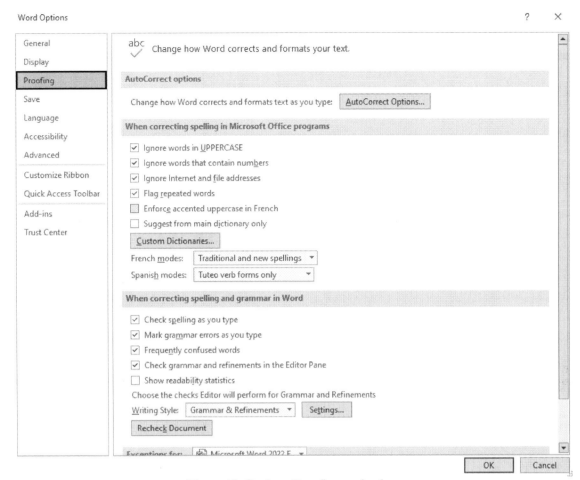

Figure 33: Options Proofing on backstage

Save

Perhaps it has happened to you: You were working on a **large** document in Word, suddenly Word crashes, and your document is gone, or perhaps you forgot to save your changes before closing Word. The information in the Save options may help you keep your sanity. This information includes:

-Where to find "Autosaved" documents (that is, drafts that Word automatically saves as you are working on a Word document)

-How often Word Autosaves our work. Consider whether the default of every 10 minutes is appropriate for you.

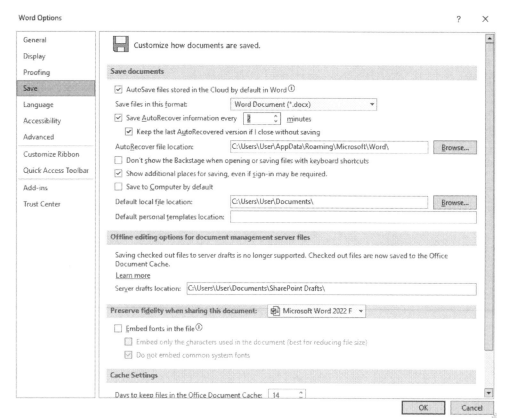

Figure 34: Options Save on backstage

Language & Advanced

We typically don't have much interest in either of these two links. The defaults tend to work well for us. Check them out for yourself, though.

Customize Ribbon & Quick Access Toolbar

Here are a couple of links with which we highly recommend you spend some time. Customizing the Ribbon may seem daunting due to all the options, but it could be well worth your time investment. Do away with the command buttons you don't use in the Ribbon and replace them with the command buttons you will use.

The same goes for the QAT (Quick Access Toolbar). See our previous discussion on the QAT for our recommendations.

Add-Ins

You're probably only visiting this page if you have an Add-In problem. Add-Ins are pieces of software that extend the functionality of the native Word application.

A note about Add-Ins: having too many enabled can slow down Word's performance.

Trust Center

Chances are you won't be spending too much time here either. If you spend time here, it will probably be within the Trust Center Settings button.

If you've used Word 2010 or later for any length of time, you've probably encountered the "Enable Content" or "Enable Editing" prompt at the top of the edit pane.

This prompt appears when you open a document from a source that Word does not "Trust." You can tell Word to trust sources using the Trust Center Settings, and more specifically, Trusted Publishers, Trusted Locations, and Trusted Documents.

The final item within the Trust Center Settings: Privacy Options. Check these out for yourself to make sure they match your privacy expectations. The "Document Inspector" feature is related to the privacy options you may wish to become familiar with.

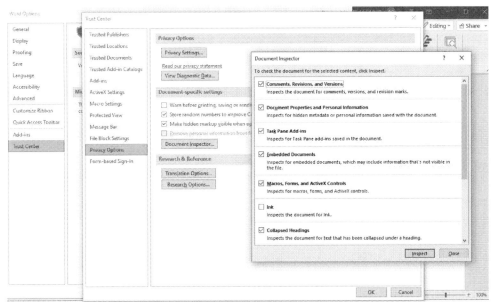

Figure 35: Document inspector

That's a wrap on our File tab discussion. Now let's talk about some of Word's document editing and content-related features.

DOCUMENT AREA

Page

The page is the white widow where all your input will be displayed. There is always a vertical blinking line on the page called **insertion point**. The insertion point indicates where text or anything you put into your document will be added. You can relocate your insertion point to the desired place by moving your cursor and double-clicking in the area.

When printed, your document will appear in the paper exactly how it appears on the page.

Scroll Bars

There are two scroll bars in the Word document area, the vertical and horizontal scroll bars. The vertical scroll bar allows you to scroll your document downward and upward, while the horizontal scroll bar will enable you to scroll your document left and right. The scroll bars only appear if all the document pages cannot be displayed on the window.

To scroll your document page, left-click on the scroll bar, hold and drag down, up, left, or right as the case may be. You can also left-click on the arrows at the terminals of the scroll bar, hold down for fast movement and click intermittently for slow movement.

Rulers

Word has two rulers; a vertical and a horizontal ruler. The horizontal ruler is used for quick indent settings (to be discussed in full later).

STATUS BAR

The status bar contains specific information about the Word document or selected text. The status bar default contains the current page, total page numbers, word counts, language, zoom slider, and page view icons.

Zoom Bar

- This bar allows you to zoom in and out of the document to make your document page appears larger and smaller, respectively, as desired.

- Drag the slider either towards the right side (+) or left side (-) to zoom in and out, respectively. You can also click on the bar to position the slider.

- Click on + and – to increase or reduce the view with multiples of 10.

- Click on the percentage tab to open the zoom window to set the page view.

- You can only set the zoom between 10% and 500%.

5   Page Dimension and Margins

Page dimension refers to the width and height of a page. You can make your document's page dimensions match the paper's size or have them follow a specific pattern. Margins refer to the space on a page's top/bottom and sides. Again, you can increase or decrease them to make your document look precisely as you want.

Page margins in Word are the spaces between your body text and the page edge. You can use these areas for headers and footers. The margins are a critical part of making your document readable. A generous margin will make your text look inviting, while a narrow margin will give reviewers enough space to write their comments. Too many words per line and long lines will make reading your document difficult. Page margins are significant for documents with many pages or facing pages. Word provides several predefined margins, including one inch on all sides. A 1-inch margin is the default setting, but you can change it to fit your needs. If you need a smaller margin, click the "Normal" button on the Page Setup dialog box, then select "Custom Margins." This dialog box will allow you to set the top and bottom margins separately. You can also change the margins individually for the left and right sides.

There are many page layout options in Microsoft Word. For example, you can customize the width of your document, its orientation, and the margins. There are also options to control the spacing of text and images. You can choose one of these options based on the document you're working on.

Margins and Making Adjustments

In Word 2022, as well as the older versions of the same application, margins are blank spaces that line your document's left, right, top, and bottom. When you type text in your document, the text does not cut into those margins. They are boundaries that your words cannot break into.

There are default margin sizes assigned for each document type chosen. In the field of books and script publications, there are standards that the manuscript's owner must maintain before his work is accepted. For instance, you have written a book in A4 Word document and then want to send it to a publishing firm for them to print it as a book for you. The publishing firm may inform you to format your manuscript in a particular margin size before they accept your work. That is a standard. So, let me walk you through how you can get to the margin section and then make the changes you need.

To access the margin of your Word document, click on the **Layout** tab of your document. When you do that, you will see some commands, one of which is *Margins*. Click on the **Margins** command to see some options in the photo below.

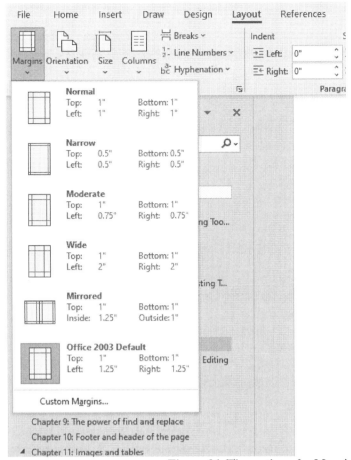

Figure 36: The options for Margins command

You will see the margins size of your document. On the other hand, you can select another new margin to form the list. There are options like *narrow, moderate, mirrored,* and the rest.

You can insert new margins if you do not want to select from the margins list. Select the Custom Margins option as you click on the Margins command to achieve that. When you do that, a dialog box will open. Type the margin sizes you want in the spaces provided for you.

Columns of Word Document and Adjustments

Just like the way you can access margin sizes, as explained in the previous subheading, you can access the column sizes of your Word document and choose something different for yourself. It is simple to do, and when you select a column different from the one assigned to your document by default, you will see the impact on your document.

To access the column of your Word document or make changes to it, tap on the *Layout* tab, followed by *columns*. This action will display some options. Click on the column you want your document to be formatted in. As you do that, you will see how it will change the layout of your document immediately.

6 Tips and Tricks for Formatting and Editing

What is style formatting in Microsoft Word 2022?

Style formatting is a way to neatly format text using one of the styles available in Word. Styles are sets of formatting instructions that can be used for different text types. To create a style, select all the text you want to use, choose Home, Styles, and type in the Style Name. Next, select Change Style and choose New or Copy to copy your selected text. Next, choose Home again and click the Close button in the upper right corner.

What is editing in Microsoft Word 2022?

Editing refers to the process of making changes to a file. You can easily edit a file in Word by selecting it and choosing Home, Edit, or clicking on the left-hand side of the status bar. The top portion of the Edit window has many tabs that help you make changes quickly and get work done faster. You can change the font or color, insert tables and pictures, or adjust margins without leaving this window.

What is a paragraph in Microsoft Word 2022?

A paragraph is a collection of words and sentences that are grouped. Paragraphs share a common topic or idea. They should be easy to read and understand. You can format paragraphs by changing the size, margins, indentation, and spacing between the lines. You can also insert special characters like em dashes instead of hyphens in your paragraphs to make them look more professional and increase their readability.

What is a font in Microsoft Word 2022?

A font is a collection of character shapes and sizes. Many different fonts are available in Word, including serifs, sans-serifs, and fancy letter styles. You can use several of them simultaneously to make your document look more interesting. According to Microsoft, fonts define a certain style of the text.

What is the font size in Microsoft Word 2022?

Text size refers to the size of the letters in a font. Font sizes are usually measured in points, which can be confusing. For example, the 10-point text is usually smaller than 12 point text. The higher the number, the larger your font will be. You can use dozens of fonts and sizes to make different sections of your document look as professional as possible or add visual interest.

What is font formatting?

Font formatting refers to changing the appearance of your selected text in Microsoft Word. For example, you can make your text bold, italic, underlined, or strikethrough by choosing a font style from the Home tab.

What is letter spacing in Microsoft Word 2022?

Letter spacing measures how far apart letters are in a font. You can increase or decrease the space between letters by turning on or off character spacing, which will cause the letter to draw closer together. This can make your document look more professional.

What is font color in Microsoft Word 2022?

Font color refers to the colors that appear in a font. You can set the colors of your font by choosing one from a black and white drop-down menu on the home tab. You can also apply gradients for more design options, but these will not appear on printed versions of your document.

What is the font color behind the text in Microsoft Word 2022?

Font color behind text refers to the ability to change the color of all or part of the text in your selected paragraph, so it appears behind text from other paragraphs. This can make your document look more professional by giving the impression that you are sending a written message.

What are uppercase and lowercase in Microsoft Word 2022?

Uppercase letters are normally printed using capital letters, but some words can use uppercase letters or other characters. Uppercasing is the process of converting all lowercase letters to capital form. Lowercase letters are normally printed using small letters, but some words can use lowercase or other characters. Lowercasing is the process of converting all uppercase letters to a lowercase form. Word automatically makes your entire document use uppercase or lowercase, but you can change this feature by selecting which type of text you want.

How to add new fonts in Microsoft Word 2022?

Go to the Home tab and choose Fonts and Text. From the drop-down menu that appears, choose Add New Font. Type in the Name of your font, Click the "Browse" button to find the font from your computer. Print screen this page to see the font on your screen. Find the font you want on your computer and print screen it. Click the OK button to add a new font in Microsoft Word for Windows. Place it under the All fonts option in the Home tab - More Fonts option of Microsoft Word for Windows.

What's compare mode and combine mode in Microsoft Word 2022?

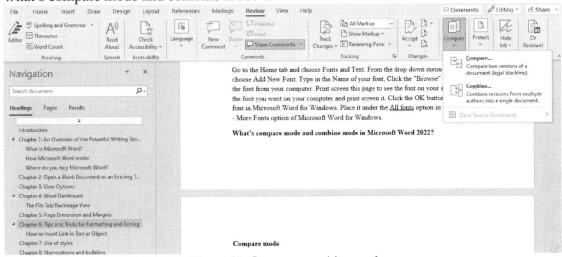

Figure 37: Compare combine modes

Compare mode

This function lets you compare two windows side by side. When you click on the 'Compare' button, the right window with the cursor moves over to the left window, and then after some time, it switches back to the original.

Combine mode

In this case, you hold the Shift key while clicking on the 'Compare' button. In this way, both windows are combined into one. After holding down the Shift key, click on Compare button again and select 'Merge.' This combination occurs only when you hold down the Shift key.

ENTERING, SELECTING, AND DELETING TEXTS

To Enter Texts into your Document:

1. Open your MS Word
2. Pick a blank document, a template, or an existing document. Word automatically sets the text insertion point at the top of the first page of any newly opened document.
3. For existing documents: Scroll down and click the point you want to enter new texts, like the last page, to reposition the insertion point.
4. Type your new texts on the keyboard, and the texts will appear at the text insertion point.

Note:

- Press the space bar using your keyboard once to put space between words.
- Do not Press **Enter** button to move to the following line. Word automatically moves to the next line when the current line is filled.
- Press **the Enter button on your keyboard only when starting** a new paragraph.
- Word automatically creates a new page once the current one is filled.

To Select Texts in MS Word:

1. Put your cursor on the texts you want to pick.
2. Left-click your mouse, holding it down, and move it across the texts.

3. Release the mouse.

OR

1. Click at the start of the texts you want to select.
2. Hold down the **Shift** button using your keyboard
3. Click at the end of the texts or **press** any arrow keys on your keyboard to select the texts in the direction of the arrow.

Some Shortcut ways of selecting Texts:
To select:

- **A word** – Double-click on the word.
- **A line** – Place the mouse pointer at the left margin and click **once** in front of the line.
- **A sentence** – Press and hold the **Ctrl** button on your keyboard, then click anywhere on the sentence.
- **A paragraph** – Place the mouse pointer in the left margin and double-click next to any paragraph line. You can Triple-click anywhere in the paragraph.
- **The whole Document** – Press the **Ctrl** key, place your mouse pointer anywhere in the margin, and triple-click or left-click once anywhere in the margin. Alternatively,

- Go to the **Home** tab, click on **Select** in **Editing** group, and **select all**. **OR**
- Press **Ctrl + A** on your keyboard.
To Select several texts that are not together:
Press down the **Ctrl** button and use any of the methods stated above to select the texts one after the other.
To Delete Texts:

1. Highlight the texts you want to delete.
2. Press the **Delete** button on your keyboard

OR

1. Move your cursor to the left side of the text you wish to delete.
2. Press the **Delete** button on your keyboard.

OR

1. Move your cursor to the right of the texts you want to delete
2. Press the **Backspace** button on your keyboard.

Deleting a Single Character
You can use the keyboard to add and remove text when you write in Word. Many keys make text, but Backspace and Delete are the only keys that can delete text. These keys become more powerful when used with other keys, or even the mouse, that help them delete large amounts of text.

- **The Delete key** deletes characters to the **right** of the insertion pointer

- **The backspace key** deletes characters to the **left** of the insertion pointer.

Deleting a Word
You can delete an entire world with the Ctrl, Backspace, or Delete keys. There are two ways to use these keyboard shortcuts. They work best when the insertion pointer is at the start or end of a word. Delete commands are only used when the pointer is in the middle of a word. These commands only delete from that middle point to the start or end of the word. The shortcut to delete is illustrated as follows;

- The word to the left of the insertion pointer is deleted when you press **Ctrl+Backspace.**

- The word to the right of the insertion pointer is deleted when you press **Ctrl + Delete.**

Note: When you use Ctrl+Backspace, delete a word to the left. The pointer is at the end of what comes before it. When you use Ctrl+Delete to remove a word, the cursor moves to the start of the next word. This is done to make removing several words in a row easier.

Deleting More Than a Word
The keyboard and mouse must work together to remove chunks of text bigger than a single letter or word. The first step is to choose a chunk of text and then delete that chunk text.

Remove a Line of Text
A line of text starts on one side of the page and goes to the other. If you want to remove the line, you can:

- Make sure the mouse pointer is next to a line of text by moving it to the left.

- Then click on the mouse.

- The text line is chosen and shown in a different color on the screen.

- Press the delete key to delete that line.

Delete a Sentence
A sentence is a group of text made up of words that start with a capital letter and end with a period, a question mark, or an exclamation point, depending on what you want to say. To do this;

- Place the mouse pointer where the sentence you want to delete lies.

- Press and hold down the Ctrl key simultaneously as you click the mouse.

- Using Ctrl and a mouse click together, you can choose a sentence of text that you want to delete.

- The Ctrl key can be let go, and then you can hit delete.

Deleting a Paragraph
A Paragraph is a group of sentences formed when you press the Enter key. If you want to delete a whole paragraph quickly, here's how to do it:

- Click the mouse **three times.** In this case, the triple-click selects the whole paragraph of the text.

- Press the **Delete button.**

Another way to select a paragraph is to click the mouse two times in the left margin, next to the paragraph, to make it select and then click on delete.

Deleting a Page
Page of text is everything on a page from top to bottom. This part of the document isn't one that Word directly addresses with keyboard commands. You'll need some sleight of hand to get rid of a whole page of text. Take these steps:

- Press the keys **Ctrl+G.**

- The Find and Replace dialogue box comes up, with the Go To tab at the top of the list of tabs.

- On the Go to What list, choose Page and then type the number of the page you want to remove.

- Click the Go To button, then the Close button. And the page shows up.

- Press the **Delete** button.

- All of the text on the page is taken off.

Split and Join Paragraphs

A paragraph, as earlier defined, is a group of sentences that all say the same thing about a thought, idea, or theme. In Word, a paragraph is a chunk of text that ends when you press the Enter key. You can change a paragraph in a document by splitting or joining text.

To split a single paragraph in two;

When you want to start a new paragraph, click the mouse where you want it to start. That point should be at the beginning of a sentence. Press the Enter button. During this process, Word breaks the paragraph in two. The text above the insertion pointer becomes its paragraph, and the text below becomes the next paragraph.

Making a single paragraph out of two separate ones

To combine two paragraphs and make them one, do this; When you place the insertion pointer at the start of the second paragraph or use the keyboard or click the mouse to move the insertion pointer where you want it to be, press the Backspace button.

This implies that you have removed the entered character from the paragraph before this one, thus making two paragraphs into one.

Soft and Hard Return

The **Return or Enter key** is pressed at the end of each line when typing on a keyboard. This indicates that you've finished one paragraph and are ready to go on to the next. However, when you set your page margins, Word knows that your text should wrap to the next line when you get to the right margin.

However, there may be situations when you want to stop writing a line before reaching the right margin. You can terminate a line in one of two ways in these circumstances. The first method is to enter where you want the line to terminate and then hit Enter. As a result, the document is filled with a **hard return.** This action (hitting Enter) signifies that you have reached the end of the paragraph and wish to begin a new one.

Another approach to end a line is to hit **Shift+Enter,** which will insert a soft return, also known as a line break or newline character, into the document. The end of a paragraph is indicated by hard returns, whereas soft returns indicate the end of a line.

A hard return displays on your screen as a paragraph mark (a backward P), while a soft return appears as a down-and-left pointing arrow.

To replace texts:

1. Select the texts.

2. Type the new texts over it.

You do not need to delete the texts; Word automatically deletes the old selected texts and replaces them with the newly typed text.

CUT, COPY AND PASTE TEXTS

Cutting text removes the text from its initial position and places it where it is **Pasted** while **copying** reproduces the text in another place.

There are various ways of copying, cutting, and pasting texts in Word; some of the top ones include the following:

Method 1:

- Pick the text you want to cut or copy.

- Click on the **Home** tab and select the Copy or Cut command as desired.

- Put your cursor to where you want to paste your text.

- Click on the **Paste** command in the **Home** tab.

Method 2:

- Select the texts you want to copy or cut.

- Right-click on the selected text.

- Select the **Copy** or **Cut** option from the menu that appears.

- Place your cursor to the desired location and right-click on your mouse.

- Select the **Paste** option with a left-click from a menu that appears.

Alternatively, you can use the shortcut commands:

- **Ctrl + C** to copy

- **Ctrl + X** to cut

- **Ctrl + V** or **Shift + Insert** to paste

Tips: You can use the **paste** option to paste the item you copied or cut last as many times and at many places as desired.

PASTE SPECIAL OPTIONS AND CLIPBOARD

Paste Special Options

While working on your document, you will likely want to copy/cut some texts that already have formatting, like font type, font size, color, etc. When you copy/cut these formatted texts into word, Word automatically reformats the texts to the destination format, which might not be what you want. However, depending on your choice, Paste Special Option is provided to help you retain the original format and paste the item as a link, picture, or plain text.

Paste Special is a word feature that provides several format options to Paste your item. The format in which you can paste your texts includes Microsoft Word Object, Formatted text, Unformatted text, Picture, file, Html format, and Unformatted Unicode Text (UUT).

To use Paste Special Options:

- Copy or cut the item you want to paste, e.g., text, picture, shape, slide, etc.

- Click where you want to insert the item in your document.

- Go to the **Home** tab in the **Clipboard** group and click the dropdown arrow under **Paste.**

- Select **Paste Special** from the menu that comes up.

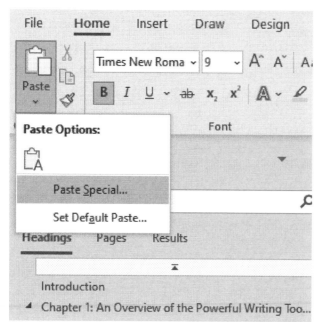

Figure 38: Paste special

- Choose one of the options from the pop-up window as desired.

Alternatively, you can use the **Ctrl + Alt + V** shortcut command on your keyboard to call the **Paste Special** window.

Note: The **Paste Special** options change based on the item you want to paste.

Clipboard

A clipboard is a location where the cut or copy texts are temporarily stored and can be recalled for use with a **Paste** command. Microsoft has a multi-clipboard that can store up to 24 items copied or cut, unlike a window clipboard that can only hold one item at a time. The **Paste** command only recalls the last item copied or cut, and you can assess the other items by opening the clipboard.

To paste any of your copied items from the clipboard:

1. Go to **the Home** tab, under the **clipboard** group.

2. Click the expandable dialog box button to display the clipboard with the list of all the copied/cut items.

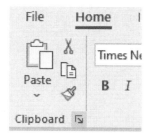

Figure 39: Clipboard paste

3. Click on the item of your choice to paste it at the insertion point or

4. Move your cursor to the item you want, and in front, you will see a drop-down button with options to paste or delete.

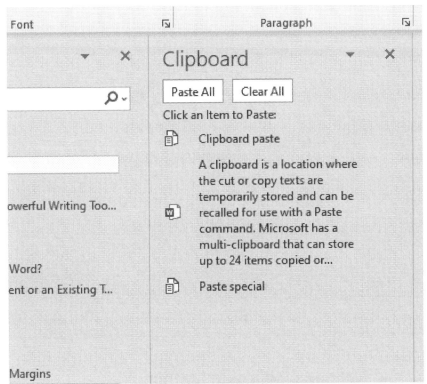

Figure 40: Items on clipboard

5.　　　Select **Paste**, and your item will be inserted into the insertion point. **Delete** and remove the data from the clipboard if you do not need it again.

Click the **x** button to close the clipboard panel and **arrow** down options to change its location (move), resize, or close it as desired.

MOVING AND DUPLICATING

Moving removes the text or object from its initial position to another location, just like cut and paste, while duplicating reproduces your text in another place like copy and paste. It is easier to move/duplicate than cut/copy and paste.

The difference between Cut/copy, and move/duplicate is that while cut/copy stores their items in the clipboard, move/duplicate never does. Therefore, using the cut/copy and paste command is advisable if you need the item later because you can easily retrieve them on the clipboard.

To move your text:

- Select the texts or items you want to move.

- Click and hold your mouse

- drag and drop the item in the desired location.

To duplicate your text:

- Select the item you want to duplicate.

- Click and hold your mouse on the item.

- Press and hold down the **Ctrl** key.

- Drag and **drop** the item in the desired location.

- Then release the **Ctrl** button last.

Note: If you release the **Ctrl** button before releasing the item in the new location, the item will be moved and not duplicated.

UNDO, REDO, AND REPEAT

MS Word keeps track of most of your tasks while working on your document until you close the document. You can undo tasks like formatting, typing, deleting, etc., and some actions like clicking on a command, saving your document, etc., you cannot undo. By default, Word can save up to **100** tasks you can undo.

To redo a task only a step back;

- Click on the undo icon [undo icon] in the **Quick Access Toolbar** once

- or even more for more steps backward.

For many steps backward;

- Click on the dropdown button in front of the undo icon;

- a list of all the tasks you have performed since you open the document up to 100 appears.

- Select a point in the list, and Word will undo everything you have done. You can only undo all the steps from the present to a point you select on the list. You cannot undo a single action that is not immediate.

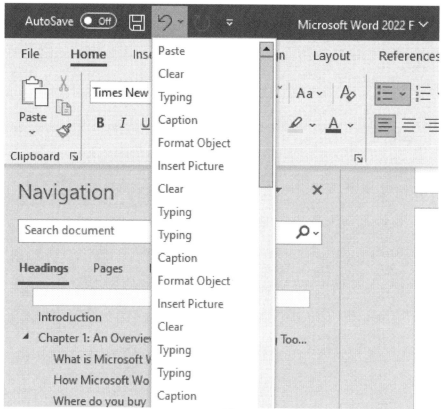

Figure 41: Undo actions

If you do not want to undo your task again, the redo command [redo icon] is also available for you to use in the **Quick Access Toolbar**. If there is nothing to redo, Words change the redo icon to repeat icon [repeat icon] for you to repeat some repeatable actions.

The redo and undo action command becomes inactive if there is nothing to undo or redo.

<u>**Keyboard Shortcuts:**</u>

Press **Ctrl + Z to undo.**

Press **Ctrl + Y to redo or repeat** as the case may be.

The Undo Command

The Undo command can undo anything you do in Word, like changing text, moving blocks, typing, and deleting text. It does this for everything you do in the program. If you want to use the Undo command, you have two ways to do it:

- The shortcut method is to Press **Ctrl+Z.**

- Alternatively, you can click the Undo command button on the Quick Access toolbar to get back to where your previous work is.

Note: In some cases, you can't use the Undo command because there's nothing to undo. For example, you can't go back and undo a file save.

The Redo Command

If you make a mistake and undo something you didn't mean to, use the Redo command to get things back to how they used to be. Suppose you write some text and then use Undo to remove the text. Then, you can use the Redo command to go back and type again. It's your choice. You can choose

- The shortcut method is to press **Ctrl+Y.**

- Alternatively, look at the **Quick Access toolbar** and click the **Redo button.**

Note: The Undo command does the opposite of the Redo command. So, if you write text, Undo removes the text, and Redo puts the text back.

The Repeat Command

To repeat what you did in Word last time, use the Repeat command to do the same thing again. This could be typing new text, formatting it, or doing many other things.

Using the Repeat command, you can keep the same picture. The Redo command turns into the Repeat command whenever there is no more to redo.

To do this:

- The shortcut method is to Press **Ctrl+Y**, which is the same keyboard shortcut as to redo something.

Figure 42: The Undo and Repeat Button

Finally, now that you know how to use the basic tools in Word to make a document, this chapter has covered some more editing tools and simple formatting effects to make a document look better. More editing tools will be discussed in other chapters.

6.1 How to Insert Link in Text or Object

I do not know your area of specialization as the reader of this book or what area you want to go into in the future. But whatever the area, I believe no knowledge is a waste. For example, in online writing (blogging), we embed links in texts and sometimes photos. When readers click on the text or photos having these links they cannot see, they are taken to a specific website. So, I will teach you how to insert links in text or photos in a Word document.

To insert the link in a text or photo, the first step you are to take is to select the text or photo. If you want to insert the link in a text, get the text selected. If you do the insertion in a photo you have in your Word document, select the photo by clicking on it once.

The next step you are to take after the selection is to click on the *Insert* tab of your Word document. Click on the dropdown at the *Link* icon indicated in the photo below.

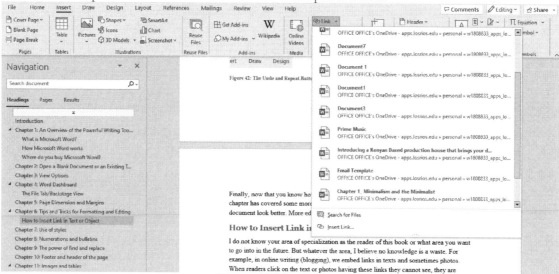

Figure 43: The Link icon

The Insert Link dialog box will open on your computer. In the *Address* space, type the link you want to connect to, for example, www.amazon.com. And then tap on the *OK* button. This last step will hyperlink the text or image you selected. Anytime a reader clicks on that text. They will be taken to the website whenever a link is added in a text, and the text color changes, usually blue, by default.
***

Hyperlinking a text turns the text into a link and makes it clickable. The link, when clicked, jumps to another location, either in the document or a different location outside the document, like a website, another file, a new email message, or any other place the text is being hyperlinked to. This feature is excellent for easy navigation of your document.

MS word automatically convert a web address to a hyperlink when you type the address and press **Enter** or **Spacebar** after the address, e.g., www.office.com

To turn your text into a Hyperlink:

1. Select the text you want to turn to a link.

2. Go to the **Insert** tab under the **Links** group. You can also right-click on the text: A menu appears.

3. Click the **Link** command.

4. Select the link destination and fill in the required information in the **Insert Hyperlink** window. There are four available options to choose from based on what you want:

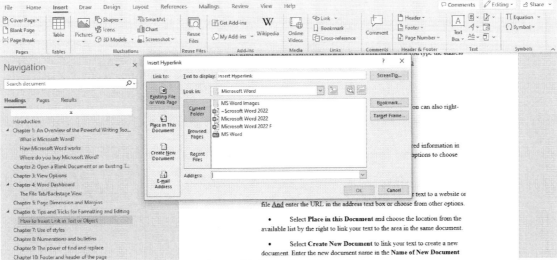

Figure 44: Inserting Hyperlink

- Select **Existing File or Web Page** to link your text to a website or file And enter the URL in the address text box or choose from other options.

- Select **Place in this Document** and choose the location from the available list by the right to link your text to the area in the same document.

- Select **Create New Document** to link your text to create a new document. Enter the new document name in the **Name of New Document** textbox, Click **change** in the **full path** section to change the new document location, and choose whether you want to edit the document now or later in the **When to edit** section.

- Select **Email Address** to link the text to send an email to a recipient. Enter the email address or choose from the recently used address.

5.   Enter **Ok** to apply, and the text now appears as a link.

To follow a link in MS word.
- Click and hold the **Ctrl** button.

- Click on the link, and it will take you to its destination.

You can edit the link by right-clinking on it and choosing from the menu that appears, based on what you want to do.

Word formats hyperlinked text differently from all other texts by default, and you can change the setting in the **Word Options.**

PAGE BREAKS AND SECTION BREAKS

When working on a document with multiple pages and many headings, it is sometimes challenging to format the document so that all chapter headings start on a new page without some beginning at the bottom. Also, when working on some types of documents with multiple sections like an article, report, paper, or book, it might be difficult to add **different** headers, footers, footnotes, page numbers, and other formatting elements.

Word duplicates the same headers, footers, and footnotes and continues numbering throughout the document. To have a separate one, document **breaks** are required.

There are two types of document breaks in Word:
- Page breaks

- Section breaks.

Page breaks partition the document's body, while section breaks partition not only the document body but also the headings (or chapters), headers, footnotes, page numbers, margins, etc.

Page Breaks are subdivided into:

- **Page break**: This forces all the text behind the insertion point to the next page.

- **Column** break: This forces the text to the right of the insertion point to the next column of the same page when working with a document with multiple columns

- **Text Wrapping break**: It moves any text to the right of the cursor to the following line and is instrumental when working with objects.

Sections are the part of Word that controls pages, headers, footers, orientation, margins, and columns on Microsoft Word. Section breaks allow you to space up your document into independent chunks. In addition, it shows which document parts have different page orientations, columns, or Headers and footers.

Uses of Section Breaks

- If your document needs different headers and footers on different pages, you will use Section breaks to do this.

- Using Section breaks, you can make a table of contents, index, and Appendices with different types of numerals.

- You'll need a section break between two pages for a document with two pages.

- If you need to mix pages that are portrait-oriented with landscape-oriented pages, you can use section breaks

- Section breaks can be added before and after Word's newspaper column feature so you can use them in the middle of a page.

- You can start page numbers again at any point in a document by putting a section break in the middle of a document.

Section Breaks are subdivided into:

- **Next Page break**: This divides the documents by creating another page that can have its special formatting. This is useful for partitioning your document into different chapters with different headers, footers, page numbers, etc.

- **Continuous break:** This divides the document into sections that can be independently formatted on the same page without creating a new page. This break is usually used to change the number of columns on a page.

- **Even Page break:** This shifts the insertion point and any text at its right to the next even page.

- **Odd Page breaks** This shifts the insertion point and any text at its right to the next odd page.

To Insert a Page Break or Section Break:

1.   Place your insertion point to where you want the break.

2.　　　　Go to the **Layout** ribbon.

3.　　　　Select **Breaks** in the **Page Setup** group.

A drop-down list appears with all the types of breaks.

4.　　　　Select from the options the type of section break you want.

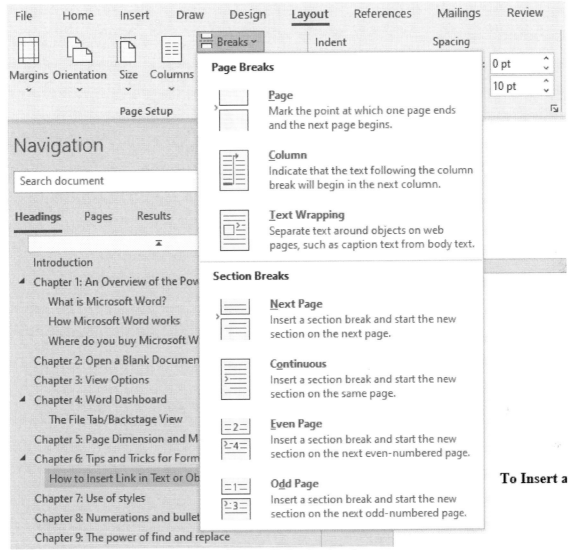

Figure 45: Section breaks

Insert a continuous section break

This is the same as above, but the section break stays on the same page; you use it if you want to do something like changing a two-column layout before going back to the normal layout.

Insert a column break

If you have a layout that uses columns and wants to force the text to move to the new column, use a column break (also in the Breaks menu).

- It can also be achieved using Ctrl + Shift + Enter.

Delete breaks

- With the non-printable symbols displayed, click in front of the jump.

- Press Delete on your keyboard.

7 Use of Styles

The user creates styles highlighting a document's structure, tone, and format. The styles that come with Word are named after the types of documents they apply to. For example, there is the Title style, which is set to bold formatting, or the Normal style, which causes no formatting. In addition, you can create your styles for documents by choosing 'New Style' from the Format menu.

A style is a collection of formatting commands under a single name. When a style is applied, lots of formatting commands are simultaneously given, and you will save yourself the stress of going to different tabs and dialog boxes to begin to format text. Styles help to save time, and they also make documents look more professional. Headings with the same style, for example -**Heading1,** all have the same look. When readers notice a form of consistency in headings and paragraphing, they will have a warm and cozy feeling about the document. They will think that whoever must have created the document knows what they are doing.

Style is a set of formatting features such as font size, color, and alignment that can be applied to text, tables, and lists to quickly change the document's appearance. Applying styles to your document helps to give it a professional look.

Why Should You Use Styles?

The following are the reasons why you need to use Styles while creating documents

- Styles give your document uniform headings and subheadings

- Styles allow for efficient formatting while working with your document.

- Applying a style in your document gives you a quick way to see the headings and subheadings on the Navigation Pane.

- Applying styles to your document gives you an easy shortcut to automatically get a table of contents and a list of tables and figures.

Components of Styles

The following are the components of Styles

- **Paragraph styles**: These paragraph styles control the formatting of a complete paragraph. The paragraph style has the following settings; font, paragraph, tab, indentation, line spacing, justification, border, language, bullet, numbering, and text effects. The paragraph style is denoted with the paragraph symbol (¶)

Figure 46: Paragraph styles

- **Character styles:** The character style can only be applied to text in a document. To apply this style, you will first have to select the text. The character style has the following settings: font name, font size, italics, bold, color, border, language, and text effect.

- **Linked (Paragraph and character)**: These style types can be applied to paragraphs and text within a document. These styles can be denoted with paragraph symbol (¶) and the letter a. Note: The Linked style must be enabled.

- **Table styles:** These control the formatting outlook of a table in a document. The table styles have the following settings borders, shadings, alignment, and fonts.

- **List styles:** These control the formatting of the list by applying similar alignment, numbering, bullet characters, and fonts.

How to See All Styles In Microsoft Word

On the Home tab, look at the style option and click on one style; for example, it will highlight all text around the style.

Microsoft word doesn't load all the styles; all you have to do is click on the small icon on the bottom right corner of the style panel (Circled in the figure below), and all the style shows up. You can further click on the options button, and you see the option select style to show. Click on all styles and click on OK. Then all styles that are missing will show up

Figure 47: Style pane arrow

Why Uses Styles in Words

i. You can be sure that all the headings, paragraphs, subheadings, etc. have the same correct, consistent formatting

ii. It is faster to apply style than doing it individually

Applying Styles to your Text or Paragraphs

You can apply styles to your text or paragraph by following the steps below

- Select the text or paragraph you wish to format (You can position your cursor at the beginning of the paragraph)

We use this paragraph for showcasing the application of styles to the text. It will provide the different aspects where all the headings, paragraphs, subheadings, etc. have the same correct, consistent formatting

at the beginning of the paragraph)

We use this paragraph for showcasing the application of styles to the text. It will provide the different aspects where all the headings, paragraphs, subheadings, etc. have the same correct, consistent formatting

- In the **Styles** group on the **Home** tab, select the **More** drop-down arrow.

Figure 48: Highlighted paragraph

- In the **Styles** group on the **Home** tab, select the **More** drop-down arrow.

Figure 49: More drop-down on styles

- Choose your best style from the drop-down menu. You can choose **Para 53**.

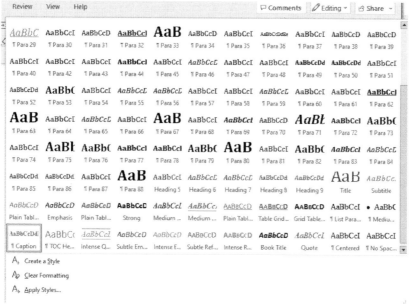

Figure 50: More styles

- The text selected will appear in the desired style selected.

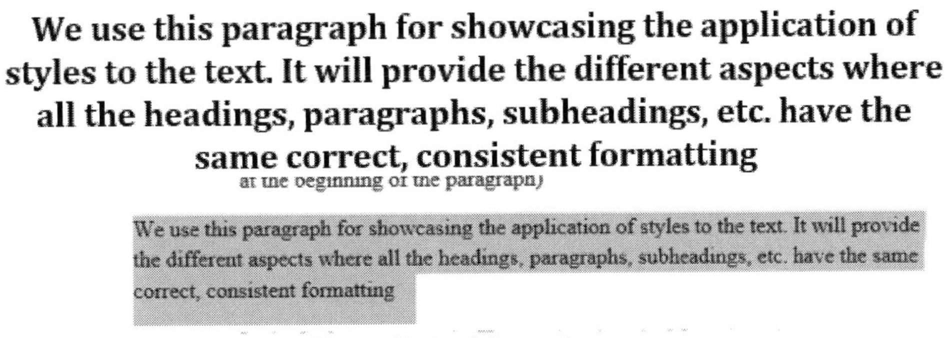

We use this paragraph for showcasing the application of styles to the text. It will provide the different aspects where all the headings, paragraphs, subheadings, etc. have the same correct, consistent formatting

at the beginning of the paragraph)

We use this paragraph for showcasing the application of styles to the text. It will provide the different aspects where all the headings, paragraphs, subheadings, etc. have the same correct, consistent formatting

Figure 51: Applying styles

Applying a Style Set

Style sets are made up of a title, headings, and paragraph styles. Style sets permit you to format all the elements in your document at once instead of modifying each of the elements separately. Before applying the Style set, you must have assigned styles to your paragraph, text, table, or list.

Follow the procedures below to apply the style set to your text or paragraph

- Click on the More drop-down arrow in the Document Formatting group on the Design tab.

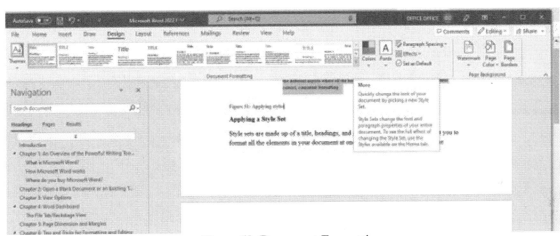

Figure 52: Document Formatting

- Choose the best style from the drop-down menu.

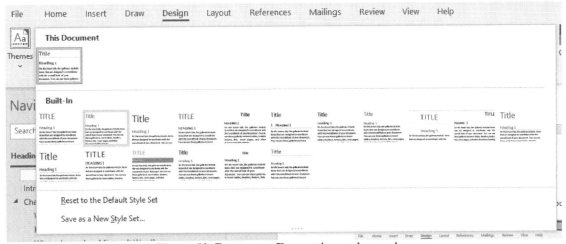

Figure 53: Document Formatting styles to choose

- The style set selected will appear on the entire document.

Creating a New Style

There are two ways to create a new style in your document: by creating it from the paragraph or from the ground up. So now, let's create a new style using the earlier two methods.

Creating a New Style from a Paragraph

To create a new style from a paragraph, follow the steps given below

- Select the paragraph you wish to change its formatting into a style

- From the **Home** tab, open the **Styles** gallery and click on **Creating a Style**

Figure 54: Creating a new paragraph style

- In the **Create New Style from the Formatting** dialog box, enter the name of the new style and then click on **Ok**

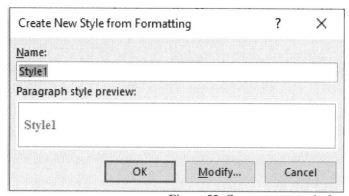

Figure 55: Create a new style from formatting

Creating a Style from the Ground up

To create a new style from the ground up, follow the steps given below

- From the **Home** tab and click on the **Styles** group button

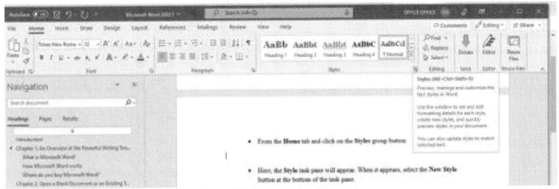

Figure 56: Styles from Home button

- Here, the **Style** task pane will appear. When it appears, select the **New Style** button at the bottom of the task pane.

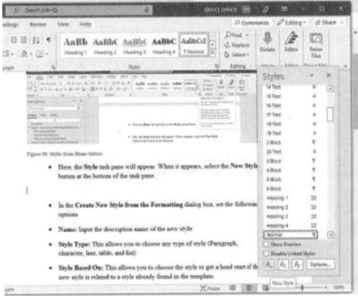

Figure 57: Create New Style from the Formatting

- In the **Create New Style from the Formatting** dialog box, set the following options

- **Name:** Input the description name of the new style.

- **Style Type:** This allows you to choose any type of style (Paragraph, character, line, table, and list)

- **Style Based On:** This allows you to choose the style to get a head start if the new style is related to a style already found in the template.

- **The style for Formatting Paragraph:** This allows you to select a style from the drop-down list if the style you are creating is related to or followed by an existing style.

- **Formatting:** This allows you to choose an option from the menu to refine your style.

- **Add to Style Gallery:** This check box allows the style's name to appear in the Styles gallery, Style pane, and Apply Styles task pane.

- **Automatically Update:** This updates the changes made to the styles in the document.

- **Only in This Document/New Documents Based on This Template:** This allows you to make your style part of the template from which you created your document and the document itself.

- **Format:** Clicking on this button directs you to a dialog box where you can create or refine the style.

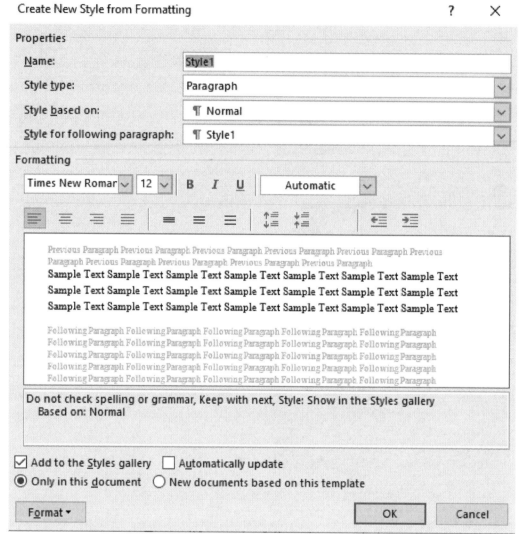

Figure 58: Creating your new style

- Then click on Ok

Modifying a Style

To modify a style, follow the steps below:

- Go to the **Home** tab, right-click on the Style you wish to change in the **Style**s group, and then click on **Modify** in the drop-down menu

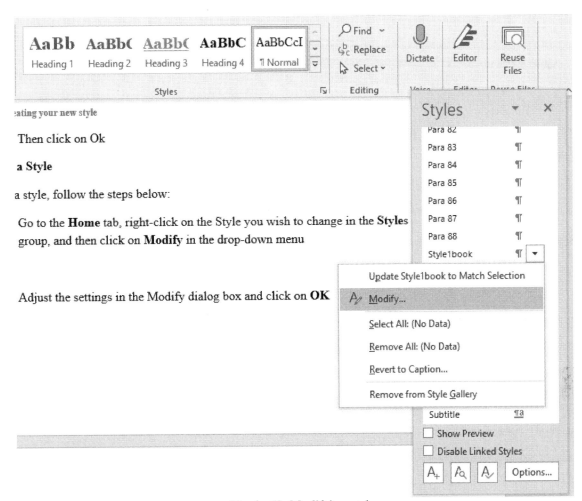

ating your new style

Then click on Ok

a Style

a style, follow the steps below:

Go to the **Home** tab, right-click on the Style you wish to change in the **Styles** group, and then click on **Modify** in the drop-down menu

Adjust the settings in the Modify dialog box and click on **OK**

Figure 59: Modifying style

- Adjust the settings in the Modify dialog box and click on **OK**

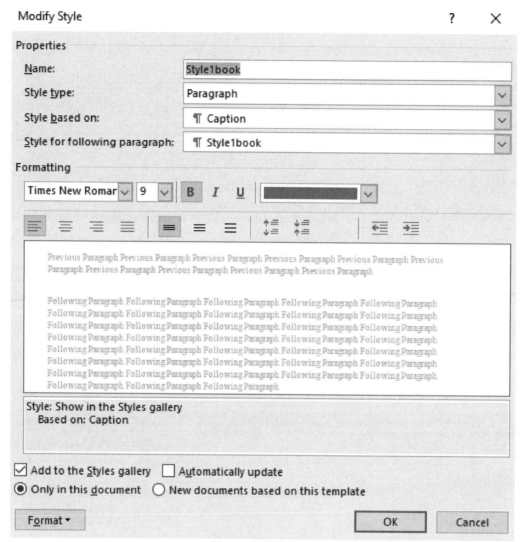

Figure 60: Adjust style settings

Renaming Your Styles

To change the name of your styles, follow the steps below

- Go to the **Home** tab, right-click on the Style you wish to change in the **Style**s group, and then click on **Rename** in the drop-down menu

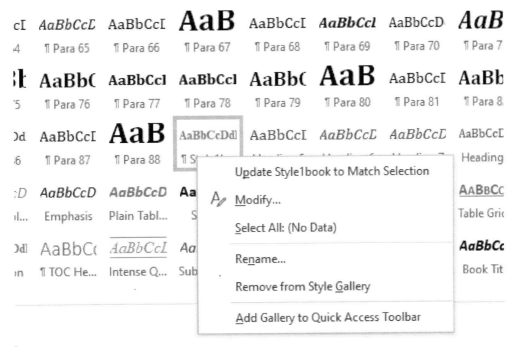

Figure 61: Renaming styles

- In the **Rename Style** dialog box, enter the name and click on **Ok**

Rename Style ? ✕

Please type the new name of the style

Style2022

OK   Cancel

Figure 62: Rename style

To use a style in Microsoft for Headings: Highlight all the different headings on your document. There is a section called styles on the home tab, as shown below. Click on the style you want, and that style will be applied to the selected headings.

Figure 63: The Style Group

Note: One great benefit of styles is that it applies to all selected headings as you make changes to a style.

iii. Helps to navigate through your document faster.

How to Delete Styles

Click on the arrow on the home tab on the style groups. Next, click on the particular style, and in the drop-down arrow, click delete. If it asks if you're sure you want to delete it, click yes. Once done, the style will no longer appear on the style menu.

Alternatively, on the style pane on the home tab, click on the managed file at the bottom of the style pane. Select the name of the style to delete and then delete. Click the yes button on the Confirmation box that appears.

However, to permanently remove the style from the template, you must take an extra step. Click on the import and export button at the bottom of the dialogue box, and on the left side, you will see a template of a document name list in the styles available in the drop-down. Choose the template name within which the style you want to delete has been saved from the styles available on the drop-down. Then in the template document name list, select the customized style to delete. On the Confirmation box that appears, click yes to the question and close.

Restricting Styles Changes on Microsoft Word 2022

To turn on style restrictions:

- Click on the **File** Tab and then select protect a document in the back icon as shown in figure 64

- On the drop-down menu, select **Restrict Editing (**Figure 64)

- Next, on the restrict editing pane, select formatting restrictions and then select the settings

- On the formatting restrictions dialogue box, check/mark "limit formatting to a selection of styles," as shown in figure 65

- Now check or uncheck the individual styles you want to allow in the document, select one of the preset option buttons or click "All" to check every style currently allowed in the document. Click on "Recommended Minimum" this option checks comment style options currently allowed in the document but unchecks fewer comments styles such as a table. "None" unchecked all style options (figure 65)

- Then check or uncheck the three optional formatting choices (i. allow other formats to override formatting restrictions; this first option implies that you should allow other formats to surpass the option selected in the formatting restrictions style or box ii. Block theme or scheme switching prevents other users from changing the document to a different theme in the design tab or a separate scheme such as the color scheme iii. And the last option is to block Quick Style set switching, which, when clicked on, helps prevent other users from using the style options on the home tab) When you're done, select Ok. This is circled red in figure 65

- A dialogue box will ask, "The Document may contain formatting or styles that aren't allowed. Do you want to remove them"? Select No if you want to keep all of your existing styles while preventing other users from using them

- Next, select yes on the start enforcement button and enter a password on the start enforcing protection dialogue box and then select OK, as shown in figure 67

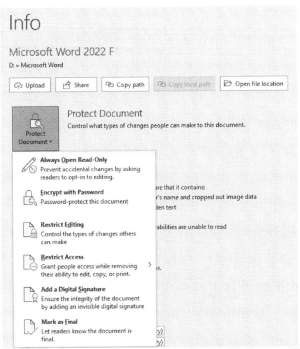

Figure 64: Protect Document Button

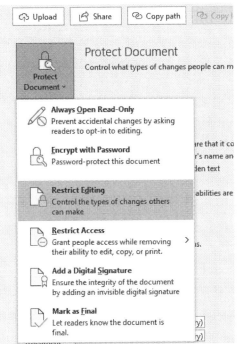

Figure 65: Restrict Editing Button

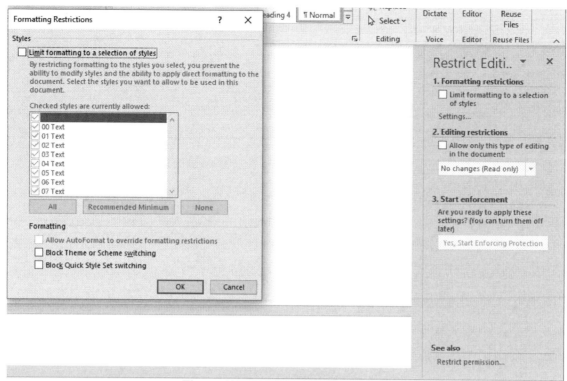

Figure 66: Formatting Restrictions Icon

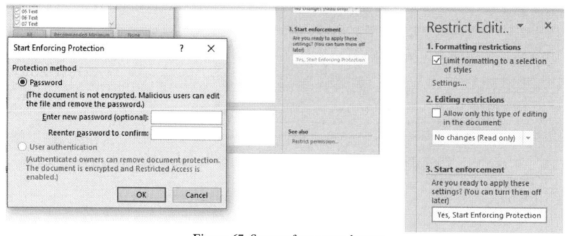

Figure 67: Start enforcement button

Turning Off These Style Restrictions

Return to the restrict editing task pane, and select the stop protection button (figure 67). Enter your password in the unprotected document dialogue box and click OK. When this is done, it turns off the style restrictions from the password-protected copy of the file you shared with other users.

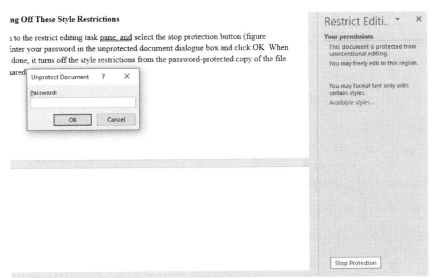

Figure 68: Stop protection button

Note: You will have to share your password with them if you would like them to turn off the protection also.

8 Numerations and Bulletins

Numeration: This refers to the numbering of a document. Word display counters for numbering, such as 1.1.2, but creating specific symbols and numbers in separate places makes it easy for users to reference. Word uses numbers in basic format: the first digit followed by a decimal point and then a second digit or number with a letter or symbol signifying the position (1, 2, 3, etc...). Bullets: This function allows users to create the 'bullets' or the numbered items in a document. Word uses bullets in different styles, but all can be customized according to the user's preference. A bullet point is a short line that serves as proof or an idea that is easy for readers to comprehend and digest.

Bullets and numbers are used to list things in the document. For example, they are used to attract the reader's attention to the pace to which something is moving or the importance attached to a specific through the arrangement of the list. Bullet and number lists are located under the paragraph section in the Home tab.

CREATING A BULLET LIST

The bullet is an icon people use to list an item in a document. The bullet can be a dot, a small square, a marked sign, and so on. When you arrange a list with a bullet, such an item will be indented. To make a list with a bullet, study the steps below:

- Place your cursor pointer to the line where you want to start the bullet list.

- Tap on the **Home tab** and move to the paragraph section.

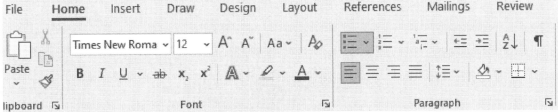

Figure 69: Home bullet option

- Then click on the **bullets down button** and select **any bullet style** you want. The bullet you selected will be reflected.

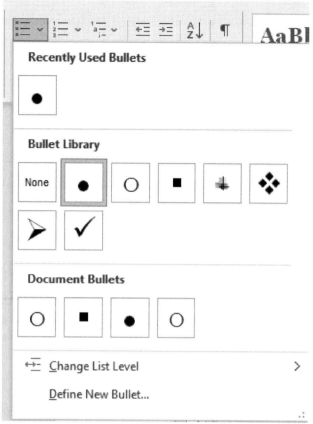

Figure 70: Bullet types

- Type whatever you want, and press **Enter** to move to the next line with an automatic bullet list. The more Enter you click, the more bullet list you will have.

Note: bullet has its paragraph and indent formatting. Click on the bullet icon again to stop the automatic bullet listing.

To customize your list bullet:

Select **Define New Bullet**

A Define New Bullet dialog box appears.

Set the **character** and **alignment** as desired, then press **OK**

- Select **Symbol** to use a symbol as your listing icon. A symbol dialog box appears. Choose your desired symbol, press OK, and your symbol will be set as your listing icon.

- Select **Picture** to use an online picture or any picture on your computer as a list icon.

- Select **Font** to set the **font style**, **size,** and the **effects** of your list icons.

CREATING A NUMBER LIST

A numbering list is a common type of listing an item of a document. To number a list, do well:

1. Place your cursor pointer to the line where you want to start the number list.

2. Tap on the **Home tab** and move to the paragraph section.

3. Then click on **numbering** and select any **numbering style** you want. The number style you selected will be reflected on the first line.

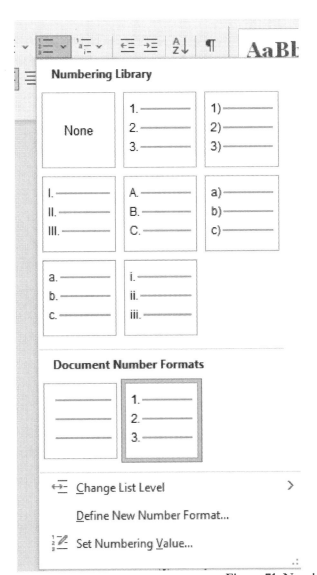

Figure 71: Numbering styles

4. Press **Enter** to move to the next item with automatic numbering; the more Enter you click the number list, the more number list you will have.

Note: click on no number to remove the number list, and click on the "number list" icon to stop automatic numbering.

To customize your numbered list:

Select **Define New Number Format**

A **Define New Number Format** dialog box appears.

Select and set the **format** /**alignment** as desired.

Selecting bullets or the numbering command will change the list style if your cursor is already in numbered or bulleted lists.

Also available is a **Multilevel list** command for you to use if your list has a sub-list.

Figure 72: Multilevel list

You can format the listing style by right-clicking on the list and selecting an option as desired.

ADDING MULTILEVEL LIST

As its name denotes multilevel, the listing is of various types. It has the main listing, sub, and sub-sub listing. Word will automatically carry out the multilevel listing for you. To do multilevel listing, study the below guideline:

1. Insert the **first item in the list** to the line without numbering it.

2. Tap on the **Home tab,** move to the paragraph section, and then click on the **multilevel menu button.**

3. Choose the **desired multilevel style**, and immediately the first number will be attached with a number or alphabet depending on the multilevel style you choose.

Figure 73: desired multilevel style

4. Press the **tab key** for the sub-listing item and **Enter another tab key** for the sub-sub listing.

Note: you will use a tab to move from main to sub and sub-sub listing. You will use **Tab +Shift** to move back from the sub-listing and main listing.

9 The Power of Find and Replace

We started looking at some of the basic ways to use your keyboard to navigate around your document in the previous chapters. In this chapter, you'll be introduced to a few more utilities you can use in Word to navigate your document and increase your efficiency when working with your documents. In addition, this chapter will concentrate on the Go to, Find, and Replace options.

Looking for a Word

When working with enormous files, you may require a quick way to get to a specific page or to replace a word in a document.

To access your "**Find**" and "**Replace**" options, click at the top of your document, then go to the **home** ribbon. Across on the right-hand side is an editing group, where you'll find them. In addition, you can see that "**Find**" has a little drop-down arrow next to it, indicating that it offers three options: **Find**, **Advanced Find**, and "**Go to.**"

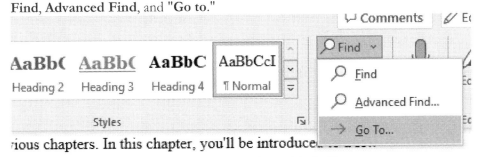

Figure 74: Go To

In this example, we'll start on "**Find**," which opens up a little navigation window on the left-hand side where you can put in exactly what you're looking for. It brings up results once you type in the term you're looking for, and you can see them listed underneath in the results section and highlighted in your document, making it incredibly easy to find them. By clicking on the cross, you can close this navigation panel. That's one approach to searching your document for a specific word.

You can go by **Section**; you'll learn how to break your text into sections in later chapters, and then you can go to any area you want.

By going to a specific line number, you can navigate by **Line**.

You can navigate via **Bookmark**; bookmarks are something we'll talk about later, but they're a way of placing a small bookmark in a specific spot on a page so you can jump to it fast.

You can also use any **Comments** you have in the text to browse.

We also have **Footnotes**, **Endnotes**, **Fields**, **Tables**, and other features. Of course, which one you use depends on what you have in your document at the time. But keep in mind that those Go to choices are still available.

Figure 75: Find results

Using advanced Find to Search Your Document

If you select Advanced Find, you'll be sent to a little dialog box that asks you what you're looking for and displays the last item you looked for. If you want to skip this one by one, you can say "**Find Next,**" which will highlight the word in the document the first time it finds it. You can then say "**Find Next**" again to step through each one in your document one at a time, and when you get to the end, it will tell you it's finished searching, and you can click OK.

Figure 76: Find Next

Getting specify With Find

The "**More**" option in this Find and Replace box is also something to be mindful of. When you click it, you'll see that you have many options. For example, you can tell it to **match the case**, meaning it will only find the word "firm" if it matches that case. So if the word "firm" is in this document with an uppercase F, it won't find it because you told it to match the case.

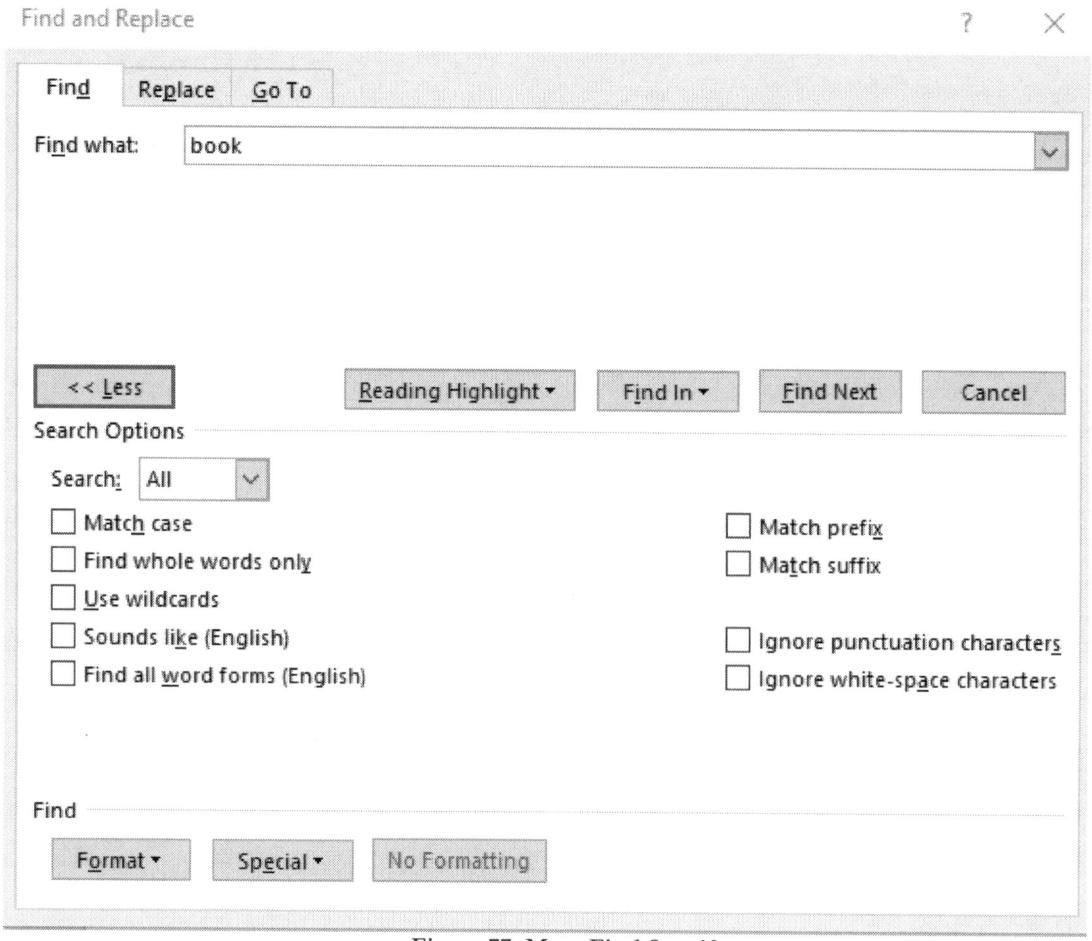

Figure 77: More Find Specify

You can choose to "**Find whole words only**," which means that if what you're looking for is a part of another word, it won't be found.

You can also say "**Use Wildcards**" and place a wildcard in front of the word, midway in the middle, or at the end. If you type in A*, for example, it will discover everything in that document that begins with an A, regardless of what comes after it. You can also include a wildcard at the start, such as *S, which implies it will look for anything that ends in S, regardless of what follows before it. It's worth noting that wildcards come in handy when looking for specific items. Another thing you can do up here is to type "A" and then two question marks (A??) to indicate that the word must begin with an A and contain no more than three characters in total. It doesn't matter what those three characters are, but they must be three.

You can also use the "**Sounds Like**" option to find words that sound similar to the one you're looking for. It might pick up words like turn, burn, study, or anything along those lines for a word like "firm," for example.

"**Find all word forms**" will find any form of that word, and you can then choose between "**Match prefix**," "**Match suffix**," "**Ignore punctuation**," and "Ignore whitespace characters," among other possibilities. Finally, remember that beneath the "More" drop-down, you have various options for customizing what you're looking for in your document, which can become very detailed.

Replace One Word with Another

Make sure you're at the top of my document and select the "**Replace**" option this time. We have "**Replace**" under "**Find**" in the editing group, which allows you to **replace one word with another**. For instance, if you want to replace the name "Smith" in your document with "Ashby," you may say find "Smith" and replace it with "Ashby," and you'll have all of the prior possibilities to choose from. If you merely want to replace Smith with Ashby, pick "**Replace all**." You'll get a little window telling you that the replacements have been made, and if you look at the document behind you, Smith has been replaced. This is a quick and easy technique to replace several words in a document.

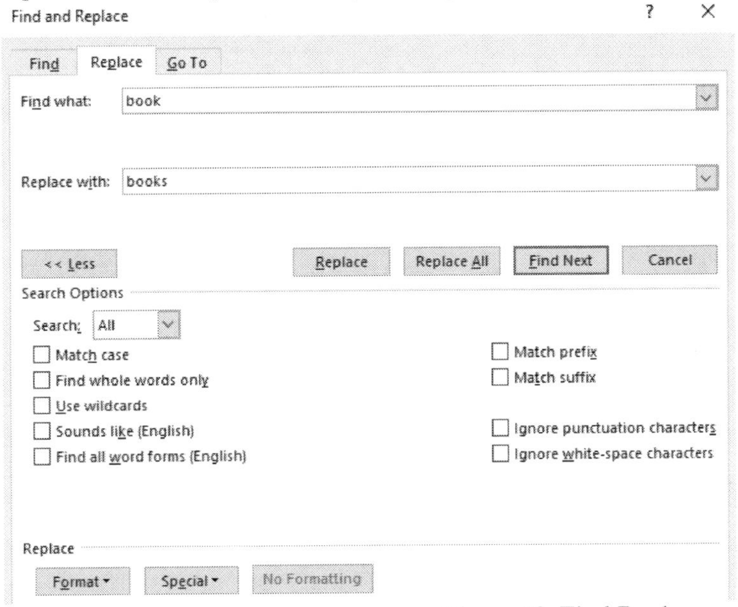

Figure 78: Find Replace

Go to any point in your document

The "**Go to**" option, which lets you perform different things in your document, is the last item you should know in this chapter. When you go to Find and select the "**Go To**" option, you'll be able to browse around your document. You can accomplish this by entering a page number and saying "**Go To**"; for example, if you input page 2 and say "Go To," it will take you to page 2.

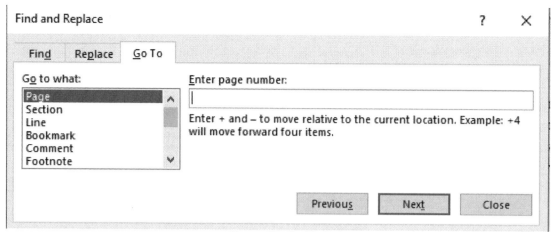

Figure 79: Go To Point

You can go by **Section**; you'll learn how to break your text into sections in later chapters, and then you can go to any area you want.

By going to a specific line number, you can navigate by **Line**.

You can navigate via **Bookmark**; bookmarks are something we'll talk about later, but they're a way of placing a small bookmark in a specific spot on a page so you can jump to it fast.

You can also use any **Comments** you have in the text to browse.

We also have **Footnotes**, **Endnotes**, **Fields**, **Tables**, and other features. Of course, which one you use depends on what you have in your document at the time. But keep in mind that those Go to choices are still available.

10 Footer and Header of the Page

Page footers:

This refers to the text that appears at the bottom of every page of your document. It includes the page number, time and date, or any other information you need. In addition, word allows you to create a custom page footer for any document. Go to the Layout tab - Page Setup and select your custom page footer under the 'Footer' option.

Header: This refers to title information usually found at the top of every page in a document. This includes the page name, title, and author name. Word allows you to set your header information with a particular font style, size, alignment, and other settings.

INSERTING HEADER OR FOOTER

A **Header** is a text added to the top margin of every page of a document. At the same time, a **footer** is a text added to the bottom Margin to give information about the document, e.g., the title, page number, image, logo, etc.

To add a Header or Footer to your document:

1. Go to the **Insert** ribbon.

2. Select **Header** or **Footer** command.

A drop-down menu appears with header or footer styles.

3. Click on the desired style.

Word activates the top and bottom margin for your header or footer insertion.

4. Replace the text with your desired text.

5. Click on the **Close Header and Footer** command when you are done.

Alternatively,

1. Double-click in the top or bottom margin to activate the header and footer area.

2. Insert your footer or header.

3. Double-click outside the margin area or press the **Esc** key to go back to your document.

You can always use the above method to edit your header or footer. Also available is a contextual **Design** tab you can use to design your header or footer.

To delete your header or footer, just delete the text and close the header and footer.

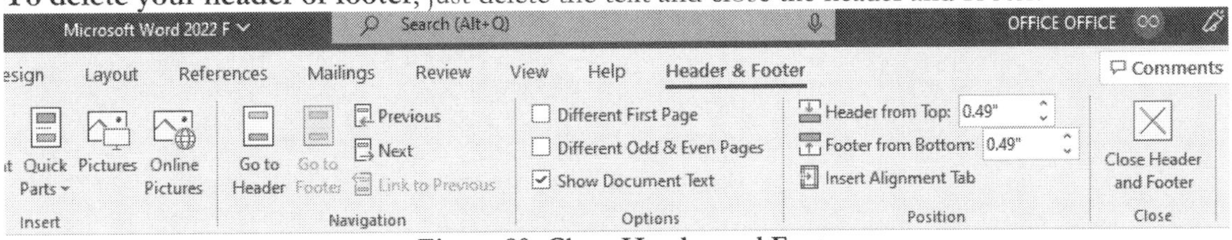

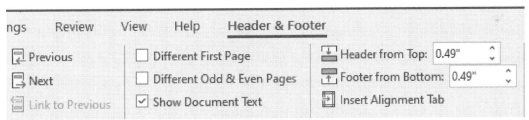

Figure 80: Close Header and Footer

Inserting Different Headers or Footers in Word

To insert a separate Header or Footer for a Separate Section:

1. Insert **Next Page** section breaks where you want different headers or footers to start.

2. Activate the headers or footers of each section.

In the **Navigation** group of the **Header & Footer** Tools ribbon;

3. Deselect the **Link to** the **Previous** button to disconnect the sections.

4. Add the header or footer for each section or chapter.

5. To put a different header on the document's first page or a section, Check the **Different First Page** box.

6. To put a right-justified header for some pages and a left-justified header for some pages, check the **Different Odd & Even Pages** box.

Figure 81: Link to the Previous

7. Close the header/footer when done with the settings.

Saving Headers or Footers for Later Use

In case you are using a particular header or footer to create so many documents, it will be advisable to save the header/footer.

To save your header or footer for later use:

1. Activate and select all the header or footer contents you want to save.

2. Click the **Header** or **Footer** drop-down button as the case may be.

3. Select **Save Selection to Header Gallery** or **Save Selection to Footer Gallery,** depending on whether you select Header or Footer.

Figure 82: Save Selection to Header Gallery

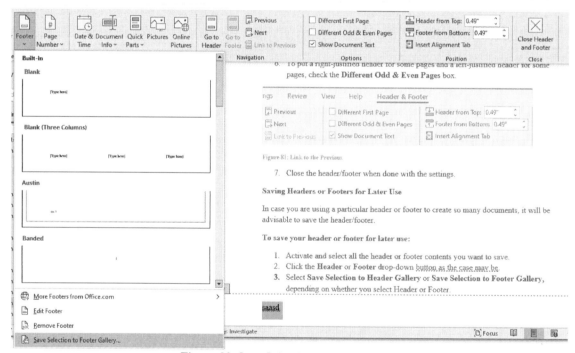

Figure 83: Save Selection to Footer Gallery

A dialog box appears.

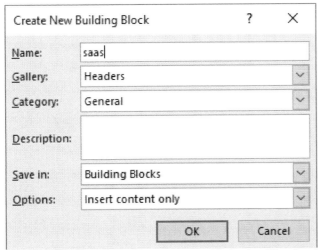

Figure 84: Saving Header Gallery Dialog box

4. Input the name you want to give the header or footer and do any other desired settings.
5. Press **OK,** and your header or footer will be saved.

You can access and apply the header or footer at any time in the drop-down list of the **Header** or **Footer** drop button. You might have to scroll down to see your preferred options.
To delete your saved header or footer:
1. Right-click on it.
2. Select Organize and Delete.

A dialog box appears highlighting the header or footer.
1. Click the **Delete** button.
2. Press **yes** to confirm the prompt that appears.
3. Press **Close** in the dialog box and your header or footer will no longer be in the gallery.

11 Images and Tables

Images and tables: how to insert them, how to add new lines and columns in an existing table, what's a caption and what are the caption types, how to insert a caption, what's the automatic updating of the number inside a caption, how to take a screenshot, what's copyright and how to choose image copyright free/public domain/royalty free, etc.
While working on your document, there are times you need to illustrate your work with shapes, pictures, or images and a movable textbox. Word provides features that enable you to do that without stress. Below are step-by-step guides on how to work with illustrations in your document.

11.1 Inserting Images

To add an image to your document:
1. Place your cursor where you want your picture to be.
2. Go to the **Insert** ribbon.
3. Click the **Picture** command in the **Illustration** group.

The **Insert Picture From** menu box appears.
4. a. Select **This Device** if your image is on your computer.

An **Insert Picture** dialog box appears.

b. Select **Online Picture** if you want to use an online image.
Your default browser opens.

5. a. Select and open the image folder. Frow the left menu, you can open another location to search for the image. Select your image.

b. Browse for your desired image.

6. Click the **Insert** button or double-click on the image.

Alternatively, copy the image wherever it is and paste it into your document.

INSERTING SCREENSHOTS

You can insert screenshots of any opened window on your system in your document.

To capture and insert a screenshot in your document:

1. Place your mouse where you want your screenshot to be.
2. Open and display the image or document you want to capture on your computer screen.
3. Click on the **Insert** tab.
4. Select **Screenshot** in the **Illustration** group.

A drop-down menu appears, showing you the available whole window screenshots.

5. a. Select the desired available screenshot if you want to capture the whole screen, and Word automatically inserts the screenshot in your document.

b. Select **Screen Clipping** to capture a part of any of the windows.
Your cursor turns to a plus icon, and your screen turns blurred.

6. Click, hold, and drag the mouse to select your desired portion of the window.
7. Release your hand when done, and Word automatically inserts your selected window portion into your document.

NOTE: To insert your desktop screenshot, close or minimize all documents that can interfere with the screen. You do not need to close the document you are working with, for Word closes it automatically when you select **Screen Clipping** as you follow the above steps.

INSERTING SHAPES

Different shapes, like circles, rectangles, lines, arrows, and more, are available in Word for your use.

To add shapes to your document:

1. Click the **Insert** tab.
2. Select the **Shapes** to command in the **Illustrations** group.

The Shapes dialog box appears with all the available shapes.

3. Click on any of the shapes as desired.

Your cursor turns to a cross.

4. Move to the location in your document where you want your shape to be.
5. Click and drag to draw the shape to the desired size.

Tips: The shape turns itself off after each use to keep it active for continuous use,

- Select and right-click on it
- Select **Lock Drawing Mode** from the menu that appears.
- Draw the shape as many times as desired.
- Press the **Esc** key or click on the shape icon again when you are done.

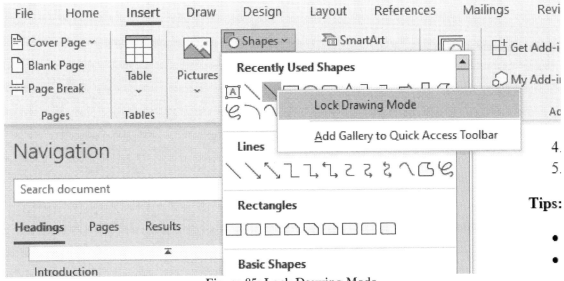

Figure 85: Lock Drawing Mode

You can as well add text to your shape.

To add text to your shape:

1. Click inside the shape.
2. Type in your text.

Format your text just like any other text in your document as desired.

ADDING SMARTART TO YOUR DOCUMENT.

SmartArt visually communicates essential ideas, information, and processes with a graphical presentation.

Word has a SmartArt gallery consisting of a list, process, cycle, hierarchy, etc., to meet your specific requirement.

To add a SmartArt to your document:

1. Place the insertion point where you want your SmartArt.
2. Go to **Insert** ribbon.
3. Click on **SmartArt** in the **Illustration** group.

A dialog box appears.

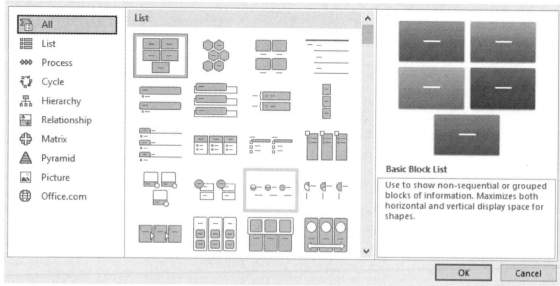

Figure 86: SmartArt

4. Click on the SmartArt type that best describes what you want to do, e.g., list, process, cycle, etc.
5. Select one of the SmartArt type varieties as desired.
6. Press **OK,** and Word inserts the SmartArt with a pane.
7. Replace the **SmartArt** pane text with your texts.

For more items, press **Enter** in the last item, and Word automatically creates more places for you to continue.

With the SmartArt is contextual **Design** and **Format** tabs for you to format your **SmartArt.**

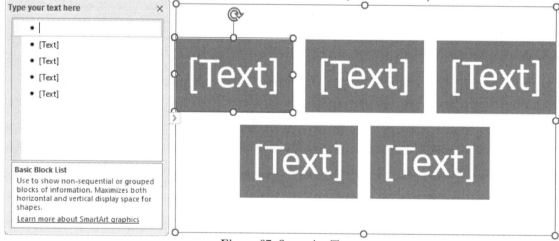

Figure 87: SmartArt Text

Designing SmartArt

Various options are available to set up, organize and design your SmartArt to your taste after inserting it.

To design your SmartArt:
1. Select the SmartArt.
2. Go to the contextual **SmartArt Design** tab.

3. Make the desired changes:

- Click on **Change Color** or the **SmartArt Styles** gallery drop-down arrow to see the list of different color templates you can select and apply to your SmartArt.

- To rearrange your points in the SmartArt, select the shape and click the **Move Up** or **Move Down** commands in the **Create Graphic** group.

- To change the list level of a selected shape or bullet, click the **Promote**, or **Demote** command in the **Create Graphic** group.

- You can change the SmartArt layout from left to right and vice visa by selecting or deselecting the **Right to Left** command.

- If you need more than the three available shapes, click the **Add Shape** button in the **Create Graphic** group to add more shapes.

- If you need more than the available bullet on the shape, click the **Add Bullet** button in the **Create Graphic** group to add more bullets.

- You can hide or Unhide the text pane on your slide by clicking the **Text Pane** button in the **Create Graphic** group.

- You can convert your SmartArt to text or shapes by clicking the **Convert** drop-down arrow and selecting the desired option.

- If your SmartArt has picture icons, click on the icon, and follow the prompt to add your desired picture.

- Click the **Reset Graphic** button to undo all the settings if you wish to.

Figure 88: SmartArt Design

WORKING WITH TEXTBOX

A textbox is an object that allows you to type your text and place it anywhere in your document. Using a textbox makes working with text flexible.

To insert a textbox:
1. Click the **Insert** tab.
2. Select the **Text box** in the **Text** group.

A dialog box appears with preformatted textbox options.
3. Select an option as desired, and the textbox appears in your document or

-Select **More Text Box from Office.com** to get more text box options on the Microsoft Office website.
Select **Draw Text Box** if you want to draw your text box to your desired size manually. Your cursor turns to a cross.

- Click the point you want to put your textbox and drag it to draw to your desired size.
4. Type in your text and click anywhere outside the box when you are done.

To Edit your text box:
1. Double click on the text box and edit like a normal word document.
2. Use your arrow keys to navigate in the textbox.

WORKING WITH WORDART

A WordArt is a form of a textbox with additional styles. Word has a gallery of WordArt with different styles that you can quickly apply to your texts to change their appearance and styles.

To use WordArt in your document:
1. Click on the **Insert** tab.
2. Select **WordArt** in the **Text** group.

WordArt drop-down menu appears.
3. Click on the desired style, which appeared in your document as a text box with the text format as the style of letter **A** in the gallery.
4. Type in your text and click anywhere outside the box when you are done.

To Edit your text box:
1. Double click on the text box and edit like a normal word document.
2. Use your arrow keys to navigate in the textbox.

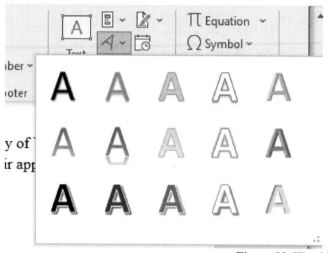

Figure 89: WordArt

OBJECT LAYOUT (MAKE OBJECT FLOATS WITH TEXT WRAPPING)

Word inserts an object **in line** with text by default, but options can change the object layout relative to the text. Using any of the **With Text Wrapping** options makes your object float, i.e., you can select and move it freely to any location, whether there is text or no text in the place. It also allows you to write on your image.

To make your object float:
1. Select the object.

2. Click the **Layout Options** icon that appears at the top right side of the object, or Go to the contextual **Format** ribbon and select **Wrap Text.**

A drop-down menu appears.
3. Select an option in the **With Text Wrapping** option depending on how you want your image to relate to the text.

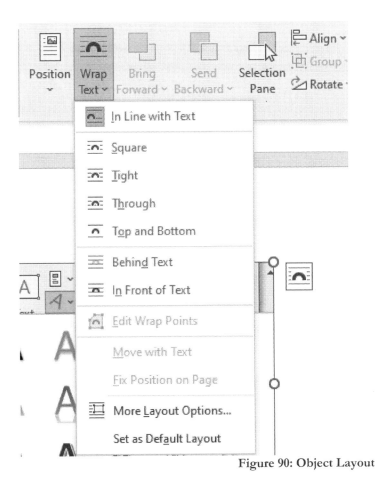

Figure 90: Object Layout

Hover on each option to see their names and how the layout works with the text with the icon. For example, this icon ⬆ called **Behind Text** shows that the object will be at the back of the text if it is moved to where there is text.

There are also two options for moving the object with text or fixing the object's position on the page. Check any of the desired options.

For more layout, select **See more**.

FORMATTING AND EDITING OBJECTS

Objects are shape, picture, image, screenshot, WordArt, Textbox, and SmartArt. When selected, any objects will have a contextual object **Format** tab that can be used to format the object. Most of the Format commands are the same across all the objects, and most are for visual effects enhancement of the object.

Selecting an Object

To format an object, the first thing you do is select the object. Follow the steps below to select an object:

- Click inside of the object.
- Move your cursor to any part of the object outline. Your cursor turns to four-headed arrows.
- Click on the outline.

Deleting an Object

1. Select the image you want to delete.

Selection handles appear around the image.

2. Press Delete or Backspace button on your keyboard, and your image is removed.

Applying Visual Effects Enhancement to an Object

MS Word has impressive features that you can use to make changes to your object after you have inserted it into your document. You can make the following changes with Word features.

For pictures and some other objects:

- **Corrections:** It adjusts your image brightness, contrast, sharpness, or softness in different proportions.
- **Color:** It changes the color of your image with different shades from color to black and white.
- **Artistic Effects:** It changes your image to look like a sketch or paint of different styles.
- **Compress Pictures:** It reduces the size of your image.
- **Change Picture:** It makes you change your picture to another one retaining the size and format of your current picture.
- **Reset Picture:** To undo all the changes you have made to the image.
- **Picture Border:** It helps to put an outline around the image, and the outline color, width, and style can be changed as desired.
- **Picture Effects:** It applies effects like shadow, reflection, glows, etc., to your image.
- **Picture Layout:** It makes your image easy to edit by converting it to a SmartArt graphic.

Figure 91: Graphic Layout

Other formatting features for most objects include:

- **Object Fill** : Selecting this command fills your shape with the default or last applied color. Click on the drop-down button to select a desired fill color in the color palette.

- **Object Outline** : Selecting this command, put borders around your object with the default or last applied color. Click on the drop-down button to select a desired outline color in the color palette.

- **Object Effect** : This gives your object some artistic effects like shadow, reflection, glow, 3-D rotation, etc. Click on the command, select from the effects option, and choose a desired version of the effects.

- **Object Style:** This contains a gallery of preformatted objects for your quick use.

Figure 92: Shape Formats

To make changes to your object using any of the features above:

1. Select the object.

The object **Format** contextual tab appears.

2. Click the object **Format** tab.

3. Select the effect you want to apply, e.g., **Corrections, Border, Artistic Effects, fill, etc.**

4. If the effect has a drop-down icon, click on it, and select an option as desired.

The object style in the **Format** ribbon depends on the type of object you inserted.

Remove Picture Background with MS Word

Word has a feature that can help you remove the background of your picture for quick use.

To remove an image background:

1. Select the picture or image. Picture Format tab appears.

2. Go to the **Picture Format** tab

Figure 93: Remove image background

3. Select the **Remove Background** command.

Word changes the color of the background it wants to remove and opens the **Background Removal** ribbon for you to adjust.

4. Click the **Mark Areas to Keep** button, go to your image and mark out some part you would like to keep if there is any.

5. Click the **Mark Areas to Remove** button, move your cursor to your image and mark out some part you wish to remove but was not highlighted if any.

6. Select **Keep Changes** to remove the background when you are done or

7. Select **Discard All Changes** to keep the picture's background.

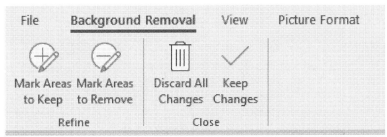

Figure 94: Background removal

Writing on an Image/Picture

To write on an image:

1. Insert your image.
2. Change your image layout to **Behind Text** in the **With Text Wrapping** option.
3. Insert a textbox or WordArt and format as desired.
4. Move your text to the top of the image.
5. Select the Image and the textbox or WordArt.
6. Group them.

Note: Consult other sections of this chapter on how to insert, text wrapping, and group objects.

RESIZING AND CROPPING OBJECT

To resize your image:
1. Select the image you want to resize.

Handle borders appear around the image.
2. Click and drag on any of the handles as desired.

The image changes size as you drag it to the left, right, up, or down.
3. Release your mouse when the size of the image is as desired.

Note: Use the corner handles for uniform increase/decrease in your image size.

7. Select **Discard All Changes** to keep the pictu

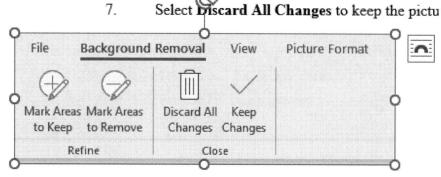

Figure 95: Image resizing

Alternatively,
1. Select the object.

2. Go to the contextual **Format** tab.

3. Enter the actual height and width in the text boxes provided (or use the arrows) in the **Size** group.

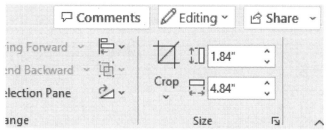

Figure 96: Image resizing (b)

Cropping
Cropping an image allows you to remove some outer parts of an image.
To crop an image:
1. Click the image you want to crop.

2. Go to the object **Format** tab.

3. Click the **Crop** button in the Size group.

A crop handle appears around the image borders
4. -Drag the **side cropping handle** inside to crop the side

- Drag the **corner cropping handle** inside to crop two adjacent sides equally and simultaneously.

- To crop two parallel sides simultaneously, press and hold down the **Ctrl** key as you drag the side cropping handle simultaneously.

     5.   Press **Esc** on your keyboard when you are done.

Figure 97: Crop element

For more cropping options, click on the **Crop** command drop-down icon and select an option from the menu.

-      The **Crop to Shape** allows you to crop your image to the desired shape from the list that appears.

-      **Aspect Ratio** gives you some ratio at which you can crop your work.

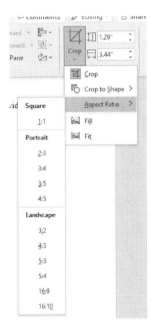

Figure 98: Aspect Ratio

Can you try something like this?
MOVING, ROTATING, AND FLIPPING IMAGE
To move your image from one place to the other:

     1.   Select the image.

Handle borders appear around the image.

     2.   Click, hold down, and drag the image to the desired location.

To copy, cut, and paste an object

     1.   Click the object to select it.

The object border appears.

  2. Click the border of the object

-Press **Ctrl + C** to copy or **Ctrl + X** to cut
Alternatively,
 -Right-click on the border. A dialog box appears.
-Select **Cut** or **Copy** as desired.

  3. Move your cursor where you want the text box to be

  4. Press **Ctrl + V** to paste the text box.

To rotate your image:

  1. Click the image you want to rotate.

Handle borders appear around the image.

  2. Select the rotating handle at the top of the image.

Your cursor turns to a circular arrow.

  3. Rotate the image clockwise or anticlockwise as desired.

Alternatively, and in other to **flip** the image:

  1. Select the image you want to rotate/flip.

  2. Go to the **Picture Format** tab.

  3. Click the **Rotate** command in the **Arrange** group.

A drop-down menu appears.

  4. Select an option.

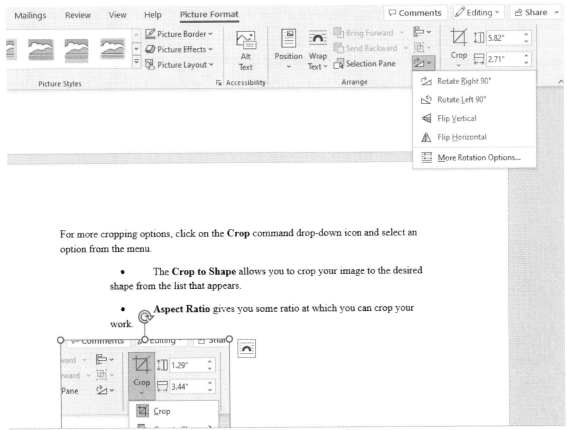

Figure 99: Image rotation

ALIGNING, ORDERING, AND GROUPING OBJECTS IN WORD

Suppose you work with multiple objects like images/pictures, shapes, textbox, and WordArt in your document. In that case, knowing how to align appropriately, order, and group objects is essential.

NOTE: To align, order, or group objects, you need to select them, and for you to be able to select multiple objects in Word, you must ensure that their layout is any of the **With Text Wrapping** options.

Aligning Objects

To align two or more objects:

1.   Hold down the **Ctrl** or **Shift** key and click on the individual objects you want to align to select them.

2.   Click on the **object Format** tab

3.   Select **Align** command in the **Arrange** group. Align drop-down options appear.

4.   Word aligns the objects in their current position by default. For example, select an option in the 3rd group to align with the page or margin.

5.   Select one of the alignment options as desired.

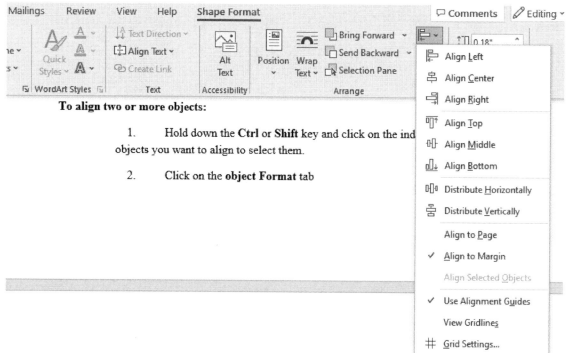

Figure 100: Align object

Note: The alignment options in the 1st and 2nd groups are relative to the 3rd group options. You can use the second group to **equally** distribute your objects horizontally or vertically in the 3rd group.

Ordering Objects

Ordering an object is essential when two or more objects will have to overlap. Objects are placed on top of one another according to the order in which you inserted them into your document, creating different **levels**. Ordering the objects means changing their levels as desired.

To change an object's level:

1. Select the object you want to change its level.

2. Click the **Format** tab.

3. Click the **Send Backward** or **Bring Forward** drop-down in the **Arrange** group.

A drop-down menu appears.

4. Select an option, and Word automatically reorders your object.

   ○ **Send Backward** and **Bring Forward** send your object one level backward and forward, respectively.

   ○ **Send to Back and Bring to Front**; send your object behind and in front of all objects.

   ○ **Send Behind Text and Bring in Front of Text** makes the text and image feasible, respectively.

Alternatively, to have more control over your ordering,
Select the **Selection Pane** command in the Arrange group.

The selection navigation pane appears on the right side of your window with the list of all the objects starting from the first object at the top to the last at the back.

. To rearrange, Select, Drag, and Drop any object to the desired level.

Grouping or Ungrouping Objects

You may sometimes want some of your objects to stay together when working on your document. This can be achieved by grouping.

To group objects:

1. Select your objects by holding the **Ctrl** or **Shift** key and clicking on the individual objects.

2. Click on the **Format** tab.

3. Select **Group** in the **Resize** group.

Then your objects will be a singular object that can be moved, resized, and formatted together like one.

To Ungroup your objects:

1. Select the grouped object.

2. Click on the **Format** tab.

3. Select the **Group** command drop-down icon.

4. Select **Ungroup** from the menu that appears

Copyrights:

Copyright laws are the rules that govern how authors and publishers distribute, sell and use their work. These laws protect authors and publishers who have created original works. For more information, check out Wikipedia.

Image copyright free/public domain:

Image copyright-free indicates images that are free of any copyright restrictions. This means that every person can use the pictures without having to pay or get permission from any other person who owns the copyright of the picture.

Image copyright free/public domain can be found in the following sources:

* Flickr.com, a marketplace for images and art created by the community

* Pexels.com, commercial-free stock photos from different sources all over the world.

* Pixabay.com is a growing collection of public domain photos uploaded by users and can be used for free under their CC0 license.

* Depositphotos.com is an excellent illustration stock photography and illustrations free of copyright restrictions.

Royalty-free or Creative Commons:

Creative Commons is an organization that provides tools for copyright-free material to be shared and distributed on the internet and also applies certain conditions regarding these sharing rights. This means that the usage of the material can be flexible. However, the third party who wants to use this material has to agree to the terms of use and license agreement.

11.2 What is a Table

A table is a grid of cells organized into rows and columns. Tables are used to organize any form of content, be it text or numerical data, for typing, editing, and formatting appropriately in your document. The following are the components of a table:

- **Cell**: This is the box formed when the row and column intersect.

- **Header row: This is the name of the label along** the top row that describes what is in the column.

- **Row labels**: These are the labels in the first column that explain what is in each row.

- **Borders**: These are the lines indicating where the rows and columns are.

- **Gridlines** are the gray lines that reveal where the columns and rows are. The grid lines do not appear unless they are enabled. To display the gridlines, go to (Table Tools) and click on the View Gridlines button.

Creating a table

We have numerous ways to create a table in Word. Below are the method of creating a table:

- Drag the table menu

- Insert the table using the Insert Table dialog box

- Draw a table

- Convert text to table

- Create a quick table

- Construct a table from an Excel worksheet.

How to create a Table by Dragging the Table Menu

You can create a table by dragging the table menu. To do this, follow the steps below

- Select the **Insert** tab and click on **Table** in the **Table** group

Figure 101: Insert table

- A drop-down menu is open containing a grid. Hover over the **Grid** to select the numbers of columns and rows you want.

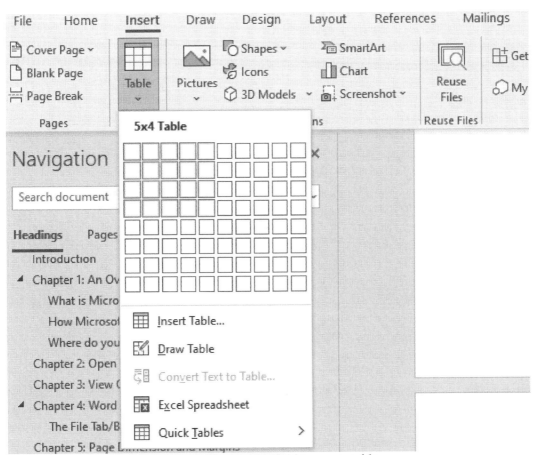

Figure 102: Grid to create table

- Click on the **Grid**, release your mouse, and the table will appear.

Inserting the Table Using the Insert Table Dialog Box

Another way to create a table is by using the Insert Table dialog box. To insert a table using the Insert Table dialog box, follow the steps given below:

- Go to the **Insert** tab and click on **Table** in the **Table** group

- In the drop-down menu, click on **Insert Table**

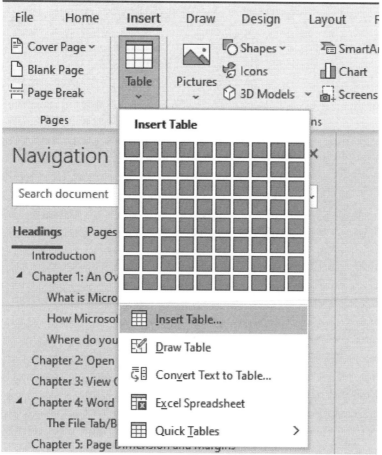

Figure 103: Insert Table Dialog Box

- In the Insert Table dialog box, enter the number of columns and rows and how you want the column to **Autofit.**

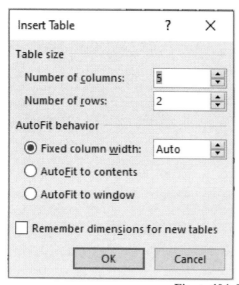

Figure 104: Insert Table Dialog Box Autofit

- Then click on **Ok.**

INSERTING TABLE

Tables give you a convenient way to display information that might otherwise be bulky and confusing.

EDITING A TABLE

The following will explain how to edit your table.

Inserting Rows and Columns

To Insert Rows and Columns;

- Move the cursor to the row or column you want adjacent to the reference. This selects the table, and the **Table Design and Layout** tabs appear.

- Select the **Layout** tab.

- Choose **Insert Above, Insert Below,** or **Insert Left** or **Insert Right** depending on where you want the new row or column.

Figure 105: Editing your table

Movement within a Table

To move within your table

What to do	What it does
To select an entire table	Go to the top left corner of a table and click on the table move handle.
To select an entire column	Drag over the column's content or Click the column top border.
To select an entire row	Drag over the row's content or Place your mouse pointer on the left margin pointing to your desired row and click.
To select a single cell	Drag over the cell's content or click thrice inside the cell.
Keyboard Arrow Keys	Arrow keys will move up and down, left and right.
Tab	The **Tab** key is used to move from left to right.
Shift + Tab	Use **Shift +Tab** to move from right to left.

Adjusting Column Width

To adjust column width;

Columns in a newly added table have the same width. However, sometimes there's the need to change the column width to accommodate the data entered.

Using the mouse:

- Place your mouse pointer on the column boundary—the mouse pointer changes to a double vertical line with the left and right arrows.

- Drag the mouse pointer to the direction you want to change the width.

- Release the mouse button when you are satisfied with the width size.

Using AutoFit:

AutoFit in Word is a feature that will automatically adjust your column width to accommodate the widest text entered in any table column. It is more advisable to **AutoFit** the entire table.

- Place your mouse pointer at the left-most column boundary; the mouse pointer appears as a double vertical line with the left and right arrows.

- Double-click on the mouse button.

Using the Table Tools:

- Click in the cell within the column to be resized.

- Click the **Layout** tab.

- In the **Width** box, click on the up (increase) or down (decrease) arrow to change the width.

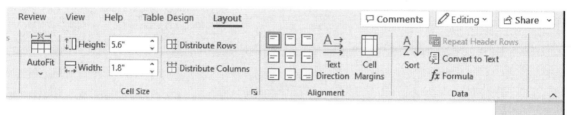

Figure 106: Using table tools

Merge Cells, Split Cells, or Table
To Merge Cells, Split Cells, or Table;
To merge cells means to combine two or more adjacent cells to form a single cell. Splitting cells is the opposite.

- Select the cells you want to merge or split or all the cells in the table boundary you want to split.

- Click **Layout.**

- Click **Merge Cells, Split Cells, or Split Table,** depending on your task.

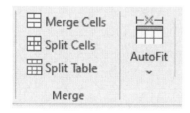

Figure 107: Merging or splitting table

Delete Cells, Rows, Columns, or Table
You may want to delete a Cell, Row, Column, or Table from your document.
To Delete Cells, Rows, Columns, and Table;

- Select the cell or cells to be deleted.

- Click the **Layout** tab.

- Click the **Delete** button. The delete options will appear.

- Choose from the available options the task you want to perform.

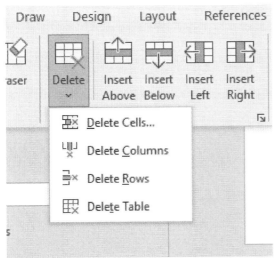

Figure 108: Table deletion actions

DRAWING A TABLE

While working with a table, you might want to add cells within a table or when you know your table is not going to be uniform.

To draw a table;

- Go to **insert**.

- Click **Tables**.

- Select **Draw Tables**. Your mouse pointer turns into a pencil tool, and you can draw within your document.

- Drag your mouse into your desired size and shape before releasing **it. Alternatively;**

- Click within the table in your document.

- Click the **Table Design** tab.

- Select **Draw Tables**.

ERASING PART OF A TABLE

To erase part of a table;

- Click within the table in your document.

- Click the **Table Design** tab.

- Select **Eraser.** Your mouse pointer turns into an eraser.

- Place your mouse over the table line to be removed.

- Drag the mouse over the line to erase. The line appears selected before you release your mouse.

- Release your mouse to erase the line.

- Repeat for as many lines as you want.

- When you are done, click **Esc**.

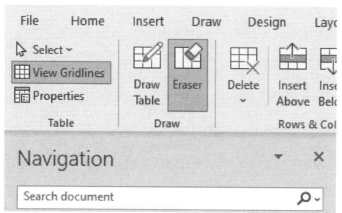

Figure 109: Erase table

FORMATTING A TABLE

While working with tables in Microsoft Word, it has several built-in table styles you can to your table for quick and consistent formatting or creates your own.

Gridline

Gridlines are borders that appear in your document when you add them while working with tables. Therefore, when working with tables, it is always advisable to put them on. Gridlines only appear as a format in your document but do not print.

To Turn On your Gridlines;

- Click within the table in your document.

- Click the **Layout** tab.

- Click **View Gridlines**. Gridlines will appear for all word documents.

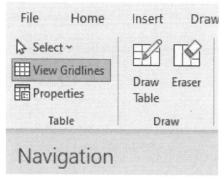

Figure 110: View gridlines

Applying Table Styles

Applying the same style to all the tables is advisable when working with multiple tables. Using the table styles rather than manually applying style to each table or direct formatting can be done. It ensures consistent formatting of your tables and saves a lot of time.

To apply a table style;

- Click within the table in your document.

- Click the **Table Design** tab.

- Click the More down arrow in the Table Styles for more styles, as shown below.

Figure 111: Table design styles

- Select from the available styles. Your table formatting will change as you hover over different table styles.

- Click your desired style to apply to your table.

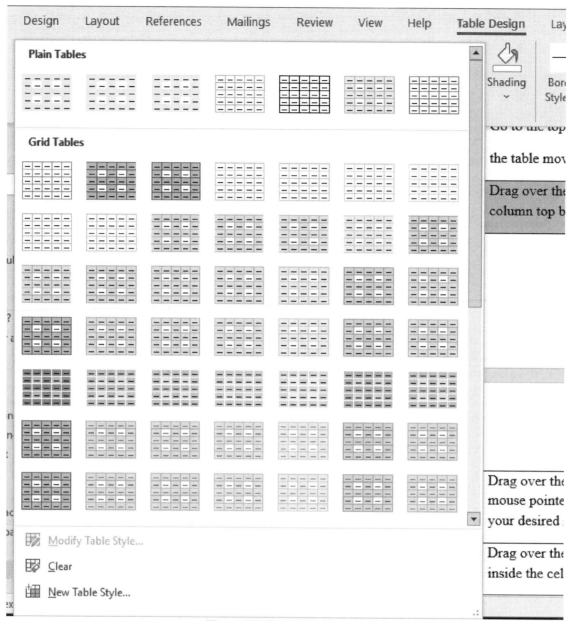

Figure 112: Desired table styles

Selecting Table Style Options

After applying your table style, there are different table options for you to select from it. These options affect the table style format.

To select Table Style Options;

- Click within the table in your document.

- Click the **Table Design** tab.

- Go to **Table Style Options**

- **Header Row**: If checked, the header row, i.e., the first row in a table containing headings for all columns, will be formatted differently from the body rows.

- **Total Row**: If checked, it will format the last row differently from the body rows. E.g., to create a row for mathematical totals.

- **Banded Rows/Columns**: If checked, format even and odd rows differently. There's alternate row/column shading, so they are easier to read.
- **First or the Last Column**: If checked, the first or last column is formatted differently from the other columns.

File	Home	Insert	Draw
☐ Header Row		☐ First Column	
☐ Total Row		☐ Last Column	
☑ Banded Rows		☑ Banded Columns	
	Table Style Options		

Figure 113: Table style options

The Table below has the above Table Styles Options

Name	Class ID	Subject

Modifying a Table Style

A style can be modified after applying it to a table. Once modified, the change will reflect all tables using that style.

To modify a table style;

- Click within the table in your document.

- Click the **Table Design** tab.

- Click the More down arrow in the Table Styles.

- Click **Modify Table Style** or Right Click a table style and select **Modify**; a dialogue box appears.

- Modify your formatting, i.e., font size, style, color, fills, etc.

- Select;

- **Only in this document** if the modified style is applied to only the current document.
- **New Documents based on this template** for the style to be modified for future documents based on the current template.

- Click **OK**.

Note: A manually or directly applied table style will likely override a modified style. If you apply a table style and the tables using that style do not change, that might be the reason. You may then need to clear the formatting before the change is applied.

Below is the Modify Style Dialog box

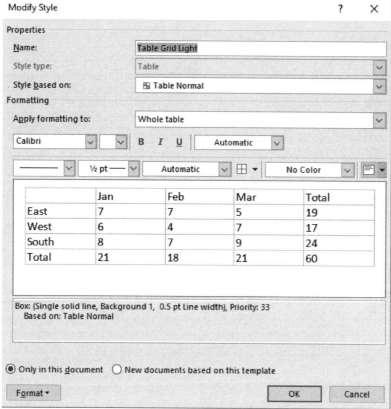

Figure 114: Modifying table style

Modifying Table Properties in a Table Style

Table properties, including cell margin, row settings, and table alignment, can be modified using **Format** in the **Modify Style.**

To change Table Properties in a Table Style;

- Click within the table in your document.

- Click the **Table Design** tab.

- Click the More down arrow in the Table Styles.

- Click **Modify Table Style** or Right Click a table style and select **Modify**; a dialogue box appears.

- Click **Format** on the bottom left of the dialogue box. A dropdown menu appears with several options.

- Click the option you want to modify; a dialogue box appears with other options.

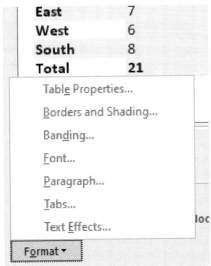

Figure 115: Modifying table properties

- Click on the **Table Properties** option, the dialogue box below.

- Select any formatting option you want to apply to your table.

- Click **OK**.

- Select whether to apply **Only in this document** or **New documents based on this template.**

- Click **OK.**

Creating a New Table Style

If you don't want to use the already built-in table styles, you can create a new or custom style for your use.

To create a custom table style;

- Click within the table in your document.

- Click the **Table Design** tab.

- Click the More down arrow in the Table Styles.

- Select a table style to apply as a base style.

- Click the More down arrow in the Table Styles.

- Click **New Table Style, and** a dialog box appears.

- Name a name for the new table in the Name box.

- Format your table accordingly.

- Select whether to apply **Only in this document** or **New documents based on this template.**

- Click **OK.**

The new style appears in the Table styles gallery under **Custom** at the top. Just right-click on the style and select Delete Table Style to delete it.

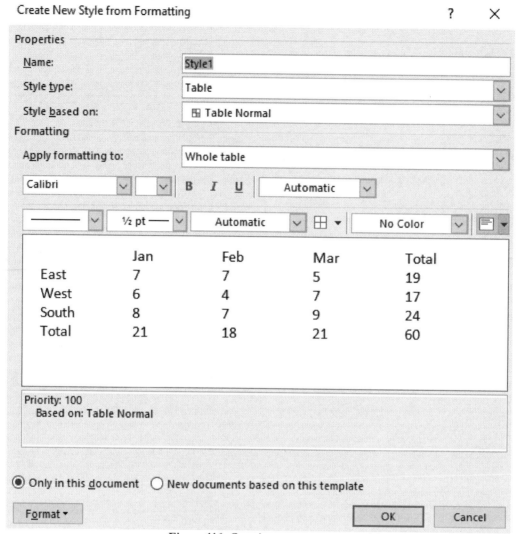

Figure 116: Creating a new custom table style

Clearing a Table Style
This is to clear a table style and remove formatting;

- Click within the table in your document.

- Click the **Table Design** tab.

- Click the More down arrow in the Table Styles.

- Click **Clear.**

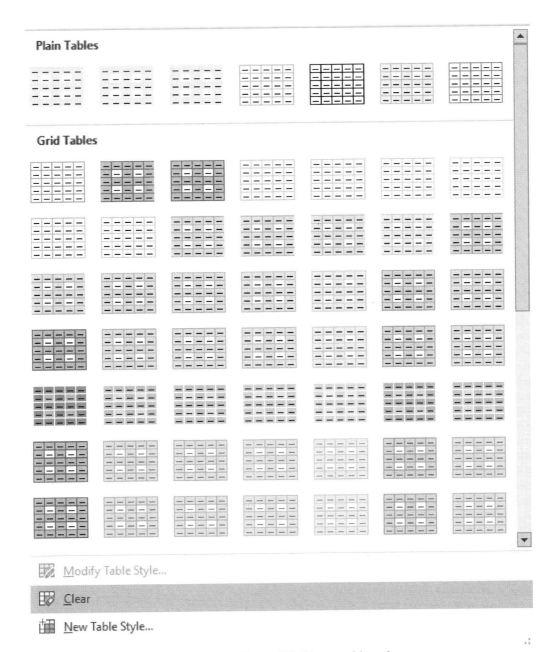

Figure 117: Clear a table style

Setting a Default Table Style

Setting a default table style means applying that style for new tables in the current document or all new documents that will come after the setting.

To set a Default Table Style;

- Click within the table in your document.

- Click the **Table Design** tab.

- Click the More down arrow in the Table Styles.

- Then right-Click the table style to be used as the default style.

- Select Set as Default from the drop-down menu. A dialogue box appears.

- Select from the options.

- Click **OK**.

12 The Graphs and Charts

The graphs and charts: what a graph, what's a chart, what are the types of graphs and charts, how to create them

INSERTING A CHART INTO YOUR DOCUMENT

A chart is another Word feature that lets you virtually present your information or data. You can insert any chart in your Word document.

To insert a chart in your document:

1.   Place your insertion point where you want the chart.

2.   Go to the **Insert** ribbon.

3.   Click **Chart** in the **Illustration** group.

Insert Chart dialog box appears.

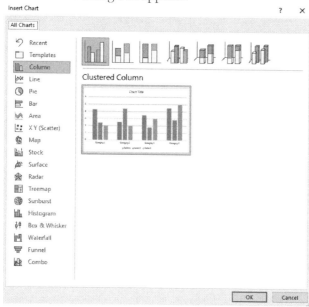

Figure 118: Insert chart dialog box

4.   Select a chart type and double-click on the desired chart.

The chart appears in your document with an excel spreadsheet.

5.   Input your data into the excel spreadsheet, and the charts update your data.

6.   Close the spreadsheet window.

FORMATTING A CHART

1.   Select the chart.

2.   Click on the plus sign at the top right corner.

3.   Check or uncheck the box of elements to put or remove them from the chart.

4.   Click on the arrow in front of any selected elements for more settings.

5.   Click on the **More Option** to have control of the element from the element Format dialog box.

Each element has its **Format** dialog box to format your chart elements fully. You can change their color, width, size, gap, etc., as the case may be. The format dialog box can also be opened by:

- Double-clicking on the element or

- Right-clicking on the element and choosing **Format Data Series** from the list of the options or

- Using the keyboard shortcut command **Ctrl + 1** on the element.

You can also format your chart in the contextual **Chart Tools** tap (Design and Format buttons) or at the brush icon , the chart style below the **+** sign. You can filter your chart using the chart filter below the chart style icon.

13 Common Problems and Mistakes

Retrieve a draft

Despite your best efforts to preserve your Word documents, a computer breakdown or power outage may prevent you from saving the most recent version of your work. If that happens, don't worry. Word may have saved it as a draft using the Automatic Repair feature.

- To find the draft, go to File > Open.

- Select Recent Documents.

- Scroll to the bottom of your recent paper's list. The Recover Unsaved Documents button is located at the bottom.

- Press the button.

- The dialog box Open will display. Select the document to be recovered, then click the Open button.

AUTOSAVE WITH AUTO RECOVER

Word has AutoRecover to recover the unsaved files, but it may not fail you if you fail to set it up accurately. To set AutoRecover to save the unsaved file, kindly;

1. Tap on the **File and select Option** from the backstage to open the Word Options dialog box.

2. Select **Save,** then choose **Save AutoRecover Information,** and **set the minutes** you want MS word to continue saving the document for you automatically.

3. Tap **Ok** and **close** the dialog box.

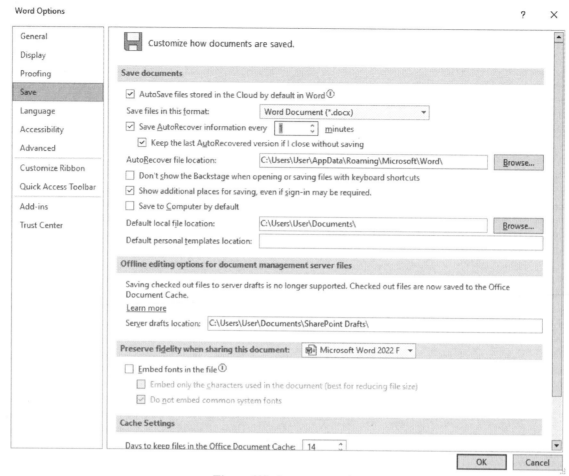

Figure 119: Autosave settings

PROTECTING YOUR DOCUMENT

The best means of restricting frustration is to adequately secure the document from other people, most times if it is a family or joint desktop. To create secure your document to a greater level, do well to:

1. Tap on **the File** and select **Info** from backstage.

2. Tap on **Protect document menu and** select the **best option** preferable to you.

Figure 120: Protecting your document

3. Supply the required information regarding the option you selected and tap Ok.

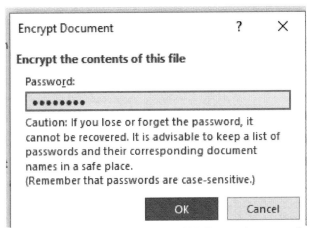

Figure 121: Protecting your document with a password

Note: take caution with whatever option you select. If you are locked out of the document, you have no other option but to reaccess the document.

14 Table of contents, Image list, Table list, Index

MAKING A TABLE OF CONTENTS

The table of contents serves as a guide to each topic you discussed in the textbook. When you prepare the table of contents, the table of contents will have a number page with each heading and subheading, provided you have numbered your document. The style that will be used for preparing the table of contents is the style. For example, heading 1 is for the chapter number and main heading. In addition, you may use headings 2 and 3 for sub-heading. If you use the heading style correctly, you won't have a problem preparing a table of contents. To create a table of contents, follow this simple guide:

1. Create a style for chapter, heading, and subheading with heading 1, 2, or 3.

2. Move to the beginning of the document and place the cursor pointer at the beginning of the first paragraph.

3. Then tap on the **Insert tab** and select the **blank page** from the page section to create a separate blank page for the table of contents at the beginning of the document.

4. Place the cursor pointer on the blank page and move to the **References tab**.

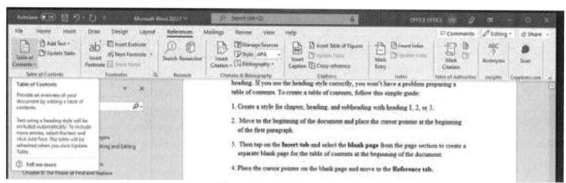

Figure 122: References tab

5. Move to the table of contents section and tap on the "**table of content**" **menu button**.

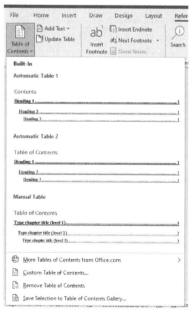

Figure 123: Table of contents options

6. Select a **preferred table of contents format** for your document; immediately after you select the format, a table of contents will be created.

Table of Contents

Introduction **5**

Chapter 1: An Overview of the Powerful Writing Tool - Microsoft Word 2022 .... **8**

What is Microsoft Word? 8

How Microsoft Word works 9

Where do you buy Microsoft Word? 9

Chapter 2: Open a blank document or an existing template **13**

Chapter 3: View options **19**

Chapter 4: Word Dashboard **26**

The File Tab/Backstage View 32

Chapter 5: Page dimension and margins **44**

Chapter 6: Tips and Tricks For Formatting and Editing **47**

Figure 124: Sample table of contents

Note: if you added an item to the table of contents by attaching more heading styles, update it to the table of contents by tapping on the Update table under the contents section, then select how to update it and tap Ok.

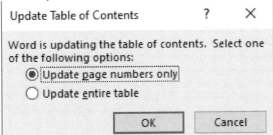

Figure 125: Update table of contents

Microsoft Word has a feature that enables you to generate a table of content automatically or manually with easy-to-use templates. To insert a table of contents automatically in your document, you must create or format your document using the Word built-in headings in the **Styles** group

To Insert a Table of Contents:

1. Ensure your document headings uses Word built-in headings styles

2. Place your insertion point where you want the table of content to be.

3. Go to the **References** ribbon.

4. Click **Table of Contents.**

A drop-down menu appears.

5. Select an option:

- The first two options automatically insert your table of contents with **all** your available headings.

- The third option inserts the table of contents with placeholder texts and allows you to replace them with your headings.

- Select **More Tables of Contents from Office.com** for more templates.

- Select the **Custom Table of Content** to customize your table. A dialog box appears; edit as desired, and press **OK**.

- If you already have a table of content in your document, you can delete it by selecting **Remove Table of Contents.**

Updating your Table of Contents

Word does not update your table of content automatically if you make changes to your document. You will have to update it manually.

To update your Table of Content:
1. Position your cursor in the table of content.

Table borders appear with buttons at the top-left.
2. Click the **Update Table** button.

A dialog box appears.
3. Click the **Update entire table**.

4. Press **OK**.

Word automatically updates your table.

Alternatively,
1. Right-click on the table of content.

A drop-down menu appears.
2. Select **Update Field.** You can also select **Update Table** in the **Table of Contents** group in the **References** ribbon.

A dialog box appears.
3. Click **Update the entire table**.

4. Click **OK**.

Note: Do not always forget to update your table after making significant changes that affect the headers or page numbers.

CREATING AN INDEX

An index is just like the table of contents, but the index goes deeper than the table of contents. The index gives clues to every item of importance in the document. To create an index, these are the route paths:

1. Select the word or group of words that you want to include in the index list

2. Tap on the **Reference tab** and move to the index group, then tap on the **Mark entry button** to open the Mark Index Entry dialog box.

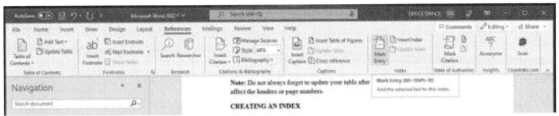

Figure 126: Mark entry index

3. Mark entry dialog box will be opened with the selected text in the main entry. In addition, you may insert a subentry for more explanation about the main entry.

4. Click **Mark or Mark all button. T**he mark is to mark only the selected item, while the **Mark is to mark all the items that match** the selected item in the document.

5. Mark all the items you want to be included in the index list inside the document and close the Mark index entry dialog box.

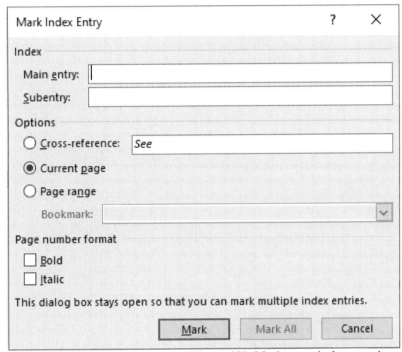

Figure 127: Mark entry index creation

6. Close the show/hide command by tapping the **show/hide button** in **the Home tab** in the Paragraph section. The show/hide command is used to show itself automatically immediately after you mark any index entry.

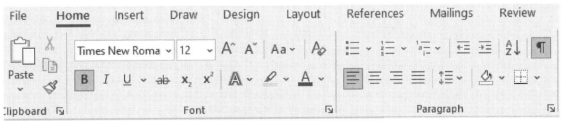

Figure 128: Show hide index button

7. Place the cursor pointer where you want to put the index list, which is proper to appear at the end of the note.

8. Tap on the **Reference tab** and the **Insert Index button** at the index section to open an Index dialog box.

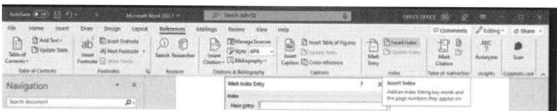

Figure 129: Insert index button

9. Make the necessary settings, such as style index in format, number of columns you want to create for the Index in the column section, and the page alignment.

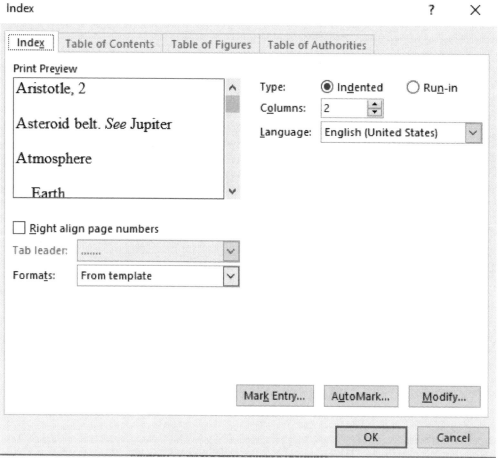

Figure 130: Insert index button dialog box

10. When you are done with the setting, tap on **Ok** to Insert the Index list into the document.

Note: Heading and subheading have to be in the Index list. You have to get them added. You can delete and amend the index if you are not pleased with the arrangement by commanding for insert index dialog box.

CREATING A LIST OF FIGURES

A "List of Figures" is mainly used to create a list of tables you caption. If you fail to prepare a caption for each table you have in the document, a "List of Figures" will not work. To create a "list of the figure," do well to:

- Tap on the **References tab** and move to the captions section.

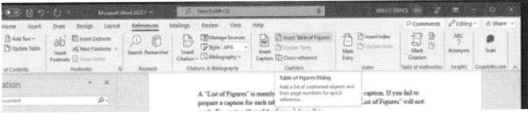

Figure 131: Insert table of figures

- Then click on **Insert Table of the figure** to open the table of the figure dialog box.

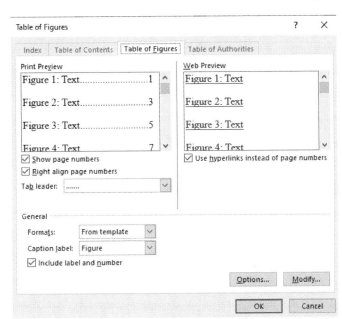

Figure 132: Insert table of figures dialog box

- But you must have created a caption for the table you have in the document.

Figure 133: List of figures

INSERTING AUTOMATIC TABLE OF FIGURES

Word has a command to automatically add a table of figures to your work, just like adding a table of contents.

To automatically generate a table of figures, you must have added captions to all the figures used in your document using the Word **Insert Caption** command.

To Insert Table of Figures:

1. Ensure you use the Word caption feature to add captions to your objects.

2. Place your insertion point where you want the table of figures to be.

3. Click the **References** tab.

4. Select **Insert Table of Figures** in the **Caption** group. Table of Figures dialog box appears.

5. Select your desired Format, make other changes, preview, and press **OK**. Your table of figures appears in your document.

FOOTNOTES AND ENDNOTES

Footnotes and endnotes contain additional notes to supplement and explain ahead of what is mentioned in the text. Footnotes will be inserted at the bottom of the page, while the Endnote will be inserted at the end of the chapter, section, and document. To make footnotes or endnotes, do well to:

1. Select the word or the group of words that you want to reference with a footnote or endnote.

2. Tap the **references tab** and select either the **footnote or endnote.**

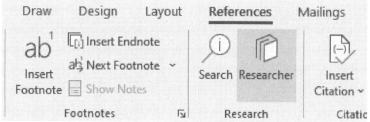

Figure 134: Footnotes and endnotes

3. Type the **footnote or endnote** at the provided place where the command transit you in the document with the superscripted number.

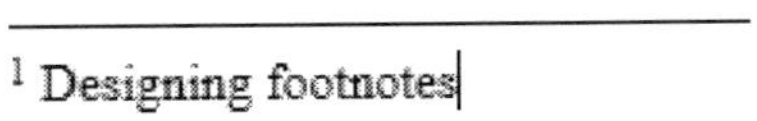

[1] Designing footnotes|

Figure 135: Footnote sample

Note: check the footnote and endnote information by clicking the superscripted number on the document's reference word (s).

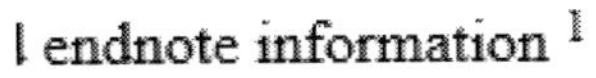

| endnote information [1]

Figure 136: Footnote wrapping text

Tip: You can check the footnote and endnote as they are arranged in the document by tapping on show notes. Once you delete the reference text, the footnote and Endnote will be deleted as well

15 Error checks

No matter how perfect and flawless you are on Word, there will always be some unavoidable mistakes or errors that occur around spelling and grammar. These errors can cost you more than you imagine, especially in business and education. To avoid these errors, that is why you need to make the best use of the Proofing Tools

The Proofing Tools

The proofing tools allow you to use the spelling and grammar checking features in Word for a wide range of languages to check for spelling errors and grammatical error

The proofing tool is in the **Review tab**, on the left-hand side under the **Proofing** category

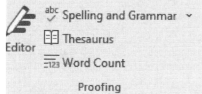

Figure 137: Proofing category

15.1 Grammar Revising

USING AUTOCORRECT IN WORD

AutoCorrect is a function found in all Microsoft products that allows you to change how words are spelled or shown in your documents, and it comes preloaded with several options.

Autocorrect is one of the amazing features of Word that fixes hundreds of common spelling errors and typos automatically. Moreover, the correction happens instantly, and you might not even notice it. For instance, you cannot type the word **help** because Word automatically corrects it to **help** by default. Let's imagine you want to spell out the word "the," but you misspelled it slightly; pressing the spacebar will automatically change it to "the." Likewise, if you type "acn" and press space, Word detects that you're probably trying to spell "can," but you've just misspelled it, automatically changing it for you. That is an autocorrect option; it will detect or recognize often misspelled words and correct them for you, which is a beneficial tool. It will also help with other subjects, such as fractions. For example, if you were typing half (1/2), pressing the space bar turns it to that fraction; similarly, if you were typing 1/4, using the spacebar converts it to that fraction. Again, Word's autocorrect option is being used. Aside from typos and spelling errors, autocorrect features helps in fixing common punctuation mistakes, automatically capitalizing the first letter of any sentence, names of days, months, and some inverse capitalization errors.

Ordinals are another example; you might see them in things like dates. For example, if you type the 1st of August and press the spacebar, the "st" becomes a superscript, bringing the date into proper format; the same goes for the 2nd, and so on.

Another example would be **Hyperlinks**. If you write in a website address and hit Enter, it will highlight the website and turn it into a hyperlink, which you can see by hovering over it. If you hold down the Ctrl key and click your mouse, it will take you to that website. This is where the autocorrect choices come in handy.

Let's look at several other autocorrect features, one of which is quite a cute little one if you've never seen it before. If you **input three dashes** (---) and **press Enter**, you'll get a continuous solid line, and the best part is that you can go up and type on the line if you want to.

continuous solid line, and the best part is that you can go up and type on the line if you want to.

Figure 138: Three dashes

You get a solid bold line if you do that again, but this time you **hold down your shift key**, do **three dashes**, and hit **Enter**; you just incorporate the shift to get that.

You get a solid bold line if you do that again, but this time you **hold down your shift key**, do **three dashes**, and hit **Enter**; you just incorporate the shift to get that.

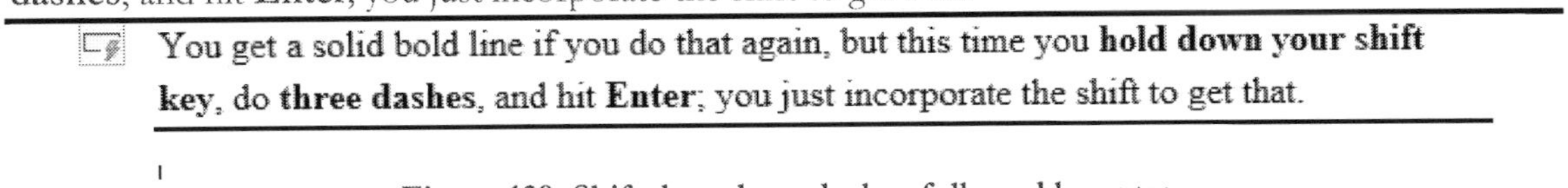

Figure 139: Shift then three dashes followed by enter

If you **press Enter** after **pressing Shift** and **three asterisks**, you'll get a dotted line, and if you press Enter after pressing Shift and three-pound symbols, you'll get a different style line.

style line.

Figure 140: Shift then three asterisks followed by enter

Many lie around in autocorrect that you might not be aware of, and they can be quite helpful if you need to get something done quickly. These are excellent illustrations of how Word's autocorrect is implemented and operates.

This Word feature also autocorrects common text shortcuts to their proper characters. So, for example, if you type -->, it automatically corrects to →, (R) changes to ®, the properly registered symbol, and so many others in the list.

But what happens if you want the word that Word has autocorrected? You can undo the autocorrect.

To undo an AutoCorrect:

- Quickly press **Ctrl + Z** or undo before typing any other characters, and if you did not catch it fast,

- Move your cursor to the blue rectangle at the bottom of the first letter of any autocorrect word and click. A menu box appears to undo the autocorrect or do other further settings.

You can edit the Word autocorrect feature, add your own always misspelled word, or remove some words from autocorrecting.

To adjust AutoCorrect Settings:

1. Click the **File** tab to go to the **Backstage**.

2. Select **Options** in the left side menu bar. The **word Option** window appears.

3. Choose **Proofing** in the left side menu.

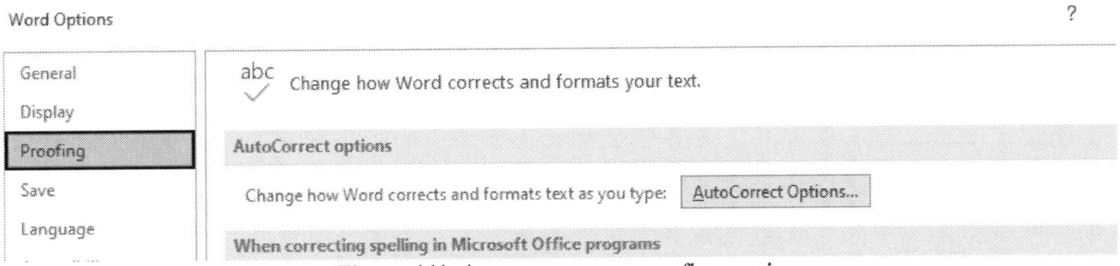

Figure 141: Autocorrect on proofing options

4. Click on the **AutoCorrect Options** button. An autoCorrect dialog box appears with the autocorrect tab active. Click on other tabs as desired.

You will see the list of all problems Word fixes for you from the dialog box.

5.   Select and press the **Delete** button to remove anyone you do not want word to autocorrect.

6.   Add a new entry using the **Replace** and **With** text boxes.

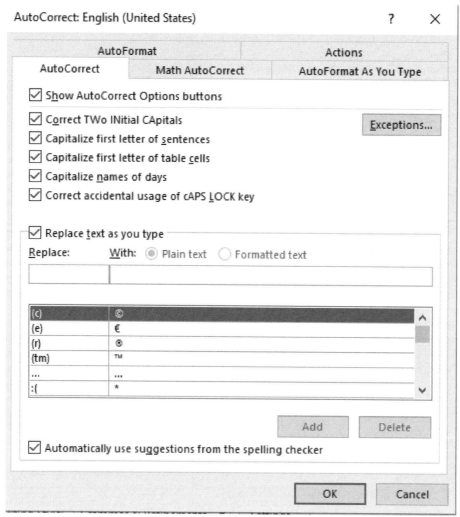

Figure 142: Adding new entry for autocorrect feature

7.   Press the **OK** button and close the dialog box.

Changing AutoCorrect's Preferences

If you want to look at how Autocorrect is set up and what autocorrect choices you have selected, go to the **File** tab in the backstage area and scroll down to **"Options"** at the bottom. Then, in the **"Proofing"** section, you'll see autocorrect options at the top. This is where you save all of the autocorrect options if you select **"Autocorrect Options."**

At the top, you have a few options to choose from; by default, they're all selected. In addition, you can **"correct to initial capitals,"** **"capitalize the first letter of sentences,"** the first letter of table cells, the names of the day, and so on by using the autocorrect settings button.

These are all checked, indicating that you want Word to do that. So, for example, if you type the word "Monday" and don't type a capital, you want it to change to a capital. These are some of the most fundamental choices, and you might want to have all of them.

Correcting Your Spelling Errors

Computer software such as Word processing has been an excellent tool for simplifying human needs. However, while trying to construct words, typographical errors can occur, which led Microsoft corporation to look for a means to reduce the possibility of typographical errors while typing. Word has several tools to help you proofread your document and correct any mistakes. However, many don't know how helpful Word 365 is regarding autocorrect and spelling checking. To understand how to autocorrect or scan your document against typographical errors, follow this step-by-step procedure below:

- Make sure you are currently on your document to be corrected

- Go to the "Review" tab

- On your left-hand side, look for "Spelling & Grammar" and click on it

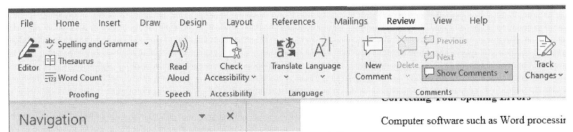

Figure 143: Spelling and Grammar

A dialog box will appear on your right-hand side, starting a spelling check from the first error to the last. For example, the first typographical error could be "Resources" instead of "Resources," so if it was intentionally typed, you click on the "Ignore" option. If not, select the corrected word in the suggestion box, then click on the "Change" option to continue to autocorrect other words.

- Once you select the right suggested words, click on the "Change" option, which will take you to the next misspelled text. Note that if the dictionary feature is installed on your Word 365 and it is a similar word in the dictionary, it will be explained below. If not, click on the "Get a Dictionary" option.

- It is important to note that the spell-checker is not perfect. Sometimes it will say a word is spelled wrong when it is not, such as people's names, street names, and other unique proper nouns. If that happens, you have a couple of different options;

  o The *"Ignore"* option will skip the word one time without changing it.

  o The *"Ignore All"* option will skip the word every time it appears in your document.

  o While the *"Add"* option will permanently add the word to your inbuilt dictionary, so it never becomes an error again. Make sure the word is spelled correctly before using any of these options.

Correcting misspellings one at a time

- Word is designed to mark spelling and grammar errors while you type. That is what the little red and blue wavy lines, as seen in the illustration, are for. Then, you can check your document manually, refer to the marks, and make corrections.

- Red means that there is a spelling error. To correct it, all you have to do is right-click, then choose the proper spelling from the menu, after which the red curly line will be erased.

- Blue means that there is a kind of grammatical error. In this example, it looks like I used the wrong word in the context of the sentence. For example, using *"their"* instead of "there."

Customizing Spelling & Grammar Check

"Word" can be pretty good at picking up on errors like this, but there are certain things that it is set to ignore by default, including sentence fragments, poor sentence structure, and other common grammar mistakes. You must adjust the default proofing settings to include these in your grammar check. To do this,

- Go to the "Backstage view," accessed through your "File menu."

- Click on "Options" on the left pane

- Then, navigate to "Proofing" in the dialog box

- To customize your grammar settings, look for "Writing Style" near the bottom of the Window. Then click the "settings" option located on the right side

- And another dialog box will appear; here, you can set it to check Grammar Only or Grammar & Style, which will cause Word to be strict about the style of your preferred choice. You can also turn specific items on or off to better suit your needs. For example, if you want Word to check for sentence fragments and run-ons, you can turn them on. Ensure you click the "Ok" button once you are through with the changes.

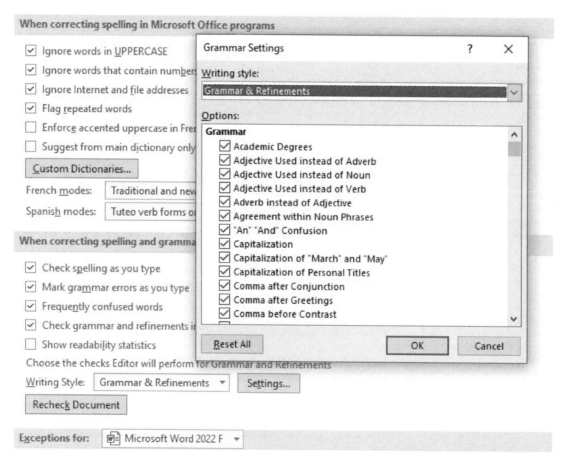

Figure 144: Customizing Spelling & Grammar Check

Preventing text from being spell-checked

- To do this, go to the "Backstage view," which can be accessed through your "File menu."

- Click on "Options" on the left pane

- Then, navigate to "Proofing" in the dialog box

- There are still lots of other ways that you can use to customize your settings depending on your preference. For instance, you can stop Word from marking spelling and grammar errors while you type.

- You can also turn off frequently confused words, like "**there** vs. **their.**" Remember that your spelling and grammar choices apply only to your Word copy. So, if you ignore any error or add a word to your dictionary (for example, your name), those wavy lines will reappear when you send the document to someone else. You can avoid this issue by hiding this document's spelling and grammar errors. Just check the two boxes near the bottom of the Window. When you are done, click "Ok"; now, the errors are hidden.

Finding the Right Word with the Thesaurus

Before I explain "Thesaurus," it is essential to know what "Thesaurus" is. Thesaurus is a tool specially designed into Word by Microsoft to get the synonyms of whatever you are looking for by giving suggestions. So, for example, you can look for "benefit," and you will be given multiple suggestions of synonyms for "benefit," such as "advantage" and "profit," with a classification of which part of speech such words fall under.

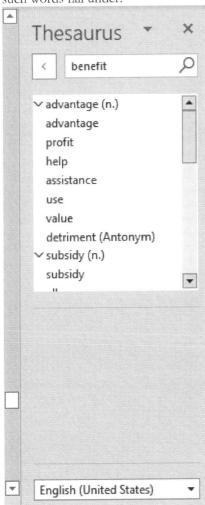

Figure 145: Use of Thesaurus

Now, how do we make use of Thesaurus? Simply follow these steps:

- Go to your "Review" tab."

Under the "Review" tab, on your left-hand side, locate "Thesaurus" and double-click on it

- A dialog box will appear on your right-hand side opposite your Navigation pane dialog box, which is located on your left-hand side if activated

- Then, you can type your word or phrase into the "Search" bar. For example, we can look for "Environment" on our "Thesaurus pane" and see what our result will be. You can also type another word of your choice and also see what your result will be

Thesaurus helps you find a word that is similar to your chosen word. Then, it suggests different ways of saying what you want to say.

Making use of the Navigation Pane

For simplicity and flexibility, it is essential to note that you can have your search bar pane through the navigation pane side by side while typing in a Word environment. Follow these step-by-step procedures to achieve that:

- Go to the "View" tab

- Under the "View" tab, on your left-hand side, look for "Navigation Pane," and make sure it is ticked. If not, do so to see the effect on your document.

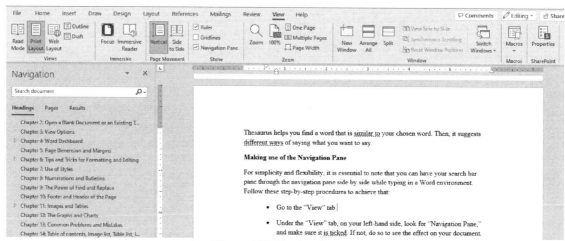

Figure 146: Navigation pane

- Here is the result; the below "Navigation" dialog box will automatically appear permanently on the left-hand side of your document, except if you untick it from the "View" tab. It enables you to see your listed "Headings," slide "Pages," and search "Result" instantly.

Choosing Language Option

- Go to the "File menu."

- At the displayed interface, click on "Options."

- A dialog box will appear on your left-hand side. Select "Language"

- Then, "Language" features will also appear on your right-hand side. You can choose from the available languages by scrolling through to see other options.

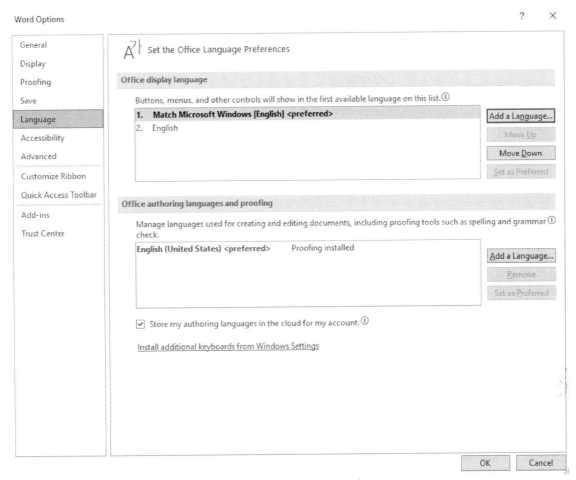

Figure 147: Language settings

- Once done, press the "Ok" option

- Then, you will be instructed to restart Office so your language changes can take effect.

- Take note of your Word 365 interface before restarting your PC. It's by default in the English language

Preventing Text from Being Spell Checked

Certain words in your documents cannot be spell-checked, especially words like address lists, lines of computer codes, and foreign languages such as French, Spanish, etc. To prevent text of this kind from being spell-checked, follow the steps below

- Select the text.

- On the **Review tab**, click the **Language** button, and select **Set Proofing Language.**

Figure 148: Set Proofing Language

- In the **Language** dialog box, click on the **Do not check spelling or grammar** check box

Figure 149: Prevent Text from Being Spell Checked

Hiding Spellings and Grammar Errors in a Document

Suppose you want to share your document with someone and do not want the person to see the red and blue lines. All you need to do is turn off the automatic spelling and grammar checks. Not only will the errors be hidden on your computer, but they also will not be displayed when viewed on another computer. To hide the spelling and grammar errors, follow the steps given below

- Go to the **Backstage view** by clicking on the **File** menu

- Click on **Options** on the left pane

- In the **Word Options** dialog box, click on **Proofing**

- Go to **Exceptions** and click on the checkboxes; **Hide spelling errors in this document only** and **Hide grammar in this document only**

Use of external tools such as Grammarly Plugin

Grammarly is an online tool developed for both web and Word, which has a free and paid version. The free version provides basic word checking, proofreading, and grammar checker, but the upgraded version costs $12.00 per month for one user. In addition, it provides more advanced editing features and allows you to check publications created by your team members in real-time.

Grammarly helps with checking and correcting grammar and spelling errors. Grammarly helps by using specialized software to check the accuracy of your written work, otherwise known as grammar. Grammarly works by detecting the errors that occur when you write sentences in a word processor. It identifies the errors and suggests corrections and fixes that can be made to rectify them. Grammarly also checks your work for plagiarism and smart punctuation. It is capable of detecting more than 250 types of grammatical, spelling, and punctuation mistakes, including improper quotation marks, apostrophes, semicolons, commas, and colon usage. Once you check your work remotely, Grammarly will notify you of grammatical or spelling errors and integrate them with your grammar style guide. It allows users to carry out various functions, such as checking for every single error, then you can learn how to correct the error. The points that help you with this are listed below.

- Grammarly has a free version that helps correct your document's grammar. The plugin is available for Microsoft Word so that it can be installed manually.

- Grammarly also integrates with Microsoft Outlook and provides enhanced grammar checking in emails. You can use this plugin with all email accounts supporting the feature.

- After you have installed this plugin, you will find a Grammarly icon on the menu bar. Click on it and select 'Check grammar, spelling, and style' from the main menu. The process is pretty simple and will take you to a page where you will be guided through the process.

- Once you have created a new document, Grammarly will check that document's spelling, grammar, and style on completion. If it finds any errors, it will highlight them for you to correct.

16 Print and Export

Page Setup

When you initially start a document, it comes with only the default pages, which are all portraits. The first thing you should look at is your **margins**. You may be okay with them by default, but some individuals like to adjust them just to vary the look of their work or to fit more content on their page. You'll be able to fit more content on the page if the margins are smaller.

Setting Up your Margins

You have two rulers in your document: one at the top and the other on the side. If you can't see your rulers, click up to **View** and check **Ruler**. You'll be able to view your margin line after that.

Remember that **your margin is the gray area**, while **your document is the white area** where your words will appear.

If you want to adjust them, go up to your ruler, and place your mouse between the gray and white sections until it changes into a **double-headed arrow**, click, and you'll see a faint line come up a vertical line, and all you have to do now is pull your margin to the right.

As you can see, this has reduced your margin and increased the amount of text on your page. You can repeat the process on the left. These arrows can get in the way, so sometimes you just have to move them out of the way; this will shift part of your text, but don't worry, just grab the margin, in the same manner we did the other side, make sure your cursor is a double-headed arrow, and drag it over to the left once more. Because your arrows up here have moved, you may notice that some paragraphs have been indented.

All you have to do now is move those back, and everything will fall into place. The left-hand half of this method is a little tricky. Moving your margins up and down to the top and bottom of your page, on the other hand, is significantly easier; you click and drag to shift those margins up or down, and you can do the same with the bottom. By decreasing your margins, you can fit more text on your website.

If none of it appeals to you, click the Layout tab and **"Margins."** Then, when you click the drop-down menu, you'll find various options.

If you merely want to decrease the size of your margins, **"Narrow"** is an excellent option, and if you click on it, it will automatically modify your margins.

Creating Your Margins

If you wish to choose your margins, navigate to **"Custom Margins."**

A dialog box will emerge when you click that, allowing you to modify the top, bottom, left, and right margins. So, you can use the up or down arrows, and as you do, a tiny little preview will appear here, showing you precisely what you're doing.

Figure 150: Custom margins

Alternatively, you can insert a figure for each of these and click **"OK"** to see how the margins have changed. Once you're satisfied with all of your margins, you can go on to your headers and footers.

How to Print Document

After creating your document by filling it with contents, you may like to print it out to have a feel or send it to someone. Whichever the reason is okay as what is more important is to know how to print your document from your PC. So the first step is to connect the printer to your computer using a suitable cable.

Click on the *File* tab of your document and then the *Print* command. The next step you are to take is to click on the *Print* button again.

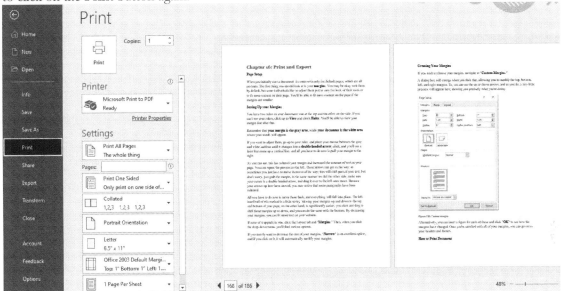

Figure 151: Print a document

Steps in printing Word document

If you want to print more than one document copy, just set it up in that print interface. Also, if you're going to change some settings, do that on that print interface before hitting the last print button. The document will start printing from your printer as soon as you do that. Alternatively, you can open the print interface by using a shortcut.

The shortcut you are to use is pressing the **Ctrl** and the **P** keys on your computer keyboard. This will bring up the print interface. You can then follow the prompts to complete the printing by clicking on the *Print* button.

How to Convert Word Document to PDF File

Although a Word document is created and saved in doc or Docx format, you can still save it in PDF format. Also, if you create a document and then decide to send it to someone, the recipient may request you send it in PDF format, so if you learn how to convert that document to PDF format, it will be a plus.

There are reasons people prefer to convert their Word documents to PDF. One of the reasons is that PDF files cannot be altered easily compared to Word. But on the other hand, PDF files are usually read-only. So it cannot be edited easily. It is like locking a file for a particular purpose.

To convert your document to PDF, the first step you are to take is to click on the *File* tab. When you do this, you will see some options. From those options, click on the *Export* command.

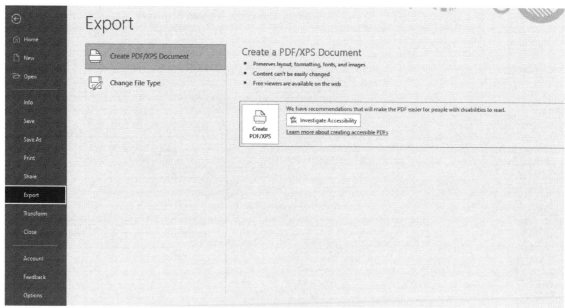

Figure 152: The Export command indicated

As you click on the ***Export*** command, click on the ***Create PDF/XPS*** button.

In the next Window, enter the name you want the document to be identified with. And lastly, click on the **Publish** button. You are done with the conversation once you do that.

Water Marks

A watermark is an image or text that appears behind the document's main text. It is always lighter than the text so you can read the document easily.

a. How to Add Watermark

- Click on the Design tab, and on the right side, you will see an option on the page design known as Watermark.

- Click on the drop-down menu, and you will see some options (Confidential, diagonal, confidential vertical, etc.)

- Click on anyone, and it shows on your document page

b. To Edit a watermark

- On the watermark options, click on the Custom Watermark, and a dialogue box shows up with different options (no watermark, picture watermark, text watermark)

- If you click on the text watermark, click the text you want, the font, the color, layout, and size, and then click on apply. An example of a customized watermark is shown in figure 9 below

- Then the text you typed is applied based on what you filled in the dialogue box.

- To add a picture watermark, select a picture from any folder on your pc, click on Insert, and then click on apply. The picture is shown on your document.

c. How to remove a Watermark

- Click on Design

- Go to watermark and click on Remove Watermark

17 Track changes

Tracking Changes to Documents

The Track Changes command allows you to make changes that can easily be spotted or identified. These changes can be reviewed, removed, or made permanent. Changes made in a document are recorded in different colors, with one color for each reviewer, new text is underlined, and deleted text is crossed out.

Turning Track Changes On and Off

To turn on the track changes, follow the steps below

- Go to the **Review tab** and click on **Track Changes** to turn it on. When turned on, the Track Changes button will appear darker than the rest ribbons.

Figure 153: Track changes

- To turn off the **Track Changes**, click on the button again. When the Track Changes is off, Word stops marking changes, but the colored underlines and strikethrough from the changes remain in the documents until they are accepted or rejected.

How to Show and Hide Track Changes

The Display for Review and Show Markup menus control how comments and edits appear

The Display for Review Menu

The Display for Review menu chooses how edits and comments are to be displayed in the document, To locate the **Display for Review** menu, go to the **Review** tab and click on **Display for Review.**

Figure 154: Display for Review

To see how edits and comments are displayed, click on the **Display for Review** drop-down menu, and the options are

- **Simple Markup**: This option displays the changes made on the document with a vertical line in the left margin as an indication.

- **All Markup**: This displays all edits and comments made in the document. New text is underlined, and deleted text is crossed out.

- **No Markup**: This displays the edited version of the document without showing any trace of visible edits or comments.

- **Original:** This displays the document's original version without edits or comments.

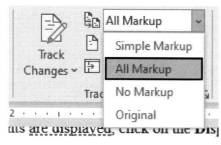

 its are displayed, click on the Dis
are

Figure 155: Markups for reviewing

The Show Markup Menu
The **Show Markup** menu allows you to choose the features the Track Changes display
To locate the **Show Markup** menu, go to the **Review** tab and click on **Show Markup**
To display all comments and edits in your document, select **Show Only Comments and Formatting in Balloons**

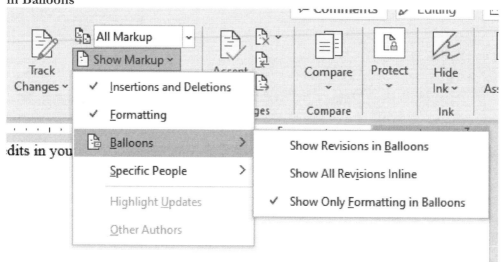

Figure 156: Markup and balloons

Deleting Text with Track Changes
To delete a text with Track Changes, follow the steps below

- Select the text you wish to delete

- Select the **Delete** key on the keyboard. The deleted text will appear with a strikethrough in the All Markup view.

Inserting Text with Track Changes
To insert text with Track Changes, follow the steps below

- Place the cursor where you wish to insert the new text

- Type the new text, and the new text will appear with an underline

Replacing Text with Track Changes
To replace text with track changes, follow the steps below

- Select the text you wish to replace

- Type the replacement text, and the original text will appear with a strikethrough. At the same time, the replacement text will appear with an underline in the All Markup view.

Changing Formatting with Track Changes

Formatting your document involves applying font style, font size, color, italics, etc.

To format text, follow the steps below

- Select the text you wish to format

- Change the format, and the Track Changes will automatically show the selected formatting applied in the document

Accept or Reject Track Changes

Changes made with Track Changes must be accepted before they become part of the document. You can either accept or reject edits individually or all at once.

To accept or reject track changes, select the change made, go to the **Review** tab, and do any of the following

- **Accept a change:** Click the **Accept** button, open the drop-down list on the Accept button, and select **Accept This Change** or **Accept and Move to Next.**

- **Reject a change:** Click the **Reject** button or open the drop-down list on the **Reject** button and select **Reject Change** or **Reject and Move to Next.**

- **Accept all changes:** Open the drop-down list on the **Accept** button and select **Accept All Changes.**

- **Reject all changes:** Open the drop-down list on the **Reject** button and select **Reject All Changes.**

18 The power of automatism

The power of automatism: what's VBA, what's a MACROs, how to register a macro to do repetitive operations quickly, where download Word templates for different needs (articles, CVs, motivational letters, contracts, book, thesis, job offer, etc.)

Understanding the Macros

Word Macros are scripts that perform actions, like running formulas or inserting templates. Creating Macros in Word is easy and requires no special skills. To begin, you must assign a key combination to perform the actions. Next, you can create and edit a macro using the VBA editor, accessible by pressing the shortcut key ALT + F11.

Macros are small pieces of code written in a programming language. They are not immune to errors or virus threats, so it is essential to use proper code. Incorrect codes will break your macros. Also, macros should not interfere with other Word commands. If you are unsure of a macro, you can search for it in the Macros dialog box.

You must enable the macro option in Word to enable macros in Microsoft Word. The macro icon looks like a tape and is blue. Clicking it will record the action you want. Once it is complete, you can then use it to edit your document. The macro icon is located in the View tab.

Macros are useful for a variety of tasks. For example, using Find and Replace to replace multiple words can be tedious. Macros make it easier for you to highlight words you use often. Whether searching for multiple synonyms or highlighting multiple words, a macro can be tailored to perform these tasks quickly.

1. Creating the Macro

You should understand the actions you wish to record before recording your macro.

Click View Tab

Click the Macros options to display a down menu

Choose Record Macro

Alternatively, enable the Developer tab. Then, go to the Code section and click Record Macro.

A Record Macro dialog box will appear. Type in your preferred Macro name. Do not use any space. Select the Button option since we will add it to Quick Access Toolbar (QAT).

    *2. **Add Macro to QAT***

Go to the Word Options dialog box and heat to Customize the Quick Access Toolbar. Next, choose the created Macro that appears on the left before clicking on Add.
You may modify the name if you wish to do so. You can also change the icon for your button.

    *3. **Once you complete, click OK.***

Select the position to save your Macro. It is stored in the Normal template by default.

    *4. **Set a description for your Macro***

In the description box, enter a descriptive term if you so wish.
Click OK, which takes you back to Word Options, where you also click Ok.

    *5. **Record the desired actions***

You will realize the cursor has a cassette tape icon. An implication is that it is the macro recording mode. Do the actions you wish to be part of your macro.

    *6. **Stop the recording***

Once you are done, click the View tab. Next, click the down arrow on the Macros button and click on Stop recording.

    *7. **Run your macro***

Open a new Word document.
Click the Article Setup button appearing on the Quick Access Toolbar.

18.1 Inserting Equations in Word Document

Word is built so that people from different areas of discipline can use it. Whether you specialize in Mathematics, Physics, or Chemistry, Microsoft Word has some already designed equations that you can insert in the document you create to communicate the information you need to your students or readers. You do not need to overthink how to create the contents of the equations individually because that has been put together for you by Microsoft in their MS Word document.

To insert an equation or equations in your Word document, click on the **Insert** tab first. This action will then display some commands. The next step you are to take is to click on the dropdown of the **Equation** command. This command is positioned in the right-hand hand corner. It is indicated in the photo below.

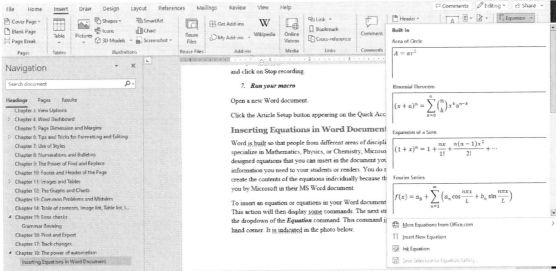

Figure 157: Inserting formulas in Word

As you can see in the above photo, some equations are displayed. You can scroll down until you get to the equation you want to use, click on it, and it will be inserted into your document.

In addition, if the equation you want to insert in your document is not found on the list as you scroll down, there are other options to display more equations. For example, as you click on the dropdown of the **Equation** command, take your cursor down and click on *More Equations from Office.com*. When you take this action, more equations will be displayed. You can then click on the one you want to be applied to your document.

If the above approach does not give you the equation for the work you want, you can click on **Insert New Equipment** or **Ink Equation**. When you select the former, you will be allowed to type or draw the equation you want by yourself. And if you go with the latter, Word will allow you to insert the Mathematical equation you need in the document through handwriting. Your equations are essential to Microsoft, which is why they provide you with many options to get the job done.

When you use the handwriting approach, as you write, it is corrected automatically to what you want. If, for instance, you write a symbol and it is changed to another one, do not be troubled by trying to correct that one that was misinterpreted. Instead, keep writing; at the end, Word will change it to what you want. It is an app that works with the help of artificial intelligence.

Using Symbols in Your Document

Symbols communicate important messages to people. For example, you may be typing on your document and, at a point, needs to insert a symbol or symbols at a spot. To achieve that, you need to know how to do it.

To insert a symbol in your Word document, click on the spot of your document where you want it to be placed. Next, click on the **Insert** tab. You will see some commands under this tab. First, drag your cursor to the top-right corner and then click on **Symbol,** which is indicated in the photo below.

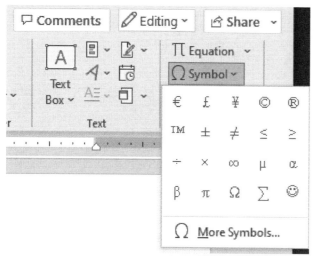

Figure 158: The symbol command

On clicking on the *Symbol* command, some symbols are displayed, which you can see in the above photo. Those displayed are popular symbols, and I use them in most cases. But, if the one you want to insert in your document is not there, click on **More Symbols**. As you take that step, you will see many displayed. Just keep scrolling until you get to the one you want to have in your document. As you get to it, click on it and click on the **Insert** button as well.

This above action will get that symbol inserted in your Word document. The last step you are to take is to close the symbols dialog box by clicking on the "X" of the dialog box.

To insert a such symbol or special character;

1. Position your cursor where you want to insert the symbol.

2. Go to the **Insert** tab in the **Symbols** group.

3. Click on **Symbol**. A dropdown menu appears.

4. Select the desired symbol if found on the list; otherwise, click on **More Symbols** for more available options.

5. Select your desired symbol.

6. Click **Insert**. The symbol will appear in your document.

7. Then Close the **Symbol** window.

For Special characters:

1. Click the **Special Character** tab in the **Symbol** window (follow steps 1-4 above to open it)

2. Click on the desired character and click the **Insert** button.

There are so many symbols that you can use in this feature. You can change the **font** and the **subset** to view them. Also displayed in the dialog box are the Unicode name and the character name of the selected symbol. You can familiarize yourself with the symbols by changing the font and the subset for you to locate anyone when needed quickly.

19 The strategic SHORTCUTS

Frequently used shortcuts

Ctrl + A	Highlight all your content
Ctrl + B	Applying bold to selected text
Ctrl + C	Copy content into the Clipboard
Ctrl + D	Font dialog box
Ctrl + E	Centralized text
Ctrl + F	Navigation for searching
Ctrl + G	Go to a page, section, line number
Ctrl + H	To replace a text
Ctrl + I	Applying italic to selected text
Ctrl + J	To justify your text
Ctrl + K	Insert hyperlink to content
Ctrl + L	Align text to the left
Ctrl + M	Move paragraph
Ctrl + N	Create a new document
Ctrl + O	Open a document
Ctrl + P	Print out document
Ctrl + R	Align text to the right
Ctrl + S	Save document
Ctrl + U	Applying underline to selected text
Ctrl + V	Paste the copied contents from the Clipboard
Ctrl + W	Close current document
Ctrl + X	Cut the selected content
Ctrl + Y	Redo the previous action
Ctrl + Z	Undo the previous action
Ctrl + [	Decrease the font size
Ctrl +]	Increase the font size
Esc	Cancel a command
Ctrl + Alt + S	Split the document Window
Ctrl + Alt + S	Remove the document Window Split

Access Keys for ribbon tabs

Alt + Q	Move to the "Tell me" or Search field on the Ribbon to search for assistance or Help content
Alt + F	Open the **File page** to use the Backstage view.
Alt + H	Open the **Home tab** to use common formatting commands, paragraph styles, and the Find tool.
Alt + N	Open the **Insert tab** to insert tables, pictures, shapes, headers, and text boxes.
Alt + G	Open the **Design tab** to use themes, colors, and effects, such as page borders.
Alt + P	Open the **Layout tab** to work with page margins, page orientation, indentation, and spacing.
Alt + S	Open the **References tab** to add a table of contents, footnotes, or a table of citations.
Alt + M	Open the **Mailings tab** to manage Mail, Merge tasks, and work with envelopes and labels.
Alt + R	Open the **Review tab** to use Spell Check, set proofing languages, and track and review changes to your document.

Alt + W	Open the **View tab** to choose a document view or mode, such as Read Mode or Outline. You can also set the zoom magnification and manage multiple documents in Windows.
Alt or F10	Select the **active tab** on the ribbon, and activate the access keys
Shift + Tab	Move the focus to commands on the ribbon.
Ctrl + Right arrow	Move between command groupings on the ribbon
Arrow keys	Move among the items on the Ribbon
Spacebar or Enter	Activate the selected button.
Alt + Down arrow key	Open the menu for the selected button
Down arrow key	When a menu or submenu is open, it's to move to the next command
Ctrl + F1	Expand or collapse the ribbon
Shift+F10	Open the context menu
• Left arrow key	Move to the submenu when the main menu is open or selected

Navigate the document

Ctrl + Left arrow key	Move the cursor pointer one space at a time to the left
Ctrl + Right arrow key	Move the cursor pointer one space at a time to the right
Ctrl + Up arrow key	Move the cursor pointer up by one paragraph
Ctrl + Down arrow key	Move the cursor pointer down by one Paragraph
End	Move the cursor pointer to the end of the current line
Home	Move the cursor to the beginning of the current Line
Ctrl + Alt+ Page up	Move the cursor pointer to the top
Page down	Move the cursor pointer by scrolling the document down
Ctrl + Page down	Move your cursor pointer to the next page
Ctrl + Page up	Move your cursor to the previous page
Ctrl + End	Move your cursor to the end of the document

20 Conclusion

Microsoft Word is a powerful tool meant for writing and editing documents. It has numerous features allow you to create or edit multiple files in just a few steps. It also allows you to insert images and embed objects from the internet or other files using hyperlinks. You can also set the header information, add comments to your document, and check grammar errors.

Microsoft Word is a complete package for any writers that use it for creating different kinds of documents. It is pretty simple and not at all varied.

Kevin Pitch

MICROSOFT EXCEL

Introduction

Have you ever wanted to play "spot the difference" with your colleagues? Or do spreadsheets seem too complicated for you to learn how to use? Do you ever feel like you're drowning in words, numbers, and percentages? Do you ever wish that there was someone to teach you the ins and outs of Microsoft Excel? Have no fear! This Microsoft Excel guide has the perfect solution! In Excel, you can make it as easy or as complicated as you want. For example, you can make a spreadsheet that only includes one column and two rows or create a complex spreadsheet that will take hours to figure out.

How? With Excel, you can create and use lists to store information. You can sort, search and filter that information. You can clean up and organize the data using formulas and functions, so your lists are in alphabetical order, or a list of numbers is automatically converted into a graph. How great is that!

If you're a beginner looking to learn the basics of Microsoft Excel, look no further than this book! This comprehensive reference guide shows you everything you need to know to create worksheets, use formulas, integrate graphs, format data, and create charts. In addition, it's easy to follow the examples, making learning easier and saving you time! The book is an ideal choice for both personal use and business purposes!

Many books claim to be your best Excel ally, but they are just a waste of your time. Unlike other books, this one is highly recommended by people of all levels, from beginners to experienced Excel users. It's also an excellent reference for people who love learning. It's thorough and research-based, ensuring that you learn everything you need to know to master Excel charts and graphs.

As a beginner, you'll find that there are many things you must learn to become an expert in Excel. For example, learning to recognize data patterns and analyze them is essential. Once you have mastered basic Excel skills, you'll be ready to apply more advanced skills, including learning to customize Excel macros. There are also many tips for advanced users.

If you're ready to move beyond basic Excel skills, this is the book. Although not intended for beginners, it assumes you have some knowledge of pivot tables and relationships. It also introduces you to advanced Excel tools. These tools are ideal for those who need to analyze complex data. You'll learn about advanced Excel techniques, such as financial modeling, which is incredibly complex.

What will you learn?

Once you have learned the basics of using Microsoft Excel, you will probably want to take advantage of its advanced features. These include writing formulas and visualizing data. While these skills may seem time-consuming at first, they can save you a lot of time in the future. Advanced Excel features blur the line between spreadsheets and code. One may use the Visual Basic for Applications, a programming language working inside Excel software, to automate tasks, create interactive forms, and coordinate changes among multiple users.

Basic skills are essential for any job, no matter the industry. You should be familiar with the UI and ribbons to create effective charts and reports. Learning to use basic macros, data validation, and graphs and charts is essential for almost every job. If you have a specific job or want to become a more efficient worker, you should take courses and practice on a project. Learning by doing is a great way to gain confidence in using Excel.

Luckily, most companies now use spreadsheets and cloud computing. Microsoft Excel is now available as a web app for mobile devices. Unlike the Excel desktop, the web app has less features, such as functions, pivot tables, and charts. Microsoft has also recently released an all-in-one office app designed to be used for spreadsheets and other office applications. Fortunately, learning to use Excel doesn't need to be difficult. Take it step by step until you're comfortable using it.

Advanced Excel training for employees improves employee productivity. More efficient employees will complete tasks faster, provide better customer service, and produce more work in less time. Advanced Excel training can result in an hour or two saved per employee, which translates to significant extra hours per week for the company. This is an invaluable investment for your career and your job security. You'll be surprised at how quickly you can increase productivity by taking advanced Excel training.

Daily challenges that require Microsoft Excel

Many books and online courses teach the basics of Excel, but true mastery of the program takes practice. Daily Excel challenges provide an opportunity for you to practice. Excel Experiences may include problems like duplicates, inconsistent formatting of cell, or incomplete data. In addition, you can download an exercise file and work out a solution for the problem on your own.

The future of technology

A new research project at Microsoft, called Calc Intelligence, aims to bring intelligence to spreadsheets and end-user programming. Rather than just extending the grid and formulas that makeup spreadsheets, it will extend them to the point where they can do end-user programming. This innovative approach was spawned from the work of researchers who have used spreadsheets as the basis for research into knowledge computing, natural language processing, software analytics, and more.

In 2021, a senior researcher at Microsoft Research Cambridge, Advait Sarkar, envisioned adding extra cells in Excel for formatting and other purposes. Programming language design is a research discipline, and he envisions more streamlined human-computer interfaces.

Adding advanced analytics features to Excel has already changed the way it works. Users can ask it to calculate average sales in each country. This feature is available only to Office ProPlus users. Access, however, has been around for years and hasn't found widespread acceptance.

One way to make Excel even more helpful is to integrate it with enterprise-level databases. Many BI Software applications already add these integration elements, including Oracle Answers. Another example is Qlikview, which supports exporting to Excel. Currently, there is no clear competition for Excel. The feature set of Excel makes it the most comprehensive and versatile spreadsheet software available. Other less popular spreadsheet applications are not fit for real-world corporate use.

While Excel will remain important for general purposes, it won't become a stand-alone big data tool. But, for high-level manipulation and management, Excel is an invaluable tool. It's unlikely to go away anytime soon. For the time being, the future of Excel is bright. So, what should it do to improve? The future of Excel should focus on its strengths. However, it should be simple but powerful.

21 What Is Microsoft Excel?

You can learn about the different features and functions of Microsoft Excel in this book. We will also cover where to buy MS Excel and the different ways to sell it. This section provides all the information you need to make the right decision. If you are considering selling MS Excel, read this section first. It will help you choose the best option for your needs. In addition, it will save you time and energy by giving you the essential information you need.

The Clear Definition of Microsoft Excel

We describe Excel as a spreadsheet application advanced by Microsoft. It is available on various platforms, including Windows, macOS, iOS, and Android. Its features include calculation abilities, graphing tools, pivot tables, and Visual Basic for Applications. In addition, it falls under Microsoft Office suite of software. But what is Microsoft Excel, and what can it do for you? Let's find out.

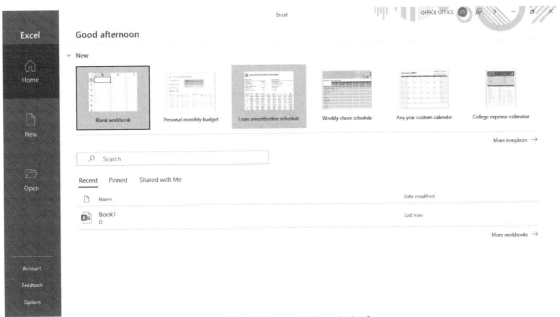

Image 1: The Microsoft Excel platform

Workbook: Every Excel document contains at least one worksheet. Worksheets are grids where you enter information. They can contain large amounts of text, numbers, and formulas. Worksheets can be renamed and have different styles and colors. They can also be organized according to data type entered. The Workbook always contains a worksheet. You can open multiple worksheets simultaneously and switch back and forth between them by navigating tabs.

Hundreds of Calculations: Excel is a great spreadsheet application. You can perform hundreds of calculations using the tool's many functions. It can perform basic math, pivot tables, charts, and more. It can even perform advanced calculations involving large amounts of data. For instance, besides numbers, you can utilize Excel to calculate angles, the tangent of angles, and pi to fourteen decimal places. You can also use this software to perform statistical analysis and report statistics.

Getting Started: Microsoft Excel can be started in either of two ways, depending on your computer setup. For Windows users, click Start button to open Start menu. Next, navigate to the Program Files (x86) folder. Double-click on this folder, and you will see the Microsoft Office folder. Double-click this folder and open Microsoft Office application. There, you've just learned a new application. Alternatively, press the Window button and type Excel in the search box (for the latest Windows operating systems). Click on the Excel icon and the app will launch.

Pivot Table: Another feature of Excel that is often overlooked is the pivot table. These can help you easily and efficiently create complex charts, reports, and calculations. This feature can save you a lot of time by automating the process and reducing the need for manual work. Lookup Formulas: Another helpful feature of Excel is its lookup function, which locates information within a workbook based on the criteria entered. You can write lookup formulas to build dashboards, interactive charts, and even complex mathematical functions.

Chart of Excel Versions

#	Name	Released
1	Version 1	1985
2	Excel 2	1987
3	Excel 3	1990
4	Excel 4	1992
5	Excel 5	1993
6	Excel 95	1995
7	Excel 97	1997
8	Excel 2000	1999

9	Excel 2002	2001
10	Microsoft Office Excel 2003	2003
11	Microsoft Office Excel 2007	2007
12	Microsoft Office Excel 2010	2010
13	Microsoft Excel 2013	2013
14	Microsoft Excel 2016	2016
15	Microsoft Excel 2019	2019
16.	Microsoft Excel 2021	2021
17.	Microsoft Excel 2022	2022

Table 1: Microsoft Excel Versions

21.1 How Does Microsoft Excel Work?

A spreadsheet program is the foundation of Microsoft Excel, which is used to make financial statements and other documents. Anyone can use Excel to create a spreadsheet. To use Excel, click "File" icon on the computer's desktop, and choose "New." You can then decide to create a new workbook in any location. You can also name the workbook and put any relevant information into the cell. After creating a spreadsheet, you can save the workbook to your chosen location.

Many businesses use Excel heavily in their day-to-day operations. They must keep track of many different pieces of information, including inventory flows. Inventory flows need to be controlled to avoid overstocking. Excel keeps track of customer and supplier transactions, important dates, schedules, and dates. Many people use Excel to manage their contacts, keep track of sales and keep track of clients and suppliers. You can even organize your client's sales and financial health with this powerful software program.

You can also enter formatting rules to make data appear a certain way. This will allow you to format a cell for specific text or a range of numbers. For instance, if one types "3/4" into a given cell, it will display as "4-Mar". You may not realize it, but you're entering a fraction. To avoid the "3/4" displayed on the screen, you'll need to format the cell before entering the data.

Learning to use the keyboard shortcuts to save time and make the most of your spreadsheet. While most of us cannot imagine living without a mouse or a touchpad, keyboard shortcuts are essential for our daily tasks. Learn to use the Ctrl + A shortcut to select all the data in a sheet. Then, insert hyperlinks with triangle-shaped button in the upper left corner. Using this shortcut, you can also find information about contacts in a list.

21.2 Where do you buy Microsoft Excel?

If you've been looking for a good office software suite, this the appropriate place. Microsoft Excel is a spreadsheet program that stores data in a special format called a "workbook." Each column and row contains data referred to as a "cell."

If you're looking for a specific Microsoft Office application, you can purchase it separately. Microsoft Excel is part of the Microsoft Office productivity suite. To use Excel's full capabilities, you'll need a subscription to Microsoft 365. This subscription bundles Excel with other Office applications and includes regular updates. A subscription to Microsoft 365 includes Excel as part of a yearly plan and will consist of other benefits, like cloud storage.

What are the possible sell options for MS Excel

In an office, the use of Microsoft Excel is a necessity. Its powerful features make it an excellent tool for managing information on people. Individuals can be tracked using a single column in a spreadsheet. Information such as name, email, start date, items purchased, subscription status, and last contact can all be tracked in one place. Microsoft Excel is widely used by companies and individuals alike for budgeting, analysis, and reporting.

In the corporate world, account managers often require MS Excel skills. This is because they handle records on customers. Microsoft Excel allows them to organize and edit those records. Employees, too, need to be comfortable using the software. In addition, employees with Excel skills are typically required to keep track of their customers' records, making the software indispensable. However, there are several alternatives available. In the case of Microsoft Excel, you should consider the following alternatives.

22 What Are the File Extensions Used by Excel?

What is an Excel extension?

File extensions are a group of letters appearing at the end of a file's name. They are usually two to four or even characters long and can be any length. Excel uses a few standard extensions. This section will cover Excel 2019 to the latest versions. It also covers XLSX files. Here are the most common file extensions used by Excel.

The XLS extension is the oldest file format supported by Excel. The XLS format is the default file extension for Excel versions 2.0 to 2003. It requires more disk space and may contain malicious VBA code. Also, the XLS format has fewer rows and columns than its newer counterparts. The XLS format is not compatible with Excel 97. Whenever you wish to use an older version of Microsoft Excel, you'll need to convert it to an XLS format first.

If you have a file in Excel, the file extension shows you its name and type. Before opening it, you should look for the XLS file extension. Before Excel 2007, it was XLS. The XLS extension was used for older versions of Excel. This format is an archive of XML documents. Unlike the XLS file format, Excel 2007 uses the Office Open XML format to save its spreadsheet information.

XLSB files are a comparatively faster version of the XLSX format. Therefore, they are often used if your Excel file contains VBA macros. Since they are binary files, XLSB files are much faster than those with XLSX or ODF extensions. Regarding file size, the XLSB extension is the best choice for large Excel files. You should use the ODF format if the file size is smaller than 10 MB.

XLS files are Microsoft Excel spreadsheets. They may contain charts, mathematical functions, and other formatting. Excel spreadsheets are often used in business contexts, where they can store financial data and perform calculations. XLSX files use the Open XML standard. Microsoft Excel 2007 and later versions support XLS format. These files can also be viewed using other spreadsheet programs. You can open XLS files with any text editor and view them on your computer.

- The .xlsx extension is commonly used in Excel to store basic data. XLSX is the current and most recent default extension for such an Excel file. This is in addition to XLS, another default extension was used until Microsoft Office 2007.

- The .XLSM is a database that may be used to store VBA code. This is solely designed for usage with macros. With the aid of extension, you can quickly determine if a file contains macros. A second file extension named (.CSV) Comma Separated Values demarcates the data, separated by commas in another file format.

- The .XLSB extensions are used for various functions such as compressing, saving, and opening. If your excel files contain a large amount of data or information, this file extension will help you by first compressing, then saving, and opening them quickly. By selecting File > Save As from Excel menu bar, you could merely save an Excel file in a different file format.

- **XLTX -**An Excel file is kept as a template that can use to create new Excel workbooks.

- **XLTM -** An Excel file with macros that are stored as a template.

- Several file formats are available in the Save As dialogue box, depending on which sort of sheet is active in the document: a single worksheet, chart worksheets, or other worksheets.

- For files that were created in a prior version of Excel or another program but are not yet in the current file format, pick File > Open using the menu bar.
- In Compatibility Mode, the workbook automatically opens when you access an Excel 97-2022 workbook. The use of Excel 2022 file format will enable you to take advantage of the new features that have been introduced to the application since its introduction.

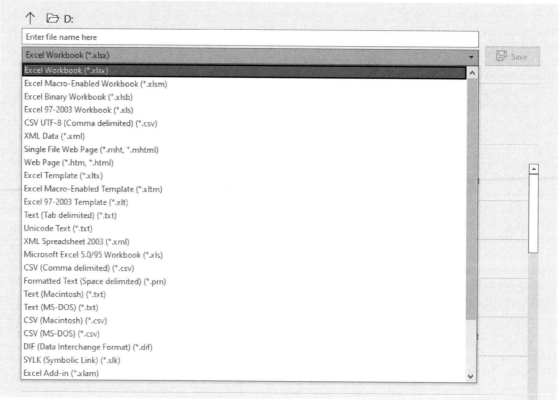

Image 2: Microsoft Excel File Extensions (a)

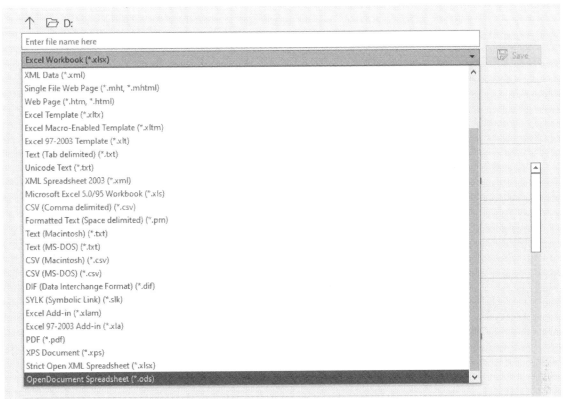

Image 3: Microsoft Excel File Extensions (b)

Where do you download Microsoft Excel Extensions?

If you wish to use a Mac version of Excel, you may wonder where to download the various Microsoft Excel extensions. The extension of an Excel file is essential because it indicates if the file has macros. When you save a document using this extension, it is protected from malicious macros. It is also reliable for security and macros, as it can accommodate large amounts of data. However, this file format can be slow to load and frequently crash.

You can also download the Office Online Extension if you own a Chromebook. This extension allows you to work on Excel files through your web browser. To install this extension, you must have an active Microsoft account. Once you log in, your Excel Online files will be stored on your OneDrive account. This makes it easy to access and edit Excel files on the Chromebook. While this extension isn't a complete replacement for Microsoft Office, it is an excellent option for those who prefer a native Windows experience.

If you can't locate the Microsoft Office Addins folder, you can use the Excel Addin Folder Path file. To find the Addins folder, open Windows Explorer and navigate to the Microsoft Addins folder. Next, click on **Insert,** then select Get Add-Ins. In the Addins dialog box that shows up, choose add-in you need and check the details. You can then click Add, Try, or Buy option.

Once done, you are now ready to use the Excel program with the latest version of Excel.

Once you've installed the new Excel version, you can install the free or paid versions of Excel Add-Ins in the same place. The Office Add-Ins Store is an easy-to-use website that offers a variety of useful Excel tools. It's run in Excel Online so you can access it from either desktop or mobile devices. You can also install the Office Add-Ins in Excel using the Start button.

22.1 Microsoft Excel vs. Google Sheets

If you compare the features of Microsoft Excel and Google Sheets, you'll discover that Google's product is much more flexible and capable. The app's online integration with other Google solutions makes collaborating with others on your spreadsheets easy. Google Sheets' formulas can also connect to other Google solutions, like Google Translate and Google Finance. In addition, Sheets can be used offline. This means that both spreadsheets are equally as useful for small businesses and large corporations.

Both programs have their advantages and disadvantages. However, there's no need to choose between the two if you don't have many documents to store. Google Sheets' free version is a boon for people who need to share spreadsheets with co-workers. The latter also offers collaboration features that Excel lacks. But Google Sheets has a lot of advantages that you should consider before choosing one or the other.

For small spreadsheets, Google Sheets is the better choice. This free tool allows you to work with multiple users on the same spreadsheet and save it in real-time. Microsoft Excel, on the other hand, does not allow real-time saving. You must save your spreadsheet on OneDrive or SharePoint to access it. Microsoft's online spreadsheet also requires you to share the file via email, which isn't ideal for collaboration. However, the free version of Google Sheets has many advantages that make it a better option for small businesses.

While both programs are very similar, one crucial difference lies in the data handling capabilities of each. While Google Sheets' maximum cell capacity is five million cells, Excel can support up to 17 million. This means that Google Sheets' maximum cell capacity is much lower than Excel's. As a result, in addition to better overall performance, Google Sheets' free version is much less user-friendly than Excel's. The same goes for formatting and editing.

If you need to share spreadsheets with a team, you'll want to use Google Sheets. The free version allows you to edit and track changes, but you'll need a subscription plan if you want to share spreadsheets with others. Microsoft Excel is available to all Google users, but many people start with Google Sheets and stick with it. Besides, Excel can also be downloaded to your system.

22.2 Microsoft Excel vs. QuickBooks

While these programs are very similar, they serve slightly different purposes. As a result, one is excellent for small businesses, while the other is best for larger enterprises. For example, small businesses can use Excel to manage their finances and monitor cash flow. Still, for larger companies, the features of QuickBooks are far more comprehensive and powerful when specializing in accounting and invoicing.

In addition to having extensive functionality, QuickBooks Online is also available on mobile devices. As a result, business owners can easily access most accounting features on the go. In contrast, Excel's mobile app is limited in its capabilities, including the ability to invoice, enter bills, and generate reports. Both programs also offer assisted bookkeeping for an additional fee.

Another benefit of using accounting software is that it eliminates the need for manual bookkeeping, saving business owners precious time. With Quickbooks, business owners no longer need to spend hours entering data into spreadsheets; the software will do it for them. QuickBooks is easy to learn and can be used by outsourced bookkeepers. Small businesses can also focus on expanding their businesses instead of managing their books manually. QuickBooks offers many customization options, making it a highly versatile option for smaller businesses.

Another benefit of QuickBooks is its ability to manage expenses. It imports data from connected accounts and digital wallets. Users can also create custom expense rules that display expenses when they run financial reports. QuickBooks mobile app lets users attach pictures of receipts to transactions. In addition, the software automatically sorts expenses to maximize tax deductions. With the help of QuickBooks, you can create shareable profit and loss reports and a cash flow statement.

23 Excel Dashboard

There are several ways to explore the Microsoft Excel interface. First, learn how to use the various tabs to access important information. Excel comes with more than a dozen different cursor shapes. You'll learn which ones do what when you explore these shapes. You can also use the mouse to select any cell in the worksheet. Clicking on a cell will make it active. A name box will appear for the active cell. Once you've changed the cell, you can save or change your work.

23.1 What is Excel Interface?

The interface is composed of several components that make up Excel. These components are the Workbook Components and the Ribbon. The Ribbon has commands, groups, and buttons. Each tab has a different function and is categorized based on its usage. For example, the Home tab has buttons for most frequently used functions. The Ribbon also has tabs for Inserting, Formatting, Data, Review, and Clipboard. The Ribbon can be used to move between different sections of the workbook or between individual workbooks.

The user interface in Microsoft Excel has a few key elements. The status bar displays some common information, and the zoom slider controls the size of the worksheet. It can also be customized. Here are some of the other components of the Excel interface. The ribbon contains tabs and other icons that control the application's functions. Once you've chosen a tab, go to its properties and choose a color scheme. You can also adjust the background of the workspace and background color.

The title bar of the spreadsheet displays the name of the active document. The upper-right corner has control buttons that allow you to change the sheet label, share it, and close the workbook. Other interface elements in Excel include the diskette and excel icon. In addition, the menu bar has commands like File, Insert, Page Layout, Formulas, Data, Review, and the Help tab with a light bulb icon. All menus have subcategories to simplify the distribution of information and calculation.

Image 4: Excel Interface

23.2 Tabs in Excel

File

There are various ways to organize the information you store on your file tabs in Microsoft Excel. For example, the Office Tab consolidates actions such as saving and closing multiple files. This tab is also used to organize the files in your Favorites Group. You can also customize the size of the tabs. You can set the length of the tabs to be automatic, self-adaptive, or fixed. The auto-adaptive option displays most file names, and the fixed option shows the same length for all tabs.

All your Excel worksheet operational aspects are here in the File Tab. The INFO section gives you a chance to set a given password to your workbook to ensure no one else can modify it when you are not around.

Use the NEW option under File to come up with a new worksheet. In addition, you may use the keyboard shortcut Ctrl+N or Command+N (for Mac users).

The OPEN option allows you to open and work on a previously saved file. Choosing the option will open a directory where you are supposed to choose your file's location.

SAVE option ensures that everything you are working on is stored and up to date every time you select the option.

Other options include share, print, close, and export.

The Quick Access Toolbar

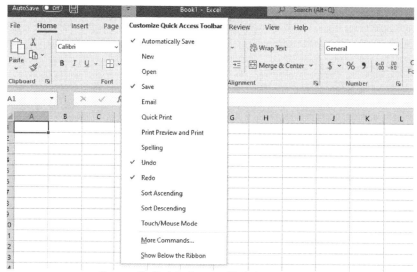

Image 5: Quick Access Tab in Windows

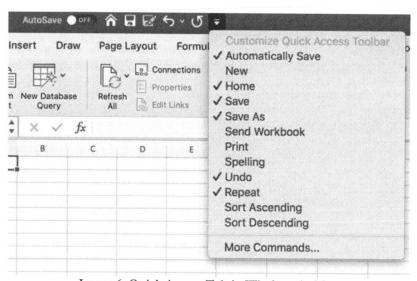

Image 6: Quick Access Tab in Windows in Mac

Quick Access Toolbar (QAT) is positioned to the upper left corner of Excel program. Save, Redo, and Undo are part of the QAT's default commands. Clicking the little downward arrow at the right end of the toolbar brings up a customization dialogue box where you may add or remove icons from the toolbar.

Tell me

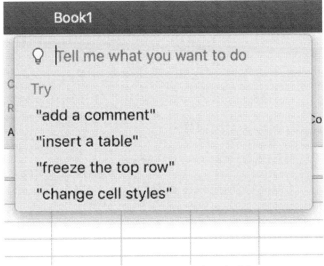

Image 7: Tell me search box in Mac

The tell me search box in the user interface allows for quick and easy locating commands without necessarily going to the ribbon tab or group. Instead, type here any command you wish to use.

Title Bar

The name presently in use is shown in the title bar at the top of excel spreadsheet program. The bar places the workbook's name at the center.

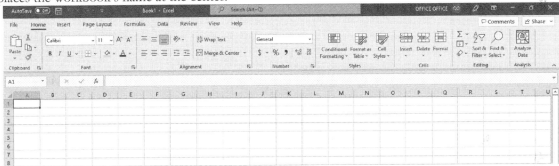

Image 8: Title bar in Windows Platform

Image 9: Title bar in Mac platform

Book1 is the name of the workbook.

23.3 Ribbon

The ribbon is the primary working element of the Microsoft Excel interface and includes all instructions necessary to do most basic operations. You will realize it is divided into tabs with a set or group of commands.

Image 10: The ribbon

Excel Ribbon Tabs

The Excel ribbon has nine tabs: File, Home, Insert, Page Layout, Formulas, Data, Review, View, and Help. You can add additional tabs with your preferred command buttons like Draw and Developer to create a customized Ribbon.

Image 11: Ribbon tabs in Windows platform

Image 12: Ribbon tabs in Mac platform

Home

Contains the most often used commands, such as copy and paste, find and replace, sort, filter, and format data. You can also meet the format painter and other clipboard functions.

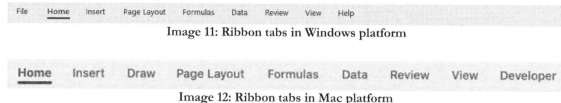

Image 13: Home tab in Windows platform

Image 14: Home tab in Mac platform

With the front ribbon, you can get font tools to tweak your font like font name and size, font color, fill color, alignment, wrap text, merge & center, number ribbon for numerical & non-numerical figures, formatting styles, the cell ribbon, and editing ribbon.

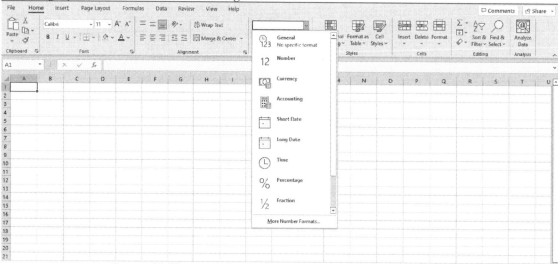

Image 15: Home tab formatting aspects in Windows platform

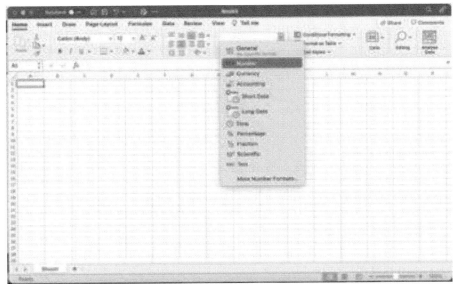

Image 16: Home tab formatting aspects in Mac platform

Commands

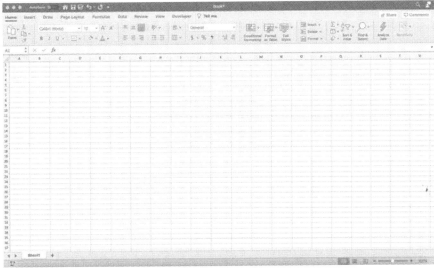

Image 17: Command groups

Commands belong to a group.

Name Box

The Name Box allows you to examine the reference (address) for a single cell or range of cells and set the name for that cell or range of cells.

Functions to Insert

It obtains the desired outcome using a particular function depending on its inputs. It is one of Excel's features.

Formula Bar

You may inspect and alter the function or formula that applies to any cell in the sheet for any calculation in the Formula bar.

The resizable bar above the columns of an Excel sheet is known as the formula bar. For better graphics, everything we enter in any cell shows above it. It's excellent for formatting formulae before pressing Enter.

The function box on its left is where you pick the kind of functions you wish to perform. For example, let's say you're looking for the average (mean), lowest (MIN), or highest (MAX) numerical values in a batch of data.

The name box is located to the left. It shows and informs you of the cell you're in, such as A1.

Image 18: The Formula bar

Row and Column Headings

The column comprises vertical light grey colored lines that carry the letters identifying each column within a spreadsheet. It has a column header at the top (above the first row). Each row in a worksheet is identified by a group of horizontal light grey colored lines with each row identified with a number. Row Heading shows at top of the page (left of first column).

The Vertical/Horizontal Scrollbar

The scrollbar is important for seeing regions of the worksheet by scrolling up, down, left, or right using the Vertical or Horizontal scrollbar.

Page View Options

Page View Options are at the screen's right side, with one on taskbar.

Normal: Default view in the worksheet.

Page Layout: Separates worksheet into many page sizes for print previewing.

Page Break Preview: Displays the worksheet as individual pages with content to examine how a page appears.

Zoom Slider/Toolbar

Zoom slider is at the workbook's bottom right corner. Used for zooming in and out the spreadsheet to appropriate size.

Select all with a single click

To select the full worksheet, click the top left below the Name Box. Ctrl + A is the same thing.

Gridlines

Horizontal and vertical light grey lines in a worksheet.

Cell

We form a cell at the point rows and columns in a worksheet intersect.

Cell Address

The column letter identifies a cell's position, while the row number is the cell address or reference.

Active Cell

A bold cell with a black outline is an Active Cell. An active cell is a distinguishable mark that allows you to input and change data.

Sheet tab/active sheet

The name of sheet tab is bold and shows in the workbook's bottom left corner while a chosen worksheet is presently being utilized.

Cell range

A range of cells is defined as more than two cells chosen horizontally or vertically in the Microsoft Excel Spreadsheet Environment.

Tabs on sheets

Sheet tabs are the sheet names that emerge from the worksheet's bottom left corner in the Microsoft Excel Spreadsheet Environment.

Insert Tab

The Insert tab is mostly used for visualizing data. Using images, charts, and 3D maps entails bringing your data to life.

Image 19: The Insert tab in Windows platform

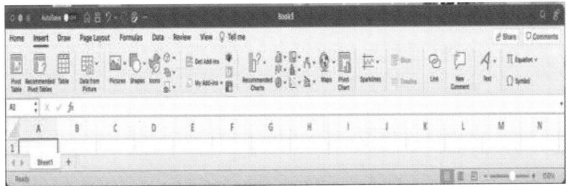

Image 20: The Insert tab in Mac platform

Page Layout

This tab is used to set up pages and print them. It controls the worksheet's layout, margins, alignment, and print area.

Image 21: Page Layout in Windows

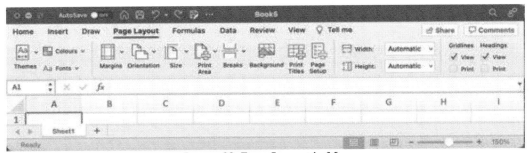

Image 22: Page Layout in Mac

Formulas

This tab allows you to enter functions name variables and change the values of calculation parameters. It is in charge of the computation choices.

Image 23: Formula bar in Windows

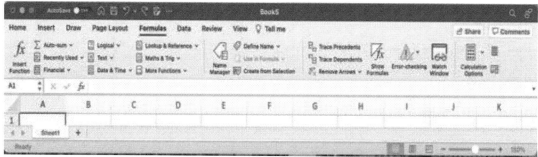

Image 24: Formula bar in Mac

Data

This tab includes controls for manipulating worksheet data and connecting to other data sources. In addition, it has features for sorting, filtering, and modifying data.

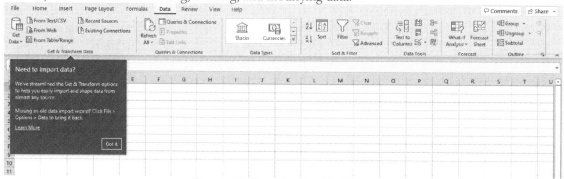

Image 25: Data bar in Windows

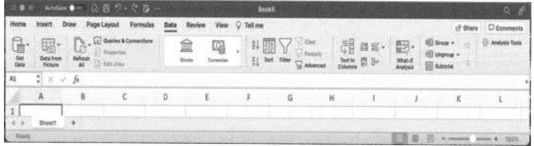

Image 26: Data bar in Mac

Review

This tab mainly provides capabilities for verifying spells, documenting changes, making notes and comments, sharing, and safeguarding worksheets in Excel workbooks.

Image 27: Review Tab in Windows

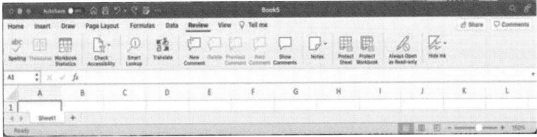

Image 28: Review tab in Mac

View

Switch between worksheets, see excel worksheets, freeze panes, and organize and manage numerous windows are all available from the View tab.

Image 29: View tab in Windows

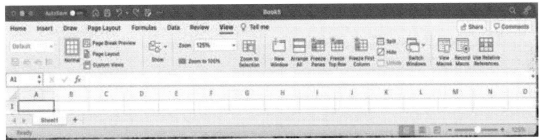

Image 30: View tab in Mac

Help

The tab opens the Help Task Pane, where you can search any term and learn more.

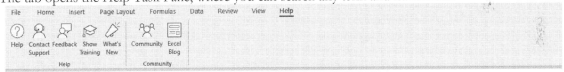

Image 31: The Help tab

The developer is the term for this. The developer tab may be accessed by selecting the File tab, then heading to Options, selecting "Customized Ribbon," selecting the developer option, ticking the box, and clicking OK.

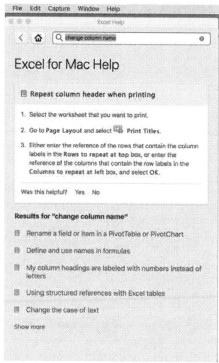

Image 32: Excel for Mac Help

24 The power of sorting and filtering

A spreadsheet is a tool that helps you organize and present data. Microsoft Excel is available for Android, macOS, Windows, and iOS. Its tools include graphing, pivot tables, calculation, and Visual Basic for Applications. It is part of Microsoft Office software suite. First, learn the benefits of filters and sorting. Then you can use them to create useful charts.

The power of sorting and filtering in Excel can assist one organize and subset data to make it easier to analyze. Most users flock to Data tab in the Ribbon and click the Sort and Filter icons. But there's a better way. Learn to use Excel's sort and filter options to create your custom filters. Here's how. But first, let's get familiar with the essential functions of these commands.

First, select the cells you want to sort. In this case, you want to sort by country. To do this, click on the data cell and choose "Cells" as the column name. Select the first column of the data column and click Sort. Now, go to Data tab and click "Filter." You can also choose to filter by date ranges. Make sure you select a date range from which you intend to sort the data.

Sorting and filtering in Microsoft Excel help you understand the data better. By removing unnecessary data, you'll be able to make better decisions. You can easily access the data that you want by using the functions. You'll notice the difference in a matter of seconds! If you're unsure how to sort your data, read the following guide. And remember, there are several ways to sort data in Excel.

Before deciding on your filtering and sorting options, know what each column of data means. Then, you'll need to decide how much information you want to filter. You can sort your data by selecting different criteria. For instance, you might wish to filter all the data corresponding to the cells' color. You can also sort by date. The key is to find out which data you want to filter based on your criteria.

24.1 Sorting data

Before sorting data, you must first decide whether to sort a cell range or the entire worksheet. One column organizes all the data on your worksheet. When you apply Sort, related information from every row is kept together. When working with a sheet with numerous tables, sorting a range sorts the data in a range of cells, which might be helpful. Other texts on the worksheet will not be affected by sorting a range.

To sort data from a Sheet

1. In the example, we alphabetically sort a T-shirt order form using the Last Name.

	A	B	C	D	E
1	**Homeroom**	**First Name**	**Last Name**	**T-Shirt Size**	**Payment Options**
2	115	Susan	Evers	Medium	Pending
3	115	Sharon	Bouvier	Medium	Check bounced
4	115	Andy	Womder	Large	Cash
5	120	George	Bluth	Extra large	Cash
6	120	Dee	Reynolds	Medium	Money Order
7	115	Mario	Bobsey	Large	Check
8	115	Luigi	Boris	Small	Check
9	120	Fred	Cartwright	Small	Cash
10	115	Ronnie	Furlan	Medium	Debit Card
11					

Image 33: Table with T-shirt orders

2. Choose a cell within column C to use for sorting. Use cell C2 as an example.

3. Click A-Z command to sort from A to Z or the Z-A command for sorting Z to A on the Ribbon's Data tab. We'll sort A to Z, for example.

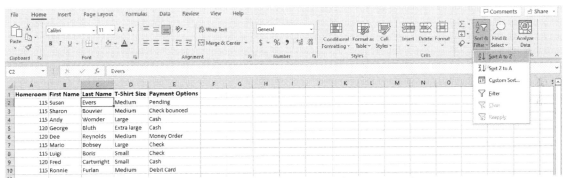

Image 34: Sorting T-shirt orders using last name column

4. The selected column will be used to sort the worksheet. The last name will sort the worksheet in the example.

	A	B	C	D	E
1	**Homeroom**	**First Name**	**Last Name**	**T-Shirt Size**	**Payment Options**
2	120	George	Bluth	Extra large	Cash
3	115	Mario	Bobsey	Large	Check
4	115	Luigi	Boris	Small	Check
5	115	Sharon	Bouvier	Medium	Check bounced
6	120	Fred	Cartwright	Small	Cash
7	115	Susan	Evers	Medium	Pending
8	115	Ronnie	Furlan	Medium	Debit Card
9	120	Dee	Reynolds	Medium	Money Order
10	115	Andy	Womder	Large	Cash
11					

Image 35: Sorted data on T-shirt orders

To sort data of Cell Range

1. Choose the cell range that you'd want to sort.

5R x 2C		fx	Class				
	A	B	C	D	E	F	G	H
1	**Homeroom**	**First Name**	**Last Name**	**T-Shirt Size**	**Payment Options**	**Class**	**Orders**	
2	115	Susan	Evers	Medium	Pending	Freshers	5	
3	115	Sharon	Bouvier	Medium	Check bounced	Junior	8	
4	115	Andy	Womder	Large	Cash	Senior	11	
5	120	George	Bluth	Extra large	Cash	Sophomore	5	
6	120	Dee	Reynolds	Medium	Money Order			
7	115	Mario	Bobsey	Large	Check			
8	115	Luigi	Boris	Small	Check			
9	120	Fred	Cartwright	Small	Cash			
10	115	Ronnie	Furlan	Medium	Debit Card			
11								

Image 36: Choosing cell range to sort

2. On the Ribbon, pick the Data tab, then Sort command.

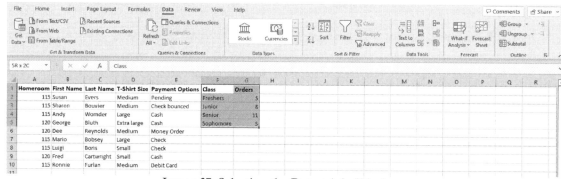

Image 37: Selecting the Data tab in Windows

Image 38: Selecting the Data tab in Mac

3. A dialogue box for sorting will display. Select the column that you'd want to sort by.

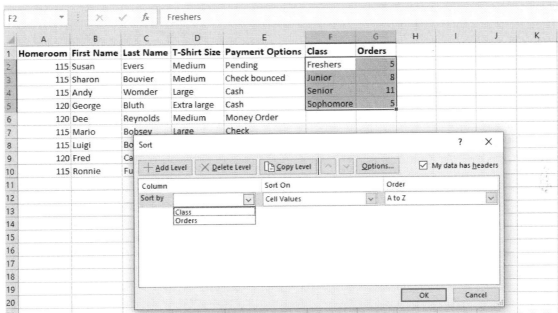

Image 39: The Sort dialogue box in Windows

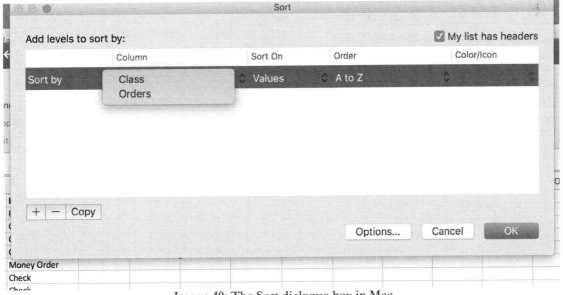

Image 40: The Sort dialogue box in Mac

4. Choose ascending/descending order.

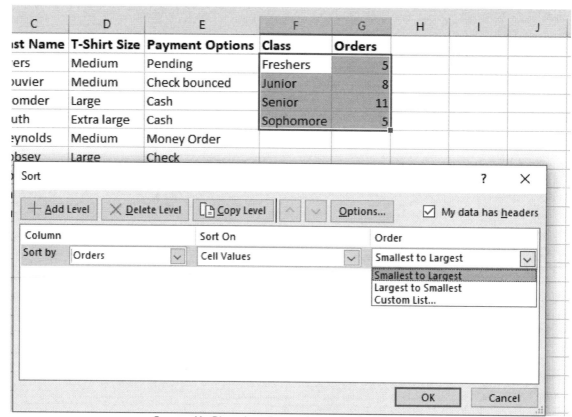

Image 41: Choosing the sorting order in Windows

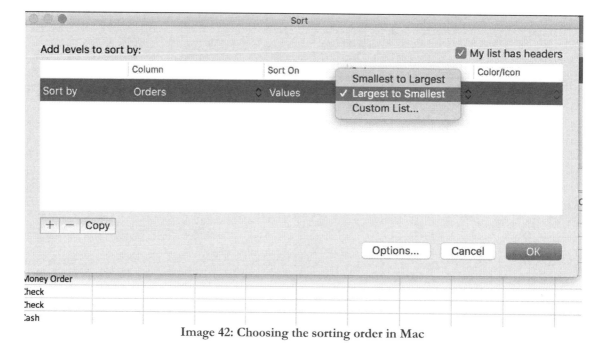

Image 42: Choosing the sorting order in Mac

5. Click OK.

The selected column will be used to sort the cell range. The Orders column will be ordered from highest to lowest, for example. It's worth noting that the Sort did not affect the rest of the worksheet's information.

To Sort Data in one column

Execute the steps below to sort on a single column:

1. Select any cell in the column to sort by clicking on it.

2. Click AZ to sort in ascending order in the Sort & Filter group on the Data tab.

To Sort Data in multiple Columns

Execute the steps below to sort on multiple columns:

1. Select Sort from the Sort & Filter group on the Data tab.

2. The Sort dialogue box is displayed.

3. From the 'Sort by' dropdown menu, choose Last Name.

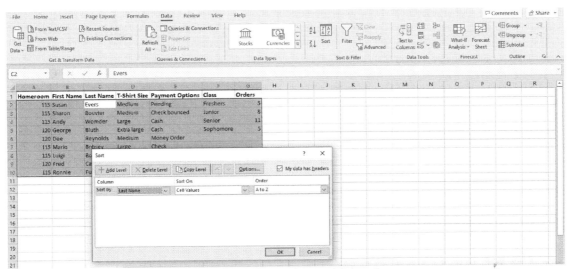

Image 43: Steps for sorting multiple columns

4. Select Add Level from the dropdown menu.

Image 44: Adding level for sorting multiple column

5. From the 'Then by' dropdown list, choose Orders.

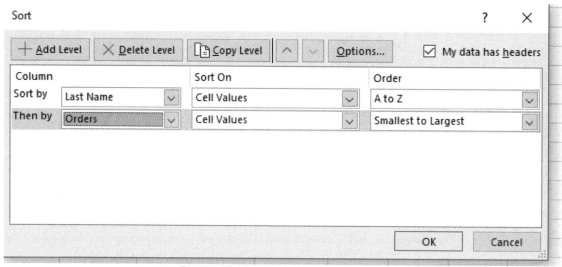

Image 45: The Then by sorting order

6. Select OK.

7. Result. The records are arranged by Last Name first, then by Orders in the example.

	A	B	C	D	E	F	G	H
1	Homeroom	First Name	Last Name	T-Shirt Size	Payment Options	Class	Orders	
2	120 George		Bluth	Extra large	Cash	Sophomore	5	
3	115 Mario		Bobsey	Large	Check			
4	115 Luigi		Boris	Small	Check			
5	115 Sharon		Bouvier	Medium	Check bounced	Junior	8	
6	120 Fred		Cartwright	Small	Cash			
7	115 Susan		Evers	Medium	Pending	Freshers	5	
8	115 Ronnie		Furlan	Medium	Debit Card			
9	120 Dee		Reynolds	Medium	Money Order			
10	115 Andy		Womder	Large	Cash	Senior	11	
11								
12								
13								
14								
15								

Image 46: Results of sorting multiple columns

24.2 Custom Sorting

The default sorting options may not always be able to sort data in the order you require. Fortunately, Excel allows you to establish your sorting order by creating a custom list.

A quick word on Custom Sort: This allows you to choose how the data is sorted within a given column. For instance, rather than sorting information alphabetically, you might wish to arrange it by size. In this scenario, you'll need to make a custom list for the sort order.

1. Select the data to sort by clicking on it.

2. Select Custom Sort from the dropdown menu after clicking the Sort command.

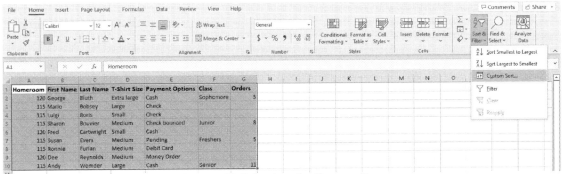

Image 47: Selecting the Custom Sort

3. The Sort window shows up, letting you choose the column and how to sort it.

4. You may use default selections (weekdays or months) or come up with a new list. Select the Custom List option from Order column, then NEW LIST to create a new list.

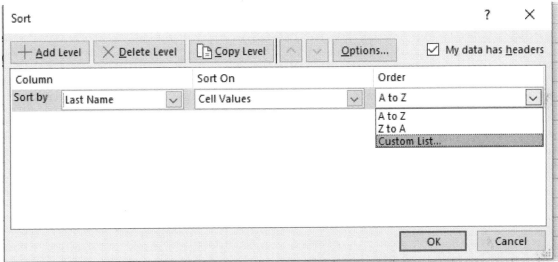

Image 48: Selecting the Custom List option

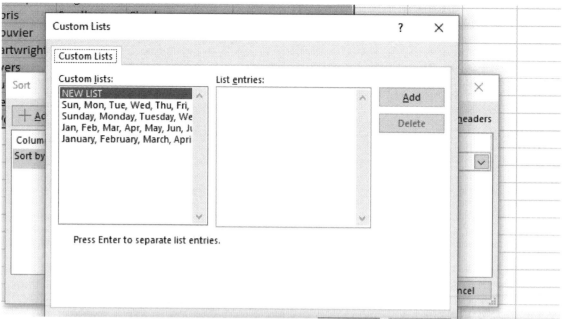

Image 49: Selecting the New List

5. If you're constructing a custom list, type the order you want the data to be sorted. An example is sorting by size from tiny to large.

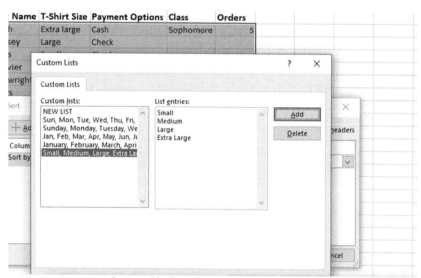

Image 50: Creating your Custom List

6. Your custom ordering list will show in original Order dropdown menu after clicking add.

7. After that, select your personalized list and click OK.

8. It will sort the data.

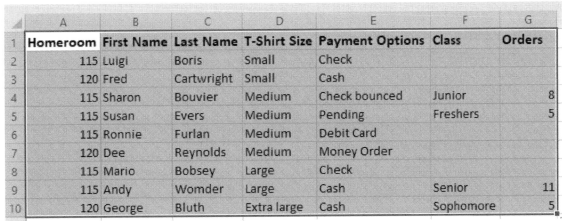

Image 51: Outcome of the Custom List

It's simple to control which column is sorted first in a multilayer sort if you need to change the order. Select the column and alter its priority by clicking the Move Up or Move Down arrow.

Sorting by Conditional formatting

A spreadsheet's most commonly used feature is conditional formatting, which allows users to apply formats to a cell or group. A set of criteria usually determines the formats. It makes it easier to spot differences in cell values at a glance. For instance, you have two entries that are either true or false. For simple identification of circumstances, you might use a custom color scheme.

Implementing Conditional Formatting to more than one cell is the same as adding one or more formulas to each cell. As a result, applying Conditional Formatting to many cells may degrade performance. When working with vast ranges, be cautious. Many datasets contain icons created using Excel's Conditional Formatting. You can sort the data in a specific order depending on these icons. Icon sets replace regular conditional formatting choices focusing on font and cell formatting modifications.

To sort data:

1. Select a range of cells.

2. Select Sort & Filter option, then Custom Sort from the Home tab.

3. Choose the column holding the conditional icons from the Column dropdown arrow.

4. Select Conditional Formatting Icon from the Sort using the dropdown arrow.

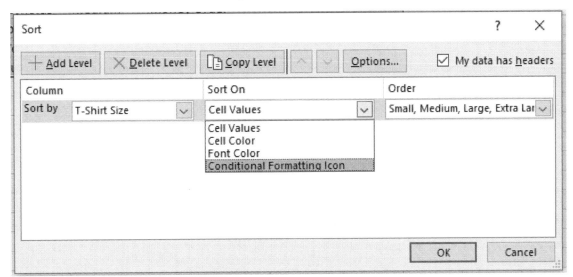

Image 52: Conditional Formatting Icon

5. Choose a color from the dropdown arrow under the order, for example, green.

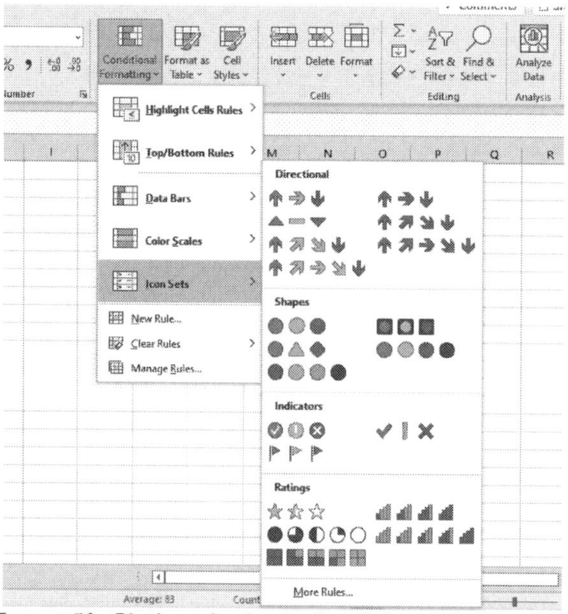

Image 53: Choice of color in Conditional Formatting

6. The color icon items you chose will be at the top of the list if you select on the top from the dropdown list next to the sort order box.

7. To add a second sort level, select Add.

8. Use the same parameters as the previous sort level, but select another color from the Order dropdown arrow. For example, choose yellow.

9. Select Create to add a third sort level, then apply the same parameters as the first two levels, but this time choose a different hue from the Order dropdown arrow, such as Red.

10. It will sort the data and close the dialogue box by selecting OK.

11. At the top of the data range, entries with the green icon are placed together, followed by entries with the yellow icon, and records with the red icon.

24.3 What is a filter?

Filtering data is a common task, but you might wonder how to create a filter in Microsoft Excel. There are several ways to create a filter in Microsoft Excel. Listed below is a sample filter formula. To use the filter, you must enter the desired criteria in the criteria range or a set of cells outside the list. The criteria range must contain the names of the fields in the list and the desired criteria in the rows below. The criteria range may span several rows, so you may want to enter your list of desired criteria in a single row.

The FILTER function takes three arguments: an array of data to filter, a cell reference, and a condition. You can filter by several criteria, including the size or number of rows or columns in the source range. Once you have determined the criteria, use the filter only to display relevant data in the result range. The filter results are dynamic and will automatically update when the data in the source range changes. When a filter is applied to a data range, it spills into more than one cell, so you may need to create a second worksheet to view the results.

A FILTER function is an array filter in Excel that filters a set of data. It belongs to the Dynamic Arrays group of functions. The result of this filter spills into a range of cells, starting from the cell in which the formula is entered. To filter data, you need to supply an array with the included criteria, or you can use text strings. Like a number, you must place text in quotation marks.

24.4 Filtering Data

The filter in Excel aids in the display of pertinent data by temporarily removing unnecessary elements from the screen. Then, the information is filtered according to specified criteria. The goal of sorting is to concentrate on the most important aspects of an information set. For example, an organization's city-level sales data can be filtered by location. Then, the user can see the sales of several cities at any one time.

Working with a large database necessitates the use of a filter. The filter, a widely used tool, transforms a complex view into one that is simple to comprehend. The dataset must have a header row that provides the name of each column to apply filters.

Working with filters is beneficial because they cater to our specific requirements. To filter data, check the boxes next to the entries you want to see and uncheck the boxes of the ones you don't.

What are the types of filter

In Excel, there are two types of filters: number filters and text filters. You can use a number filter to only display data that matches specific criteria, while a text filter lets you hide the data from any column. The difference between these two types is the way they work. A number filter lets you specify which column or row contains a specific character or word, while a text filter lets you select the range of values it includes.

The first type of filter is the basic, or default, filter. The second type is the advanced filter, which lets you specify complex criteria for filtering data. The advanced filter is a more advanced type, allowing you to compare a filtered list to the complete one. You can even copy a list you create with a filter to another worksheet. These are both useful in many situations, and you can find the one that's right for your needs the easiest.

The criteria range is a range of Excel cells containing the criteria you'd like to compare. It can be located outside the list itself. In this case, the criteria range must contain the names of the list field and the desired criteria in the cells below. Sometimes, the criteria range spans several rows. It is possible to have multiple criteria in the same row, called compound criteria. It is not necessary to use all three types of criteria.

The advanced text filter allows you to exclude certain words or dates from the list. It helps search for specific records, such as the top 5,000 in column B. The advanced date filter allows you to select a particular period. This type of filter lets you specify whether you want the filter to be applied only to records that are higher than $2,200. If you are unsure of the best filter for your data, you can always use the advanced date filter.

How to smartly use Filters

To effectively filter data, you must know how to apply filters. You can apply multiple filters to multiple columns, but this section will focus on using just one. Then, you must sort the results using the options in the top-right corner of the pop-up window. Then, choose the condition, value, or color filter. Once you've selected the filter, select it and click OK. Once your filters are in place, select a data range.

In modern versions of Excel, you can define parts of a worksheet as Tables. Although Tables don't look like ordinary cells, they can enable advanced features. You should note that if you sort a range of cells inside a table, the Filter and Sort options will be grayed out. You must first look for the Table option on the Ribbon to identify whether the cells are part of a table.

The filter you apply to a column will only show data within the specified range. Therefore, if your workbook has rows and columns that span multiple sheets, it may not work. To avoid this, use the Go To Special feature. You can use the filter to select a range of cells or apply the filter to one cell range and ignore the rest. If unsure, use the arrows to indicate where to apply the filter.

In addition to using filters to narrow the range of data, you can also utilize advanced Excel formulas to analyze filtered data. These include pivot tables and pie charts. This will help you analyze and visualize your data, and you can apply and remove filters quickly and easily. You will be amazed by the number of possibilities! The best part is that Excel has so many filters that you're bound to find one that suits your needs.

How to add a filter

To add a filter in Microsoft Excel, click the Advanced tab. You will then see the drop-down arrow in the column header. To clear the filter, click the range's name and OK. The filtered data will be displayed in the sheet. You can click the Clear Filter button if you don't want to see any filtered data in the sheet. To add a filter in Excel, follow the instructions below.

When creating a filter in Microsoft Excel, the first step is to create the desired range of data. If the filter is based on cell value, you can attach the criteria to the cell. For example, if you need to view employees' hours, you can select the employees who work full-time. Click OK to hide other information. Click the Filter icon to apply the filter. You can also use the Advanced Filter option to add a date range filter in Excel.

The FILTER function is a formula entered in a spreadsheet cell. This differs from the filter commands on the toolbar or the pop-up menu. The FILTER function filters a range of data and only shows rows/columns that meet the condition. The source range can be a single column or a list of several columns. To use the filter in Excel, type the FILTER function in the appropriate cells, click on "Data" along the top toolbar, and then click on "Filter."

Before adding a filter, you must add a header row on the table to indicate column labels. Once this is done, you must click "Filter" in the Sort & Filter group. Then, you can sort the data and choose the boxes you want to display. When you've selected the data, the arrow button will turn into a "Filter" button, and your filter will be applied to all the rows.

The following are the three methods for adding filters to Excel:

- Under the Home tab, there is a filter option.

- Under the Data tab, there is a filter option.

- Using a shortcut key

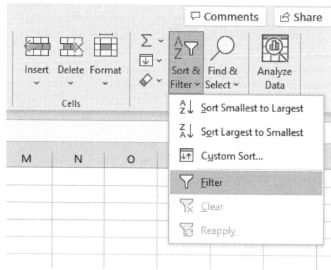

Image 54: The filter option

Method 1:

1. Under the "Sort and Filter" dropdown, select the data and click Filter in Home Tab.

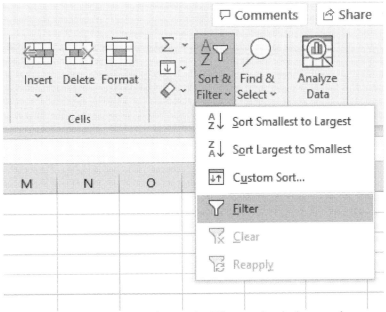

Image 55: Maneuvering to the Filter option in home tab

2. The filters are applied to the data range that has been chosen. Filters are the dropdown arrows within the red boxes.

	City	Invoice Value	
1	City	Invoice Val	
2	Bangalore	213572	
3	Delhi	291927	
4	Mumbai	123579	
5	Bangalore	230687	
6	Delhi	148527	
7	Mumbai	233898	
8	Bangalore	186534	
9	Delhi	239509	
10	Mumbai	119729	
11	Bangalore	177820	
12	Bangalore	101673	
13	Delhi	218910	
14	Mumbai	153982	
15	Bangalore	182091	
16	Delhi	106532	
17	Delhi	228725	
18	Mumbai	100928	
19	Bangalore	209817	
20	Bangalore	114894	
21			
22			

Image 56: Filter dropdowns columns

3. To see the different names of the cities, click the dropdown arrow in the column "city."

Image 57: Filtering by city

4. Select "Delhi" and uncheck all other boxes to get only the invoice values for "Delhi."

Image 58: Choosing the Delhi option

5. Filtered and showed statistics for the city of "Delhi.

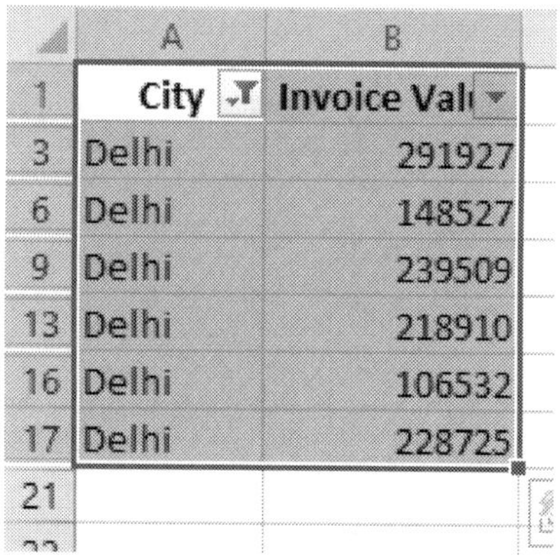

	A	B
1	City	Invoice Valu
3	Delhi	291927
6	Delhi	148527
9	Delhi	239509
13	Delhi	218910
16	Delhi	106532
17	Delhi	228725
21		

Image 59: Results of filtering by city

Method 2:

Under the "sort and filter" area of the Data tab, select the "filter" option.

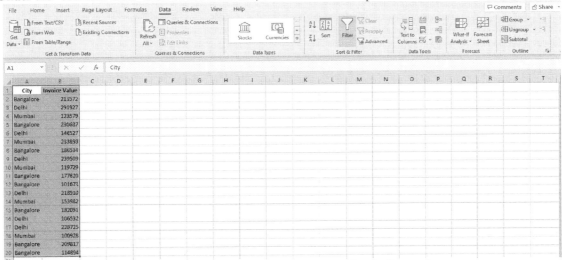

Image 60: Maneuvering to the Filter option in Data tab

Method 3:

Keyboard shortcuts are an excellent method to make everyday tasks go faster. Using one of the shortcuts below, select the data and apply the filter:

Press the keys "Shift+Ctrl+L" at the same time.

How to Add Filters

Advanced strategies are used to filter numbers. Let's look at some examples to grasp better how Excel filters function:

Number Filters Option

Examples:

- To find integers larger than 100000 in column B (invoice value).

- Use the filter to find numbers greater than 100000 but smaller than 200000 in column B.

Use a filter with a number larger than 100000.

Step 1: Click on the filter symbol in column B (invoice value) to open the filter.

Step 2: In the "number filters" section, select "greater than," as seen in the image below.

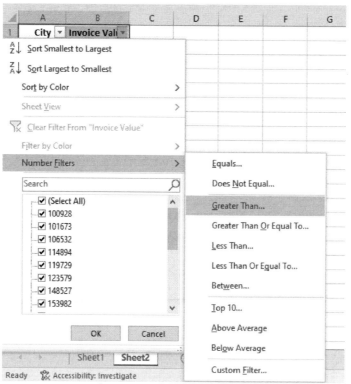

Image 61: Number filtering

Step 3: A box called "custom auto-filter" appears.

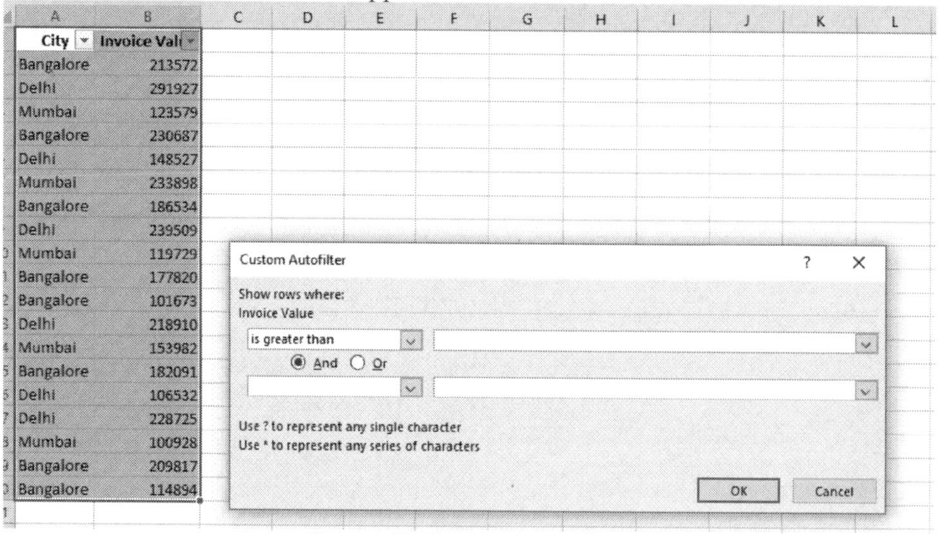

Image 62: Custom auto-filter

Step 4: In the box to the right of "is greater than," type 100000.

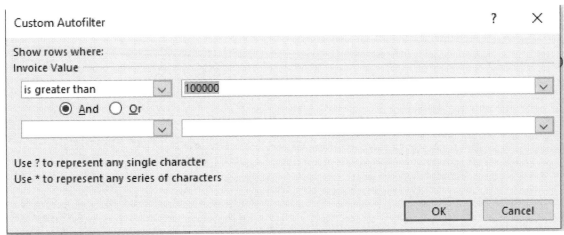

Image 63: Is greater than option

Step 5: The invoice values above 100,000 are displayed in the output. The filter icon is the symbol within the highlighted box.

City	Invoice Valu
Bangalore	213572
Delhi	291927
Mumbai	123579
Bangalore	230687
Delhi	148527
Mumbai	233898
Bangalore	186534
Delhi	239509
Mumbai	119729
Bangalore	177820
Bangalore	101673
Delhi	218910
Mumbai	153982
Bangalore	182091
Delhi	106532
Delhi	228725
Mumbai	100928
Bangalore	209817
Bangalore	114894

Image 64: Results of is greater than option

And the filter has been applied to column B, as indicated.

Filter numbers larger than 100000 but fewer than 200000.

Step 1: Select "greater than" from the "number filters" menu.

Step 2: Select "is less than" in the second box on the left-hand side of the "custom auto filter" box.

Step 3: In the box to the right of "is greater than," type 100000. In the box to the right of "is less than," type the number 200000.

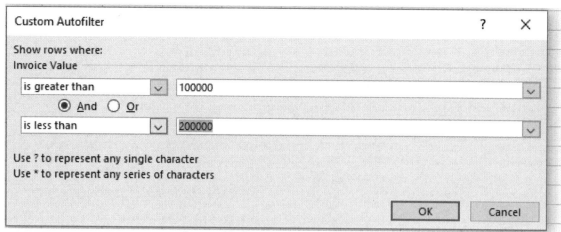

Image 65: Greater than and less than

Step 4: The invoice values larger than 100,000 but less than 200,000 are displayed in the output.

	City	Invoice Valu
4	Mumbai	123579
6	Delhi	148527
8	Bangalore	186534
10	Mumbai	119729
11	Bangalore	177820
12	Bangalore	101673
14	Mumbai	153982
15	Bangalore	182091
16	Delhi	106532
18	Mumbai	100928
20	Bangalore	114894

Image 66: Results of greater than and less than

"Search Box" Option:

Example:

For example, the first column (city) with product IDs is replaced while working on the data under the preceding item to filter the product ID "prd 1" 's details.

The following are the steps:

Step 1: Filter the "product ID" columns and "invoice value" with filters.

Image 67: Applying filters with search box

Step 2: Type the value to be filtered into the search box. So, type "prd 1" into the box.

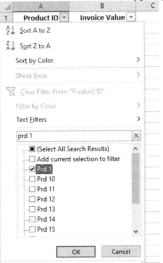

Image 68: Typing in the filter search box

Step 3: As seen in the accompanying image, the output only shows the filtered value from the list. As a result, the billing value of the product ID "prd 1" may be shown.

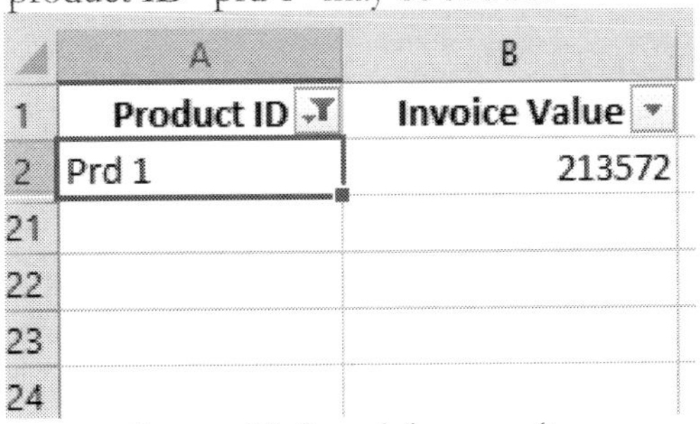

	Product ID	Invoice Value
1	Product ID	Invoice Value
2	Prd 1	213572
21		
22		
23		
24		

Image 69: Search box results

Text Filters

Text filters are used when you wish to filter a column by a specific word or number; when filter cells start or end with a particular character or text; when filter cells are based on whether or not they contain a specific character or word in the text.

Text filters are used when cells are identical to or not equivalent to a detailed character.

Example:

Let's say you wish to apply the filter on a single item.

1. Select equals from the text filter by clicking on it.

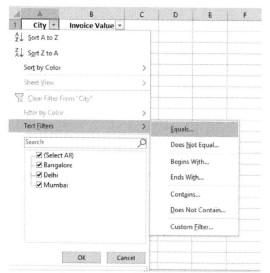

Image 70: Equals text filter

2. It gives you a single dialogue box with a Custom Auto-Filter dialogue box.

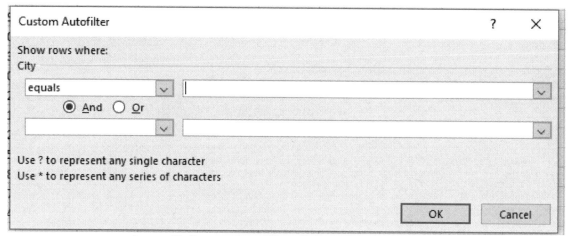

Image 71: Custom Auto-Filter dialogue box for text filter

3. Select Bangalore from the dropdown menu and click OK.

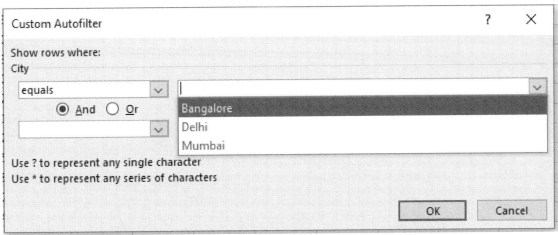

Image 72: Selecting options in Custom Auto-Filter dialogue box

4. Now you'll only see data from the Bangalore category, as seen below.

	A	B
1	City 🔽	Invoice Value 🔽
2	Bangalore	213572
5	Bangalore	230687
8	Bangalore	186534
11	Bangalore	177820
12	Bangalore	101673
15	Bangalore	182091
19	Bangalore	209817
20	Bangalore	114894

Image 73: Data displayed from text filter

Colors can filter data if your data has rows with different colors or cells filled with different colors. Use the "Filter by Color" option.

Grouping and ungrouping lines and columns

You must create a group to create a hierarchy between lines and columns. You can do this by using the Outline class. Then, click on the group, and you'll see an outline around the grouped lines and columns. This outline can have up to eight levels. Once you have created a group, you can use the same method to hide and show individual rows and columns.

To create a group, click the first sheet tab, and all sheets between that tab and the last will be included in that group. You can also ungroup sheets by clicking on one outside the group or right-clicking the grouped tabs and choosing Ungroup Sheets from the pop-up menu. You can also create a group by adding page breaks and formulas. In Excel, the Advanced tab contains more options to create a group, such as page breaks, gridlines, row and column headers, and zeros values.

One way to create a group is by joining rows and columns together. Grouping a sheet is helpful if you want to compare similar content or collapse data areas. For example, group the data by month if you compare monthly sales figures. Or, you can select only the last row and group it by month. To get a clearer picture, you can use a filter.

Another option for grouping and ungrouping lines and columns in MS Excel is to use the Outlines section. Click the "Group" button or the "Subtitle" row to highlight the entries to group rows and columns. You can also click the "Ungroup" button on the data toolbar to remove the grouping. This process is a great way to organize large data sets.

What is conditional formatting in Microsoft Excel?

This formatting function allows you to change how a cell looks based on its values. For example, it can separate dates, hide certain cell contents when printed, and highlight weather descriptions and temperatures. This feature can help you create visually appealing worksheets. You can download example data and practice using it.

The conditional formatting feature in Excel lets you highlight specific text. It is possible to use conditional formatting in highlighting text based on a value greater than ten, a range of values, or a top-bottom rule. You can type in the value field or use cell references if you need to highlight a specific cell. You can apply this style to any cell in an Excel document. To apply it to multiple cells, choose one rule per cell and select another.

One thing to remember when using conditional formatting is that multiple rules can conflict. If multiple rules evaluate true for the same value, the newer rule will always take precedence over the old one. However, you can change the order of the rules by selecting the Manage Rules dialogue box. Also, if you want to apply more than one rule, you can use the 'This Sheet' option to pull up all lists applied to the current sheet.

Conditional formatting helps you identify and highlight important data. Whether you're highlighting budget constraints, tasks, or budget constraints, conditional formatting can help you make the most of your data and boost productivity. Learn how to apply conditional formatting to your spreadsheets and make your work easier and more effective! This guide will walk you through some of the most commonly used conditional formatting options.

Once you've created a conditional rule, click the "Edit" button next to it. The Conditional Formatting Rules Manager window will open. Click Edit Rule in the Formatting Rules Manager to edit or delete the rule. If a condition is false, click the "Stop if true" check box to cancel the conditional formatting. Alternatively, you can click the 'Stop if false' checkbox and OK.

Creating drop-down menus

There are several ways to create drop-down menus in Microsoft Excel. One way is to manually enter the list into the Source box of a cell. To make this work, you must ensure that the cell's column headings are comma-separated and select the option "My table has headers." In addition, to create a drop-down list, you must create a named range.

Once you have selected the cells to include in the drop-down list, go to Data tab. Select Data Validation option from Data tab. This will validate your data and make it more reliable. Once you're done with the Data tab, you can move on to the next step of creating drop-down menus in Excel. Input Message: Type the message you want to display to the user who will be selecting a cell in your drop-down list. The message will appear in a yellow pop-up sticky when the cell is selected. You can also display an error message if the data entered is invalid. However, invalid data will not be displayed. To prevent this from happening, check the Show Error Alert option.

Dynamic Dropdown Menu: You can create dynamic drop-down lists in Microsoft Excel with the use of named ranges. In creating a dynamic list, you must make a cell with a named range containing the items in your drop-down list. Make sure the name of the range contains an equals sign. This will enable a dynamic drop-down menu to update automatically as an item is added or removed.

Removing duplicates

If you have many duplicates, you can remove them from your spreadsheet using the Remove Duplicates feature. This feature will check multiple columns for duplicates. The dialogue box will also tell you how many values are duplicates and how many remain. After removing duplicates, you should recheck your data to ensure that it's accurate. The next time you're working with your spreadsheet, you can use this feature to remove duplicates.

The first step in removing duplicates in Excel is to select the data set you'd like to deduplicate. You'll see a list of duplicate values highlighted in a yellow box. Click "Delete" to remove the duplicate values. The second step involves checking the unique value column to see if it contains a duplicate. If the cell's value is not a duplicate, Excel will highlight it and give you a summary of the values that are removed.

Once you have selected the data, you'll have a list of all the columns you'd like to remove. Then, choose the Remove Duplicates tool. This tool will keep the first instance of a column and delete the rest. After removing all duplicates, you can filter, sort, and summarize your data. Selecting the columns to use in the duplicate removal process is a simple process that will save you a lot of time and trouble. The next step in removing duplicates in Microsoft Excel is to find the column containing the duplicates. To find the duplicates, look for a small square with a downward-pointing triangle. Select the filter icon next to every title to show the list of rows and columns. Then uncheck the checkbox corresponding to the number one. Then, select the rows and columns where the duplicates occur. To remove duplicates from your table, open Power Query editor. Click the left direction arrow button to select the entire dataset. This pop-up menu will hide duplicate data columns. Press CTRL+C to copy the data. Then press CTRL+V to paste it. Then, select the Data tab in the top menu and click Remove Duplicates icon. Once you've selected the column, click OK to close Power Query editor. Once you've finished, you'll be left with a new table free of duplicates.

25 Power of Automatism

What is a formula?

You may be wondering: What is a formula in Microsoft Excel? A formula is an expression that works on the values in a range of cells. If the formula contains an error, it will still return a result, which makes it extremely handy for quick calculations. For example, formulas can be used to calculate addition, subtraction, multiplication, division, and percentages and manipulate date and time values. The most basic type of formula in Excel is a mathematical equation. You can use the standard operators, such as the + and - signs and asterisks (*). You can also use parentheses to surround the part of the equation that you want to calculate first. For example, to change the operation from addition to multiplication, you can replace the (+) sign with parentheses (*).

Another type of formula is a function. We define a function as a predefined formula that performs an action based on specific values. For example, all spreadsheet programs include functions that you can use to find ranges of cells quickly. To use these functions effectively, you need to understand their different parts. Cell references and arguments are essential, as they will guide you through using them correctly. And remember: a formula can only perform certain operations.

How to insert formula

When you're new to Excel, you might wonder how to insert a formula in a cell. You can learn how to do so with the help of the Insert Function wizard, which is located on the formula bar. First, click on the button on the left side of the formula bar and type the function's name in the cell. Then, click on a function in the dialog box, and you'll be presented with a list of related functions. From here, click on the function that you want to insert.

You can also copy the formula by dragging it to another cell. You can copy a formula in Excel using the cell's bottom-right corner. Excel will automatically copy it and adjust the cell references to match the other cells. This is the easiest way to insert a formula in Microsoft Excel. When you copy a formula, Excel will automatically adjust the references, so you'll have no problems with formatting.

To insert a formula in a cell, you need to select it. If you have a range of cells, you can select a cell and insert the formula into that range. The SUM function will calculate the sum of the cells in the range A1-A2 if you select them. If you have more than one cell in the range, you can switch the reference type by pressing F4 or Ctrl+V.

Importance of the language of the formula

The importance of the language of formulas in Microsoft Excel is widely recognized. However, people who are not proficient in computer programming have difficulty creating complex formulas in Excel. One option to deal with this issue is copy-pasting formulas from other programs into cells. But copy-pasting formulas will lead to large formulas, and errors are often undetected. In contrast, the language of formulas in Excel can benefit from the dataflow programming model and the Excel application's IDE capabilities.

The order of calculation is another important factor when it comes to creating an Excel formula. The formula must start with an equal sign (=). On creating a formula using a web browser, the characters following the equal sign are interpreted as a formula. In Excel for the web, the operands, or values to be calculated, are separated by calculation operators. In Excel for the web, it is essential to note that formulas are calculated from left to right.

A formula may be a single cell or a whole column or row. It can refer to multiple values. Typically, a comma or a semicolon is used to separate arguments in a formula. In some countries, the comma acts as a Decimal Symbol. In European countries, semicolon acts as a List Separator.

Importance of the language of the settings

Changing the language of the settings in Microsoft Excel is not as complicated as in earlier versions. Excel used to support only one language for the main interface and multiple languages for proofreading functions. Today, however, it has become much more complex. Fortunately, there are still several options for changing the language of Excel. Most languages are supported automatically, while others may require downloading a language pack. Once you've selected your language, Excel will change its language settings accordingly.

To change the language, go to the Options menu. Click on the Language option. Select the language from the drop-down menu under Choose Editing Language. Left-click on the language, and then click "Set as default." You can also add additional languages to your Excel workspace. This way, you can view your spreadsheets in a language that suits you best. You may want to change your default language to another one, but you should set the correct one for all work with the program.

To change the language of the settings in Microsoft Excel, you need to edit your personal Microsoft account settings. After changing the language in Excel, change the settings in other Office Online products. It is important to note that you can change the language of the settings in Office 365 products, such as Dropbox and SharePoint. Make sure you change the language of all these settings to have the best product experience.

Most common function to use inside the formulas

One of the most common functions in Excel is SUM function. This function adds the values or ranges of cells, returning the sum of the values. To use the sum function, type the =SUM() or =SUM(a1:a10) or +SUM(B3-B13) into the cell and drag the mouse down the column. The AVERAGE function is also very useful for finding the average value.

To sort data, drag the mouse down a column. The MIN function returns the minimum value in a column, and MAX finds the maximum value. Both these functions are helpful when you need to find a high or low value in a data set.

Another useful function to use inside a formula is the lookup function. This function returns a value based on data in a specific cell. The lookup value must be in the table's leftmost column. Usually, it will be in cell B2.

You must specify the cell reference when using the TODAY or NOW function. For example, the NOW or HOME function must be entered in the home cell (A1) or cell A1. In addition, the cell reference must be set to date format if you are using the TODAY function inside a formula. Otherwise, the function will not update when you recalculate the spreadsheet. For example, type =TODAY() into cell A1 to change the format of the TODAY function.

If you want to combine two data records, the most common function to use inside the formulas in Excel is the =CONCATENATE function. It joins two cells or fields with different data types. For example, you can join two records with the same zip code if one is for a city and the other is for a state. The CONCAT function is also useful for combining multiple values.

The order of operations in a formula is also essential. Multiplication is always performed before addition, but you can change this order by using the parentheses symbol. The dollar sign tells Excel to change the cell reference when the formula is moved. The formula itself can be as simple or complex as you want. It's a quick and easy way to calculate numbers. It will not cost you a cent to use Excel's built-in functions.

The TRIM function in Excel is a useful tool for removing extra spaces or padded text. If you need to add numbers to a row, you can use the =TRIM(text) function to get the result without spaces. This function can also remove extra spaces in the middle of words. This is useful when emailing or file-sharing data. Rogue spaces in the formula can mess up the results when a formula is added to multiple rows of numbers.

Remove the formula but keep the result

There are a few ways to remove the formula from an Excel document. The first way is to right-click the cell you want to remove the formula from, then press "Enter." To add a part of the formula to a new cell, press "Return." Then, select the part of the formula you want to add. Note that you can also leave the formula in a partially-formatted state. You can change the calculation settings in your workbook to the manual, such as removing the check mark from the "Recalculate before saving" check box. Changing the behavior of formulas can be useful when you need to hide a formula from someone else. Another way to remove a formula but keep the result in Microsoft Excel is to select the cells you want to change. Sometimes, you can't see the cell when you're trying to remove the formula, so it's better to highlight the cells containing the formula. You can also click the cells containing the formula and highlight them. A2 is the first cell with data and is the easiest to work with.

Another way to remove the formula in Microsoft Excel is to copy the cells where the formula is and paste it as a value. To do this, you must select the cells containing the formula and paste the values you want to change. Once you've copied the cells, you can use the To Actual utility to remove the formula from those cells. It's a great way to save time and reduce the file size.

Autofill

The Autofill feature in Microsoft Excel allows you to fill cells with data based on the patterns in adjacent cells. You can even use this feature to fill more than one row and column at a time. You simply enter the first day of the week and drag the fill handle to the cell you want to fill. You can also use the Smart Tag to fill formatting only.

The Autofill feature is particularly useful when working with dates and extending a series of numbers, days or months. Excel recognizes dates and times and adds the first two amounts to the range. You can even go back in time by changing the date or year of a date. You can also select an exact number by specifying the initial value in two neighboring cells. This way, you can use Autofill to automatically fill in complex patterns, such as dates, numbers, and more.

Autofill in Microsoft Excel allows you to fill in a range of cells based on a pattern. Select a cell from the list and drag it into another range. This feature also allows you to use the same pattern in multiple cells. For example, if you wanted to fill a cell with a number, you could hold down Ctrl and drag the fill handle to the selected cell. This action will copy the value into the range. Afterward, you can click on the Fill Handle to select additional cells.

Access AutoFill by using Fill handle (the small square to the cell's bottom-right corner that gives the opportunity of filling adjacent cells).

Using AutoFill to Enter a Series of Values

AutoFill command will recognize a given pattern and complete more values. Let's use this to complete days of the week.

- Select cell containing first value for the series (**Monday**)

- Hover your mouse towards the cell's bottom right corner until it forms a black plus symbol.

- Click without releasing and drag either across or down the cell you intend to fill

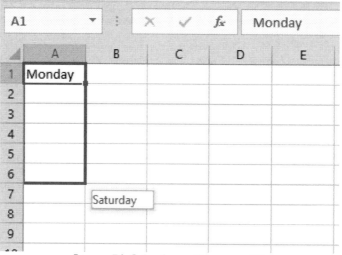

Image 74: Selecting cells to autofill

- The AutoFill will complete days

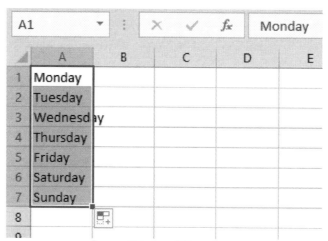

Image 75: Autofilling days

Applying AutoFill in Copying Data

AutoFill Command allows one to copy and paste their data to other cells of the same worksheet. Here are the steps.

- Select cell with the data to copy

- Hover mouse to form the black plus sign

- Click and drag across or down

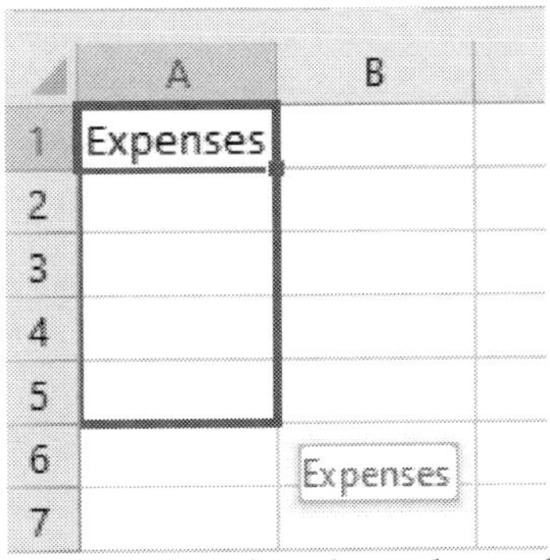

Image 76: Copying through autofill

- AutoFill will copy the data into intended cells.

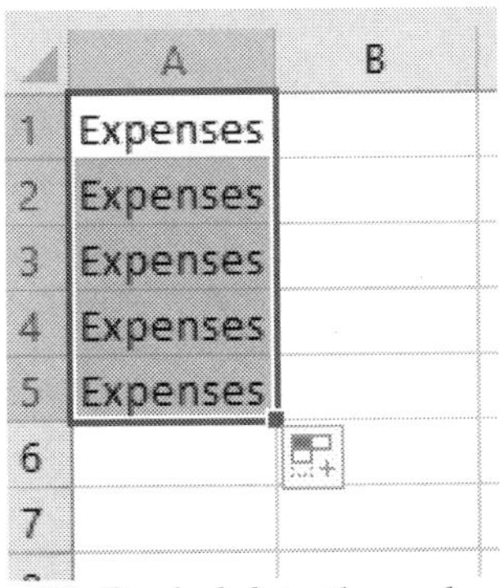

Image 77: Copied data through autofill

What are VBA and MACROs

What are VBA and MACROs? Both are programming languages for Microsoft Excel. Macros allows one automate almost any task within the program, from creating customized charts to performing data-processing functions. Often, these languages are used by programmers to create advanced tools that do not come with the Excel program itself. In addition, VBA is also used to work in non-Microsoft environments, such as in commercial or proprietary applications.

VBA (Visual Basic for Applications) is a programming language that automates tasks in Excel and other Microsoft Office applications. Macros are collections of instructions or code that Excel reads to perform tasks. In addition to automating simple tasks, these programs can create shortcuts for specific functions. Learning the basics of VBA and MACROs in Excel will streamline your work processes.

MACROs allow you to automate repetitive tasks within Microsoft Excel, such as adding values to a list or entering data in a database. You can create custom functions using VBA, but remember to use a unique name for each. Macros are not permitted to share the same name as other macros or Excel functions and properties, so giving them unique names is essential. You can also use a macro to record a specific task that you perform regularly.

To start coding a macro, open the VBA editor by pressing Alt + F11 in Excel. This will show you the code for all open workbooks. You can also view the code by double-clicking an object. Remember, recorded macros always appear in modules. So, before you begin coding, you should define all variables used in the macro. In addition, make sure to save your workbook as a Macro Enabled Workbook.

Where to download excel templates for different needs

A resource library is a great place to start downloading templates. These templates come in various categories, such as business, financial management, planners, and trackers. By selecting a category, you'll be able to see all of the templates that fall under that category. You can then download a template based on its purpose. For example, you might want to create a calendar or a sales report. The resource library will have dozens of calendar templates to choose from.

SpreadsheetZONE is another resource where you can download Excel templates. You can either browse the collection by category or search for specific templates. The templates are alphabetically organized and updated often. Some templates that can be downloaded from the site are Invoice & Inventory Management Tool, Temperature Conversion, Professional Invoice, Global Industry vs. Agriculture Dashboard, and more. This resource is excellent for anyone who needs a spreadsheet for a specific need. It is important to note that SpreadsheetZONE has ads, so you may not immediately see every template you need.

Once you get the template you're looking for, you'll need to enter it into the Default personal templates location field in Microsoft Excel. This will allow you to choose the template appearing automatically each time the program opens. Then, you can use it to create a personalized calendar. Another useful resource is Wincalendar, which offers a calendar for different occasions. There's something for everyone: a graph paper template, a fitness chart for a man, and even a weekly meal planner. Other resources include the default Excel Templates Gallery you access when you open the Excel application to create a new workbook, Microsoft Office Resource Library, Spreadsheet123, Vertex42, and Template.net.

What are TRUE and FALSE

What are TRUE and FALSE in MS Excel? TRUE and FALSE are two logical functions that indicate whether or not something is true. In other words, if a cell contains 'True' and 'False,' the cell is TRUE. These functions are needed to make the spreadsheet compatible with other software. While they don't expand the abilities of logical tests, they can be extremely useful for calculating several conditions simultaneously.

This formula compares text values character-by-character in alphabetic order. For example, if cell A1 contains 'ag,' it will return TRUE. On the other hand, if cell A1 contains 'p,' it will return FALSE. In other words, if cell A1 is 'agave,' it will be true, and if cell B1 contains 'p,' it will be FALSE.

To create a logical equation or formula, you must understand how the two functions work. TRUE indicates the logical value, and FALSE indicates the logical opposite of it. So, for example, if you want to create a chart in Excel that contains all the phone numbers of different organizations, you'll need to understand how the two functions work. In addition, you need to understand how these logical operators work in Microsoft Excel to use the formulas effectively.

The formulas in Excel are flexible enough to handle Boolean values. By default, TRUE and FALSE values are numbers, but you can use them in formulas without double quotation marks. If you're wondering how to use these values in Excel, check out the sample file below. You'll learn the basics of using the COUNTIF and COUNTIF functions in Microsoft Excel.

25.1 Cell Referencing

We define a cell reference as an alphanumeric data or value in excel to identify or locate a cell in the worksheet. The cell reference comprises one or more letters for columns and a number for the row, e.g., **A1**. You can locate the data you wish to calculate using the cell reference. The cell reference is also known as the cell address.

Cell Reference Types

Knowing the types of cell references is pertinent to understanding better how to use the cell references together with formulas. So now, let's quickly examine the types of cell references.

Relative References

By default, the cell references in the Excel worksheet are relative. When the cells are copied across multiple cells, the cells change based on the relative position of rows and columns. For instance, when you added =**B3+C3** in cell **D3** and copied it to cell **D4**, the formula will change to =**B4+C4.** The relative references are best used when replicating the same action across multiple rows and columns. To create and copy formula using the relative references, use the following procedures

- Click cell **(D2)** to enter the formula and type in the formula =**(B2*C2)** in the cell to get the anticipated result

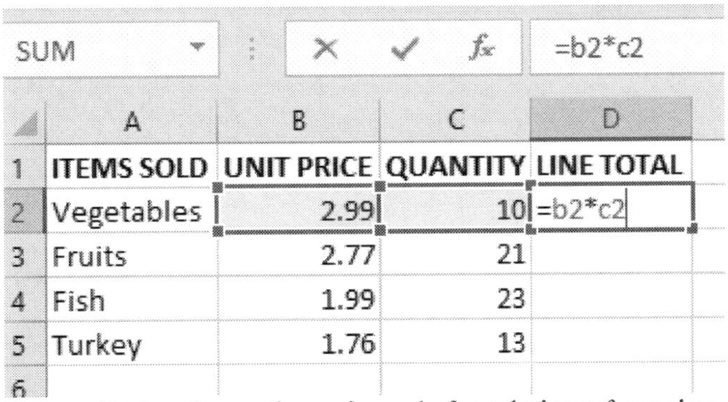

Image 78: Implementing a formula for relative referencing

- Press the **Enter** key, and formula is executed and will show results

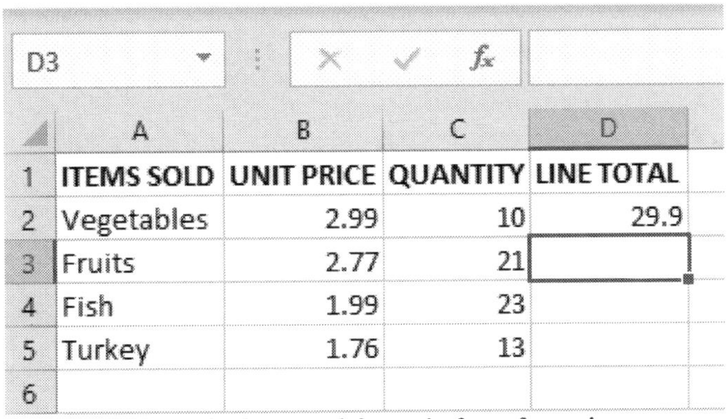

Image 79: Executed formula for referencing

- Identify the **Fill handle** at lower part of **D2**, click and drag down to **D5.**

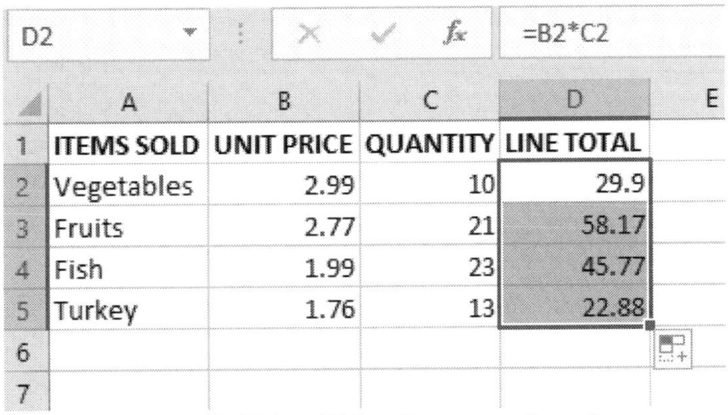

Image 80: Using fill handle to copy formula

- The formula is copied down and the results will show in each cell.

Absolute Cell Reference and Multiple cell Reference

An absolute cell reference stays locked on a specific cell or cell range, even if the formula is changed, making use of the dollar sign ($).

Multiple cells use the dollar sign to keep the row or column constant.

A3	Both column and row won't change on copying data
A$2	**The row remains constant when copied**
$A2	**The column remains constant**

Table 2: Using dollar sign to reference cells

In the example below, we will be using cell D1, which contains the tax rate of 8%, to calculate the sales of each item in column E. However, we must make the D1 constant when we copy the formula to fill other cells. If the D1 is not constant, the following result will be obtained.

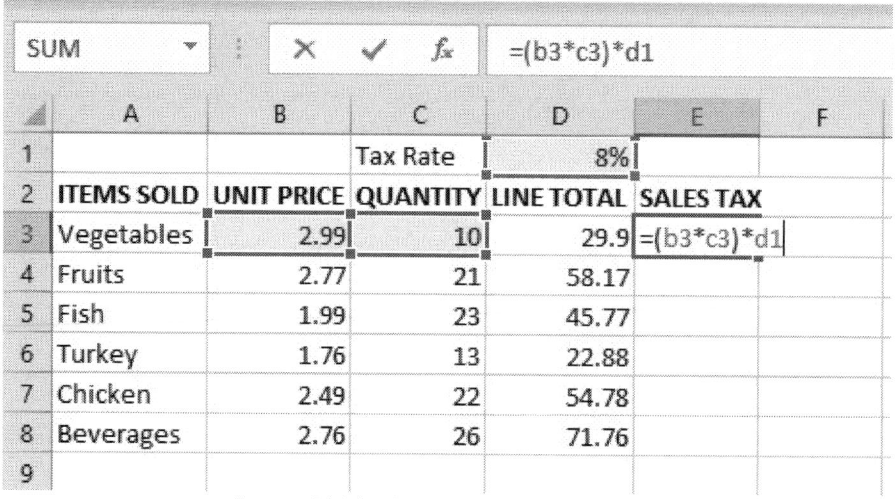

Image 81: Tax implementation formula

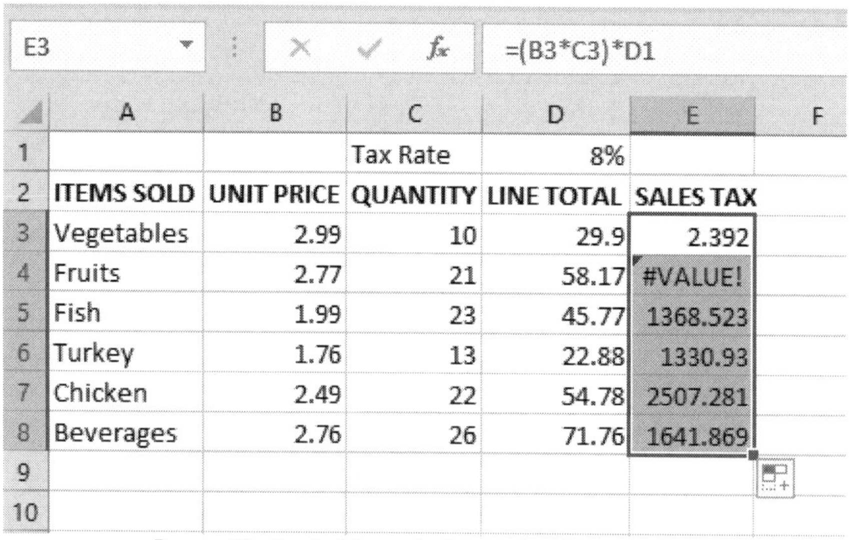

Image 82: Copied formula for tax implementation

To avoid getting the result shown in the table above, follow these steps using the dollar sign

- Click on the cell **(E3)** where the formula will contain and type in the formula **=(B3*C3)*D1** in the cell to get the anticipated result.

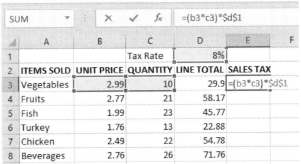

	A	B	C	D	E	F
1			Tax Rate	8%		
2	ITEMS SOLD	UNIT PRICE	QUANTITY	LINE TOTAL	SALES TAX	
3	Vegetables	2.99	10	29.9	=(b3*c3)*d1	
4	Fruits	2.77	21	58.17		
5	Fish	1.99	23	45.77		
6	Turkey	1.76	13	22.88		
7	Chicken	2.49	22	54.78		
8	Beverages	2.76	26	71.76		

Image 83: Using the dollar sign to avoid errors

- Press the Enter key to execute the formula, showing the outcome in the cell.

	A	B	C	D	E
1			Tax Rate	8%	
2	ITEMS SOLD	UNIT PRICE	QUANTITY	LINE TOTAL	SALES TAX
3	Vegetables	2.99	10	29.9	2.392
4	Fruits	2.77	21	58.17	
5	Fish	1.99	23	45.77	
6	Turkey	1.76	13	22.88	
7	Chicken	2.49	22	54.78	
8	Beverages	2.76	26	71.76	

Image 84: Outcome of the formula with the dollar sign

- Use **Fill handle** on cell **E4** and drag upto cell **E8**.

- Release your mouse and you will see the result in each cell

E3 f_x =(B3*C3)*D1

	A	B	C	D	E	F
1			Tax Rate	8%		
2	ITEMS SOLD	UNIT PRICE	QUANTITY	LINE TOTAL	SALES TAX	
3	Vegetables	2.99	10	29.9	2.392	
4	Fruits	2.77	21	58.17	4.6536	
5	Fish	1.99	23	45.77	3.6616	
6	Turkey	1.76	13	22.88	1.8304	
7	Chicken	2.49	22	54.78	4.3824	
8	Beverages	2.76	26	71.76	5.7408	
9						
10						

Image 85: Autofill results without errors of the formula

26 Graphs and Charts

26.1 What is a graph?

Using graphs in Excel is simple, quick, and useful for many calculation purposes. The chart feature of Microsoft Excel offers several different graph types. While a chart represents values, a graph represents the relative percentage of data in a set of values.

Line graphs are popular with Microsoft Excel users. This type shows changes over time and can be used to compare trends. For example, you can plot an employee's compensation or the number of hours they worked in a week against their annual leave.

A graph in Excel is a representation of data in a worksheet. A graph represents a network consisting of a finite set of vertices and edges. Graphs have many real-life applications and represent various networks, including telephone networks, circuit networks, and city paths. Graphs are also used in social networks such as Facebook, representing each person as a vertex, with a corresponding node containing their name, gender, and location. It allows users to analyze data more efficiently. Graphs in Excel are easy to create and can represent a variety of metrics. The first step is to know your data. Then, you can sort the data before making a graph and add a border to separate the data points.

In a presentation, a graph can be a huge impact. You can choose from many different graph types to make your presentation look good. Make sure to understand all the different graph types and find the one that fits your needs.

What are the types of graphs?

A line graph is one of the simplest and easiest to read. It is also helpful in displaying changes over time. Line graphs also have the benefit of displaying multiple results with different lines. For example, if you compare three different types of smartphones, you could use a line graph with different colors for each. As you can see, there are many graphs in MS Excel. However, choosing the right one for your project depends on your data and the argument you're trying to make. So the first step is deciding what you want to display, then arranging and formatting the data.

Line Graphs

The line graph is the most common, straightforward, and fundamental type of chart graph. This is the most effective way of displaying many closely related data series. In addition, because line graphs are incredibly lightweight (they are made up of mere lines, as opposed to more sophisticated chart types, as seen below), they are great for achieving a minimalistic style.

Tips:

- Eliminate all gridlines

- Eliminate all shading and borders

- Each series should be highlighted with a different color.

Column Graphs

Observers may also use column graphs to see if parameters shift over time. If only one data parameter is included, they are called "graphs." When several parameters are active, users cannot gain much input into how every parameter has improved. When the avg. No. Of hours worked /week and the avg. No annual leaves are plotted side by side. As seen in the Column graph below, the avg number of hours worked/ week, and the avg number of Annual leaves do not have the same consistency as the Line graph.

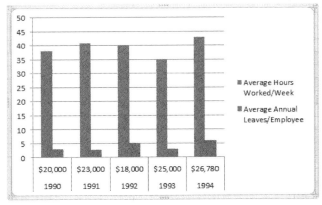

Image 86: Column graph

Bar Graphs

These are identical to column graphs in that the constant variable is allocated to Y-axis, and the parameters are measured against the X-axis. When displaying a single data series, bar graphs (or columns) are the most effective representation method. Because bar charts are heavier than line graphs, they are more successful at emphasizing a point and standing out on a page than the other two.

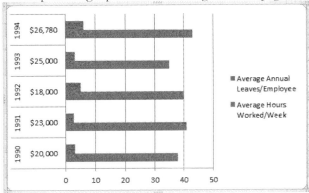

Image 87: Bar graph

Tips

- Eliminate all gridlines
- Reduce the width of the space between bars

Combinations graphs

Combining the two graphs above results in a combo chart containing bars and lines of different lengths. In the case of two data series that are on entirely different scales and may be expressed in completely different units, this is incredibly useful. For example, the most frequently used illustration is a bar graph with money on one axis and percentages on the other.

Tips

- Eliminate all borders and gridlines.
- Include a legend
- Reduce the breadth of the bars' gaps.
- Axis adjustment

How do you create graphs?

For example, if you are a movie theater owner, you may want to keep track of ticket sales of older movies. You can choose the names of the movies to show in column A, the number of tickets sold each month in column B, and so on. You can also add bold headings to make the chart more readable.

The type of graph you choose depends on your data, including how many parameters you wish to include.

Another popular type of graph is a line graph. This graph can show data in a specific period, from one day to five years. The line graph is the most basic type and is available in all versions of MS Excel. It is possible to make a variety of different types of line graphs, depending on your needs.

To create a graph in Excel, you first must import data into the spreadsheet. Then, you can either type in the data manually or copy and paste it. Then, you need to assign the correct data type to each column. If the data isn't formatted properly, your graph will not show up.

Another method of creating a graph in MS Excel is to save it as a picture or insert it into a visual template. To do this, you can right-click on the chart and click on "Save As Picture." You can give the picture a name and select the file type from there. The file type is JPEG. Click on "Save" when finished.

Microsoft Excel is still the favored tool among finance and accounting professionals for many activities, and data visualization is no different. MS Excel provides the ability to create a wide range of charts and graphs. In addition, the templates are easily modifiable, allowing you to improve the financial models. Finally, graphs and charts created in Excel can be exported to other applications to be included in your report or presentation.

How to Create a Graph in Excel: A Step-by-Step Guide

The following section explains how to create any type of chart in Microsoft Excel:

- When entering the data, Microsoft Excel should be utilized. Another feature of Microsoft Excel is importing data from other apps.

- Check that the data is organized in a table format and that all variables are labeled accurately.

- Select the data that will be used to construct the graph. Make sure to include the labels, as well.

- Select the appropriate data and select Insert -> Charts from the menu bar. Using one of the templates will save time if you are definite about the type of graph that would be most useful for your project. If you're unsure which graph type to use, you can look at the Recommended Charts section. Excel will then give you a plethora of appropriate graph options for your data.

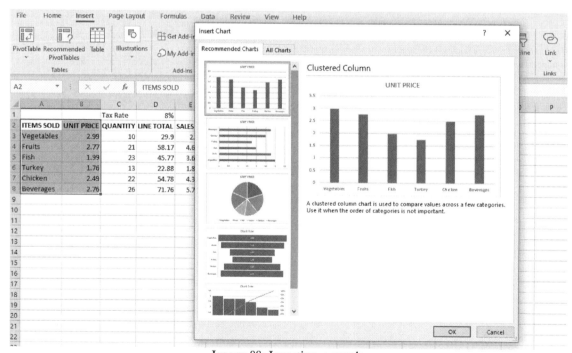

Image 88: Inserting a graph

26.2 What is a chart?

The first step to creating your chart is giving it a name. This is a simple process and can be fun. The default title of the chart will probably be "Chart Title," but you can change it to something more meaningful to you. You can also change the size and color of labels.

A chart is an excellent way to represent data visually. In Excel, data can be challenging to interpret, so a chart can help make it easier to make sense of the information. In addition, using Excel's built-in charts makes the data analysis process easier and faster. There are many charts, each with different functionality and presentation styles.

In business presentations, most presentations feature charts to help audiences remember information. Charts can help businesspeople visualize key data and take action based on the findings. As companies become more data-driven, they're becoming more essential. For example, department heads use charts to assess the effectiveness of new marketing campaigns or strategies. For example, a chart can help show how many orders are fulfilled at a warehouse per hour. When used in business presentations, charts can help executives visualize data more easily and make their presentations more memorable.

Charts help people understand complex data. They allow people to easily see trends and patterns, and they can tell stories. For example, a column chart may show the number of unique visitors to Computer Hope over time. As sales increase, the bar lengths increase, indicating an increase. There are many types of charts available to display data. Listed below are some of the most popular ones supported by various programs. You can find one that suits your needs and will help you explain complicated data in an easy-to-understand way.

There are various types of charts in Excel one can create depending on the data you're working with. You can create pie charts, scatter plot charts, and bar charts. Once you've decided on the chart type, you can use the Chart Design tab.

Column charts are one of the most common charts used in presentations. These types of charts compare multiple values in a single column. They are best used when there are several data sets and you want to compare multiple variables simultaneously. You can also create combo charts by combining a series with multiple values.

A column chart can use pictures or numbers. For example, a pictograph can show how many calories a cheese and bacon hamburger has. A pictograph showing the number of calories in beet greens is another example. A chart that shows stock market data is another type of chart. Stock market charts can display information about stocks or the volume of shares traded over time. Excel has several different types of charts, and each shows different information.

26.3 Types of charts

Several different charts are available in MS Excel, including line charts, column charts, and pie charts. Each of these types of chart can be used for different purposes. A line chart, for example, may show the number of times a value occurs. A column chart, on the other hand, may show information about two discrete objects, such as stocks, prices, or profits.

A pie chart is a basic chart, but more advanced versions are available for more complex applications. For example, a university might use a pie chart to show the racial makeup of its students. A doughnut chart lets you visualize a single data series in a pie chart format. It also enables you to add additional data sets in layers to the chart. The best use for this type of chart is to compare two different sets of information.

Another chart type in Excel is the area chart. This has the same pattern as the line chart and is a better choice for indicating the change between different data sets. Similarly, the pie chart and doughnut chart help show percentages, while the surface chart represents an optimum combination of two data sets. Again, excel makes these charts and graphs very easy to create once you've mastered a few basic steps.

Column Charts

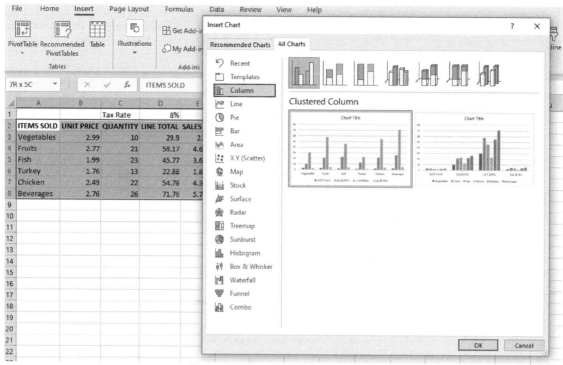

Image 89: Column chart selection

These charts represent data with vertical bars. They are important when comparing groups of data. To use the column charts:

- Highlight your data

- Select the option for **Columns** and then **Clustered Columns** in the chart menu.

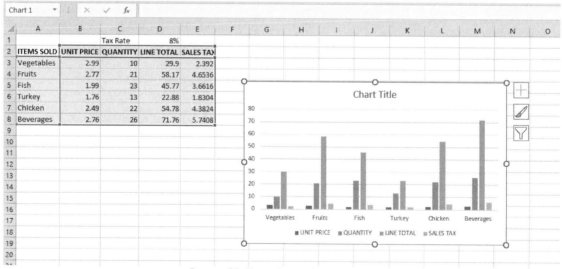

Image 90: Inserting column chart

Bar Charts

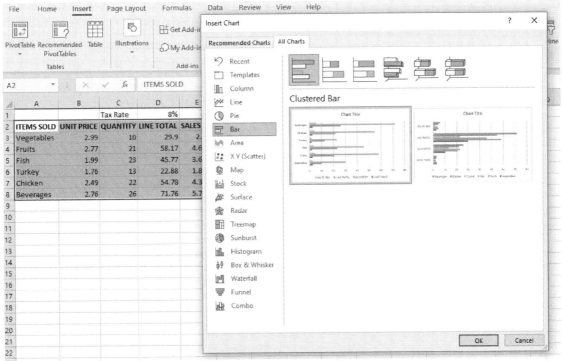

Image 91: Bar chart options

You can also use them for comparing a group of data. They differ from column charts because they represent data with horizontal bars. To use column charts:

- Highlight your data set

- Select the option for **Columns** and then **Clustered Bars** in the chart menu.

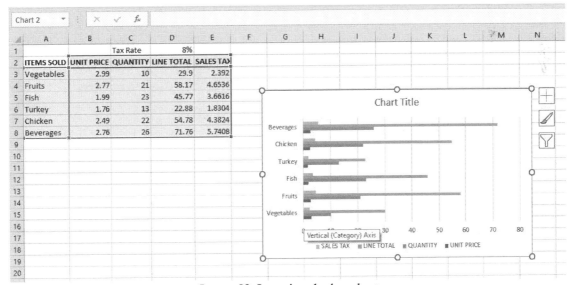

Image 92: Inserting the bar chart

Line Charts

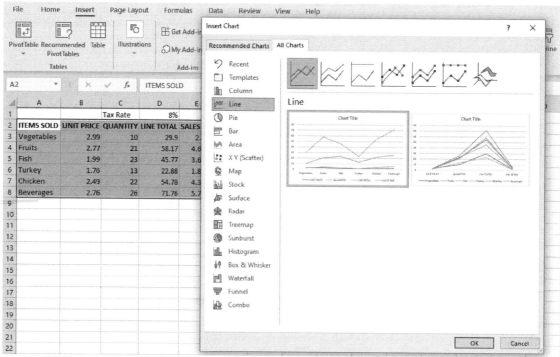

Image 93: Line chart options

These are used for showing data progression or trends. To use line charts:

- Highlight your data

- Select the option for **Lines** and then select any style for the chart.

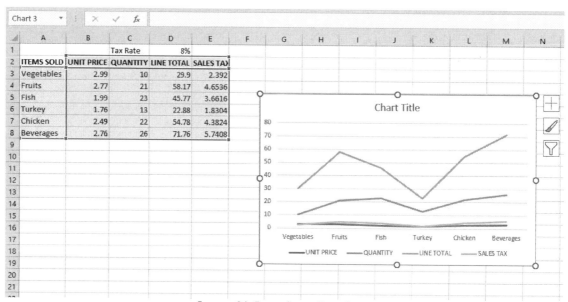

Image 94: Inserting a line chart

Pie Charts

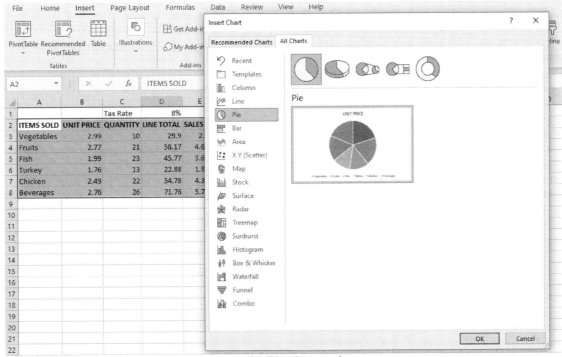

Image 95: Pie chart options

These are used for showing data in sections. To use pie charts, highlight your data and then select the option for **Pie Charts.**

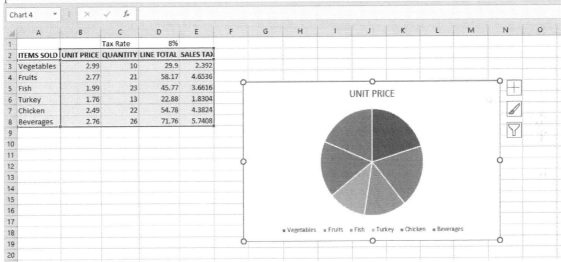

Image 96: Inserting a pie chart

Scatter Plots or XY Charts

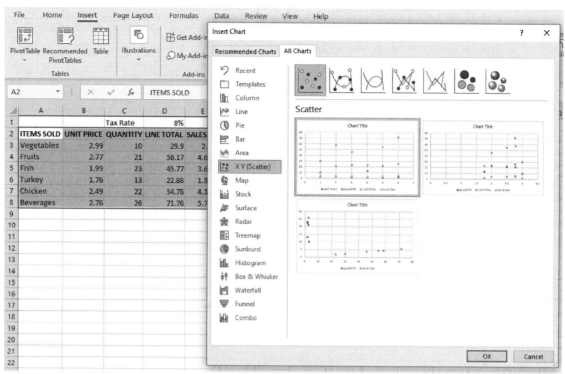

Image 97: Scatter plot options

These are used when finding how X affects Y in a data series. To use scatterplots, highlight your data and select the option for **Scatter.**

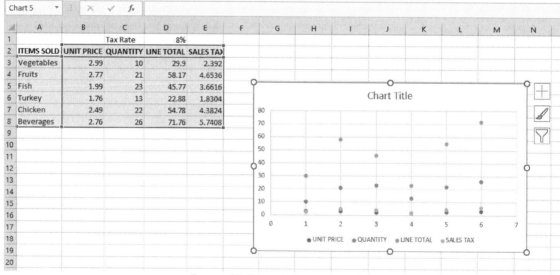

Image 98: Inserting a scatter plot

Area Charts

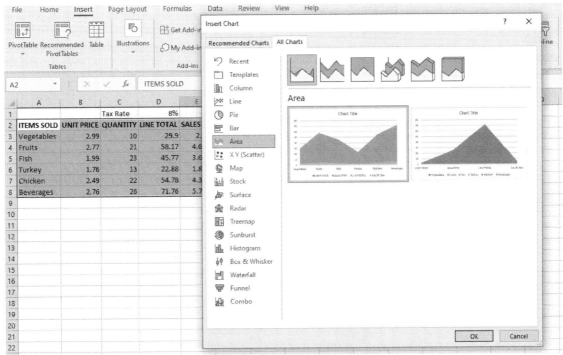

Image 99: Options for area charts

These represent data in filled colored areas. They can be inserted by selecting the **Line** chart option and then choosing **Area** under area for 2-D options.

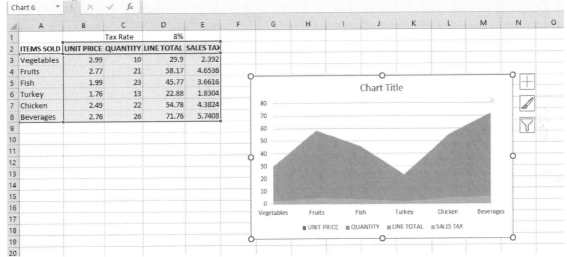

Image 100: Inserting area chart

Radar Charts

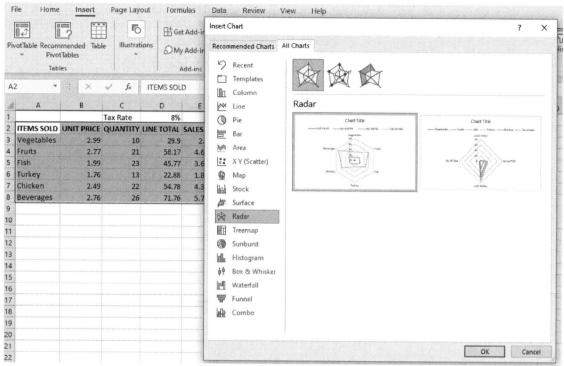

Image 101: Radar chart options

These charts compare multiple items in 2-D representation in a data set. They are otherwise known as Spider Charts. Radar charts can be added to your worksheet by selecting the option for additional charts in the **Insert** menu and choosing appropriately after highlighting your data.

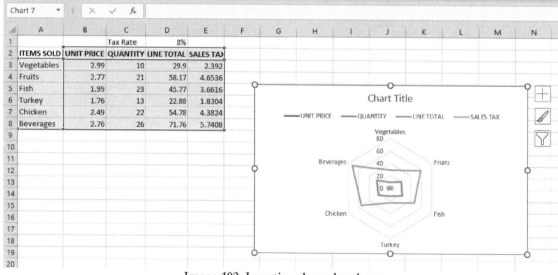

Image 102: Inserting the radar chart

Surface Charts

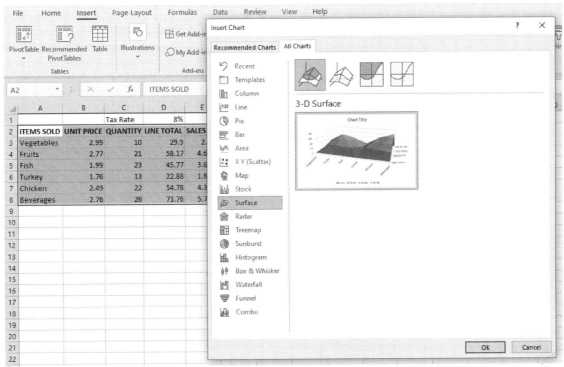

Image 103: Surface chart options

These represent your data in clear 3-D formats. They can be inserted by selecting the option for additional charts in the **Insert** menu and choosing appropriately after highlighting your data.

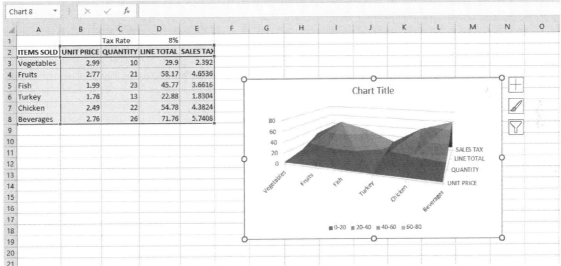

Image 104: Inserting the surface chart

Stock Charts

Just as the name implies, they are best used for representing stocks in a data set. They can be inserted into your worksheet following the same procedure as Surface charts.

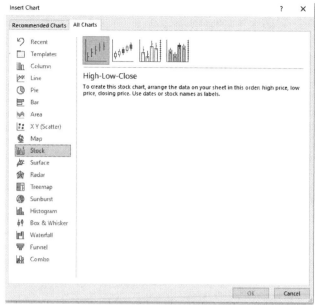

Image 105: Stock charts

Bubble Charts

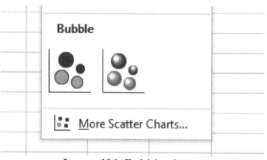

Image 106: Bubble charts

Highlight your data, select the option for additional charts, and select **Bubble** charts.

OTHER TYPES OF CHARTS IN EXCEL

Histogram

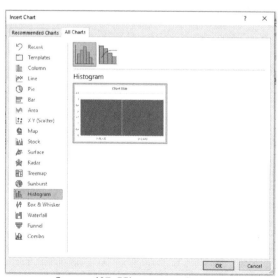

Image 107: Histogram element

This chart shows how often an event or item occurs in a data set. Insert histograms by selecting the option for **Static Charts** on the **Insert** menu and then choose the **Histogram** option. Do not forget to highlight your data. You can format the bars by right-clicking on the chart and selecting the format option.

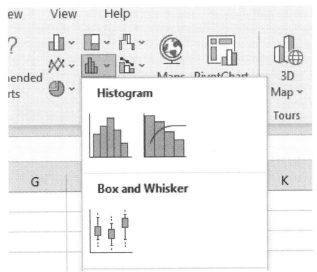

Image 108: Inserting the histogram

Waterfall Charts

- Highlight your data

- Select the option for **Stacked Columns** in the **Insert** menu

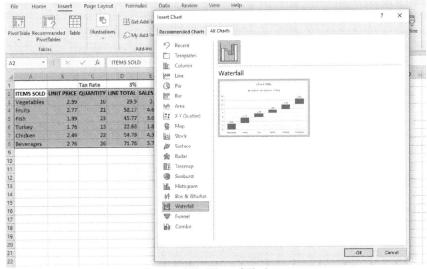

Image 109: Waterfall charts

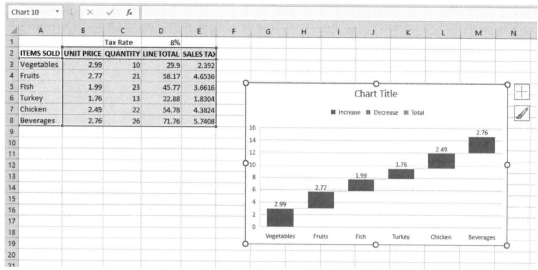

Image 110: Inserting the waterfall chart

- Right-click the inserted chart and choose the format option

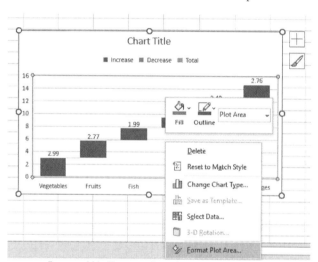

Image 111: Formatting the waterfall chart

- Select the options to remove fill and borders in the **Format** window

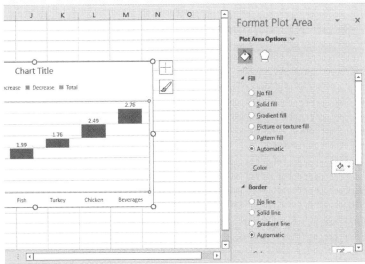

Image 112: The Format Plot Area

Waterfall charts show graphically how data flows in a data set.

Box and Whisker Charts

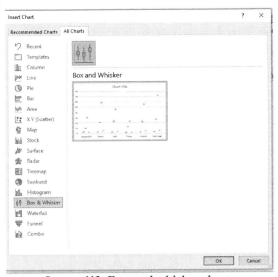

Image 113: Box and whisker charts

These show specific values of your data. Insert box and whisker charts by first highlighting your data, selecting the option for **Static Charts** on the **Insert** menu, and then choosing the appropriate option.

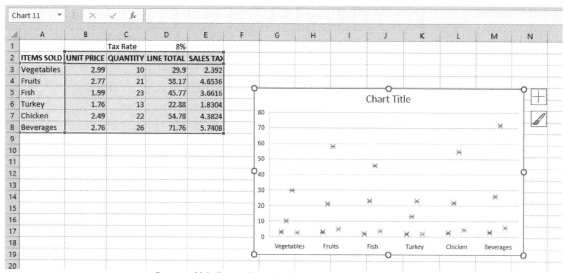

	Tax Rate	8%		
ITEMS SOLD	UNIT PRICE	QUANTITY	LINE TOTAL	SALES TAX
Vegetables	2.99	10	29.9	2.392
Fruits	2.77	21	58.17	4.6536
Fish	1.99	23	45.77	3.6616
Turkey	1.76	13	22.88	1.8304
Chicken	2.49	22	54.78	4.3824
Beverages	2.76	26	71.76	5.7408

Image 114: Inserting the box and whisker chart

Sunburst Charts

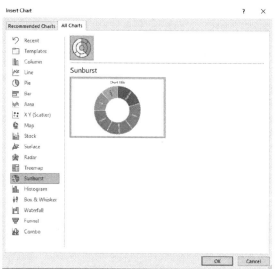

Image 115: Sunburst chart

- Highlight your data

- Navigate to the option for Hierarchical charts

- Select **Sunburst** charts

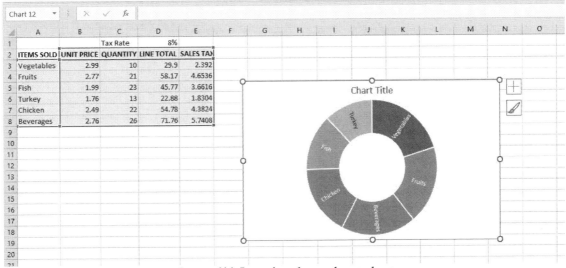

Image 116: Inserting the sunburst chart

Treemap Charts

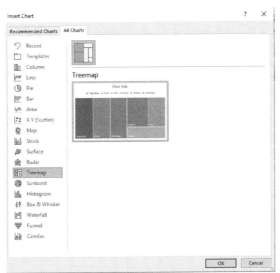

Image 117: Treemap chart

- Highlight your data

- Navigate to the option for Hierarchical charts

- Select **Treemap** charts

Funnel Charts

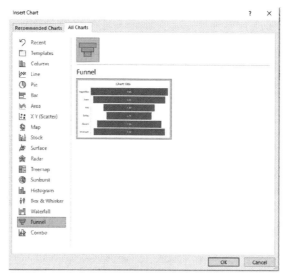

Image 118: Funnel chart

- Highlight your data

- Navigate to the icon for **Waterfall** charts

- Select **Funnel** charts

Map Charts

Image 119: Map chart

- Select your data

- Navigate to the **Maps** option and select **Filled Maps**

How do you create charts?

Charts in MS Excel can be formatted to look just the way you want them to. To change the look of a chart, you can change the style and colors of each element. You can also change the data that you are plotting. The chart can look as complex as you want it to be or as simple as you want it to be.

The next step in creating a chart is choosing which cells you would like to include in the chart. You can highlight cells and then drag the cursor from the top left cell to the bottom right cell. You can also choose what kind of chart you want to create from the charts group on the ribbon. You can also click on a specific cell to display its description.

There are several ways to create charts and graphs in MS Excel. Column charts display categorized data, while bar charts show data arranged horizontally. A column chart is more suitable for showing data about a single category, while a bar chart is better for a group of categories.

Another option is to format individual data as a table. This makes it easier to update the data range. When you add more data, Excel automatically updates the table and chart.

27 Microsoft Excel Data Analysis

If you are a business person, you are probably familiar with Microsoft Excel Data analysis. But if you have never performed any analysis in Excel, you may be wondering what it is all about. This chapter will explain this type of analysis, how to do it, and which functions to use to create your analysis. First, learn why it's important to perform Excel data analysis. You can begin by exploring the Data Analysis ToolPak in the Tools menu.

What is Excel Data analysis?

When analyzing data, using Excel is an excellent choice. You can get data from many sources, including financial records, sales figures, and customer reviews. Excel has many features that make it easier to analyze the data and find patterns.

Histogram: Use the Histogram function on the Data Analysis menu to create a histogram. If you have three adjacent cells with data, enter the numbers in these cells. If the values are missing, Excel will accept blank cells. For other missing values, enter 0,1,2 or the range of three adjacent cells. This function will not label the output based on column and row numbers, which can be confusing when working with many variables.

=FIND: The =FIND function helps find the values that meet a condition. The COUNTIFS function can determine the number of cells that satisfy certain conditions. It also does not require a sum range. The COUNTA function is a useful data analysis function because it can identify if a cell is empty. You can use this to analyze gaps. This function can also help you identify patterns and anomalies.

Spikelines: MS Excel offers a visualization feature called sparklines. Sparklines are mini-graphs that can be inserted within cells. Sparklines are excellent for visualizing trends. You can add one or multiple sparklines to a data range, so you can easily see which ones are trending the most. You can even use Excel to create graphs that look like a stacked area chart. And the possibilities are endless.

Sorting: Sorting and filtering data in Excel allows you to visualize the important values. For example, in conditional formatting, you can color-code cells and place symbols next to values. Conditional formatting allows you to exclude duplicate rows and sort them by color. You can also sort data by a specific rule or a color scale. You can also use the "Subtotal" function to ignore hidden rows. It can even create heat maps.

How to do Excel Data analysis

Whether you're looking to analyze your data for a business presentation or just interested in making your spreadsheets look nice, you'll find that the tools in Excel can help you perform various functions. For example, you can sort data in descending or ascending order, filter, highlight records that meet criteria and create charts. In this book, we'll go over some of the more important Excel tools and how to use them for data analysis.

Sparklines are little line charts that display data from a range of values. They are a great way to identify trends and highlight high and low values. Moreover, you can use these charts to perform a what-if analysis, which lets you create different scenarios and compare the results. The Excel Goal Seeker can be another useful tool for analyzing data in Excel. You can find a great example of this in the following video.

What-If Analysis involves exploring different scenarios by changing formula values. Solver, an add-in program for Excel, can help you perform this type of analysis by locating the optimal formula value for an objective cell, subject to other constraints and limitations placed on other formula cells. This function is particularly useful for data analysis. These tools can help you visualize huge data sets. They are an indispensable tool in any business's arsenal. But it's only the beginning of what Excel can do for you.

Sorting is another way to analyze data in Excel. For example, if you have a dataset that includes people with allergies, you can either manually count them or use an Excel formula to calculate them. Then, you can choose the specific cells you want to analyze and use the Quick Analysis feature or CRTL + Q. This feature helps you create charts that show trends and analyze smaller data sets.

Pivot tables are one of the most powerful features in Excel when it comes to data analysis. Pivot tables, also called cross-tabulation, help you summarize and slice data so that you can focus on specific aspects of your data. Pivot tables are easy to create, and you don't need to learn complex formulas to build one. You can also blend the information, such as the percentages of different factors in an industry. Pivot tables can also help you identify trends.

Functions to use in Excel Data analysis

You can use various functions to manipulate data in a Microsoft Excel Data analysis. The LOOKUP function, for example, returns a value from a column to a row. The SELECT function combines two functions, allowing you to combine and summarize data from several ranges. In addition to these functions, Excel also provides lookup functions, such as Vlookup and Hlookup, which you can use to find the values in a column.

The Median function is a useful formula for finding an array's middle number. To use this function, sort your data into ascending order. The formula performs this automatically. You can use the standard deviation function if you need to find the most common value in a data group. Finally, the SUM() function returns the sum of the numbers that have passed. However, make sure that you sort your data first.

One of the most useful Excel functions is =RANK, which allows you to show values in either ascending or descending order. This function is often used in data analysis to determine which clients order the most of a certain product. You can also use =RANK to display the values in order of popularity. For instance, if you sell coffee, you can use =RANK to see which client orders the most. There are more than 20 types of charts in Microsoft Excel. Although most people get by with a Line chart, Bar chart, and Pie chart, you can also try a Scatter chart, which requires two sets of corresponding data. Regardless of your business, you should consider using Excel for data analysis. The benefits are endless! Just learn the correct way to use these functions in Microsoft Excel.

If you need to calculate how many values of a certain type are in a cell, you can use the COUNTIFS function to perform the calculation. This powerful function allows you to count the number of values that match the criteria. The result is a set of values for which you can calculate an average. This is a powerful function that can help you analyze large data sets with ease. When used correctly, this function will help you find the most relevant information in the data.

Importance of Excel Data Analysis

The Importance of Excel data analysis for businesses can't be underestimated. Its advanced features help analyze large volumes of data with ease. It also lets you sort data, both in ascending and descending order. In addition, you can apply various filters to data, including a 'What-If' analysis to determine the effect of changing formula values. The Solver add-in uses operations research methods to find optimal solutions to decision-making problems. It even comes with its analysis tool, Analysis ToolPak, an add-in to Excel.

If you're new to data analysis, you may be wondering how you can begin with this method. While many programs can analyze large amounts of data, Excel is a powerful tool for creating reports and data analysis. It doesn't require previous experience and doesn't require you to download any software or install any programs. To use the Excel data analysis ToolPak, search the Help for "Data Analysis Tools." One thing you should know about Excel is that it only accepts data in blank cells if there are no missing values. Often, the same data arrangement won't work for different types of analysis.

The Importance of Excel data analysis continues to grow. Despite the recent advancements in data analysis software, many Excel users still use old versions of the program. Using the Quick Analysis feature in Excel can help you analyze data quickly, with minimal work. The ability to add beauty to a report is also crucial. Before you start editing your workbook, you should turn off Auto Refresh. This will prevent your table from refreshing whenever you make changes.

A pivot table in Excel can make analyzing data easier. For example, the What-If analysis feature lets you highlight specific cells based on their values. You can also use the "what-if" function to find duplicate rows. This feature enables you to shade a row if it has a duplicate value. Another useful feature in Excel is the Conditional Formatting feature, which allows you to ignore rows with no data. You can even use the Conditional Formatting feature to generate Heat Maps.

28 Common Problems and Mistakes with Microsoft Excel

A few of the most common mistakes and problems people encounter with Microsoft Excel are listed below. Each problem and mistake has a solution. For example, learn how to unlock an excel with a password or where to locate temporary Excel files. If you have ever encountered this error, this book is here to help you! It will show you how to quickly fix them and ensure you don't make any more mistakes. So read on to discover the most

What are the common problems and mistakes

While Excel is one of the most widely used data processing and spreadsheet applications, it rarely develops severe errors. But even when it does, it can still cause problems with its performance and usability. There are many reasons why users experience these problems, such as missing DLL files, corrupt workbooks, or macros. In addition, there are also instances where users encounter malware or infection. To understand why this happens, you should first know how to identify the root cause of the error.

The #NUM error occurs when a formula or function contains invalid numbers. Excel can't display the values if the formula doesn't specify the right width. Check if the number contains text, blank cells, or special characters. If you find such errors, you can fix them by replacing the values. Remember that the types of inputs that cause Excel errors can save you from having to redo your work.

Another common mistake is circular references. Circular references can occur for various reasons, but the spreadsheet's creator easily fixes most. To avoid this problem, you should ensure that the name of the cell is correctly spelled. Also, ensure that you use quotation marks around any text in the formula. Keeping the names of formulas short and simple will help you avoid these problems. Moreover, it will save you time when solving errors in your work.

A list with problems and solutions for each one

A list of common problems and solutions for Microsoft Office applications is a must-have for any Excel user. It's an excellent tool for simple lists, but it can become a complex project if you're using it for macro programming or automating data processing. Listed below are some of the most common problems you may encounter when using Excel to create a project. These problems can affect performance, stability, and development.

You should first check your software if you're experiencing freezing issues when using Microsoft Excel. This could result from failing to install the latest update, an add-in conflicting with Excel, or another process using it. You can usually fix this problem by uninstalling the add-in or reinstalling the program. Also, you should make sure to install the latest update for Microsoft Office so it can fix any loopholes and replace outdated files.

There are many reasons that Microsoft Excel can freeze, including outdated antivirus software, an erroneous add-in, or a faulty program. The most common solution is to start Excel in safe mode. Otherwise, you may need to install the latest update to resolve the issue. However, it may be necessary to uninstall the add-in first. If the issue persists, you might need to restart Excel using the safe mode.

How to unlock an excel with a password

If you've ever been caught trying to unlock an Excel spreadsheet, you probably know how frustrating it can be. Fortunately, you're not the only one who has encountered this problem. Here are a few common mistakes when unlocking Excel documents with passwords. Using a simple password cracking application can significantly speed up the process. But remember to always re-save your spreadsheet after cracking a password, and you can re-use it with a password.

You may have made a mistake when you set up the password, causing the file to become unusable. Therefore, you should always write down the password and store it in a safe place, so you don't forget it. Alternatively, a password-protected file may be impossible to open. However, fortunately, there are solutions available. Excel File Repair Tool (EFRT) is one such program. It can help you fix corrupt Excel files, preview them, and save them.

The first mistake is to open the workbook with the worksheet that has been password protected. If you don't have this permission, you can still use the method by saving it in an older version. To do so, open the workbook and select "Excel 97-2003" (*.xls) when you save it. After saving the workbook, you should follow the prompts to edit or download the protected sheet.

Where excel saves temporary files

Where does Excel save its temporary files? In most cases, Excel stores all its files in C:UserscyAppDataLocalMicrosoftOfficeUnsavedFiles. But if you accidentally delete a recent Excel file, you won't know where to find it. If you're a Mac user, you can find your unsaved Excel file in the temporary files folder. Then, you can copy it to another location and open it in Excel. Alternatively, you can save it through the app instead of Excel.

Regardless of where the Excel temporary file is stored, you can still open it as an actual workbook. This way, you can recover unsaved workbooks. But there are a few tips you can follow to ensure that you don't delete the files by accident. First, open Microsoft Excel and change the file extension to xls or xlsx. Secondly, you can choose to hide these files by checking the "Hide" option when you right-click on them.

In addition, you can recover unsaved Excel files by reopening the program. After reopening Excel, you should see a sidebar with your available files. Select the AutoSave Excel version from the list. Next, navigate to the Temp folder. This folder will store the temp files of your work, so it's important to note that these files don't contain all your work.

The Document Auto Recovery Command

This feature allows one to recover documents when incase there is a computer failure, crash or power failure leading to data loss. Auto Recovery is automatically saves changes you make to your workbook. Enable Auto Recovery command

- Click **File** tab and choose **Options**

Image 120: First step to setting Auto Recovery

- Click on **Save** in the **Options** dialog box that pops up.

- Key in minutes for the interval within **Save AutoRecovery Information Every** box. Could be 1 or 2 minutes

- click **Ok**

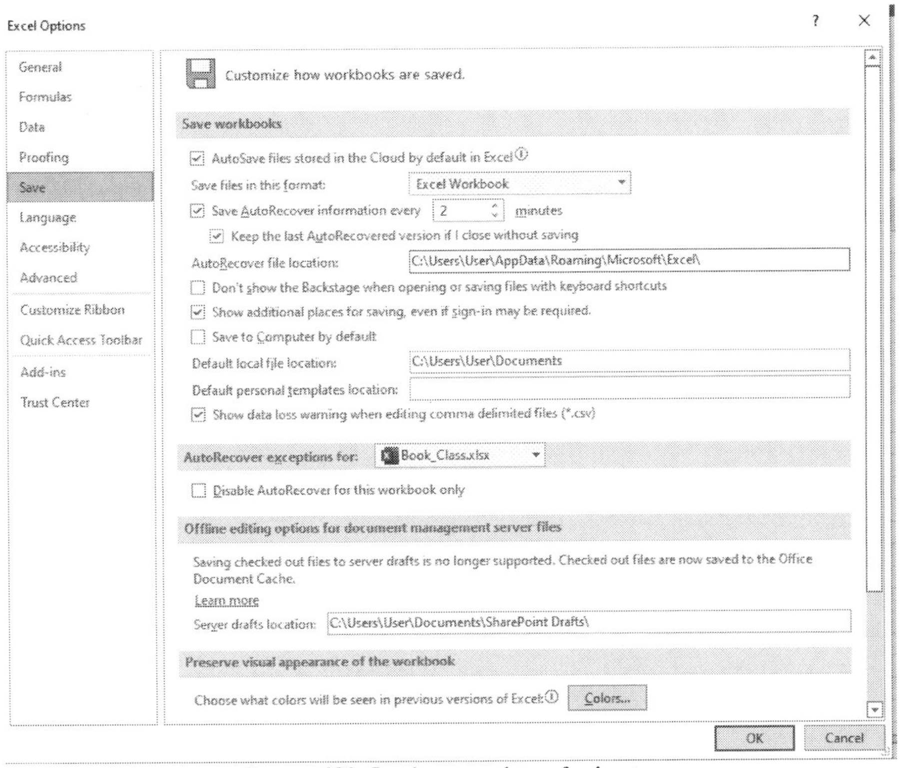

Image 121: Setting number of minutes

How to recover corrupted files

You're not alone if you're unsure how to recover corrupted Excel files. This corruption can be caused by viruses, system errors, or even unidentified reasons. If you've ever encountered this problem, you may wonder how to recover corrupted Excel files and restore lost data. The good news is that recovering corrupted files is not as difficult as it seems. Below are some techniques to use to recover corrupted Excel files.

The first step in fixing a corrupted Excel file is to open it. To do so, open the file in Microsoft Office Excel, or use the repair tool. If this method fails, save the file in another format. It's important to remember that this process is a bit risky and will lose formatting and formulas. The best method to fix corrupted Excel files is to use an alternative file format that the operating system can open.

To open a corrupted.xls file, you must first install a Microsoft Office Excel converter. Otherwise, you won't be able to open it in Word. Then, to fix a corrupted.xls file, you need to change the format to a newer, more compatible format. For example, if you've saved the file in the XLSX format, you need to change it back to the older XLS file format to use the same file.

How to set autosave

To avoid losing data, you must set AutoSave in Microsoft Excel to save your work in the right place. By default, the program saves your work in a temporary file with an arbitrary name and then gives it a more meaningful name when it saves it. However, this feature can be hindered by various obstructions, including accidentally deleted files in the Recycle Bin. It also generates various errors when it tries to access the file.

To enable AutoSave, go to File tab, then select Options. Click Save tab. In Save tab, click AutoSave files and set AutoRecover information every X minutes. Enter a time that you want the program to save your changes. You can also select the file location and specify exceptions. If you accidentally delete an important document, you can restore it by choosing the AutoRecovery option.

In addition to misplacing the autosave option, you can accidentally delete the temporary file that Excel creates. This may occur if you are using an external hard drive. Sometimes, the error is caused by deleting or renaming a temporary file. In such cases, Excel will try to save the file without autosave, resulting in an error message that says, "Cannot access the document because it is read-only."

Which Excel has lookup

VLOOKUP is one of the many features of Microsoft Excel. This function searches data in a column for an identifier similar to the lookup value. This function searches in columns that are listed vertically. It also searches to the right of the old data to find new data to the right of the old. In addition, VLOOKUP requires that the data be listed in ascending order.

However, sometimes the lookup function returns incorrect results. In such cases, you should first sort the lookup ranges to contain the data you're looking for. Otherwise, the function will return results that are not relevant. In such cases, you can combine the IF() and EXACT() functions to get the desired results. While these functions may seem the simplest way to search for data, they're not.

When using a lookup function in a cell, you need to specify which type of match you want. You can use an exact or non-exact match, but you'll need to remember to enter the values in ascending order. Also, remember that an array formula requires multiple cells. If you're a beginner, this method might be too complex for you to try. You can also use an INDEX. This function helps search an array.

29 Personal Finance Use

How to Use Microsoft Excel for Personal Finance

If you want to use Microsoft Excel for personal finance, here are some tips to get you started. You will learn how to efficiently keep track of your earnings and expenses, create a budget, and analyze your financial situation. You'll also learn how to synchronize your financial accounts with other apps. And since Microsoft isn't responsible for your personal financial information, you can trust that your information will remain private. You can even use it for tax purposes.

Keeping track of earnings and expenses Efficiently

Keeping track of your earnings and expenses is essential for planning cash flow, maximizing the use of loans and credit, and ensuring that you pay the right amount of tax. Detailed records can also help plan your cash flow and help you prepare accurate financial statements. In addition, tracking your earnings and expenses can help you find ways to save money and make more informed business decisions. Even though you can keep track of all transactions manually, it's best to consider an accounting software solution that automates this process.

Using Microsoft Excel to track expenses is easy to keep tabs on your spending. A dedicated income and expense worksheet will make it easier to enter transaction data. It also has a tab for common expenses, such as rent and mortgage. An expense tab can be tailored to your specific needs. Keeping track of personal expenses is crucial during college, when time and distractions may cause you to spend more than you intended. If you'd like to create a spreadsheet to keep track of bills and income, you can download the free Monthly college budget workbook. You can upload it to OneDrive to access it online or print it for manual tracking.

There are many free spreadsheet alternatives available, including Google Docs and OpenOffice. While Excel is not free, it's easy to use, and you can make it work for your needs. In addition to using the Microsoft Excel software, you can also download a free Excel budget template. Excel templates are available online and can be customized to suit your specific needs. With a little effort, you can create and maintain a budget spreadsheet that can track your earnings and expenses in a way that is convenient for you.

While tracking your income is essential, it's not enough to have it tracked. You should review your expenses regularly and look for inconsistencies or inefficiencies. Doing so can ensure that your finances are under control and help you set goals. For example, suppose you have an irregular income. In that case, you may be able to identify any cash flow shortfalls before they happen and use your extra money for debt repayment or savings.

Creating a budget

If you're looking to create a budget, you'll find that a spreadsheet is your best bet. Microsoft Excel has several features to customize and create a budget workbook that suits your needs. For instance, you can create columns to track income and expenses by category and totals and labels. Once you've established your monthly budget, you can make it more visually appealing by using border colors, fonts, and formatting options.

Microsoft Excel is a great way to start if you're just budgeting. There are many budget templates available on the Microsoft Office Template website. You can search for the template that best suits your budget needs, downloads it, and use it. This can save you time by calculating your finances without spending hours each month on the project. Moreover, these budget templates are free, so you don't have to worry about investing large amounts of money to get started.

Even though budgeting is tedious, it is vital to track your income and expenses and set aside a portion of your salary for designated savings. This way, you increase your chances of meeting current needs while planning for future goals. Creating a budget is an excellent idea, even if you're on a modest income. It can also improve your financial position. So, how do you create a budget using Microsoft Excel?

Creating a budget spreadsheet with Microsoft Excel is easier than you might think. You can simply input estimated amounts into columns, drag them to the desired location and enter the totals. This way, the spreadsheet will look more attractive. You can also use formatting functions to make the spreadsheet more visually appealing. If you're not a computer geek, you can also download and install a free trial of Microsoft Excel.

To create a budget spreadsheet, use a template to track your income and expenses. In Excel, you can label each row with a different color. You can also use the Fill tool on the menu bar. It looks like a paint can tipping over and pouring out. Click the Fill button and select the color you want to add to each row. Avoid dark or bright colors, and be sure not to use too many.

Debt Management

Money in Excel is a financial management tool that works within Microsoft Excel. You can link your various financial accounts into your spreadsheet and view all their information in one convenient location. The tool also gives you insights into your spending habits, including monthly expenses. This feature was designed to replace Microsoft Money but was recently upgraded. Using Microsoft Money, you'll probably want to upgrade to the new version. For more information about Money in Excel, visit the Microsoft website.

Money in Excel has some notable benefits. It's extremely secure, backed by Plaid, which all the major financial institutions use. It delivers a ton of information. The Recurring Expenses template shows recurring charges across various credit cards. While some credit card companies offer similar features, many people do not have one comprehensive view of all their cards. The Money in Excel software lets you easily sort your expenses, categorize them, and set priorities for spending.

Financial Analysis

If you are interested in personal finance analysis, you may want to try using Microsoft Excel. There are numerous benefits to using Microsoft Excel for personal finance analysis. It is highly secure and a solution used by many financial institutions, including banks and credit unions. You can view a wealth of information about your finances, including recurring expenses on different credit cards. This template is beneficial because many credit card companies have similar features, but most people don't have one comprehensive view of all their credit card usage.

To begin using Excel for personal finance analysis, download a free template. This template works with both Excel online and desktop software. You'll find two separate worksheets: the Expense tab and the Summary tab. Once you've logged in, you can compare your monthly income and expenses to see how they compare. The Summary worksheet automatically displays your cash flow status. The spreadsheet contains standard expense categories and subcategories for each category. There are also tabs for filtering and sorting to get a quick overview of your finances.

Another great way to use Excel for personal finance analysis is to subscribe to a service like Tiller, which automatically populates spreadsheets with automated data feeds. This service was developed for Google Sheets but recently made its way to Microsoft Excel. Microsoft recently recommended Tiller to subscribers of its Microsoft 365 service. You can try it for free for 60 days and pay $79/year afterward. There are also many other features to choose from.

Money in Excel is an Excel add-in that connects your financial accounts to your spreadsheet. With this tool, you can track your spending habits and generate a budget based on your spending habits. Money in Excel will also let you view your monthly expenditures by category. And it's compatible with over 10,000 financial institutions. If you don't want to use Money in Excel, you can use another personal finance analysis software, like MSN Money.

30 Engineer and Statistician Use of Microsoft Excel

Engineers and statisticians extensively use Microsoft Excel and other statistical tools to improve the accuracy of repetitive calculations. These programs also help engineers collect data and create statistical charts that display their findings. Learn how to use Microsoft Excel for your next engineering or statistical project. This section will explore Essential formulas to learn, functions that connect numbers and search for data in a specific column, and how to perform Engineering Analysis with Numerical Solutions.

Essential formulas to know

You need to know some essential formulas in Excel for engineers and statisticians, but not everyone knows what they are. There are many formulas in Excel for engineers, including basic arithmetic and calculus. This book is for you if you want to learn to use these in your work. The book will take you through the basics of Excel and then teach you how to use these formulas to solve engineering problems.

For example, the MROUND function lets one to round a number to a specific multiple. It is also possible to use the FLOOR or CEILING functions in rounding a number to the nearest integer. Lastly, the COUNTIF function counts the number of cells meeting the given criteria. You can use this formula to compute a group's average number of shareholders. However, you should use quotation marks when using the COUNTIF function.

When using Microsoft Excel, you will want to know what functions you can use to solve technical problems. Using these functions will help you calculate numbers more quickly. In addition to basic math operations, you can also use Excel to manipulate date and time values. You can even create tables, graphs, and other types of data to visualize the results of your calculations. The more you know about formulas, the more confident you will be with the program.

Using the CONVERT function to convert between complex units is also a helpful skill. It is also valuable for converting complex units like decimals and kiloliters. Data Validation is located under the Data tab of the ribbon. You can also use Named Ranges to eliminate the pain of referencing Excel cells. You can also use the LOOKUP and HLOOKUP functions to look up data by column or table. Suppose functions are helpful for logical tests. They test more than one condition and return a value if it's true or false. The IF functions are essential for data analysts because they automate decision-making. However, they are difficult to use, and if you're not sure what to use, try searching online. A basic understanding of Excel formulas is essential for many careers in today's world.

Functions connected to numbers for approximation

The Excel formula COUNTIFS is a way to calculate the number of places in a fraction, decimal, or percentage. The exponent "E" stands for the number of decimal places. This method is sometimes less accurate, but generally, it is the same. The difference is the way the calculator treats numbers over 15 significant figures. It treats a number differently if it is more than 15 significant figures, and this difference can sometimes be beneficial.

The second type of function, TCROUND, can display arbitrary sums and 3-D references to other sheets or files. The TCROUND function can also display arbitrary numbers, although it cannot integrate results from a think-cell round. Integrating a formula with multiple decimal digits is also impossible using TCROUND statements. The results of TCROUND statements are treated as separate problems and can be used as input for other formulas.

VLOOKUP function is another function used for data extraction. It locates content in Excel table cells by searching for cells with the specified range. This search method determines if a particular value appears more than once. In addition, it helps parse data into similar categories. The XLOOKUP function is similar to VLOOKUP but has more flexibility. It allows the user to perform advanced operations and search across many columns.

Rounding is another common function used for approximation. It can be used to reduce long decimal numbers to smaller fractional numbers. It can also be used to round currency values. Microsoft Excel offers different rounding functions, including ROUNDDOWN. The functions are explained with examples. You may want to use these functions as they are often helpful in specific applications. Learning about Excel functions is essential before implementing them into your spreadsheet.

Functions to search data in a specific column

The VLOOKUP function in Microsoft Excel is a powerful tool for finding information in a table's cells. The search range and syntax determine whether a particular cell contains an exact or approximate match. Statisticians and engineers use these functions to draw insights from spreadsheet data. XLOOKUP is similar to VLOOKUP but offers greater flexibility. Here's how to search data in a specific column using the two functions.

VLOOKUP searches data in a specific column by performing a vertical lookup in the leftmost column. For instance, if you are working with a budget for home supplies, you can use VLOOKUP to find the serial number for any item in the same row. This function allows it to manipulate data using Excel's functions rather than the usual formulas. Functions are more accurate and productive than formulas and will allow you to analyze data more quickly.

EXACT (text1, text2) will compare two text strings and then return TRUE if the values are identical. Otherwise, it returns FALSE if they are not identical. The EXACT function is often used to perform complex tasks but isn't used alone. For example, the EXACT function can search for data in a specific column. However, a similar search in a different column requires using the EQ function.

VLOOKUP is the most commonly used function in Microsoft Excel. It searches one or more columns for data, while IFNA searches only one. The VLOOKUP function is a powerful tool that can also return #N/A. The IFERROR function, which searches multiple columns, will be used when the function fails. However, the VLOOKUP function is still more powerful than INDEX, but it can sometimes return an error message.

Engineering Analysis with Numerical Solutions

A literature review of the application of spreadsheets in engineering fields reveals several examples. The spreadsheets were used for different individual applicants but are equally effective in implementing numerical solutions for physical problems. This paper demonstrates how to use Excel as an engineering tool to solve problems. It uses its facilities to calculate integrals and derivatives, which are mathematical operations commonly used in engineering software. Students can perform central differences, calculus, and other analysis procedures using an Excel spreadsheet.

This textbook is filled with examples and includes over 100 end-of-chapter problems. It is ideal for graduate and undergraduate courses and does not require programming knowledge. It also allows practitioners to conduct most calculations using their familiar spreadsheet package. The corresponding textbook is a helpful resource for students and researchers in engineering and science fields. This text demonstrates using Microsoft Excel to solve complex engineering problems and create parametric reports.

Although Excel provides several functions for analysis, these tools do not always meet the requirements of scientific applications. However, some features are essential for engineers. For instance, DIAdem provides hundreds of calculations for engineering and scientific analysis. Furthermore, these functions can be customized and used without programming, providing full previews. In addition, there is a framework for developing domain-specific calculations, which is extremely useful for engineers.

In addition to its many capabilities, Excel includes the CONVERT function that allows users to convert complex units from one type to another. This feature is especially useful in engineering, where the units are often converted to another. Named Ranges, meanwhile, eliminate the pain of working with Excel cell references. The Excel spreadsheet can also be customized to meet your specific engineering needs. So, start analyzing and creating numerical solutions with Excel today!

31 How Can Business and Management Use Microsoft Excel?

Advanced Excel training can increase employee productivity. Highly-trained employees will finish their tasks faster, offer better customer service, and produce more work in less time. Moreover, advanced Excel training can save up to half an hour per employee, which translates to many extra staff hours a week. And when it comes to the business world, this amount is no joke. So how does advanced Excel training benefit you? Read on to learn more.

People management

One of the most actual applications of Excel in the company is managing people.

Employees, clients, sponsors, or training participants may all be organized in MS Excel.

Personal data may be saved and accessed effectively with Excel. For example, a spreadsheet row or column may include an individual's name, email address, employee start date, purchases, subscription status, and last contact.

In business and management, Microsoft Excel can help you manage huge amounts of data, including human resources functions. With a human resources tool such as Excel, you can record employee data, including their work hours, vacation time, and even their subscription status. The human resources tool also helps you stay on top of your day-to-day tasks and keep track of turnover. In addition, you can use the program to track employee information, such as birthdays and other important dates.

When it comes to the day-to-day operations of any business, nothing is more important than people. And the most challenging thing to manage is people. You can't afford to be mediocre in this area. That's why you need to know how to handle people well and keep them happy. You can create pivot tables, understand customer and sales data, and analyze employee costs and productivity.

Office administration project management

You may not realize it, but Microsoft Excel is an excellent tool for office administration. Not only is it useful for project management, but it also supports invoicing, paying bills, and contacting clients and suppliers. It is the all-purpose tool you need to manage all office aspects. You can use Excel to manage your office activities, whether you are an administrative assistant, administrator officer, or supervisor. Here are some tips if you want to use them for project management.

Excel is a powerful tool for complicated things but can also be prone to errors. While several tools manage projects, Excel remains a popular choice in most industries. While it may have some limitations, it is universally accessible in organizations using Microsoft Office. You might need to import or export data from other tools depending on your needs. Be sure to know the compatibility of Excel with other tools before you start working.

In addition to combining Microsoft Office apps with Excel, MS Project is an excellent tool for contract administrators. Contract management templates are easily customizable and allow you to record contract details in a simple, no-fuss manner. You can even customize the templates to suit a particular contract lifecycle stage. Account managers, in particular, should be skilled in Excel since they deal with customers' records. A simple template for this can save you a lot of time and effort.

Accounts management

You may have heard about its capabilities if you're interested in using Microsoft Excel for business management and accounting. This tool allows you to create charts of accounts and manage your financial data. You can add any number of accounts to your chart of accounts and create them in one convenient location. Accounts management in Microsoft Excel is an essential part of any business. However, it can be challenging to manage your accounts correctly without the right tools.

The software comes with various pre-built templates for financial records, including balance sheets, accounts payable, and accounts receivable. There are also specialized templates available for purchase and download from third-party vendors. In addition to pre-filled spreadsheets, you can also create your accounting templates. To get started, download free accounting templates and create the financial reports you need. Whether you need a simple balance sheet, a detailed balance sheet, or a detailed accounting report, Excel can make the process a breeze.

With the help of an Excel add-on, you can create graphs of historical data. In addition, you can perform complex mathematical calculations. You can also use the data in Excel to make business decisions. This tool is the preferred choice for many business owners. Microsoft Excel also offers several features that make it ideal for business accounting. This includes graphs and pre-made templates for the most common accounting functions.

Excel is an efficient tool for handling people's information. You can create spreadsheets with personal details such as name, email, start date, last contact, and more. Using Excel, you can manage people by keeping track of their transactions. A column can include information about individual employees, clients, and suppliers. Excel can even track critical dates and schedules. So, you'll never have to worry about not getting the data you need for strategic analysis.

Projections and forecasting

A financial business forecast relies on a method known as forecasting, which involves predicting future sales based on historical data. This allows business owners to calculate other factors such as overhead expenses and staffing. The first step in using a forecast is to choose the appropriate historical data. Most businesses will select three to five years' worth of sales data. After choosing the necessary data, adjust the variables that drive the forecast calculation. The forecast sheet will then appear in a new worksheet.

Financial projections can be prepared in Microsoft Excel using the Exl-Plan template. These templates can be customized to include the name of the business, starting date, minimum monthly amount, and other factors. In addition to preparing financial forecasts, these templates can also be used for budgeting and business planning. These tools also contribute substantial spreadsheet know-how. You can download the free trial versions of these programs for a limited period to see how they work. Financial projections are often inaccurate and must be adjusted based on actual information. However, good planning begins with realistic expectations, and Microsoft Excel is an essential tool for this purpose. Excel's powerful data visualization capabilities and useful insights guide management. Excel-based forecasting tools can help you see the road ahead and avoid pitfalls. And with the right data, the Excel tool can be used to model financial scenarios, making it easier to manage your business.

While small business owners might not be in the market to secure bank loans or attract investors, they can still use financial projections to chart their growth potential and create budgets. Financial projections help a business survive and thrive. No matter your business type, Excel can help you with your financial management. And whether you are in the beginning stages or have been in business for years, financial projections are an essential part of any business plan.

32 Most Helpful Formulas

FIND

The FIND function is used to locate where a given text substring occurs within another string or range of text strings. The answer is returned as a number signifying the position at which the first character of the string occurs. That sounds a bit complicated in theory, so let's look at a practical example.

If the string of text "Microsoft Excel" is in cell A1, and we wish to know how far into that string the word "Excel" begins, we can use the function:

=FIND("Excel", A1)

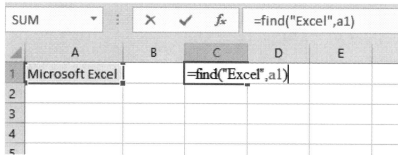

Image 122: The FIND formula in action

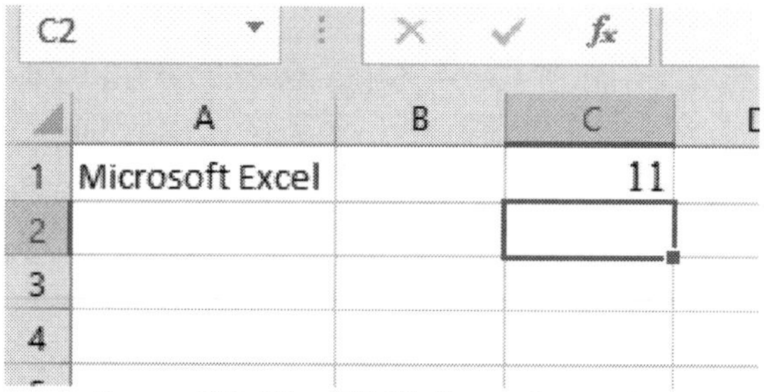

Image 123: The FIND Formula results

This will return an answer of 11. This means that the "E" at the beginning of "Excel" is the 11th character in the string of text "Microsoft Excel."

The FIND has a general structure during its use as shown below:

=FIND(find_text, within_text, starting_position)

The first argument, find_text, is the substring we are searching for. The within_text argument denotes the larger string of text throughout which we are searching. The final argument, starting_position, is optional, hence its omission from the earlier example. This argument allows you to choose where in the string you would like to search from. For example:

=FIND("o", A1, 6)

This function would skip the first "o" present in the string "Microsoft Excel" by beginning its search at the 6th character and would return a value of 7, signifying the position of the next "o" as the 7th character.

It is important to note that the FIND function is also the case- and punctuation-sensitive. Therefore, not only must your search criteria be appropriately capitalized and punctuated, but you must also remain mindful that spaces will be included in the character count.

HYPERLINK

As expected, the HYPERLINK function enables you to embed clickable links in your Excel worksheet. This can be useful if you are referencing external data and must declare your source.

The structure for the use of this function is:

=HYPERLINK(link_location, link_name)

The link_location argument should contain the URL for the website that you wish to include. The link_name is an optional argument, but I recommend its use as it enables you to include a shorter clickable title on the embedded hyperlink.

For instance,

"http://www.websitename.com/a_really_long_link_with_lots_of_numbers123456789_and_symbols% #:~:%.pdf" is a long and unwieldy title to include in a single cell. We can instead include this link and call it "Click Here For More Info" using:

=HYPERLINK("http://www.websitename.com/a_really_long_link_with_lots_of_numbers123456789 _and_symbols%#:~:%.pdf", "Click Here For More Info")

This will present the link much more tidily and explain to external readers why the link has been included.

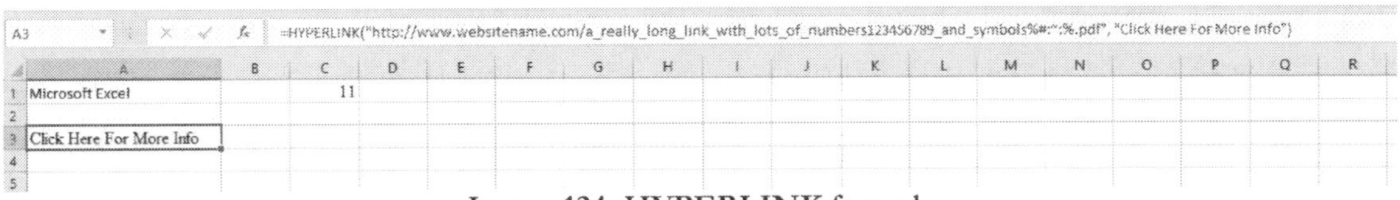

Image 124: HYPERLINK formula

IF()

It is common to use this function when it is essential to sort data following a specified logic setup. This is the most beneficial aspect of the IF formula since it enables you to include formulas and functions inside the formula itself.

- =IF (C2<D3, 'TRUE,' 'FALSE') is an example.

Comparing the two numbers can determine if the value at C2 is less than the value at D3. Ideally, the cell value should be TRUE if the logic is accurate; otherwise, the cell value should be FALSE.

IF functions have two potential outcomes: the value assigned if the test returns as true and the value assigned if the test returns as false. Therefore, their general structure is:

=IF(logical_test, value_if_true, value_if_false)

These kinds of functions can be applied to many situations. For instance, if you are tracking your diet and exercise in an Excel worksheet, you may wish to allow yourself 10% more calories on the days you exercise for an hour or more. The function of your daily caloric allowance might look like this:

=IF(Exercise>59, AvgAllowance*1.1, AvgAllowance)

Suppose functions can also be combined to create more complex logical tests. For example, we may wish to increase your daily caloric allowance by 15% if you exercised for an hour or more at the gym, wish to increase it by 10% if you exercised for an hour or more at home, or increase it by 5% if you completed any form of exercise for less than an hour. These more complex functions will be covered in a later chapter.

LOOKUP

The LOOKUP function searches a row or a column for a value that matches its search criteria. Before using this function, it is advised that you sort your data into ascending order, as described later in this chapter. For now, let us look at the LOOKUP function's structure:

=LOOKUP(lookup_value, lookup_vector, result_vector)

The lookup_value gives the information for which we are searching. This can be a number, a string of text, a cell reference, etc. The lookup_vector argument should contain the data that we wish to search. This data can only be one-dimensional, i.e., spread across a single row or column and composed entirely of neighboring cells. The result_vector is an optional argument and denotes the list of data from which we would like to pull our return value. For instance, if we are looking up Seán's monthly sales, we would search the employee column for Seán's name but would wish to return a value from the monthly sales column. It is important to note that the result vector should be the same length as the lookup vector for the function to operate.

This is possible if you wish to search a two-dimensional range of cells using the LOOKUP function, but the arguments are slightly different.

=LOOKUP(lookup_value, array)

When searching a range of cells across a selection of rows and columns, it is impossible to specify a separate return array. Therefore, the resulting value will be present in the last cell of the same row or column as the discovered lookup value.

HOOKUP

HLOOKUP is for Horizontal Query, and you can use it in obtaining data from a given database by scanning a row to identify any matching data and then print the results coming from relevant column. HLOOKUP checks for a certain value within a row, while VLOOKUP checks for a certain value within a column.

Formula: **=HLOOKUP(value to look up, table area, row number)**

LOWER

The LOWER function converts a given text string to its strictly lowercase version. This can be useful for data commonly presented all in lowercase, such as email addresses. The structure for using this function is quite simple as it only has one argument, the string of text in question.

=LOWER(text)

Since the LOWER function deals exclusively with text, numerical characters and punctuation will remain unaffected by its application. Therefore, you need not fear receiving an error code if your text argument includes numbers and punctuation; the function will simply ignore them.

MATCH

The MATCH function is similar to FIND function in that it searches for a given value and returns its position. However, unlike the FIND function, MATCH does not search a single cell or string of text. Instead, it searches a range of cells, or "array." The structure for the use of the MATCH function is:

=MATCH(lookup_value, lookup_array, match_type)

The lookup_value argument is, of course, the criteria that we are searching for. In a list of groceries, this might be "bananas." The lookup_array is the range of cells we wish to search for our lookup_value, e.g., A: A, which denotes all of column A. The match_type argument is optional and has three potential values. This is another area in which the MATCH function operates differently to FIND. When the match type is set to equal one, if the function cannot locate an exact match to lookup value, it returns the position of the closest match below the lookup value. When you use this option, please ensure that the range of cells being searched is sorted in ascending order, as this will impact what is decided to be the closest match. This is the match type that the function will default to when the argument is omitted, so it is best to sort your list anyway. How to do this is covered later in this chapter.

If the match type argument is set to equal zero, an error will be returned if an exact match cannot be found. This is the only match type in which the search array's order is irrelevant. If the match type is set to equal -1, the function will return the closest match above the lookup value. Therefore, the array of cells being searched should be in descending order.

PROPER

The PROPER function is used to capitalize the first letter in each word in a string of text. Businesses often use this to ensure that their customer names are appropriately capitalized before any communications are sent. For example:

=PROPER("john a. smith")

This function will return "John A. Smith." More commonly, the argument for the PROPER function is a cell reference. This will allow the function to be dragged and copied along entire sections of the worksheet.

PROPER also converts all other letters in the text string to lowercase, so the common internet-joke typing style of capitalizing every second alphabetic character, such as in "aRe YoU oKaY?" can be easily converted to "Are You Okay?"

However, one issue to keep in mind is that Excel reads any letter occurring after an apostrophe (') as the start of a new word. This is great if you are trying to capitalize Irish and Scottish last names like O'Hara, but not so ideal if the text in question reads, "Mike'S Butchers." So, when using the PROPER function, tread carefully where apostrophes are concerned.

SUBSTITUTE

The SUBSTITUTE function replaces text string(s). This is regularly useful if the data imported from an external source is in an incompatible format for the operations we have in mind. The structure for using this function is:

=SUBSTITUTE(text, old_text, new_text, instance_num)

The text argument refers to the cell or range of cells in question. The old_text argument is obviously the text string we wish to replace. As with all text strings used as part of a function, ensure that you surround this argument with quotation marks during use. The new_text is the replacement text that we wish to substitute in place of the old text. The instance_num is the only optional argument in this function. It can specify a specific occurrence of the old_text argument we wish to replace, e.g., "1" would cause the function only to replace the first instance in which the old text occurs. If this argument is omitted, it is assumed that we wish to replace *all* instances of the old text.

Remember that the SUBSTITUTE function *is* case-sensitive, so replacements will only be implemented where the old text is the same as the old_text argument.

UPPER

Like its LOWER counterpart, UPPER converts a string of text to contain capital or uppercase letters entirely. For instance:

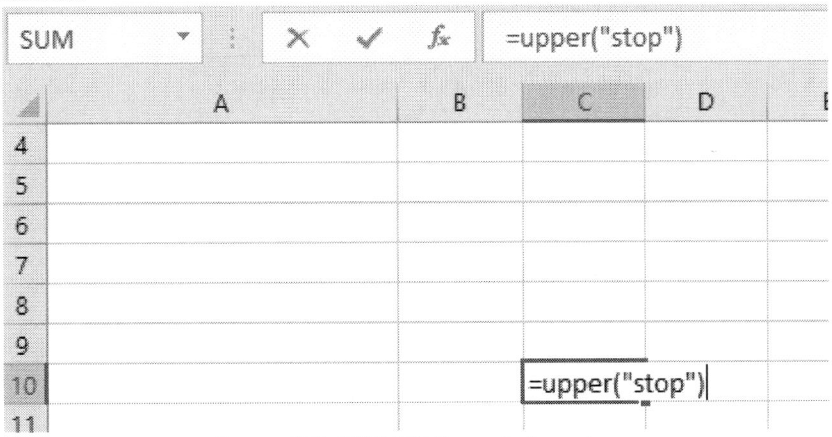

Image 125: UPPER formula in action

=UPPER("stop")

This function will return the word "STOP" entirely in capital letters. More commonly, the function's argument references a cell in which a text string is contained rather than the text itself.

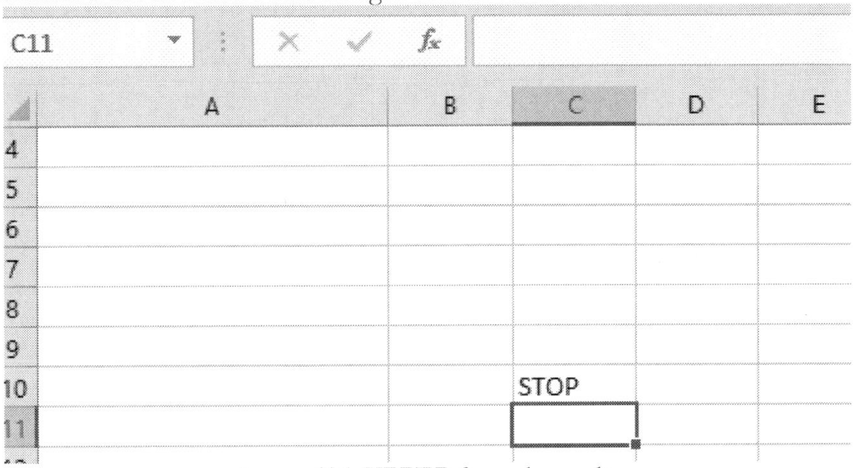

Image 126: UPPER formula results

Remember that the UPPER function deals solely with text and, therefore, will ignore numbers and punctuation present within the text argument in question.

EXACT

The EXACT function compares two or more strings of text. Imagine, for instance, that a business wants to compare the address of a customer entered into a mailing list with that pulled from a database. The EXACT function might be used. The name of this function is not an exaggeration; it will only match text strings that are the same, meaning that it is sensitive to case, punctuation, and spacing. Therefore, "101 S. Blank St." will return a FALSE response when compared against "101 s blank st," "101 s. Blank St.," or "101 S Blank St." using the EXACT function.

For this reason, EXACT is more commonly used to compare case-sensitive data, such as passwords, or unpunctuated data, such as product or item codes. The structure for the use of this function is a simple one.

=EXACT(text1, text2, text3…)

Each argument can be either a string of text contained by quotation marks or a reference to a given cell.

32.1 Upgraded Function in Excel 2022

Average

The AVERAGE function calculates the average of the cell values in a specified range. For example, to obtain the average total sales, just enter "AVERAGE(C3, C4, C5)," as shown in the sample below.

Image 127: Average formula in action

It calculates the average automatically, and you may save the result anywhere you choose.

Image 128: Average formula results

Sum

As the title suggests, this function returns the total value in the supplied cell range. It does addition as if it were a mathematical operation. Here's a sample of what I'm referring to:

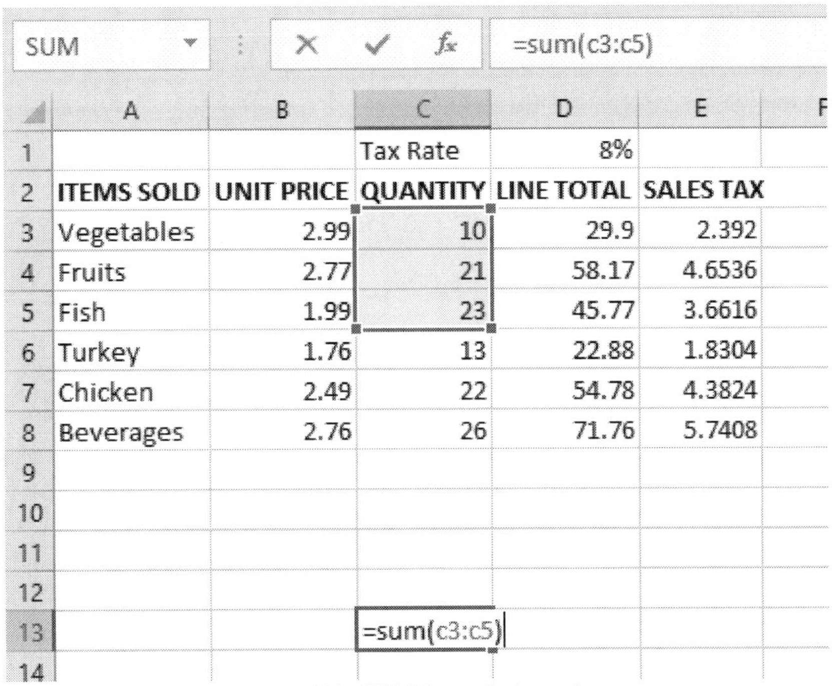

| | SUM | ▾ | ⋮ | ✕ | ✓ | *fx* | =sum(c3:c5) |

◢	A	B	C	D	E	F
1			Tax Rate	8%		
2	ITEMS SOLD	UNIT PRICE	QUANTITY	LINE TOTAL	SALES TAX	
3	Vegetables	2.99	10	29.9	2.392	
4	Fruits	2.77	21	58.17	4.6536	
5	Fish	1.99	23	45.77	3.6616	
6	Turkey	1.76	13	22.88	1.8304	
7	Chicken	2.49	22	54.78	4.3824	
8	Beverages	2.76	26	71.76	5.7408	
9						
10						
11						
12						
13			=sum(c3:c5)			
14						

Image 129: SUM formula in action

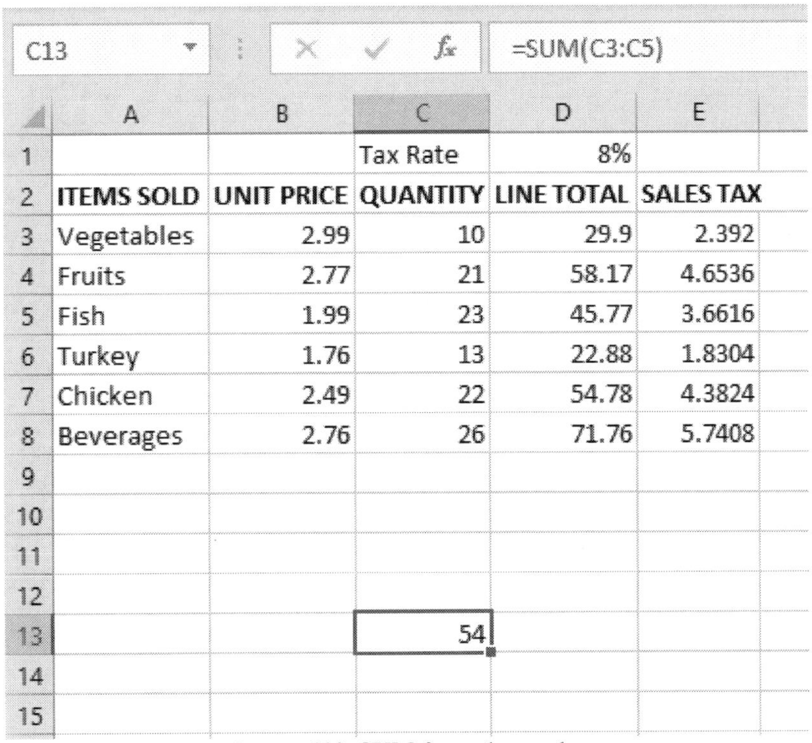

| | C13 | ▾ | ⋮ | ✕ | ✓ | *fx* | =SUM(C3:C5) |

◢	A	B	C	D	E	
1			Tax Rate	8%		
2	ITEMS SOLD	UNIT PRICE	QUANTITY	LINE TOTAL	SALES TAX	
3	Vegetables	2.99	10	29.9	2.392	
4	Fruits	2.77	21	58.17	4.6536	
5	Fish	1.99	23	45.77	3.6616	
6	Turkey	1.76	13	22.88	1.8304	
7	Chicken	2.49	22	54.78	4.3824	
8	Beverages	2.76	26	71.76	5.7408	
9						
10						
11						
12						
13			54			
14						
15						

Image 130: SUM formula results

We just wrote in the method "=SUM(C3:C5)" to get the total quantity, as you can see. C13 is where the result is stored.

Subtotal

Let's have a look at how the subtotal method works now. The SUBTOTAL() method returns a database's subtotal. Depending on your needs, you may choose between average, count, total, minimum, maximum, secs, and others. Let's focus on two instances of this.

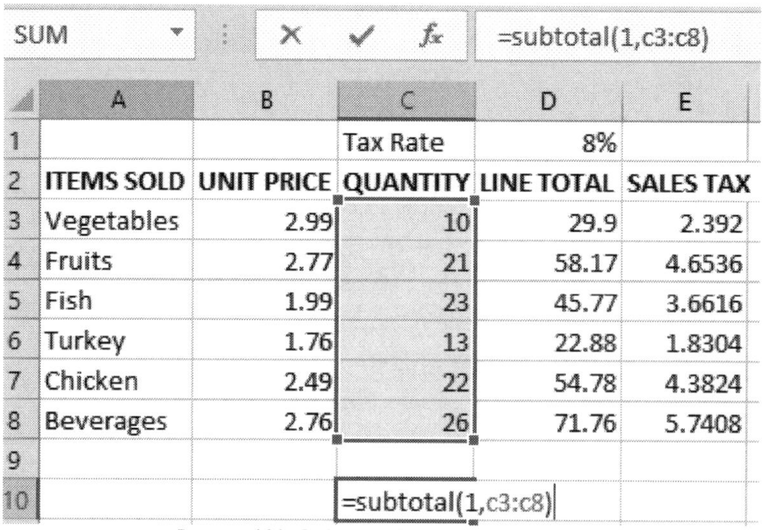

| SUM | ▼ | : | × | ✓ | *fx* | =subtotal(1,c3:c8) |

▲	A	B	C	D	E
1			Tax Rate	8%	
2	ITEMS SOLD	UNIT PRICE	QUANTITY	LINE TOTAL	SALES TAX
3	Vegetables	2.99	10	29.9	2.392
4	Fruits	2.77	21	58.17	4.6536
5	Fish	1.99	23	45.77	3.6616
6	Turkey	1.76	13	22.88	1.8304
7	Chicken	2.49	22	54.78	4.3824
8	Beverages	2.76	26	71.76	5.7408
9					
10			=subtotal(1,c3:c8)		

Image 131: Subtotal formula in action

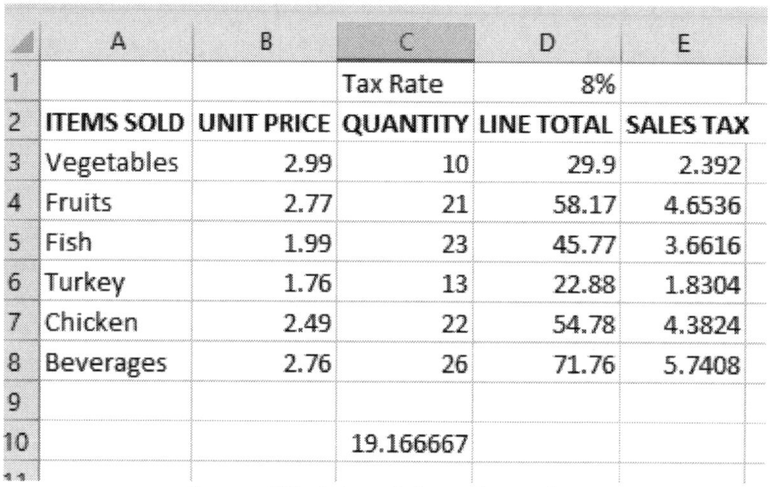

▲	A	B	C	D	E
1			Tax Rate	8%	
2	ITEMS SOLD	UNIT PRICE	QUANTITY	LINE TOTAL	SALES TAX
3	Vegetables	2.99	10	29.9	2.392
4	Fruits	2.77	21	58.17	4.6536
5	Fish	1.99	23	45.77	3.6616
6	Turkey	1.76	13	22.88	1.8304
7	Chicken	2.49	22	54.78	4.3824
8	Beverages	2.76	26	71.76	5.7408
9					
10			19.166667		

Image 132: Subtotal formula results

In the preceding example, we calculated the subtotal on cells spanning from C2 – C8. As you'll see, the method used is "=SUBTOTAL(1, C2: C8)," where "1" refers to the average in the subtotal list. As a result, the method mentioned above will return the mean of C2: C8, with response 19.166667 being put in C10.

"=SUBTOTAL(4, C2: C8)" picks the cell with the highest value between C2 and C8, which is 26. The maximum result is obtained by including "4" in the function.

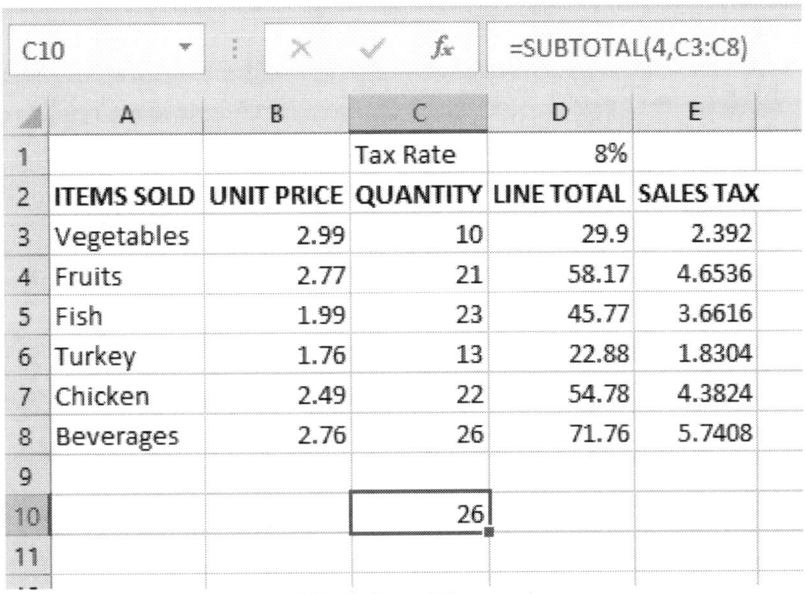

Image 133: Subtotal for maximum

Count

This calculates the number of viable cells in a region containing a number. It excludes the empty cells and those that contain data in some other format than numeric.

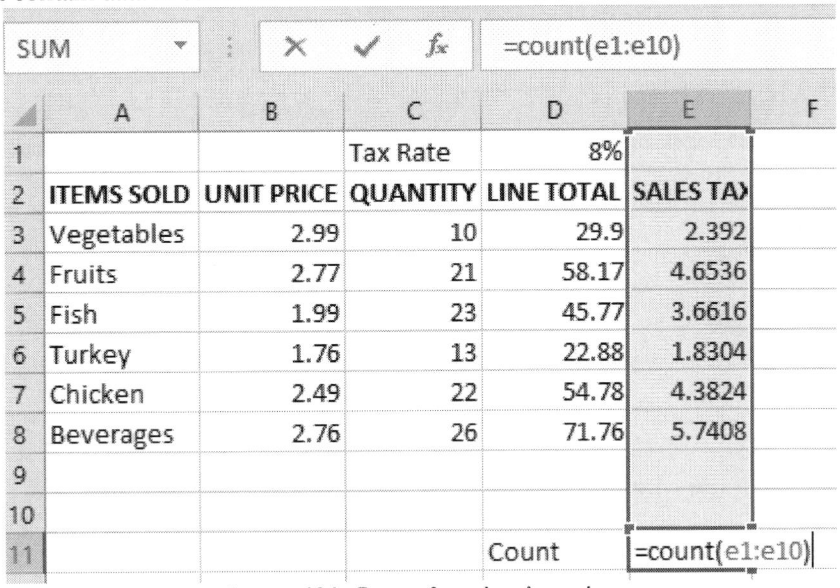

Image 134: Count function in action

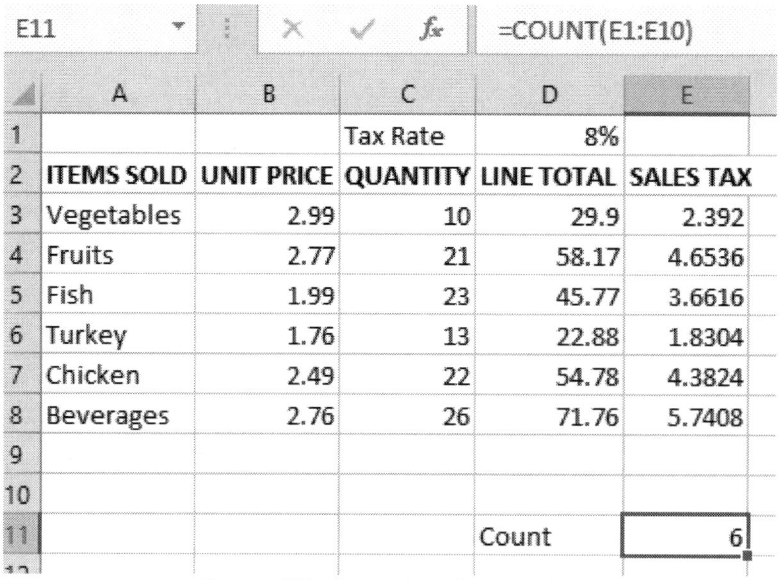

Image 135: Count function results

As you've seen, we're counting from E1 to E10, a total of 10 cells. The result is 6 since the Counts method only examines cells with quantitative data, and the cell with "Sales Tax" is ignored. If you ever need to collect all the cells with numeric values, text, or other data types, use the method 'COUNTA.' COUNTA, but on the other side, it does not include any blank cells in its calculations. COUNTBLANK is a function that counts the number of blank cells in a given cell.

MODULUS

When a divisor subdivides a given integer, the MOD() function returns the residual. Now, for a better understanding, consider the instances below. We divided 10 by 3 in the first case. The remainder is computed using the "=MOD(A2,3)" function. The outcome is saved in B2. We may also use the shortcut "=MOD(10,3)" to get the same result.

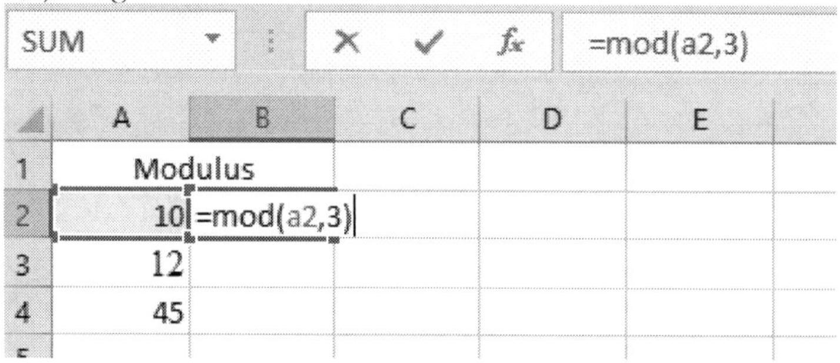

Image 136: Modulus function in action

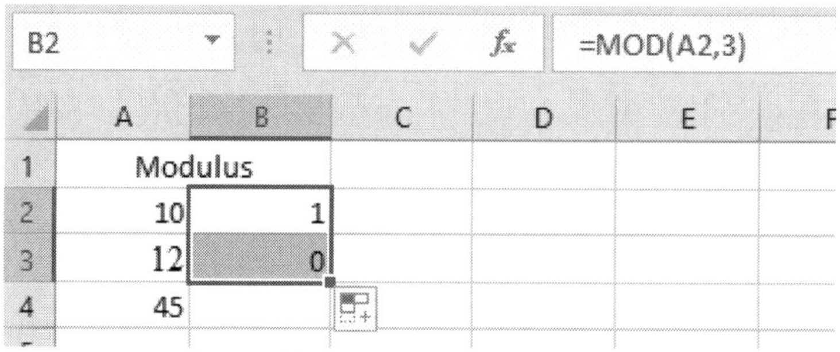

Image 137: Modulus function results

Likewise, we've split 12 by 4 in this case. 0 is remaining, which is saved in B3.

CEILING

Then there's the ceiling function. The CEILING() function takes an integer and rounds it up to the next significant multiple.

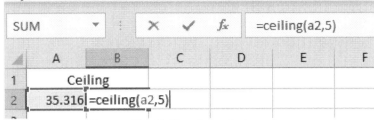

Image 138: Ceiling formula in action

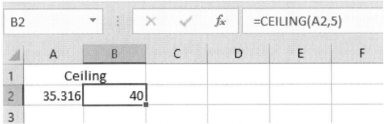

Image 139: Ceiling formula results

For 35.316, the biggest multiple of 5 is 40.

POWER

The "Power()" method produces an output of raising an integer to a given power. Take a look at some of the examples below:

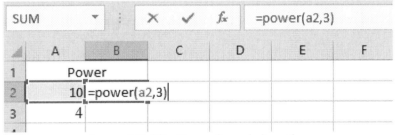

Image 140: The Power formula in action

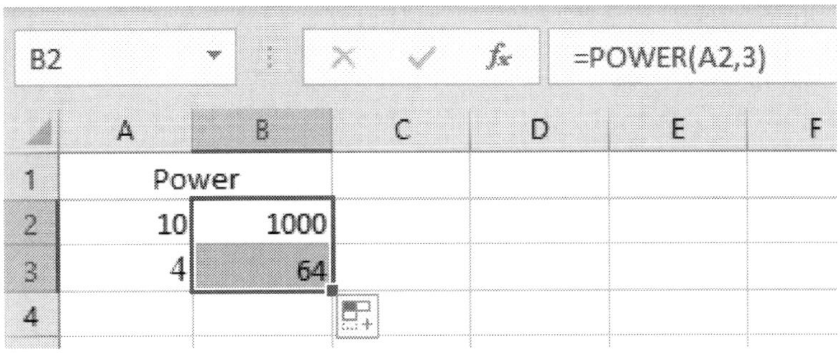

Image 141: Power formula results

As you can see, we need to enter "= POWER (A2,3)" to discover its power of 10 contained in A2 increased to 3. This is how Excel's power function works.

FLOOR

The floor function rounds a given number down to the nearest multiple of significance.

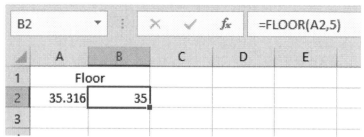

Image 142: Floor formula

Considering 35.316, the minimum multiple of Five is 35.

LEN

LEN() calculates the total quantity of letters in a file. As a result, the whole number of characters, comprising spaces and special characters, will be counted. An illustration of the Len method is shown below.

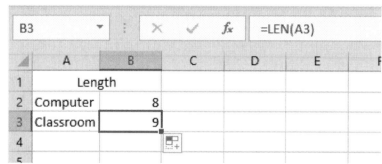

Image 143: LEN formula

CONCATENATE

This method connects or merges several text data into a single string. The many methods for performing this function are listed below.

- We have used the notation =CONCATENATE in this example (A2, " ",B2)

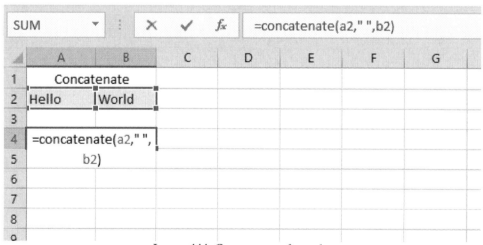

Image 144: Concatenate formula

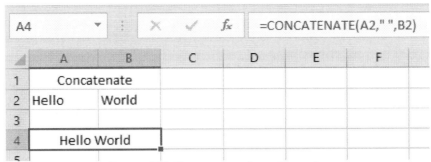

Image 145: Concatenate formula results

- We have used the notation =CONCATENATE in this sample (A2&" "&B2)

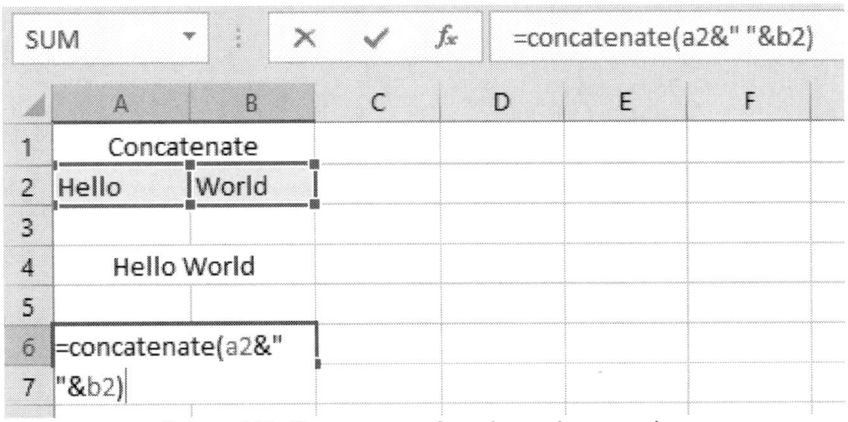

Image 146: Concatenate function using notation

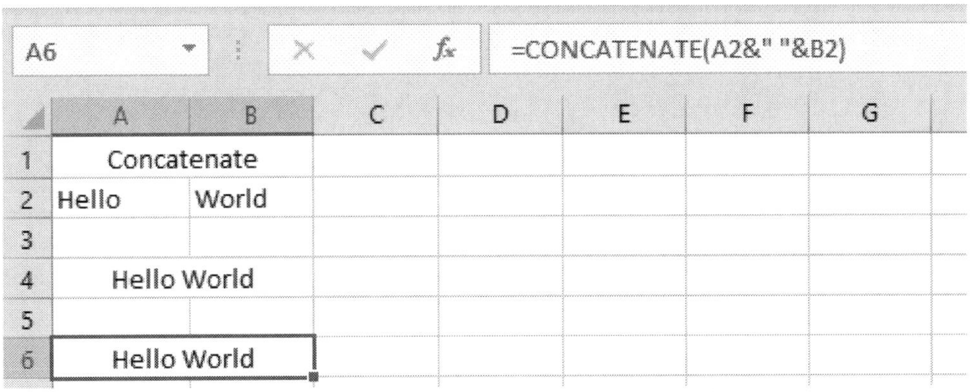

Image 147: Results of using Concatenate function using notation

The concatenation function in Excel may be done in two different ways.

REPLACE

The REPLACE() method replaces a section of a string of text with another text string, as its name implies.

"=REPLACE(old text, start num, num chars, new text)" is the syntax. The index point at which you wish to begin replacing the characters is denoted by start num. The amount of characters you wish to replace is indicated by num chars.

Let's glance at how we can take advantage of this feature.

- By entering "=REPLACE(A15,1,1,"B")" we are substituting A101 with B101.

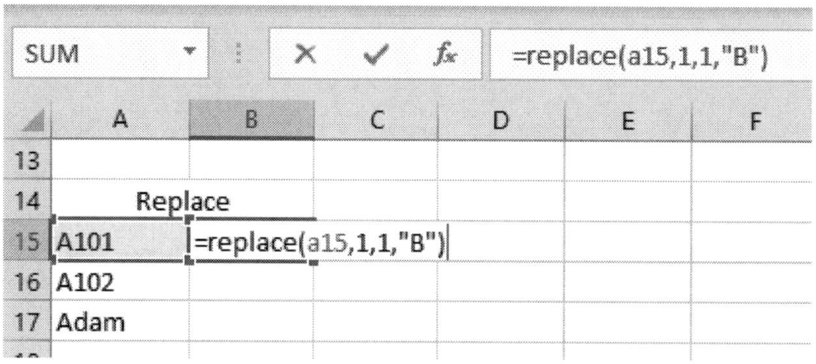

Image 148: Writing the REPLACE formula

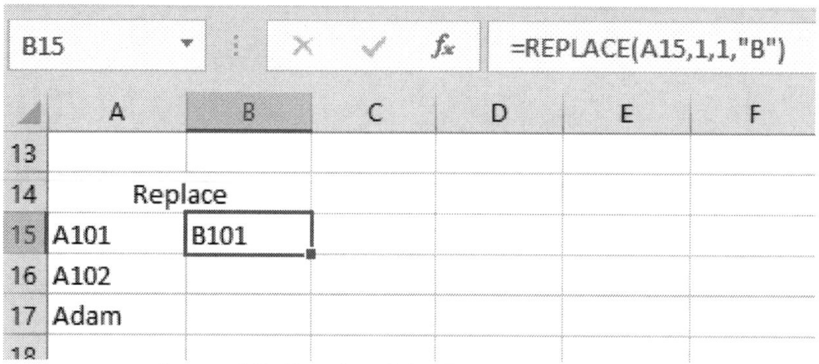

Image 149: Results of the REPLACE formula

- Next, we type "=REPLACE(A16,1,1, "A2")" to replace A102 with A2102.

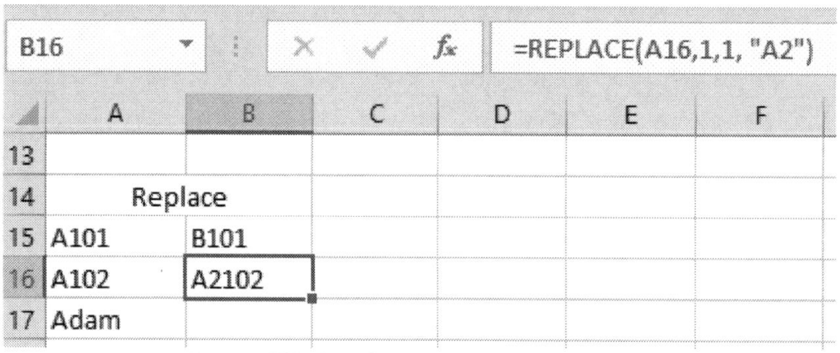

Image 150: Another way of using Replace

- Lastly, we type "=REPLACE(A17,1,2, "Sa")" to replace Adam with Saam.

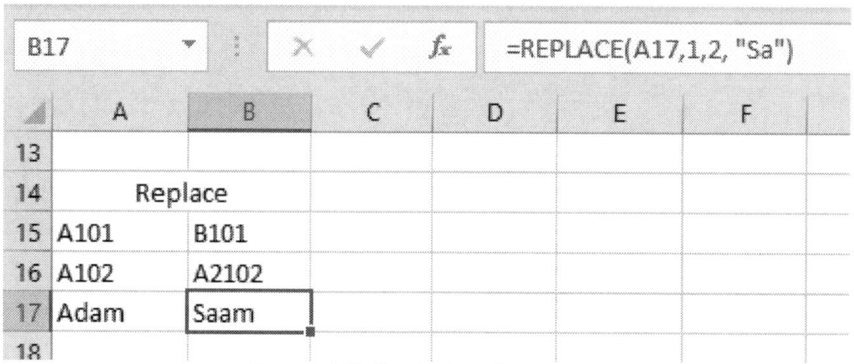

Image 151: Replacing first letter

After all this, we will move toward the following function.

LEFT, RIGHT, MID

The LEFT() method returns the set of characters in a text string starting from the leftmost character. Meanwhile, the MID() method, given a starting location and length, retrieves the words from the center of a text string. Finally, the right() method returns the number of characters remaining after a text string has been terminated.

Let's look at a few instances to comprehend these functions better.

- In the example below, we use the method left to get the leftmost item on the phrase in cell A5.

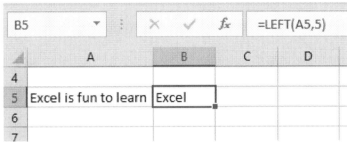

Image 152: LEFT formula

An example of how to use the mid method is shown below.

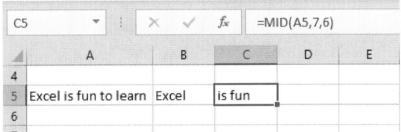

Image 153: MID formula

- Here's an illustration of how to use the correct function.

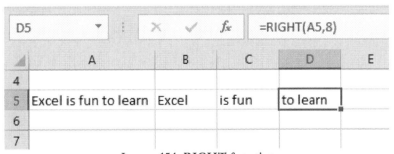

Image 154: RIGHT function

Trimming the Data (TRIM)

With the TRIM function, you can be confident that your routines will not cause errors due to disordered gaps in their input. It ensures that all empty spaces are filled in this manner. While other activities are capable of acting on many cells at the same time, TRIM is limited to working on a single cell, as opposed to other functions that are capable of acting on multiple cells at the same time. The drawback of this method is that it introduces duplicate data into your spreadsheet as a consequence of this.

- =TRIM (text)

Example:

Trim(A2) eliminates any blank spaces from the value in cell A2 by using the TRIM() function.

TODAY ()

The TODAY() method returns the current date and time on the system.

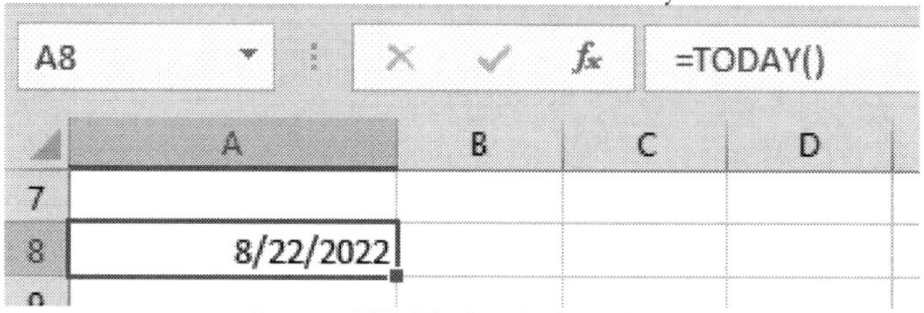

Image 155: Today () function

The DAY() method returns the current month's day of the week. It will be a number ranging from 1 to 31. The start day of the month is January 1, and the end day of the month is December 31.

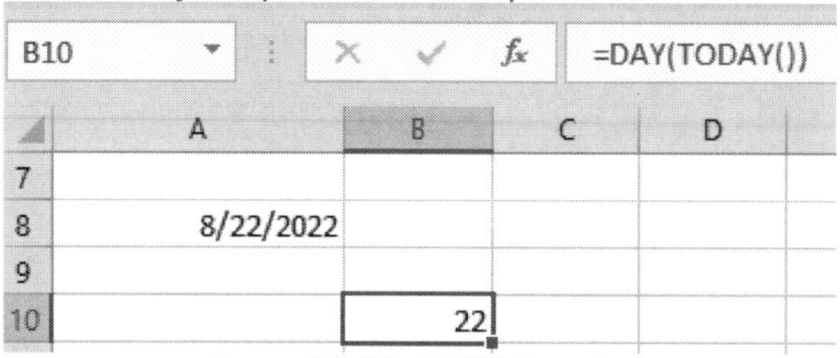

Image 156: The DAY() formula

The month is returned by the method MONTH() as a number between 1 and 12, with 1 representing January and 12 representing December.

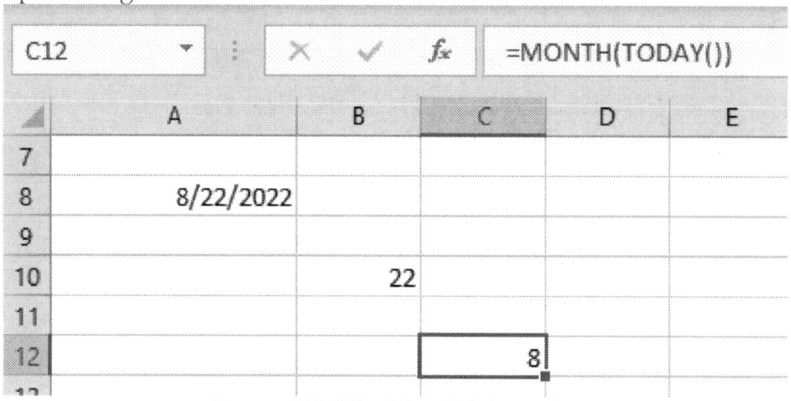

Image 157: The Month() formula

When a date value is provided, the YEAR() method returns the year, as the name implies.

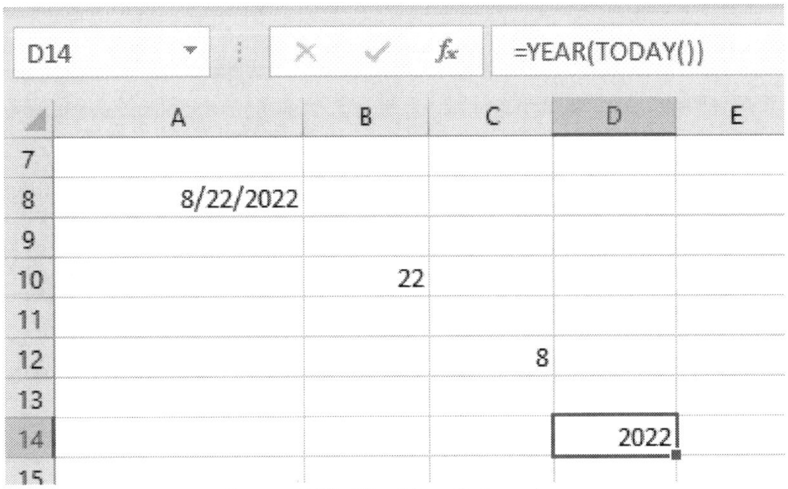

Image 158: The Year() function

DATEDIF

The DATEDIF() method calculates the difference in years, months, or days between two dates by comparing the dates in question.

A DATEDIF function, as seen below, calculates a person's current age from the person's birth date and the date of the current calculation.

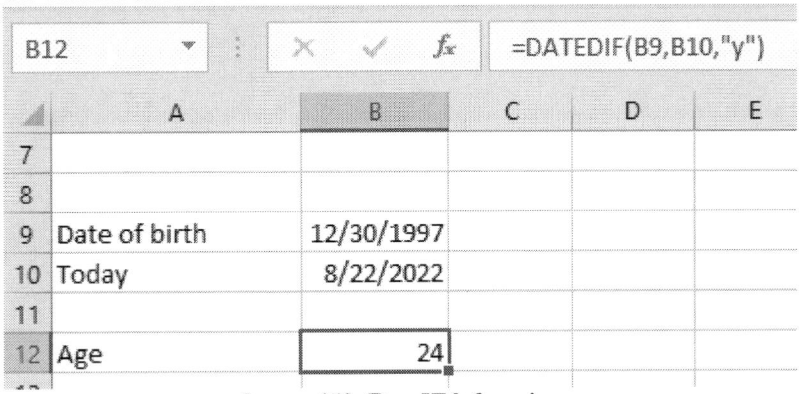

Image 159: DateIF() function

Now, let's look at a few of the essential advanced Excel functions often used to analyze data and generate reports.

VLOOKUP

The VLOOKUP() method is the next subject in this section. This is a vertical lookup function for searching a specific value in the table's leftmost column. The function returns a value from a column in the same row you specified. The following are the parameters of VLOOKUP function:

- The lookup value - It is the value you must search for within the table's first column to complete the operation.

- Table - This displays the name of the table from where you obtain the value.

- Col index - The index of the table column from which you retrieve the value.

- Range lookup – The TRUE = approximate match in the range (default).

- FALSE indicates that there is an exact match.

The VLOOKUP function will be shown with the help of the following table.

	A	B	C	D	E
1	First Name	Last Name	Department	City	Date Hired
2	Ben	Zamba	HR	Boston	10/11/2015
3	Stuart	Carry	Marketing	Chicago	9/8/2011
4	Jenson	Button	Operations	Ohio	7/3/2017
5	Lucy	Davis	Sales	New York	10/1/2019
6	Trent	Patinson	IT	Kansas	5/4/2020
7	Johnny	Evans	Sales	Houston	2/3/2018
8					

Image 160: Table to use for VLOOKUP

You might use the VLOOKUP function to determine which department Stuart is a member of, as seen in the following example:

Here, 0 represents the range lookup, A11 represents the lookup result, A2:E7 represents the table array, and 3 represents the column index number containing department information.

C11				f_x	=VLOOKUP(A11,A2:E7,3,0)	

	A	B	C	D	E	F
1	First Name	Last Name	Department	City	Date Hired	
2	Ben	Zamba	HR	Boston	10/11/2015	
3	Stuart	Carry	Marketing	Chicago	9/8/2011	
4	Jenson	Button	Operations	Ohio	7/3/2017	
5	Lucy	Davis	Sales	New York	10/1/2019	
6	Trent	Patinson	IT	Kansas	5/4/2020	
7	Johnny	Evans	Sales	Houston	2/3/2018	
8						
9			Vlookup			
10	First Name	Last Name	Department	City	Date Hired	
11	Stuart		Marketing			
12						

Image 161: Vlookup function in action

On pressing the Enter key, the program will return the word "Marketing," indicating that Stuart is a member of the marketing department.

HLOOKUP

HLOOKUP(), also known as horizontal lookup, is a function that functions similarly to VLOOKUP(). The HLOOKUP function scans the first row of a table or array of benefits to find a value. Then, it returns the value from a specific row in the same column that has been supplied.

The following are the parameters of the HLOOKUP function:

- This is the value to lookup in the lookup table.

- Table - This is the table where you must extract information.

In this case, the row index specifies the row number from which the data will be fetched. If the match is exact, this value is true; otherwise, it is false. Range lookups are Boolean value that shows whether the match is precise or approximate. The default result is TRUE, which implies that there is a good match in this case. Let's look at how to utilize the HLOOKUP function to locate the city of Jenson in the table above.

`=hlookup(H8,G1:M5,4,0)`

D	E	F	G	H	I	J	K	L	M
			First Name	Ben	Stuart	Jenson	Lucy	Trent	Johnny
			Last Name	Zamba	Carry	Button	Davis	Patinson	Evans
			Department	HR	Marketing	Operation	Sales	IT	Sales
			City	Boston	Chicago	Ohio	New York	Kansas	Houston
			Date Hired	10/11/2015	9/8/2011	7/3/2017	10/1/2019	5/4/2020	2/3/2018
			First Name	Jenson					
			City	=hlookup(H8,G1:M5,4,0)					

Image 162: Hlookup in action

In this example, H8 contains the lookup value, i.e., 4 represents the row index number, Jenson, G1:M5 represents the table array, and 0 represents an approximation match. Once you press the Enter key, the word "Ohio" will appear.

G	H	I	J	K	L	M	N
First Name	Ben	Stuart	Jenson	Lucy	Trent	Johnny	
Last Name	Zamba	Carry	Button	Davis	Patinson	Evans	
Department	HR	Marketing	Operation	Sales	IT	Sales	
City	Boston	Chicago	Ohio	New York	Kansas	Houston	
Date Hired	10/11/2015	9/8/2011	7/3/2017	10/1/2019	5/4/2020	2/3/2018	
First Name	Jenson						
City	Ohio						

Image 163: Results of Hlookup

INDEX-MATCH

The INDEX-MATCH function matches a value in the left column to a value in the right column. On the other hand, the VLOOKUP function does not allow you to return an assessment from a column to the right. In addition, index-match benefits VLOOKUP in that VLOOKUP demands more processing capacity from Excel.

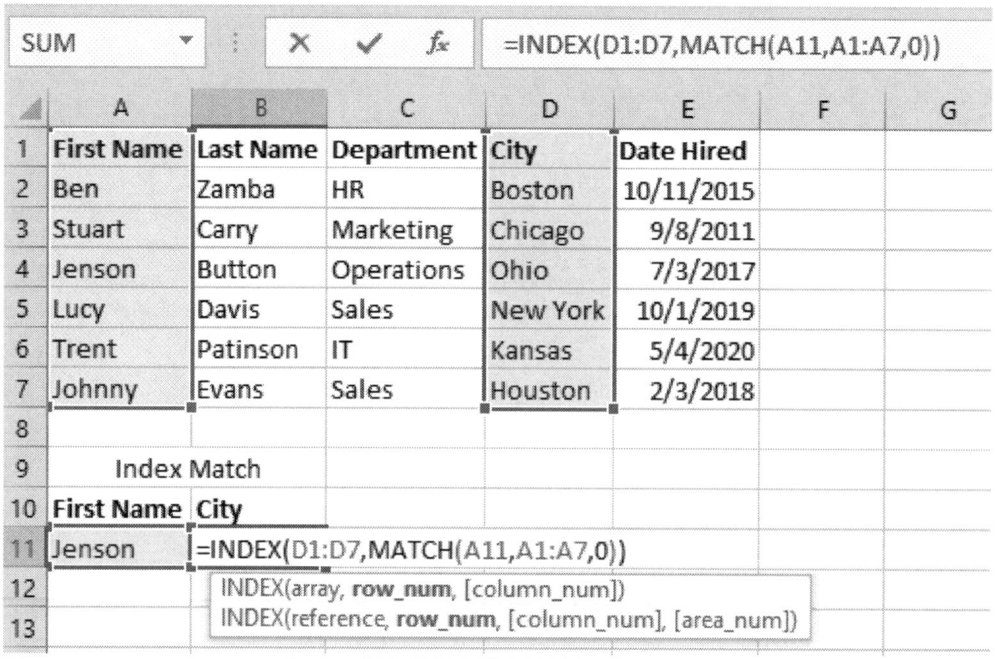

SUM | =INDEX(D1:D7,MATCH(A11,A1:A7,0))

	A	B	C	D	E	F	G
1	First Name	Last Name	Department	City	Date Hired		
2	Ben	Zamba	HR	Boston	10/11/2015		
3	Stuart	Carry	Marketing	Chicago	9/8/2011		
4	Jenson	Button	Operations	Ohio	7/3/2017		
5	Lucy	Davis	Sales	New York	10/1/2019		
6	Trent	Patinson	IT	Kansas	5/4/2020		
7	Johnny	Evans	Sales	Houston	2/3/2018		
8							
9	Index Match						
10	First Name	City					
11	Jenson	=INDEX(D1:D7,MATCH(A11,A1:A7,0))					
12		INDEX(array, row_num, [column_num])					
13		INDEX(reference, row_num, [column_num], [area_num])					

Image 164: INDEX-MATCH function

This is because it must assess the whole table array you picked, which is time-consuming.

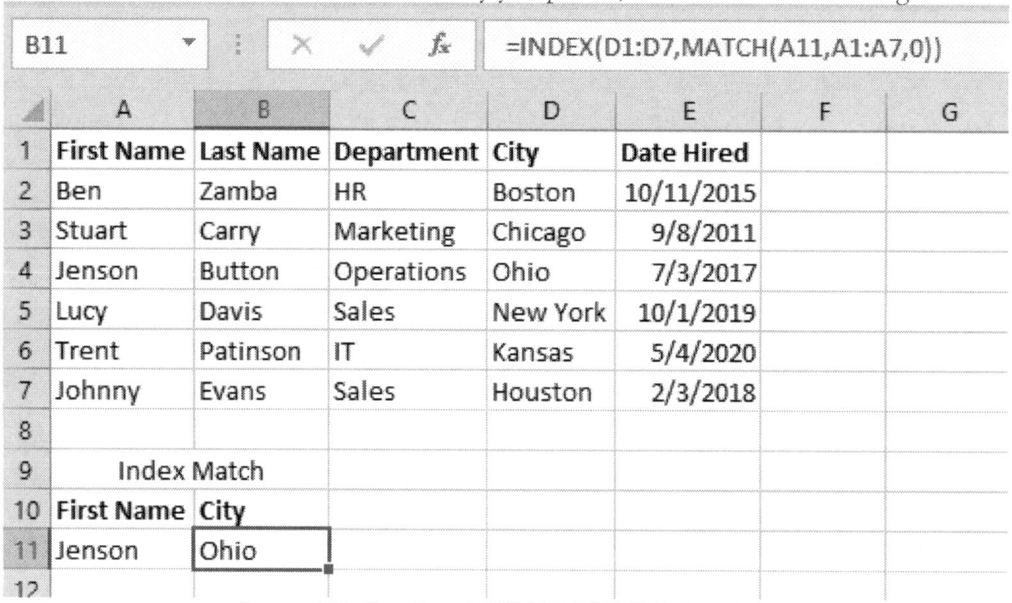

B11 | =INDEX(D1:D7,MATCH(A11,A1:A7,0))

	A	B	C	D	E	F	G
1	First Name	Last Name	Department	City	Date Hired		
2	Ben	Zamba	HR	Boston	10/11/2015		
3	Stuart	Carry	Marketing	Chicago	9/8/2011		
4	Jenson	Button	Operations	Ohio	7/3/2017		
5	Lucy	Davis	Sales	New York	10/1/2019		
6	Trent	Patinson	IT	Kansas	5/4/2020		
7	Johnny	Evans	Sales	Houston	2/3/2018		
8							
9	Index Match						
10	First Name	City					
11	Jenson	Ohio					
12							

Image 165: Results of INDEX-MATCH function

With the INDEX-MATCH function, Excel has to take into account the return column and the lookup column.

COUNTIF

COUNTIF() is a function that counts the total number of cells in a range that meet a condition. It counts the total number of cells in a range that satisfies a condition.

SUMIF()

SUMIF() is a function that adds cells specified by a criterion or condition to the total.
SUMIFS() is a function that adds the cells indicated by a set of criteria or conditions to the end of a string.

33 Writing Text in Microsoft Excel

To write text in Microsoft Excel, you can take a few steps to format your data. Before entering data, you can format the cells with text or numbers. To format the entire column, you should right-click and select Format Cells on Number tab. Then, on the Home tab, choose Text format. The default text format is Number, so you can change it to another type to make it easier to sort. You can also change a single entry to text format by typing an apostrophe (') in front of the data.

Aligning text to the left

To align text to the left in Microsoft Excel, select the Helper column of the cell you'd like to align. Type the original string in the helper column. If necessary, add leading spaces to it. To calculate the number of spaces to align text, subtract the position of the aligning character from the maximum number of characters before it. Then, click the Align Text button to apply the change.

Using the Format Cells dialog box, you can also choose to align numbers and text to the bottom-left corner of cells. First, click on the Align Text or Align Numbers option. Next, select the desired option and then click OK. The options for alignment will change. To align text, you can also adjust the indentation of the cell by using the Format Cells dialog box or the shortcut keys Alt+H.

Formatting text

You're not alone if you're looking to format text in Microsoft Excel. Many people struggle with this task. Fortunately, you can take some easy steps to make your work much easier. You can choose from several preset styles to make formatting your text a breeze. Listed below are a few tips for formatting text in Excel. Once you've learned them, you'll be on your way to writing effective and professional documents in no time.

The first step to formatting text in Excel is selecting the text you want to format. Use the font group on the Home tab and click the arrow in the bottom-right corner of the text group. In the Font tab, you can change the font style and color of your text. After you've made your selections, click the "Apply" button to save the changes. You can then format the text by right-clicking the cell.

Checking for errors

One way to detect errors when writing text in Microsoft Excel is to use the IFERROR function. The IFERROR function checks for errors in a VLOOKUP formula and returns user-friendly error text when there is a problem. You can also use the IFNA function to trap #N/A errors if an error is detected. The IF ISNA formula traps only #N/A errors.

The warning icon or green triangle in the upper left corner of a cell indicates an error. The error is caused by a faulty formula or a reference to a cell that does not exist. However, some errors are more serious and may even break the fundamental laws of mathematics. An example of an error in a formula is that the column is too narrow to fit the data. If the column width is too small, you can simply resize the column, and the error will go away automatically.

Changing the font type

You can change the font type in Microsoft Excel to any other font you want. The fonts available in Excel typically range from 8 to 72 points, but you can change the size of each font by selecting "Custom." To revert to the default font, you must restart Excel. Otherwise, you can change the font size by clicking "No Formatting."

After you change the font, Excel will revert to the default settings for the font used for cell entries. You can change this setting in Excel 2010 without affecting your existing workbooks. Before making a change, you may want to preview the fonts in a worksheet first to ensure they look right. For accessibility purposes, you may want to use a larger font size. Changing the default font is a simple way to add style to your spreadsheet and give it a professional appearance.

Changing the font size

If you're writing text in Microsoft Excel, you may wonder how to change the font size. Excel specifies font size in points equal to 1/72 of an inch. To change the font size, use the toolbar. Next, click the point size tool to the left of the text-attribute tools. From there, select the font size you'd like. Excel will then display a drop-down list of options.

You can also change the font size by using the arrow keys. In the arrows, you can scroll through the font size list and change the size of your text. By increasing the font size, you'll get a bolder font, while decreasing it will result in a smaller font. Changing the font size can be tricky, but if you follow a few simple steps, you'll have no trouble making changes.

Changing the color of the text

The first step to changing the font color in Microsoft Excel is to select the cell in which you want to change the font. On the 'Home' tab, click the 'Font' button. From the dropdown menu, select a font size from the color palette. Click OK to apply the change. You will then be able to select a new font color. Changing text color in Microsoft Excel is easy once you know how.

The next step is selecting the text's color in the cell. Click the Format button in the lower section of the formula, which contains cell A1. Then, click the Font tab, where you can select a color. Click OK to apply the selection. The formatted text in Figure A is now red. In Figure B, you can see the formatted text and formula. After this, click the Font tab again to choose a color for the font.

FUNCTIONS FOR TEXTS IN EXCEL

These functions are used in text data. Their presence in your formula allows Excel to concatenate, switch text cases, find and extract specific parts of the indicated text, etc.

Function to Combine Strings of Text

The **CONCATENATE** function is used for combining multiple strings of texts in Excel. An example is **=CONCATENATE(D1, F1).**

The operator to perform a similar operation is the ampersand (**&**) symbol.

Switching Texts to Sentence Cases

The function **PROPER** is used for this operation. Other functions to switch text cases are the **UPPER** function for capital letters and the **LOWER** function for small letters. Examples are:

=LOWER(A2)
=UPPER(A2)
=PROPER(A2)

Image 166: Proper function in text

Deleting Excess Spaces in Strings of Text

Excess spaces can be removed from your texts using the **TRIM** function. E.g. **=TRIM(C2)**

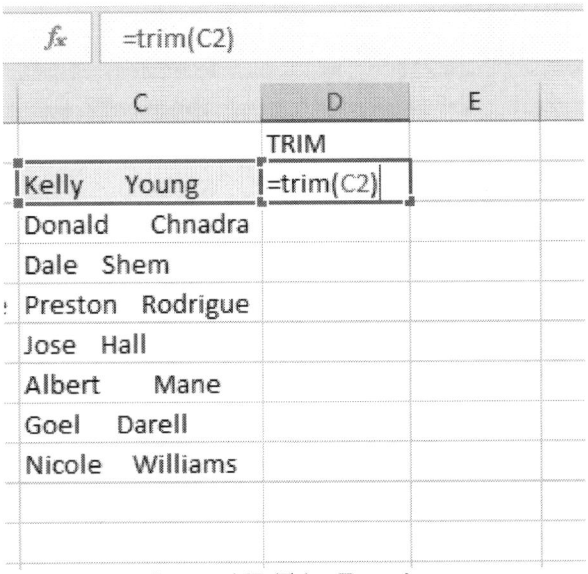

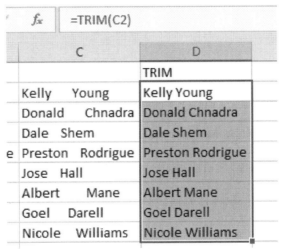

Image 167: Trim Function

Image 168: Trim results

Discovering Parts of a String of Texts

Various functions are available to extract specific parts of your texts. These include:

- **The LEFT Function**

This function finds characters starting from left side of your text. The syntax for the formula is as follows:

=LEFT(cell_text, num_chars)

cell_text argument denotes the cell holding the text, and **num_chars** denotes the number of characters to be extracted. E.g: **=LEFT(B2,4)**

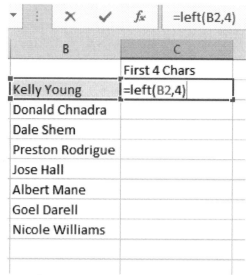

Image 169: Left function for text

Image 170: The Left Function results

- **The RIGHT Function**

This function finds characters starting from your text's right side. The syntax for the formula is as follows:

=RIGHT(cell_text, num_chars)

E.g: **=RIGHT(B2,4)**

Image 171: Right function in text

- **The MID Function**

This function holds an addition argument to tell Excel where to start and end its extraction operation.
=MID(text, starting_num, num_chars)
E.g: **=MID(B2,6,3)**
This formula above tells Excel to start its extraction from the 6th character and then extract the next three characters.

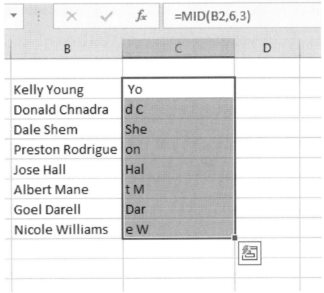

Image 172: MID function in text

Extracting Texts Before and After Particular Characters
The **LEFT/RIGHT** functions and the **SEARCH** function are used as suitable.
For extracting texts before the character, use the following syntax for your function:
=LEFT(cell_text, SEARCH("char", cell_text)-1)
The **char** argument denotes the character to be used as the reference point. Example includes:
=LEFT(C2, SEARCH("-",C2)-1)

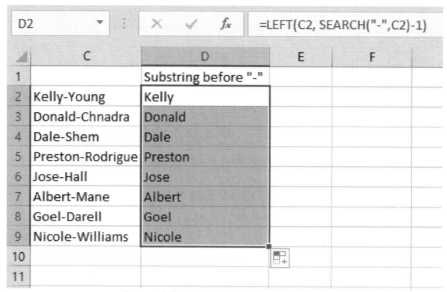

Image 173: Extracting the text before

For extracting texts after the character, use the following syntax for your function:
=RIGHT(cell_text,LEN(cell_text)-SEARCH("char", cell_text)).
Example includes: **=RIGHT(C2,LEN(C2)-SEARCH("-",C2))**

D2			fx	=RIGHT(C2,LEN(C2)-SEARCH("-",C2))			
	C		D	E	F	G	
1			Substring after "-"				
2	Kelly-Young		Young				
3	Donald-Chnadra		Chnadra				
4	Dale-Shem		Shem				
5	Preston-Rodrigue		Rodrigue				
6	Jose-Hall		Hall				
7	Albert-Mane		Mane				
8	Goel-Darell		Darell				
9	Nicole-Williams		Williams				
10							
11							

Image 174: Extracting the text after

Searching for Specific Text Characters in a String
The **SEARCH** or **FIND** functions are used for this operation. The syntax is as follows:
=FIND(find_character, within_text) or
=SEARCH(find_character, within_text).
For example: **=FIND("e", "fine")** or **=SEARCH("wash", "carwash")**
Searching for Second Occurrence of Specific Text Characters in a String
This operation uses the **FIND** function. Where the specific character is first found is indicated in the formula. E.g: **=FIND("-","POWER-2-BIG", 7)**
This formula tells Excel to search for the **"-"** character and begin its search from the 7th character since the character is first found in the 6th character.
Replacing Content of Texts
The **SUBSTITUTE** function is applied with the following syntax:

=SUBSTITUTE (cell_text, old_text, replacing_text).

E.g: **=SUBSTITUTE(D5,"c","b").** This formula replaces every "c" character with "b."

If you want only to replace specific characters, you can add another argument to denote this:

E.g: **=SUBSTITUTE(D5,"c","b", 2).** This tells Excel to only replace the second "c" character with "b."

Calculating Number of Times a Given Character Appears in a Certain Text

This operation uses the **LEN** and **SUBSTITUTE** functions. Example includes:

=LEN(D2)-LEN(SUBSTITUTE(D2,"A","")).

This formula calculates the number of times the character "**A**" appears in the text.

Starting Lines of Formulas on New Lines

- Place your mouse blinking cursor at the start of the argument where the new line would begin

- Press key **Alt** and press **Enter**

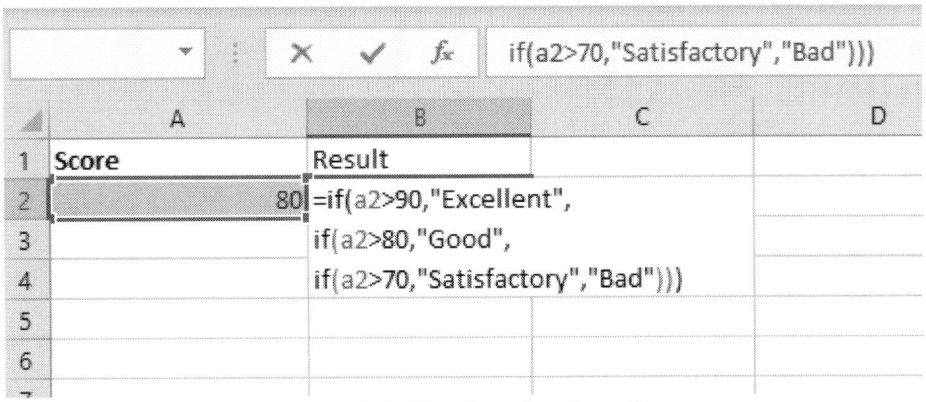

▼	⋮	✕ ✓	*fx*	if(a2>70,"Satisfactory","Bad")))

◢	A	B	C	D
1	Score	Result		
2	80	=if(a2>90,"Excellent",		
3		if(a2>80,"Good",		
4		if(a2>70,"Satisfactory","Bad")))		
5				
6				

Image 175: New lines in a formula

Erasing Unwanted Characters from Fields for Text

Follow this syntax to clean up unwanted characters in your texts:

=SUBSTITUTE (Cell_Text , "char_to_be_removed", "replace_with").

E.g: **=SUBSTITUTE(D3,"!"," ")**

This formula replaces the "!" character in cell D3 with a space.

Formatting Numbers by Adding Zeros

The **TEXT** function is used in this case. E.g. **=TEXT(B2,"0000000000")**

The dialogue box for customizing numbers can also be used.

- Highlight the cells to be formatted

- Right-click on these cells and select the option to format them

Image 176: Steps for formatting text

- Navigate to the option for **Custom** in the dialogue box

- Type in multiple zeros as desired and select the **OK** button

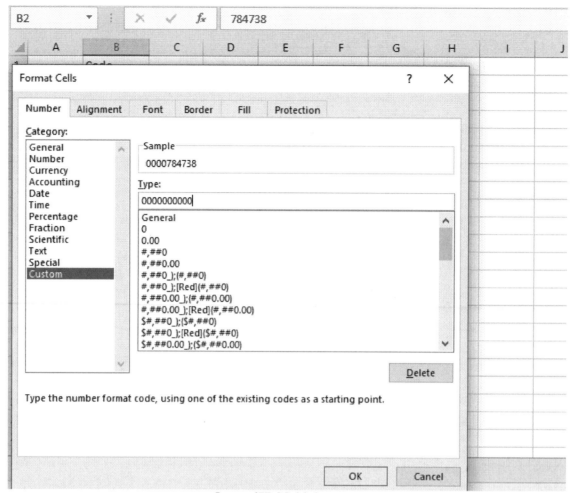

Image 177: Multiple zeros

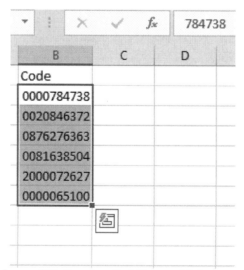

Image 178: Results of adding multiple zeros

Formatting Numeric Values in Strings of Text

This operation includes the concatenation operator and the **TEXT** function for combining text and numeric values. Formatting the numeric values follows the syntax:

=TEXT (cell_reference, required_formatting)

E.g. **=B5&": "&TEXT(C8, "$0,000")**
This formula combines the text in cell B5 and the formatted currency value in cell C8.

Applying the DOLLAR Function

This function changes numeric values to text, as mentioned in the previous section for formatting numbers in texts. Example includes:

=DOLLAR(259.99) that gives a result of **$259.99**

Combined with text, for instance,

="Radio price is "&B6 would give a result of **"Radio price is 99."**

Including the **DOLLAR** function:

="Radio price is "&DOLLAR(B6) would give a result of **"Radio price is $99.00."**

34 Using Images and Shapes in Microsoft Excel

If you're unfamiliar with using Images and Shapes in Microsoft Excel, then you've come to the right place. Learn how to add clip art or shapes to a document, worksheet, or spreadsheet. Using these tools is quick, easy, and will help you make your documents and spreadsheets stand out from the crowd. This section will walk you through the process from beginning to end. Using Images and Shapes in Microsoft Excel will make your documents look stunning and enhance your data entry efforts.

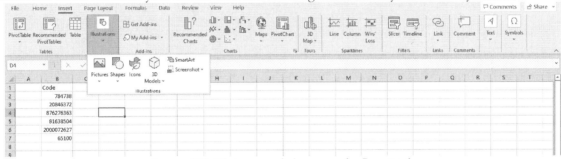

Image 179: Pictures and shapes under Insert tab

Formatting images and shapes in Microsoft Excel

There are several ways to resize and format images and shapes in Microsoft Excel. Most images and shapes move with the cells in the spreadsheet. However, your images and shapes can stay in place by locking their size. To do this, right-click on your object and choose the "Size and Properties" category. The Properties menu is located on the left side of the window. After formatting the objects, you can click the Save button.

Select a picture in your Excel spreadsheet. You will then see a text box over the image. It is possible to alter font, size and color of the text. You may click "Picture" button as well to change the shape's appearance. The task pane also allows you to resize and reposition the object. It will remain centered when you reposition the image.

Adding clip art to a spreadsheet

Adding clip art to a spreadsheet in MS Excel is a simple process, as long as you know how to use the program. The clip art is a collection of readymade illustrations that can be used within Microsoft Office programs. The clip art is divided into several categories, and you can easily insert them into your spreadsheet by using the tool that comes with Microsoft Excel. To insert clip art, simply type the name of the image into the search field and click "Insert." This will show you a list of results, and you can then select the image you want to insert into your document.

There are two ways to insert a picture into your spreadsheet. First, you can insert a picture by dragging it into your spreadsheet or selecting a picture and inserting it. Once you have the picture, you can move it to another location. If you move the picture, you must recreate the link. The second way is to browse the file that contains the picture. In the "File name:" field of the Insert Picture dialog, type the picture's name. Then, choose the option of Paste to paste the picture into the sheet.

Adding a shape to a worksheet

In Microsoft Excel, adding a shape to a worksheet is a fairly straightforward process. To add a shape, select it and right-click it. Then, you can choose from the shape's Styles options to choose a style for your shape. The Intense Effect style will add a shadow to your shape and gives it a 3D look. You can also change the Theme setting to choose a beveled effect instead.

Adding a shape in Microsoft Excel is easy - just select the Insert tab and the Shapes or Illustrations option. You'll then be able to click on the desired shape and drag it to the desired location on the worksheet. Shapes can be tied to cells in the worksheet, updating the text as the worksheet is calculated. They can also be drawn with the mouse pointer. To use shapes in Excel, you need to know that you can add several shapes to a worksheet.

Adding a shape to a document

Adding a shape to a document is an excellent way to add visual appeal and clarity to your work. You can use it to create graphs, charts, and maps and add them to email correspondence or slide shows. Shapes are also great for separating names and addresses. In addition to adding visual appeal, shapes can help you organize your work by making it easier to read. The shapes you can add are called SmartArt graphics, and they can be used in various ways.

You can also use the Shape tool to add text to your shape. You can type text inside a shape and change the font and color to suit your document. You can use the Text tool to add meaningful text when adding text to a shape. You can find text formatting options on the Home tab. In addition, you can lock the drawing mode to resize and position the shape easily.

34.1 Using Smart-Art in Microsoft Excel

If you want to add visual flair to your spreadsheets, you can use SmartArt in Microsoft Excel. Here are some tips and tricks. You can also add text or bullet lists to SmartArt. First, let's take a look. Using SmartArt in Excel is easy once you understand how they work. Once you've mastered the basics, you can start creating your SmartArt! You can even change the look and feel of your SmartArt by adding different shapes.

Adding a shape to a SmartArt

To add a shape to a SmartArt in the text pane, select the graphic. You'll notice two contextual tabs at the bottom of the window. Select the Design tab and click the Add Shape button. This brings up a drop-down gallery of shapes to add to the graphic. Then, you can select a shape and click OK to make it the new default one.

You can also change the colors and styles of your SmartArt graphic. Click the "Change Colors" button on the "SmartArt Tools" ribbon. Hovering over the options gives you an idea of which colors you want. Click OK to commit your changes. Now, you can add text inside the shape or beside the bullets in the pane. You can also change the shape and fill color.

Here is the step-by-step guide:

Go to INSERT tab.

Select illustrations then SmartArt.

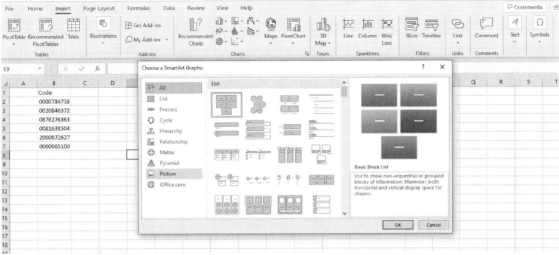

Image 180: SmartArt in Excel

Choose your preference the list then click OK

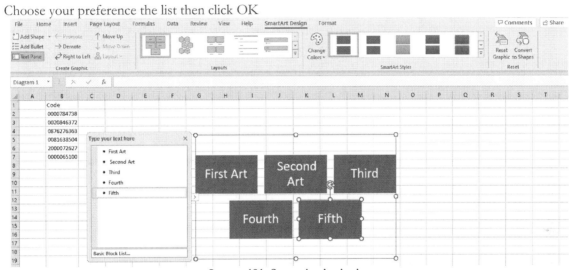

Image 181: SmartArt in Action

Modifying the look and feel of a SmartArt

In Microsoft Excel, the SmartArt object starts as a simple blue diagram. In the Design tab, you can customize the look and feel of the SmartArt with one of the several available color styles. SmartArt also has a color palette and supports adding pictures and text. In addition, the Colors and Styles group contains more than 30 color schemes. To choose a style, click the Change Colors or SmartArt Styles button.

You can change the look and feel of a SmartArt by changing the shapes and text. Changing the font, color, and size of a SmartArt is simple. To change the layout, click on the Shape toolbar and select a different color. You can also change the look and feel of a SmartArt by ungrouping it. Creating separate SmartArts is also a great way to make the graphics look more professional.

Adding text to a SmartArt

The first step in adding text to a SmartArt is to insert a new shape. You will notice that as you add more shapes, the size of the SmartArt will decrease. To resize the SmartArt, simply drag the border out of the shape's borders. Excel will adjust its dimensions to the new dimensions. You can then add text inside the shape or beside the bullets in the pane.

If you're using a SmartArt, it's vital to note that you can add multiple shapes and text to the graphic. The shapes can be of any shape, such as a line, a triangle, or a circle. This makes it easy to make the

SmartArt graphic look more professional. The text boxes can be resized, rearranged, or formatted in any way you desire.

Adding a bullet list to a SmartArt

You will need to find the right one to add bullets to a SmartArt graphic. First, click on the Insert tab and select the SmartArt Illustrations group. From the list, select the SmartArt Graphic you want to use. Then click OK. Once inserted, you can change its color or shape using the Format tab. In the following steps, you will learn how to add a bullet list to a SmartArt graphic.

The next step is to copy the bullet symbol and paste it into the text box. If you do not have a numeric keypad, you can activate Num Lock by pressing Shift + Fn. Alternatively, you can simply click and drag the fill handle to the desired location. If you want to repeat a list of bullets, you can repeat the steps above. You can also copy the bullet symbol and paste it into another cell.

35 Basics of Data Validation in Microsoft Excel

If you are creating a report in Microsoft Excel, you may be interested in knowing more about data validation. This feature is used to specify which types of data and values are allowed. Depending on the data you are calculating, data validation may restrict the values you can enter in fields such as drop-down lists, whole numbers, decimal numbers, lists, and text length. This section will cover the basic types of data validation and how you can apply them to your report.

List validation

There are many ways to use list validation in Microsoft Excel. First of all, you need to know that list validation is not foolproof, and you can get around it by pasting data into a cell or selecting Clear>Clear All on the Ribbon's Home tab. The easiest way to keep a list of options is to type them on the worksheet. You can create a drop-down list on the same worksheet if you need to have several options at once.

It is possible to specify an optional message for users when using drop-down lists. This message will appear when a user selects a cell having a drop-down list. This message will be displayed on the user's screen and will inform them to enter valid data. You can also use the Input Message tab to customize the error message. Once the message has been created, click OK. Then, close Data Validation window.

The Drop Down List within a Cell

You may name an item based on a specified Excel table to build a drop-down menu in Excel. And use that item as the Data Integrity drop-down list's source. If you don't wish to build a named table, see the named range paragraph below for details.

Creating a Drop-Down List

You may build a drop list of choices in a cell with the use of Data Validation. There are three simple steps to follow:

- Make a table of contents OR a list

- Give the List a Name

- Make the drop-down menu

Make a title for the list — In this case, the employees. Type the items you wish to view in the drop-down list in a single column immediately below the header cell. Between the entries, do not leave any blank cells.

	A	B	C	D
1		**Employees**		
2		Luigi		
3		Fred		
4		Sharon		
5		Susan		
6		Ronnie		
7		Dee		
8		Mario		
9		Andy		
10		George		
11		Lou		
12		Kim		
13		Jesse		
14				
15				
16				

Image 182: Table to use in creating drop-down list

- Click on the insert and then click on the table

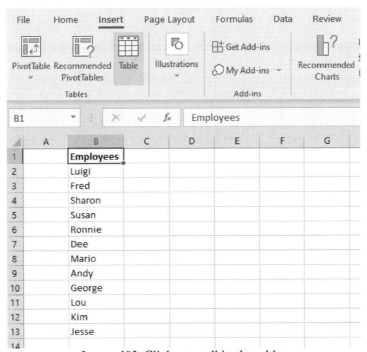

Image 183: Click one cell in the table

- Check the box

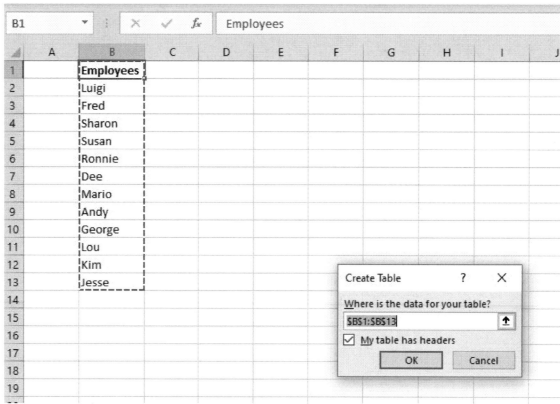

Image 184: Creating table with headers

In this way, you can name the table.

You may use a named range to construct a list inside one or even more cells now that you've generated one. Choose the cells where you would like this same drop-down list to appear.

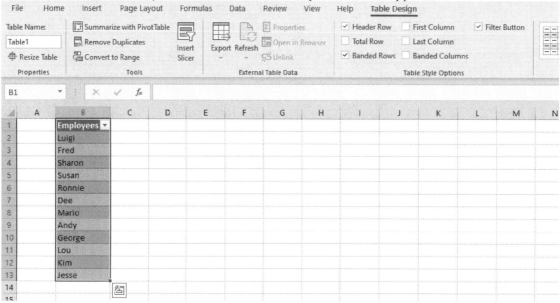

Image 185: Drop-down list

Checking for duplicates

You might have trouble finding duplicate values in your data, but you can easily filter the data by using the "Check for Duplicates" tool in Microsoft Excel. This feature helps you identify any row, column, or cell with duplicate data and displays a duplicate symbol if it exists. You can also delete duplicates, copy them, or move them to another row or column. Read on to learn how to operate.

You can check for duplicates in a data table by applying a formula to the data. Then, depending on the data set, you can apply a filter on a cell header or column content to find duplicates. Once you have the formula applied, you can delete the duplicate data. To perform this operation, select the data set and the range that includes the duplicate data. You can then use the COUNTIF function to get the number of duplicate values in each cell.

Checking for intersections

There are several ways to check for intersections in Microsoft Excel data validation. The intersect operator returns the intersection of two lists. This operation can be performed on single or multiple rows. In the example above, the intersect operator returns the value 11 if cell E4 is the only cell in both ranges. Differently, you can check for intersections using named ranges. For example, if you want to test whether a product is available during a particular month, you can use the intersect operator.

Using the intersecting reference is a much simpler way to check for intersections in your Microsoft Excel data. You can create a rule that will filter all intersections of two ranges based on their labels. You can also use an intersection reference to specify a specific department or period for combining the cells. Using an intersection reference makes the consolidation process faster and helps you maximize the amount of information available.

Creating a rule for data validation

Creating a rule for data validation in MS Excel requires some technical knowledge. To get started, create a named range. Named ranges are always absolute, so the names of cells in that range will never change. To create a named range, simply enter the name of the range in the Names field of the workbook and then click the Add button. Once you have created the rule, you should click the Data - Validation tab to open the Settings tab. In the List, select Allow, and then enter your criteria for data validation. It's important to remember that Excel does not differentiate between uppercase and lowercase names, so make sure you enter the correct name.

Data validation rules are a useful feature of Excel 2016. They prevent data entry errors by telling users what to enter and what not to enter. Data that does not meet these rules will be flagged as incorrect. This helps keep the data clean and prevents it from being contaminated by mistakes. In addition, data validation rules help prevent sloppy data entry and itchy feelings. For example, you can create a date-validation rule that requires the date of birth to be within a specific range. You can also create a numeric rule to check if a number falls within a specific range.

36 Using Pivot Tables in MS Excel

If you are working with data you want to analyze in a pivot table, you will need to organize it. Separate data into columns and rows and group similar data together. Make sure to format column headings differently from the data. Bolding and centering them can help differentiate data. Create data islands if necessary to separate data. You can choose a Pivot Cache or Report filter for more advanced users.

Advanced Pivot Tables

There are several ways to use advanced pivot tables in Microsoft Excel. First, you can sort items by descending or ascending values by clicking the More Sort Options button. This will open a filter menu and display options to sort values by columns, rows, or totals. The values in the data table are default sorted by column headings. For example, to sort by percent, choose % Difference From or % Sum of Columns.

You can also add color scales to your pivot tables. Select Styles > Color Scales to add them. Then select or choose color option that you wish to use. You can create your own if you don't find one you like. You can also add icon sets to indicate changes in your pivot table. For example, if you wanted to show how many sales increased or decreased in a particular quarter, you could create a color scale for the entire range.

Report filter

There are a few ways you can customize your report filter in Microsoft Excel. One of the most powerful options is the ability to sort items by descending values or ascending values. This option is found in the filter menu. You can choose to group or ungroup items by using the options on the right. To sort an item by descending value, click on the More Sort Options button. Then, select the value field you'd like to sort by.

To use the Report filter, drag the Region cell to the filter area. Then, you can choose Northeast as the criteria. After this step, the filter will be added to the pivot table. This option works like any other filter but is easier to use. The following section will show you how to make your filter more intuitive. However, before using it, ensure you understand how the report filter works. If you're using the Report Filter to create a report, you should make sure you understand the limitations of the Report filter.

Show Values As

If you have calculated fields with division operations, you may see errors such as "#DIV/0!." The value will appear in the value field as "0," but the error message will not be helpful for your audience. To correct these errors, you can change the value field settings by clicking "Analyze" on the ribbon and then selecting the little down arrow in the Value Field settings.

The default value for column A/row 1 is "A." This is the top-left-most cell of your sheet. Click this cell to select the value of that column. After you've made your changes, you'll see a new table with the values you want. You can also change the columns and rows by rechecking the "Edit" button at the top of the new window. This is the default value for columns in Microsoft Excel pivot tables.

Pivot Cache

To create separate caches in Microsoft Excel, you can use a table. Simply click on the Table button on the Ribbon. Select your data source you wish to work with. Once you have chosen the data source, Excel will open the Design tab and prompt you to name the table. Type a descriptive table name and click OK. Your table will then be saved as a separate cache. You can remove the cache if you want to reduce the size of your Excel file.

You must have a calculated field in your workbook to use a calculated field in your pivot table. Creating a pivot table from this field is easy - open the data source and select it from the list of options. You can then sort the data by ascending or descending values. In the Value Fields tab, click on the drop-down menu to ascend or descend.

36.1 How to create your first pivot table

Pivot tables work best with transactional data. Raw data files are obtained straight from your company's IT department.

To generate the greatest pivot tables, make sure your data adheres to the following guidelines:

- Make certain that each column has a one-cell header. Use different headers for each column; don't use the same heading for two columns. If you want your headers to display in two rows, enter the first word, press **Alt+Enter**, and then write the second.

- If a column should include numeric data, no blank cells should be allowed in the column. Instead of blanks, use zeros.

- Avoid using blank rows or columns.

- Remove any totals that are incorporated in your report.

- Make sure the worksheet is not in Compatibility mode. When the worksheet is in Compatibility mode, several pivot table capabilities from Excel 2007–2019 are disabled.

- When you add any new data to bottom of your monthly data set, you should consider converting it to a table using **Ctrl+T**. After a refresh, pivot tables generated from tables instantly take up new rows copied to the bottom of the tables.

- Whether your data contains months split over multiple columns, return to the source software program to check if an alternative representation of the data with months running down the rows is available.

This data collection contains two years' worth of transactional data. The customer has a single text column. There is just one date column. Quantity, Revenue, COGS, and Profit are all numerical columns.

	A	B	C	D	E	F	G	H
1	Region	Product	Date	Customer	Quantity	Revenue	COGS	Profit
2	East	XYZ	1/1/2022	Microsoft	954	22810	10220	12590
3	Central	DEF	2/3/2022	TellTale F	118	2256	948	1308
4	East	XYZ	4/4/2022	Design So	426	9140	4070	5070
5	East	DEF	4/7/2022	Compuy F	773	18502	7987	10515
6	East	ABC	8/5/2022	Oxygen Lt	407	8470	3589	4881
7	East	DEF	9/2/2022	Fotr Logist	1067	21800	9978	11822
8	Central	ABC	1/7/2022	Data Solve	355	46800	6653	40147
9	West	DEF	4/4/2022	Amazon	1820	33091	2200	30891
10	East	ABC	3/9/2022	Oxford	809	8809	3492	5317
11	West	XYZ	8/3/2022	Cambridg	649	9003	2820	6183
12	West	XYZ	2/6/2022	Jade	998	7323	1729	5594
13	Central	DEF	6/6/2022	Rux	849	8661	1309	7352
14	West	ABC	9/2/2022	Juke	1289	13892	3309	10583
15	Central	DEF	3/7/2022	Wetin	1354	36781	6720	30061
16	East	XYZ	9/1/2022	Oficia	1098	14602	4679	9923
17	Central	DEF	10/10/2022	Dolce	1134	22589	11980	10609
18	West	ABC	11/2/2022	Sdata Vad	682	67227	28928	38299
19								
20								

Image 186: Table to use in creating Pivot table

Begin with a blank pivot table

The typical way to make a pivot table is to start with a blank one. Select one cell from your data. From the Insert tab, choose PivotTable. The Create PivotTable dialog box appears in Excel.

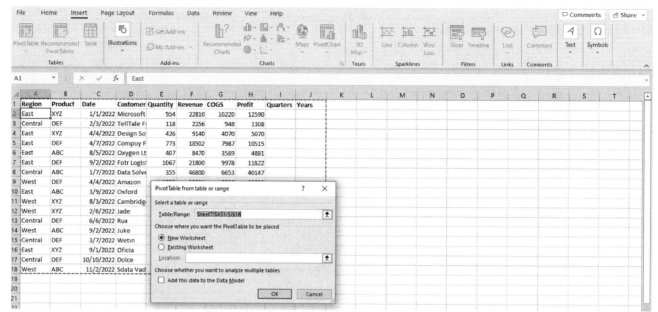

Image 187: Starting a blank table

This dialog box validates the data range. Excel usually does this properly if there are no blank rows or columns.

You can create the pivot table on a new blank worksheet or in an existing place by using **Create PivotTable dialog box**. For instance, if you want to create a dashboard with many pivot tables, you may place the pivot table in J2 on this worksheet or adjacent to another existing pivot table or pivot chart.

You can create a pivot table from a relational model by clicking the Add This Data to The Data Model check box.

Using the field list to add fields to your pivot table

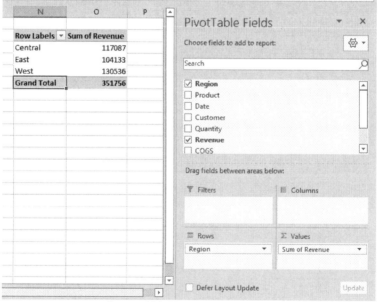

Image 188: Using the field list

If you begin with a blank pivot table, you will see PivotTable Fields. At the top of the PivotTable Fields section is a list of fields from your original data collection, and at the bottom are four drop zones. To create your report, drag and drop fields into the drop zones at the bottom.

Using the field list to modify the pivot table report

Examine the Region, Product, and **Revenue sections**.

When you choose a text or date field, it goes to the Rows drop zone in the PivotTable Fields list. When you check a numeric field, it goes to the Values drop zone, and the field type is changed to Sum of Field.

You can view the Sum of Revenue by Region and Product by selecting **Region, Product, and Revenue**.

You may further personalize the pivot table by rearranging the fields in the drop zones. Drag the Region field, for example, below the Product field in the Rows drop zone.

How to rearrange a pivot table

The following are the drop zone parts of the PivotTable Fields list box:

- **Filter:** This part is used to filter the report to just specified criteria. The slicer function effectively replaces this part.

- **Rows:** This part contains fields that display on the table's left side. When you pick the check boxes at the top of the field list, all text fields are moved here by default.

- **Columns:** This part contains fields along the top rows of your table's columns. *(NB: This is a crosstab report by old database experts)*.

- **Values:** This section contains all the numeric fields summarized in the table. Most values are automatically summed by default, but you may modify the computation to an average, minimum, maximum, or other calculation.

(NB: You can add fields to a drop zone by dragging them from the top of the PivotTable Fields list or from one drop zone to another. Drag a field from a drop zone to the outside of the PivotTable Fields list or uncheck it from the field list to remove it from the drop zone).

Calculating and roll-ups with pivot tables

Pivot tables provide many more calculation choices. One of the most fantastic features is the ability to roll daily dates up to months, quarters, and years.

Daily dates are organized into months, quarters, and years

Good pivot tables begin with high-quality transactional data. That transactional data is almost always recorded with daily dates rather than monthly summaries.

Follow these steps to create a summary by month, quarter, and year:

1. Begin with data, including daily dates. Next, create a pivot table with daily dates in the row field, regions in the columns, and the sum of revenue in the value area.

2. Choose a cell that has a date. Select **Group Field** from the PivotTable Analyze tab.

3. Select Months, Quarters, and Years from the Grouping dialog box. Click the OK button.

Follow these steps to create an intriguing alternative to the report:

1. To eliminate the **Region and Quarter fields** from the report, uncheck the boxes next to them.

2. Move the **Years field** from the Rows to the Columns area by dragging it from the Rows to the Columns area.

You now have a pivot table that displays totals by month and quarter and compares years throughout the report. You'll see that your pivot table field list contains three date-related fields: The years and quarters fields are both virtual. The months are included in the original Date field. Microsoft made a good design move by allowing years and months to be pivoted to various areas of the pivot table.

Adding calculations outside the pivot table

However, after you've grouped the dates in the pivot table, you won't be able to add a calculated field inside the pivot table. Thus you'll have to use ordinary Excel to give the percent Growth column.

The most common stumbling block is step three. Take the following steps:

1. In D4, right-click the **Grand Total** and choose to **Remove Grand Total**.

2. In D4, create a heading called percent Growth.

3. Enter =C5/B5-1 in cell D5. If you utilize the mouse or arrow keys while creating the formula, you will get stung by the GetPivotData issue.

4. Cell D5 should be formatted as a percentage with one decimal point.

5. In D5, double-click the fill handle to copy the formula to all rows.

Changing a field's computation

By default, a numeric column with the default calculation of Sum will be added to the pivot table. Excel has ten more computations, including Average, Count, Max, and Min.

The figures in this part begin with an entirely new pivot table. You may follow along by doing the following:

1. Remove the pivot table from the previous examples' worksheets. This memory clears the pivot cache.

2. Choose one cell from the Data worksheet.

3. Select **Insert > PivotTable**.

4. Mark the Region, Product, and Revenue fields with a check.

5. Move Revenue to the Values section two more times. *(NB: They will display as Sum Of Revenue2 and Sum Of Revenue3 in the pivot table)*.

6. Select **Report Layout > Show In Tabular Form** from the Design tab.

7. Select **Report Layout and Repeat All Item Labels** from the Design tab.

How to sort a pivot table

Customers are displayed alphabetically in all pivot tables in this chapter thus far. In each case, the report would be more interesting if it were provided and arranged by revenue rather than client name. When you click the AZ or ZA icons on the Data tab, Excel creates rules in the Sort and More Sort Options dialog boxes.

*   Open a row field drop-down box and choose **More Sort Options** to retrieve these choices later. More Sort Options may be accessed by clicking the **More button** (Customer).

How to filter using slicers

Slicers are visual filters that make it simple to do a variety of ad-hoc analyses. While slicers are simpler to use than the Report Filter, they have the advantage of filtering numerous pivot tables and charts built from the same data source.

Adding slicers

Follow these procedures to add default slicers:

1. Choose one cell from your pivot table.

2. Select **Insert Slicer button** on PivotTable Analyze tab.

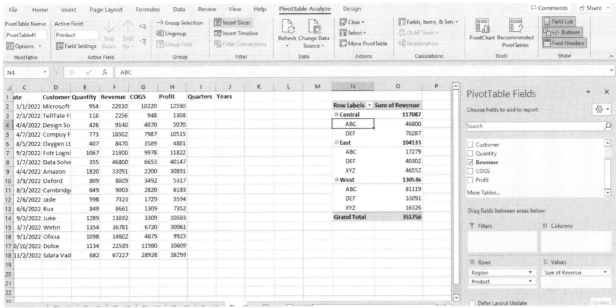

Image 189: Inserting slicers

3. Select any fields that would make good filter fields. The region, product, and years are chosen. Months, quarters, and dates would also work.

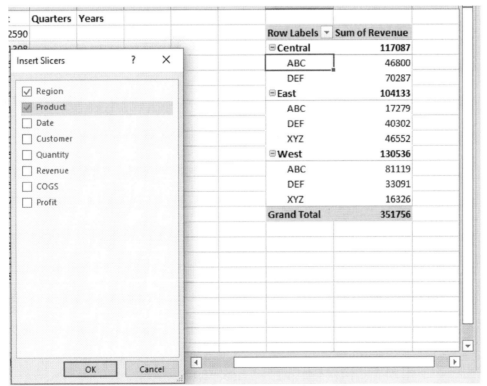

Image 190: Fields to add to pivot table

4. Click the *OK button*.

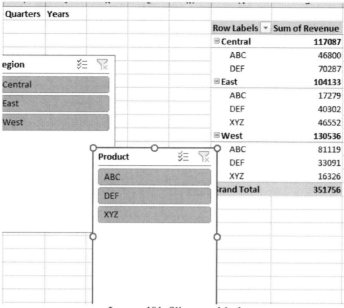

Image 191: Slicers added

Arranging the slicers

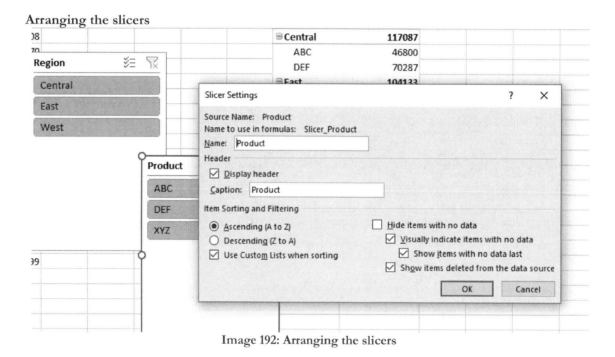

Image 192: Arranging the slicers

The slicers may be repositioned and resized. Choose a logical configuration for the slicers. Here are a few instances.

Short entries can be found in the Region and Product slicers. Extend the width of each slicer and then use the Columns option in the **Slicer Tools Options panel** to increase each slicer to three columns. The Year slicer is broader than necessary. There are also two more items in the slicer (1/1/2024 and >12/31/2025) that are Auto Group leftovers. These may be disabled in the Slicer Settings dialog box. Choose Slicer Settings after selecting the slicer. Hide Items With No Data is also enabled.

Using Excel's slicers

Choose that item to choose a single item from a slicer. Then, to multiselect in Excel, select the symbol with three check marks at the top of the slicer. Each item may now be selected by clicking on it.

You can also use the **Ctrl key** to pick several objects that are not adjacent or drag the mouse to select items that are nearby.

Items in other slicers may become inaccessible due to selections in one slicer. The items are pushed to the bottom of the list in this situation. This indicates visually that the item is not accessible based on the current criteria.

To remove a filter from a slicer, click the **Funnel-X symbol** in the slicer's upper right corner.

Slicers can be set up to filter many pivot tables and pivot charts at once. For example, if both pivot tables use the same data source, the slicers will affect both pivot tables.

If there are numerous pivot tables, proceed as follows:

1. Choose a slicer.

2. Select **Report Connections** from the ribbon's Slicer Tools Options menu.

3. Choose which pivot tables should be filtered by the slicer.

Using the row label filter to filter

To proceed, open the 16-Slicers.xlsx file and create a new pivot table. Examine Customer, Date, Quantity, Revenue, COGS, and Profit fields. Next, open the Report Layout drop-down menu from the Design tab. Select Tabular form, then Repeat All Item Labels. On the Design tab, tick the Banded Rows box. You will get the pivot table as a result.

This drop-down menu has four distinct filter mechanisms:

- For fields with text values, the Label Filters fly-out menu shows. You may use this fly-out to find client names that include specific words, begin, end, or fall between letters.

- The Value Filters fly-out menu lets you filter consumers based on values in the pivot table. Use the Value Filters fly-out if you only want orders above $20,000 or if you only want to view the Top 10 clients.

- Excel 2010 introduced the Search box, which is comparable to Label Filters but quicker.

- Use the check boxes to exclude specific consumers, or use Select All to clear or select all customers.

Clearing a filter

To clear all filters in the pivot table, click the **Clear button** in the Data tab's Sort & Filter group. To remove filters from a single field in the pivot table, enter the filter drop-down menu and pick Clear Filter from **"Field."**

Using check boxes to filter

The Customer drop-down menu lists all of the customers in the database. Clear their check boxes in the filter list if you need to exclude a few particular consumers.

The **(Select All) option** restores any previously cleared boxes. If all boxes are already checked, selecting **(Select All)** clears them all.

Because it is simpler to choose three clients than it is to clear 27 if you need to delete the majority of the items from the list of customers, you can do it by following these steps:

1. If any customers have been cleared, choose Select All to reselect all of them.

2. Tap **Select All** to delete all clients.

3. Choose which consumers you wish to see.

37 How to Use a Microsoft Excel Named Range in Formulas, Cells, and Formulas

If you've ever used a Microsoft Excel Named Range, you've probably wondered how to use it. But you're not the only one. You can use it in Formulas, Cells, and even Formulas! Here are a few tips to get you started. The name of a named range will always be case-sensitive, so it's crucial to know how to type it correctly. You can also find the range's name in the Name Manager and use it in your formulas.

The dynamic named ranges

You may create a dynamic named range by using a formula. It works just like a column or row. Firstly, you need to define the width and height of the range. Height and width determine the number of columns and rows you wish to include. After that, you simply need to define the first_cell. Similarly, the offset_cols will tell the function where to place the upper-left cell.

If the data you wish to add to a named range is changing in a short period, you can create a dynamic named range. If you don't wish to edit the formula, use the OFFSET function instead. However, you should note that this volatile function will slow down your Excel workbook. A better option is the INDEX function, which is semi-volatile and will not affect the speed of the workbook.

Case-insensitive names

If you're trying to use a named range in Excel, you might wonder how to specify a case-insensitive name. First, it is a good idea to remember that your name can contain up to 255 characters, but it can't be longer than that. Second, Microsoft Excel also doesn't distinguish between lowercase and uppercase letters, so if you enter the first name incorrectly, Excel will automatically replace it with the second. What are the steps of creating named ranges using Excel?

1. Go to the formula bar and select Define Names
2. A dialogue box will pop up where you will type your desired range name. a scope dropdown will always be set to a given workbook.
3. Select cell range in the other field
4. Click OK to finalize the changes and save.

Note: If you choose an absolute reference, Excel creates a name with the range scope of the workbook. If you want a relative name, remove the $ sign.

Formulas that can be created with named ranges

There are many advantages to using named ranges in your Excel workbooks. First, they make it easier to navigate the workbook. Using a named range will make navigation easier, as you can click the range's name and go to it. This makes it easier to type formulas and troubleshoot errors when creating or editing ranges. In addition, named ranges are easier to understand and write, making them easier to use. When creating a new named range, you can give it a descriptive name that refers to its contents. Named ranges are often used for multiple Worksheets, such as quarterly figures or annual reports. Named ranges can make it easier to remember which cell ranges are involved in formulas. Creating a named range is as simple as typing a descriptive name in the Name box.

Creating a named range in Excel

Creating a named range in Excel is easy. Simply navigate to the Formulas tab and click the Define Name button. In the Name box, enter a name for the range. This name will appear in the cell reference box. After entering the name, click OK. The Name box will contain the cell reference and the name. Type in any other name for the range if necessary. The Name Box will appear in the upper-left corner of the spreadsheet. The default scope is the workbook or worksheet.

Creating a named range in Excel makes it easy to manage and change the contents of your workbook. Named ranges are particularly useful in conditional formatting. Advanced and intermediate Excel courses cover the topic extensively. By creating and naming a range, you avoid physically selecting the cell range. The Name Box feature makes it easy to navigate to named ranges. Names must not be longer than 255 characters and contain no spaces.

38 How to Use the Microsoft Excel Lookup Function

If you've tried using the LOOKUP function in Microsoft Excel, you probably wonder whether it works. There are several reasons why it may not. For one thing, you may be asked to specify an exact or approximate value. Either way, Excel will automatically return the value closest to what you're looking for. The more advanced XLOOKUP function is another way to use the LOOKUP function.

LOOKUP function

You can use the LOOKUP function when you want to perform a lookup in Microsoft Excel. This function finds data that matches a value in a particular cell. There are a couple of different types of lookups. First, VLOOKUP searches for values in a column that matches a specific value. This function is best used when the data is organized by time and is large. Otherwise, you can use the HLOOKUP function.

Excel will use the lower value if the lookup value is between two values. If the value is smaller than the first column, it will return an error message. A table array is created with the Price column. The cell value in the second column is the Price. Therefore, Excel uses the Price table in cells A17 to B24. Using this table array, the LOOKUP function in Excel will return the value of the Price from column A17 to B24.

Range_lookup

The Range_lookup function in Microsoft Excel allows you to look up data in a column by cell reference. You can use this function in all versions of Excel. The lookup_value argument can be a number, cell reference, or text string. In either case, you must include the column index number to get a match. If you don't include it, an approximate match will be returned. The Range_lookup function can only look at the first column in an array, so you will need to use an index or match formula to find a value in the left column.

The VLOOKUP formula has an optional argument for range_lookup, which matches two values based on the range. In this case, the function will find the closest match value. Otherwise, it will look for the next largest value less than the lookup value. The lookup column will return a #N/A error if the match does not exist. Alternatively, the VLOOKUP function can apply range lookup to larger tables.

Returns 0

If you receive an error message like "Microsoft Excel Lookup Function returns 0," it is likely that your data is incorrect. The reason is fairly simple. The Lookup function looks up a cell value that matches a specific text string. You should type the value in cell D14 in the first column. In the second column, type the word "cereal" to search for the value of "cereal."

This function searches a specific cell's value, either an exact or relative match. The default match mode is exact, which returns a #N/A error if no matches are found. The match_mode argument can be any number between 0 and 1 (exact match).

Errors

Sometimes a VLOOKUP formula will fail to work, and you're not sure what the problem is. In such cases, you can try using the INDEX or MATCH functions. These functions will work similarly but search for values to the left of the range. For example, Microsoft Excel Lookup Function errors occur when numbers are formatted as text, such as when you import data from an external database or type an apostrophe before a number to show the leading zeros.

The most common error in the VLOOKUP formula is the space character, which is a common occurrence. You will receive an error message with the code #N/A if this happens. You can use the TRIM function to remove spaces from the lookup values and VLOOKUP, which works similarly. The ISERROR function will detect errors and render output based on a logical test.

Using it to retrieve a value from a list or table

To use the lookup function in Excel, you need to create a formula containing a cell with a value present in the list or table you wish to find. This function is called a VLOOKUP. It looks for a value based on a unique identifier in the list and table. This information can be a product code, stock-keeping unit, or customer contact.

Using the VLOOKUP function can be tricky. The problem can arise from the formula's syntax and the value referenced. When a VLOOKUP fails to locate a value in a column, it returns a #N/A error. If you have a table where the columns are sorted in alphabetical order, ensure you align the values vertically.

39 Macros In MS Excel

A macro in Excel is nothing more than a set of instructions that are repeated over and over. Following the creation of a macro, Excel will step-by-step carry out the instructions on whatever data you supply. Let's consider this example. We create a macro for giving instructions to the program where it picks a number, adds 3, multiplies by 5, then returns the modulus of the number.

- Now, whenever we instruct Excel to carry out the macro execution, it becomes an automatic process by Excel without the manual step by step.

- A macro can be used to record almost any type of information. As a result, it's possible to perform numerical computations, text operations, formatting, and cell movement in any way you can.

- When you continuously repeat the same steps, you save time when you use macros. While this may not seem like much initially, it can add up over time.

- If you're formatting raw data, filtering and sorting data, or simply repeating a sequence of functions and actions on your sheets, you're on the right track.

- You can easily share macros across your colleagues to carry on with the project since they are stored within a spreadsheet.

How to create a macro in Microsoft Excel

- Before you can utilize Excel macros to automate your chores, you must first "record" a macro in Excel.

- Excel should take steps when the macro is executed can be specified by recording the macro.

- Additionally, whereas Visual Basic for Applications (VBA) can be used to construct a macro, Excel allows you to record an Excel macro using standard commands rather than Visual Basic for Applications (VBA).

Consider the following straightforward example. We have a list of names in our spreadsheet, as well as a list of their monthly sales:

	A	B	C	D	E
1	Name	Sales			
2	Luigi	$ 12,967.00		Highest sales:	
3	Fred	$ 17,526.00		Name:	
4	Sharon	$ 14,625.00			
5	Susan	$ 14,088.00			
6	Ronnie	$ 11,973.00			
7	Dee	$ 10,726.00			
8	Mario	$ 18,923.00			
9	Andy	$ 15,636.00			
10	George	$ 10,819.00			
11	Lou	$ 13,728.00			
12	Kim	$ 16,514.00			
13	Jesse	$ 19,382.00			
14					

Image 193: Creating a macro

- Let's create a macro to rate the sales from the highest to lowest and goes through the information to come up with name of salesperson who beats the record with the most highest sales.

- Customizing the ribbon requires one to select File > Options. From the sidebar appearing, choose Customize Ribbon. Ensure you check the Developer Add-in in the Main Tabs:

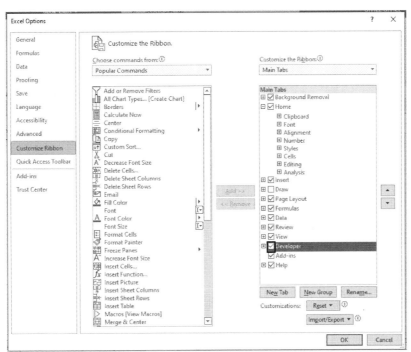

Image 194: Customizer ribbon in action for macros

- Click OK to ensure the tab shows in main window. You'll notice a Record Macro button.

- Simply click that button to begin recording a macro.

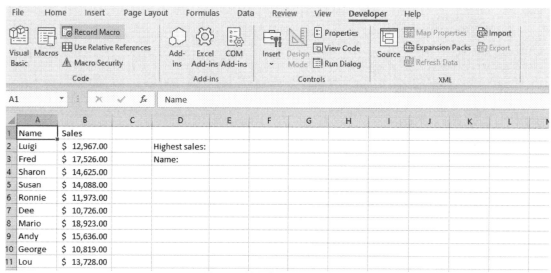

Image 195: Record Macro

- If you wish to provide a name to the macro (for this case we used "HighSales") and come up with a shortcut key, there will be a prompt requesting for that information.
- Avoid overwriting the default Ctrl-based shortcuts that people use on a frequent basis.

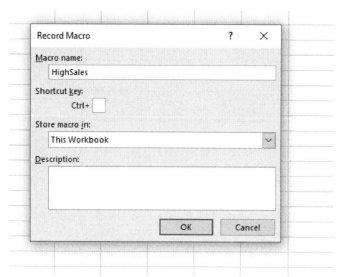

Image 196: Giving a name to the macro

- 3 options are available where one can store their macro: store in new workbook, current workbook, or in an existing macro workbook.
- This workbook (Book_Class.xlsx) contains macros that can be executed on any workbook that you can access in Excel.
- You can use it to store all of your Excel macros in a centralized location for easy access.
- If you're building a macro that will only be used in this spreadsheet, save it there. If, on the other hand, you believe you may need to reuse the macro in another worksheet, save in a macro workbook.

- Click OK and Excel will always execute as per the steps.

Let's follow these steps:
Apply filters to your columns
For column B, we sort it from highest to smallest figures
Copy cell B2
Click cell E2 and paste the copied content
Copy cell A2
Click cell E3 and paste the copied content
Make E2 & E3 **bold**

- To record a macro, simply click Record Macro, follow the on-screen instructions, before clicking Stop Recording.

- Once you start recording, Record Macro button is replaced by the Stop Recording button, which you can use to end the recording.

- Each of those activities is standard; for example, clicking Filter button, sorting using the dropdown filter arrow, and copying the cell with the Ctrl + C keyboard shortcut.

- This is what it will look like after we are finished:

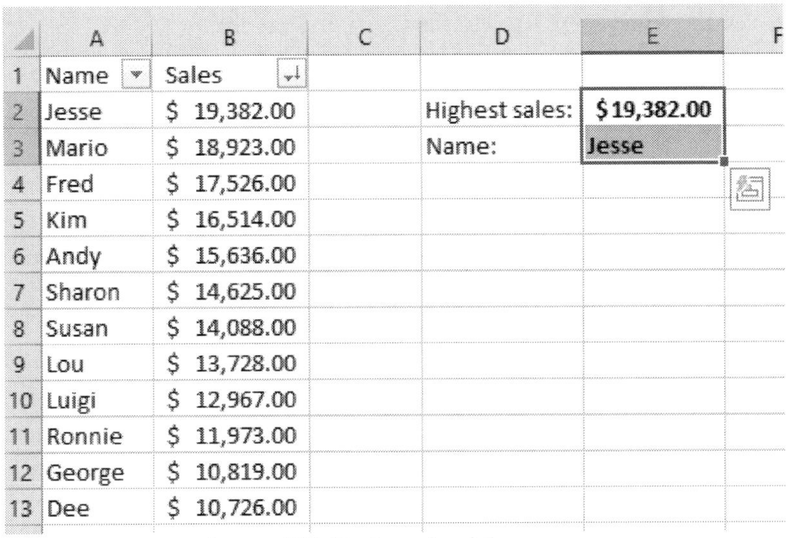

	A	B	C	D	E	F
1	Name	Sales				
2	Jesse	$ 19,382.00		Highest sales:	$19,382.00	
3	Mario	$ 18,923.00		Name:	Jesse	
4	Fred	$ 17,526.00				
5	Kim	$ 16,514.00				
6	Andy	$ 15,636.00				
7	Sharon	$ 14,625.00				
8	Susan	$ 14,088.00				
9	Lou	$ 13,728.00				
10	Luigi	$ 12,967.00				
11	Ronnie	$ 11,973.00				
12	George	$ 10,819.00				
13	Dee	$ 10,726.00				

Image 197: End result of the macro

- A macro can be created using just this information! Press the record button, conduct some actions, and then press the stop button.

Running a macro

After saving your macro, you can execute it in various ways.

- To get started, you can launch it immediately from the Ribbon menu. A Macros button can be found on the application's View and the Developer tabs. To view the macros, click on corresponding icon.

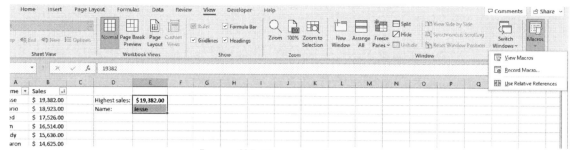

Image 198: Executing the macro

- The resulting window shows all saved macros. Select the one you need and click Run to execute.

- Excel will retrace the steps you took throughout the record-keeping session.

- To ensure it was successful, unbold E2 & E3 and delete them in the sample worksheet, and then arrange the names alphabetically in the new worksheet.

- Execute your macro and check if you get same results.

- The shortcut key that you used to save your macro can also be used to run it. For example, ctrl + the key combination you entered in the save box.

- Adding a shortcut key afterward is as simple as navigating to View Macros, selecting the macro, and selecting Options. Creating a new shortcut key will be an option when you log in.

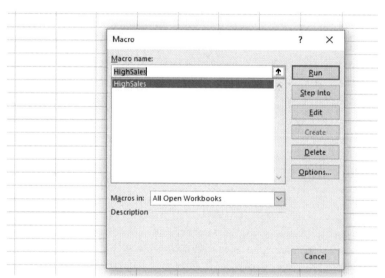

Image 199: Running the macro

- Add a shortcut key by heading to View Macros, choose your macro, click Options. Then, create a new shortcut key available to you after the installation is complete.

You can create a button to execute your macro if you regularly run a complex macro or share your spreadsheet with others.
This is how you do it.

- To begin, create a form; in this case, a rectangle with rounded corners will suffice.

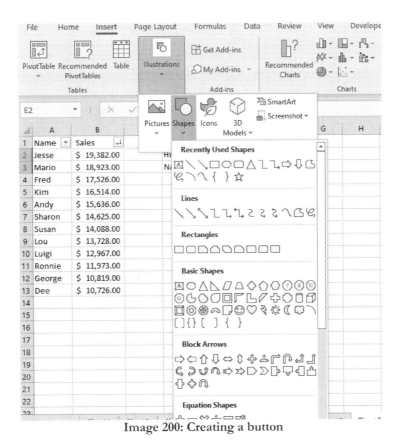

Image 200: Creating a button

- In the Shape Editor, right click and choose Edit Text to add describing text to your shape.

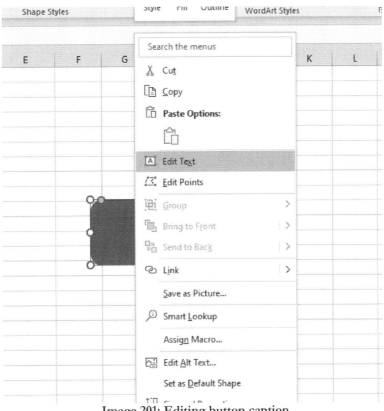

Image 201: Editing button caption

- Now, right-click the shape and choose Assign Macro from the context menu.

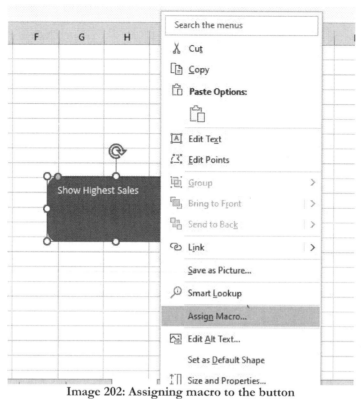

Image 202: Assigning macro to the button

- After selecting the corresponding macro from the subsequent window, click OK to confirm your selection.

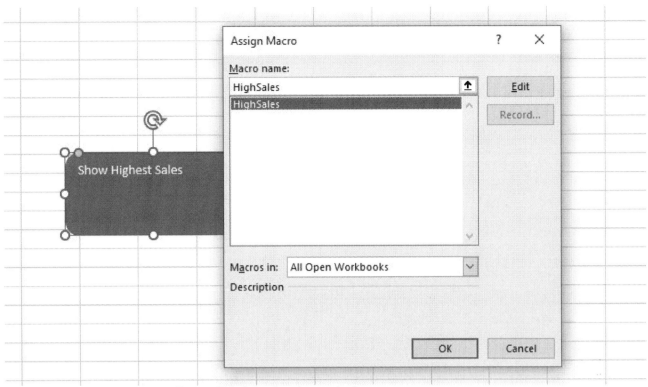

Image 203: Selecting the particular macro

- After that, clicking the shape will execute the pre-recorded macro.

Let's see how to directly run your macros using the QAT (Quick Access Toolbar).

- Before you can use the macro, add View Macros button to QAT.
- Select File > Options from the menu bar, and then Quick Access Toolbar from the left-hand pane:
- Scroll down and choose View Macros, followed by the Add >> button.

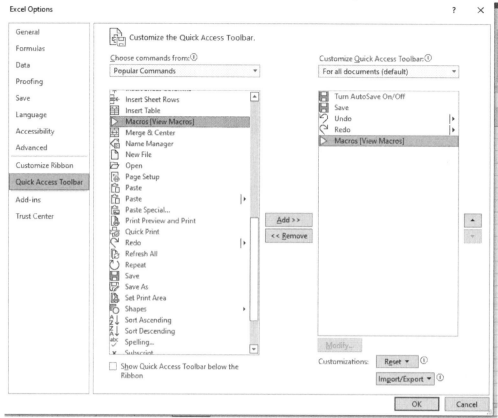

Image 204: Running macro added to QAT

- Click on the OK button.
- Simply click the macros button at the top of the Excel window to start a macro right away:

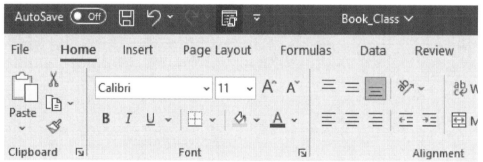

Image 205: QAT with the macro icon

40 Printing

How to work with page breaks
Page breaks fall into two:

- Automatic page break – Excel automatically goes to next page one it hits the bottom/right margin of your physical page.

These page breaks vary automatically when you modify the margins, add or remove rows, or change the height of specific rows on the page.

Initially, the spreadsheet does not display automatic page breaks. However, if you exit Print Preview and return to Normal view, automatic page breaks are shown in the document as a thin dashed line. Page Layout view and Page Break Preview mode both show automatic page breaks.

How do you disable page breaks? Click File then Options. Head to Advanced and select Display Options for This Worksheet. Ensure Show Page Breaks is unchecked. If you do this regularly, the shortcut keys **/fta** followed by **Alt+k** will bring you there.

- Manual page break

You can manually insert page breaks where you wish to start a new page in rows or columns. For example, at the beginning of a new part of a report, you may wish to place a manual page break. A manual page break does not alter in response to changes in the worksheet's rows.

Adding page breaks manually

Follow these procedures to insert a page break at a specific row manually:

1. Click the row number that should be the first row on the new page to choose a full row. Alternatively, choose the cell in that row's column A.

2. Select **Page Setup, Breaks, and Insert Page Break** from the Page Layout tab.

Follow these procedures to insert a page break at a specific column manually:

1. Click the letter above the column that should be the first column on the new page to choose a whole column. Alternatively, choose row 1 from that column.

2. Select **Page Setup, Breaks, and Insert Page Break** from the Page Layout tab.

Note: When you insert a page break when the cell pointer is outside row 1 or column A, Excel simultaneously inserts a row page break and a column page break. This is rarely what you desire. Make careful to insert a row break by selecting a cell in column A or a column break by selecting a cell in row 1.

Manual versus automatic page breaks

There is a small visual difference between manual and automated page breaks in Normal mode. The dashed line indicating a manual page break is more apparent than the line indicating an automated page break.

To have a clearer view of page breaks, go to **View, Page Break Preview,** and choose **Page Break Preview mode**. Automatic page breaks are shown as dotted blue lines in this mode. Solid lines represent manual page breaks.

Making adjustments using Page Break Preview

Page Break Preview mode allows you to move a page break by dragging the line connected with the page break. When you drag an automated page break to increase rows or columns on a page, Excel adjusts the Scale % for all pages.

Remove manual page breaks

To do away with a manual page break for a row, do the following:

1. Place cursor on the row below the page break.

2. Select **Page Setup, Breaks, and Remove Page Break** from the Page Layout tab.

To remove a manual page break for a column, do the following:

1. Set your pointer in the column to the right of the page break.

2. Select **Page Setup, Breaks, and Remove Page Break** from the Page Layout tab.

(NB: Select Page Setup, Breaks, Reset Any Page Breaks from the Page Layout tab to eliminate all manual page breaks. It's worth noting that removing the page breaks returns the scale to 100%).

How to find print settings

It is possible to alter the print settings or page setup in Excel at least nine times. The most frequent duties may be found in a variety of areas. You may, for example, modify the margins in five of the nine spots. In addition, four of the nine locations allow you to adjust the paper size and orientation. When you get to the more esoteric settings, you may only be able to discover them in one or two locations. You can find out where you may be able to adjust the setting for every specific job. Here's where you can locate each location:

- **File > Print:** To show the **Print panel**, open the **File menu** and choose **Print**. This panel contains Printer and Page Setup options in the middle and a huge Print Preview on the right.

- **The Ribbon's Page Layout Tab:** Choose the Page Layout tab in the ribbon. Printing is divided into three categories: **Page Setup, Scale to Fit, and Sheet Options**.

- **Page Setup Dialog:** To open the classic **Page Setup dialog box**, click the **diagonal arrow** icon in the lower-right corner of the three groups in the **Page Layout ribbon tab**. There are four tabs in this dialog box. The tab is identified by the superscript next to each bullet: 1 for Page, 2 for Margins, 3 for Header/Footer, and 4 for Sheet. This dialog box may also be accessed by selecting the Print Titles button in the Page Layout tab of the ribbon.

- **Page Layout View:** On the View tab, choose **Page Layout**. This indicator may also be seen in the bottom right corner of the Excel screen.

- **Header & Footer Tools Design Tab:** On the **Page Layout view**, select one of the three header or footer zones on any page to bring up the **Header & Footer Tools Design tab** in the ribbon. It is important to note that to leave the Page Layout view, you must first click outside of the header or footer zones. Although this is the most concealed option, it provides a more convenient approach to adjusting headers and footers.

- **Preview of Page Breaks View:** On the **View tab**, choose **Page Break Preview**. This symbol may also be seen in the bottom right corner of the Excel window.

- **Printer Properties Dialog:** To open the **Print panel**, use **Ctrl+P**. Just below the printer name, a link to Printer Properties appears.

- **Excel Options:** Select **Options, Advanced from the File menu**. After you've done a Print Preview, this is the sole area where you may disable the display of automatic page breaks.

- **Print Preview Full Screen:** Drag this icon to the **Quick Get Toolbar** to access a full-screen version of Print Preview akin to prior Excel versions.

Printing with a single click

If you're a keyboard fanatic, you may be annoyed that **Ctrl+P** in Excel brings you to the Print panel rather than completing a rapid print. However, Quick Print can be restored to Excel in a few simple steps.

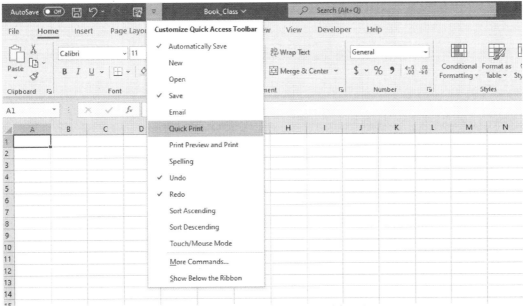

Image 206: Printing using the QAT option

The Quick Access Toolbar (QAT) is a row of tiny icons immediately above or below the ribbon. A drop-down menu appears to right side of this toolbar. To show a brief list of common commands, use the drop-down menu at the right edge of the Quick Access Toolbar. Select **Quick Print**.

When you click the **Quick Print button**, Excel sends one copy of the current worksheet to the last printer you used. The worksheet is sent to the default printer if you have not previously printed it in this Excel session.

Although this restores Quick Print as a mouse click, it is still inconvenient for keyboard-centric users. On Excel, pressing and releasing the **Alt key** displays a row of shortcuts for the first nine items in the Quick Access Toolbar.

Using the File menu to print

To reach the Print panel, select **File > Print, or you may press Ctrl+P**. The resulting panel combines options from the Print and Page Setup dialog boxes in the screen's center and Print Preview on the right. As you change the settings in the screen's center, Print Preview changes, allowing you always to see the most recent preview.

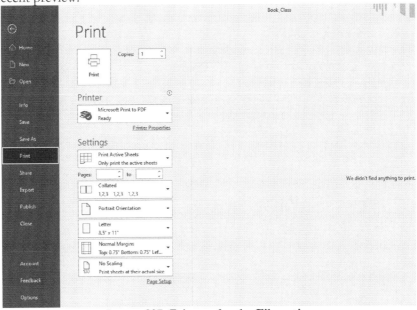

Image 207: Print under the File option

A huge Print button dominates the screen's left side. To print your document, click this button. You can adjust the number of copies printed by spinning the spin button next to the Print button.

(NB: The remainder of the left panel is devoted to a new kind of gallery. Without opening the gallery, you may view the current selection. There is no need to access the drop-down menu if the relevant printer is already chosen).

Choosing a Printer

Excel shows all the existing printers and indicates whether or not the printer is presently online and accessible when you enter the Printer drop-down menu. This useful enhancement lets you identify whether the department printer is jammed and print to a new printer.

Viewing the Page Layout

The Normal view is the default view when you start Excel. The only options in previous versions of Excel were Normal view and Page Break Preview mode. However, starting with Excel 2007, Microsoft introduced the **Page Layout view**, which is useful when preparing a document for printing. *(NB: The three views in Excel may be found on the View tab or the right side of status bar).*

You have a fully functional worksheet in the Page Layout view. The formula bar, for example, works, and you can browse around the worksheet. However, the following are the distinctions between Page Layout and Normal view:

- On each page, white space appears to illustrate the margins. This is typically advantageous since you can see page gaps between columns or rows. If you wish to conceal the white space, right-click it and choose **Hide White Space**.

- A ruler appears underneath the formula bar, which you can use to modify margins by moving the ruler's gray regions.

- Areas are labeled **Add a Header and a Footer by clicking the Add a Header and Add a Footer buttons**. Whereas headers and footers are hidden in previous versions of Excel, they are visible in the **Page Layout view** of Excel.

- Click to **Add Data** is shown in areas of a worksheet that are not in the data area. One issue with the Page Break Preview mode was that sections outside the data area were grayed out. *(NB: The Click to Add Data Labels option enables you to continue adding pages to your spreadsheet).*

(NB: The sole downside of using Page Layout view is that it disables your Freeze Panes settings. Excel alerts you to the fact that this is occurring. Excel employs this to underline the distinction between Print Titles and Freeze Panes).

How to choose what to print

Active Sheets, Entire Workbook, and Selection options are available in the Print What gallery. You can further customize these options by selecting Ignore Print Area.

When you pick **Active Sheets**, the currently chosen sheet is printed. If you specify a print area, just that range is printed; otherwise, Excel displays the whole document's usable range. However, when you pick several sheets in Group mode, all of the chosen sheets print.

Image 208: Printing active sheets

When you choose the Entire Workbook option, all no hidden worksheets in the workbook are printed. One benefit of this choice is that the pages are sequentially numbered as the printing progresses from Sheet1 to Sheet2.

By selecting the Selection option, you can temporarily override the print area. For example, if you need to print a tiny portion of a huge report, choose that portion and then choose the Selection option in Print What gallery. *(NB: This saves you from changing the Print Area repeatedly).*

The **Ignore Print Area option** instructs Excel to disregard any previously set print zones. The full utilized area of the worksheet is printed as a result of this.

Using the Pages spin buttons, you may print selected pages. Key in page number in both the Pages and To boxes to print a single page.

Changing Printer Settings

The remaining galleries on the left side of the Print panel are repainted once you choose a printer. Use the gallery to pick each choice if you print to an office printer that supports collating and stapling. Excel does not display the galleries if you print to a home printer that does not have these settings.

Changing a few of the Page Setup options

Despite their appearance, the final options on the left side of the Print panel are used to manage portrait vs. landscape, paper size, and margins. If you modify it here, it will be reflected in the Page Setup dialog box.

If you're wondering why these settings are duplicated here, you may also be wondering why your preferred Page Setup options aren't. Although it is convenient to go from portrait to landscape mode here, it would be much more convenient to be able to modify the Page Scaling or **Rows to Repeat At Top options**. However, this is impossible since such adjustments need closing the **Print panel** and using the ribbon's **Page Layout tab**.

Exploring other page setup options

Other page layout options can be found throughout the various interface areas. Although some of these are obscure, you may need to use them in certain circumstances.

Printing gridlines and headings

Select **Sheet Options > Gridlines > Print from the Page Layout tab** to print the gridlines on a worksheet.

You can also print the A-B-C-D column and 1-2-3-4 row headings. To do so, go to the Page Layout tab and select **Sheet Options, Headings, and Print**. This option comes in handy when printing formulas with the FORMULATEXT function and the need to see each cell's cell address.

Centering a small report on a page

Small reports printed in the page's upper-left corner may appear out of place. Instead of expanding the margins, you can center the report horizontally or vertically on a page.

To open the **Page Setup dialog box**, choose **Page Layout, Margins, and Custom Margins**. Two check boxes at the dialog box's bottom allow you to center the report on the page.

Replacing error values when printing

Excel computations may sometimes produce mistakes such as **#N/A! or DIV/0.** Although these error numbers assist you in determining how to correct the issues, they seem out of place on a printed page. You have the option of replacing any mistake cells with a blank or two hyphens.

To access the Sheet tab of your Page Setup dialog box, choose **Page Layout and Print Titles**. Then, select **blank> or — from the Cell Errors As drop-down option**.

Printing comments

Cell comments are often shown as a little red triangle in a cell. After your report, you can print a table with all the comments. Then, choose **At End Of Sheet** from the **Comments And Notes drop-down menu** on **Sheet tab** of Page Setup dialog box.

Excel produces your report and then opens a new page with each comment/note listed. The new page displays the cell and the comment/note content.

The other option for printing comments and notes is to print any visible ones that are currently visible where they are displayed. Select **Review, Notes, and Show All Notes** to see them all. You can drag them to a new location when visible so they do not obscure important cells.

Controlling the first-page number

You may be putting a printed Excel spreadsheet amid a printed Word document. If the Excel worksheet appears on the tenth page of the Word report, for example, you'd want the Excel page numbers to begin at ten rather than 1.

Select the **dialog box launcher** from the Page Layout tab at the bottom right of Page Setup group.

The **Page tab** of your Page Setup dialog box is displayed in Excel. The last option is First Page Number, set initially to **Auto**. For instance, enter 10 in this field, Excel will print the Excel worksheet with page numbers 10, 11, 12, and so on.

41 Excel Shortcuts

There are so many shortcuts in Excel. However, I will be introducing you to some shortcuts that are mostly used in Excel

Editing Shortcut

Shortcut Keys	Functions
F2	For editing cell
Ctrl + C	For copying cell content
Ctrl + V	For pasting cell content
Ctrl + X	For cutting cell content to another cell
Ctrl + D	To fill down
Ctrl + R	To fill right
Alt+ E+ S	Paste special
F3	For pasting the name into a formula
F4	Toggle reference
Alt +Enter	For starting another new line within the same old cell
Shift + F2	For inserting or editing a cell comment
Shift + F10	For displaying a shortcut menu
Ctrl + F3	For defining the name of a cell
Ctrl + Shift + A	For inserting arguments names with parentheses for a function after typing a function name in a formula
Alt + I + R	For inserting a row
Alt + I + C	For inserting a column

Table 3: Table with editing shortcuts

Navigation Shortcuts

Shortcut Keys	Functions
Arrow	For moving from one cell to the next
F5	Go to
F6	For switching between the worksheet, the Ribbon, the task pane, and the Zoom controls
Home	To go to the beginning of a row
Ctrl + Home	For moving to the beginning of a worksheet
Ctrl + End	For moving to the last cell that has content in it within the worksheet
Shift + Arrow	For selecting the adjacent cell
Shift + Spacebar	For selecting an entire row
Ctrl + Spacebar	For selecting an entire column
Ctrl + Shift + Home	For selecting all to the start of the sheet
Ctrl+ Shift + End	For selecting all to the last used cell of the sheet
Ctrl + Shift + Arrow	To select the end of the last used row/column
Ctrl + Left Arrow	For moving the word to the left while in a cell
Ctrl + Right Arrow	For moving the word to the right while in a cell
PageUp	For moving the screen up
PageDown	For moving the screen down
Alt + PageUp	For moving the screen to the left
Alt+ PageDown	For moving the screen to the right
Ctrl + PageUp/Down	For moving the next or previous worksheet
Ctrl + Tab	To move to the next worksheet while on the spreadsheet

Shortcut Keys	Functions
Shift + Tab	For moving cell to the right
Tab	For moving to the next cell

Table 4: Table with navigation shortcuts

File shortcuts

Shortcut Keys	Functions
Ctrl + N	New
Ctrl + O	To open
Ctrl + S	To save workbook
F12	Save As
Ctrl + P	Print
Ctrl + F2	For opening the preview print window
Ctrl + Tab	For moving to the next workbook
Ctrl + F4	For closing a file
Alt + F4	To close all open Excel files

Table 5: File shortcuts

Formula shortcuts

Shortcut Keys	Shortcuts
Ctrl + Shift + Enter	To enter an array formula
Ctrl + /	For selecting array formula range
Ctrl + '	To copy a formula from a cell and edit
Ctrl + [	For selecting all precedents cells
Ctrl +]	For selecting all dependent cells
F4	For changing the type of cell reference from relative to absolute
Alt + =	Sum range
F3	For displaying the range of names

Table 6: Formula shortcuts

Paste special shortcuts

Shortcut Keys	Functions
Ctrl + Alt + V+T	Paste Special formats
Ctrl + Alt + V+V	Paste Special values
Ctrl + Alt + V+F	Paste Special formulas
Ctrl + Alt + V+ C	Paste Special comments

Table 7: Paste special shortcuts

Ribbon Navigation shortcuts

Shortcut Keys	Functions
Alt	To display the Ribbon shortcut
Alt +F	To go to the File tab
Alt + H	To go to the Home tab
Alt + N	To go to the Insert tab
Alt + P	To go to the Page Layout tab
Alt + M	To go to the Formulas tab
Alt + A	To go to the Data tab
Alt + R	To go to the Review tab
Alt + W	To go to the View tab

Shortcut Keys	Functions
Alt + Q	To put the cursor in the Search box
Alt + JC	To go to the Chart Design tab when the cursor is on a chart
Alt + JA	To go to the Format tab when the cursor is on a chart
Alt + JT	To go to the Table tab when the cursor is on a table
Alt + JP	To go to the Picture Format tab when the cursor is on a picture
Alt + JI	To go to the Draw tab
Alt + B	To go to the Power Pivot tab

Table 8: Ribbon Navigation shortcuts

Clear shortcuts

Shortcut Keys	Functions
Delete	For clearing cell data
Alt+ h + e + f	For clearing cell format
Alt+ h + e + m	For clearing cell comments
Alt+ h + e + a	For clearing all data formats and comments

Table 9: Clear shortcuts

Selection shortcuts

Shortcut Keys	Functions
Shift + Arrow	For selecting a cell range
Ctrl + Shift + Arrows	For highlighting a contiguous range
Shift + Page Up	For extending selection up one screen
Shift + Page Down	For extending selection down one screen
Alt + Shift + Page Up	For extending, selection left one screen
Alt + Shift + Page Down	For extending selection right one screen
Ctrl + A	For selecting or highlighting all cells in the worksheet
Ctrl + Space	To select the whole column or row
Shift + Ctrl + Space Bar	For selecting table
Alt + ;	For selecting visible cells
Shift + Home	For selecting a range from the start cell too far left
Shift + End + Arrow	For selecting a range from the start cell to the direction of the arrow
Ctrl + *	For selecting a continuous range of data
Ctrl + Shift + 0	For selecting all cells with comment
F5 + Alt +S +K + Enter	For selecting all blank cells

Table 10: Selection shortcuts

Data editing shortcut

Shortcut Keys	Functions
Ctrl + D	To fill down from the cell above
Ctrl + R	To fill right from cell left
Ctrl + F	To find and replace
F5 + Alt + s +o	For showing all constants
F5 + Alt + s +c	For highlighting the cell with comments

Table 11: Data editing shortcuts

Data editing (inside a cell) shortcuts

Shortcut Keys	Functions
F2	For editing the active cell

Enter	To confirm a change in a cell before opting out of that cell
Esc	To cancel a cell entry before opting out of that cell
Alt + Enter	To insert a line break within a cell
Shift + Left/Right	For highlighting within a cell
Ctrl + Shift + Left/Right	For highlighting contiguous items
Home	To move to the beginning of the cell contents
End	For moving to the end of a cell content
Backspace	For deleting a character from left
Delete	For deleting a character from the right
Tab	For accepting autocomplete suggestions
Ctrl + Page Up/Down + Arrows	For referencing a cell from another worksheet

Table 12: Data editing (inside a cell) shortcuts

Other shortcuts

Shortcut Keys	Functions
Ctrl + Z	To undo the last action
Ctrl + Y	To redo the last action
Ctrl + 9	To hide any selected rows
Ctrl + 0	To hide any selected rows
Ctrl + Shift + (	To unhide any hidden rows in a given selection
Ctrl + Shift +)	To unhide any hidden columns in a selection
Ctrl + ;	To enter date
Ctrl +:	To enter time
Ctrl + '	To show formula
Ctrl +]	For selecting an active cell
Alt	To drive menu bar
Alt + Tab	To open the next program
Alt + =	To autosum

Table 13: Other shortcuts

42 Conclusion

The new Microsoft Excel 2022 is equipped with a whole lot of new features and enhancements much more than its predecessor (Microsoft Excel 2021). This version of Microsoft Excel comes alongside Microsoft Office 365 and its collaboration makes Excel 2022 a very unique software.

In this guide, users will learn the fundamentals regarding Excel like creating pivot tables, learn about worksheets and workbooks, creating links between worksheets, use formulas to join text use keyboard accelerators, using date math, how to use AutoSum and so much more.

At the end of this guide, users will fully understand Microsoft Excel 2022 and get to begin using the software on their own and with their companies. Going further, this User Guide includes updated information and an up-to-date step-by-step guide to make your adventure of acquiring and learning Excel 2022 functionalities more enjoyable.

If you are a business or individual worker who wants to learn how to create tables, organize, and manage data, you need to purchase this Guide and start your incredible journey.

MICROSOFT POWERPOINT

INTRODUCTION

Microsoft PowerPoint 2022 brings many new features to present your ideas and data. For example, you can now use the slide transitions feature to change from the current slide to the next. Moreover, this software also allows changing the transitions for all the slides. Likewise, you can now customize the look and feel of your presentations with the new layout.

How PowerPoint works basic of the algorithm work

PowerPoint is a presentation software that lets users create and present visuals in various formats. The new PowerPoint 2022 includes new features to help you create presentations that impress your audience. For example, you can add multiple shapes to your picture, ensuring that they will not scatter across your slide. Doing so improves the clarity of your image and keeps it from being imbalanced when copied.

In Microsoft PowerPoint, you can easily add text to your slide. You can do this by choosing the Notes option at the bottom of your PowerPoint environment. You can also use the Auto Content Wizard to see a content sample. You can also choose to group shapes and move them together as one. You can also select a group by holding the Shift key and then clicking on each shape. You can then move each shape inside the group.

The Zoom control is another feature that lets you zoom in and out of your presentation. You can find it near the slide view, near the Zoom Control shortcut option. The Zoom Control meter has a range of 10 to 400. Most people keep it set to about 69% or 71% for readability. PowerPoint users can also encrypt their files with passwords to protect them from unauthorized access. To do this, you must choose a password and confirm it.

PowerPoint works by being a presentation graphics software allowing one to create professional-looking electronic slide shows. These slide shows are composed of slides that demonstrate the graphical interpretation of data. That means they can deliver information more creatively. In addition, PowerPoint allows you to use shapes, charts, and other elements to create impressive slides.

When working on a presentation, you want to ensure that you're using the latest version of PowerPoint. If you're not sure, click on the About Window to find out the version you're using.

What is a Slide?

In Microsoft PowerPoint, a slide is a single page in a slideshow. The term slide also describes a set of slides, or a "slide deck," in a slide show. It can be a single page developed in a presentation program or a document using a document markup language (DML). Microsoft PowerPoint provides two ways to design a slide: you can maximize the slide or scale the content to fit the page. The former blows up the slide to the size you specify, but the slide's content may fall outside the frame. The latter option scales the content to fit the page and can help you save time when creating a presentation. PowerPoint allows you to format your slides in landscape or portrait orientation. The slide sizes are also adjustable. You can select from three different slide sizes. To format your slides, click File>New. You can easily locate the Slide Show tab at the top of the screen. Use the options on the ribbon to change the size of your slides.

Where to Buy Microsoft PowerPoint

Microsoft PowerPoint is one of the most popular business programs in the world. While it was initially designed for business use, the software has many communities and school applications. The first package was a stand-alone product but became part of the Microsoft Office suite. Because of its popularity, Microsoft has secured a near-total market share in the presentation software space.

The first version of PowerPoint was released on April 20, 1987. The software was initially called presenter, and its name changed later in the 1980s. Originally, PowerPoint was only available for Macintosh, but Microsoft eventually purchased Forethought and released a Windows version a year later.

Microsoft PowerPoint is a presentation package that makes it easy to present your ideas to an audience. Its built-in tools and features allow even the most novice users to create professional-quality presentations. It also has live collaboration and co-authoring capabilities. In addition, it has accessibility options that enhance the experience of those watching. So whether you're trying to sell a product, present a business plan, or give a presentation to your co-workers, PowerPoint is the perfect presentation program to use.

If you need to upgrade to the latest version of PowerPoint, the best option is to purchase it directly from Microsoft. You can also subscribe to Microsoft 365, which provides access to the latest versions of the Office applications, including PowerPoint. This service costs an annual fee, and you'll get the newest software version and any updates. However, remember that you'll need to renew your subscription each year to continue using the latest version of PowerPoint.

Office 365 offers a cloud-based storage service called OneDrive. It comes with 1 TB of free storage space, and users can access it from any platform. Furthermore, it can be used on mobile devices such as iPads and smartphones. Through this feature, you can access your presentations on the go.

What's the student version & where to download it legally?

The student version of Microsoft PowerPoint is in the Microsoft Office 365 suite. The software is free to download and is available for eligible users. It allows students to make presentations with text, images, graphics, diagrams, and sounds. You can also add complex and simple animations to your presentations.

43 KICK-START

You can choose to open a new document or an existing template to get started.

Figure 159: Opening MS PowerPoint app

Advantages

PowerPoint is one of the most utilized presentation software applications, and most people are familiar with its essential features. Its rich multimedia features help keep audiences engaged and add visual impact to your presentation. In addition, the program comes with an extensive library of templates that make it easy to create professional presentations. However, PowerPoint is not a replacement for the presenter's voice, so you'll still need to deliver the presentation in person. One advantage of PowerPoint is that you can store it on a USB flash drive or in a cloud storage app. Doing so makes it easier to share and access your work from any location. Nowadays, people work from home more often, and tools that facilitate remote collaboration are in demand. PowerPoint has considered this trend and has created a feature that allows co-authors to edit a presentation simultaneously, without the need to send it anywhere. One of the other main advantages of PowerPoint is that it supports collaborative work, especially in office settings. Many users can work on the same presentation and leave notes for clarification. With the new feature, you can even write your presentation with a stylus.

44 WHERE TO DOWNLOAD POWERPOINT EXTENSIONS FOR MICROSOFT POWERPOINT 2022

If you're looking to learn how to create PowerPoint presentations, you've come to the right place. Through this book, we will teach you how to create attractive presentations using the Microsoft

PowerPoint application. This book includes project-based learning as well as hands-on project development. You'll learn everything from formatting shapes to using Format Painter, Animation Painter, Quick Access Toolbar, and Presenter View.

What is a PowerPoint extension?

You can install a PowerPoint extension to add more features and options to your presentations. This tool allows one to change the slides' font, size, style, color, and more. Thousands of add-ins are available for free or on trial accounts. Almost anyone can use them.

Office Timeline is a PowerPoint add-in that lets you create beautiful timelines, Gantt charts, and Swimlanes. It also offers animation controls and a library of instructional slides. You can even embed a video or audio file into your presentation. You can add a voiceover to your presentation with the Speech-Over Professional add-in.

Another popular add-in for PowerPoint is the MLC PowerPoint Add-in, which helps you swap shapes and create presentations faster. This add-in is available for PowerPoint 2007, 2010, and 2013 and will let you make changes to your presentations without using special software. It also allows you to set the Branding Colors for your slides. Another helpful tool is HTML5Point, which converts PowerPoint presentations to HTML5 content. It also preserves fonts, rich media content, and most animations. Microsoft PowerPoint is now available for mobile devices, as well as on tablets. This application allows you to make presentations no matter where you are. Moreover, it supports rich animation, cinematic motion, and 3D models. With these features, you can easily create an excellent presentation.

One of the most popular presentation software, Microsoft PowerPoint, is free for personal and business use. The new version provides a web interface that lets you access the program through any web browser. It also offers more than 700,000 stock photos for your presentations. You can also get a subscription to Envato Elements and access hundreds of templates and stock photos for your presentations.

Where to download PowerPoint Extensions

If you are designing your next presentation, you may wonder where to download PowerPoint Extensions for Microsoft PowerPoint 2022. After all, it can take a lot of time and effort to create a compelling and appealing presentation. Fortunately, many free PowerPoint add-ins can help make the process easier. One of these is PowerUser, which allows you to add charts, graphs, and more to PowerPoint presentations. It also includes an extensive library of stock images and icons.

Another helpful PowerPoint add-in is Office Timeline. This program helps you create beautiful timelines, Gantt charts, and Swimlanes. The program also features a microphone recording tool and enables you to add voiceover to your presentations. This tool is handy for creating training videos and eLearning courses and is compatible with PowerPoint 2007 and 2010. It also supports Office 365 and 32-bit editions.

Depending on your needs, PowerPoint add-ins can enhance your presentation and make the development process more manageable. Some of the best add-ins are free, and you can download them from official sites. iSpring Suite is the most popular PPT add-in for eLearning, while the free version offers similar features.

The Symbols and Characters PPT add-in can be downloaded from the Office Store. This add-in makes it easy to use diacritics and special characters in PowerPoint. It also provides an easy search function that helps you narrow your search by language. Symbols and Characters can also be used in simulations to emphasize the real-world connections between different subjects and languages.

Another excellent option for PowerPoint add-ins is SlideHub. This add-in offers thousands of professionally designed slides for business use. It also includes more than 10 million license-free stock photos. This add-in also helps you insert your company's color palette for consistency across your presentations. Using this feature saves you time while creating your presentation.

Another helpful feature of PowerPoint is its ability to recover unsaved presentations. Its Recover Unsaved Presentations option allows you to view your presentation by double-clicking on its icon. Of course, you'll need to enable the file extensions in Windows Explorer to access these files.

PowerPoint vs. Google Slides

PowerPoint and Google Slides are both presentation tools that offer much customization. PowerPoint has a vast selection of professional designs and thousands of visual elements. Google's new offering, Slides, is a free alternative that promotes collaboration and sharing.

Google Slides also features version history, which is helpful if multiple people are editing the same File. It records any changes you make and allows you to restore previous versions. This feature is beneficial for presentations where several people edit the same document. Google Slides' version history also means you can access earlier versions of a presentation if someone accidentally changes something.

Google Slides is incredibly easy to use and has a simple interface. It can be viewed on a variety of devices. It also has an Explore mode, which allows you to search through images from Google. Google Slides has many similarities to PowerPoint, although the former has a steeper learning curve. It is also more customizable and offers a broader selection of templates.

Google Slides is the modern cloud-based alternative to PowerPoint. Although PowerPoint has some limitations, Google Slides is a fully cloud-native application. That means you can access it on various devices, including tablets. The only downside to Google Slides is that it is not available offline, but Google Chrome users can easily store their files in the cloud. Otherwise, it offers the same user interface and functionality as PowerPoint. It lets you edit your decks on as many devices as you wish.

Google Slides is a free alternative for PowerPoint. It allows you to edit your presentation even when offline. It requires a Chrome extension and is downloadable. Unlike PowerPoint, it also has a built-in auto-save feature, which ensures that your presentation is always saved.

Google Slides allows you to collaborate with multiple users. That means multiple employees can edit a single document simultaneously, while you can share a single presentation with many. You can also share your presentation online with as many people as you want. You can also share the presentation with others by email if you'd like. Google Slides also allows comments, so you can easily share them with your audience.

PowerPoint vs. Canva

One of the critical differences between PowerPoint and Canva is that Canva allows you to download individual slides, whereas PowerPoint does not. You may also have to download or install specific fonts to use Canva. You can also move objects in Canva, but you may not be able to do that in PowerPoint. One of the most impressive things about Canva is its incredible font selection. You can download fonts from many online sources, but PowerPoint does not. While both programs are great options for presentations, Canva provides more features and is easier to use. For example, it has a broader selection of fonts and ready-made templates. It also has a drag-and-drop design feature that is more intuitive. As a result, Canva has a solution for everyone, whether you need a professional design or a simple one to share on social media. Another essential advantage of Canva is its ability to be used for printing. With just one click of a button, users can create professional-looking presentations. This feature is handy for flyers, business cards, and other items. And Canva claims to be ethically produced, so it may be a good choice for those who have a desire to print their designs. However, this feature doesn't work well for anyone with an extremely slow Internet connection. As a result, elements may take some time to load. On the other hand, a desktop app would display selected elements right away. As such, Canva isn't a perfect replacement for PowerPoint, but it is a powerful app in its own right. However, it does not compare favorably to the "real" presentation apps and isn't designed to replace PowerPoint in the business world.

Moreover, both PowerPoint and Canva have a vast library of templates that make design-related tasks easier for their users. For example, there are templates for social media graphics, presentations, eBooks, posters, and cards. You can also create your slides from scratch. Then you click elements and drag them into the editor. Similarly, you can add text, photos, and highly customizable videos. Using these tools will help you create a professional-looking presentation.

45 TIPS FOR MICROSOFT POWERPOINT 2022

Knowing a few tricks and tips will make the process much easier if you create a PowerPoint presentation. For example, you can lock the aspect ratio and proportion of images in PowerPoint to avoid distortion. By doing this, users can easily create a more appealing, engaging presentation. You can also use SmartArt and Background graphics to spice up your presentation and add some extra color to it.

Slide master controls the design of your PowerPoint presentation

If you want your slides to have the same appearance throughout your presentation, you must set up a slide master before you begin creating your presentation. The slide master defines the overall design of your presentation and is linked to all other slide layouts. When changes are made to your slide master, they are reflected on all following slides automatically. To modify the appearance of your presentation, you can add components to the slide master and modify the layouts of individual slides. The Slide master is an essential PowerPoint feature. You can use it to modify the text's color, font, and positioning. You may also alter the background color of each slide using a theme. Each theme has a unique slide master. Utilizing a theme will save you time and make your presentation more uniform. The slide master is the simplest approach to establishing the layout for all slides in a presentation. It controls every aspect of the appearance of your slides. Any changes to the master will affect every slide in your presentation. You can choose a template, a style, and an overall layout for all your slides. Doing so will save you time and ensure your presentation is professional and polished. Then you can focus on creating the best possible presentation for your audience. After creating a slide master, you can save it as a template and share it with other people. To do this, simply click the File tab and choose "Save as." The file will have the master layout and the slide layouts. The dotted lines will show the relationships between the master layout and the slide layouts. If you wish to change the default slide layouts to reflect your company's brand style, you can make changes in the Slide Master by clicking the "Change Master Layout" button.

Slide transitions

If you wish to add sound to your slide transitions, you've come to the right place. This feature lets you add sound to your slides, and you can control its speed. For instance, to alter the transition's speed, click "Duration" spinner and enter the duration you want. You can also enable slide transitions that advance to the next slide whenever a user clicks the mouse. Morph transitions are perfect for comparing elements between different slides. The transition makes the elements on the slide larger or smaller. These transitions are often suitable for text and chart elements. Your presentation can highlight other text or chart elements once or twice. You can also use varying shapes for the transitions. Slide transitions are easy to apply to your PowerPoint presentations. They are available in many styles and can be as subtle or flashy as you want them. You can change the speed and direction of your transitions by selecting them in the slide navigation pane. The effect options command will also give you a preview of your transition. Once you've selected the transitions, you can set the speed and type of sound you want to add. There are also almost 50 different transitions available in PowerPoint. Among them are "Push" and "Origami," which fold a slide into a paper crane and fly off-screen to reveal the next slide. You can add object animations to your slide, too. PowerPoint includes many animations for objects. The options are available in the Transition to This Slide menu. You can also use several other animations, including fading, dissolving, and wiping. The objects can also be animated with sound, which you can turn on or off as you wish.

SmartArt

SmartArt for Microsoft PowerPoint 2022 offers a new way to create attractive slide designs with text, pictures, and more. To create your SmartArt, select the text you wish to use. Left-click your mouse and hold, then drag the cursor over the text. Then, click the "Convert to SmartArt Graphic" button, which is in the "Paragraph" section of the "Home" tab. The button has the same icon as the "SmartArt" function in the Insert tab. SmartArt for Microsoft PowerPoint 2022 features a new "Text Pane" tool that makes editing text easy. To change text, click the tiny arrow in the center of the SmartArt graphic. The "Text Pane" features different sections for each SmartArt box.

Once you make the necessary alterations, click "Ok" button to save the changes. SmartArt allows you to insert and customize the text in many ways. Its sizing controls enable you to resize individual shapes and add text and images to them. SmartArt graphics can also be repositioned within a larger graphic. That means you can quickly change the appearance of your slide without any additional software. Another SmartArt tool allows you to create a timeline graphic in your presentation. Doing so will show essential milestones or events in a project. You can also change the timeline graphic with the help of SmartArt tools in the Design tab. There are many ways to make a timeline graphic. You can copy and paste it from the design tool to the slide or use a dedicated tool to create a timeline graphic in PowerPoint. Another option is to subscribe to Office 365 for a monthly fee to access a collection of PowerPoint templates. This subscription service includes PowerPoint templates and apps. For those unfamiliar with SmartArt, you should look at the infographic templates in Office 365. These infographic templates allow you to create stunning presentations using data and images.

Background graphics

The latest version of Microsoft PowerPoint offers several new features, including background graphics. The background graphics in your slides are easy to edit and can be locked in the slide master view. Doing so allows you to edit and modify your images without affecting the rest of the presentation. First, select the element you wish to edit to edit the background graphics.

For more customization, you can also use the set transparency tool to make all or part of the background image transparent. This feature can also be used to hide individual PowerPoint backgrounds. You can also add watermarks to each slide. Make sure you click on Apply to All to save your changes. The "Format Background" panel allows you to select a picture from your computer and fill the background of the slide master and any layout masters below it. You can also choose to use a "Watermark" effect, though you may need to adjust the transparency percentage to achieve the desired result. In 2022, people will be more natural. That means that the best backgrounds for PPT will be natural-looking and unobtrusive. This approach allows you to engage with your audience in an authentic way. In addition, bright colors and natural images will make your slide more appealing and help you connect with your audience. Another option is to use grayscale pictures as backgrounds. These images are easier to read and provide more contrast between text and image.

Adding audio

Adding audio to Microsoft PowerPoint 2022 can be done by choosing from various options. First, you can choose to play audio from the file you've created or from iTunes. Then, once you've added audio, you can modify its appearance with the Audio Options tab. For example, you can pause, rewind, or continuously play the audio. Other options include letting the audio play automatically whenever a slide is on display and looping the audio.

Once you've added audio, you can start playing it on the PowerPoint slides. You can do this by inserting an audio file or recording it. The music player has playback and pause buttons and several other options. You can even customize the player settings. If you don't have a music player, a temporary "Playback" tab appears when PowerPoint opens. This tab provides you with handy tools to work with audio files.

In Microsoft PowerPoint 2022, you can add a customized delay for the audio's start and end time. However, if you aren't interested in adding a delay, you can leave out this field. You can also choose to start and stop the audio at specific intervals. Then, you can add a caption or a subtitle for the audio. Adding audio to Microsoft PowerPoint is easy. First, you need to plug in your microphone. Once you've done this, click on the Recording tab and choose "Audio" or "Record Sound" from the navigation bar. You can also add audio to the video if you've recorded audio using the microphone. You can control both the volume and playback of the audio in PowerPoint.

46 OPEN A BLANK DOCUMENT OR AN EXISTING TEMPLATE

Create a New Presentation

You can utilize a template if you want to come up with a PowerPoint presentation. Each template in PowerPoint has its font, colors, and slide layout. To create a new presentation, you can use any of the following templates;

- The Blank Presentation Template

- The Built-in Template

- Online Template

Using the Blank Presentation Template

Follow the following steps to create a new presentation using the blank presentation template.

- Go to **File** tab

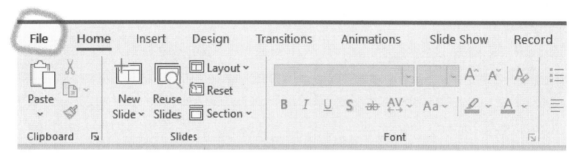

Figure 160: The file tab for creating blank presentation

- Select and click **New**, and then click **Blank Presentation**.

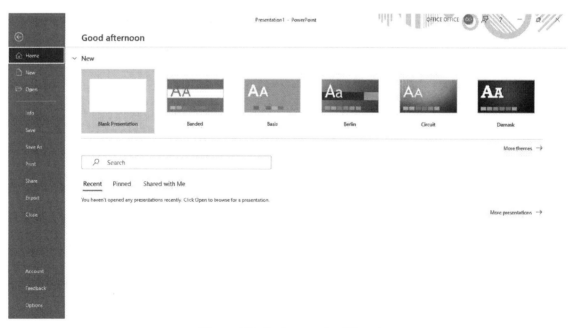

Figure 161: Options under File tab

- A new presentation is displayed.

Using the Built-in Template

The built-in templates are redefined templates created by Microsoft. These templates comprise custom formatting and design that help save time and stress. To use the built-in template, follow the steps provided below.

- Go to the **File** tab

- Click on **New**, and then click on any of the built-in templates.

- Here, a preview of the template comes up with information on the slide layout and themes that come with the template and how they can be used.

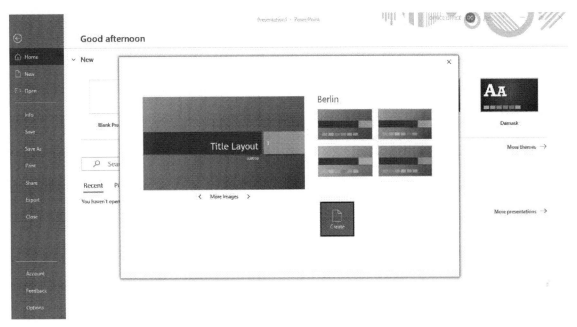

Figure 162: The Berlin template information

- Click the **Create** button to use the template you selected to create a new presentation.

- A new presentation is displayed.

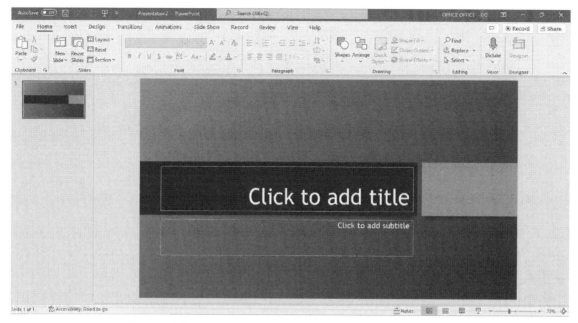

Figure 163: Creating a presentation from the Berlin template

Using the Online Template

Rather than using the blank template or built-in template, you can decide to get your templates online. These templates are refined, and you can download them to your computer. To use the online template, follow the steps given below.

- Go to the **File** tab

- Click on **New** on the left side of the window, and then enter the template you wish to find in the search bar.

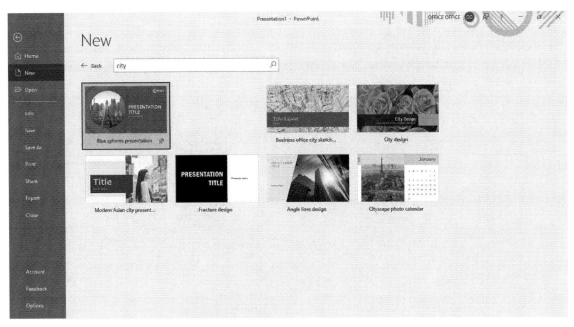

Figure 164: The online templates

- In any of the templates that pop up, select the template you desire

- Here, a preview of the template comes up with information on the slide layout and themes that come with the template and how they can be used.

- Click the **Create** button to use the template you selected to create a new presentation.

47 POWERPOINT DASHBOARD

The Backstage View

Figure 165: The backstage view

With the Backstage View, you will be exposed to frequently used features to manage files and data. These features are fourteen, and they are listed below.

- Home

- New

- Open

- Info

- Save

- Save As

- Print

- Share

- Export

- Close

- Account

- Feedback

- Option

Opening **Backstage View**

- Click on **File tab**

- When Backstage view is displayed, you can select any of the fourteen options you wish to use

- To go back to the **Normal** view from the **Backstage** view, click on **Back** arrow button at the very top of your interface.

Understanding the PowerPoint Ribbon Tabs

The Ribbon Tabs are a group of commonly used commands used to perform an essential task. For example, the following are the tabs in Excel:

Figure 166: PowerPoint Ribbon Tabs

- **Home Tab**: This is the tab that contains features such as Cut, Paste, Font, Paragraph, and other elements that are necessary to add and organize slides in the presentation.

- **Insert Tab**: This tab allows you to add objects, such as pictures, shapes, charts, links, text boxes, videos, etc., to your slides.

- **Design Tab**: This tab allows you to add a theme or color scheme to your slide or format the slide background.

- **Transitions Tab**: This tab allows you to set up how your slides change from one to the other.

- **Animations Tab**: This tab allows you to maneuver the movement of things or objects in your tab. With this tab, you can use several animations in the gallery found in the Animation group.

- **Slide Show Tab**: This tab allows you to set up or arrange your presentation for others to see.

- **Review Tab**: This tab allows you to add comments, run spell-check, or compare one presentation with another.

- **View Tab**: This allows you to view your presentation using the different views (Normal, Reading View, Slide Sorter, & Slide Show)

- **File Tab**: This tab allows you to view the Backstage of your presentation to access features such as Home and New. Open, Info, Save, Save As, etc.

- **Tool Tabs**: There are six Tool tabs, namely, Drawing Tools, Picture Tools, SmartArt Tools, Chart Tools, Table Tools, and Video Tools. The most commonly used Tools tabs are the Drawing Tools tab and Picture Tools tab. The Drawing Tools tab appears when you select a shape or text box, while the Picture Tools tab emerges when you click on a picture in your presentation.

PowerPoint has six (6) views you can use to view your task. The view will change in respect of the activities you are carrying out on the file; each view has its benefit over others depending on the job you are doing. The default view you will be working on as you launch into the PowerPoint application is the Normal view.

Switching to Different Views Switch

You can change to a different view on PowerPoints from two places, which are:

1. **The View bar:** there are **five views** in the presentation view group and **three views** under the master view group. They are located in the upper right corner of the panel.

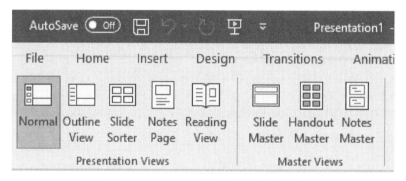

Figure 167: The different PowerPoint views

2. **The Status bar View button** has four frequently used views on the status bar. These views are in the middle of the status bar at the bottom of the window application.

Figure 168: Status bar views

Knowing The Ideal Time to Switch to Different Views

Knowing when it is right to switch to various views based on the task you are doing or the task you are about to do will be of great importance. For example, some views help create a presentation, while some are useful for delivering a presentation. So let us check when each view should come to action:

1. **Normal view (Default View):** it is the default view because it is the view that comes with your application at any time you launch into PowerPoints. It is the best view that helps you view the presentation slide as the thumbnail in the slide plane. The actual slide will appear in the screen's center for slide editing and examination. The thumbnail slide grants you easy navigation within the presentation and allow you to conveniently manage the slides, such as addition, deleting, and arrangement.

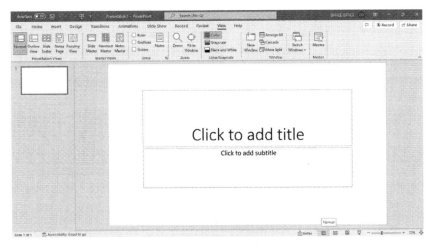

Figure 169: Normal view

2. **Outline view:** this is the view that works well with the text. It helps you direct your attention to the text, especially when you are about to type or read it.

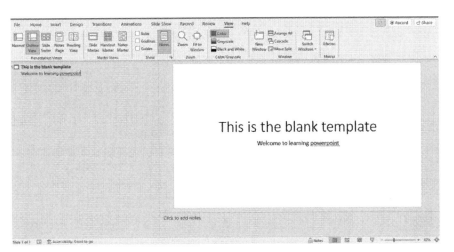

Figure 170: Outline view

3. **Slide sorter view:** This is the view that appears on the main screen and allows you to sort and arrange the sequence of slides as you design and print the presentation. It presents you with the actual shape of each slide.

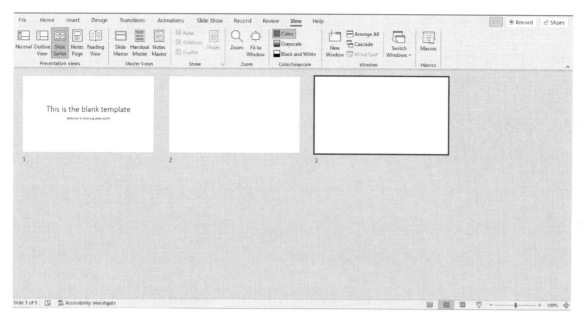

Figure 171: Slide sorter view

4. **Reading view:** a reading view is used to view one's presentation in a single slide on a window with easy control for review. Reading view is the needed view when you want to review your presentation to check an area that is necessary for amendment. It ensures you amend essential parts before delivering the presentation from slide to slide. It is not used to deliver the presentation but to review it for necessary corrections. To amend the contents of the presentation when you are in the reading view, kindly switch to another view and correct it because the reading view does not permit alteration.

Figure 172: Reading view

5. **Slide show view:** this is the view to be used when it is time to deliver a presentation to the audience. The view occupies the entire screen. It is similar to giving an actual presentation to the audience; you will see everything, such as timing, graphics, transition effect, and animation, just the way it will come when you are giving an actual presentation.

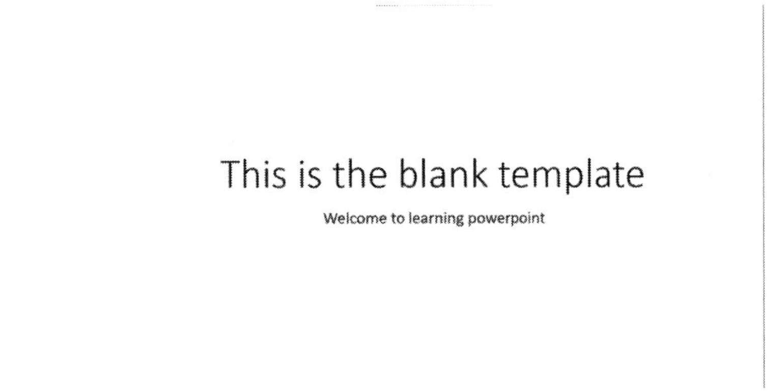

This is the blank template
Welcome to learning powerpoint

Figure 173: Slide show view

6. **Notes page view**: this is the view that permits the insertion of notes and views them to support you during the presentation, provided you add any notes.

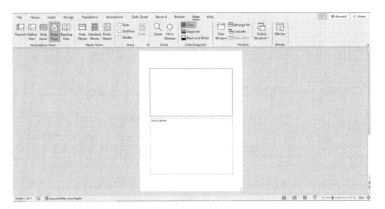

Figure 174: Notes page view

Note: Note page view and normal view (default view) allow insertion and viewing of presenter notes.

7. **Master views** involve three modes: notes master, handout master, and slide master. They are advanced views that require a higher level of expertise for a more accurate presentation. We will discuss them in length in the subsequent chapter.

Slide Master
Handout Master
Notes Master
Master Views

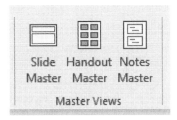

Figure 175: Master views

48 TIPS AND TRICKS FOR FORMATTING AND EDITING

Font Formatting

Font formatting changes the appearance of a group of PowerPoints or characters individually. Most of the commands used for font formatting are available in the **Home** ribbon in the **Font** group. In addition, you can explore additional commands by clicking the launcher option .

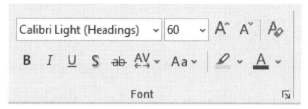

Figure 176: Font formatting

To format text:

1. Choose text you wish to format.

2. Then, go to **Home** ribbon.

3. Select as desired:

- **Font** dropdown list to alter the shape of the text.

- Number dropdown list or the **Increase and Decrease** buttons to alter font size.

- **Bold** for making the text darker and thicker.

- *Italics* to slant the text.

- **Underline** to underline the text with a single black line. Click the dropdown button in the front to choose the underline color and style.

- **Strikethrough** to draw a line through the text.

- Text Shadow to apply shadows to the text.

- Character Spacing to set the space between each text's letters. Click on the dropdown button and select an option. Select more options to have complete control of the spacing. The text can be either expanded or condensed.

- **The Font Color** feature changes the color of the text. Use the dropdown icon to select the desired color.

- **Text Highlight Color** for changing background color of the text. The last color you selected will be applied to your text; use the dropdown icon to change the color.

- 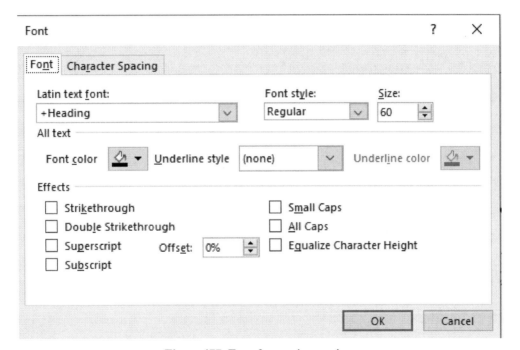 To clear all the text formatting.

- **Change Case** to choose from one of its five options:

  o **Sentence case** capitalize only the first letter,

  o **lowercase** puts all the text in lower letters,

  o **UPPERCASE** capitalizes all the letters of the text,

  o **Capitalize Each PowerPoint** capitalizes only the first letter of each PowerPoint of the text, and

  o **TOGGLE CASE** put only the first letter in lower case and all others in uppercase.

4. For more options, click the dialog box launcher. A font dialog box appears.

5. Make changes as desired and press **OK**.

Figure 177: Font formatting options

Setting Line Spacing

Line spacing is simply the vertical distance between lines.

To set your presentation line spacing.

1. Select the entire presentation.

2. Click the Home tab

3. Click the line spacing icon in the **Paragraph** group.

A dropdown list appears.

4.   Select your desired number spacing.

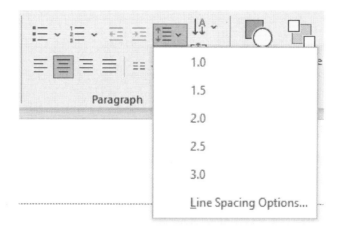

Figure 178: Line Spacing

PowerPoint affects the spacing as you hover over the numbers. Therefore, before choosing, you can check how it looks if you do not have a number in mind.

Text Alignment

Text alignment is a formatting attribute that determines the appearance and location of texts on a slide concerning the textbox. The primary text alignment in PowerPoint are:

- **Left alignment:** It aligns your text to the left side of the textbox.

- **Center alignment**: It aligns your text at the center of the textbox.

- **Right alignment**: It aligns your text to the right side of the textbox.

- **Justified**: It aligns your text to the right and left sides of the text box and adds extra spaces where necessary, except for the last line.

- **Align Text:** It enables you to align your text to the text box's top, middle, or bottom.

Left alignment is PowerPoint's default alignment and is appropriate for most situations. For example, you can use center alignment for headings, right alignment for a date, and justified if you want a smooth look of your presentation edges.

To align your text:

1.   Select the entire text or the whole slides you wish to align.

2.   Then, go to the **Home** tab.

3.   Click on any of the desired alignment commands in the **Paragraph** group.

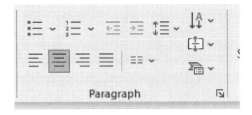

Figure 179: Paragraph group

Indentation

Indentation is used for shifting the edge of a list or line inward or outward, as the case may be.

The **indent** command button is available in the **Home** tab in the **Paragraph** group as two buttons:

- **Increase List Level** and

- **Decrease List Level**

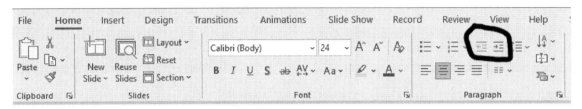

Figure 180: Indentation list

To add indent to a list or text:

1. Position your cursor in any place within your text or highlight the list you wish to add indent.

2. Go to the **Home** tab.

3. Click on the **Increase List Level or Decrease List Level** commands as the case may be.

These buttons decrease or increase the indent by **5"** per click. If you want to set the desired indent,

4. Hit the dialog box launcher in the **Paragraph** group. **A paragraph** dialog box appears.

5. Input the desired value in the **Before text** box and click **OK**.

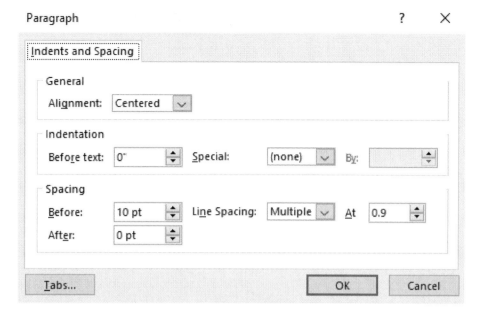

Figure 181: Indentation setting

Designing Your Presentation with Themes

Themes is a powerful PowerPoint feature that you can quickly and easily use to create a professional-looking presentation. A theme is a predefined set of fonts, effects, colors, and backgrounds that work well together. The theme changes the entire look of your presentation or some selected slides when applied.

Whenever you create a presentation in PowerPoint, you use the default theme, the Office theme. **However,** PowerPoint has a gallery of themes for your quick use. Given below are how to apply, modify and create themes.

Applying Themes

To change the theme of your entire presentation:

1.   Click the **Design** tab.

2.   Select your desired themes in the **Themes** group. Then, click on the scroll-down button to see more options.

Figure 182: Working with themes

3.   Hover your cursor over the themes to preview them live in your presentation.

4.   Click your desired theme to apply it.

To change the theme of a or some slides:

1.   First, select the slide(s) you want to add to the theme.

2.   Next, go to the **Design** tab.

3.   Right-click on the theme you want to apply.

4.   Select **Apply to Selected Slides** from the menu box that appears.

Each theme has four color variants you can choose from in the Variant group.

Customizing your Themes

Customizing a theme involves changing any of the theme's elements to create a unique look for your presentation.

To change themes colors:

1. Go to **Design** tab.
2. Click **Variants** group scroll button.
3. Choose **Colors** command. A color palette appears.
4. Select the desired color set or click **Customize Colors** to combine your colors.

To change a theme font:

1. Go to **Design** tab.
2. Click **Variants** group scroll button.
3. Select **Fonts.** A font list menu appears.
4. Select your desired theme fonts or

Select **Customize Font** to customize your font. Set your desired font in the dialog box that appears, rename, and press **Save**.

To change a theme background:

1. Go to **Design** tab.
2. Click **Variants** group scroll button.
3. Select **Background Styles.** A list of backgrounds appears.
4. Select the desired background.
5. Select **Format Background** to set your background's color, gradient, and properties in the right **Format Background** pane.

Figure 183: Changing theme background

You can save your current or customized theme for later use.

To save a theme:

1. Click **Design** tab.

2. Click on **Themes** scroll-down button.

3. Choose **Save Current Theme**.

4. Input a file name for your theme and press **Save** in dialog box that appears.

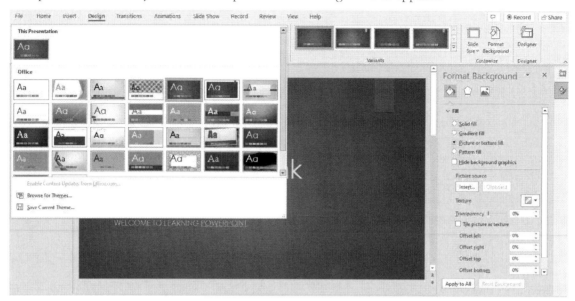

Figure 184: Saving a theme

FORMAT PAINTER

When you want to format a section of your presentation just like you have formatted one, PowerPoint has a special command called Format Painter. Instead of going through the stress of doing the formatting all over again. **Format Painter** copies the format of one and applies it to the other.

To use a Format Painter:

1. First, select the text that has your desired format.

2. Next, head to **Home** tab and Clipboard group.

3. Finally, click once on the **Format Painter**.

Figure 185: Format Painter

Your cursor turns to a paintbrush.

4. Move your cursor to the text you want to format.

5. Select the text.

PowerPoint automatically formats the text like the one you copied.

Unfortunately, format Painter turns itself off after each use. To keep it active for continuous use,

- Double-click on it.

- Press the Esc key or click on the icon when you are done.

49 NUMERATIONS AND BULLETINS

PowerPoint allows you to highlight your points using numbered or bulleted lists. A bullet or number makes your list distinct and easy to present. In addition, you can customize your list by editing or formatting the bullet/number font, color, icon style, and alignment. When the order of the items on your list is important, use a numbered list. Bulleted lists, on the other hand, are useful when the order of the items in your list is irrelevant.

To create a bulleted list:

1.   Highlight the list you want to add bullets to **or**

Set the cursor to where you want the bullet to begin.

2.   Go to **Home** tab.

3.   Click **Bullets** dropdown button within **Paragraph** group.

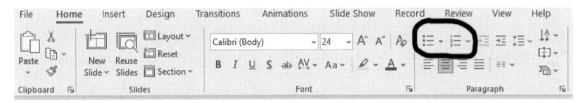

Figure 186: Bulletins and numbers

A dialog box with a list of bullet styles will appear.

4.   Select your desired bullet style, and it appears in your presentation.

To create a numbered list:

1.   Highlight the list you want to add numbers to **or**

Place the cursor where you want the numbering to start. Set the cursor to where you want the numbering to begin.

2.   Go to the **Home** tab.

3.   Click on the **Numbering** dropdown button in the **Paragraph** group.

A dialog box will then emerge with the list of numbering styles.

4.   Select your desired numbering style, and it appears in your presentation.

To customize your list icons:

1.   Select your list.

2.   Head to **Home** tab and then the **Paragraph** group.

3.   Click **Bullets** or **Numbering** dropdown button. A menu appears.

4.   Select **Bullets and Numbering**

A dialog box with two tabs pops up.

5.   Make your desired settings:

-To alter the sizes of the icons, use **Size** box or its arrow buttons

-To alter the icon's color, use **Color** dropdown button,

-To alter the icons to symbols, click the **Customize** button and choose your desired symbols in the dialog box.

-To use any picture as the icon, click **Picture** button and follow prompts.

6.   You can also click on the **Numbered** tab to use numbers of any format.

7.   Click **OK** when you are done with the settings.

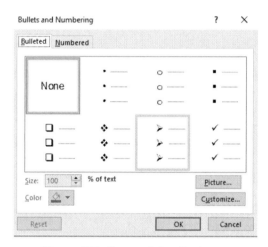

Figure 187: Customizing list icons

Tips:

- To create different levels of bullets, press the Tab key to indent the points.

- Selecting the bullets or numbering command will change the list style if your cursor is already in a numbered or bulleted list.

Bullets and numbering are the keys that PowerPoint employs in arranging its list in any of the text boxes **(text box and text frame).** Bullets and numbering are of great use in PowerPoint as they allow easy listing of steps, ideas, and instructions in the perfect order of sequence they should follow. Both bullet and numbering are in the paragraph option. Visit them to make your list more professional.

50 THE POWER OF FIND AND REPLACE

Find command is a PowerPoint feature that allows you to find text in your presentation. Also available in PowerPoint is **Replace** option, which will enable you to find words and replace the word with another word. With these fantastic features, you can also find a font type and replace it with another font.

Using the Find feature in PowerPoint.

Find command can search through your presentation in seconds and find a given word or character for you. You can search through either a section of your presentation or the entire presentation.

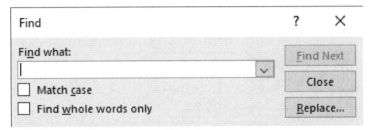

Figure 188: Find command

To find text:

1. Go to the **Home** tab.

2. In the "**Editing group**," click the "**Find**" button. A Find dialog box is displayed.

3. Click and type in the Find textbox, the word, or the phrase to search.

4. Click **Find Next** button.

5. Select any of the displayed text to use.

6. To close the pane, click the X button in the upper-right corner.

How to streamline your search

PowerPoint also allows you to customize your search to eliminate too many irrelevant findings.

To customize your search:

- Check the **Match case** box. If you want the text in the exact case you typed, i.e., searching for **Learn** will not bring **learn** if you select this option.

- Check the **Find whole words only** button if you want text not being part of another different word, i.e., when you search for **'in'** you won't find '**instance**.'

- Hit the **OK** button to exit the current window.

Using the Find and Replace Command in PowerPoint.

PowerPoint provides an option not only to find a text but also to replace the text with a desired one.

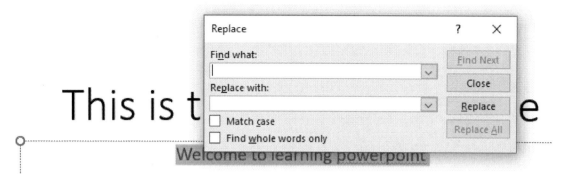

Figure 189: Find and replace

To find & replace text:

1. Go to **Home** tab

2. Click **Replace** button within **Editing** group.

Find and Replace dialog box appears. Alternatively, use **Ctrl + H** to launch this box.

3. Click **find What** text box and type the texts you wish to search.

4. Click **Replace With** textbox and input the text to replace what you input above.

5. Select any of the below buttons:

- **Replace** to replace the text that is currently highlighted.

- **Replace All** to replace all matches in the entire presentation.

- **Find Next** to replace all the matches, starting from the current position of the cursor position to the end of your presentation.

PowerPoint automatically replaces the word or phrase

6. To exit the dialog box, hit the **Close** button or **X** icon.

51 SHAPES, IMAGES, AND TABLES

Creating Table to Display Information

One of those powerful tools to display information in PowerPoint is a table. The table is the arrangement of cells in the form of rows and columns. Tables are used to accommodate both alphabetical and numerical data. PowerPoint has four methods of creating data. Briefly, we will be checking them out.

Dragging on the Table Menu

To create a table by dragging the table menu, follow the steps below

- Go to the **Insert** tab, and click on the **Table** button to select the rows and columns you want in your table

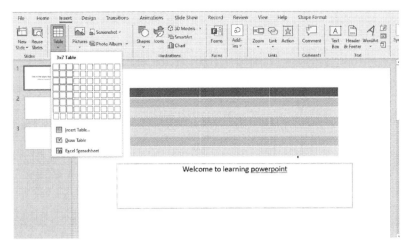

Figure 190: Inserting a table

Clicking on the Table Icon

Another way of creating the table is clicking on the Table icon in the placeholder frame. The Table icon is displayed amidst other contents in the Master slide.

To create a table here, use these steps

- Click on **Table icon**

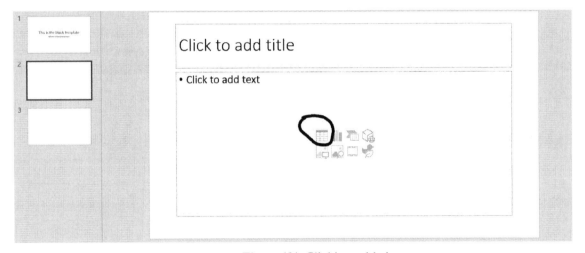

Figure 191: Clicking table icon

- In the **Insert** dialog box, Input the number of columns and rows you want in the table, and click on **Ok.**

Using the Insert Table dialog box

To create a table using the Table dialog box, follow the steps below

- Go to **Insert** tab, click **Table** button

- From dropdown list, select **Insert Table.**

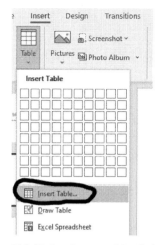

Figure 192: Using insert table dialog box

- In **Insert** dialog box, Input the column and row numbers you want, and then click on **Ok.**

Drawing a Table

To draw a table, follow the steps below:

- Go to **Insert** tab, click on **Table** button

- From the dropdown list, select **Draw Table**

- When the pointer changes to a pencil, draw the table on the slide with the pencil.

Applying Table Styles

To change the table styles in your slides, follow the steps below:

- Select any cell in the table

- Head to the **Design** tab and find the **Table Styles** group to click on the **More** dropdown arrow, which will display the available table styles.

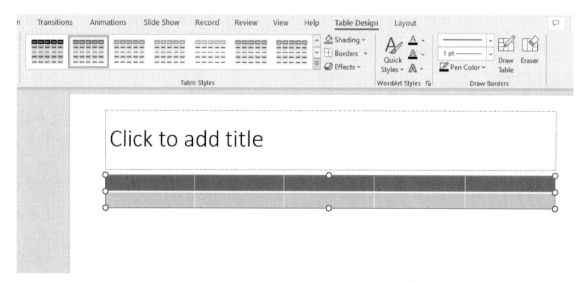

Figure 193: Table styles

52 THE GRAPHS AND CHARTS

Getting Familiar with Charts

Before we learn how to apply charts to presentations, it is pertinent to understand the jargon under charts. The main reason behind this is to familiarize you with charts as you begin to use charts to represent numerical data in your presentation.

The following is the jargon under the chart:

- **Graph or Chart**: A chart or graph is a set of numbers that change into a picture.

- **Chart type**: There are different chart types; pie charts, column charts, scatter charts, etc.

- **Chart Layout**: This contains components such as headings & legends that provides an opportunity of crating a simple and standard chart.

- **Chart Styles:** This is what contains the formatting elements that are responsible for how a chart appears in your presentation.

- **Datasheet:** These are where the charts created are being derived. Don't forget, a chart or graph is a set of numbers changed into a picture.

- **Series:** Series can be defined as the collection of similar or related numbers to form a chart.

- **Axes:** These are lines found on the edge of a chart. The axes fall under two categories; the x-axis at the chart's bottom. And the y-axis at the left edge of the chart.

- **Legends:** These boxes show the different series plotted on the chart.

Below is a small description of the main chart categories. Have a look at each one in PowerPoint as you read down the list:

- **Column:** data represented by vertical columns (see bar chart).

- **Line:** data points joined by lines.

- **Pie:** data making up slices of pie.

- **Bar:** data represented by horizontal columns (see column chart).

- **Area:** data represented by lines but with shaded areas underneath.

- **XY Scatter:** data plotted as points, but points are not joined.

- **Map:** This chart plots the data on a map for geographical data.

- **Stock:** data plotted as vertical lines showing high/low/close values. If you're familiar with stocks and shares style charts, you'll be accustomed to the "candlesticks" produced in this chart style.

- **Surface:** these are similar to line charts but represented in 3D.

- **Radar:** there is no X-Y axis. The data you plot here is relative to a central point.

- **Treemap:** hierarchical data displayed as nested rectangles.

- **Sunburst:** hierarchical data displayed as concentric rings.

- **Histogram:** similar to a "column" chart but a histogram plots a distribution of data.

- **Box & Whisker:** these charts show data distribution using boxes with a vertical line (the "whiskers") representing the median value. The whiskers show variability outside upper and lower values.

- **Waterfall:** a column chart representing data as vertical bars (left to right). It highlights change and shows a breakdown of that change.

- **Funnel:** Horizontal bars stacked over each other from widest at the top to narrowest at the bottom, giving a funnel-like appearance.

- **Combo:** combine different charts onto the same axes.

To insert a chart in your presentation:

1. **Place your insertion points** where you want the chart. Put the chart's anchor points where you want them to be.

2. Go to the **Insert** ribbon.

3. Click **Chart** in the **Illustration** group.

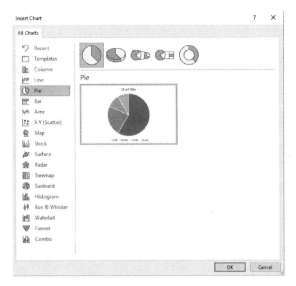

Figure 194: Insert chart

Insert Chart dialog box pops up.

4.   Select a chart type and double-click on the desired chart.

The chart appears in your presentation with an excel spreadsheet.

5.   Input your data into the excel spreadsheet, and the charts update your data.

6.   Close the spreadsheet window.

Formatting a Chart

1.   Choose the chart.

2.   Click on the plus sign, which is at the top right corner.

3.   Check or uncheck the box of elements to put or remove them from the chart.

4.   Hit the arrow in front of any selected elements for more settings.

5.   Click on **More Options** to have control of the element from the element Format dialog box.

Each element has its Format dialog box to format your chart elements fully. You can change their color, width, size, gap, etc., as the case may be. The format dialog box can also be opened by:

- Double-clicking on the element or

- Right-clicking on the element and choosing **Format Data Series** from the list of the options or

- Using the keyboard shortcut command **Ctrl + 1** on the element.

You can also format your chart in the contextual **Chart Tools** tap (Design and Format buttons) or ✎ the chart style below the **+** sign at the brush icon. You can filter your chart using the chart filter ▼ below the chart style icon.

Applying Chart to a Presentation

To apply the chart within the presentation, follow the steps provided below:

- Head to **Insert** tab and press the **Chart** icon in **Illustration** group

- Choose the desired chart in **Insert Chart** dialog box and press **Ok.**

NOTE: You may use alternative ways of inserting charts into your presentation

- Ensure to create a new slide whose layout contains a **Content placeholder.** Then click on **Chart** icon that appears with other icons in the Content placeholder.

Applying a New Slide with a Chart

You may need to apply a new slide with another chart in your presentation. All you need to do is follow the simple steps provided below:

- Select the slide you want next one to follow.

- Go to **Home** tab and select **New Slide** button in **Slide**s group.

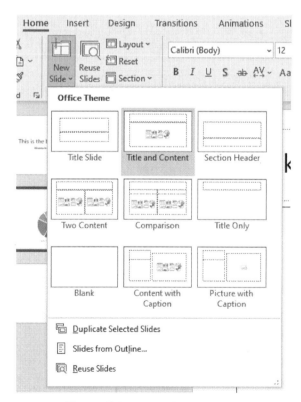

Figure 195: New slide with chart

- Here, a list of slide layouts pop. Click on anyone whose Content placeholder has an icon for inserting a chart.

- When the slide layout is inserted, click on the **Chart** icon that appears with other icons in the Content placeholder.

- Choose the chart you wish to use before clicking **OK**

- Finally, you can edit the sample data displayed in the chart in separate worksheet windows at the top of the slide that looks like an Excel to the data you have in mind or desire.

NOTE: Whatever changes are made in the separate worksheet automatically appear in the chart.

Applying Chart to a Current or Existing Slide

To apply a chart to a current or existing file, follow the steps below:

- Head on to the slide you wish to insert the chart

- Head on to **Insert** tab and press the **Chart** icon in the **Illustration** group,

- In **Insert Chart** dialog box, choose the desired chart and press **Ok**

- Finally, you can edit the sample data displayed in the chart in a separate worksheet window at the top of the slide which looks like an Excel to the data you have in mind or desire.

Altering the Chart Type

To change chart type in your slide, follow the steps below:

- Click on the chart you wish to change its style and go to the **Design** tab

- Select desired chart type by clicking the corresponding **Change Chart Type** button.

Manipulating Chart Data

In a separate worksheet are the data that gives the numbers used to plot charts in PowerPoint. In this session, we will deal more with how to change the chart data by using the Chart Design tab. The Chart Design tab allows you to execute operations such as switching rows & columns, altering the selection of data, refreshing your chart and editing source data.

Switching Rows and Columns

The first option in the Chart Design tab is the Switch/Row Column. As the name implies, this changes the row or column. To switch Rows or Column, use the following procedure:

- Choose the chart you intend to swap rows and columns

- Select Switch Row/Column in the Design menu.

Change your Data Selection

Using the chart's Select Data button, you can alter the displayed data set. For example, to change the data selection, do the following.

- Choose the chart you intend to change the data selection

- Select the Data option under the Design menu.

The following options will appear in the resulting dialog box:

- Change the data range

- Switch rows and columns

- Modify ranges and series

Editing Source Data

To effect any change on your data which is where your chart is derived from, you need to click on **Edit Data** found in the **Data** group when you go to the **Chart Design** tab. Each time you click on this option, a small excel window shows the chart where any change you desire can be made. Then, when you return to PowerPoint, the changes will auto-update in the chart.

Changing the Chart Layout

It's possible to create a basic and standard chart with the help of the chart layout, which includes elements like headings and legends. Follow these instructions to modify your chart's presentation:

- To modify a chart's appearance, pick it and then click the Design tab.

- Pick out your preferred layout by visiting the **Quick Chart Layout**.

Changing the Chart Style

The changing Chart Style feature is what contains the formatting elements that are responsible for how a chart appears in your presentation. There are several numbers of chart styles made available by Microsoft where you can select from

Here are the actions you need to take to modify the chart type used in your presentation.

- Choose the graph whose appearance you want to alter.

- Head to the **Design** tab and select the style you wish in the **Chart Styles** group.

Elaborating the Chart

With PowerPoint, you can add superfluous or adventitious elements, such as titles, labels, legends, etc., to your chart. One of the easiest ways to add these elements to your chart is to apply chart layout to your chart.

You can also add these elements to your chart one after the other. To do this, make a selection on the chart and click on the **Chart Elements** button.

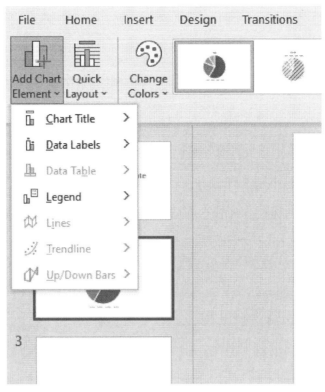

Figure 196: Chart elements

The followings are the elements that can be added to your charts

- **Axes**: These are lines found on the edge of a chart. The axes fall under two categories; the x-axis at the chart's bottom. And the y-axis at the left edge of the chart.

- **Axis Titles**: These elements explain the meaning of axis on the chart. The Primary Horizontal and Primary Vertical Axis Titles are the two types of axis tiles commonly used in almost all charts.

- **Chart Titles**: This is what talks about the chart's content. It can be dragged to any place on the chart.

- **Data Labels**: With this option, you can add labels to data points on your chart.

- **Data Table:** Here is the presentation table from which the chart was derived.

- **Error Bars**: This helps to add a graphical element that displays the values of all the points.

- **Gridlines**: These are light lines displayed behind the chart to trace the location of any line plotted, bar, or dot, by the chart.

- **Legends**: This helps to categorize the data series found in the chart.

- **Trendline**: The trend of the data points can be shown with the help of line elements, and many methods of trend calculation can be used to do so.

53 INSERT VIDEOS AND AUDIO

Creating Audio with Your Presentation

With PowerPoint, you can insert audio into your presentation to spice it up. The audio can be in the form of sound effects, background music, or recording.

Inserting Audio File

To insert an audio file on your slides, follow the steps given below:

- Head on to **Insert** tab and select **Audio on My PC** in **Audio** drop-down list under **Media** Group

Figure 197: Insert audio

- In **Insert** dialog box, locate and select audio file before pressing **Insert.**

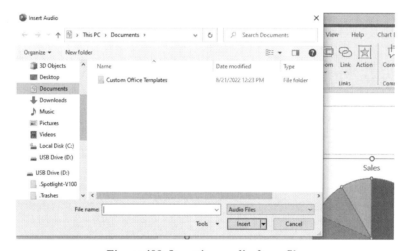

Figure 198: Inserting audio from file

- The audio is then displayed on the slide.

Recording Audio to Your Slides

Rather than insert audio to your slide, you can decide to record audio. To do this, follow the steps below:

- Head on to **Insert** tab and press **Record Audio** in **Audio** drop-down list under **Media** Group

- In your **Record Sound** dialog box, set the name of the recording within the **Name** box.

- Hit **Record** button to start recording.

- When you are done recording, hit the **Stop** button on the screen, and click on the **Play** button to preview your recording.

- Finally, hit **Ok** button to insert the recorded audio into the slide.

Trimming Your Audio File

Probably your audio file is longer than the presentation, and if you wish to make it correspond with your presentation, all you need to do is trim the audio file. To trim an audio file, follow the steps below:

- Click audio file you wish to trim, go to **Playback** tab and press the **Trim** command in the **Editing** group.

- In the **Trim Audio** dialog box, drag **green handle** to configure start time and **red handle** to configure end time.

- Utilize the **Play** button to preview the trimmed audio file, and press **Ok** button when you finish.

Previewing Your Audio File

To preview an audio file before playing it on the slide, follow the steps below:

- Select the audio file by clicking on it

- Click on the **Play/Pause** button below audio file, and the audio file will begin playing

- **To navigate from anywhere in the audio file, click on the** timeline to the desired place you want.

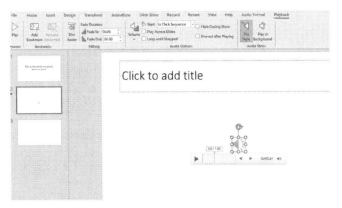

Figure 199: Working with audio

Applying Fade In and Fade Out to Your Audio File

To apply fade in and out to your audio file, follow the steps below:

- The Fade In and Fade Out fields can be found in the **Editing** section of the **Playback tab** after selecting the audio file.

- Enter the values you want in the **Fade In** and **Fade Out** fields or you can use the **Up** and **Down** arrow in the **fade In** and **Fade Out** fields.

Adding Bookmark to Your Audio File

To add a bookmark to your audio file, follow the steps below

- Use the timeline to locate where the bookmark will be added to the audio file

- The **Add Bookmark** command may be found in the **Bookmarks** sub-group of the **Play tab**.

- A circle indicates the bookmark's location in the timeline.

Deleting an Audio File from Your Slide

Slides with embedded audio can be removed by selecting the file, then erasing it with the Delete key.

NOTE: To move the audio file, click and drag it to where you want it to be on the slide

Working with the Audio Options

The Audio options allow you to coordinate how and when the audio file on your slide will be played during the presentation. To locate the **Audio Options** group, go to the **Playback** tab.

The following are the tools available in the **Audio Options** group

- **Volume**: Use this to adjust the volume of the audio in the slide

- **Start**: Use this to determine if the audio file in the slide will play automatically or when you click the mouse.

- **Hide During Show**: This allows you to hide audio icon while displaying your slide show.

- **Play Across Slides**: Playback of the audio file can be spread over numerous slides rather than just the one you're now viewing.

- **Looped until Stopped**: This puts the audio file in repeat mode until you stop it.

- **Rewind after Playing**: This option allows you to take the audio to the beginning after it must have finished playing.

Playing Videos on Your Slides

Apart from inserting audio files on your slides, you can also add videos to make them livelier and more interesting to the audience.

Inserting a Video on Your Slides

To insert videos on your slide, follow the steps below:

- head on to **Insert** tab and press **Video button** in the **Media** group

- In the Video drop-down list, choose any of the below options

  o **Online Video**: Select a given video from YouTube or embed it by pasting the video's URL into Insert dialogue box and clicking on **Insert Video**.

○ **Video on My PC**: Here, go to the **Insert** dialog to identify and select video file, then press click on **Insert**.

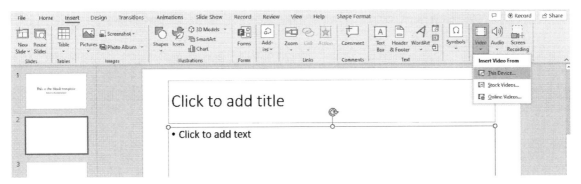

Figure 200: Inserting video

- Finally, the video will display on the slide.

Previewing the Video

To preview a video before playing it on the slide, follow the steps below:

- Select the video by clicking on it

- Click **Play/Pause** button appearing below the video and the video file starts to play

- To navigate from anywhere in the video, click on the timeline to the desired place you want.

Deleting a Video from Your Slide

To delete a video from your slide, click on the video file and press **Delete** or **Backspace**.

NOTE: To move the video file, click and drag it to where you want it to be on the slide

Trimming Your Video

To trim an audio file, follow the steps below:

- To trim a video, you must select it, navigate to the **Playback tab**, and finally use the **Trim Video** command found in the **Editing group**.

- To adjust the beginning and ending times of the clip, use the **green** and **red handles**, respectively, in **Trim Video** dialogue box.

- Utilize the **Play** button to preview the trimmed video file, and press the **Ok** button when you finish.

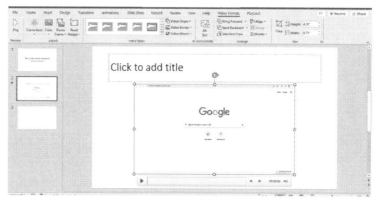

Figure 201: Video elements

Applying Fade In and Fade Out to Your Video File

To apply fade in and out to your video file, follow the steps below:

- Fade in and out fields can be found in the **Editing section** of the **Playback tab** after selecting the video file.

- Enter the values you want in the **Fade In** and **Fade Out** fields or you can use the **Up** and **Down** arrow in the **fade In** and **Fade Out** fields.

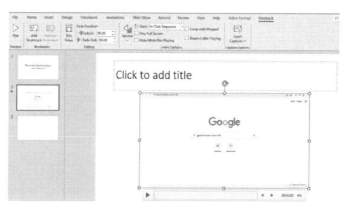

Figure 202: Fade in fade out

Adding Bookmark to Your Video File

To add a bookmark to your video file, follow the steps below

- Use the timeline to locate where the bookmark will be added to the video file

- Navigate to the **Play tab** and select the **Add Bookmark** command from the Bookmark group.

- The bookmark appears like a circle in the timeline.

Working with the Videos Options

The Video options allow you to coordinate how and when the audio file on your slide will be played during the presentation. To locate the **Video Options** group, go to **Playback**.

The following are the tools available in the **Audio Options** group

- **Volume**: Use this to adjust the volume of the video in the slide

- **Start**: Use this to determine if the audio file in the slide will play automatically or when the mouse is clicked on.

- **Play Full Screen**: With this option, your video can occupy the entire screen when it is playing.

- **Hide While Not Playing:** This allows you to hide the video when it is not playing.

- **Looped until Stopped**: This puts the video file in repeat mode until you stop it.

- **Rewind after Playing**: This option allows you to take the audio to the beginning after it must have finished playing.

Modifying the Outlook of Your Video

Just like the pictures, PowerPoint allows you to modify your video's outlook. For example, you can apply or add video styles, borders, shapes, etc.

Creating a Poster Frame

The poster frame is a frame extracted from the video on the slides. The poster frame becomes the first thing the audience will see before the video is played.

To create a poster frame, follow the steps below

- Click on the timeline in your video

- In the **Format** tab above the video, click on Poster Frame and choose **Current Frames**.

- Here, the current frame becomes the poster frame.

NOTE: To use an image from your computer, click on **Image from file.**

To insert a Video on your slide:

1. First, choose the slide you want your video to be.
2. Next, go to the **Insert** ribbon.
3. Next, click the **Video** command in the **Media** group.

Finally, the **Insert Video From** menu box appears.

4. Select an option:

a. Select **This Device** if your video is on your computer. An **Insert Video** dialog box appears.

b. Select **Online Videos** to insert online video. Your default browser opens.

5. If you choose;

a. Select and open the video folder. You can open another location to search for the video from the left menu. Select your video.

b. Browse for your desired video.

6. Click the **Insert** button or double-click on the video.

To Insert an Audio into your presentation:

1. First, select the slide you want your video to be.

2. Next, go to the **Insert** ribbon.

3. Next, click the **Audio** command in the **Media** group.

Finally, the **Insert Audio From** menu box appears.

4. Select an option:

a. Select **Audio on My PC…** if your audio is on your computer. An **Insert Audio** dialog box appears.

b. Select **Record Audio** to record your voice or audio. A dialog box appears.

5. If you choose;

a. Select and open the audio folder. You can open another location from the left menu to search for the audio. Select your audio. Click the **Insert** button or double-click on the video.

b. Click on the red record icon to start recording and press **OK** when done.

Alternatively, you can copy the video or audio wherever it is and paste it into your presentation.

Your audio or video appears on your slide with a control bar containing buttons to play, pause, stop, adjust volume, and so on.

Trimming Audio or Video

PowerPoint has a feature to help you trim your audio or video. You can even purposely insert an audio or video to trim in PowerPoint and resave the file as media.

To trim a video or audio:

1. Choose Audio or Video for your slide. The contextual **Playback** tab is displayed.

2. Select the **Playback** option.

3. Select **Trim Audio** or **Trim Video** in the **Editing** group. A dialog box appears.

4. Select and drag any of the sliders on the bar to the right or left to mark the start and end points. Or,

5. Set the Start and End times in the boxes below.

6. Use the play button to make sure you trim as desired.

7. Click **OK** when done.

Tips: To save your media as stand-alone:

-   Right-click on it then select **Save Media as**. You will see dialog box popping up.

-   Rename as desired, and press **Save**.

54 THE MAGIC OF ANIMATIONS

Transition and Animations are beautiful PowerPoint features that give life to your presentation. Transition is a visual effect that happens when you change from one slide to another during a presentation. On the other hand, the animation is a motion effect that you can apply to the slide objects like text, images, charts, tables, etc. Transition is applied to slides, while an animation is used to slide objects.

ADD TRANSITION TO YOUR SLIDES

To add a transition to your slide:

1. First, select the slide you wish to add the transition.

2. Then, go to **Transitions** tab.

3. Click drop-down arrow within the **Transition to This Slide** gallery to see the list of all the available transition effects.

4. Select your desired transition effect.

Transition Effect Options

For some of the transition effects, there are different effect options to choose from. The available effect options depend on the type of effect you choose.

Figure 203: Transition styles

To change the transition effect options:

1. First, select the slide you have added as a transition.

2. Next, go to the **Transitions** tab in **Transition to This Slide** group.

3. Next, select **Effect Options**. A drop-down list appears.

4. Select your preferred transition effect.

Any transition effect you select will apply to your current slide only. To apply the effect to all slides, click **Apply To All** button in **Timing group**.

Transitions Settings

- **Duration:** All transition effects have their default duration, which might be too fast or slow for you. To set your desired effect duration, click within **Duration** text box, input your value directly, or use up or down arrow.

- **Sound:** It is possible to add a sound effect to the transition in the Sound drop-down button during the presentation. There are some available sounds you can select from. You can also choose any sound from your computer. To choose a sound from your computer, click the **Sound** drop-down button and press **Other Sound.** A dialog box appears. Navigate through your computer to locate the sound, select it, and press **Open.**

- **Trigger:** Slides changes on mouse click during the presentation by default. If you want the slide to change automatically after some set time, uncheck the **On Mouse Click** box, check the **After** box, and put the time in the text box directly, or use the up or down arrows. If you check both boxes, the first occurrence will change the slide, i.e., if you click the mouse before the set time, the slide will change, and if there is no mouse click, the slide will change at the specified time.

Transitions Preview

Anytime you apply a transition to your slide, you can see the effect live on your slide by default. You can always replay the preview with the **Preview** command in the **Transitions** tab.

Animating Text and Object

PowerPoint animations are in 4 categories, namely:

1. **Entrance:** Such animations determine the way an object appears on a slide.

2. **Emphases:** These animations affect an object or text on the slide, usually used to draw attention to the object or text.

3. **Exit:** The animations determine the way an object leaves the slide.

4. **Motion Path:** These animations determine how an object moves around on a slide, e.g., an object can move from left to right.

To add animation to a text or object:

1. First, select text or object you want to animate.

2. Then, go to **Animations** tab.

3. Select your desired animation effect in **Animations** group. Then, use the animation gallery drop-down arrow for more options. For even more options, press the **More --- Effects** at the bottom of the lists.

Figure 204: Animations settings

4. Select your preferred option from the dialog box that appears and simultaneously see the preview on your slide.

5. Press **OK**.

Animation Effect Options

You can choose from different effect options for some of the animation effects. The available effect options depend on type of effect you desire. For example, the default **Fly In** effect option allows the object to fly in from the bottom. You can change this setting from the top.

To change the animation effect options:

    a)   First, select the object you have added an animation.

    b)   Then, in Animation group, navigate to **Animation** tab.

    c)   Next, click on **Effect Options**. A drop-down list appears.

    d)   Select your preferred animation effect.

For more animation effect options, press dialog box launcher in **Animation** group.

Animations Preview

Anytime you apply an animation to your slide, you can see the effect live on your slide by default. You can always replay the preview with the **Preview** command in the Animations tab. Click the Preview drop-down button and uncheck the AutoPreview command to turn off the auto preview.

Tips:

- You can always tell the object that has an animation with a small number that appears on its left-top side, one for each effect. The number indicates the effect position on the mouse click in the slide.

- The slide's thumbnail with an animated object(s) will also have a star icon.

- You can preview a slide animation and transition by clicking the star beside the slide left side thumbnail.

55 COMMON PROBLEMS AND MISTAKES

How to unlock a PowerPoint file with a password (online and offline)? Where does PowerPoint save temporary files to refind them if the file is corrupted? How can it be recovered?

It can happen that you mistakenly close your presentation without saving your last changes; the good news is that PowerPoint has an **autosave** feature that allows you to recover your file with the previous unsaved changes.

To recover your unsaved presentation:

1. Proceed to the backstage view by pressing on **File** tab.

2. Click **Open** tab.

Open pane appears.

3. Click **Recover Unsaved Presentations** button at the bottom of the recently opened presentation list.

Figure 205: Recovering unsaved presentations

There is a list of unsaved presentations in the location dialogue box.

4. Select the likely presentation. You can check the date to know the likely one.

5. Press the **Open** button.

Your presentation opens.

6. Save the presentation accordingly.

Alternatively,

1. Proceed to the backstage view by clicking on **File** tab.

2. Click **Info** tab.

The info pane opens.

3. Choose the **Manage Presentation** drop-down.

4. Click the **Recover Unsaved Presentations** menu that appears.

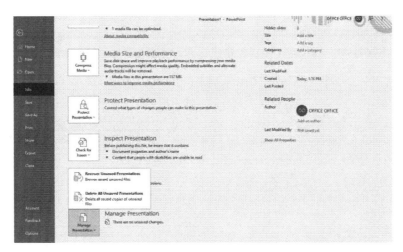

Figure 206: Recovering unsaved presentations alternatives

The location dialog box pops with the list of unsaved presentations.

5. Follow **steps 4-6** above.

56 ERROR CHECKS

One of the essential features in PowerPoint is the Proofing feature. The Proofing feature allows you to avoid or minimize errors while preparing your PowerPoint presentations. In addition, the Proofing feature contains some options that will enable you to punctuate and capitalize the words in your presentation appropriately. Not only that, you get to correct your spelling mistakes even before you make them.

In this session, we will tour how the Proofing feature will help you create a seamless and flawless presentation.

Check Your Spelling as you Prepare your Slides.

One of those mistakes you don't want to make is spelling errors. Guess what? You don't have to finish your presentation before you begin to correct your spelling errors. As you go, the Proofing feature does that for you. The Spell Checker displays any incorrectly spelled word with a wavy red line underneath it. When the wavy red line appears, you can do any of the following.

- Type in the correct words

- Right-click on the word and a menu will show up listing suggested words that match the incorrect phrase.

- You can ignore the missing words and continue with your work.

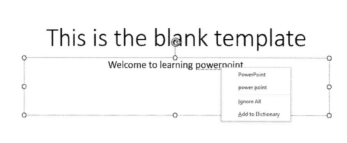

Figure 207: Error checking

Checking Spellings for an Entire Presentation

Rather than correcting spellings one after the other while working, PowerPoint allows you to correct them after you finish. To check the spellings in your presentation, follow the steps provided below:

- First, go to Review tab. Click on Spelling button.

- A spelling pane will pop up on the right-hand of the PowerPoint.

- Here you can choose one of the following options (**Ignore Once, Ignore All, Add, Change, Change All**)

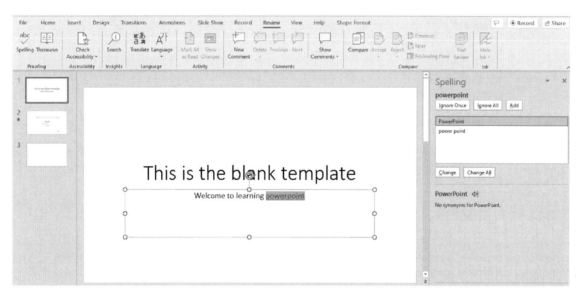

Figure 208: Spell check

Using the Thesaurus

Thesaurus is another feature for proofing in PowerPoint that allows you to check the synonyms and antonyms of words. With Thesaurus, you can locate the correct words for some terms in your PowerPoint.

To use Thesaurus, follow the steps provided below:

- First, select a word, right-click on it and click on **Synonyms.**

- Then, in the contextual menu displayed, click on **Thesaurus**.

- Here, the Thesaurus task pane will pop up on right-hand side of the PowerPoint with a list of related words.

Capitalizing the Correct Way

Capitalizing the correct way is one of the features of PowerPoint. With the Change Case command, you can capitalize the slides the right way. To do this, follow the following steps:

- Select text to capitalize

- Proceed to **Home** tab and click on **Change Case** button

- In the **Change Case** button, you can select any of the following options:

- **Sentence Case**: This option capitalizes first letter in a sentence, and every other word is in lowercase

- **Lowercase**: This option changes all the words to lowercase

- **Capitalize Each Word**: This option capitalizes the first letter of each word in a sentence.

- tOGGLE cASE: This option changes lowercase words to uppercase and vice versa.

Getting Familiar with the AutoCorrect Feature

One of the features you should joke with while proofing your slides is the AutoCorrect feature. The AutoCorrect feature automatically corrects the following while typing.

- Spelling errors

- Styles errors

- Incorrect capitalization of words

To determine how the AutoCorrect feature operates, follow the steps provided below:

- To do this, go to the File menu and then to the Backstage view.

- Click the **Proofing tab** to left side of **Options** dialog box, then press **AutoCorrect Options** button on the right side of the same window.

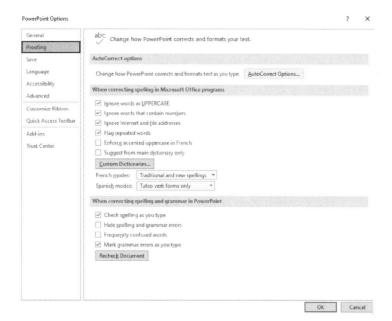

Figure 209: Autocorrect options

When AutoCorrect dialog box pops up, select any or all of the checkboxes as displayed in the image below:

- **Show AutoCorrect Options Buttons**: When selected, AutoCorrect button will appear underneath the revised text.

- **Correct TWo INitial CApitals**: This feature looks for words with two initials and converts the second one to lowercase. For some reason, it disregards words with three beginning letters and assumes this is on design.

- **Capitalize First Letter of Sentence**: This option allows capitalizing the first word of all the sentences in your slides.

- **Capitalize First letter of The Table Cells**: This option allows capitalizing the first letter of the cells in a table.

- **Capitalize Names of Days**: This helps to capitalize the days of the week, such as Monday, Tuesday, etc.

- **Correct Accidental Use of Caps LOCK KEYS**: This option helps to correct every word capitalized backward.

- **Replace Text as You Type**: It is among the major options in the AutoCorrect feature. This option encompasses words that are incorrectly used from time to time and the words used to replace them.

To add your own words, go to the **Replace** text box and enter the term you wish to replace, move to the **With** text box and enter the word to replace the one in the Replace textbox, and then click on **Add**.

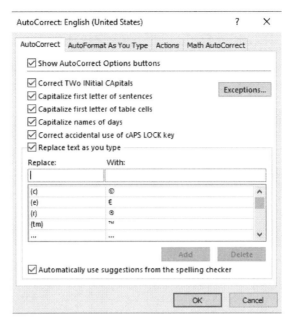

Figure 210: Autocorrect elements

57 PRINT AND EXPORT

You can get a hard or paper copy of your presentation by printing it.

To print your presentation:

1. Ensure you connect your computer to a printer.

2. Ensure you load your printer with the right size paper.

3. Hit the **File** tab to go to the PowerPoint backstage.

4. Select **Print** in the left side pane.

The print pane appears to your right.

5. Input the number of copies you want directly or with the arrows in the **Copies** box.

6. Select a printer in the **Printer** drop-down if you connect your computer to more than one printer.

7. Under **Settings**, each box shows the default settings. To make changes to any, click the drop-down in front of the one you want to change and select your preferred option in the drop-down menu.

- You can print specified slide numbers by inputting the numbers and separated by a comma in the **Slides** textbox.

- Collated style is applicable when you want to print more than one copy of the presentation.

8. Preview your work in the right section of the **Print** pane to see how it will come out. Then, make use of the scroll bar to go through the pages.

9. Click the **Print** button.

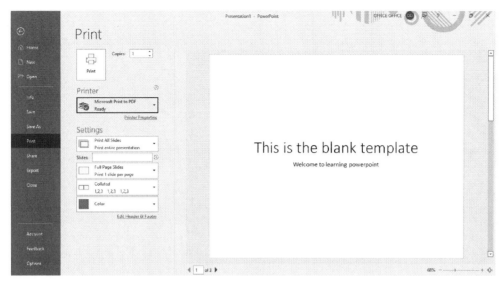

Figure 211: Print options

58 THE IMPORTANCE OF SECURITY

After devoting your time and energy to creating your presentation, it will be necessary if you protect your sensitive presentation from plagiarism, stealing, indeliberate editing, and so many forms of security threats. PowerPoint has impressive security features to help you secure your presentation based on how sensitive the presentation is.

To secure your PowerPoint presentation:

1. First, go to the PowerPoint Backstage by clicking the **File** tab.

2. Next, click the **Info** tab in the left side pane.

The info pane appears on the right side.

3. Finally, click the **Protect Presentation** button.

A dialog box appears.

Figure 212: Protecting your presentation

4. Select an option from the list.

- **Mark as Final:** This makes your presentation read-only (i.e., typing, editing, and proofing capabilities disabled), with a message at the top of the presentation screen informing the reader that the presentation is final. However, any reader can still edit and resave the presentation by clicking the **Edit Anyway** button in the top message. Select this security feature only if you need to notify the reader that it is the recommended final version of your presentation or to discourage editing.

- **Add a Digital Signature:** Protecting your presentation with a digital signature has several benefits, like maintaining proof of presentation integrity, signer identity, and others. However, you must purchase a digital signature from a verified Microsoft partner to use it. Selecting this option for the first time will prompt you to where you can get one.

- **Restrict Access:** This gives people access to your presentation but restricts them from copying, editing, sharing, or printing it. You will have to connect to the Information Right Management (IRM) server to help you secure the presentation. Selecting this option will prompt you to connect and lead you through the process.

- **Restrict Editing:** This is a flexible way of securing your presentation from any editing and giving control over the type of editing that the allowed people can do. This option opens a pane to the right of the presentation for you to set **formatting and editing restrictions** and **start enforcement**.

- **Encrypt with Password:** Adding a password to your presentation is a vital form of protection, and you can give the password to only those you want to provide access to your presentation. Nobody can open your presentation without the password, not to talk about editing. Selecting this option, PowerPoint asks you to enter a password and to re-enter it for confirmation.

- **<u>Always Open Read-Only</u>:** This feature prevents your presentation from accidental editing by always opening it as read-only. A dialog box appears each time you want to open it, notifying you that the presentation will be opened as read-only. Press **Yes** to continue and **No** if there is a need to make changes.

5. Follow all the prompts based on your choice and press ok.

6. Close your presentation for the security setting to take effect.

59 THE STRATEGIC SHORTCUTS

Keyboard Shortcut Commands

Working with Keyboard shortcut commands can reduce your stress, save your time and increase your productivity to a considerable extent. Below are the top shortcut commands you can use to work smartly in PowerPoint.

Shortcut Keys	Functions
Ctrl + A	For selecting all contents of a slide or text placeholder.
Ctrl + B	Make bold the highlighted texts
Ctrl + C	For copying the selected item.
Ctrl + D	For duplicating the active slide.
Ctrl + E	For center aligning the text you select.
Ctrl + F	For opening **Find** dialog box.
Ctrl + G	For grouping selected items
Ctrl + H	For opening **Replace** dialog box.
Ctrl + I	For italicizing highlighted text
Ctrl + J	For justifying (alignment) selected content.
Ctrl + K	For opening **Insert Hyperlink** dialog box.
Ctrl + L	For aligning text to the left.
Ctrl + M	For inserting a new blank slide.
Ctrl + N	For creating a new blank presentation.
Ctrl + O	For opening an existing presentation.

Shortcut Keys	Functions
Ctrl + P	To go to **the Print** tab in backstage view.
Ctrl + Q	For closing your presentation.
Ctrl + R	For aligning your text to the right.
Ctrl + S	Save your presentation.
Ctrl + T	For opening Font dialog box.
Ctrl + U	For underlining the selected text.
Ctrl + V	For pasting what you copied last.
Ctrl + W	For closing your presentation.
Ctrl + X	Cutting selected items.
Ctrl + Y	Redo the last action.
Ctrl + Z	Undo your last activity.
Ctrl + Shift +C	To copy Format
Ctrl + Shift + G	To Ungroup Selected items
Ctrl + Shift + F	For opening Fonts tab of the **Format Cells** dialog box.
Ctrl + Shift + >	For increasing font size of selected text
Ctrl + Shift + <	Decreasing font size of selected text
PgDn	Moving to the next slide.
PgUp	Going to the Previous Page.
Shift + F3	To toggle the selected text cases.
Shift F10	To display the context menu.
Esc	To cancel an active command.
F1	To open Microsoft PowerPoint **Help**
F5	To go to the slideshow view of the presentation

Shortcut Keys	Functions
F7	To open the Spelling checker pane.
Alt + F4	To Exit your presentation
Alt + W + Q	To open the Zoom dialog box.
Alt + Shift + V	For pasting the formatting only to a different Shape.
Alt + Ctrl + Shift + >	Superscript selected item
Alt + Ctrl + Shift + <	Subscript selected item
Alt + F	Going to **File** tab.
Alt + H	To go to **Home** tab.
Alt + N	To go to **Insert** tab.

Shortcut Keys	Functions
Alt + G	To go to **Design** tab.
Alt + T	To go to **Transition** tab.
Alt + A	To go to **Animation** tab.
Alt + S	To go to **Slideshow** tab.
Alt + R	To go to **Review** tab.
Alt+ W	To go to **View** tab.
Alt + Q	To search item

60 CONCLUSION

What have you mastered? Take action by practicing and learning on Microsoft PowerPoint.

MICROSOFT TEAMS

INTRODUCTION

Microsoft Teams launched in September 2016, offering organizations a chat-enabled collaboration service for medium to large teams. Microsoft Teams is designed to enable you to manage and provide easy access to conversations easily. With the integration of Office 365 Groups, Microsoft Teams can be an option for company-wide communications and collaboration on any number of channels, from a team chat room to a single-user channel. Learn how Microsoft Teams can enhance your productivity by giving employees the tools they need to communicate more easily and collaborate more efficiently. Microsoft Teams is a proprietary business communication platform, belonging to the Microsoft 365 family of products. Its features include workspace chat, file storage, video conferencing, and application integration. While it can be confusing initially, the software has many advantages and is an excellent choice for most businesses.

1.1 What is Microsoft Teams?

Microsoft Teams is a collaboration and communications tool available as a stand-alone app or as part of a bundle. It offers several features, including chat, video conferencing, and file sharing. It also lets users create a shared background and avatar. In addition, Microsoft Teams includes reports and analytics that help users track usage statistics.

Microsoft Teams is part of Microsoft 365, which includes other productivity tools, like Outlook, and comes with security features. It costs $5 per user per month. It supports up to 10,000 participants. It also offers integrations with popular third-party apps like Trello, Asana, and Zoom.

Adoption is key to Microsoft Teams' success. Once a team has accepted the new features and processes, real results can be achieved. But it's crucial to remember that a company cannot expect all employees to switch overnight. Therefore, it's essential to consider any potential issues that might arise as the new software is adopted.

Teams features include built-in online meetings and audio/video conferencing. Meetings can last up to 60 minutes. Teams also offers unlimited storage for personal files. Users can also integrate Office apps with the service. Developers can also build custom apps for Teams. Microsoft has also partnered with hardware vendors to provide video conferencing hardware.

Microsoft Teams integrates with all of Microsoft's other apps and services. For example, you can create files right in Teams channels. You can also work with team SharePoint sites through Teams. In addition, Teams is tightly integrated with Microsoft Power Apps, which allows you to create and share low-code apps. The platform can also help you organize your conversations by letting you create and manage conversations in channels.

1.2 Basic algorithm work of Microsoft Teams

We refer to Microsoft Teams as a team collaboration platform offering a variety of features. These features are divided into different user groups. Each group has its purpose and has its preferences. Understanding how these user groups interact with the platform is crucial to creating a successful collaboration experience. Here are a few things you should know.

Microsoft Teams has two different network protocols, UDP and TCP. UDP has a higher MOS score and is less likely to have a high down count. Both protocols can be affected by low bandwidth. Therefore, choosing the proper network protocol for your specific needs is crucial.

1.3 Where can you buy it or download

Microsoft Teams is a collaborative messaging software you can use to communicate with other team members. The program is available for desktops and mobile devices and is compatible with most App Stores. A free trial is an excellent option if you're unsure whether you want to buy a license.

Microsoft Teams is a versatile messaging app that organizes tasks and initiates team conversations. It also offers features such as video conferencing and shared workspaces to help you collaborate with coworkers and clients from any location. You can also perform collaborative tasks like sharing files, hosting meetings, and setting up tasks in real-time.

You can download the Teams app from the Microsoft Store. It is available for Windows 10 and 11. Although you can download the Teams app from the Microsoft Store, it will not be included in the Office 365 bundle.

Microsoft Teams is a collaborative workspace for Windows computers. It syncs data across platforms so you can use it on a desktop, mobile, or tablet. It also integrates with Office 365 and OneNote to make it easier for you to work with others. So if you're considering using the program to improve your business, it's worth trying.

Microsoft Teams offers essential features, including video conferencing, file sharing, and chatting. It also has tools for sharing ideas, assigning tasks, and moving projects off a whiteboard. In addition, you can sync Microsoft Teams with your Exchange calendar, so it will automatically show up in Outlook.

1.4   How do we get MS Teams free?

It is possible to access the Teams interface minus subscribing to the Microsoft 365 plan. The only disadvantage is that the free version of the Microsoft Team is not packed with many of the benefits of the premium versions – but you will still get some basic features you can relate with. Intimate yourself with the steps below to get access to a free version of the Team interface;

- Navigate to your favorite browsing apps (preferably Chromes) on your computer, and type https://www.microsoft.com/en-us/microsoft-teams/free.

- Once the address has loaded, tap the ***sign up for free button***

- You will be prompted to enter your e-mail address. You can sign in with the Microsoft account you had previously created or even create a new account entirely. Verification will be required if you are utilizing Microsoft service for the first time. To verify your mail, enter the code sent to your mail into the box provided.

- After the Account verification and you have successfully signed in to your Microsoft account, you either download Teams app using your PC or to start using it via the web.

- Tap the web-based option if you are interested in using the web-based version of Teams. On tapping, you will be taken to Teams web portal (https://teams.microsoft.com).

- The "how to invite people to Teams" page will be displayed next. Select "got it" and you then have access to Teams workspace. A congratulatory message will pop up, welcoming you into the Teams world.

1.5   Getting Teams through the Microsoft 365

Signing up to your preferred Microsoft 365 business plan automatically gets Microsoft Teams included. Users can still enjoy a free version of Microsoft 365 without using their money to subscribe, but it does not come with the Microsoft Team. Let us take a look at how you can get access for free.

- Navigate to your preferred web browser from your desktop, and visit https://www.office .com/.

- Tap the "Get office icon."

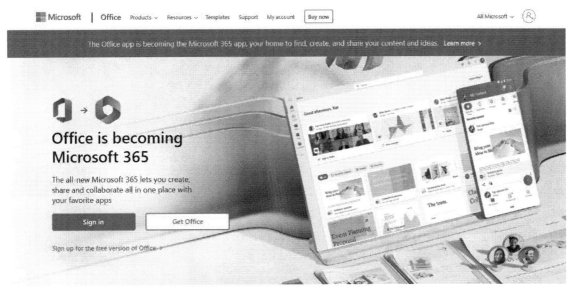

Figure 213: Welcome to Office

- Once you tap the "get office icon" you will be redirected to https://www.microsoft.com/en-us/microsoft-365/buy/compare-all-microsoft-365-products?tab=1&rtc=1, where you can compare between existing Microsoft plans. There are two tabs; ***Home plan and business plan***.

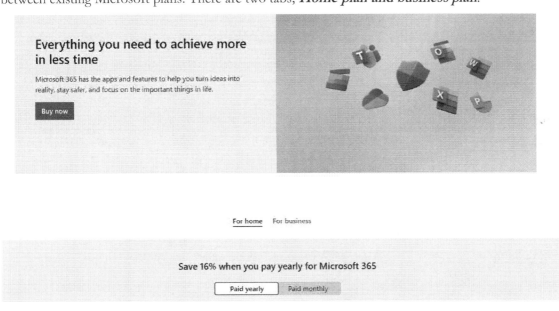

Figure 214: Find the right solution for you

- Select "***For business***" tab to get started and choose your plans.

- When you click the "***For business***" *tab*, you can choose between the four available plans. The business basic also features Microsoft Teams.

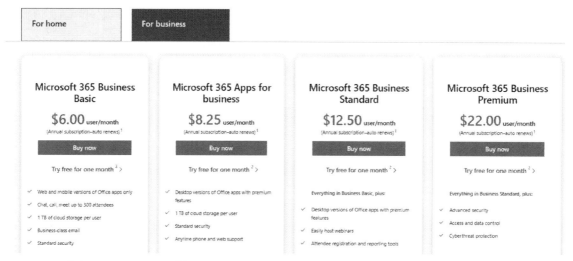

Figure 215: For Business Packages

- Navigate the page to the bottom and select **_"Try free for one month"_** as an option of the Microsoft 365 business basic or any other plan that suits you.

- A page where you will be required to answer some basic questions and provide some information will be prompted.

- Provide each piece of information carefully, and the last step will get you set for your selected plan.

- Immediately after you provide all the information, your free trial will be ready, and you can tap on the **_"Get started icon"_** to continue.

1.6 Where can you use it?

You can use Microsoft Teams to collaborate with your coworkers. To start using it, you must sign in to the Microsoft account. To sign in, visit Microsoft's Teams website and click sign-in button. Select appropriate username and choose if you want to use Teams for business purposes. You must also agree to Terms of Service and Privacy Policy.

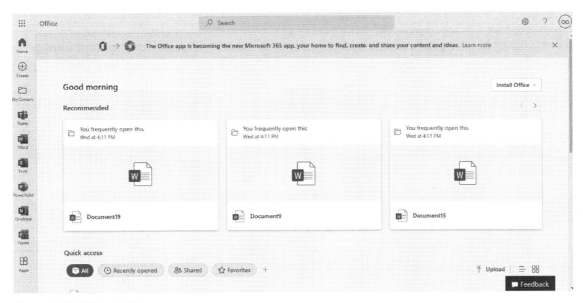

Figure 216: Office Online

Microsoft Teams also lets you invite people to join a meeting. You can send out invites to people using a shareable link, your e-mail contact list, or a direct e-mail. If you're using the web version, you'll need to allow permission for people to join the meeting. Once they're in, they'll receive notifications. They'll also be prompted to provide their camera and microphone access.

Microsoft Teams also lets you share documents and media with others. You can also screen share, whiteboard, or breakout into virtual rooms. It also supports enterprise security and compliance. The app also includes a default document library folder. If you're using the app for business purposes, you should set permissions to restrict access to sensitive information.

Microsoft Teams is integrated into Windows 365 and Azure Virtual Desktop. It has many business benefits and integrates with popular desktop and mobile devices. It is also compatible with many third-party meeting room devices. Microsoft has also integrated Teams with HoloLens, a headset that lets you see experts in real-time.

Microsoft Teams is a productivity application that integrates apps and tools in one place. It enables collaboration with others on projects and improves productivity and efficiency. The app also integrates information from Microsoft Outlook and SharePoint lists into the workspace. It also allows you to schedule meetings, video chats, and file sharing with colleagues and friends. The service is compatible with multiple operating systems, and you can install it on your computer, tablet, or mobile device.

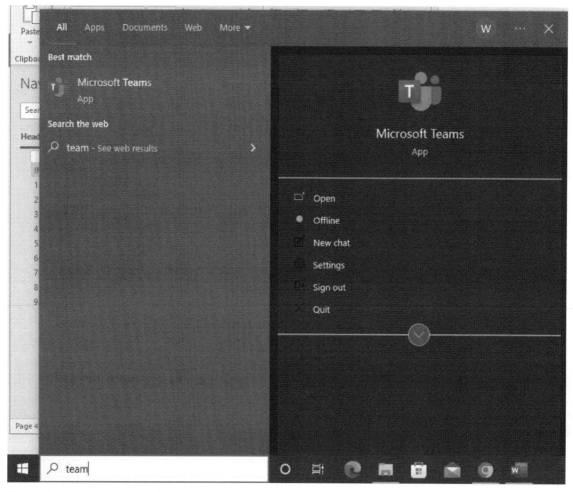

Figure 217: Accessing MS Teams

1.7 MS Teams extension and where to download them

Many useful extensions are available whether you're using MS Teams for teamwork or as an enterprise tool. Bonusly, for example, makes it easy to express appreciation to coworkers. With its easy-to-use interface, you can grant colleagues a bonus, review their performance, and see the latest achievements. Another helpful extension is Tactiq, which lets you take screenshots during meetings and export transcripts. This extension connects with your Microsoft Teams account and displays the meeting transcript in real-time. You can also take notes on sentences in the meeting and save them later for future reference.

Microsoft Teams users can also use Polly, which allows them to create surveys using Microsoft Teams. Polly helps you to collect opinions from your team and votes on questions quickly and easily. To use this extension, add the question and answers you want to ask and mention the @polly in the chat.

2 MICROSOFT TEAMS COMPARISONS

You're probably curious about how these tools compare if you're comparing Microsoft Teams with Slack, Skype, or Google Meet. These comparisons will give you an idea of what you can expect from each application. But before you choose a platform, you should know that these products don't have the same features.

2.1 Microsoft Teams vs. Slack

Microsoft Teams is a chat-based workspace available in Office 365 and is an excellent choice for large organizations. It integrates Skype and other services and includes private group chats. Slack, however, focuses on bringing all team communication into one place. While Teams is more complex to setup, it does offer some advanced features that other messaging apps don't. For example, it allows users to change the font color and add bullet points to their messages.

Microsoft Teams and Slack offer many features that make them useful for large enterprises. For example, Slack offers video conferencing but can only support up to 25 users simultaneously. Unlike Slack, however, Microsoft Teams offers screen sharing on all plans, including free. In addition, Teams supports live events and captioning of videos.

Teams and Slack are great options for small businesses, but the two have some differences. Microsoft Teams has more features and is cheaper. It also offers more options, including unlimited message history. Teams also allows teams to screen-share and can be more flexible for teams that don't use Microsoft 365.

Microsoft Teams is the market leader for collaboration. Both tools have a good user experience and advanced security and compliance features. Microsoft Teams is also GDPR and DLP-compliant.

2.2 Microsoft Teams vs. Skype

While Microsoft Teams is not a direct replacement for Skype for Business Online, it provides several features that make video chat and phone calls easier. In addition, teams bring together various tools such as chat, calls, file sharing, and third-party apps into one seamless experience. As a result, Teams meet the diverse communication needs of distributed workplaces.

Teams is a powerful communication tool that integrates with dozens of third-party apps. It is also customizable and can be used for collaboration. For instance, you can embed games and other applications into your workflow. However, Skype doesn't support such integrations. For business use, Teams has more business-oriented features.

Microsoft Teams is designed to foster collaboration. On the other hand, Skype for business was originally intended to be a communications platform. Collaboration features were added almost as an afterthought. Microsoft Teams enables meetings with up to 250 participants. It also has advanced video conferencing capabilities. Additionally, you can share your desktop, screen, and single applications with team members. You can also use advanced features such as transcription and translation.

Teams offers more features than Skype. It has a more intuitive interface and supports more collaboration. Teams also have a more robust search feature and bookmarks. It also supports Microsoft Cloud architecture, which ensures excellent security, zero downtime, and customizable data governance policies.

2.3 Microsoft Teams vs. Google Meet

One of the biggest differences between Microsoft Teams and Google Meet is that Teams runs in a Microsoft 365 environment. As a result, your team can collaborate on files, presentations, and other items. On the other hand, Google Meet lets you share your entire screen, browser tabs, and individual files. In addition, Google Meet is a browser-based service that is much easier to use than Microsoft Teams.

Another significant difference between Google Meet and Microsoft Teams is that Google Meet allows you to keep a live video feed on screen while presenting. In contrast, Microsoft Teams will enable you to disable it. Google Meet also lets you customize your background and connection quality. Despite the differences, each platform offers plenty of features to boost collaboration.

Google Meet has a more streamlined interface and fewer buttons. The two programs also share similar video-conferencing features. Google Meet also offers a variety of integrations, including integrations with Microsoft Office, Gmail, and Zapier. You can also dial into a meeting via phone.

Google Meet is free for small businesses and individuals, but it's also available to anyone with a Google account. It allows you to have 24-hour 1:1 calls and 1-hour-long group meetings with three or more users. You might want to consider Zoom if you're not a business user. Microsoft Teams is a better choice for large teams.

3 SOFTWARE INTERFACE AND USE

3.1 Screen sharing in Microsoft teams

Regular screen sharing involves showing presentations or participants via a process or tool. All partakers, except unconfirmed guests, are in a position to share the screen. Unconfirmed guests will be offered a number and should wait in the lobby until the organizer grants them access.

Begin sharing the screen

Screen sharing can happen in a conversation, meeting, or call.

- Click screen share icon during a call, meeting, or chat.

- You may choose to share:

The entire desktop

Only one screen/window

Whiteboard

A PowerPoint presentation

3.2 Scheduling a Meeting

Scheduling a meeting in Microsoft Teams is a straight forward process. To schedule a meeting:

1. First, you need to click on the purple "Schedule a Meeting" button.

2. Next, create a title for the meeting and enter all relevant information.

Note - If you don't specify the location of the meeting, it will be displayed as a Microsoft Teams meeting, so you may choose to leave the location field blank.

3. The next thing you want to do is invite your attendees, and to do this, enter their names into the "Invite People" section.

Note – You can find the scheduling assistant very useful here, as you can use it to see if the individual you're inviting is available for the meeting.

4. Finally, Click "Schedule."

5. You will see a pop-up with the details of the meeting you just scheduled. From the pop-up, you can join the meeting, cancel the meeting, and chat with participants (this will open a separate chat window). You can also edit the meeting information, close the window, and return to Microsoft Teams.

3.3 Joining a Meeting

Joining a Teams meeting is a straight forward process. You can decide to join the meeting via your Outlook calendar or your "Meeting" tab on Teams. If you are joining from the Outlook Calendar, just click on the link "Join Microsoft Teams meeting," or if enabled, dial the toll-free or local number and type in your given conference ID number when requested.

If you are joining the meeting directly from Teams, locate your "Meetings" tab, click on the meeting, and finally, click the "Join" tab at the top-right corner of your screen.

3.4 Share and control the screen

To share the screen with other participants in the first call, click Share screen button located towards the bottom and select the screen you want to display in the group. By doing this, other users will see and follow the screen without having to leave the video call.

Other users can control your screen if they get permission. You can let other participants control the screen by selecting their names in the bar at the top of the call.

3.5 User Availability (Status)

Before you call someone, it is possible to check if they are available, away, busy, or do not disturb mode. On the Calls tab, you notice a colored circle next to the profile picture of the person. The color is a representation of their current state.

If you call a member who cannot answer the call while busy, you may choose to notify them when their status comes to On. Remember that availability does not necessarily mean that they can call you. Other tasks may need their attention, though such an announcement can be a temporary guide to the best time to contact individuals.

- Click the person's icon/profile picture you wish to monitor on your status screen.
- A pop-up window will appear with more information about the contacts. Click on the chat icon. The private conversation opens.
- On the screen's left side, you will notice a list of used conversations. Right-click or click the ellipse button on the desired person's name.
- Click report when available. Whenever available, you will note a pop-up appearing on the screen.

Monitor their status

- You should right-click (or click the ellipse button) the person's name on the chat screen.
- Click Disable Notifications.

3.6 How to React to chat messages

It is possible to react to someone's message without responding. You may use an emoji like thumbs up, surprise emoji and more.

To do so, hover the mouse over the message or you may select the ellipsis against the message to see the reaction options. You then choose the appropriate reaction you desire.

The more people react to a message with same emoji, the number of such reaction increases. Reactions can be significant in recognizing a message without typing out a reply.

Once you are comfortable with the Interface and the capabilities, using Teams and navigating around it is relatively straightforward.

- Toolbar- On the left side, we have the toolbar, which has a variety of functions. In addition, we have:

- *Activity*-It demonstrates every single item of your areas of interest as well as what you must be aware of that has taken place.
- *Chats*-It gives you the ability to send messages to your fellow contemporaries. You can select specific individuals or a number of them to start a conversation.
- *Teams*- You can construct channels here and check out the different groups you're a part of.
- *Meetings*- Here, you can launch a session and immediately continue to schedule a meeting.
- *Calls*-Here, you can easily make calls directly from your contact list.
- *Files*-You can share data and upload files to the 'OneDrive'cloud.
- *[...]*- The three dots enable you to add more functions from the toolbar. For example, you can extend Microsoft Teams depending on your requirements.
- *Apps*- here, you will obtain additional applications for your Teams.
- *Help*- Help provides more information about the operation of the Teams application.
- *The Channel Bar* -the channel bar provides you with more possibilities whenever you've chosen one of the tools for use. Additionally, it facilitates the organization of conversations when making use of the Meeting tool.

- Command/Search Box -the command box is at the very top of the application. You can use it to locate contacts and perform actions quickly at the beginning of an application when you input a slash "/."

- The Tabs-The tabs enable you to navigate between Team pages more efficiently. Additionally, you can add a tab using the + sign.

- The Conversation box -outlines your online interactions and talks with different individuals and organizations.

- Chatbox - using this will allow you to perform text-based communication within Teams.

4 TEAMS AND CHANNELS

Create a New Team

Follow the steps below when you need to create a new team.

- Open MS Teams software.

- Select Teams icon located to the left file tab.

- Click "Join or Create a Team" link. Consider the goals for the new team. Put in mind what the leaders for the new team intend to achieve, if you already had another team with similar goals. Are members same as those for the previous team or there are new ones?

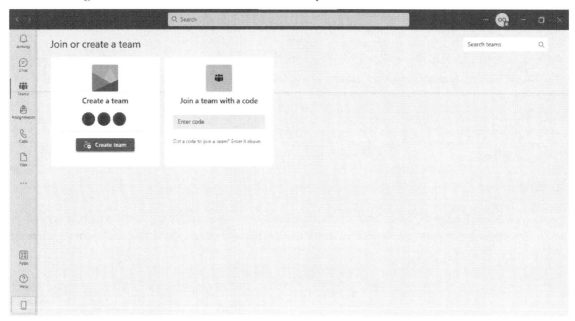

Figure 218: Create a Team

Decide the kind of team to set up.

- Private: Members will seek permission to join the team.

- Public: Anyone can join this team. It is open to everyone.

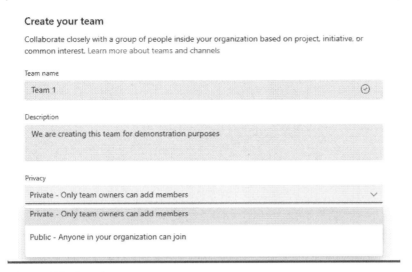

Figure 219: Creating your team

Type the name and summary of your new team, and then press Build. Teams will take a few moments to do their job by building a new team for you. Once done, your new team shows up in your list of teams to the left file tab. Note that when a new team is formed, a channel named General is created instantly.

4.1 How to Invite People to Your Team

- Create your new team.

- Choose the private or public privacy type of the group. You will get a dialogue box giving you an opportunity to welcome people to join once the team has been set up.

- In the search box, type the names of the people to add to your team. Your search feature immediately scans and populates a text box depending what you type. The results happens in real time as you type.

- Once the right person appears in the list, select the individual's name before selecting Add.

- Add as more members to the team as you wish.

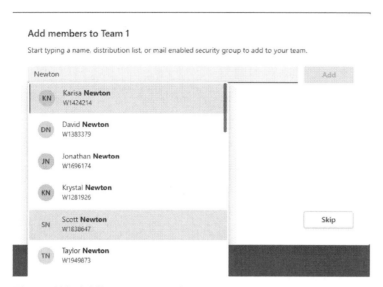

Figure 220: Adding team members

All invited users will get a notification about their team membership.

Follow these steps when you wish to invite individuals to a public or private team once it is already created:

- To see a summary of your teams, click the Teams symbol in the left file tab.

- Tap the ellipse beside the team name you want to ask somebody to join. It will open a drop-down menu with some options.

- Choose Add Member from the drop-down menu that shows. Next, the Add Members dialogue box should appear.

- In the text box, simply type names of people you wish to add to the team.

- Once you find the right person, click the names of the people and Add. The users will be notified depending on how alerts have been set up.

4.2 Creating a New Channel

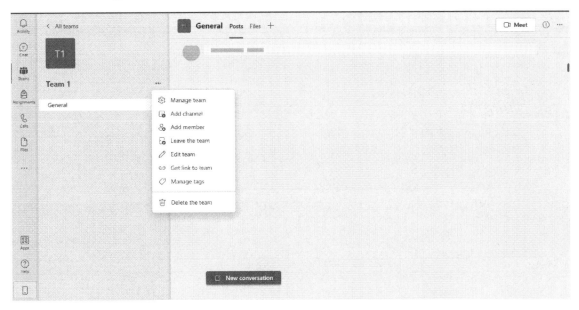

Figure 221: Adding a Channel

At the heart of a team are channels. Teamwork and communication happens inside channels. Channels sit inside a team; therefore, a team is made up of one or more channels. A channel acts as a single place where team members can share messages, files and tools.

- You can organize a channel depending the project, group or relevancy.

- It is possible to make changes on how they get the notifications from a channel.

- Threads are good for side conversations that focused & organized within given channels.

Every team begins with the default "**General**" channel. Such is there to discuss general topics related to the purpose of the team. You can have a wiki page as a general landing page for your team. For each other topic, i.e., project, task, etc. create a new channel.

The best approach is to bundle all related content in one place – under a channel. There is a limit of 200 channels per team – currently, including deleted channels.

4.3 Create a channel

1. You Click the **ellipses** icon for more options to the right of the team in question in the "**Teams**" pane.

2. You Click the "**Add channel**" option in the pop-out menu to create a channel.

3. You Enter text in the "**Channel name**", "**Description (optional)**" fields, Select from the "**Privacy**" drop-down field and check the "**Automatically show this channel in everyone's channel list**" tick box.

Lastly, you Click the "**Add**" button at the bottom to complete the channel creation on the "Create a channel for '[team name]' team" screen.

Note: *You can always "**Edit this channel**" and change the "Channel name" and the "Description" text box fields, and the "Automatically show this channel in everyone's channel list" tick box.*

*You cannot change the "**Privacy**" field after the channel has been created. You will need to create a new channel with new privacy settings.*

4. You will see your channel's landing page on the larger right pane of the TEAMS App window as illustrated below in Figure 42. The new channel also has the name of the team member who created it followed by the phrase "**[Full Name] set this channel to be automatically shown in the channels list**" from the Selection previously made when creating the team.

5. You Click the **ellipses** icon to the right of your channel and Select the "**Hide**" option from the pop-out menu to hide your team.

6. You Click the "**# hidden channel**" link (in the "Teams" pane) to view the hidden channel(s). This can easily be missed.

7. You Click the "**Show**" option to the right of the channel in question to show that channel.

Tip: *Once your channel has been hidden, the text formatting of that channel will change to italic text. When you Click away from your channel, it will be hidden under the link something like "**# hidden channel**".*

8. You Hold down the left mouse button and move the team in question up or down in the "Teams" pane. Figure 45 below illustrates the "**Communications**" team dragged from bottom to top of "**Your teams**".

Note: *When it comes to ordering your channels; you should practice naming your channels with a number prefix. Renaming a channel retrospectively however does not rename the SharePoint Online folder – you will have to rename the folder on your SharePoint site also.*

Tip: *You should create a channel only if it is required (as you would when you create a team). This means that you create a channel when there is a requirement for it or that you have use for it.*

9. You Create a Private channel as you would anyone channel, except for the "**Privacy**" drop-down field, you Select the "**Private – Accessible only to a specific group of people within the team**" option. You Click the "Add" button at the bottom to finish creating the private channel where the new channel will have a padlock icon to the right of that channel's name.

4.4 CALENDAR

The Calendar function is one of the many tools included in Microsoft Teams. These tools help in boosting productivity and improving communication amongst staff members. It is possible for team members to schedule meetings directly within the Microsoft Teams app, specify the meeting's details, and add other team members so that they are not only informed of the event but also have it added to their synced Microsoft Teams calendar. The shared calendar within Microsoft Teams facilitates this.

How the Microsoft Teams Calendars Function

Microsoft Teams is a collaboration tool that is designed for companies or groups, and as a result, it is organized with a group, or team, as its primary point of emphasis. You sign into MS Teams group using your email address, but in most cases you may not. You will use the enterprise email address provided for you to access Teams as well as any other Microsoft 365 apps or services relevant to you. Additionally, the MS Teams app includes only one primary calendar shared among all the team members. Group affiliates may add events or meetings to this calendar. Such additions will immediately appear on other group members' calendars. If you expect a person to attend an event or forum on the calendar, you can add them to the event or meeting.

The Step-by-Step Guide to Creating an Event on the Shared Calendar for Microsoft Teams

In this section, we'll go through the steps to take when creating an event known as a meeting in MS Teams.

Please follow the instructions below to create a shared calendar event in Microsoft Teams.

1. Launch the Microsoft Teams software.
2. Click the Calendar option.
3. Select the "New meeting" option from the menu.
4. Use the drop-down option at the top of your page to select appropriate time zone for your location.

NOTE: You do not need to be concerned about your team members' different time zones because the start time of your meeting will automatically adjust depending on their time zones.

5. Give your meeting a name in the "Add title" section.
6. Put the names of the people whose attention you would like to draw to the upcoming event in the section labeled "Add required attendees."

You can share this calendar event with other individuals who are not members of your MS Teams group or who may not even use MS Teams at all by typing their complete email addresses in place of their name.

By selecting 'Optional,' you can add group members you wish to inform about the meeting but must not necessarily attend.

After setting up the meeting, each of the invited parties will receive an invitation at the email address associated with their account.

7. The next step is to determine when the meeting will begin and end.

8. If the meeting is to occur on a regular basis, proceed by clicking on the option that says "Does not repeat" to access the menu and select the options that best fit your needs to turn the meeting into a recurring event. Choose the "does not repeat" option if you don't want the meeting to happen again in the near future.

9. If you want to restrict the meeting to a specific channel, click Add channel button to pick the channel you want to use. You might, for instance, wish to make it in a manager's channel to ensure only the team members subscribed to the channel are aware that there is a planned meeting.

10. The next field is the one where you add the location. In spite of its name "Location Selection," this does not actually involve choosing a physical location. It helps in selecting a room system enabled with Microsoft Teams and linked to the internet.

11. In the meeting field, located towards the bottom of your screen, enter the relevant information about the meeting.

12. When you are through, click the 'Send' button to add event to the calendar for MS Teams and invite the people added to the team.

5 COMMUNICATE VIA CHAT AND VIDEO CHAT OUTSIDE YOUR ORGANIZATION

5.1 Chatting With External Users and Guests

In a typical organization, an external user is a partner or a customer with whom you must communicate or collaborate. In Microsoft Teams, there are two types of external users: federated users and guests. The first category refers to users from another domain trusted by your organization. The second refers to users added as guests to your organization's Active Directory using their (personal or professional) e-mail addresses. You can chat with an external user or a guest like you chat with a colleague.

Your administrator must turn on external access, so you can call, chat, and schedule meetings with external (federated) users. Unlike guests, federated users do not have access to teams and channel resources and cannot be added to a group chat. For more details on what external and guest users can and cannot do, visit Microsoft's website at: https://docs.microsoft.com/en-us/microsoftteams/communicate-with-users-from-other-organizations.

6 THE BEST TEAMS APP

Apps in MS TEAMS are small applications or tools you use to do your job or complete a task. That is communicating and keeping in touch with your colleagues, teammates, or guests outside your organization – keep track of your work or tasks, add-ons to existing apps that add a new feature, and over-added value.

AttendanceBot is a Microsoft Teams App for managing staff timesheets, sick days, paid time off, and vacations. Its simple clock-in and clock-out messages allow you to keep track of employee time within Microsoft team meetings. It also exports timesheets, enabling you to monitor time spent on particular clients. You can then view the data on a dashboard.

6.1 Popular apps from third-party companies

If you're looking for ways to maximize your Teams productivity, you should consider downloading one of the many MS Teams apps. These tools allow you to organize and share your workspace with your entire team, and some of them are even free. Some of these applications are management-related, while others are simply for personal use. For instance, attendance bots like AttendanceBot let you track the hours that your team members work. They're easy to set up and require no technical knowledge. Another great integration is with YouTube. You can search for and share videos using the Teams app. It's easy to create a playlist, add a link, and share the results. You can also pin the videos to your team channel tab for easy reference. These apps can even help you keep track of staff training videos. If you're looking for a new way to get the most out of your Microsoft Teams experience, consider one of these third-party apps.

Another useful tool is Remind. Remind allows you to set reminders from groups, channels, and personal messages. The interface is very easy to use, and you can set up recurring reminders and snooze alerts.

6.2 Freshdesk and Zendesk

Both Freshdesk (https://freshdesk.com/) and Zendesk (www.zendesk.com) have a variety of features and functions to improve customer service. They both have a comprehensive support page with a knowledge base, FAQ repository, and training videos. They both feature a quick-search bar, which is useful in locating specific information quickly. Freshdesk also lists an 800 number for last-minute support needs.

While both services offer basic ticket management features, Zendesk is more flexible with features such as view-based organization, custom conditions, filtering, and grouping tickets. Zendesk also offers pre-built dashboards that display business data in a clean and simple manner. In addition to ticket management, both services offer tools to manage people and collaborate in real-time.

Zendesk is more enterprise-friendly, however, and provides enterprise-grade support and a dedicated customer success team. However, it is important to note that both services have limited phone and live chat features.

Both have a Teams app that lets you get notified of the tickets delegated to you and your team.

6.3 Asana and Trello

Trello (https://trello.com/) and Asana (https://asana.com/) are the best Microsoft Teams apps to use when you need to collaborate on projects. They are easy to use and provide a great user experience. Users can create project templates and color-code tasks. Both tools help teams visualize project status and track progress.

Both Trello and Asana offer a free subscription. Trello is easier to use than Asana and is more visually oriented. Projects in Trello resemble a bulletin board with virtual cards that represent tasks. When a user clicks on a card, they can see information about the task, including the due date, checklist, and comments. Trello also allows you to drag and drop tasks and even customize the background to make them more personal.

Trello and Asana give team members a clear view of all project tasks. Teams can create all-team discussions and announcements and manage their projects in one place. Both apps make it easy to create and manage teams. Users can even create teams based on criteria, job roles, and more. Asana also allows you to collaborate with guest users and share your calendar.

6.4 Dropbox and Google Drive

Dropbox and Google Drive are both cloud storage services. Both of them offer similar functionality but differ in their user experience. Dropbox is more intuitive, and it has a desktop-like directory structure. You can access all your files from your desktop, and the file system is accessed quickly. Dropbox is a good option for people who work with large files, while Google is better for those who need access to documents from different locations.

Dropbox is a good choice for marketing workflows because it supports a variety of file types and features. For instance, Dropbox allows you to write content, review files, add comments, and deliver the final product to clients. It also allows you to easily store and share documents. It's also a good choice for content collaboration in Google Cloud, as it supports rich media and makes it easier to share content.

Dropbox is also great for collaboration, which is essential in today's remote-working world. If you need to access files from different locations, you can easily switch between desktop and mobile using your Dropbox account. Dropbox is also compatible with Microsoft Teams' mobile app, which allows you to collaborate with colleagues without leaving your office.

6.5 Twitter

You will keep up to date with Twitter (https:/twitter.com) without anyone ever leaving Teams when you enable the Microsoft Teams Twitter app. When you install the Twitter app, you'll get a channel connection to get tweets and follow hashtags on Twitter.

Another Twitter alternative is MailClark. This app acts as a shared inbox for messages sent to and from Microsoft Teams. This is useful for many different purposes, including customer support, marketing, recruitment, and sales. While Twitter is a popular social media site, it may not be the best choice for every company.

Adding Twitter to Microsoft Teams is easy. You can use the social networking site to share company updates and employee accomplishments. You can also add third-party Twitter apps to extend Microsoft Teams' features.

6.6 Salesforce

If you're looking for a way to seamlessly integrate Salesforce (www.salesforce.com) with Microsoft Teams, you've come to the right place.

Salesforce and Teams can be integrated to track and collaborate on opportunities. Opportunity feeds let team members view details of deals, players, and potential sales. Customer Support channels store contact information, and Salesforce integration allows team members to quickly collaborate with customers and respond to any issues. Similarly, Microsoft Teams and Salesforce can be integrated with a variety of other applications, including Microsoft Planner.

Microsoft and Salesforce both have loftier ambitions for their collaboration products. Both are trying to be the de facto collaboration platform for enterprises. However, each company has different goals for its customers. Salesforce has an enterprise-grade focus on quick messaging, while Microsoft focuses more on systems that can support the bulk of daily work. Application providers are also building productivity features into their own products, which challenges Salesforce's vision for the future of the collaboration market.

6.7 Kronos

Kronos (www.kronos.com) is a business collaboration software that helps organizations manage their team members. It provides real-time alerts, centralized policy management, and staffing forecasts through advanced optimization algorithms. It also includes self-service capabilities for employees, including instant access to project lists. This is a great choice for organizations of all sizes, including small and medium businesses.

The main feature of this Microsoft Teams app is that it is fully integrated with the Microsoft Teams platform. It helps teams keep track of upcoming meetings and allows participants to add notes, assign presenters, and set objectives. Users can also share agendas and vote, and the app syncs with Microsoft Planner. This makes it ideal for teams that meet on a regular basis.

Kronos has a variety of business-specific solutions for time and attendance management. It integrates with existing time clock systems, as well as mobile apps. It also offers a time-off management system and a physical time clock. Kronos' InTouch time-clocks feature a 7-inch touchscreen that allows employees to punch in and out with a swipe of their badge. Employees can also view their schedules and request time off, and review their work schedules.

6.8 GitHub

The GitHub app for Microsoft Teams recently entered the public preview phase. The app offers new features, including subscriptions and comment threading, that make it easier to collaborate on coding projects. According to the company's blog post, the app will help developers manage and coordinate coding projects without leaving Teams. It also includes a subscription feature, which lets you set notifications for pending pull requests, issues, and commits.

The GitHub app for Microsoft Teams connects with the two most important work spaces: GitHub and Microsoft Teams. This makes it easier to collaborate and monitor work. The app also includes a threading feature, which groups all pull requests and issues under a single primary card, displaying the latest status and meta-data. You can also create, close, and reopen issues with the GitHub app. It also sends push notifications to help you stay updated.

Another great feature of GitHub is its ability to connect with other apps. It is a popular source-code repository that gives developers access to tools to build better software. With GitHub and Microsoft Teams, developers can collaborate on code, chat, and share files easily. This means that they can get their work done more quickly and efficiently.

6.9 Connectors in TEAMS

Users use connectors to subscribe and receive messages and notifications from web services. Connectors automatically update the team with current content direct to a particular channel. Such updates can be from services like GitHub, Twitter, SharePoint, Azure, Trello, etc., in the conversation feed – in the post tab of a channel.

1. You Click the **ellipses** for "**More options**" on your chosen channel and Click the "Connectors" option from the pop-out menu.
2. You Click the "**Add**" button next to the connector you wish to add on the pop-up page starting with the title "Connectors for…".
3. You Click the "**Add**" button again on the pop-up page for that connector, for instance, the "**RSS**" connector, as illustrated below.

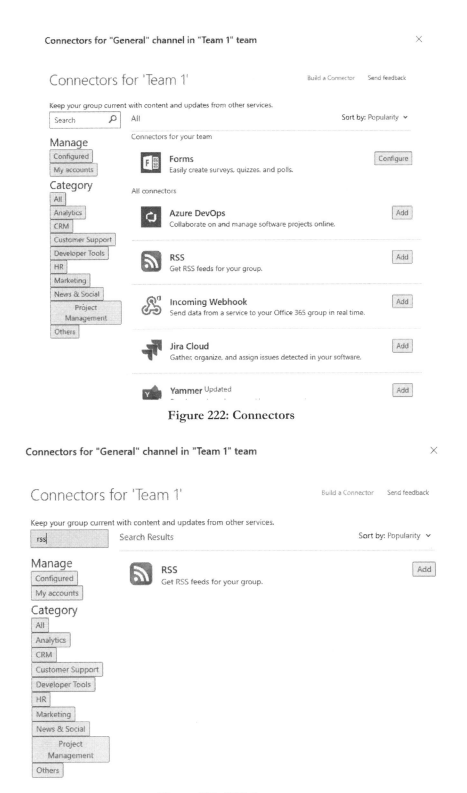

Figure 222: Connectors

Figure 223: RSS Connector

There are many apps that you get notifications from in a channel. One such app is SharePoint News, as illustrated below in Figure 86. The news feature on your SharePoint site keeps your team engaged with important or interesting stories. When you add the "**SharePoint News**" App connector to your channel, a notification message is sent each time a new News post is published on your site.

> **Note:**   *The "**SharePoint News**" App shows news from your SharePoint site in your conversation feeds in your channel's "Post" tab. You can configure an app after you have added it.*

When you create a connector for SharePoint News, the "SharePoint News" connector listens for any news published on the SharePoint team site for a given team. When there is new news content, this connector will publish a message in the "Post" feed to that news article in the connected channel.

7 TIPS, TRICKS & FAQ WITH COMMON PROBLEMS AND SOLUTIONS

Microsoft Teams have several skills, and using the tips and tricks provided in this section can enhance the use of Teams.

Stay in the Activity Warning Loop

The Activity tab will alert you when someone @mentions you, likes something you've written, or addresses a thread you've started. The Operation Bell number shows how many alerts you've been waiting for. The Activity tab is located at the top of the navigation panel on the left. So what's going on with your activity feed?

Using Immersive Reader to allow text to get narrated to you

One of Microsoft teams' most overlooked features; the immersive reader lets you read the text aloud at varying speeds. This function is useful when your eyeballs are busy elsewhere, but you still need to catch the textual details you get.

Click on the 3 dots on any message to start the immersive reader, and pick the reader from your drop-down menu.

Find Relevant Data By Cutting through Clutter With @Mentions

You can cut through the clutter and filter the content you see with @Mentions when a communication explosion occurs in various channels. It can differentiate your text and to-do lists from the other conversation

Visit a specific content Later by using the bookmark feature

Microsoft Teams allows you to bookmark certain content that you can later revisit. This way, when you need it, you will spend less time searching for essential data despite less relevant information.

Using slash commands to work quickly

Agile navigation is necessary if you want to get the job done quickly. Microsoft Teams allows this by giving you the option to use slash commands. For example, you can use /WhatsNew to test whether you have not missed out on something new. This command will carry you through the T-bot channel to the Release Notes Tab. Several of the slash commands most widely used in Microsoft Teams include:

- /Files – Latest files exchanged with you can be viewed
- /GoTo – you can enter a channel right away
- /call – launches a call with other leaders on the team
- /help – enables you to get help through T-bot
- /Saved- Directs you to your saved messages

Build a special working experience by using a Personalized View of Applications and Contacts

Each employee has a host of favorite apps to get the job done. In addition, you can build a special working environment just for you using Microsoft Teams.

You can see the tasks and things allocated to you from the planner, Jira cloud, etc., by accessing Personal App Space

Use the hide and show feature in teams to remain organized

Working through a sorted list of channels makes it easier to get the job done. Microsoft Teams let you pick the channels and teams you want to see and hide. Tap on the three dots next to a team or channel, and then press on more. Clicking on hiding will hide the team or channel.

Have company wikis in one location to boost collaboration

Wikis is an excellent feature inside Microsoft teams that enhances collaboration. In the left-hand menu, click on the three dots, and select the Wiki option. It will take you to the homepage of the Wiki, where you can take notes. You may also receive a list of all wikis about you by clicking on the All tab.

To translate non-English communication, use Inline Message Translation

This feature enables you to translate any message that you receive into any language other than English.

Grant access to people outside the company to communicate with others

When you want to communicate with a member outside your organization, you can use Microsoft teams to provide them with safe guest access. Guests are also permitted to attend meetings and view documents.

MS App Studio To Get Applications Made For Your Need

You can use MS App Studio to get unique applications that match your needs. It helps businesses to use Teams terminology to create their tools

Use bots for Microsoft teams to boost work by using some automation

MS teams have some pre-made bots for getting work done quickly. Some of the common ones are:

- Polly: this bot lets you keep track of employee engagement and poll members.
- WhoBot: this bot will let you know your colleagues.
- Grow bot: this bot lets you exchange kudos with members of the team
- Stats Bot: This bot delivers scheduled reports from outlets like Google Analytics.

Analyze Microsoft Team Usage By Members By Using Analytics and Reports

You can use the report feature to monitor how workers use Microsoft Teams. It will give you more visibility into the tool's most-used functionality and applications. By visiting the admin center of Teams, you will access files. Click Analytics and Reports button and choose the report to preview. In Teams, only the service admin can pull a report.

Record meetings for later access or share on all groups at a go

Microsoft Teams provides the option of recording meetings and screen sharing. The recorded meetings can be saved on Microsoft Stream. Recording can be done by clicking on the three dots in the channel and choosing Start Recording.

Prioritize shifts By using the shift function to control first-line staff

Shifts functionality helps managers to fix issues surrounding job shifts. With this function, they can schedule where a particular team's support is required in excess. You can access this function by clicking on the three dots and selecting Shifts.

Using Proximity Sensing to join A Meeting

This feature will detect Microsoft team room systems for the teams within your device's Bluetooth range. This way, you'd be able to find a place to get on a meeting collaboration easily. You can do this by going through available room systems near you after launching the team meeting.

8   ADMINISTRATOR TEAMS

If you are your organization's admin, you might be required to help your organization set up the Teams interface. Setting up the Teams interface might entail assigning moderators to channels, updating the teams for more effective collaboration, and assigning team owners to teams that don't have owners. The MS Teams admin center allows you to manage the team in your organization and control all that is happening within the team just by clicking or tapping some essential features. As an admin, you can check admin center through https://admin.microsoft.com. Only the Global administrator or the Teams service administrator can access the admin center to use most of the available tools.

The organization's admin can manage meeting settings from the MS Teams admin center by going to *Meetings* and tapping on *Meeting settings.*

✓   **Allow anonymous users to join the meeting:** When the anonymous join is enabled, anybody can join team meeting as anonymous member by using the link present in meeting invitation. The admin can allow anonymous join using the Microsoft admin center by following these steps;

- Visit the admin center, which is accessible at https://admin.teams. microsoft.com.
- From admin center's left navigation pane, visit **Meetings,** and tap on **Meeting settings.**

- Scroll to **Participants,** and toggle ON the ***anonymous can join*** header.
- You can toggle off the settings if you don't want an anonymous identity to enter your meeting.

✓ **Customizing meeting invitations:** You can add any other information when sending a meeting invitation. Your organization can add its logo, other websites, or product links to the invite sent out. To customize your meeting invitation, follow these tips

- Visit the admin center, which is accessible at https://admin.teams. microsoft.com.
- In the admin center on the left navigation pane, visit **Meetings,** and tap on **Meeting settings.**
- Scroll to the **E-mail invitation,** and carry out the following actions;
    - **Logo URL:** You can type the address where you save the organization's logo.
    - **Legal URL:** Fill in the URL if the company has a website people can visit for any issue relating to legal concerns.
    - **Help URL:** People can visit this link for help with any issues.
    - **Footer:** Enter a footer message.
- Tap **Save** to finish.
- Wait for some time for these settings to take effect. Then you can try to send out an invite to preview what the meeting invite will look like.

Team overview grid

To access all the management tools for Teams, the administrator should swipe to the Team node in the admin center by selecting ***Teams*** and then tap on ***manage Teams.***

The Microsoft grid has the following features embedded;

- **Team identity:** This is usually the team's name designated by the admin.
- **Channels:** This shows you the number of channels that have been created.
- **Team members:** This displays the total number of members in the team.
- **Owners:** The total number of teams' owners in the team. Team owners can be more than two.
- **Guests:** Indicates the number of guest users in the team.
- **Privacy:** Shows the kind of access type the backing Microsoft 365 group has.
- **Status:** Shows either archived or active condition of the team.
- **Description:** This tells you information about the Microsoft 365 plan from which the particular Microsoft Teams you are using has been unboxed.
- **Classification:** This tells you information about the classification of the Microsoft 365 plan from which the particular Microsoft Teams you are using has been unboxed.
- **Group ID:** This shows the distinctive Group ID of the Microsoft 365 plan from which the particular Microsoft Teams you are using has been unboxed.

Note: Sometimes, you might not see all of these features in the admin center grid, but you can tap the *"edit column icon* and then toggles on/off any feature you want to add from the column. Tap *"Apply"* when you are done to effect the change.

Adding a new Team

Select *"Add"* when you need to add a new team. The *"Add a new team"* page will be prompted, where you can assign names and descriptions to the team. Set the group to private or public, depending on what you want. Also, set the team's classification.

Editing the team

To edit any group and carry out some team-designated settings, tap any team you want to edit and select edit by the left of the team's name.

Archiving a team

The admin can archive the team by setting the team into a read-only mode.

Deleting a team

Once you delete the entire Microsoft 365 package, Microsoft Teams will be deleted. A deleted team can be restored because it is only soft-deleted for 30 days before you can no longer have access to it. For example, you can restore a deleted account as an admin by navigating to the admin center. Tap the *"expand groups icon"* and select *"Deleted groups."* Choose the group you wish to restore, and then tap *Restore groups.*

Searching the Teams

You can search the team name field by deploying the string *"Begins with"*

Making adjustments to Teams

Right from team profile page, you can have access to change any of the following features or settings;

Members: the admin can add or remove any member he wishes, even promote a group member as owner, or stripe a group owner with his permission.

Channels: The Admin can create a new channel and remove or edit any previously created channel. The default general channel cannot be deleted.

Team name: The Admin can alter the team name to edit it or give it another name entirely.

Team description: The Admin can alter the team description to edit it or write another description for the team entirely.

- **Privacy:** The Admin can decide whether the team should be private or accessible to everyone.
- **Classification:** The Admin can choose any of the three classifications, which include; Confidential, highly confidential, and general.
- **Conversations settings:** The Admin can decide whether to allow members to edit and delete messages from the group.
- **Channel settings:** the admin can decide whether to allow group members to create a new channel or edit a previously created channel.

Troubleshooting Teams

- Sometimes, minor errors can occur during the process of operating Teams. These minor errors can be corrected by changing some of the settings within the Microsoft 365 groups or the Team interface. Check the following troubleshooting strategies;
- Team members missing from the grid: This can be caused by incorrect team profiling by the system. This can lead to a missing property before the system can recognize the team. You can solve this by setting the missing property to the actual value using MS Graph.

From The Admin's Perspective

For this, you need to enter the Microsoft 365 admin center and go down into Microsoft Teams. Before you go there, flip over to "**Teams & groups,**" then "**Active teams & groups,**" and locate the team you just created.

You can see that it's created a Microsoft 365 group for that team. If you click on the group here, which is quite essential that you do, and click on "**Members,**" it shows you all the members, but if you go into "**Settings,**" this is important; if you want the team to be contactable externally, then allow external senders to e-mail this group, send copies of group e-mails, and you can change the privacy here as well. Now the one thing that you cannot change is once it becomes a team, that's it. Essentially a team is an extended Microsoft 365 group. It is extended because you can use third-party products here as well.

Administering the team templates

In your admin center, you're going to click on the drop-down arrow for Teams, and here, you're going to come into "**Teams templates.**" Here is a complete list, and this is useful because you get a description of exactly what the team is. You can see who published the team template (now there are hundreds of templates out there, and several third-party providers are also providing these templates). It shows you how many channels, how many apps the team had, and when it was last modified. So, you can see that you've got the same templates here, and you may be wondering if it is easy to create a template here.

Click on the "**Add**" button, and just as you saw in Microsoft Teams, you can create a new template, use an existing template or start with an existing template.

You can go ahead and create a new template. Give it a name, put a little description in here, and you can specify the locale; if your demo tenant is in the US, you would need to use a US-based tenant. Click on "**Next**" to proceed. Note that if you try and click on next and don't have a description, you need to go ahead and put that in before proceeding.

Now, you're going to enter how many channels you want. So, you'll click on "**Add**" and enter the channel(s) details. Then, you're just going to apply that and add that channel to the template.

You can also add apps as well if you want to. So, you can bring in an app by simply typing the app's name. Any app that's grayed out shows me that the app is already in there, so you get that by default, but if there are any third-party ones, then, of course, you would go ahead and add those.

So, go ahead, click on "Submit," and see that you've created this template. Any templates you create will go straight to the top of the list, which is very similar to other Microsoft products.

So that's typically how you create the templates. If you go back to one of the other templates here, you can see that this tells you a little bit about the template; you've got an excellent description here, the number of channels and apps, and each template has its unique ID here. It shows me which channels have got which apps applied to them, so some planning is often helpful here. Finally, you can go into the apps; it shows you which apps are here, and you can click on them to get more details.

Next in your journey of administering templates is called "**Template policies**." Again, there is a global policy that contains pretty much all the templates, but you might want to create your template policy and then assign that policy along with those templates to your users.

What you can do is go ahead and add a Template policy. Then, you can decide which templates you want to show and hide. Notice that you're not deleting the template; all you're doing is you're just hiding that specific template here. Again, you can put in a description, and once you've done that, you can scroll down and see that it gives you a list of those hidden templates. So, you click on "**Save**," and now that this is selected, you can decide if you want to assign this template to any particular user.

When you search for names in teams, you need to search for a minimum of three characters. This is because when the users log into teams, these templates will be the only two templates they see, and it shows you which templates have been distributed and how many users have been applied there.

The other thing we have here is "**Teams update policies**," If you go into the default settings here, this means how often you want Teams to be updated. This used to be in organizational-wide settings, but it's worth mentioning here because if you enable the "**Office preview**," you'll get new features updated, including Teams templates.

9 THE STRATEGIC SHORTCUTS

Save time with keyboard shortcuts

Using keyboard shortcuts can be faster than using a mouse or touch screen and is especially useful for disabled users. The list is broken down by category, including General, Guide, Messages, Meetings, and Calls, so users can easily find the shortcuts they need.

General

Function	In Desktop application
Display keyboard shortcuts	Ctrl + (.) period
Display commands	Ctrl + (/) slash
Initiate a chat	Ctrl + N
Access a specific channel or team	Ctrl + G
Open **Search**	Ctrl + E
Access filter	Ctrl + Shift + F
Access settings	Ctrl + (,) comma
Access apps flyout	Ctrl + (`) accent
Zoom out (Enlarge)	Ctrl + (-) Minus
Zoom in (Diminish)	Ctrl + (=) Equals
Reset zoom to default	Ctrl + (0) Zero
Access help	F1
Close	Esc (Escape)

Messaging

Function	In desktop application
Initiate a conversation	Ctrl + N
Access compose box	Alt (left) + Shift + C
Enlarge compose box	Ctrl + Shift + X
Go to new line	Shift + Enter
Send message	Ctrl + Enter
Search current channel or chat messages	Ctrl + F
Reply to a thread	Alt (left) + Shift + R
Mark important message	Ctrl + Shift + I

Navigation

Function	In Desktop application
Access **calendar**	Ctrl + 4
Access **Files**	Ctrl + 6
Access **Chats**	Ctrl + 2
Access **Calls**	Ctrl +5
Access **Teams**	Ctrl +3
Access **Activity**	Ctrl + 1
Shift selected team up	Ctrl + Shift + Up arrow
Shift selected team down	Ctrl + Shift + Down arrow
Access previous list item	Alt (left) + Up arrow
Access next list item	Alt (left)+ Down arrow
Return to previous section	Ctrl+Shift+F6
Proceed to next section	Ctrl+F6
Access the **History** menu	Ctrl + Shift + H
Get an open app	Ctrl + F6

Calls and Meetings

Function	In desktop application
Initiate audio call	Ctrl + Shift + C
Initiate video call	Ctrl + Shift + U
Receive audio call	Ctrl + Shift + S
Receive video call	Ctrl + Shift + A
Dismiss audio call	Ctrl + Shift + H
Dismiss video call	Ctrl + Shift + H
Refuse call	Ctrl + Shift + D
Raise your hand	Ctrl + Shift + K
Lower your hand	Ctrl + Shift + K
Call out raised hand	Ctrl + Shift + L
Mute	Ctrl + Shift + M
Unmute	Ctrl + Spacebar
Toggle video	Ctrl + Shift + O
Initiate screen share session	Ctrl + Shift + E
Access sharing toolbar	Shortcut not available

Function	In desktop application
Admit screen share	Ctrl + Shift + A
Refuse screen share	Ctrl + Shift + D
Screen Current list	Ctrl + Shift + F
Access Background settings menu	Ctrl + Shift + P
Let in people from lobby announcement	Ctrl + Shift + Y
Send or Save meeting request	Ctrl + S
Check day	Ctrl + Alt (left) + 1
Check week	Ctrl + Alt (left) + 3
Check work week	Ctrl + Alt (left) + 2
Proceed to next day or week	Ctrl + Alt(left)+Right arrow
Return to previous day or week	Ctrl + Alt(left) +Left arrow
Access current time	Alt (left) + (.) period
Schedule meeting	Alt (left) + Shift + N
Join through meeting details	Alt(left) + Shift + J
Move to suggested time	Alt(left) + Shift + S

10 CONCLUSION

Microsoft Teams is an excellent option for businesses of all sizes and can help enhance employee collaboration. While adding Microsoft Teams may be more time consuming than other functionalities in Office 365, the added functionality it enables can be worth it. It can be an effective way for businesses to communicate. It also provides a more streamlined experience when communicating with customers, reducing the number of communications that need to be handled. As a business grows and the number of employees and customers increases, it becomes increasingly difficult to manage communications on multiple channels. Using Microsoft Teams, you can easily enable commercial communications while standardizing your messaging protocol.

MICROSOFT OUTLOOK

INTRODUCTION

The Microsoft Office suite includes a personal information manager called Microsoft Outlook.

What is Microsoft Outlook?

It is primarily an e-mail client but can also be used for web browsing, note-taking, contact management and task. It also has various other features, including the ability to create and edit a calendar.

You'll find a list of all your Outlook accounts in the Personal Folders File section of the Outlook window. Each of these accounts has its folder, and messages are stored there. In addition, you can see a preview of your e-mails in the To-Do bar or your Tasks, or you can see them on your calendar. You can also find different e-mail options through Quick Parts, which are like organized galleries. These features make it easy to organize your workspace and manage your e-mails.

Microsoft Outlook is a proprietary email client with built-in calendar, contact, and task management, as well as industry-leading support for Internet standards-based messaging platforms. Microsoft Office, Microsoft Exchange Server, and Internet Explorer are also integrated. This ensures that all your Microsoft applications work well together, and you won't have to worry about mismatches between applications. Plus, the Outlook interface is consistent across all platforms so that you can see all your information in one place.

Microsoft Outlook is available for Windows, Mac, mobile phones, and the web. You download the software from the Microsoft website and follow the installation instructions. The installation wizard will guide you through setting up the software. You can also get an Outlook CD-ROM if you want to install Outlook offline.

Where to buy or download

Microsoft Outlook is an e-mail application that can be downloaded and installed on computers. It is compatible with Mac and Windows computers and can also be used for webmail. This e-mail application has an integrated calendar, contact management features, and an address book. It syncs with other devices and includes a virtual sticky note tool for storing notes. It can also be downloaded on Android and iOS devices. It can also be integrated with many business applications.

You can buy Microsoft Outlook as a standalone application or download it from the Microsoft website. After downloading the application, follow the prompts to install it. A wizard will walk you through the installation process. You can download Outlook to your computer using a CD-ROM if you don't have an Internet connection.

Microsoft Outlook is a highly-rated e-mail client. It comes with excellent features and is easy to use. It also offers easy-to-read message previews, a side-by-side calendar, and other features. In addition, it's a secure application that won't sell or share your personal information with advertisers.

It's also a popular choice for professionals. Many businesses use Outlook, which easily manages calendars, to-do lists, and contacts. Outlook is also part of Microsoft's 365 suite of productivity applications. If you aren't sure whether Microsoft Outlook is right for you, try out the free 30-day trial before making a decision.

Where to use Microsoft Outlook?

Microsoft Outlook has many useful features for managing your e-mail. Its calendar feature helps you track meetings, appointments, and work tasks. Outlook can also help you organize your to-do list. It can also help you send e-mail appointment requests and meeting invitations. Outlook does all of these functions without requiring you to open separate applications. You can use Outlook's calendar to view events for the whole day or up to five days.

Microsoft's support center has a vast knowledge base that contains helpful articles about all Microsoft products, including Outlook. In addition, you can also find videos and walkthroughs on how to use Outlook on Windows 10, Mac, mobile devices, and the web. These resources are free to download and can be found by searching for Outlook on any device.

Outlook is a powerful e-mail application that is part of the Microsoft Office suite. It can be used on your personal computer or a business network. It offers an e-mail calendar, contacts, and task management and is part of Microsoft Office 365. You can also use it on mobile devices like Windows phones and tablets. Using Microsoft Outlook in a business environment, you'll find many ways to collaborate with co-workers and customers.

One of the most important things when using Outlook is organizing your e-mails. A cluttered inbox can make it hard to find essential e-mails, so an intuitive folder system can help you organize your e-mails easily. This will save you hours of searching for e-mails. You can also use Outlook's e-mail templates, which make it easy to send and receive e-mails.

Microsoft Outlook Vs. Other Applications

Microsoft Outlook is the premium e-mail application that comes as part of Microsoft Office. Despite its high price tag, Microsoft has improved Outlook over the years and has been designed to increase productivity. Windows Mail is fine for daily e-mail check-ups, but if you want to check your e-mail more often, Outlook is the way to go.

Microsoft Outlook vs. Gmail

Microsoft Outlook has long been the king of business e-mail solutions, but Google has revamped the industry with innovative services. While Office has been a desktop-centric software suite, G Suite is designed for the cloud. As a result, both programs can respond to customer feedback faster and roll out new features more quickly.

While apps take over real-time communication, e-mails are still king in business. However, if you use both, it is essential to know the pros and cons of each. So let's look at the pros and cons of Outlook and Gmail. Which one is right for you?

Both e-mail services have different features and layouts. Gmail's interface is cleaner and more intuitive, while Outlook's is more customizable. While Gmail is free for individuals, working professionals may require a paid account. Outlook's interface is instantly familiar to those familiar with Microsoft Office. Both e-mail programs offer built-in spam detection.

Gmail has more features, including advanced search. For example, Gmail allows you to search for messages based on their categories. Microsoft Outlook lets you carpet messages with different colors, but Gmail enables you to mark important messages with stars. You can also apply descriptive tags to messages. This feature allows you to follow up more thoroughly on client conversations.

Outlook offers a more traditional file system for e-mail organization and is easier to use for new users. Gmail relies on labels to organize e-mail messages, but users must create labels for each. As a result, Gmail's feature can benefit some people, but it cannot be very clear for others.

Microsoft Outlook vs. Apple Mail

Microsoft Outlook is one of the leading e-mail clients available for Mac users, but Apple Mail is free and comes with the Mac operating system. Both e-mail clients offer the same functionality, but Apple Mail has unique features and is much easier to use. For instance, it allows you to set VIPs, which means you will get priority mail from them. Moreover, the Apple Mail interface is simple and intuitive, so beginners will likely prefer it.

Apple Mail can only be used in the Apple ecosystem. Unlike Outlook, Apple Mail is only available for macOS, iPhone, and iPad users. Because of its Apple-only nature, it's not universally compatible with other operating systems. On the other hand, Outlook can be used on Mac OS, Windows, and Android. This makes it an excellent choice for Mac users.

Outlook offers more features and is more stable and secure. Compared to Apple Mail, it is more streamlined and easy to use. It is also available as part of Office 365, with several other features that make it a more professional application. Both are good choices for business users, and users may want to decide based on their individual needs.

Both Apple and Microsoft mail have their advantages. Apple mail has many features that Mac users can't get on an iPhone or iPad, but the user interface is similar, which makes it easier to use. However, Outlook is more complex than Apple Mail and uses more CPU resources. However, it offers many features, including a calendar, task list, and to-do list.

Microsoft Outlook vs. Thunderbird

Microsoft Outlook and Thunderbird are two of the most widely used desktop email programs. Both have a wide range of features and have different strengths and weaknesses. Thunderbird has an easy-to-use interface, while Outlook has a more robust feature set. Microsoft Outlook is the better choice for businesses since it has a better link to Microsoft Exchange servers.

Thunderbird is an excellent choice if you use several e-mail accounts. It allows you to manage an unlimited number of e-mail accounts without switching between multiple e-mail programs. It also features a unifying view, which is convenient when managing multiple accounts. However, Thunderbird has some limitations, and you may have to reset the application after installing add-ons. Thunderbird is an open-source e-mail client that can be downloaded for free. In contrast, Microsoft Outlook requires a subscription to Microsoft Office. Thunderbird is available for various platforms, including Linux and Mac OS X. The Thunderbird Foundation continues to develop the e-mail client. This allows it to be accessible on more computers than Microsoft Outlook.

Microsoft Outlook has many advanced features, such as spam filters and firewalls. However, Thunderbird is a free, cross-platform e-mail application. So regardless of the operating system, Thunderbird can make life easier for businesses.

61 SOFTWARE INTERFACE AND USE

The Microsoft Office suite includes a personal information manager called Microsoft Outlook. The application is most commonly used as an e-mail client but includes other features such as calendaring, contact management, task management, and web browsing. Learn how to organize and manage your e-mails and other important information using these features.

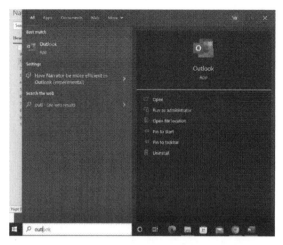

Figure 224: Accessing MS Outlook from Start Menu

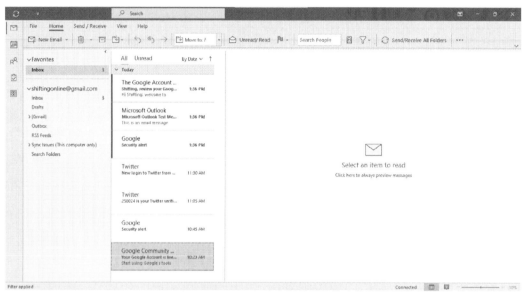

Figure 225: The Outlook Platform

61.1 What is cc in Microsoft Outlook?

CC stands for carbon copy, whereas BCC stands for blind carbon copy. This allows you to send one e-mail to multiple recipients and hides their e-mail addresses. CC is used when you want to send a copy of the message to more than one recipient, but BCC is used when you want to send the message only to certain people

The Cc field is used when you want to send an e-mail to someone else but does not want the recipient to read it. For example, when sending an e-mail, you can add as many people as you like in the To field. However, you don't want to add so many people to your e-mail that it makes your recipients feel like they must do something. By using Cc, you can ensure that all recipients receive your e-mail. Additionally, it enables you to send courtesy copies to parties with whom you may not be in direct communication.

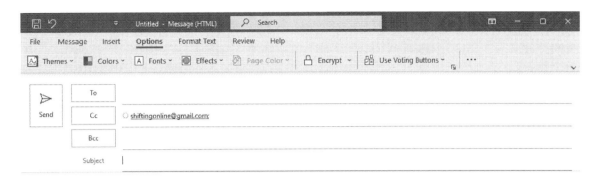

Figure 226: The CC and Bcc features

While CC and BCC are often debated, they are similar in their functionality. BCC stands for "blind carbon copy." When you send an e-mail to your manager, you can specify BCC to send a copy to the manager, for example. The CC and BCC fields will automatically appear each time you send an e-mail message.

The Cc field can also help protect your privacy. The Bcc recipient cannot see your replies unless they are on the Bcc line. However, you should remember that BCC recipients are often spammers. For this reason, most e-mail service providers limit the number of people they allow on BCC. Therefore, it is best to ensure the people you want to send e-mails to are on your safe sender list.

61.2 What is ccn in Microsoft Outlook?

Ccn is a common feature in Microsoft Outlook that allows you to send a message to a selected group of recipients. Using this feature is useful when you need to send a message to many partners with different addresses. In addition, this feature protects your contact information from being sent to the wrong people.

Adding a new contact group in Microsoft Outlook is simple. First, open Outlook. Then click on the "Add Group" tab. Next, click the "+" sign next to the group you wish to add. You will then be given a list of the groups available to you. Once you've added your groups, you can remove the duplicates.

You can also automatically include BCC recipients in your e-mails by installing the Compliance Copies add-in. This add-in works similarly to the Always BCC feature. However, it uses a more complicated set of rules to determine who to BCC. You can also set exceptions for this feature.

Another new feature is called @mentions. This feature will help you manage tasks and e-mails with more ease. For example, you can click the @mentions button in the reading pane to let the sender know that you liked the e-mail. This can be particularly useful if you have an e-mail from your manager saying you've done a great job on your TPS reports. Instead of typing "thanks," you can press the "+" button to let your manager know how much you appreciate their feedback.

61.3 What is reply to all in Microsoft Outlook?

You can use the reply All feature when you reply to multiple people. This will enable you to include all recipients' e-mail addresses in your reply. However, it is essential to note that Outlook does not automatically include the address that sent the message in the reply. It assumes that the sender has access to the original attachments. If this is an issue, there are workarounds.

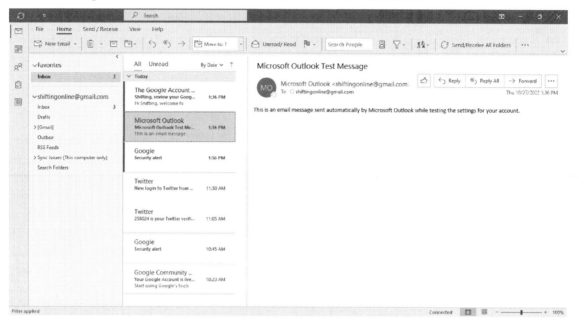

Figure 227: The Reply All feature

If you want to prevent the feature from being used by others, you can disable the "reply to all" feature. You can do this through the Developer tab on the ribbon. In the Developer tab, select "Design a form." Then, select "Reply to All." In the Properties window, uncheck "Enabled" and click "OK." Reply to all has caused plenty of drama in offices. According to the VoloMetrix email-timing company, office workers spend as much as 15 percent of their time replying to e-mails. And about 5 percent of those e-mails contain "reply-all" messages. That's a staggering amount of time, costing a company tens of millions of dollars every year.

While reply-all users have been abusing the feature, servers are now better able to handle the traffic. This change was made to combat this behavior. However, users still abuse reply-all to a large extent. This problem has plagued Microsoft for years.

61.4 Creating a signature

Outlook.com allows you to create only one signature, which you can include when you want. For instance, you might use a very grand and formal signature for business to impress lackeys and sycophants and intimidate enemies. Unless, of course, you only have lackeys and sycophants as friends, in which case you should leave it off your messages. You certainly should go heavy on the praise, Your Royal Highness!

Following these steps will allow you to add a signature to Outlook.com:

- At the top of Outlook.com Mail, click the Settings icon.

- Click View Full Settings at the bottom of the pane.

- A dialog box appears.

- Select Compose and Reply from the middle pane.

- A box appears for the signature.

- Fill in the signature field with your text.

- Format your text as desired using the tools above the box.

- You can now click "Save."

The Settings dialog box is closed.

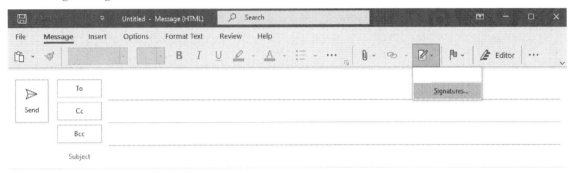

Figure 228: Signatures

How to Include E-mail Signatures

Make your signatures to add to your e-mails' bottom lines. Text, pictures, a symbol, an online commercial card, and even a picture of your scribbled signature are all acceptable forms of a signature. To create a signature, follow the steps below:

1. Select signature> Signatures in a new e-mail.

2. Select New from the E-mail Signature section.

3. Enter a username, then hit OK.

4. Do the following under Choose default signature:

   - Select an e-mail account linked to the signature from the list of available accounts.

   - Select the signature you wish to permanently apply to every new e-mail response from the list of new messages. You can disregard this option if you don't wish to automatically sign your e-mail letters because (none) is the default selection.

- Select the signature you wish to be automatically inserted (auto-signed) when you respond to or forward e-mails from the Replies/forwards box. Alternatively, choose the default choice of (none).

5. Enter the signature beneath the Edit signature, after which hit OK.

6. Select the signature in a brief message, then pick the desired signature.

To add a command from the ribbon to the Quick Access Toolbar

1. Choose one of the following options:

- Right-click a ribbon command and choose to **Add to Quick Access Toolbar**. You may add any command, including a drop-down menu of selections or a thumbnail gallery.

- Click the **Customize Quick Access Toolbar button** at the right end of the Quick Access Toolbar. Next, select a command to add from the selection of frequently used commands.

To open the Outlook Options dialog box's Quick Access Toolbar page

1. Complete one of the following tasks:

- Click the **Customize Quick Access Toolbar button** at the right end of the Quick Access Toolbar, then **More Commands**.

- Select the **File tab**, then select **Options** in the Backstage view's left pane. **Next, click Quick Access Toolbar** in the left pane of the Outlook Options dialog box.

- Right-click any ribbon tab or space, then choose Customize Quick Access Toolbar from the context menu.

From the Outlook Options dialog box, add a command to the Quick Access Toolbar

1. Open the Outlook Options dialog box and the Quick Access Toolbar page.

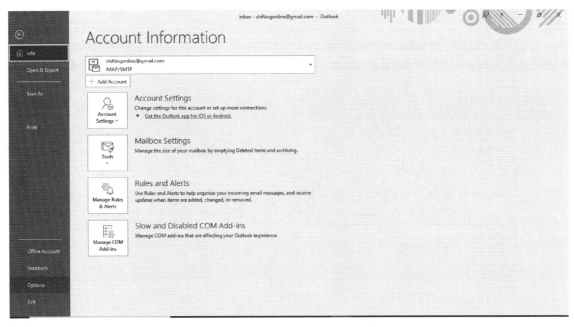

Figure 229: Heading to the Outlook Options

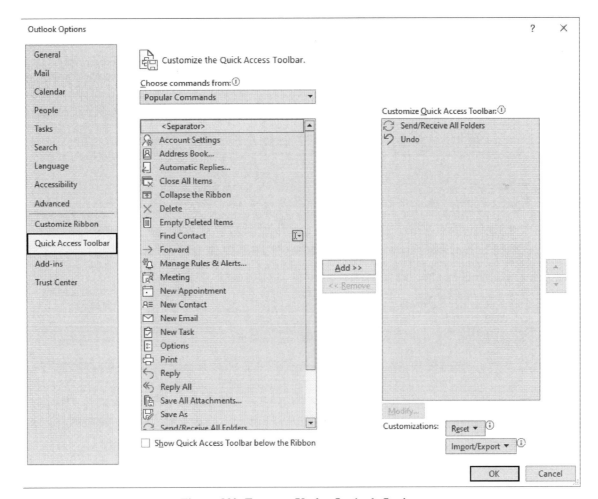

Figure 230: Features Under Outlook Options

2. Pick the tab the command appears on in the Choose commands from list, or click **Popular Commands, Commands Not on the Ribbon, All Commands, or Macros**.

3. Locate and click the command you wish to add to the Quick Access Toolbar in the Choose **commands from the window**. After that, press the **Add button**.

Display a divider on Quick Access Toolbar

1. Open the Outlook Options dialog box and the Quick Access Toolbar page.

2. Click the command you wish to enter the separator after in the right pane.

3. Choose one of the following options:

   - Double-click Separator> on the left pane.

   - In the left pane, choose separator, then click the **Add button**.

To move the Quick Access Toolbar's buttons

1. Open the Outlook Options dialog box and the Quick Access Toolbar page.

2. Click the button you wish to move in the right pane. Then, drag the button to the desired location using the Move Up or Move Down arrows.

To relocate the Quick Access Toolbar

1. Choose one of the following options:

   - Click the **Customize Quick Access Toolbar button** at the right end of the Quick Access Toolbar, then Show Below the Ribbon or Show Above the Ribbon.

   - Open the Outlook Options dialog box and the Quick Access Toolbar page. Next, select or clear the Show Quick Access Toolbar below the Ribbon check box in the space below the Choose **commands** from the list check box.

How to restore the Quick Access Toolbar

1. Open the Outlook Options dialog box and the Quick Access Toolbar page.

2. **Click Reset** in the lower-right corner, then choose one of the following options:

   - Only the Quick Access Toolbar should be reset.

   - Clear all personalizations.

3. **Click Yes** in the Microsoft Office dialog box that confirms the modification.

62 CONTACTS

People are the collective noun for the individuals and organizations that make up your professional and social networks. The only constraints that could apply to who you could or cannot add as a contact are those you or your employer impose. Whoever you include as a contact is entirely at your discretion. For instance, your organization may have policies regarding communication with particular external e-mail accounts.

62.1 How to create a contact

Contact may be as straightforward as a username and an e-mail account, or you could include more information, such as physical addresses, numerous telephone numbers, a photo, and anniversaries. Your contacts are located in the People section of the favorites menu in the Outlook window's lower left-hand corner. Go to People and select New Contact. You can also use Ctrl+Shift+C to establish contact from any folder.

Get a list of the contacts in your Outlook address book

It's a good idea to have a duplicate of your friends in your contact list. You may save a comma-separated value (.csv) document of your friends to your phone and access it in Excel.

- Select File > Open & Export > Import/Export to open Outlook.

Figure 231: The Open & Export Feature

- Select Export to a folder > Proceeds in the Exports and Imports Wizard.

- Select Contacts as the file to download for your account after selecting Comma Separated Values on the Export to a File screen. Ensure the Contacts folder you select is linked to your e-mail address before continuing. This is crucial if you are executing these actions on someone else's PC.

- Go to where you wish to put the comma-separated values (.csv) file after selecting Next > Browse.

- After entering a file name, select OK > Next.

- To begin the export procedure, select Finish.

- Remember: Outlook does not provide a notification whenever the export procedure is finished.

Finding a contact from any Outlook module

You'd like to search for a person, but you're currently using another module. That's fine. Any Outlook module can be searched using the Search People box on the Home tab on the ribbon.

The steps are as follows:

- Find people by clicking on the "Seek People" box on the right of the "Home tab" of any Outlook module.

- Type the name of the contact.

- To open that contact's record in Outlook, press Enter.

- When you enter only a few letters of a name, Outlook lists names that contain those letters, so you can choose the contact you had in mind. For instance, with the word "Wash," you can search for Sam Washburn, George Washington, and any other people on your list that include "Wash."

- To view a contact record, double-click its name.

63 E-MAIL ORGANIZATION

63.1 Organizing Folders

By now, you are most likely used to arranging items into various folders. Windows helps to arrange all the other documents into unique folders. Outlook will also do the same. Create a folder and move your stuff into it.

Create a new e-mail folder

The simplest and most direct way to organize and manage emails is to archive them. Before filing a message, at least one folder wherein the file will be stored will be created. The folder is there for life unless you decide it is no longer needed, and delete it. After that, you can create as many folders as you need.

To create a folder, follow the steps below:

- Locate the Mail Module, choose the inbox option in the folder pane, or press the Ctrl + Shift + I buttons. If you were not doing some other thing before, the inbox should be selected by default when Outlook is opened.

- Choose the Folder tab and select the New Folder button on the ribbon. This will open the Create New Folder dialog box.

- In the Name text box, enter a name for the new folder. You can choose to use any name that suits you. You can also make as many folders as possible. There shouldn't be too many folders, either, to avoid confusion.

- Click on the OK button. The new folder will then be displayed in the Folder pane.

63.2 Move your messages to another folder

Filing messages can be as easy as moving them from their folder into another folder where you prefer them to be. All you need to do is open the box once they arrive and move each message to the desired folder. For another method of moving the messages to a different folder, follow the steps below:

- Locate the mail module > click on the message title that should be moved. The message will then be highlighted.

- Choose the Home tab option and click the Move button on the ribbon. The move drop-down menu will then be open.

- Choose the name of the preference folder to which the message should be moved.

63.3 Organize E-mails with Search Folders

You can sort your Outlook inbox and other folders using the search folders. The Search Folder offers one space where a specific type of message can always be found. A search will not move messages; it just creates a kind of imaginary section for messages. This way, you check through one message type at a time.

When MS Outlook is initially opened, there is no display of search folders in the folder pane. Therefore, if there is a need to use search folders, there will be a need to include one of the default search folders or make a search folder of your choice.

64 CALENDAR

On the other hand, the Microsoft Outlook calendar enables you to manage your work and home appointments simultaneously. So, it becomes beneficial if you frequently have work meetings at home. In addition, it helps in many ways, such as reminders, recurring appointments, and notes.

Outlook calendar lets you make a custom view of your calendar, which helps keep track of your appointments easily. Apart from this, the calendar allows you to add events from e-mails, which is more convenient. It also shows your most recent e-mail, phone calls, messages, and tasks. Moreover, it comes with new features that help you manage your schedules.

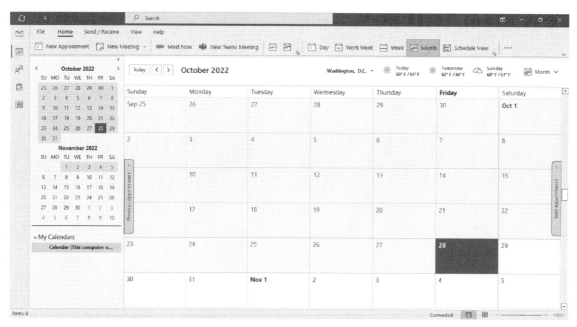

Figure 232: The Calendar Feature

The basic features of the Outlook calendar are highlighted below:

- Create an appointment on the go

- Manage appointments, meetings, tasks, and other items at the same time

- View your schedule at the same time as your team

- Share your calendar with your team

- Calculate a new appointment

- Create an event

- Create recurring appointments

- Calculate the due dates of your tasks

- Add comments to your events

Also, it allows you to share your e-mail with colleagues and clients. It also integrates with Windows, Mac OS, iOS, and Android platforms.

Moreover, you can edit your calendar directly in Microsoft Word and Google Sheets. Also, it has built-in integration with popular websites such as Google Drive, Facebook, Twitter, LinkedIn, Google Calendar, and others.

To start, open Microsoft Outlook and click on the "**Calendar**" tab. This will open up your calendar view, where you can see your upcoming events. If this is your first time using Outlook Calendar, it may be empty right now. To add an event, click on the "**New Event**" button in the top left corner of the calendar view. This will open up a new event window where you can enter all of the details for your event.

You'll first need to give your event a name and choose a date and time for it. You can also select which calendar this event should belong to (more on calendars later).

Next, you'll need to decide whether this is an all-day or half-day event by checking either the "**All Day**" or "**Half Day**" box next to "**Duration**."

In addition to setting a date and time for your event, you can also set a reminder for it by clicking on the "**Reminder**" tab near the top of the window. Here, you can choose how far in advance before the start time of your event you would like Outlook Calendar to remind you about it.

You may also want to invite people other than yourself to attend your event. To do so, click on the "**Invite Attendees**" button at the bottom of the **New Event** window. A new window will pop up where you can type in the e-mail addresses of any attendees you would like to attend your event with you.

The first field in this window allows you to specify whether or not these individuals are required to attend; check off the "**Required**" box next to their name if needed. Then, once everything looks good, click "**Send**."

Now that we've gone over adding basic information about an event let's discuss some advanced features available in Outlook Calendar. One such feature is recurrence; with recurrence enabled, you can manage your time by automating recurring tasks. For example, you can use recurrence to create appointments, reminders, and tasks that repeat at fixed intervals or on specific dates.

To create a recurring appointment, reminder, or task, open the relevant window in Outlook and click on the "**New**" button. In the resulting dialogue box, select "**Recurring**" from the list of options and specify how often you want the task to repeat. You can also choose to have Outlook remind you before each task occurrence.

Once you've created a recurring item, it will appear in your calendar or task list with an orange bar, indicating that it's scheduled for recurrence. To change any details about how often the item repeats or when it occurs, double-click on it and make your changes in the resulting dialogue box.

64.1 How To Insert Calendar To E-mail

There are a few ways to insert a calendar into an e-mail in Microsoft Outlook. To start, open the e-mail you want to send and click on the "**Insert**" tab. Then, select "**Calendar**." This will open up a new window for choosing which calendar to insert.

If you have an appointment or meeting that you want to include in your e-mail, click on the time slot, and it will automatically be inserted into the body of your e-mail. You can also add text around it if desired. If there is more than one event happening at that time, Outlook will give you the option of which event to include in your message.

If you want to send someone a link to your calendar so they can view it online, go back to the "**Insert**" tab and select "**Link**."

In the window that pops up, type in https://calendar.google (or whatever web address for your specific calendar) and hit **enter.** Your recipient will then be able to see and edit any events on your calendar.

64.2 How To Create an Appointment

Microsoft Outlook is a program that allows you to manage your e-mail, calendar, and contacts. You can create appointments from your e-mail by following these steps:

Step 1: Open Outlook and click on the Calendar tab.

Step 2: In the Calendar pane, click on **New Appointment**.

Step 3: The Appointment window will open. In the Subject field, type in a brief description of the appointment.

Step 4: In the Location field, type in where the appointment is taking place (if applicable).

If you want to invite people to attend this appointment

 Step 5: To invite people to attend this appointment:

i) Click on Add Attendees

ii) A list of all your contacts will appear

iii) Select which contacts you would like to invite

iv) Click OK

v) Repeat if necessary

vi) When finished adding attendees, click Close.

Step 6: Now we'll set up what time this appointment is happening:

i) Under Start Time, select AM or PM

 ii) Use the drop-down menu next to End Time or enter a specific time manually

Iii) Click OK

iv). When setting up the date and time information for your new appt., click Close.

Step 7: Finally! Give your new appt some details

i) For the location, enter any pertinent info about where/when this meeting will take place

ii) For Description, give more details about what this meeting entails - be as specific as possible!

iii) If there are any attachments associated with this meeting (e-mail drafts or documents), attach them here

iv) Once everything looks good, hit Save & Close.

64.3 How To Create A Meeting

It's simple to set up a meeting in Microsoft Outlook. By selecting **"Meeting"** from the **"Create"** menu or by clicking the **"New Meeting"** button on the toolbar, you can create a meeting. When you create a meeting, Outlook will ask you for some information about the meeting.

The first thing you'll need to do is choose who will attend the meeting. To do this, click on the "**To**:" field and enter the names of all attendees. You can also type in e-mail addresses or names of groups if you want to invite everyone to a specific department or Office.

Next, you'll need to choose a date and time for your meeting. To do this, click on either of the two date fields and select a date from the calendar that pops up. Then, use one of the two-time fields to select an appropriate start time for your meeting.

Finally, you'll need to give your meeting a name. This is optional, but it's helpful if you have multiple meetings with the same group of people. Once you've filled out all the information, click **OK** to create your meeting.

64.4 Microsoft Outlook: Share

Microsoft Outlook also includes features that allow users to collaborate with others by sharing calendars, contacts, and tasks.

To share your calendar in Microsoft Outlook:

Step 1: Open Microsoft Outlook

Step 2: Click on the "**Calendar**" tab

Step 3: In the "**My Calendars**" section on the left-hand side of the screen, right-click on the calendar you want to share and select "**Share Calendar**" from the menu that pops up.

Step 4: A new window will open, asking who you want to share your calendar with. You have three options: "**Public Folder,**" "**Specific People,**" **or "Groups**." Selecting one of these options will populate a list of people or groups you can share your calendar with below. If you choose either of the first two options, you'll need to provide at least one name for it to be shared successfully. For example, if you choose Groups, type the group name into the text box provided and hit enter/return on your keyboard). After selecting who you want to share your calendar with, click on the OK button at the bottom of the window.

Step 5: The window will close automatically after a few seconds, and your selected recipients will now have access to view (and optionally edit if permissions are granted accordingly) your shared calendar!

65 SECURITY

Microsoft Outlook has security measures that can be applied to prevent your e-mail from getting into the wrong hands. If you are receiving unwanted e-mails or links, these measures can help secure your e-mail account. Here are a few steps Outlook takes to protect your e-mail account: Save attachments to the hard drive before opening them. If you don't have an OLK folder, Outlook will create one. If you receive a message from an e-mail address you don't recognize, do not open it and don't click on any links.

65.1 What is a spam or junk folder?

To protect your account from unwanted messages, Microsoft Outlook Security includes the Junk E-mail Folder feature. These e-mails are sent when an account is modified or changed. You can turn this feature off or enable it depending on your needs. In addition, you can use filters in the Spam or Junk folder for additional security.

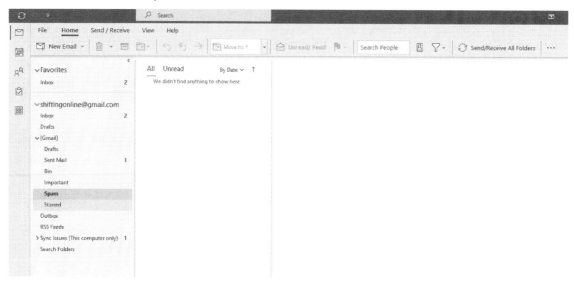

Figure 233: The Spam Folder

Junk e-mail messages are often classified as spam and are automatically placed in the junk folder. You can change this setting by checking the box next to No Automatic Filtering. However, higher protection levels may move legitimate messages to the junk folder. You can also set the Junk E-mail Filter to be more aggressive.

65.2 Filtering junk e-mail

The Junk E-mail Filter examines each new message received and determines, based on several criteria, whether or not the message might be considered spam. For example, both the time at which the message was sent and the contents of the message itself might be included in this category. The Junk E-mail Filter has its protection level set to Low by default and is switched on by default.

To set up the spam filter for Outlook.com, please do the following:

- Visit the **Settings** menu.
- Make sure that View all Outlook settings are selected.
- Go to the Mail menu.
- Choose the Junk e-mail option.
- In the column titled "Filters," check the box labeled "Block attachments, photos, and links from anybody who is not on my Safe senders and domains list."...
- Pick "**Save.**"

66 THE BEST OUTLOOK APPS/PLUGINS

Many users prefer using Outlook as their e-mail client and personal information manager. Over the years, as part of the Microsoft Office Suite, Outlook has proven to be a standard solution (in conjunction with the Microsoft Exchange Server) for both public and private organizations. Even though without a doubt, Outlook is the option to beat, many freelancers and small companies cannot afford solutions intended for larger businesses. Still, there are lots of e-mail management programs aside from Outlook that can be used for free. Some of these are

66.1 Postbox

One-time Mozilla employees created this program, and hence was based on Thunderbird. About ten years later, the software has developed into an autonomous and extremely effective mail client. The design of its interface is like that of other solutions, and it is also easy to use. Users who want a unique look can adjust themes or design their templates.

For a more efficient operation, postbox makes use of different shortcuts. For example, users can access the Quick Bar via hotkey so that messages can be moved or categorized quickly. In addition, when creating an e-mail, a signature can be entered using the Quick Bar without the mouse.

There are lots of benefits when writing e-mails in the postbox. The software has various templates and text blocks that can be used to write cover letters and replies in a placeholder that can be added and created where the receiver's name is always added automatically.

66.2 Thunderbird

For both private users and those in companies, Thunderbird is one of the most preferred options as an alternative to Outlook. The open-source solution is also available for free. The program's free version is streamlined and offers only the most basic functions. One significant advantage is the addition of various add-ons. This means that there is room for expansion of the e-mail program. However, the add-ons and extensions are made to suit their respective versions. Therefore, if you need to update your version of Thunderbird, the add-ons must also be updated.

66.3 Spike

Spike was released in the year 2013, and it combines certain functions of classic e-mail programs with those that are used in modern messenger apps. For example, elements like subjects or signatures are no longer necessary immediately after a private mailbox is linked to the application. At the same time, the basic mail client functions, which include the central inbox or contact management, will be integrated into the modern messenger environment. It is also not coincidental that the creator of spike described it as a conversational e-mail application. Note that audio and video calls can also be made via the software.

The spike depends on modern standards in terms of security. For example, communications that include attached files can be encrypted with a single click. This way, you can be sure your messages are fully protected against unwanted access. Spike is free for private users; however, monthly fees are charged when business e-mail accounts are added.

66.4 Mailbird

Mailbird is an Outlook alternative that is only free in the test version. This e-mail solution combines messages and contacts from different accounts into just one box. The interface can be designed with different free themes as it best suits you.

Mailbird offers different interfaces to various applications and also enhances the mailbox with helpful features for better interaction and teamwork. For instance, Twitter, Whatsapp, Calendar, and Dropbox can be integrated into the mail to change it into a multi-functional program.

66.5 Integrating MS Outlook With Google and iCloud

Integrating MS Outlook with Google and iCloud is now possible. However, you need to take a couple of steps to make it happen. The first step is to paste the iCloud calendar link into Outlook. After you've pasted the link, Outlook will open its dedicated calendar feature. You can then choose between different options for importing your calendar. For example, to import your iCloud calendar, select the "from Internet" option and paste the URL into the appropriate box. Outlook will then sync your iCloud calendar with your Outlook account automatically.

66.6 Integrate Outlook with Google

Integrating MS Outlook with Google and I Cloud a great way to keep your calendar up-to-date on all your devices. You don't need to re-sync every time you make changes to your calendar; any changes you make are synced to all your devices. If you want to integrate iCloud Calendar information with Outlook, you can do it through the iCloud website

If you don't already have a Gmail account, you can set it up in Outlook for Windows. Then, you can synchronize your calendar and contacts with your phone via iCloud. You can also add your Gmail account to the Mail mobile app. Apple has a helpful guide for this process.

Integrating MS Outlook with Google and iClool is a great way to sync your calendars and other information across multiple platforms. In addition to keeping your calendars up-to-date across devices, you can also use iCloud to store and share data with others. Besides that, you can also integrate your contacts with HubSpot, a marketing e-mail tool.

If you're having issues integrating your calendars with iCloud, check if the calendars are being synced on your phone. If they're not, you'll need to stop the iCloud sync and restart Outlook. You can also try signing out and back into your iCloud account. If the problems persist, you can repair the Outlook application from Control Panel or the Programs and Features menu.

66.7 Integrate Outlook with iCloud

Integrating MS Outlook with Google and iCloud takes a few extra steps. First, you have to export your calendar from iCloud. This can be done through the iCloud app or the iCloud website. If you are using a Mac, you must first sign out of your iCloud account and then sign back in. This will allow you to sync your calendars, contacts, and e-mails.

iCloud works well with Microsoft Outlook. It supports the most recent versions of Outlook and Office 365 subscriptions. However, it's not a good fit for everyone, especially if you have POP3 e-mail accounts on multiple computers. Also, to use iCloud, you'll have to have a 64-bit version of iTunes, which is not included with Outlook.

To sync your calendar from iCloud to Outlook, you must log in to your Outlook account. First, click the Calendar tab and then click "From Internet." Next, paste in the URL of your iCloud calendar and press "Sync." Your iCloud calendar will now be synced with your Outlook account.

Integrating MS Outlook with Google and iCloud can be done in just a few steps. First, install the iCloud app on your computer. After installing the app, enter your Apple ID and password. You should then be able to check your e-mail and add appointments to your calendar. In addition, you can synchronize your contacts between Outlook and iCloud.

66.8 How to Integrate Microsoft Outlook With Your iPhone and iCloud

After downloading the Outlook app to your iPhone, you need to integrate it with your Google and iCloud accounts. Thankfully, there are several ways to do so. Here's a look at a few of them. Syncing iCloud calendar and contacts with Outlook is one such way. You can also sync your contacts and calendars from your iPhone with Outlook.

Syncing iCloud calendar with Outlook

To sync the iCloud calendar with Outlook, you must download the iCloud Control Panel from the Apple website. Once you have the panel, log into your Apple ID and password, and select "Mail, Contacts, Calendars and Tasks With Outlook." The data sync may take a few minutes, depending on your network speed. The new data will be applied to your iOS device the next time you open your calendar.

You can also try to sign out of your iCloud account. This will stop syncing the iCloud calendar with Outlook, but you should still be able to access all your information. Once you're done logging out, sign in to iCloud again. This should resolve the problem.

Next, connect your iPhone to your PC via a USB cable. In the "Info" tab, select "Sync Calendars with Outlook." You can choose to sync all calendars or just the one you want to sync. After choosing a calendar, click "Apply" to begin the process of syncing. Note that you may have to disable iCloud while syncing the calendars.

Syncing calendars with iPhone

The first step in syncing calendars between an iPhone and Microsoft Outlook is to connect your iPhone to your computer. To do this, you must have the iTunes app installed on your computer. If your iPhone is not running the iTunes app, you must first turn off iCloud. Next, open the iPhone and connect it to your computer using the USB cable. After connecting your iPhone to your computer, the iTunes app should open automatically.

You can sync your iPhone with your Outlook calendar by connecting them to the same iCloud account. If you already have calendar events on your iPhone, you can choose to keep them on the iPhone. However, be aware that this may cause duplicate calendar entries on your iPhone. This is why it's essential to use a calendar backup tool, such as TouchCopy, which can copy all data on your iPhone to your PC. TouchCopy is free and can be downloaded from the TouchCopy website.

67 TIPS, TRICKS & FAQ WITH COMMON PROBLEMS AND SOLUTIONS

Ways to Resolve Microsoft Outlook Password Issues

Password issues are very common in Microsoft Outlook. Here are some reasons why you may be caught up in a password error loop:

- Outlook is not configured to remember passwords.
- The password for your e-mail address differs from the version Outlook has stored.
- Your Outlook login has become invalid.
- The program is broken and out-of-date.
- Outlook is unable to operate correctly because of security applications.

You may take several actions to prevent that and ensure that Outlook always remembers your password.

Method 1: When prompted for a password, click Cancel. This is the simplest solution that has, in some cases, been effective.

Method 2: Relaunch the laptop. Rebooting frequently resolves puzzling problems like this, so while it's not the fastest repair, it is one of the simpler ones to try. Restarting Outlook will enable you to reopen it from scratch and stop any potentially problematic background activities.

Method 3: By de-selecting, the 'Always' request for the login details box in the settings, you can force Outlook to store your login. If, after logging into the system, everything continues to function fine for a time, but later, you are prompted for it again, this is perhaps the most likely solution.

Method 4: Outlook's login for accessing your e-mail should be changed. If you change your login information but don't modify Outlook, the software asks for the username since it has no idea what it is. Also, if the e-mail address you're attempting to access requires two-factor verification, you may have to make a unique password only for Outlook.

Method 5: Access the 'Credential Manager' while Outlook is inactive, then clear out all the accounts related to Outlook/Office. First, select Windows Credentials, then click 'Remove' under the desired login details.

Method 6: While utilizing Outlook, log out from the Microsoft Office account you are currently registered with. This will not work for everyone because it could not be the identical e-mail experiencing the password problem. Sign out by selecting 'File'> 'Office Account.' After that, restart Outlook and sign in using that same interface.

Method 7: Install the most recent version of Outlook. Sometimes, a problem could be to blame, and the most updated version might fix it.

Method 8: Upgrade Windows if there are any newer versions. Some of these might have an impact on Outlook. After that, make sure to restart the laptop.

Method 9: Turn off all security features, such as antimalware software. If, after completing this, Outlook no longer requests the login information, you are aware that a privacy rule or program incompatibility is at issue and may check into it further. For instructions, go to how to turn off the Windows firewalls.

Method 10: Outlook should be launched in standby mode to stop add-ins from running. This is a bit of a stretch because all this procedure will establish the improbable scenario in which an add-in is at fault. However, if the login loop persists, it's simple to fix and will give you some guidance.

Method 11: Investigate a sluggish internet service. When you've been experiencing intermittent service, the login question can result from a lag in communication with the e-mail system. Again, moving nearer to the access point is the simplest approach to improve the Wi-Fi signal while utilizing a wireless connection.

Method 12: By selecting 'File' > 'Account Settings' > 'Manage Profiles' > 'Show Profiles' > 'Add,' you may create a new Outlook login. You may add the e-mail address again, presumably without the credential problem.

Method 13: Create a brand-new user account. Head To settings in Windows 10, for instance, and select 'Accounts' > 'Family & other users' > 'Add account.' Beginning afresh with a fresh user account has worked for some people to resolve the password reminder problem. Neither Outlook nor your existing user account will be deleted due to this.

Method 14: Activate Microsoft Support & Recovery Assistant (SaRA). This program does several tests to determine what might be incorrect with Microsoft Office and Outlook and, if feasible, will provide some fixes. When installing the application, select Outlook from the main menu, select Outlook, continue to ask for my login, and proceed according to the remainder of the on-screen instructions. This file is a ZIP format. After downloading the ZIP, extract its contents and launch SaraSetup to begin the setup procedure.

Method 15: Reinstall Outlook before attempting one more. There isn't much more that can be done to have Outlook recall your login now that a brand-new client account from the previous step and a brand-new Outlook setup has been created.

67.1 Threats to Avoid on Microsoft Outlook

Many people use Outlook as their main e-mail program. As a result, it poses a significant risk for malware, scams, and fraud. You may have read terrible stories of individuals forced to pay thousands of dollars to have their systems wiped out after becoming infected with malware, worms, and other terrible things. Unfortunately, both the threat and these tales are true. However, you may take a few simple steps to reduce susceptibility to such threats.

Here are some threats on Microsoft Outlook:

- *Spoofing (sometimes called phishing)*: These e-mails seem authentic but contain fake links to other websites designed to fool you into divulging private information like credentials and banking information. Once they have your identification, the thieves can deplete your bank balances using this data.

- *Viruses*: These downloadable files (also known as program files) can damage a drive or erase system files. Beware of files ending with ".exe."

- *Bugs*: Without your understanding or cooperation, these software files or scripts utilize your internet to process bulk e-mails containing spam.

- *Exploits*: These software files or scripts take advantage of security holes in your computer to send spam or carry out other malicious activities. These typically originate from obscure tools that certain websites have incorporated.

- *Spyware*: These covert applications track your online activities (perhaps even the passwords you write) and send the information back to their creator.

- *Adware*: These covert applications cause your browser to behave in a way that displays its adverts or pop-up advertisements on your screen.

- *Inappropriate search taskbars*: These add-on toolbars substitute a company's sponsored search engine for your default search engine so that the outcomes of your queries display their promoted websites.

Such things threaten you. Now consider how to defeat them. Below are the top suggestions:

1. Windows Defender is the default antivirus application, but you may wish to upgrade to one with extra features and e-mail checking. Symantec (Norton) Antivirus, as well as McAfee VirusScan, are two widely used. Most comprehensive antivirus solutions provide e-mail screening for both incoming and outgoing messages. Keep that function activated. You will be shielded against the majority of email-attached malicious programs.

2. Whenever you receive e-mails that have an attachment, be wary of it. Before you view the attachment, make sure the following:

- Is it coming from a familiar person?

- Were you hoping for a file from them?

- If the response to either inquiry is no, get in touch with the sender and ask what the e-mail is before you view it.

3. Always check any attachments that include the EXE, COM, BAT, or VBS data formats as an ending.

4. Be extremely wary if you receive a message with a ZIP-encoded attachment. (A ZIP file includes more resources.) One typical worm infection, for instance, disseminates itself via a ZIP file labeled as a digital greeting card.

5. Be extremely wary if you receive e-mail communication from your institution or a government organization. Most government and bank agencies avoid using e-mail for sensitive transactions. Instead, enter the web address into your internet browser to get straight there. Please refrain from clicking the message's link.

6. Be skeptical if you receive an e-mail from eBay or PayPal. These businesses occasionally do send out valid e-mails. However, phishing websites frequently pose as such websites. So avoid clicking the hyperlinks in the e-mails; instead, use your web browser to go straight to PayPal or eBay. It's more likely fraudulent if it doesn't address you by name in communication from PayPal or eBay. But this isn't a specific method to know.

7. Place the mouse cursor on links in e-mails that you're unsure about. The exact URL that the link points to is displayed in a ScreenTip. Again, it's likely a phony if it doesn't reflect the wording in the link.

8. Malicious search toolbars might deceive you into adding them to the program installation process. Typically, you may remove them via Windows' Control Panel. (Right-click Start, select Control Panel

and then select Uninstall an application under the Programs heading. Next, remove any installed apps that have "toolbar" in the name by scrolling throughout the menu of installed applications.

9. Yahoo! and Google toolbars are OK to maintain because they are authentic. Although they are optional, many individuals feel that any proprietary toolbar ruins the user experience of their browser.

68 ADMINISTRATOR OUTLOOK

To become a Microsoft Outlook Administrator, you must have basic knowledge of Outlook. There are many different ways to do this, including using the Outlook admin center. This article will help you navigate the admin center and configure Outlook. Once you know what to do, you will be well on becoming a Microsoft Outlook Administrator.

Knowledge to become an MS Outlook Administrator

MS Outlook is a popular e-mail program for many businesses. It can sort e-mails, locate colleagues, and set automatic replies when you're out of the Office. It can also manage your calendar to help you organize events. However, to become an effective administrator, you should know how to set up the software properly and learn how to customize it to meet your specific needs.

Outlook admin center

If you're having trouble accessing your e-mails, use Outlook on the web or the mobile client. The Outlook admin center is also where you can set the default signature for new e-mails.

Admins can set permission levels and assign end-user roles. These roles, which begin with the prefix My, enable administrators and specialist users to assign rights to end users. The admins can then control which settings end-users can access, change, or delete. The admins can also modify these policies by creating new ones.

69 THE STRATEGIC SHORTCUTS

SHORTCUT KEYS	FUNCTIONS
Ctrl + 1	Switch to the Mail app.
Ctrl + 2	Switch to the Calendar app.
Ctrl + 3	Switch to the Contact app.

SHORTCUT KEYS	FUNCTIONS
Ctrl + 4	Switch to the Task app.
Ctrl+5	Switch to the Note app.
Ctrl+6	Switch to Inbox Folder.

SHORTCUT KEYS	FUNCTIONS
Ctrl + Y	Go to the Folder dialog box.
Ctrl + Shift + B	Open your Contact Address book.
Ctrl + Shift + M	Open a new E-mail Message.
Ctrl +Shift + A	Open a new Calendar Appointment.
Ctrl + Shift + Q	Open a new Meeting request.
Ctrl + Shift + C	Open a new Contact.
Ctrl + Shift + L	Open a new Contact group.
Ctrl + Shift + K	Open a new Task.
Ctrl + Shift + N	Open a new Note.
Alt + Q	Open a Search Box.
Ctrl + Alt + K	Search the current folder.
Ctrl + Alt + A	Search all the folders.
Ctrl + Shift + F	Open the Advanced Search.
Ctrl + R	Reply to a received e-mail message.
Ctrl + Shift + R	Reply All to a received e-mail message.
Ctrl + F	Forward an e-mail message.

SHORTCUT KEYS	FUNCTIONS
Ctrl + Alt+ F	Forward an e-mail as an attachment file.
Ctrl + U	Mark a received message as unread.
Ctrl + Q	Mark a received message as read.
Ctrl + Shift + G	Flag a message with a follow-up.
Ctrl + Alt + J	Mark a message as "not junk."
Ctrl + Alt + 1	Show today's date.
Ctrl + Alt + 2	Show the current workweek.
Ctrl + Alt + 3	Show the current week.
Ctrl + Alt + 4	Show the current month.
Ctrl + P	Print an item.
F1	Help window.
Esc	Cancel a current task.
Ctrl + F1	Collapse or Expand the ribbon.

70 CONCLUSION

Microsoft Outlook 2022 is a powerful e-mail client with many features to help you manage your e-mail communications. In this user guide, we have introduced you to the basics of using Outlook 2022. Then, we have shown you how to create and send messages, manage your contacts, and schedule appointments. In this final chapter, we provided tips on making the most of Outlook 2022.

One of the great things about Outlook 2022 is that it can be customized to meet your specific needs. You can change the way it looks and behaves to match your preferences. For example, if you want more space in your inbox, you can adjust the settings so that messages are displayed in a list instead of in a column format. Or, if you prefer not to see images in e-mails, you can disable image loading for all or individual senders.

Another great thing about Outlook 2022 is its ability to integrate with other applications and services, such as Skype for Business or Microsoft Teams meetings. This allows seamless communication between co-workers or clients without having multiple applications open simultaneously. For example: While composing an e-mail message within Outlook, Right-click on the "To" field and Select "Add Participants" then, A window will appear with suggested participants from either skype/teams meeting roster OR contact list; from there, you can select one or more people from either list and Click "add" Message composition will now continue as normal, When ready click send as usual that's all. In addition to integrating with other Microsoft Office applications such as Word or Excel, Outlook also offers a variety of tools that allow users greater control over their schedules and time commitments. These tools include; The ability to set up task reminders which will notify users via pop-up notification/sound alert /e-mail message when tasks are due, The ability to create OneNote notebooks explicitly related to tasks assigned within Outlook, and The ability to track time spent on various activities by recording start & finish times against each task And finally the calendar sharing between multiple people use when working collaboratively on projects involving multiple deadlines.

MICROSOFT ACCESS

INTRODUCTION

While alternative databases are expensive, Microsoft Access is comparatively cheap. Additionally, it is a component of the Microsoft 365 software package. You may already own Microsoft Access, but if not, you can purchase it separately. The software is available in various editions, including standalone and free versions. You can also use Microsoft Access with other Microsoft programs, like Excel and Word. There are many ways to use Microsoft Access to develop database applications. You don't need to be an expert to utilise it, and no programming skills are required. Instead, find out what it is, how to use it, and where you can purchase or download it. This book will cover the most critical aspects of using database software.

Microsoft Access is a business, personal, and academic database management system. It is the most widely used database in the world. Microsoft Access has a lot of features that make it easy to use. The software also has a lot of templates that can be customized to suit your needs.

We term MS Access as a relational database management system (RDBMS) initially designed for Windows. It offers a wide range of features, including data security and ease of use. As a database software, Microsoft Access helps users to manage and store information in a structured way. Many companies and organizations, including the US government, have used it. You can use Microsoft Access for personal and business purposes. It helps you to combine the information to create your database.

Microsoft Access is one of the world's most widely used software and has become an essential tool for many users. Individuals use Microsoft Access, small businesses, large corporations, and governments to manage their information.

Microsoft Access is a simple yet powerful tool that combines the information to create your database. Microsoft Access can help you create your database quickly and efficiently without much hassle. The software has a guided way of teaching new users how to use it and an algorithm that will help you optimize your task and project. It also guides how to combine information to create your database and optimize your tasks and project.

Access can be used in many ways, such as creating a database, importing data, or exporting it to other programs. It also offers a wide range of features that make it easy to do tasks like finding duplicates or calculating averages.

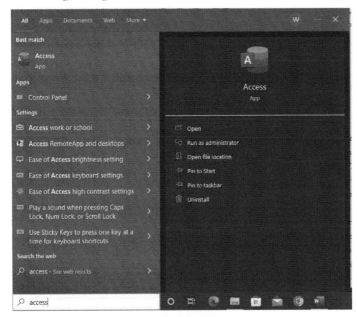

Figure 234: Navigating to MS Access

What is database & database development?

Microsoft Access provides a powerful tool for creating database objects. It offers various templates you can use as a starting point for your project. These templates are pre-built with the tables, forms, queries, and macros you need to create a custom database. You can use these templates to manage contacts, issues, or other information. Some of these templates even have sample records to help you get started.

The main purpose of a database is to organize data. Many people create databases in Access or Excel for personal use. These applications typically have short life cycles and are meant to be easy to manage for their creator. As such, most personal databases are not developed with advanced database concepts and are built by non-programmers. These databases are low-end, easy to maintain, and an excellent option for rapid application development.

While Access does not provide the utmost flexibility, it does provide many valuable tools to solve common database problems. It is also cheaper than more complex solutions and offers increased performance. The cost of a database solution can be a significant factor for an organization. However, it is essential to remember that different problems require different solutions.

Organizations change their database needs over time. The Microsoft Access platform is the most popular database application, and it can solve many problems for large and small organizations. But it is not a good database solution for every situation. Ultimately, Microsoft Access should be a part of an organization's overall database strategy.

Where can I buy or download Microsoft Access

Microsoft Access is a good choice if you're a business owner who needs to build database-heavy applications. It offers several tools and templates that let you build and edit apps easily. Access also allows you to automate various processes. It also integrates with Microsoft Azure, SQL Server, and Visual Basic. It's a powerful program that will enable you to create scalable and secure database management applications. It is beneficial for small and medium-sized businesses.

However, the program isn't free. You'll need to purchase Microsoft Access for your PC to use it. In addition, there is a challenge using the web app for this program, so you'll need a desktop computer to use it. You can also sign up for a Microsoft 365 subscription, allowing you to use Access for free for a certain period.

You may consider downloading the trial version if you're not a business owner but still want to use Microsoft Access. The software comes with many templates and comes with premium support. In addition, you can also access video tutorials and informative guides. Additionally, there's a frequently asked questions section that you can refer to for answers to common questions.

Microsoft's Office productivity suite has evolved over the years, and Microsoft Access is no exception. Microsoft Access was released back in 1992 and is among the most popular desktop database management systems (DBMS). It took Microsoft several years to develop and market a desktop database management system, but purchasing FoxPro helped accelerate the development process. In addition, by continuing to market FoxPro, Microsoft could use the database engine's source code and streamline the development process.

Where you can use Microsoft Access

Microsoft Access can be invaluable if you've been tasked with creating and maintaining business databases. This database software makes creating and maintaining a database a breeze, thanks to its easy-to-use interface. Users can import and export data easily with the help of the wizard built into the program. The wizard will also save the operation's details in a specification. Microsoft Access also includes templates to help users create and manage their databases.

Microsoft Access is available for download from Microsoft's website. Once you've downloaded the software, follow the installation steps. This database program is extremely powerful, making it ideal for organizing large amounts of data and creating custom forms and reports. Microsoft Office 365 subscribers can also use the Microsoft Access web app, which lets you work with your databases on any computer.

Microsoft Access is also helpful in schools, where it can simplify student information management. For example, it can send students emails, manage schedule changes and cancellations, and more. It can also be used to schedule and contact substitute teachers, which can help schools run more smoothly. The options are practically endless with Microsoft Access. This tool can help you organize your daily activities with ease. In addition, it is a powerful database management system that will help you run your business efficiently.

Microsoft Access allows you to integrate data from several sources, including Microsoft Office applications, SQL Servers, and Azure servers. It also offers many integration options with many other programs. If you are looking for an affordable database program, Access is a great option.

71 SOFTWARE INTERFACE AND USE

Ribbon

The ribbon contains a progression of order tabs containing the order. In Microsoft Access, the essential order tabs are Record, Home, Create, External Data, and Database tools. Each of the tabs contains a social event of related orders, and these get-togethers surface a piece of extra UI parts. The Tabs in Ribbon likewise mirror the right now dynamic article or data.

The Microsoft Access ribbon is found unequivocally on the Windows' top bar. It contains tools organized by Tabs with a gathering of buttons that assists you with dealing with records. The ribbon has the essential tabs, comprising the generally utilized orders; different tabs seem to be when you can utilize them.

A few buttons on the ribbon give decisions, while others send off an order. One essential advantage of the ribbon is consolidating those tasks or segment centers in a single spot that requires menus, task sheets, toolbars, and other UI parts to show. You additionally have one spot where you search for orders instead of looking through many spots.

Figure 235: The Ribbon Items

Ribbon Tabs and Components

The ribbon contains a movement of order tabs containing other orders. Access chief order tabs are Document, Home, Create, External Data, and Database Tools. What's more, every Tab contains social events of related orders, which surface a part of the extra new UI parts, for instance, the show, and one more kind of control that brings about choices.

The orders available on your ribbon similarly reflect the by-and-by unique article. For instance, if you have opened a table in Datasheet view and select the structure on Create tab in Structures pack, Access creates the Design considering the powerful table. That is, the name of your unique table is put in the new construction's Record source property. Furthermore, a number of ribbon tabs appear in unambiguous settings.

- **File**: File tab takes you to Backstage view with Open, Create, Save and more.

- **Home Tab:** Has frequently used commands. Create a different view, commands for text formatting, finding records, copying and pasting, rich text formatting to a memo, and more.

- **Create Tab:** Allows you to create and design Access elements like tables, forms, modules, queries, macros and reports.

Figure 236: The Create Tab

- **External Data:** This Tab provides commands that enable you to connect to other data sources. In this Tab, you can export or import data to/from file formats like Excel and CSV files (comma-separated values), databases like Access, SQL Server, Azure, ODBC data sources, and web services like SharePoint.

Figure 237: External Data Tab

- **Database Tools:** This Tab contains commands related to an Access database's inner workings. You get commands that enable you to compact & repair databases, create macros, create table relationships, analyze and tune your database performance, and move your database to different files like a backend Access database or a SharePoint server.

Figure 238: Database tools tab

- **The Backstage View**

Clicking **File** tab takes you to Backstage view. It offers menu options and commands to manage the current database and configure general Access settings. The Back button takes you back to the Access workspace.

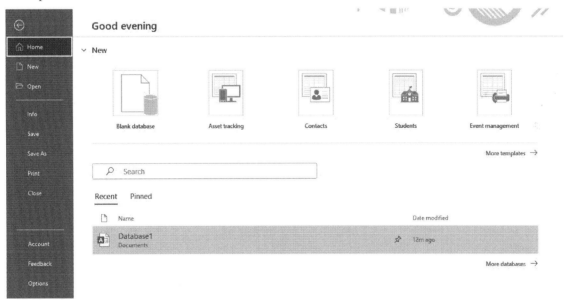

Figure 239: The Backstage View

An overview of the menu options in the Backstage view:

- **Info**: This option enables you to view and edit various properties of the current database, compact & repair the database, and encrypt the database with a password.

- **New**: This option enables you to create a new blank database or one from a predefined database template.

- **Open**: You can use this option to open your existing database, including viewing other recently opened databases.

- **Save**: This option takes you back to the Access workspace, where you can save individual Access objects.

- **Save As**: This menu option allows you to save or convert the current database. For instance, you may save the database with a different name, in which case, a copy of the database will be created. You can also convert the database to another Access format, as an object, or save it as a PDF or XPS file.

- **Print**: You can use this option to:

  - **Quick Print**: Directly forward the object to your default printer triggering any changes.

  - **Print**: Configure various printing options then print.

  - **Print Preview**: Gives you a preview of your document and allows you to change the pages you want to print.

- **Close**: Closes current database but leaves Access open.

- **Account**: View and manage information relating to the current Office user. Most of the options and settings here affect all Microsoft 365 applications installed on the computer, not just Access. For example, changing the Office Theme here will change it for all Office applications on the machine.

- **Options**: Launches the Access Options dialog box, which contains a series of settings you can use to customize Access, for example, language, display, proofing, the Ribbon, the Quick Access Toolbar, and other settings.

- **Feedback**: This allows you to provide feedback and suggestions to Microsoft and to explore the feedback from others.

72 LET'S START

CREATING A DATABASE TABLE

As I have said earlier, the most crucial part of constructing a database starts with table creation and entering data into the table. Kudos to Microsoft Access as it permits its user to create a database table with three different approaches, as I listed below:

- Creating database table from scratch.

- Creating a database table with the In-built template.

- Importing table from another database table.

CREATE A DATABASE TABLE FROM THE SCRATCH

It means you are creating a blank database table in which you will have to enter each field one after the other. Kindly open a database file and observe the itemized methods to create your database from scratch:

1. Tap **Create tab** and click on **Table Design** command to access the blank table.

Figure 240: The create table

2. The database blank table will come forth, giving you options to enter fields into your table.

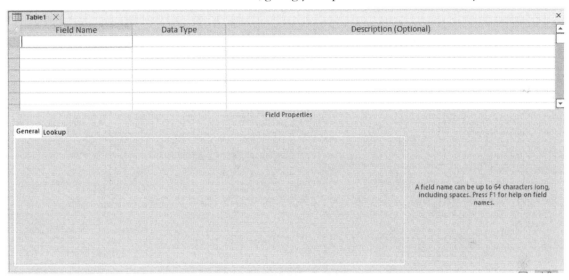

Figure 241: The table design

CREATE A DATABASE TABLE WITH THE IN-BUILT TEMPLATE

A template makes database table creation easier. It involves little modification. Nevertheless, any user who wants to use a template in creating a database table must be proficient in Microsoft Access and know how to manipulate access gadgets. You have to pick one of the parts of the template in creating a database table, as you can see below:

1. **Contacts:** This is ideal for creating a database table related to contact addresses and phone numbers.

2. **Users:** it is the database that deals with email address storage.

3. **Tasks:** monitoring the project, such as the status and condition of the project.

4. **Issues:** it is concerned with a database table structured to deal with issues based on their importance.

When you create tables with templates, there are preformatted queries, forms, and reports you can attach to the tables. Observe the following steps in creating a database table with a template together with the preformatted forms, queries, and reports:

1. Kindly close all the **Open Objects** if any object is opened in the database working area when right-clicking any **open object title** and choosing **close All** on the drop-down list.

2. Once you close all the objects from the working area, tap on **Create** tab and click on the **Application Parts** menu.

3. Select template parts from the Application drop-down list under the QuickStart heading **(Contacts, Issues, Tasks, or Users).**

4. Create relationship dialog box will come forth asking you the pattern of relation you want. This warning will come if you have any other table in the database. Immediately you see the warning, kindly click "There is no relationship" and tap on **Create** Button.

5. The new table has been created with an in-built form, query, and report. You may have to click on design view at the status bar to view the table, field, and data type for any modification; modifying the template field name is another topic in this section.

IMPORTING A DATABASE TABLE FROM ANOTHER DATABASE TABLE

The easiest method to create a database table is importing from another. It gives you work-free effort in creating a database table, just like copying and pasting. To import a database table, ensure compliance with the following guidelines:

1. Tap on the **External Tab** and click on the **New Data Source** menu, then pick **From Database** menu on the drop-down list and lastly, pick **Access** from the fly-out list.

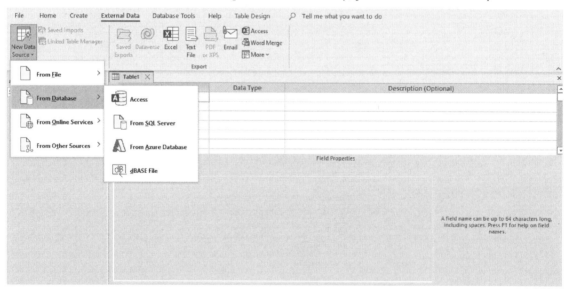

Figure 242: Importing a database

2. The Get External Data-Access Database dialog box will come forth, then Click **Browse** button to access File Open dialog box.

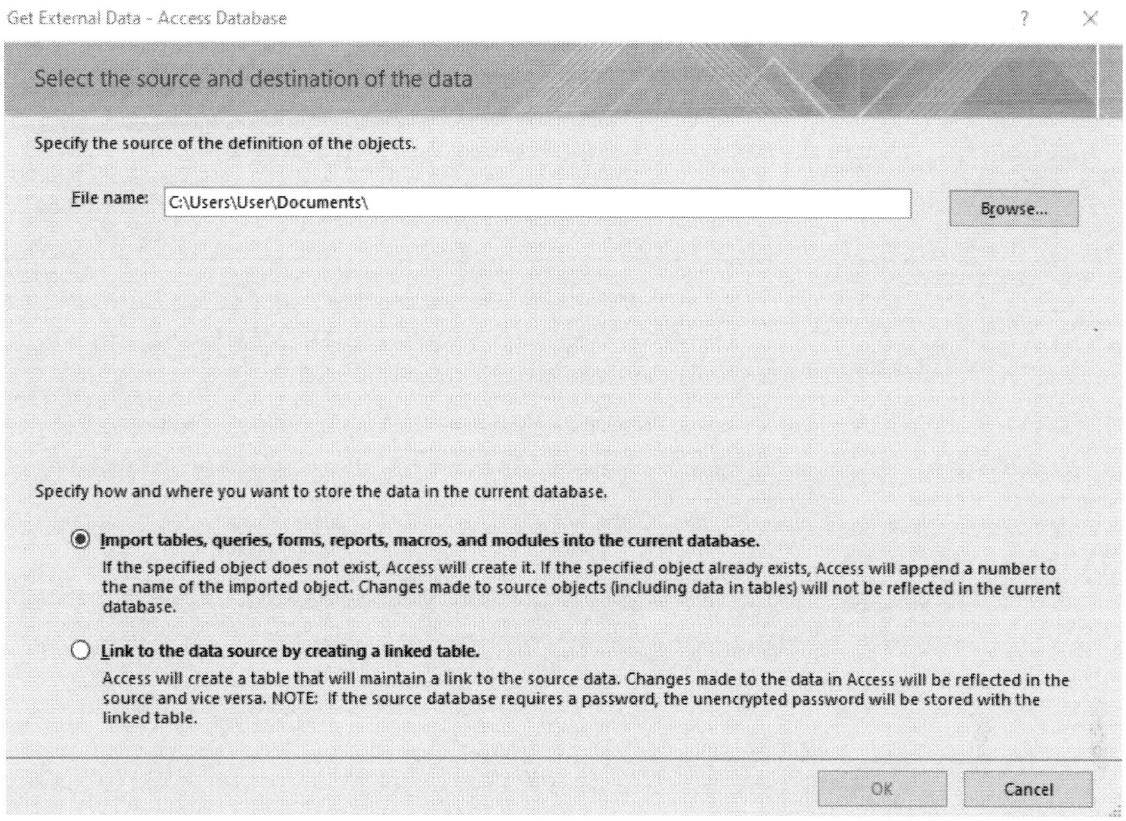

Figure 243: Importing an external database

3. Choose the **database file** with the database table you want and tap on the Open button to access Get External Data-Access Database dialog box.

4. Pick the first option with inscription(**Import Tables, Queries, Forms, Reports, Macros, and Modules into the Current Database**) and tap **Ok** to access dialog box for Import Objects.

5. Select the **database table(s)** you need with **Ctrl + click** for multiple selections under the Table tab (you have the option to "import table fields, format, and data" or "table fields and format only" by clicking on the Options button and select either Definition and Data or Definition only respectively under import tables.

6. Then click ok for authentication.

Note: you will be provided with a save import dialog box. Click on the close button. If your table to import has lookup fields, the imported table will automatically consist of lookup fields.

DATA TYPE	DESCRIPTION	SIZE
Short Text	It can be used to store all forms of Text that can't be used for calculation, such as addresses, telephone numbers, names, and so on	Ability to hold 255 characters.
Long Text	It is designed to store large forms of Text; only a few users use this type of data type	Ability to hold 63,999 characters.
Number	It is used for storing numerical data that can be used for calculation and currency computation.	Up to 16bytes
Large Number	It is used for storing very hefty data of numerical numbers for calculations and computations	Big Integer of about 450 bytes
Date/Time	It is used for storing date and time, and this can as well be used to determine the range of calculation	8bytes
Currency	It is used in storing monetary data for calculation	8bytes
Auto Number	It is used to store numbers in a particular sequence depending on how you set Auto Number, and you can assign it as the primary key provided there is no unique data in the database tables	4 bytes to 16 bytes
Yes/No	It is used to store logical values like yes/no, true/false, etc.,	At most 8bytes
Attachment	It is used to store files, charts, and images. In addition, you can use it to attach files to the database table just the same way as attaching files to the email.	About 1GB
OLE object	It is used to insert database file links into another application file, such as a Word document	About 2GB
Hyperlink	It is used to store data that has a webpage format.	Maximum of 2048 characters
Calculated	It is used to store mathematical values from one field to the other.	Not much dependent on the data to be calculated
Lookup wizards	This is mainly used to create a drop-down list from which the worker can use to enter data in a way to eliminate the error of data entering	About 200 byte

How to export files from Access to Excel

- Select your table or database object you wish to export.

- Select "External Data" tab ribbon.

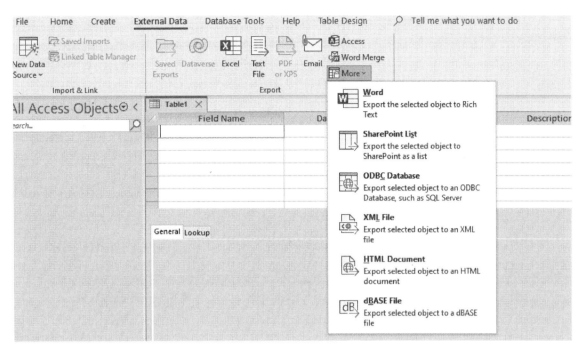

Figure 244: Exporting an item

- In Export group, select Excel. The wizard opens.

- Enter a name for the record (if you enter a comparable name as an ongoing activity manual in the goal, you will be incited to replace it), and snap on the Scrutinize button to pick a region for the report. Next, pick various decisions in the wizard, including planning, assuming you want to open the goal archive and export isolated or picked records. The record ought to be closed first on the off chance that you are replacing an ongoing activity manually.

- Select ok. Excel will consequently open if you have decided to open the objective document when complete. While naming the Excel workbook during this cycle, you might need to remember a date for the name if you want to hold duplicates of the information for precise dates. Toward the end of the cycle or when you return to Access, a dialog box will seem to inquire whether you need to save the export steps. If you are exporting consistently, you can save the Export ventures for reuse.

BUILDING DATABASE TABLES RELATIONSHIP

Table relationships indicate the connection between two selected database tables following the same information they have in them. The major means of creating the relationship is to use one table's primary key field against the other's foreign key fields. Commit these two rules to memory any time you want to create a relationship between two tables:

- A relationship is only permitted within two related tables in the same database. For instance, the number field can't be compared with the text field with which they are unrelated. It must be a related field.

- Using Primary and foreign keys, you can tell Microsoft Access how the two tables will be related.

CATEGORIES OF RELATIONSHIPS

Database relationship is of three categories. Each category depends on the number of fields you want to relate with others in both tables. The following are the categories of database table relationship:

A One-To-Many Relationship

This is the most used relationship among the categories of tables relation. It is carried out by connecting one unique record (primary or indexed field key) field in one table against many records in other tables.

For example, consider a database for tracking orders with tables for customers and orders. A customer may place any number of orders. So, the user may reflect numerous orders in the Orders database for each customer represented in Customers table. Therefore, Customers table and Orders table are related one-to-many times.

To depict a one-to-many connection in your database architecture, add the primary key from the "one" side of the relationship to the "many" side of the relationship's table as an extra field(s).

In this case, you may, for example, add a new column to the Orders database called Customer ID, which is the ID field from the Customers table. Then, using the Client ID number in the Orders record, Access can locate the appropriate customer for each order.

A Many-To-Many Relationship

This establishes a relationship in both tables with more than two fields in each table; none of these fields is the primary field key.

Let's look at the connection between a product table and an Orders table. The user may include more than one product in a single order. Conversely, a single item may show up on numerous orders. As a result, each record in the Orders table may have multiple records in the Products database.

Furthermore, for each entry in the Products database, there may be many records in the Orders table. This is a many-to-many connection.

Because it breaks the many-to-many relationship into two one-to-many relationships, a third table, commonly known as a junction table, is necessary to represent a many-to-many relationship. The next step is adding the third table's primary key to each of your first two tables' primary keys. So, third table keeps track of each instance, or occurrence, of the relationship.

The One-To-One Relationship

Each record within first table can only have one matching record within your second table, and vice versa. Such kind of relationship is not very common.

A one-to-one connection can be used to segment a table with many fields, isolate a database area for security purposes, or store data specific to a subset of your main table. Both tables must include the same field if you locate such a relationship

You may create explicit table associations in the Relationships window or by dragging a field from the Field List pane. When using tables, Access searches for table connections to discover ways to link the tables. Before creating additional database objects like queries, forms, and reports, you should create table relationships for several reasons. Check them out:

- Table relationships help you construct effective queries.

- Your form and report designs should include table relationships.

- Table relationships enforce referential integrity, thus, avoiding orphan records. For instance, an order record referencing a different record but doesn't exist is called an orphan record; an example would be an order record referencing a non-existent customer record.

- A primary key can be identified as a unique identifier assigned to each table when creating a database. Next, you assign foreign keys to associated tables using the primary keys as references. These primary key-foreign key references must remain in sync. Reference synchronization is supported by referential integrity that depends on your table relationships.

73 LET'S EXPLORE THIS IN DETAIL

Field Properties

Attributes describe the nature and behavior of data contributed to a field. More focus of a field is the data type that defines the nature of the data you can store there.

To set a field property, you must first locate the desired field's specific property on the tabs. The property you want to change is typically found under the "General" tab. The "Lookup" tab is only used when manually configuring "lookup" field attributes that display values from another table or list.

In the table's design view, you may modify the attributes of the custom table fields you create. When tables are opened in design view, the table design grid, which spans the top half of the screen, displays field names and data types. Below that, in the "Field Properties" section, on the two tabs labeled "General" and "Lookup," you can modify the properties of the field that is presently selected in the table design grid.

You can adjust the size, presentation, default values, and various other elements of the selected field by using the field properties on the "General" page. In the "Field Properties" section's right pane, you can hover the cursor on a property box to learn details about its use or purpose. You can Select the property box if you need further clarification on how to set the value of a specific property and then hit the "F1" key to get more help. A second window containing the help file will open, allowing you to read and print it as needed.

Field Size Property

- In a text field's "Field Size" property, you can specify the number you enter as the field's maximum character limit. In addition, the quantity of data that one can enter into the field can be limited. As the default field size, Access sets a text field's character limit at 255.

- Additional field characteristics can be added after a field is created and its data type is chosen. For example, you may customize field size to depend on the field's data type with extra features. For example, you may change the size of a Text field by modifying its Field Size attribute.

- When the "Field Size" is specified, number fields are distinct from text fields in that you select the type of numbers that the field can store before setting the field size. The possible sizes include "Byte," "Single," "Double," "Integer," "Long Integer," "Replication ID," and "Decimal."

- A long Integer is the standard field size for numbers. One of the most significant field sizes is this one. You can choose a smaller field size if you'd like because Access works better with smaller objects, so you can. If not, don't be concerned; you probably won't experience significant performance issues. Keep in mind that you should leave the setting at "Long Integer" if you are linking the "Number" column to an "AutoNumber" field in a table relationship.

- The Field Size property is particularly crucial for Number and Currency fields since it establishes the field values' range. For instance, a one-bit Number field can only store integers between 0 and 255.

- Each Number field value's required amount of disk space is likewise determined by the Field Size parameter. The number can utilize precisely 1, 2, 4, 8, 12, or 16 bytes, depending on the size of the field.

Note: The field value sizes for the Text and Memo fields are adjustable. Field Size determines how much space can hold a single value for various data types.

Field Caption Property

- When the Hyperlink Address or Hyperlink Sub-Address property is set for the control, the Text of the Caption property serves as the hyperlink display text for label or command button controls.

- The string expression for the Caption property has a maximum character count of 2,048.

- When dragging a field from your field list to create a control, the field's "Field Name" property setting is copied to control's Name property box. They will also reveal in label of the newly created control if you haven't provided a Caption property setting for your field

- The control's label caption or column header in the Datasheet view will be decided by the field's "Field Name" property setting if no caption is supplied. If the query field caption is left blank, the underlying table field caption will be used. Form1, for example, will be given a unique name by Microsoft Access if you don't define a caption for a button, form, or label.

- If you want an ampersand to appear in the caption text, enter two ampersands (&&) in the setting for a caption. For instance, enter Save && Exit in the Caption property box to display Save & Exit.

- Use the Caption attribute to attach an access key to a label or command button. The character you intend to use as an access key should be preceded by an ampersand (&) in the caption and usually underlined. Hit Alt and the underlined character to switch the attention to a control on a form.

Default Value Property

- You can set a field's default value, which will be applied to all new records. If necessary, you can modify the default value of a field when adding another entry.

- You can establish a default value by entering the desired value in the Field Properties' Default Value field. For example, the default text you enter for a Text field should be exemplified in quotes ("); for example, "Net 30." Likewise, date field values should be delimited by a number sign (#); for example, #1/15/95#. Access will naturally enter the number signs if you don't enter them.

- For instance, if a table has client names and addresses, and most of those locations are in Denver, you can determine Data as default value for State field. The Express field's value can be changed only for the new record you make for an occupant client of Nairobi. A table's default value can't be changed after creation.

Required Field Property

- Use the needed attribute to specify whether a field must contain a value. If this attribute is set to Yes, all fields and controls associated to the field must contain a value; null values are prohibited.

- For instance, you could wish to confirm that each record's Last Name control contains a value. On the other hand, suppose you want to allow Null values in a field. Then, you must explicitly mention "validation rule Or Is Null" in the Validation Rule property setting and set required property to No.

Note that the required property does not cover AutoNumber fields.

Input Mask Property

- You can specify exactly the way data should be entered into your database using an input mask. It is an expression that details the formatting requirements for data when entered into the system.

- The format in which a phone number should be entered is specified below. Nine is optional, and the suffix "0" is required, implying that the area code is not compulsory here.

- An example of an input mask is given below:

(999) 000-0000

- Table fields, queries, forms, and report controls can all use input masks. The small dotted icon that looks like this can be Selected to start Input Mask Wizard:

Note that applying an input mask eliminates the need for using the wizard. You can enter the input mask straight into its cell if you know how to get it done. The only action taken by the input mask wizard is to create a suitable mask and insert it into the same cell.

Also, remember that you cannot apply an input mask to a field with a Date Picker on it.

Custom Input Mask

In line with the above discussion, you can create input masks in two ways:

Create using Input Mask Wizard (fastest way and easy).

The Input Mask Wizard's one limitation is that you may only use it to build input masks for fields containing ZIP codes, phone numbers, SSN, and timestamps.

By entering a string of characters in your Input Mask box, you can create the input mask on your own (the more difficult way). By looking at the table after this session, you can see what you need to enter to build an input mask if you wish to use this method.

FORMS

We have been manually inserting and entering data directly into our tables. Meanwhile, think of a situation where you need to have other individuals in your company add data to your table; it may not be as user-friendly to them as it is to you. The way out is to create a form making it pretty easy for other people in your organization to add data.

To **add a form**, firstly, select the desired table to create its Form by double-clicking on it.

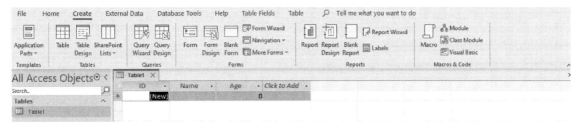

Figure 245: Creating a form

Now, click the **Create** tab and observe the **Forms** group. In the Forms group, we have different options to help you create a form.

However, clicking on **Form** is the easiest way to create a form.

Then, you are presented with a new form, and inside it is what your table looks like. Beneath the Form is the other table, which shows because we have linked the two tables together.

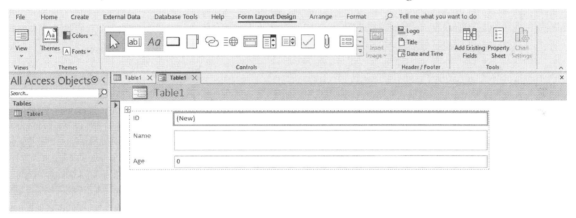

Figure 246: Form layout

You can use buttons at the Form's bottom to move from one Form to another and add a new (blank) record.

Customizing Forms

You can change the appearance of your Form by adding themes, colors, controls, logos, and more in the Design tab.

Design View

Just as we have Design View in tables, we also have Design View in forms. Click **Design View** button at the bottom right corner.

In the Design View, you can move different elements around and design the Form depending on how you want it to look.

Form View

The **Form View** button is at bottom right corner, which will allow you and other people to add records to your table. When you need to **add a new record** to your table through the Form, go to the lower part of your Form and click the **New (blank) record** icon. After clicking on it, you can fill out the Form and do the same for the linked table. After changing and customizing your Form, the next thing to do is save and close the Form. Then, click the **Save** icon to save and give it a name. Then, right-click your Form at the title bar and choose **Close**.

You should now notice a new category on your navigation panel, which says **Forms**. And in Forms, we have the Form we just created. You can double-click on it to open it.

74 REPORTS

This chapter will examine how you can create a basic report and add some features. Then, you'll see how to do some calculations in your reports and how you can do a specific report based on a query.

What is a Report?

A report is a way to organize or summarize the data so that it can be printed.

If you have a table with lots of data and have to print it just like that, it would be challenging to see all the data. It isn't very easy seeing it in that table format, especially if you're presenting that printed document to someone else. So instead, you can take that table and the data in that table or a query and base a report on it to make it look a little bit better.

The report is very similar to Forms, except you're just doing it in a printed format instead of a form.

Some Terminologies

At the top of a report, we put the **Labels** for the fields so that you know what each column is about, and then the section below contains the **Textboxes** that will contain the data from the table or the query that you are referring to.

You'll see a page header with labels that'll display as it is so that you can change those and it won't affect anything. However, the detail section has text boxes with the actual link to the fields in the table, so whatever is in the table will be displayed there. But, again, you can't change these because it will show the value for the fields.

You'll notice in your report that there are many blocks for each row in the design view. It only shows one, and it will just repeat this detail section again and again until it gets to the bottom of the page, and then it will recreate the page with a brand-new page header and then continue with those details.

Controls in Reports

You can add some controls to reports similar to what we did in forms. You can add a label, and if you want to specify other information on the report, you can use a label. You can use an image component if you connect to an image or show a little picture. If you wish to draw a line or separate something with a line, you can use the line component. You can use all these options, and we'll try them now in the report.

Creating A Report

Using our database from the previous examples, we're going to create a new report. To do that, click on **Create** and go to the **Report** options. You can design a report, have a blank report, add values, or use the **Report Wizard**. For this illustration, we are going with the last option.

After clicking on that option, you can specify the values you want in your report and the fields you want.

When you click "**Next**," it'll ask if you want to do a grouping. We'll talk about grouping as we proceed.

Next, specify if you want to sort data by a particular field.

You can also select the layout for your report.

Lastly, you will be asked to give your report a name or title. Again, remember the naming conventions; since this is a report, you can use "Rep" as your prefix to know the difference between the table data and the report data.

Click on "**Finish**," and it will show the Design and display the Form for you.

This opens up in the Print preview option, where you can see what each page will look like, and you can go straight to printing, but if you're not satisfied with the report, you can edit it to look better. To do this, go to the design view, and now you can change things over here.

If you notice that the birth date doesn't fit, you can change the report's layout, so look at the options at the top and work with those options.

If you see hashes on your report, you can't see the data in that field because it's not big enough. So to avoid that, you can rearrange some of these fields to make them spaced out and a little bigger.

If you want to make it justified or you want to make it left-aligned or right-aligned, you can do all those types of things by selecting Home and seeing all the options over here.

You can change the labels, and it won't affect the data but for the text boxes, leave them as is because that's going to fetch the data from the table and repeat this detail section.

You can also do other features to your report, such as adding another label at the top or editing a particular label. For example, let's say you want to put a line between each record. In that case, click on the Line icon under your Design tab at the top, which will put a nice line across. Then, you can right-click on that line, go to Properties, and see other options specific to that line. Please note that anything you do in detail will be repeated for each displayed record.

Calculations In Reports

Before we continue, you must know which control you may use to enter these formulas, and that control is the Text box. When designing your report, you may include a text box and then enter the formula within the text box. You cannot use standard Text in a text box; if you wish to enter standard Text, use a label.

So, what are the types of calculations that you can use?

If you want to add up all the values in a particular field, then you will use Equals sum (**=SUM**), and then in brackets, you will write down the name of the field that you want to do the summing on. This is very similar to Excel, except that instead of cell references like A1 to A10, you'll write the field name you are referring to. You'll notice that the field name is in square brackets; that's the format. If you do not have spaces in your field names, then you can write them just as is, and they will put the square brackets in for you but if you have spaces, use a square bracket. Another is the "**MAX**," which finds the biggest value out of that particular field. Then, there's the "**MIN**," the smallest value. And then there's the "**AVG**" if you want to find the average amount paid.

There's also a "**COUNT**" where you can count how many records there are so that you can count all the emails, for example, but because you're counting all the records, you don't need to specify a particular field. Instead, you could use a *****.

The first four functions can only be used with numerical fields or fields that have numbers. For instance, it is possible to find average amount paid or the sum of all the outstanding amounts, so for anything that has to do with currency or numerical value, you can use those first. **Conversely, COUNT can be used in any field, so when you use the COUNT, you can use any field in it or a ***.

Please note that these functions cannot be used in the header or footer of a page. This is because you can't find the sum of all the values on a particular page or some or the max of all the values on a particular page. So these will not work in the page header and footer, so don't put them there.

If you wish to include a formula in the page header or footer, you may use the current page number. To do this, say = **[PAGE]** keyword, which will give you the current page number. If you want the total number of pages, that'll be = **[PAGES]**.

If you want to use the NOW field, which is =**NOW ()**, that will give you the current date and the time, and then you can format that to display just the time or the date.

So, let's go to the report we designed earlier. Right-click on it, and go to the design view so you can change the details of your report. You'll notice that by default, it's already added a couple of options like **"Now"** and that of the pages.

Let's say you want to find the average of everything in the report. Ideally, you put that in the report footer. But first, click on the text box, which will give you a label and a text box. For example, to find the sum of all the "Paid," that will be written as **=SUM(Paid)**.

Notice that there are no square brackets because you typed just as it is. However, it will put the square brackets in for you. Remember to give it a label as well.

You could also put it in the report header, but that's not a great place to keep in mind that we put all our formulas in the report footer.

Next, go to view; in this case, use Report view, and when you scroll down towards the bottom where you have report footer, you can see that the total amount paid is now included.

If you need to make changes, go back to your design view, **right-click**, and go to Properties. For example, you can change it to currency or add decimals to make it look better.

Remember to always put in the correct spelling, and you can't put the title in a text box. You can only do that in a label because you want the Text to be displayed as it is. This is a basic calculation that you can perform on your reports. To gain full mastery, you can practice with the other formulas.

75 QUESTIONS AND ANSWERS

How do you query a Database?

A database query solicits information from a database, the item program that stays aware of data. A query response regularly returns data from various tables inside your database. You can query to recover some data or alter information in your database, for instance, adding or dispensing with data Users can pick how to use that information reasonably when they get a query response. The real job of a database query is to recuperate information from a database for the user. A database query has several other vital functions, including

- Compiling information
- Presenting results clearly
- Filtering data
- Adding criteria

The two standard sorts of database queries are select queries and action queries.

Benefits of using a Query

- Use verbalizations as fields.
- View records that meet the models that you decide on.
- Accumulate information from a couple of information sources. A table ordinarily shows information that it stores.
- View information just from fields you have more interest to preview. Once a table is opened, you can see each field. A question is a useful strategy for saving a determination of fields.

Creating Basic Queries

To create a Simple Query, follow the procedure below:

On the create tab, identify the Query Wizard.

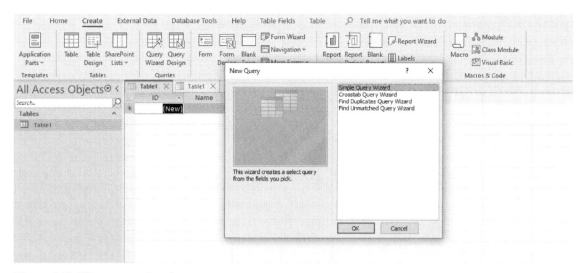

Figure 247: The query wizard

Click Ok.

Addition of field allows you to add up to 255 fields from multiple table or queries.

For each of the fields:

- Under the Available Fields, select your field for easier addition to Selected Fields list. Next, use the double right arrows (>>) to move the field.

- Under Tables/Queries, select table or query containinf the specified field.

- Then click next.

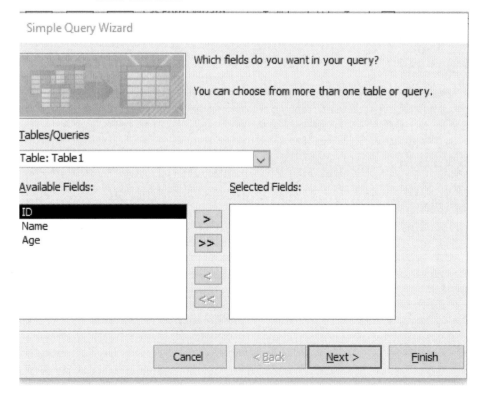

Figure 248: Addition of fields

The wizard will inquire whether you believe the question should return subtleties outline information. Select Summary, and then choose Summary or detailed option Options depending on the user.

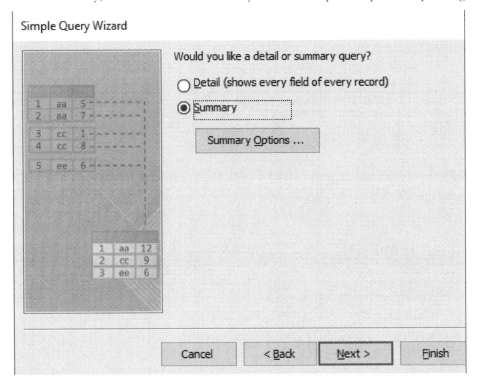

Figure 249: Choosing summary

Show the fields that need a summary and define ways of maintaining that data in summarized form in the dialog box.

You may choose the following for each of you number field:

- **Max**: Query will bring the most significant value within your field.

- **Avg**: Results to average of your values.

- **Sum:** Sums up the values.

- **Min**: Brings the smallest value.

 Pick the proper Include records in the database name check box.

Select OK. You may provide a title to the query, decide if you should open or alter your query and the click Finish.

- **Working with "AND" and "OR" conditions**

An AND operator allows a query to match two conditions, for instance, which people are entrepreneurs and have a vehicle.

An OR operator allows a query to match only a rare example of the situation, for instance, what people go to the office or work from Home.

Sorting and Filtering Data in Queries

Access empowers you to work with huge data measures; sorting and filtering let you change how you coordinate and see your data, making it more beneficial to work with, which suggests it will generally be trying to learn anything about your database by just checking it out.

Sorting and filtering are devices that permit you to coordinate your data. Filtering data permits you to hide insignificant data and spotlight the data you're enthused about. At the point when you sort data, you are dealing with it.

Sorting Data

Records are put legitimately after being sorted with data assembled. Accordingly, sorted data is regularly simpler to scrutinize and comprehend than unsorted data. Access sorts records by their ID numbers. In any case, there are various elective ways the client can sort records. For example, the client could sort the data in a database having a spot with a baked good shop in different ways:

- Clients could be sorted by name, city, or postal division where they dwell.

- The client could sort orders by request date/time or by the username of the clients who presented the solicitations.

- You can sort Text and numbers in two ways: in rising and dropping requests. Rising means going up, so a climbing sort will coordinate numbers from humblest to generally critical and Text from beginning to end.

- Things could be sorted by name, classification (like pies, cakes, and cupcakes), or cost.

To Sort Records:

Choose a field you need to sort.

Choose the Sort & Filter group on the home tab.

Selecting either Ascending or Descending button.

To save the sorted group, select the save option.

After you save the sort, the records will stay sorted until you play another sort or wipe out the continuous one. To wipe out a sort, select the Remove Sort order. **Filtering Data**

Filters permit you to see just the data you need to see. When you make a filter, you set standards for the data you need to show. The filter then, at that point, look through each of the records in the table, track down the ones that meet your hunt measures, and briefly conceals those that don't.

Filters are valuable since they permit you to focus on detailed records without being diverted by the data you're uninterested in. For example, assuming you had a database that included client and request information, you could make a filter to show clients living inside a specific city or orders containing a particular item. Seeing this data with a filter would be more helpful than looking for it in an enormous table.

To apply a filter:

Select the drop-down arrow close to the field you want to filter.

A drop-down menu with a checklist will appear and deselect everything the option needed to filter. Select OK.

Toggling your filter permits you to turn it on and off. To see the records without the filter, Select the Toggle Filter order. To re-establish the filter, select it once more.

Creating Filter from a Selection

Filtering by determination licenses you to pick itemized data from your table and find data that is relative or not the slightest bit like it. Making a filter with a choice can be more beneficial than setting up a good filter on the off chance that the field you're working with contains various things. Assuming you were working with a confectionary store database and expected to search for all things whose names contained the word chocolate, you could pick that word in one thing name and make a filter with that determination. For instance,

- Does Not End With consolidates regardless of records from those whose data for the picked field closes with the pursuit term.

- Does Not Contain involve regardless of records from those with cells containing the picked data?

- Closes With consolidates simply records whose data for the picked field closes with the inquiry term.

- Contains consolidates records with cells that contain the picked data.

76 THE BEST ACCESS PLUGINS

If you're looking for a better way to customize your Microsoft Access applications, you may want to look into UI Builder. This product offers a wide variety of features that nearly every Access user can benefit from. It allows you to focus on your primary needs while offering powerful features that would otherwise be time-consuming to create. It's also user-friendly and includes powerful features experienced software contractors and developers need.

Access SQL Editor is an add-in for Microsoft Access that enables you to save SQL with syntax highlighting and formatting. It also has features such as regex search-and-replace and automatic code formatting. You can also find and replace objects and design time properties in any Access form. Total Access Analyzer is another excellent Access plugin for improving database performance. It analyzes database objects, detects 280 errors, and applies Best Practices. It can also create right-click menus, reveal database object dependencies, and create modern dialogs. Total Access Detective is available in free and paid versions, so you can try it out without paying a single penny.

MS Access is one of the most popular DBMSs used by small and medium-sized businesses and private individuals. Because it's user-friendly and doesn't require extensive programming skills, it's ideal for beginners and those with little experience in database management. However, you should know that other DBMSs work similarly; some are free.

77 TIPS, TRICKS & FAQ WITH COMMON PROBLEMS AND SOLUTIONS

Whether you're developing a business or personal database, finding a solution for a common problem with Microsoft Access is possible. Some solutions can solve these issues, from data entry errors to broken database links. In addition, Microsoft Access has many useful features that make it easier to work with the data. For instance, you can create a search field to find records in one or more of the tables. Once you've created a query, it is possible to save it for future use. Alternatively, you can choose to view the values of database fields.

Learning how to use Microsoft Access can be difficult. This program has many features, and it can seem overwhelming. However, there are plenty of tips and tricks for Microsoft Access that can make your life easier. Let's take a look at some of them. Using these tips, you'll maximize productivity and make the most out of the software.

When you use the program, keep a current backup of your data before making any changes. When using the program, you may accidentally delete a field. Then, Access will remove that record from the table. If this happens, it won't let you undo your changes.

Another tip is to hide the ribbon. Many people hate the ribbon in Access, but hiding it isn't that difficult. You can do it with a few easy steps. First, double-click a tab to minimize its visibility, and Access will remember that you don't want the ribbon to open. Another easy tip for minimizing disk space is choosing the data type optimized for the data. This will save on storage space and processing time. Selecting the smallest data type is best, but you can also use secondary indexes with a large table. These secondary indexes provide performance gains of an order of magnitude.

DO AWAY WITH DATA MISMATCH

Data mismatch means entering data into a field different from the data type you specify for the field or having different data types between primary and foreign key that connect the two tables you put into the relationship. Data mismatch prevents you from establishing a relationship between the table you put to the relation window or query design window, affecting your query result.

WRONG CRITERIA BRING WRONG OR NO QUERY RESULT

Make all necessary efforts to enter the correct criteria into each field you put to the grid field, and do not make the mistake of entering criteria into the wrong field. These two mistakes are the consequences of wrong or no query results.

THERE SHOULD BE A LINK BETWEEN THE TABLES IN THE RELATIONSHIP

It is of great importance for the tables in relationship to have a direct link, which means there should be "implement referential integrity" between the tables in terms of recorded data and the data type in them.

EACH TABLE SHOULD HAVE A PRIMARY KEY, AND IT SHOULD BE A NUMERIC DATA TYPE

It is the principle of the database table to have a primary key that should uniquely identify other data in the field to make the relationship between tables convenient. However, it is not about having a primary key field only. The field should be a numeric data type to make that uniqueness an easy task, such as AutoNumber, ID, which should be numeric, and so on. On the other hand, using no numeric data type renders the uniqueness of the primary key field meaningless such as city name, first name, etc.

VALIDATING ACCESS DATA TYPE

The simplest and easiest way to restrict wrong data into the database table is to program the data type with validation field properties. This command issues a warning error anytime there is an attempt to enter data different from the programming data through the validation rule in the field properties.

Encrypting an Access Database

In earlier MS Access versions (before 2007), it was possible to create user accounts with different permissions to different sets of objects, which was called multi-user security. That feature is no longer available in the .accdb versions (2007 and later). In the current version of Access, each user will use the same Password to access the database in a multi-user environment.

Be careful when encrypting and always remember the password. You can't decrypt the database without your Password. Hence, it would help if you were careful when creating a password for your database. You don't want a situation where you cannot access important data because the Password has been lost. For that reason, only set a password if necessary for your working circumstances.

To encrypt an Access database with a password, follow the steps below:

Step 1: Open your database in the Exclusive mode.

1. Open Access.
2. Access opens to the Backstage view.

    Note: If you already have another database open, click the **File** tab to display the Backstage view.

3. In the Backstage view, click **Open > Browse**.

4. In **Open** dialog box, navigate to database you wish opened and choose the file.

5. Click drop-down arrow near **Open** button and select **Open Exclusive** from the pop-up menu.

Step 2: Encrypt the Database with a password.

1. With the database now open in Exclusive mode, click **File** tab to return to Backstage view and select **Info > Encrypt with Password**.

Access displays **Set Database Password** dialog box.

2. In the **Password** box, enter your desired password. Repeat in **Verify** box to confirm it clicking **OK**.

3. Click **OK** at the next prompt to encrypt the database with a password.

4. Close and then reopen.

Access will display **Password Required** dialog box.

5. Enter your Password, and click **OK**.

Access will decrypt and open the database.

Important: You mustn't forget your Password. To be on the safe side, before you protect your database with a password, ensure you've written down the Password and stored it in a safe place where it can be retrieved if necessary. Unfortunately, Microsoft does not provide any methods to access a password-protected Access file where the Password has been lost.

78 THE STRATEGIC SHORTCUTS

SHORTCUTS FOR ENTERING DATA IN DATASHEET VIEW

KEYBOARD SHORTCUTS	DESTINATION
↓	Moving to next record of the same field
↑	Moving to previous record of the same field
Enter or Tab or right arrow	Moving to next field in the same record.
Shift + Tab or right arrow	Moving to previous field in the same record.
Home	Moving to first field of current record.
End	Moving to last field of the current record.
Ctrl + Home	Moving to first field in the first record.
Ctrl + End	Moving to last field in the last record.
Page up	Moving up one screen.
Page down	Moving down one screen.

GENERAL SHORTCUTS

KEYBOARD SHORTCUTS	PURPOSES
Ctrl + O	Open an existing database
F11	Show/ hide navigation pane
F2	Switch between edit mode navigation mode in the datasheet and Design view
F1	Open the Help window
Ctrl + F1	Expand/collapse the ribbon
Ctrl + S	Save the database objects
Ctrl + X	Move selected content to clipboard
Ctrl + C	Copy selected content to clipboard
Ctrl + V	Paste clipboard content to selected cells or sections.
Ctrl + F	Open Find in find and replace dialog box in both views
Ctrl + H	Open Replace in find and replace dialog box in both views.

GRID PANE SHORTCUTS

KEYBOARD SHORTCUTS	PURPOSES
Arrow keys, Tab, shift + tab keys	To move among cells
Ctrl + Spacebar	To select an entire grid column
F2	To switch between edit mode and navigation mode
Ctrl + X	Move selected content to clipboard
Ctrl + C	Copy selected content to clipboard
Ctrl + V	Paste clipboard content into the selected cells or sections.
Ctrl + Home	Moving to first field in the first record.
Ctrl + End	Moving to last field in the last record.

79 CONCLUSION

Can you now see the efficacy of Access? Access is here to help you more than Excel or Word can do for you, Access main focus is to fill up the weakness of Excel by managing large arrays of data. Managing large arrays of data involves entering unlimited data, querying the data, and then using the query result to generate a professional report for the user. This is the best option for whosoever wishes to learn Access, does not know where and how to get started, or you have little experience but wish to dig deeper to know more about Access. This book is ideal for all levels of users, including those who have learned Excel before. However, your Excel experience is not enough until you know how to match your Excel work hand in hand with Access.

This manual user guide is adequately prepared to expose you to the mystery that guides the management of databases and to put you on the easy track for learning the use of Access in creating a perfect database. Happy exploration.

MICROSOFT ONEDRIVE INTRODUCTION

OneDrive is a popular cloud storage service that has recently become very popular. The MS OneDrive is a cloud storage service allowing users to access their files from any device. It is used by millions of people worldwide and is available on Windows, Linux, and Mac OS X, as well as on iOS and Android. OneDrive allows users to store all their files in one place, so you don't have to keep switching between different devices. OneDrive also allows users to sync their files across all their devices, so you don't have to worry about losing your files when you switch between your laptop and your phone. To use OneDrive, you need to have an active Internet connection. If you're not sure you're connected, check on a computer turned on in the background. If it's still turned off or if you can't see it, plug it in and try again in a few minutes.

OneDrive for business is a version of Microsoft's Office 365 business suite that can be installed on-premises. In addition, it provides access to files and storage from the Office apps that are unavailable on-premises. The cloud storage service is integral to the Microsoft Office 365 suite.

The cloud is the biggest threat to data storage, and companies not prepared for this will be left behind. Cloud storage and data security are hot topics these days. The problem is that there is no single standard for cloud storage, which varies from company to company. This may confuse customers unaware of the different types of cloud services available in their market and what they offer.

What is Microsoft OneDrive?

Microsoft OneDrive is a file hosting service that was first launched in August 2007. This service allows registered users to synchronize and share files. It also works as a storage backend for Microsoft Office. Its functionality is vast, and its popularity has only continued to grow. It's an excellent service for storing and sharing files.

OneDrive offers several options for sharing and limiting access. It has different permission levels for different users. For example, if you share a file with a colleague, you can control access and set restrictions. For instance, you can control who can view and edit the file. You can uncheck the box next to Allow editing to limit access to specific users.

OneDrive is available on many devices, including Windows and Mac computers. It lets you store and share files from any computer. You can access the files on your laptop, desktop, or mobile device.

OneDrive even synchronizes data with your PC and mobile devices. This is an extremely convenient feature, especially for those with limited storage.

OneDrive also integrates with Microsoft apps. Professionals who use Microsoft Word and PowerPoint often may find OneDrive extremely useful. It's also useful for professionals in customer service, freelance writing, transcription, and bookkeeping. Educators and students can also find OneDrive helpful.

OneDrive also offers cloud storage solutions for businesses. It has quickly become the cloud storage service of choice. You can even integrate it with Office 365 and OneNote. However, be wary of sharing sensitive data. OneDrive has strict privacy and security policies, and users should consider this before using it for personal purposes.

OneDrive can help you access your files across all your devices. It also lets you synchronize your system preferences and settings across devices. OneDrive also offers Files On-Demand, which allows you to access your files without downloading them. It also supports data recovery if the need arises. You can store up to 5 GB of files free of charge. You can also buy additional storage for a fee. OneDrive is a cloud storage service provided by Microsoft. To access this service, you must sign in with your Microsoft account. OneDrive will then display a folder where your files will be synchronized. You can also choose to sync your work files or just a few.

What's New in OneDrive for Business?

OneDrive for Business is Microsoft's new cloud storage service. It offers many advantages to users, such as the ability to create, edit and share files from anywhere and sync files across multiple devices. OneDrive for business also has some new features. One of these features is OneDrive Files On-Demand (ODFO). With ODFO, you can access your files from any device running Windows 8.1 or the latest, including your smartphone, tablet, or laptop. You can also access your files on your PC if you have an Internet connection - even offline! File on-demand is a feature that you can use to access your files. Here's how it works: You create a OneDrive folder somewhere on your PC. Then, from this one drive, you can access files from any other computer or device running Windows 8.1 or the latest.

Why You Need Microsoft OneDrive

To share files with colleagues, you should sign up for Microsoft OneDrive. It's a cloud storage solution that lets you collaborate on documents with other people in real-time. When a single person changes a document, all collaborators will be notified immediately, and changes can be tracked. It also has a built-in image scanner that lets you scan documents, photos, and business cards. OneDrive is a cloud storage service that syncs and stores files on multiple computers. You can also use OneDrive to backup and synchronize Office documents. The service is compatible with a variety of Microsoft products. OneDrive also makes it easy to collaborate with others. You can set up your OneDrive accounts on as many computers as you wish, and the service will automatically synchronize files from each machine.

OneDrive's feature of "files-on-demand" makes it easy to back up and sync your files. Of course, you'll need an internet connection to access your files, but the service automatically backs up your files and subfolders. That way, you don't have to worry about saving space.

Another great feature of OneDrive is that it integrates seamlessly with Microsoft's apps and services. This makes it ideal for multi-device use. Moreover, OneDrive allows you to store files online and access them on any device. You can also share files with others and save changes to your files. OneDrive is a free service, but it comes with some limitations. The service only offers limited free storage space. There are also restrictions when sharing files with others. For instance, Microsoft reserves the right to scan OneDrive files for objectionable content. The service also has several problems, including sluggishness and a lack of security.

OneDrive also offers mobile apps. It is available on iOS, Android, and macOS devices. It also supports Xbox devices. There are several storage plans available, including a free 15 GB option. The service also offers a web interface and is accessible on any platform. Whether you're working on a laptop, iPad, iPhone, or Android phone, OneDrive is easy to use and is available on many devices.

OneDrive is a cloud storage service that lets you sync and share files across computers. The program works with Windows 10 and 11 and supports a variety of multimedia and document formats. It is also compatible with Mac and Linux, allowing you to access OneDrive files from a PC or mobile device. If you're working on a project, OneDrive will enable you to work on the project from multiple time zones and even share your inspiration with others.

Among the other benefits of OneDrive, is its simplicity makes it easy to share documents with others. All you have to do is enter the URL of the document, and the recipient will receive it. That way, you can easily share documents without any worry that you won't be able to view them.

Microsoft OneDrive has strong encryption for your data. Although it's not 100% secure, it does protect your files against unwanted prying eyes. In addition to being a secure cloud storage solution, OneDrive allows you to set up two-factor authentication to protect your identity.

Another downside of OneDrive is its poor support. While it does offer a helpline, it lacks live chat. Other cloud storage providers offer live chat support. You can try community forums or search through how-to articles if you run into trouble. However, if you need help, you can only contact the support team via e-mail. Support response times were reasonably fast, but sometimes they took more than two hours to answer your query.

Another positive of OneDrive is its high level of integration with Microsoft's suite of productivity products. For example, if you use Microsoft Office products, you'll be able to access your OneDrive folder from any device. Another advantage is that you can set different levels of sharing and editing permissions for documents. This makes it easy to collaborate with others within and outside your organization.

OneDrive offers unlimited cloud storage. It is easy to setup and use. The OneDrive folder will automatically appear on your computer. Once you have logged in with your Microsoft account, you can add files to OneDrive and begin using the service. You can also share files with other OneDrive users. You can even use the OneDrive search feature to find files within folders.

Is Microsoft OneDrive free?

Microsoft OneDrive is free online storage that keeps your files safe and synced. It has an app that lets you share, view, and back up files. OneDrive also backs up your photos automatically. OneDrive can be used on Windows PCs, Macs, and Android devices. Getting started is easy; all it takes is a few clicks. You can also backup your phone's pictures and videos to OneDrive. You can get up to five GB of free storage for your files when you sign up. You can opt for a Microsoft 365 subscription with up to 100 GB of storage space if you want more storage.

When using OneDrive, you can easily back up, sync, and share files with your team. The program also provides e-mail support and two-factor authentication. This means that your data is secure, and you will receive a notification if there is a security breach. OneDrive supports in-transit AES 256-bit encryption, which means that your files will be encrypted while they're in-transit.

Another feature of Microsoft OneDrive is that you can receive up to 10GB of free storage if you sign up for the service. OneDrive also offers rewards for inviting new users to your account. If you have friends using the program, you can invite them to sign up. The more friends you invite, the more free storage you can get. You can also sign up for Office 365, which provides unlimited storage space.

The downside of OneDrive is that it only offers a limited amount of free storage. If you have a lot of files, you might find that the limit is too low. This is especially true if you use the program on multiple devices. If you only use one computer, the program will be more than enough to accommodate your files.

OneDrive is available for PCs and mobile devices, so you can easily transfer files between different devices. It is compatible with different operating systems and supports different documents and multimedia. You can access your files on your phone or tablet from anywhere. OneDrive also supports your Xbox console.

What happens if I turn off OneDrive?

Microsoft OneDrive is an integral part of the Microsoft Office suite. However, it can also cause your computer to slow down. Disabling the OneDrive application will allow you to free up RAM and CPU, which can be used for other tasks. However, it is essential to note that OneDrive will continue to run when you turn off your PC unless you turn it off yourself.

If you want to unlink your computer from OneDrive, you can do so through the settings tab. There are four options available. The first is to disable syncing. The second option is to unlink your PC from OneDrive completely. This will ensure that your files will no longer be synced with the OneDrive service.

OneDrive is a system service that is installed by default on Windows computers. Many users have objected to this inclusion, and disabling it is a simple and permanent solution. It has many advantages but also disadvantages. One of the main advantages of disabling OneDrive is that your local files will remain in place.

If you're concerned about security, you can disable OneDrive using the UAC feature. This option is more secure than the uninstall option. Nevertheless, you should choose a safe method before removing OneDrive. If unsure about the steps, follow the steps below to disable OneDrive.

You can also choose to pause OneDrive's syncing. This will allow you to work on other tasks while OneDrive is off. You can also use the pause feature to edit your files without constantly resyncing. This will also free up your PC's internet bandwidth.

Another way to turn off OneDrive is to unlink your PC and account. This will prevent OneDrive from syncing your files with the cloud. Although you'll still see the OneDrive icon on your PC's taskbar, it will not sync your files. The next time you log in to OneDrive, your files will automatically start syncing again.

Another way to stop Microsoft OneDrive is to disable it from starting on Windows. To do this, you can either uncheck the "Start OneDrive automatically when Windows signs in" option or disable the entire OneDrive startup process.

To learn more about OneDrive, keep reading! You'll find answers to frequently asked questions. For instance, is OneDrive free?

The introduction should start with a brief overview of what is happening in the industry, why it's important, what problems it solves, and some of its benefits.

The main topic should be: "What happens when your business needs more storage space than you can afford? What if you could buy cheap or free group-wide storage from an external source? What if you could get unlimited free usage of your data?"

80 SYNCHRONIZATION

What is synchronization?

Synchronization is a term that describes one of two concepts: the synchronization of processes and data. While the two are closely related, they are not the same. To fully understand the difference, we must first define what synchronization is. Here are some basic terms that describe synchronization. Synchronization occurs when two nonidentical oscillators begin oscillating at the same frequency. This frequency is called the common frequency. The common frequency is typically between and. If the frequencies are nonidentical, then the phase and amplitude will differ. In the case of two different oscillators, synchronization occurs when the coupling strength exceeds a critical threshold.

There are various examples of synchronization, from orchestral instruments playing the same tune to an automated assembly line in a car factory. In any case, synchronization involves matching the speeds of the two components. One common example of synchronization is the synchronization of the alternator in an electric power system.

Synchronization also occurs in the context of multithreading. Multithreading uses two or more threads to execute a single piece of code. Each instruction sequence has its unique flow of control. By using the synchronized keyword, one thread can call another synchronized method. This allows the thread that holds the lock to access the synchronized method. The following example shows how this works. In this program, a number is passed as an argument to the synchronized method. Then, squares of the number are printed until the upper limit is reached.

In computing, synchronization is the process of coordinating parts of a system. It ensures that they are executed in the right order and don't encounter unexpected race conditions. This process is used in many systems in our lives. GPS time-keeping systems and digital signals enable us to do this globally. Synchronization helps organizations protect data against potential data breaches. Data leakage or breaches can harm a company's reputation and revenue. A synchronization tool keeps data safe and synchronized according to each system's security requirements.

Where to use OneDrive - Desktop or Mobile or Web

OneDrive offers various services and features to users, from backing up files to syncing them and sharing them with others. While this service is available on various platforms, there are some downsides. First, the support is very limited. You can only get in touch with a customer service representative via e-mail or a general support line, which is disappointing given that many other cloud storage providers have a live chat. If you do have a problem, you can check the community forums and search for how-to articles. You can also e-mail support; the response time is usually quick, but the average was over two hours.

OneDrive is easy to set up and includes pre-installed software on Windows computers. While other cloud storage services can be complicated to install, OneDrive is much easier to install and use. After downloading and installing the program, OneDrive appears as a folder on your computer. To access your files, sign in with your Microsoft account.

You can also access your OneDrive files on your mobile device. A free OneDrive application is available for iOS, Android, and Windows 10 mobile devices, as well as Windows Phones. To download the app to your mobile device, visit the app store or the Microsoft website.

OneDrive also offers many options for sharing links and setting restrictions, depending on your account type. For example, you can share your files with your team via the OneDrive app or a link. You can specify "Public" as the link recipient in both cases.

If you don't already have a Microsoft account, you can sign up for one. This way, you can use OneDrive on all your devices. You can also use OneDrive for Business on iOS or Android mobile devices. After creating your Microsoft account, you can access your files through the OneDrive website and upload and view them.

OneDrive is an excellent way to backup your data across all your devices. However, if you sign out of your online account, you may have difficulty recovering your OneDrive password. However, you can use OneDrive on demand, which lets you save files in the cloud and only download them when needed.

What are the Plans for OneDrive?

OneDrive is a cloud storage service that allows users to access various data from anywhere. The program offers file synchronization, tagging, and more. It also allows users to download specific files when needed. This is useful for people who have limited storage space. Users can also set up restrictions on their data and file access.

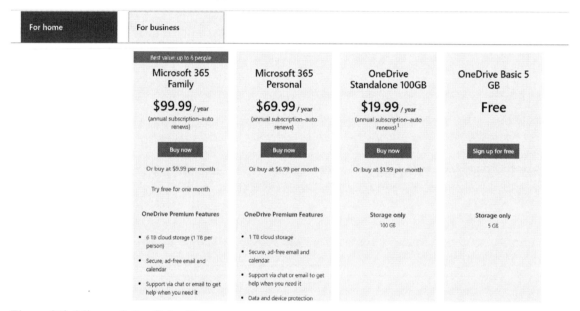

Figure 250: Microsoft OneDrive Plans

In June, Microsoft announced new storage plans for OneDrive. For those who subscribe to Office 365, OneDrive storage will increase to 1 TB. This will cost $1.99 monthly, and users can change the plan anytime. Microsoft initially said these plans would be available in the coming months. However, today, the Microsoft Store has listed them.

OneDrive is compatible with Microsoft Office 365, Outlook, and OneNote. It also offers e-mail support and is protected by two-factor authentication. However, OneDrive does not offer zero-knowledge encryption. However, users can enable in-transit AES 256-bit encryption for their files. For business users, OneDrive business plans offer greater benefits than personal plans. They offer unlimited storage, advanced security, and compliance features. However, unlike personal plans, business users can share files with others, so personal use plans aren't a good option if you're working alone.

OneDrive for Business allows businesses to access files and collaborate on projects from anywhere. They can also share files and assign permissions. The service is a good replacement for the 'My Documents' folder on a local computer. For only $10 per month, business users can get unlimited storage for their files. Additionally, they can eliminate the risk of data corruption due to hardware failure.

Microsoft has added various features to OneDrive, including creating and editing files on demand. In addition, OneDrive is also privacy-conscious, offering various sharing options. Users can choose whether to keep their files in the cloud or locally.

Microsoft OneDrive also offers business plans for businesses, with features including file auditing and user management. Plans one and two cost $5 per user per month but do not include Microsoft 365 apps. Business Plan 2 gives business users unlimited individual cloud storage and advanced security.

81 MICROSOFT ONEDRIVE VS OTHER APPLICATIONS

Microsoft OneDrive is a cloud-based service that lets you store, share, and access files on your computer from anywhere. You can access your files from any computer with an account, such as a work or school. OneDrive can be a great choice if you need to share files with coworkers or students.

OneDrive vs. Google Drive

Microsoft OneDrive is a cloud storage program similar to Google Drive. However, its features are limited compared to those of Google. For example, you can no longer collaborate in real-time on your Google Drive documents and must give everyone permission to edit your work. Also, OneDrive's search engine is not as effective as Google's.

The cost of using OneDrive is slightly lower than Google's. OneDrive offers two types of plans, one for free and one for a small fee. Google Drive has a free tier that allows you to upload up to 15GB of files. However, you have to pay a monthly subscription to access unlimited space. Unlike Google Drive, Microsoft OneDrive has no limit on how many files you can store, and you can upgrade at any time without worrying about your storage limit.

OneDrive also has an app that allows you to work offline. The app will enable you to sync your files with multiple devices. It can also be accessed through the web. Both programs allow you to create folders and store files. They are both compatible with many file formats. They also provide you with access to other applications and hardware.

Microsoft OneDrive is a cloud storage option that allows you to store personal information and exchange files. It is similar to Google Drive, but Microsoft OneDrive offers more storage space. OneDrive is great for projects that involve large amounts of files. To use OneDrive, you must sign up for a Microsoft account and download the desktop and mobile apps. The files sync automatically across all your devices without interruption.

Another essential aspect to consider when comparing Google Drive vs. OneDrive is security. The higher the security, the less likely a data leak or account compromise will occur. However, there is no 100 percent security guarantee when using a public cloud storage service, so you must trust the service provider.

Microsoft OneDrive is a cloud storage service that integrates well with Microsoft apps and integrates easily. It also syncs information between accounts, making sharing files with other users easier. However, Google Drive is widely used, and its free version is very generous. Both options are useful for file sharing and collaboration.

OneDrive vs. SharePoint

OneDrive and SharePoint are widely used document management systems, but their functionality differs. While SharePoint helps businesses improve their workflow and ensure regulatory compliance, OneDrive suits individuals and personal users more. Read on to learn more about the differences between these two cloud storage services. And keep reading for a comprehensive OneDrive vs. SharePoint comparison. You'll be glad you did! Here's how to choose the right one for your needs! Both services offer centralized storage for personal and work-related files. SharePoint allows users to share files with multiple people, while OneDrive will enable users to edit data only if they have administrator permissions. This feature is ideal for storing first drafts and other personal files that others won't access.

OneDrive is ideal for individuals who want to store documents in a secure online folder. However, it is not ideal for business users, as it's not designed for sharing with external users. In addition, OneDrive users are limited to 1TB of storage, which limits its ability to be used for projects in a business setting. However, users can pay for additional storage to increase their storage capacity. SharePoint can handle up to 15TB of data.

SharePoint is a more effective tool for collaboration than OneDrive, allowing entire offices to create online workspaces. With SharePoint, users can manage their projects through calendars, status updates, and deadline notifications. However, OneDrive and SharePoint also offer some unique features, making them distinctly different. For example, OneDrive is primarily used to share private files, while SharePoint is a hub for collaborative work.

SharePoint is a cloud-based storage service designed to allow teams to collaborate. OneDrive is best for personal use, while SharePoint is a popular cloud-based solution for business use. For personal use, OneDrive is better if you use Office or Windows for your business. In addition to sharing files, OneDrive also offers co-authoring and version history. OneDrive supports mobile devices and syncing files across the internet.

Microsoft OneDrive is cheaper than SharePoint. SharePoint online costs $5 per user per month for individual users and $10 per user per month for a small enterprise. For larger businesses, SharePoint is included in the Office 365 E3 suite, which costs $20 per user. OneDrive starts at a basic plan of 5 GB for individual users. Two plans are also available for businesses, and OneDrive for Business costs $5 per user per month.

OneDrive vs. Dropbox

Microsoft's OneDrive offers a much more flexible subscription plan. For example, for $10 a month, you can get unlimited photo storage. OneDrive also provides an impressive list of apps and is part of Microsoft's Office 365 suite. If you want to share large files, both services offer flexible sharing options, including the ability to add an expiration date.

OneDrive provides a synchronized file system that you can access from any computer. It also allows for secure file transfer and version history. For added security, it also offers archival recovery and password protection. It is also easy to use. OneDrive is particularly useful for businesses and students who need a convenient cloud storage service.

The primary differences between OneDrive and Dropbox are their storage capacity and features. Dropbox is free for individuals, while OneDrive is a paid service. Businesses can get unlimited space by paying a monthly subscription. Dropbox's free plan only offers 500 GB of space. Depending on the size of your files, you may need to pay more for storage space. If you're looking for a cloud storage option for your organization, OneDrive is the better choice.

OneDrive is more secure than Dropbox. Both services use AES 256-bit encryption to keep your files safe and secure. OneDrive's encryption is effective both in in-transit and at rest. Both Dropbox and OneDrive also offer two-factor authentication to protect your files. Whether you're storing your files in the cloud or on your device, encryption is the key to protecting your data.

Dropbox is a popular cloud storage service and has over 200 million users. Its simple interface makes sharing files a snap. Dropbox also includes a collaborative document tool called Dropbox Paper. While Dropbox Paper isn't a replacement for native office apps, it does offer an additional security layer. Dropbox offers a rewind feature, allowing users to restore a previous file version. Unlike Google Drive, however, Dropbox has a limit of 30 days on which you can restore a file. Dropbox does not have an e-mail client or office suite, but it does offer other features, such as a note-taking app, document signer, file transfer service, and a password manager. Dropbox also lets you take screenshots.

OneDrive vs. iCloud

OneDrive is a cloud storage service that comes pre-installed on Windows and Mac computers. Users can sign in and access files stored in OneDrive by using their user accounts. This makes the service an excellent choice for both personal and business use. OneDrive also offers the added benefit of being convenient and cost-effective.

While iCloud works better for users of Apple devices, OneDrive is designed to work with any device. It has more options for mobile use than iCloud and comes with a generous five-gigabyte free storage plan. You can also pay for up to one terabyte of storage for a fee.

Despite its simplicity, OneDrive is not without its drawbacks. While the OneDrive app is convenient, it lacks zero-knowledge encryption, so Microsoft can share your encryption keys with third-party providers and authorities. However, if you use OneDrive, you will be notified of any data breach as soon as possible. You can then change your password and turn on additional security features. Microsoft OneDrive has several downsides over iCloud, but if you're an Apple user, iCloud is the better choice.

If you own an iPhone or Mac, you can easily activate iCloud on all your devices. Your back-ups are instantly synchronized with all your Apple devices, and your files are accessible from any device. However, iCloud is more convenient for iPhone and Apple users because it's compatible with Windows devices.

When it comes to security, iCloud is superior to OneDrive. It offers two-factor authentication and encryption, but you must pay to enable it. This makes it much harder for unauthorized users to access your files. You must back up your data regularly with these two cloud storage services.

In general, OneDrive and iCloud both offer solid cloud storage solutions. However, you should choose based on your personal needs. For example, if you don't own an iPhone or an iPad, you may find OneDrive a better choice.

82 SOFTWARE INTERFACE AND USE

The MS OneDrive software interface and use

OneDrive is a cloud storage service from Microsoft. It requires a Microsoft account, but once you have one, you can easily access it from any device. In addition, you can also use OneDrive on your Xbox console. Once you have created an account, you can visit the OneDrive website and upload or download files.

To download OneDrive, you can download the app from an app store or go directly to the Microsoft website. You'll also need your Microsoft account details, as well as your Microsoft password. You can create an account for free or pay a monthly fee. The interface will automatically save your documents, and you can access them anytime.

Another feature that you can use to save space is Files on Demand. When you don't have access to the internet, you can use OneDrive to edit your files offline. OneDrive will automatically store changes. It's helpful if you're on a limited amount of storage. This feature also means that you can access your files on any device that can access your Microsoft account.

Figure 251: Files on Demand features

MS OneDrive is pre-installed on Windows computers, making it more convenient. It's also easier to set up than other cloud storage services. Once you've installed it, you'll see a folder on your computer called "OneDrive." After logging in with your Microsoft account, you can upload files to OneDrive. Another great feature of OneDrive is the ability to secure your files. It uses two-factor authentication, so you can use your fingerprint to sign in. You can also add a phone or e-mail code as an extra security measure. Lastly, OneDrive users can create a personal vault to store sensitive files.

OneDrive is also convenient for file sharing. If you're working with a team, you'll find that OneDrive is an excellent choice for sharing files. OneDrive's left sidebar makes it easy to check which files are shared and toggle who can view them. You can also send a link to a contact or copy a link to share files with others.

Is Microsoft OneDrive software?

Microsoft OneDrive is a file hosting service that was first launched in August 2007. It allows registered users to store, share, and synchronize files. It also functions as the storage backend for Microsoft Office. The service is free and easy to use. It is an excellent alternative to a traditional hard drive and is an easy way to backup important files.

OneDrive integrates with Office, Skype, OneNote, and Outlook. It is also very fast. The only drawback is that it doesn't yet support zero-knowledge encryption, although Microsoft is working towards implementing this feature. There are plenty of other benefits to using OneDrive. If you're worried about security, you can always turn off automatic syncing and store files on your PC.

OneDrive's best feature is its ability to integrate with Microsoft's other products and services. OneDrive is best for users with multiple devices. With OneDrive, you can store, access, and share your files on your devices. OneDrive can also synchronize your browsing history and passwords.

You can download the OneDrive client from the Microsoft website if you don't have a desktop app. After downloading, double-click the offline installer to install the software. You can download the OneDrive client from the Mac OS X website if you don't have a Windows PC. The Mac installation process will be slightly different than the Windows version.

OneDrive also has a Personal Vault, which allows users to store sensitive files in a separate, encrypted location. It uses a combination of fingerprint recognition, face recognition, and PIN for security. Users can also receive a code via SMS or e-mail to unlock their accounts. Another helpful feature is the ability to backup your camera roll. When your phone is connected to Wi-Fi, it automatically backup your photos. You can then view these photos in the cloud.

OneDrive also offers desktop and mobile apps for Windows, Android, and iPhone. These applications work the same way as the Windows File Explorer and have many of the same limitations as the desktop version. However, the OneDrive app is an easy and convenient alternative if you have a Windows device.

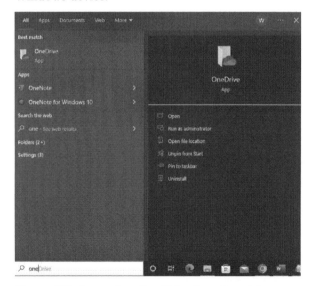

Figure 252: Accessing OneDrive from Start Menu

The basic terms of OneDrive

Microsoft OneDrive is a file storage service that lets you synchronize your data in a secure and convenient location. The service uses a world-class data center and strong encryption. As a result, your data is protected from external attacks and internal unauthorized access. However, sometimes, OneDrive may not be secure enough for your needs. You should be prepared to find alternative storage solutions for your data in these cases.

OneDrive has a feature that is very useful for desktop computers. It allows users to synchronize their files and folders across multiple computers and devices. It's similar to other cloud storage services, such as Dropbox and SugarSync. Microsoft used to offer separate services for syncing and storage, but with OneDrive, these features are combined into a single cloud service.

OneDrive offers a large amount of storage. Its storage space defaults to 15GB, equal to Google Drive. In addition, OneDrive offers 15 GB of camera roll storage for mobile devices. In November 2015, the company increased the storage capacity to 1 TB for Office 365 subscribers. The company also reduced the price of OneDrive storage subscriptions.

OneDrive also allows for easy file management and collaboration. OneDrive folders are easily accessible from any device and can be shared with other users. Sharing files on OneDrive is as simple as dragging and dropping them into another folder. OneDrive also provides backup protection for your files. As a result, OneDrive is a handy tool in many business settings.

Figure 253: Setting up your OneDrive

By signing up with your Microsoft account, you can use OneDrive on your desktops or mobile devices. The OneDrive app is pre-installed on Windows and Mac computers. You can also download it from the Apple App Store or Microsoft's website. OneDrive's interface is easy to navigate and has fields for documents, e-mails, and music.

OneDrive offers the advantages of cloud storage and synchronization, making it ideal for people with work files, large media, and research materials. OneDrive offers free and paid versions and can be used with Office 365 subscriptions. The significant advantage of using OneDrive for your computer is its ability to integrate with your existing software.

Some Signs on OneDrive and Their Meanings

You must have seen some signs or symbols on your OneDrive, but you do not know what they mean or what they stand for. In this part of my teaching, I will have the photos of these signs and inform you what they stand for. I have been using OneDrive for over 11 years and have seen some signs on the OneDrive main icon.

Two Rotate Signs on OneDrive

When you see the sign above on your OneDrive account, it means that a file you uploaded on your OneDrive is uploading to Microsoft cloud. So, you must wait until that sign clears and see only the OneDrive icon. By waiting, I mean your computer should be connected to the internet until the file is uploaded fully.

Grey OneDrive icon

The grey OneDrive icon appearing in taskbar implies that the user has not signed in or OneDrive setup did not complete.

Pause Symbol Over OneDrive Icon

When you see the sign above your OneDrive icon, it means your OneDrive is not syncing. Sometimes, you can see the above pause sign over the main OneDrive icon. There may be a reason for that. It can be because the Wi-Fi you are connected to is metered. As a result, it is configured so that OneDrive cannot sync using the data of the Wi-Fi.

Also, the pause sign can be because your computer battery has gone down and automatically turned to battery-saving mode. When the battery is in this mode, OneDrive is paused to sync automatically, irrespective of the fact that the computer is connected to the internet.

As a user of OneDrive, you can put your OneDrive in pause mode. I have done that before.
Sometimes, users do that because they are connected to the internet with their mobile data. As a result,
they do not want to be charged more data from their mobile data.

If you want to pause your OneDrive desktop app and, in return, have the pause sign on it, these are the
steps you need to take:

Right-click the OneDrive icon on the taskbar of your computer. This action will display some options.
The options are displayed in the photo below.

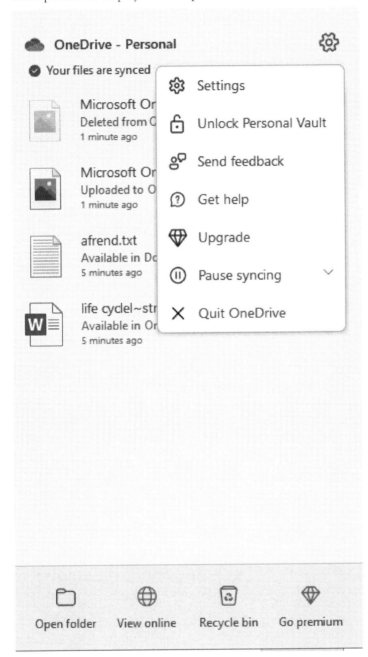

Figure 254: Options displayed when the OneDrive icon at the taskbar is right clicked

From the options you see when you right-click the icon, select **Pause syncing,** followed by how long you want the software paused. And immediately that is done, you will see the pause sign appear over the OneDrive icon. It implies that the OneDrive software cannot upload any file on Microsoft cloud in that state. Everything is put on pause.

But what if you want the software to start syncing files again? It is possible to bring OneDrive software back to its work mode. And for you to do that, you need to right-click the OneDrive icon on your computer's taskbar. This will display some options. Just click the pause mode for it to be disabled. You can also click Resume syncing for it to be out of the pause mode. These are all on the pause over the OneDrive icon. We move…

Warning on OneDrive Icon

When you see this icon on your OneDrive icon, it does not tell something good. Any time you see that warning triangle on your OneDrive account or the OneDrive icon, your attention is needed on your OneDrive account. So, click that sign as it appears on the icon to see the next action you must take for the issue to be resolved. In the end, the challenge will be fixed. But know that your computer must be connected to the internet for any action you want to take to be successful.

Red Circle with Slant Crossed Lines

That sign above does not commonly appear on the OneDrive icon in your computer's taskbar section. But in general, it can appear. For example, it can appear on the file you uploaded to the OneDrive folder. When you see the sign, it implies that a folder or file in your OneDrive account cannot be synced. In addition, this can appear when you delete a file or folder from OneDrive. To find out how the challenge may be resolved, click the notification and follow the guide you are given.

No Entry Sign on OneDrive

This sign may appear on your OneDrive icon, which you need to understand. When you see that sign over your OneDrive icon, Microsoft has blocked your OneDrive account. Again, you can appeal by contacting OneDrive to see if the issue may be resolved, and you then have your account back.

People icon appearing beside a file or folder

This means the file with the people icon beside it has been shared with others.

The Blue Cloud icon

If this icon should appear next to a folder or file on OneDrive, it simply means that the file cannot be accessed offline.

Green tick icon

This indicates that an online-only file has been downloaded to your device and is now accessible without the internet.

The green circle with a white checkmark

This indicates that files will always keep on your device even when you free up space. They are always available offline on your device.

Padlock icon

The padlock icon appearing next to sync status means that the folder or file has settings that do not approve syncing.

The Flashing OneDrive icon

This is common in Android phones. It appears briefly as a normal part of the uploading process.

Three little blue lines

They appear like glimmer marks on a file or a folder, meaning that the file or folder is new.

Available edit OneDrive options

To edit a document on OneDrive, first sign in with your Microsoft account. You will be asked to enter an e-mail address and password. Once you have signed in, you will be taken to the OneDrive web application, where you can edit your document. Once logged in, you can click on the document and edit it as necessary.

The OneDrive cloud icon will appear on your Menu bar. Click on it to open the Preferences window. From here, choose Files On-Demand. You can select "Download files as you need " or "Download all files at once." You can also mark items as offline or online only in Finder.

83 LET'S START

Creating New Folders

- Select the option for **New**

- Select **the folder** from the drop-down menu

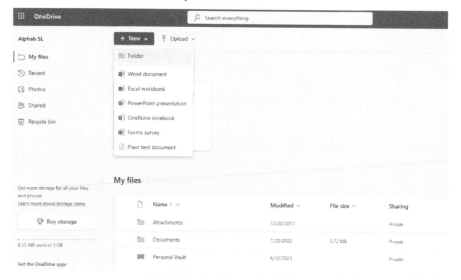

Figure 255: Creating new Folder

- Type in a name for the newly created folder and select **Create**

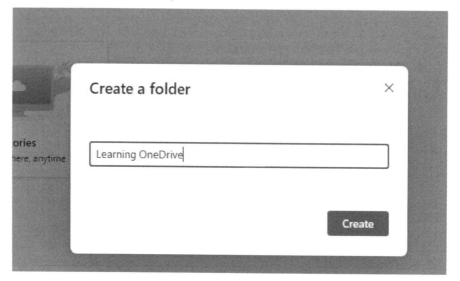

Figure 256: Naming the Folder

OPENING DOCUMENTS ON ONEDRIVE

- In the **Files** window, select the document to be opened; for instance, a PowerPoint file

- In the **Preview window** of the selected document, select the **Edit** drop-down option

- Select **Edit in a Browser**

The document is then opened and can also be edited.

- Select **OneDrive** at the top of the opened document to close the document

Creating a Folder in a Folder

Yes, creating a folder in an already created folder is possible. Let me assume that you are a book writer. As a writer, you first created a folder named "BOOKS." Inside that folder, you gave the name "Books," you have book files you published in different years. For example, you may have published books in 2013, 2014, 2015, 2016, 2018, 2019, 2020, and 2021. Irrespective of the fact that these books are inside one folder you named "BOOKS," you can decide to organize the books year by year. It means I need to create folders inside that "BOOKS" folder with names such as 2013, 2014, 2015, 2016, 2018, 2019, 2020, and 2021. All the books I published in 2013 will be inside the folder named "2013". All 2014 books will be put inside the folder named "2014," and so on.

To create a folder in an already created folder, the first step you need to take after signing into your OneDrive account is to click My files tab and then click that parent folder where you want to create a new folder. Then, as that folder opens, click

When you click the **New** command, select **folder** from the list of options. As that command is selected, type the name you want the folder to bear, followed by the **Create** command. That is all on how to create a folder in already existing folder.

Downloading Files from OneDrive

Have you been in a place where you needed a document urgently? In that situation, since you did not have your personal computer to have that document, the only option left was to download that file from your OneDrive account and then print it from any cybercafé closest to you at that moment. With OneDrive, you can download the document you saved there on your mobile phone or any computer and use it for what you want. I remember years back when I needed to submit my Curriculum Vitae (CV) to a company, which came unplanned. When I saw that opportunity, I did not have my personal computer. What I did was I looked for a nearby cybercafé and logged into my OneDrive account. From there, I could download the document and then print it out. I went ahead and submitted the file.

When you want to download any existing file in your OneDrive account, log into that your OneDrive account. Next, click the **My files** tab to see all the files in your account. Next, locate the file you want to download and get it selected. And lastly, click the **Download** button, which appears above the file.

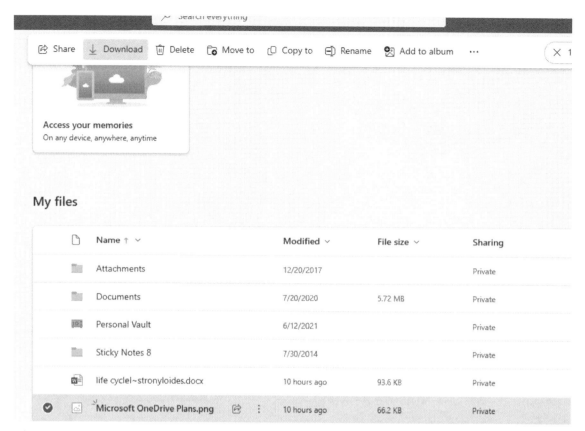

Figure 257: About to download a file from OneDrive

If you are downloading it on a computer, the system will ask you if you want to open the file or save it on your computer. In most cases, I choose the option to save it on my computer. Once the file is downloaded, you can find the file on your computer. If you have not changed the default section where files downloaded in your computer are saved, you will see the downloaded file in the download folder of your computer.

Opening Documents in OneDrive with the OneDrive Desktop Version

- Select the document to be opened and make a right-click

- Select the option to **Open the Document in PowerPoint**

    FILE AND FOLDER SHARING IN ONE DRIVE

- Rest your cursor on the file or folder to be shared and select the **check** sign that appears

- Select the **Pane for Info** button on the top corner on the right of the screen

- Locate the **Sharing** menu and select the option for **Adding People**

- In the resulting window, select either **Generate a Link** or select **E-mail**

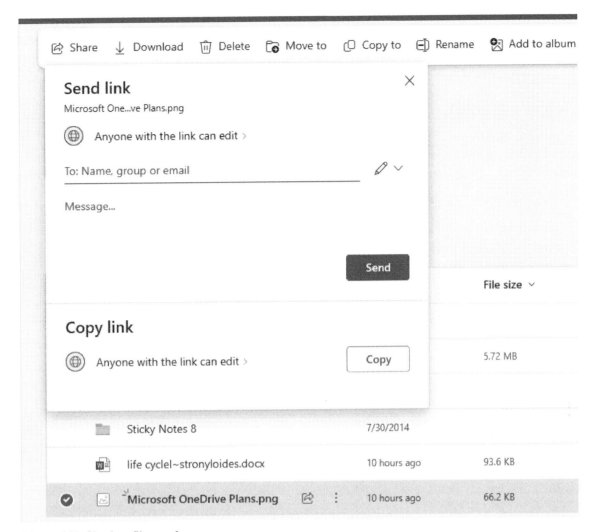

Figure 258: Sharing files or documents

- If **E-mail** is chosen, enter the e-mail address of the person the file is to be shared with and then select **Share**
- Permission of a shared file can be edited from the **Sharing** menu.

Depending on the permission granted to whom a file is shared, they can access and make changes to it at any time. In addition, they can edit and access the file if shared with multiple people. Whenever a person is working on a shared file, others can see the name of who is editing at the moment and a blinking cursor that shows the exact point the person is in the document.

Comments can also be written about shared documents. These comments are visible to all who have access to the document.

84 HOW TO BACK UP FILES WITH ONEDRIVE

Now that you are familiar with the workings of OneDrive, you've done so many things using OneDrive; you need to know that it can also be used to recover relevant files or folders. First, you will enter the OneDrive program window, click on a tab that indicates **backup,** then choose Manage backup. It is possible to back up pictures, desktop, and documents folder. First, you must select the items you want a back-up, after which you click on a tab labeled **Start backup**.

Automatic Syncing

You should also be familiar with setting up a location on your computer that can automatically sync the files with your OneDrive outline. This will cause it to take all of the files from a particular location on your file and upload them to OneDrive in the manner previously described.

You can do this by clicking the "Get the OneDrive applications" link in the screen's bottom left corner.

You will click on it, and if you are using Windows 10, you should already have it installed on your computer. However, if you do not already have it installed on your computer, you can go through the download process and install it on your computer. This will also function well on your Mac.

Right now, you will click the "Start OneDrive" button, and then you will hit the **"Open"** button.

At this point, all you need to do is enter your address and sign in for it to go through and connect.

Your folders in OneDrive will become accessible after you do this. If you click on your OneDrive and simultaneously open up this folder, you will see that the contents stored here are the same ones on your OneDrive, and you will also notice that everything is beginning to sync. Additionally, if you see the green check mark right here, it indicates that it has already been synchronized, which means that it is present in both locations, namely on your local computer and in the cloud. If it just shows the cloud, it is only stored in the cloud and has not yet synchronized. However, if it shows a double arrow, it indicates that it is now syncing.

You will notice that you have these Clouds if you go down in Windows and look at this section. They may be hiding in your Hidden Icons folder. If you want to view them quickly, you can drag them onto your taskbar. If it is synchronizing, you will notice that it is not blue yet; clicking on it will show you what is occurring. If you choose **"View online,"** you will just be sent back to the online version of OneDrive.

If you open the folder, anything you save inside will automatically be uploaded to your OneDrive account. So, for instance, if you copy a file from your computer and drop it into your OneDrive Personal, the file will be copied into that location. At that moment, it will say that it is syncing because it is going through, and when that becomes a green check mark, that will show up over your OneDrive Online; therefore if you refresh it, you will be able to determine whether or not it has synced yet.

Keep in mind that whatever you save in the personal folder of your OneDrive will automatically be uploaded to the Online version of your OneDrive, where it will be accessible to you.

You can now see that you have several different options available if you right-click on any of the files located in the personal folder of your OneDrive.

This is where you can work from the online environment and on your personal computer. When you install this on a computer, it will bring all of your information from your OneDrive. If you install this on three or four different computers, it will sync all of these different ones up, which means that you will have your information living in different places. If this is what you want, then it is fine to do so as long as you have enough space.

85 HOW TO TURN OFF AUTOMATIC SYNC IN ONEDRIVE

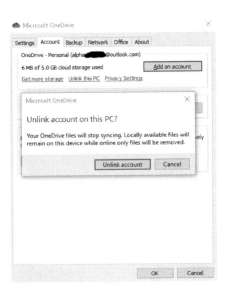

Figure 259: Unlinking an account from PC

If you have probably disconnected your computer from your OneDrive account, then you first need to ensure that all files you want have been synced to your particular computer. This can be done by accessing the OneDrive tray icons. Next, go to **Settings > Account > select folders**. Finally, check your box to ensure you sync every file and folder in **the** OneDrive, where you have unchecked any files or folders.

Our action so far will automatically download several files from the OneDrive account that have not existed on your computer. The procedure takes a while, but it is possible to examine the success when you right-click **OneDrive System tray icon** to check the process level and the time left on it.

So far, all your files are already backed up to your computer. Next, you right-click **OneDrive System tray icon** > then choose Settings. On that Settings tab, uncheck the box indicating Start OneDrive automatically once you sign in to your Windows. Click **Account tab** and **Unlink the PC** connection. On very quick notice, you click on **Unlink account** button. Your system stops syncing with your OneDrive account.

86 COLLABORATION FUNCTION

Working together in real-time

With Microsoft 365, you can now work together on files in real time. File collaboration allows you to edit, comment, and share files with others. You can also easily see the changes that others make to your files and who made them. In addition, Microsoft OneDrive has collaboration functions for iOS and Android devices.

Collaborating online in real-time can benefit your team, even if you are not in the same Office. It allows everyone to view and comment on the same document, which helps you improve knowledge sharing. Many collaboration tools are available online, including desktop sharing, document sharing, and online whiteboards.

Microsoft Teams is another way to collaborate and share documents. The Teams app allows you to collaborate with your team members. For example, you can work on documents using a live chat application and share them with other team members. You can also use Microsoft Teams to share and edit files with others.

Microsoft 365 has many collaboration features, and OneDrive is a significant component. In addition to providing a collaborative environment, Microsoft 365 also provides features to help users keep their data secure. For example, you can control the amount of sharing, which can help you create a collaboration space and protect intellectual property.

Family Editing OneDrive document simultaneously

Using a Microsoft Account, you can share a file with more than one person. This way, several people can edit the same document simultaneously. Click the Share button on the document's list, and check the box next to the file. This option is not available if you have a personal OneDrive account.

All group members need to be Microsoft OneDrive users to use group sharing. After the document is shared, you can set the permissions to allow other people to view and edit the file. You can also allow them to view and edit comments. In addition, you can create groups based on the people in your family.

Friends and Teammates

Microsoft OneDrive offers its users a great way to collaborate on documents. Users can create rich documents by adding files, YouTube videos, and social media posts. Once they're finished editing the documents, they can send them to other people. Users can even create groups to share their documents with others. This allows them to manage who has access to specific files and collaborate with them in real-time.

Can users share and edit documents on OneDrive?

OneDrive has a handy feature that allows people to share files and folders with other people. Once a recipient signs in with a Microsoft account, they can view and edit the file. If recipients wish to change permissions, they can do so in the Sharing options section.

You can share documents on OneDrive with any of your contacts. The app has a button on the right side that lets you select whom to share files and folders. To share files and folders with others, open the document, select Sharing, and then select the option to "Add People." You can also share files with e-mail addresses or social media.

If you want to share a document, you must have Microsoft Office on your computer. After you share the document, you can open it in the desktop Office application and edit it as if it were in the desktop Office program. The changes you make will be saved in OneDrive.

Once you've shared a document, you'll receive an e-mail notification from the recipient. You can enter their e-mail addresses in the e-mail address field or select their contact list. You can also select whether to give these people the right to edit the document. Alternatively, you can remove the sharing link.

Choosing the right setting for your document is very important. For example, in Microsoft OneDrive, users can limit the ability to share certain documents with specific people. The default setting is "Allow editing," but you can change this setting if you want to restrict access to the document.

87 PROTECTION AND RESTORATION

Managing the security of your OneDrive folder is essential if you wish to maintain your data. You can also restore your files and photos if necessary. This chapter will also show you how to identify and recover files infected by ransomware. In addition, you will learn about backup facility options.

Managing Security

Managing Microsoft OneDrive security and restoration is essential in protecting your company's data. While it's not possible to guarantee 100 percent protection against malware, you can at least protect yourself from losing your company's data in the unlikely event of an attack. One of the most effective ways to do this is to back up your data. This will ensure that your data remains safe, even if your company's servers are offline.

While OneDrive provides built-in security protections, you should also implement strong security policies. First, use strong, long, and complex passwords. You should also enable multi-factor authentication. Secondly, you should ensure that your employees are regularly trained to protect sensitive data, especially against phishing scams. Finally, you should have clear policies in place regarding data sharing.

Microsoft OneDrive is a powerful cloud storage platform that is fast, easy to use, and secure. OneDrive offers in-transit and at-rest encryption and ransomware detection and protection. In addition, its backup and restoration tools, like NAKIVO Backup & Replication, protect OneDrive environments and reduce the risk of data loss or ransomware attacks.

Microsoft is continually monitoring the systems supporting its OneDrive for Business services. Security teams work diligently to detect and fix any vulnerabilities that could compromise data integrity. In addition, they monitor traffic in and out of OneDrive to prevent unauthorized access. They also detect any suspicious sign-in attempts and notify users of suspicious activity.

You can select the files you want to back up or back up all files to OneDrive. OneDrive also offers features for version history. This allows you to identify which files have been edited. OneDrive can also back up your files after they have been accidentally deleted.

The Backup Facility

The Backup Facility for Microsoft OneDrive Protection and restoration is critical to protecting your OneDrive data. OneDrive is a cloud-based storage service that provides multiple benefits, including convenience, cost efficiency, and security. The files you upload to the service are stored in remote computers and servers in various regions. Users access these servers via the Internet.

This service allows users to schedule recurring backups to protect important files. Users can also manually select folders to sync and hide those not in use to free space. OneDrive users can also set automatic back-ups of every captured screenshot or connected external device. OneDrive's backup facility can protect up to 1 TB of data per user.

IBM Spectrum Protect Plus Online Services is a software-as-a-service solution that supports Microsoft 365 SharePoint, Exchange, and OneDrive. It provides granular recovery capabilities and is easy to use. Companies can protect their OneDrive data with this service while extending their client base and revenue opportunities. It also manages backups on multiple devices and data types, making it ideal for businesses.

A third-party backup provider can help you implement a cloud-to-cloud solution that ensures data integrity and security. These services are highly customizable and can meet a variety of SLA requirements. Moreover, these services can help you meet compliance regulations such as PCI and HIPAA. In addition, they provide secure encryption of data between your data center and their facility.

The restore options for your files and photos

Microsoft OneDrive Protection and Restoration offers a few ways to recover your files. First, you can restore files from a backup. Second, you can restore files that have suffered unwanted changes. And third, you can restore files that have lost partial data. In addition, OneDrive gives you a detailed log of disk usage activity to see if something abnormal is going on.

Lastly, if you accidentally delete something, you can restore it from your recycle bin. This is where you can find deleted files, photos, or documents. Depending on your settings, restoring a particular file might even be possible. Once you've located your files, click the "Restore" button to restore them. Once you've restored your files, you can access them on your other devices. To do this, download the OneDrive app from the App Store or Google Play Store. The app will appear on your device's taskbar or bottom-right corner. Next, click on the OneDrive icon. This will take you to the OneDrive Settings page. Finally, select a folder or file to back up.

Another step to protect your files is to enable two-factor authentication on your OneDrive account. By doing this, you can prevent unauthorized access to your OneDrive files. In addition to that, you can choose to prevent OneDrive from automatically syncing files and folders. You can also enable encryption on your mobile device, protecting your files even if your device is stolen or lost.

OneDrive offers at-rest and in-transit encryption. However, the encryption keys remain with Microsoft. Moreover, the software does not offer zero-knowledge encryption, so anyone could theoretically read and unlock your files without your permission.

Ransomware detection and recovering your files

You probably want to protect your files if you've recently encountered ransomware. One of the best ways to prevent ransomware is to protect the files you need most. Luckily, there are several ways to protect your files. The first is by limiting the types of files you can access. Ransomware can target all PCs, from home computers to enterprise networks and government servers.

OneDrive is a helpful tool to protect your files against ransomware because it keeps previous versions of your files. You can easily restore older versions of your files if needed. OneDrive's version history feature also lets you view older versions of your files. However, it will not restore the original file name. Instead, the ransomware will show a fake name and a useless extension. This means you will need to rename the file to restore it. OneDrive can protect your files against ransomware, but it doesn't protect all types of files. Ransomware can also affect documents from Office, photos, videos, and music collections.

OneDrive offers essential protection against ransomware, which is free. But this protection doesn't stop ransomware from doing damage. The malware can install on your computer by hacking the administrator's account. If you're worried about the security of your data, you can run a scan on your computer using an antivirus. Alternatively, you can use Microsoft Security Essentials or the Malicious Software Removal Tool to remove the ransomware.

Ransomware attacks your OneDrive account by encrypting the files. The attacker can then demand a ransom for the decryption of your files. This malicious software has been around for several years, but its use has increased due to the popularity of cloud storage services.

Can users share and edit documents on OneDrive?

OneDrive offers several options for sharing and editing files. For example, you can share any document with a selected group. You can also share folders. You'll need to add appropriate permission for each recipient if you're sharing files. To set permission levels for recipients, click on 'Share' and select the permission you'd like to give.

OneDrive only allows others to edit documents if they also have a Microsoft account. People with Edit permission can copy and move items if you've shared a folder. This makes it easier to work on documents while offline. The changes will sync to the recipient's OneDrive account.

You can use the "Share" option in the left nav to share a folder or file with other users. This will display any documents that you've shared with others. You can also change the sharing permissions for the folders you've shared. You can even switch between direct access and view and edit permissions. You can also stop sharing your files entirely. You can also set permission levels for specific people.

To share a folder or file, you must enter an e-mail address. Then, the recipient will receive an e-mail containing a link to the file. After the recipient receives the e-mail, they can choose whether to allow the document to be shared with them or not. Moreover, you can change the permission settings and remove the link.

If you wish to share your documents with other users, you can give them access to the same OneDrive account. However, the recipients must sign in using their Microsoft account to view the document. Moreover, the recipient must sign into the Microsoft account to make permission changes.

HOW TO RESTORE FILES

This feature in OneDrive gives you to restore any files you have lost for about 30 days. For you to choose a better time to recover your file, OneDrive will provide you with a histogram that evaluates the activity of the file for you to make a proper suggestion of the exact time you want to recover your files. After that, click on the file history and select the ones you wish to restore and any other options.

The following are the steps to restore your file on OneDrive:

1. Go to the OneDrive web page
2. Select "Recycle Bin"
3. After that, you will select the file to restore.
4. Click on the "Restore" option.

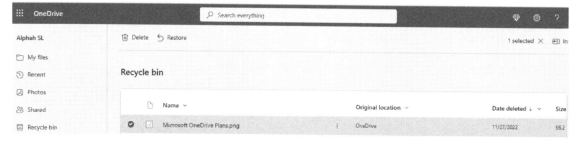

Figure 260: Restoring a deleted file

5. After doing that, your file will automatically be restored.

88 TIPS AND TRICKS

OneDrive is one of the most popular cloud storage services. Previously known as SkyDrive, Live Folders, or Essentials, OneDrive offers an excellent range of file management options and a natural integration with Microsoft Office. In addition, the program provides a range of helpful tips and tricks. This section will show you how to manage and share files on OneDrive. You'll also learn how to protect every version of a file.

OneDrive sync client

To avoid OneDrive syncing problems, follow Microsoft's guidelines for file paths, which limit them to 255 characters. When a file's path is long, it is harder to sync with OneDrive. To fix this, you can rename it to make it shorter.

If the problem persists after the above steps, you might not be connected to the correct Windows network or the Microsoft account you're using. To fix this, sign in to your account in Windows Settings. You can then choose which files you'd like to sync. Alternatively, you can let Windows sync your files automatically. Only your main folders are synced by default, but you can designate specific folders when setting up the app.

Another tip is to sync files from File Explorer to OneDrive. This will automatically sync your files from the Desktop, My Documents, and Pictures folders. However, you should consult your IT team before enabling this feature, as it can affect your bandwidth usage. It will also create a new folder on your desktop.

If you encounter conflicts between files, you can try to resolve them by resetting the OneDrive sync client. If this doesn't help, you can try restarting your router or contacting your service provider to resolve the issue. Otherwise, you may need to reset the settings and setup the OneDrive app again. The OneDrive sync client is very easy to use. The main difference between a standard client and a custom client is the size and number of files that can be synced simultaneously. OneDrive for Business sync clients can download many files at once, which can use up a lot of bandwidth. To prevent this, you can enable Files On-Demand to limit the initial bandwidth hit. Known folder moves can also affect network performance.

OneDrive sync client has several useful features. One of them is restoring previous versions of files. This can be done by right-clicking any file on OneDrive. Another handy feature is embedding files from OneDrive on a website. Finally, you can also view files in the Recycle Bin.

Sharing files in OneDrive

Microsoft OneDrive lets you share files outside of your organization. You can choose who has access to shared files, set the expiration date, and specify other recipients. In addition, you can increase your sharing limit if you need to share more files than the basic OneDrive limit. However, you should remember that OneDrive, including EXE files, does not support certain file types. You may also need to validate your account, which you can do through the OneDrive website.

When you're ready to share a file or folder, you'll have to sign in to OneDrive. You'll need your work, school, or personal credentials to sign in. Once you've signed in, you'll see a list of all the folders and files in your OneDrive account. You can select multiple items by holding down the Command or Ctrl keys.

Sharing files in OneDrive is very easy and convenient. To share a file or folder, click on its name or click "Share" at the top of the sharing dialog box. The recipient will receive an e-mail link to the file or folder. If you'd like to grant someone editing access, enter their e-mail address in the "Edit" field.

You can change the permissions if you've made a mistake when sharing a file. You can also set the expiration date for a file to prevent accidental sharing. Once you've done this, you can access the file with an Internet connection from any device. If you're unsure how to share files in OneDrive, you can ask the file owner to remove them.

You can share files and folders in OneDrive with different people. You can also create links for forwarding. You can also create folders for different purposes. If you're looking for a simple way to share your files with co-workers, OneDrive is a great option. OneDrive also provides high security, so you can keep your data safe.

When you share a file or folder, you should choose the "share" or "private" option in OneDrive's sharing dialog box. Then, you can change the permissions for the files or folders by clicking "Manage Access" on the Share dialogue box.

Managing security groups in OneDrive

Managing security groups is a helpful way to control access to OneDrive. Depending on your organization's needs, you can create different groups for different roles and people. For example, you can create a security group for new employees, legal review team members, vendors, and alliance partners. By defining different security groups, you can automatically protect certain content and prevent access by anonymous users.

Once you've created security groups, you can manage their membership. Click the "Members" tab and click the "Manage Members" option. This will display all security group members and allow you to add or remove them. You can also add resources to each security group.

Groups are also useful for managing access to SharePoint sites. Security groups are easy to create and maintain. The group users with similar permissions so that you can assign access to them once. To create a security group, visit the admin center in Office 365. You can also assign users to a security group in SharePoint.

OneDrive security groups allow administrators to restrict access to data from specific locations. Using location-based policies will ensure that only trusted devices have access to data. You can also set up multi-factor authentication for workers and guests. Microsoft Endpoint Manager (Microsoft's endpoint management tool) is an excellent choice for organizations concerned about unauthorized access to company data. Using this software, admins can take stock of their entire endpoint environment, including bring-your-own-device scenarios, and take appropriate action to prevent data breaches. One of the most common OneDrive security threats is human error. Users make mistakes and share their files with the wrong accounts. This can lead to data loss, unwanted changes, or malware infections. When using Microsoft OneDrive, you should use complex passwords and password protection to ensure your data remains safe.

Security groups in SharePoint are a great way to control access and permissions. By using security groups, administrators can manage group members centrally. In addition to SharePoint sites, security groups can control access to files on file shares, SharePoint lists, and more. Groups are also helpful for e-mail distribution. In addition, security groups eliminate the need to manage individual users. SharePoint groups automatically remove members when they leave the security groups.

Protecting every version of a file

When it comes to protecting your files on Microsoft OneDrive, there are several things you can do to help keep them safe. Using two-factor verification, which requires an extra security code when you sign in, is a great option. This way, you can be sure that your files will not be accessed by anyone else. OneDrive also recommends encrypting your files when you store them on your mobile device. As a result, your files will remain safe even if you lose or steal your device.

Microsoft OneDrive supports version history for all file types. You can create a different version for each if you have more than one file. This will give you a greater chance of protecting your files from ransomware. It will also help if you need to recover your files in case of accidental deletion or corruption. Using version history also gives you the advantage of easily recovering old files.

Another option is to redirect known folders back to your PC. For instance, you can protect the Temporary Internet Files folder so people cannot edit your file. That way, only people with the right permissions can edit the document. However, if you trust the folder's contents, you can allow them to edit the document.

89 MICROSOFT ONEDRIVE COMMON PROBLEMS AND SOLUTIONS

OneDrive users who experience problems with their storage space may need to free up some space by deleting old files, using an external hard drive, or shrinking the file size using compression tools. It is also important to wait until automatic sync is started before deleting old files. OneDrive users utilizing an organization's server may also encounter problems. In this case, users must contact their IT departments for assistance.

File paths should be shorter

One of the biggest problems with Microsoft OneDrive is that file paths aren't always short enough. Long file paths can cause your OneDrive account to crash. Luckily, there are several ways to make file paths shorter. You can start by renaming your files. This will shorten them to a single letter.

Having a long file path can also prevent your OneDrive files from syncing. To fix this problem, you can rename or move the target file in OneDrive, or shorten its file path. You should also avoid having too many subfolders in your OneDrive account and file types that are not supported.

Another way to shorten file paths is to follow Microsoft's documentation on naming files, paths, and namespaces. You can also use the subset command to shorten file paths. This can help prevent files from exceeding 255 characters, the maximum length for a file name in Windows.

OneDrive users often complain about long folder names. Long folder names make it difficult to copy or backup files. Therefore, it's a good idea to change the Organization name in OneDrive to shorten the folder name. To change the Organization name, you can go into the Settings menu and click on the Account tab. Then, you should change the name of your organization to another one.

Internet connection speed affects synchronization

If you've had trouble synchronizing your OneDrive account with your other devices, you may have an issue with your Internet connection. Microsoft OneDrive is deeply integrated into the Windows ecosystem, and signing in is essential when you first use the service. If you're not signed in, the OneDrive icon in your Windows taskbar will be greyed out. To sign in, click on the OneDrive icon and enter your e-mail address.

If your Internet connection speed is slow, you may experience problems with OneDrive synchronization. First, ensure your Internet connection speed is high enough to transfer large files. If you're unsure whether your Internet connection is fast enough, ping Microsoft's servers. This will give you an idea of how much your Internet connection can transfer. If your connection is slow, you can temporarily pause the synchronization process. If it still takes too long to sync, you can restart your PC. Lastly, don't attempt to synchronize too many files or folders simultaneously. If you do, you may pause the syncing process if you need to move or delete files. You can also check your Internet connection speed by checking your upload and download rates. For example, when synchronizing OneDrive, you can pause syncing if you experience slow to upload or download rates.

Then, try to unlink the OneDrive account that is causing problems. To unlink your OneDrive account, you will need to sign in again. You can search for solutions on the Microsoft forums if that doesn't work. Alternatively, you can always try contacting your service provider.

Another thing you should check is your CPU usage. OneDrive will use CPU and RAM when it synchronizes data, so if your internet connection is slow, it can slow down your computer. By opening the Task Manager, you can also check how much of your computer's resources OneDrive uses.

If this does not work, you can move problematic documents outside the syncing folder and restart syncing. In addition, if the files sync slowly, you may have a bandwidth throttle set up on your account. To turn off this option, open the OneDrive settings window.

Another way to improve OneDrive synchronization is to delete the files causing the issue. You can also unlink your PC and account from OneDrive. This way, you can still use OneDrive by saving files locally. However, this can be a painful experience, so you should investigate your options before trying anything else.

Resetting OneDrive fixes problems

If your OneDrive account isn't syncing correctly, you can reset it by choosing the "Unlink this PC" link in the "Account" tab. Once you've done this, you should see the OneDrive icon again. If you don't see it, click "Add an account." Then, follow the instructions to synchronize your data.

You may have to resync manually if you have multiple files in OneDrive or have large files to sync. First, you need to check the OneDrive app. Ensure you're running the latest Windows update if it's not running. If that doesn't solve the issue, restart the program.

The OneDrive app should appear again after a few minutes. You can also try re-establishing the connection by pressing the Windows + R keys. You may need to update your OneDrive account manually if it doesn't. Once the OneDrive app is back up and running, you can try using MobileTrans - Back-up by Wondershare.

OneDrive users often experience problems with syncing their files. To resolve this, ensure your files do not exceed 100GB for personal accounts and 15GB for work or school accounts. You can also try zipping your files to sync them. Finally, you can check if any of your files have been accidentally saved, moved, or deleted.

If you can't log into OneDrive, check your internet connection first. OneDrive will send you an alert if it can't connect. Then, restart your router or contact your service provider if the problem persists. Finally, if you are still experiencing problems, you should periodically check OneDrive to see if the problem is fixed.

If you cannot sync your files with OneDrive because of a poor internet connection, restarting the OneDrive app may solve the issue. In addition, restarting Windows is another way to fix OneDrive problems. This way, you can restore the original settings and restore synchronization. You can also try installing updates to your computer to prevent recurring problems.

If your OneDrive account is frozen, follow the steps in the following article. You should follow the instructions provided by Microsoft to fix frozen accounts. If you can't find any instructions, you can look for help in Microsoft's forums. These forums contain hundreds of posts. Alternatively, you can create a new post and look for information about your problem.

Some users report problems syncing OneDrive files after updating their OS. This can be due to large files or a bad connection. In this case, it's recommended to rename files using shorter file names. Renaming folders on the OneDrive directory to be shorter than the original name will ensure that the file paths are shorter.

The troubleshooting app will ask you to enter your Admin password to begin the scan. First, ensure that your computer is connected to the internet to connect to the Microsoft servers. Otherwise, the troubleshooting app won't work correctly. If the troubleshooting process fails, likely, your OneDrive is not connected to the internet.

90 CONCLUSION

Microsoft OneDrive is one of the most popular cloud storage solutions for businesses. It allows users to store and access their files anywhere, on any device. The company has been working hard to make it even more convenient for our daily lives and the productivity needs of our organizations. As a result, Microsoft OneDrive is expected to come with several new features, including a redesigned UI and more.

MICROSOFT ONENOTE

INTRODUCTION

Microsoft OneNote is one of the most popular note-taking applications available today. It is a digital notebook that allows users to capture ideas, store information, and manage tasks in one central location. With OneNote, users can organize their thoughts, ideas, and tasks more efficiently and productively than traditional paper notebooks.

It is available for both Windows and Mac users and mobile devices. It can take notes, store images, create to-do lists, share information with others, and more. The interface is user-friendly and intuitive, making it easy for users to get up and running quickly.

Developed by Microsoft, OneNote is a note-taking application that helps users organize their notes and other information. It also allows users to add multimedia files. This includes audio and video recordings. The application is also designed for mobile devices.

Whether you are a business owner, a college student, or simply looking for a way to organize your life, Microsoft OneNote can help. You may have heard that OneNote is available for desktop computers and mobile devices, but you may not know where to start. This book will discuss OneNote, where to get it, and why you should use it.

What is Microsoft OneNote?

Probably one of the most powerful applications in Microsoft's suite, OneNote is an all-in-one notetaking, research, and project management application. The program can be downloaded for free from the OneNote website. The software also offers a variety of premium plans.

OneNote allows you to take notes and add images, videos, and other media. The program is also great for teamwork, as you can share notes and files with others.

OneNote is a powerful note-taking application that people across different industries can use. It is an ideal tool for managing information, creating presentations, and managing teams. It is also an excellent tool for teachers, who use it to create lesson plans. OneNote is also great for schoolwork and lesson plans. For example, a teacher can use OneNote to take notes, assign students, and keep up with class work.

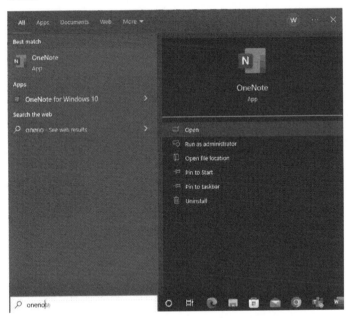

Figure 261: Searching for OneNote from Start Menu

The program is also great for research, as you can save web pages, research articles, and other information. In addition, OneNote lets you embed images and audio recordings from online sources. The program also allows you to create a screen grab and add annotations to a video.

OneNote also has a history feature, which helps you keep track of changes you've made to notebooks. This makes it easy to see which notes are the most important and which haven't been looked at. The app also has a "quick links" section, which can be shared with other users.

OneNote is also great for collaboration, as you can share notebooks with others and have them add their notes. For example, a teacher can use the "quick links" section to share notes with students. In addition, OneNote allows you to share individual pages by sending them as links in an email.

OneNote can be used for recording audio and video notes. The application also supports importing images and videos from online sources. It also allows users to create and organize pages. The application is compatible with desktop and tablet devices. Its history feature will enable users to trace the changes made to their notebooks.

OneNote is a very popular tool that over 10,000 companies use. Its freeform entry method allows users to type, draw and annotate notes. It also allows users to share and share their notebooks. It is compatible with all devices, including smartphones, and has a web version. This makes it very convenient to use. It is also helpful for teachers and students.

OneNote allows users to save and share information through the cloud. It also allows users to share individual pages through email.

Why use Microsoft OneNote

Microsoft OneNote offers several benefits that make it a valuable tool for users. It is user-friendly and intuitive, making it easy to get up and running quickly. It is also highly customizable, allowing users to tailor the application to their specific needs. It is also free with a Microsoft account and integrates with other Microsoft products, making it easy to move information between applications.

OneNote is part of the Microsoft Office suite and is available as a stand-alone application. It is free with a Microsoft account and can be used without an internet connection. It also integrates with other Microsoft products, such as Word and Excel, allowing users to move information between applications easily.

Whether you are a student or a teacher, Microsoft OneNote can be a helpful tool to help you stay organized and productive. It has many features, including an input device that allows you to write with a stylus and a powerful set of drawing tools.

Organizing your notes using OneNote is easy. The program makes use of tags and sections to keep your notes organized. OneNote can also be synchronized across multiple devices, including desktops and tablets. Using OneNote can save you time and allow you to access your notes from anywhere.

OneNote has a variety of features, including a cool translation feature. You can use the AI-powered Microsoft Translator service to translate text from English to your native language. You can also use OneNote's data encryption features to protect your information. It is also possible to password-protect individual notebooks. You can even use OneNote to search through recordings.

OneNote has other features, including creating tables and embedding files from other applications. It also has a nifty chart feature.

OneNote also has a Class Notebook feature. This allows teachers to create assignments and manage student notebooks. You can also use OneNote to create a "wish list" of items you'd like to do. You can also use the app to record and playback audio.

OneNote can be a fun way to take and share notes with others easily. You can even add images and audio.

Features of Microsoft OneNote

Microsoft OneNote has several features that make it a powerful note-taking tool. It allows users to capture ideas, stores information, and manage tasks in one central location. It also offers several features that make it easy to organize information. These include adding tags and labels, creating notebooks and sections, and adding audio and video recordings.

OneNote also offers several features that make collaboration easier. For example, it allows users to share their notebooks with others and comment and edit notes. It also provides a real-time collaboration feature, which allows multiple users to work on the same document simultaneously. This makes it easy to collaborate on projects with others.

Where you can use it - desktop

During the past year, Microsoft has made some changes to its OneNote desktop app for Windows. These changes include a new navigational user interface. In addition, Microsoft has added dictation support to the desktop app.

The OneNote desktop app is available to download from Microsoft's official website. It can be downloaded as a standalone app or as part of Microsoft 365. Both versions are free.

OneNote has a variety of apps that run on different operating systems, including iOS, Android, and Windows. It also supports Dropbox as a cloud-based storage option.

Microsoft plans to ship software updates for its OneNote desktop app in the coming years. These updates will include new navigational user interfaces and other user experience improvements. This should help bring the OneNote desktop app and the built-in Windows 10 apps closer to feature parity.

The OneNote desktop app is also available as part of Microsoft 365. Microsoft 365 subscriptions include premium features like monthly updates. If you don't have a Microsoft 365 subscription, you can still download the OneNote desktop app for free.

The OneNote desktop app is part of the Microsoft Office suite. It can be installed alongside Word, Excel, and PowerPoint desktop apps. The desktop app can store notes in the cloud or on a local hard drive. It also features a full Office ribbon interface.

OneNote also includes a Zoom feature, allowing users to view notes in more detail. However, the Zoom feature is not available in OneNote for the web.

Mobile app

Whether working on a home project, managing your school workload, or just wanting to keep track of your family's activities, OneNote can help you get organized. This versatile note-taking app can be used on desktop, Android, iOS, and Windows Phones.

OneNote offers a variety of features, including the ability to record video, record audio, record audio notes, create drawings, and attach files. It can also be used for group collaboration. You can create different sections for different purposes and lock each section with a password. It also allows you to search for notes, photos, and audio files.

The app also offers many other features, including a built-in spell checker, quick access to your most recent notes, and the ability to sync your notes with free Windows Live online storage. You can also store multiple OneNote notebooks.

OneNote is free for a limited time. You can also purchase a premium version that includes extra features. However, it may take a while for OneNote for Android to appear in the Android Market app store in your region. If you can't wait, check out the OneNote Web App, free with a Windows Live ID. It requires an Internet connection, and it works with any browser.

The app also supports two-step verification to reduce the chance of unauthorized access. Its other features include offline storage, search capabilities, and text formatting options.

Web

The Microsoft OneNote web version is not entirely up to par with the desktop version. However, key features are expected to be introduced over the next few weeks. These features include enhanced copy-and-paste functions, zooming capabilities, and better integration with Teams. These features will benefit OneNote users.

OneNote for the web allows you to clip images and videos from web pages, edit them, and resize them. You can also import Visio diagrams and Excel spreadsheets into OneNote. You can also use OneNote to create visual bookmarks for web pages. You can also share your notebooks with others. It even allows you to receive edits from other authors.

OneNote for the web includes a new mode switcher, which allows you to toggle between editing and viewing modes. You can also use your finger or a stylus to ink and draw. The app also checks to spell as you type. You can also turn off the spelling checker for the selected text.

OneNote for the web allows users to turn off author tags, which remove an author's initials next to a new note. Users can also choose proofing language. The web version of OneNote also includes a new feature called the Web Clipper, which lets you quickly enter new notes.

The OneNote web version also features improved copy-and-paste functions. For example, you can copy and paste tables and lists and use a new mode switcher to toggle between editing and viewing modes.

Can you use it offline?

Whether you're an educator or a student, Microsoft OneNote is an excellent tool for organizing notes, ideas, and lesson plans. Initially designed for the desktop, OneNote has also been remade for the mobile era.

You can save handwritten notes to OneNote and convert them to text. You can also label your notes and check off your to-do lists. OneNote also allows you to mix and match different types of notes. You can even draw ideas.

OneNote also has a powerful search. It can even search across notebooks, pages, and text. OneNote's search can help you find important stuff quickly. You can even mix and match text, images, and web clippings.

You can even save your screen clip with annotations. OneNote even allows you to share files with students and colleagues. So whether you're a student, a teacher, or an administrator, OneNote can help you organize your work.

You can also manually sync your notebooks to OneDrive. You can do this by adjusting the location of your notebooks or by syncing them using a keyboard shortcut. Alternatively, you can choose to sync all notebook pages with attachments. You can also purchase more OneDrive storage space.

OneNote has a small local cache that you can use to store some of your notebook files locally. However, the local cache is fragile and can be erased with future app updates.

If you're using OneNote on a Mac, you won't have access to offline file storage. If you use the Windows version, however, you will have access to the same files.

91 COMPARING MICROSOFT ONENOTE TO OTHER NOTE-TAKING APPLICATIONS

Whether looking for an application on your Windows or Mac computer, you may wonder if OneNote is the right choice for your needs. For those who need to keep track of their thoughts and ideas, a variety of note-taking applications are available today. Microsoft OneNote is a popular choice, but many others exist as well. This section will compare Microsoft OneNote to other popular note-taking applications, such as Evernote, Google Keep, Notability, Apple Notes, and Notion. We will explore each application's features and advantages so that readers can decide which application best suits their needs.

Microsoft OneNote vs. Evernote

Whether looking for a note-taking app for business or education, OneNote and EverNote are excellent options. OneNote is better for office junkies, while EverNote is lighter on computer resources. The two note-taking apps are available on various platforms, including Windows, Android, and iOS.

Microsoft OneNote and Evernote are two of the most popular note-taking applications available. Both offer a wide range of features and advantages, and both are great options for those who need to take notes and keep track of their thoughts and ideas.

One of the biggest advantages of Microsoft OneNote over Evernote is its integration with Microsoft Office. As a result, Microsoft OneNote can be used to create documents, presentations, and spreadsheets, This makes it an excellent option for those who are already using Microsoft Office, as it allows for easy and convenient note-taking within the same platform.

Evernote, on the other hand, does not offer this level of integration with other programs. However, it offers a wide range of features that make it an excellent option for those who need to store and organize their notes. For example, Evernote offers a web clipper, which allows users to quickly and easily save webpages, and a variety of templates, which can be used to create notes quickly. Evernote also offers a variety of organizational features, such as tags and notebooks, which can be used to find and access notes easily.

OneNote is a note-taking app that supports handwritten text, images, and tables. It also supports video, audio, and other media types. You can search for specific tags and keywords in your notes. It also allows you to share notes with other users. The app supports encryption at rest and can sync data across devices. It can also be used in a private environment.

OneNote supports the ability to synchronize notes with Evernote. It also lets you back up your notes to OneNote. OneNote is also compatible with many pen tablets. The interface is also intuitive. However, the app doesn't have the same features as Evernote.

EverNote is an online note-taking app that is free to download. However, the premium version is available for a subscription. Its free version allows you to store up to 100 notes. In addition, you can filter notes by note type, period, and keyword. It's also compatible with macOS and Windows. OneNote also comes with free storage. You can store unlimited notes, but the freemium account limits the file size to 25MB per note. The premium plan also includes an ink reply and a researcher. It also offers OCR functionality.

In addition to its note-taking capabilities, EverNote is also a scrapbooking and GTD tool. It offers notes as webpages, pictures, audio, and task management pages. It also has a freemium account that allows you to store up to 100,000 notes. It's compatible with most pen tablets and is easier to use than OneNote.

Microsoft OneNote vs. Google Keep

Whether you need a note-taking application for work or play, Google Keep or Microsoft OneNote might be just what you need. Both powerful applications allow you to record your thoughts, audio, and videos and organize your notes.

Google Keep and Microsoft OneNote are note-taking applications that offer a variety of features and advantages. Google Keep is a note-taking application that captures text, images, web pages, and even voice notes. The app is integrated with the rest of Google and allows users to send copies to other apps, share notes with friends and family, and even convert notes to Google Docs. The app can be used on any device and is available as a web or mobile app.

OneNote offers a variety of features, and you can create internal links. For example, this feature allows you to insert links within the note and emphasize points with a bulleted list. You can also use OneNote's "Alt Text" feature, which will enable you to insert text from an image.

OneNote has some cool features, but it can have a few hiccups. For example, the search tool is a bit slow, requiring you to click many buttons to get to the right page.

OneNote also offers a cool link feature to create internal links between notebooks. You can add a date, location, or text to the link. OneNote also has an option for synchronizing notes across different devices. You can choose which notebooks you want to view on each device.

OneNote has a few features that you won't find in Google Keep. For instance, the app is compatible with Bing image search and can support digital whiteboard features. It also offers a variety of widgets and can be used on Android.

Microsoft OneNote offers a wide range of features, such as integrating with Microsoft Office and creating documents, presentations, and spreadsheets. It also provides various organizational features, such as tags and notebooks, which can easily find and access notes.

Google Keep, on the other hand, does not offer the same level of integration with other programs as Microsoft OneNote does. However, it provides some advantages over Microsoft OneNote, such as quickly and easily sharing notes. Google Keep also offers a variety of templates and customization options, which can be used to create notes quickly.

In addition to its sharing and customization features, Google Keep also offers a variety of organizational features, such as labels and reminders, which can be used to find and access notes easily. Google Keep also offers a wide range of integrations with other Google services, such as Google Drive and Google Calendar. This makes it an excellent option for those already using Google services.

Microsoft OneNote vs. Notability

Microsoft OneNote and Notability are note-taking applications that offer a variety of features and advantages. Microsoft OneNote offers a wide range of features, such as integrating with Microsoft Office and creating documents, presentations, and spreadsheets. It also provides various organizational features, such as tags and notebooks, which can easily find and access notes.

On the other hand, Notability does not offer the same level of integration with other programs as Microsoft OneNote does. However, it does offer some advantages over Microsoft OneNote, such as the ability to draw and annotate notes. It also provides a variety of templates and customization options, which can be used to create notes quickly.

In addition to its drawing and customization features, Notability also offers a variety of organizational features, such as folders and tags, which can be used to find and access notes easily. Notability also provides many integrations with other services, such as Dropbox and Google Drive. This makes it an excellent option for those already using these services.

Using the right note-taking application can make taking notes more productive. OneNote offers a wide range of tools to help you organize, write, and edit your notes. The software is free to download. You can also purchase a premium subscription to add more features.

OneNote is available for Windows, Mac, iOS, and Android. You can also create templates, customize navigation space, and store ideas in one location. The application also allows you to store images, audio recordings, and PowerPoint lectures.

Notability is also available on iOS and Mac. Notability offers a variety of pens and tools to help you organize your notes. It is also an OCR tool that can convert handwritten notes into texts in 22 languages. It can also identify text in images. It also has stylus support and a zoom feature. The application has a wide range of dividers, custom colors, and an eraser. It also supports AirDrop and Dropbox.

Notability's interface is more elegant and user-friendly than OneNote's. The application also has an immersive reader that allows you to adjust the screen size. You can also rotate notes to any angle. The software also supports audio recordings and handwriting-to-text conversion.

Notability also has a powerful eraser that lets you pixel-by-pixel erase your notes. However, it is not as intuitive or flexible as OneNote's eraser. It also takes up a lot of space for notes.

Notability has more advanced features than OneNote. For example, it can convert handwriting into text and fix errors before the conversion. Notability also allows you to rotate notes and resize equations. It also has an OCR tool that will enable you to search your notes from your email or Dropbox.

Microsoft OneNote vs. Apple Notes

Microsoft OneNote and Apple Notes are note-taking applications that offer a variety of features and advantages. Microsoft OneNote offers a wide range of features, such as integrating with Microsoft Office and creating documents, presentations, and spreadsheets. It also provides various organizational features, such as tags and notebooks, which can easily find and access notes.

On the other hand, Apple Notes does not offer the same level of integration with other programs as Microsoft OneNote does. However, it does offer some advantages over Microsoft OneNote, such as the ability to sync notes across multiple devices. It also provides a variety of templates and customization options, which can be used to create notes quickly.

In addition to its syncing and customization features, Apple Notes also offers a variety of organizational features, such as folders and tags, which can be used to find and access notes easily.

Apple Notes also provides many integrations with other Apple services, such as iCloud and Messages. This makes it an excellent option for those already using Apple services.

You can easily download and install OneNote if you are an iPhone or Android user. The full-featured app offers several tools and features to meet your note-taking needs. For example, you can add images, drawings, checklists, tables, and text to your notes. You can also tag and comment on images and other items in your notes.

Notes are divided into notebooks or high-level organizational categories. These can be combined into smart folders that filter by tag. You can also search for text and attachments.

OneNote is also password protected. Users can lock their notes with TouchID or scan documents automatically. Users can also use the app to share notes with other people. You can also classify items in multiple notebooks and tag them for contextualization. You can add images, scanned documents, and more to your notes.

Taking notes in OneNote is free. However, there are also premium plans that give you extra features. These include admin tools, permission settings, and the ability to remove the 1,000-block content limit. You can also access OneNote on the web.

OneNote has a very powerful search engine. You can search for text, images, attachments, and note links. It can also look for text that was copied into a note.

You can use the app to create notes in your free account, and you can link notes to other notes using internal hyperlinks. However, you cannot export notes. Unless you are on the iCloud tier, you must export your notes to the Files app and email them to yourself. You will also need to add an email address to your account.

Apple Notes is easy to use. You can add content directly from the iPad or use the iPhone to take pictures and documents. Unfortunately, Apple Notes does not have a native app for Windows or Android, but you can access it through iCloud.

Microsoft OneNote vs. Notion

Whether you're looking for a free note-taking app or a paid product, there are many choices. OneNote and Notion are two examples of these apps.

OneNote is a note-taking application that is part of the Office family. It offers various note-taking features, such as drawing on notes, pin plain text, and adding images. It's also got an easy-to-use interface.

The notion is a note-taking application with many similar features to OneNote. However, Notion has a lot more templates and features. This includes creating a template, customizing fonts and colors, and creating content blocks.

Notion offers advantages over Microsoft OneNote, such as creating databases and collaborating with others in real time. It also provides a variety of templates and customization options, which can be used to create notes quickly.

In addition to its collaboration and customization features, Notion also offers a variety of organizational features, such as boards and lists, which can be used to find and access notes easily. The notion also offers file sharing, multiple notebooks, and encrypted notes in transit. It has a free plan that allows you to upload up to five MB of files. However, you will need a premium subscription to upload larger files. The free plan also includes unlimited blocks to have as many pages as possible. You also get a nifty web clipper that works on Chrome and Edge.

The notion also includes the ability to share files and wikis. It allows for synchronous editing of documents in real-time. However, you can only share with up to five guests.

Notion is easy to learn, but it may take time to master the features. There are many online tutorials if you're unsure how to get started. Luckily, there are also apps for mobile devices.

Notion is a note-taking app that also functions as a task management tool. It integrates with various apps, including Slack, Asana, Google Drive, and Trello. It also allows you to embed external websites and databases into your pages. This makes it an excellent option for those already using these services.

92 SOFTWARE INTERFACE AND USE

1. OneNote User Interface

On your computer, the OneNote user interface opens when you first search for and select OneNote (the desktop version), allowing you to open or create a notebook. The work area in OneNote has several tabs, ribbons, commands, etc., as seen and described below.

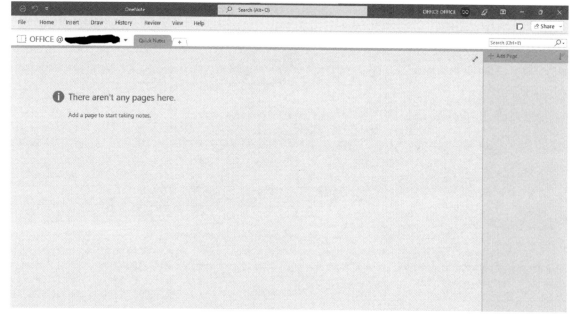

Figure 262: OneNote Platform

A blank user interface OneNote for Desktop

Note that when you create or open a notebook, the buttons in the above diagram will become active.

The user interface is displayed below when you create and open a notebook.

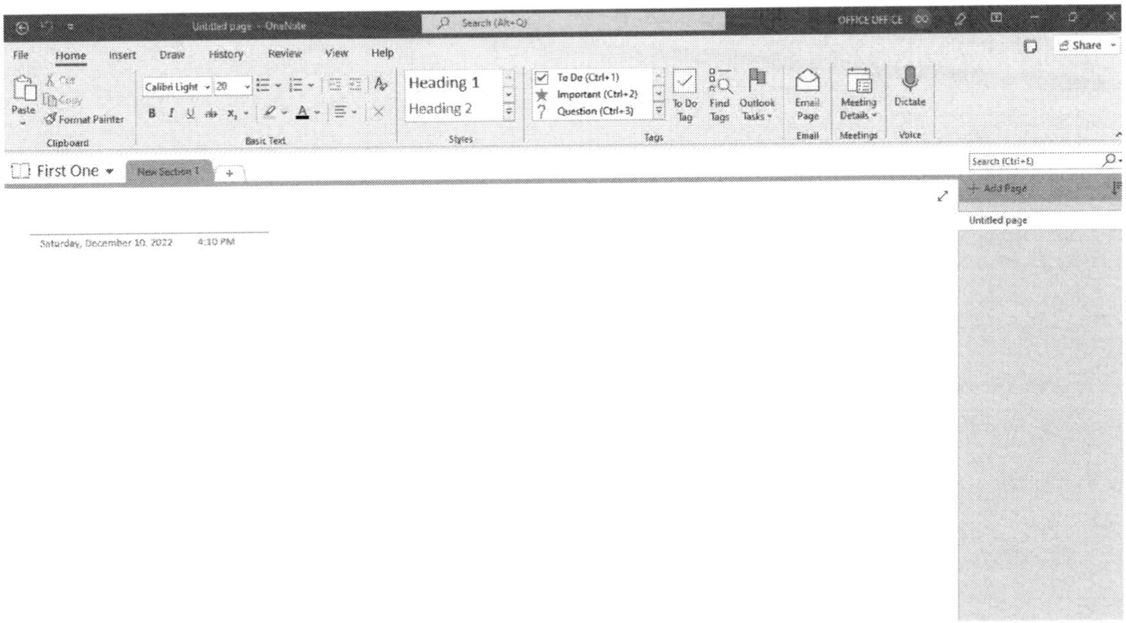

Figure 263: A Created New Notebook

Although the user interfaces of the various OneNote versions vary, they are all built around the same framework.

As it relates to the diagrams mentioned above, the user interface of the OneNote desktop version will be explained in other sections of this chapter.

2. Title Bar

The title of the opened notebook page is displayed in the Title Bar. When you give your notebook page a name, OneNote will replace the Untitled page's default title. No title will be shown if you have not opened or created any notebooks.

The OneNote window can be closed, minimized, or maximized using the buttons on the window control bar to the right of the title bar. Additionally, it has a button for the ribbon display settings, which lets you manage how the ribbon systems are displayed.

3. Quick Access Toolbar

The most frequently used OneNote commands, such as Save, Undo, Redo, etc., are all represented by icons in the Quick Access Toolbar (QAT).

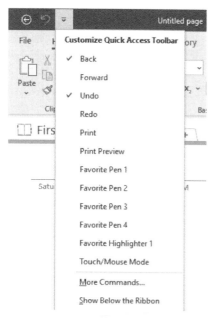

Figure 264: Quick Access Toolbar

Customizing the Quick Access Toolbar

Add your often-used command to the quick access toolbar to personalize it.

To customize the quick access toolbar:

1. Click the drop-down button at the far right of the toolbar, and check or uncheck any commands to add or remove them as desired.

2. Alternatively, you may add to Quick Access Toolbar by right-clicking the relevant command in the Home ribbon or any other tab ribbon.

Alternatively,

1. You can also right-click the quick access toolbar.

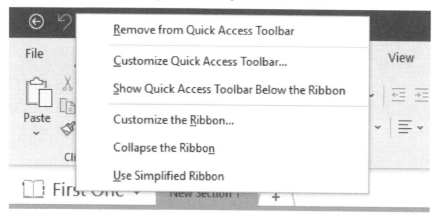

Figure 265: Right-click the quick access toolbar

2. From the list of options that appears, choose Customize Quick Access Toolbar.

OneNote Options pops up in a new window.

3. Use the left-side pane to search for and choose the desired commands.

4. Select Add from the menu.

5. Click OK.

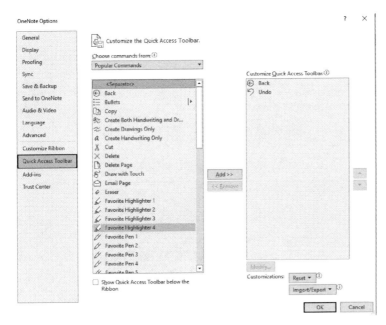

Figure 266: Customize the QAT

Right-click the tool and select Delete from Quick Access Toolbar from the list to remove any Quick Access Toolbar commands.

4. The Ribbon System

OneNote features many functions that are orderly and arranged into what is referred to as the ribbon system. Therefore, the user can easily find any command with the help of this system.

Ribbon Tabs, Groups, and Commands

There are three parts to the Ribbon system:

- **Ribbon Tabs:** These are buttons with clear names that let users rapidly find and use a collection of commands to carry out a particular operation. Examples include Home, which has sets of commands that are often used. Insert is a tool for adding various things. Draw, study history, etc.

Contextual tabs only show up when a table, image, picture, figure, chart, etc., is placed or chosen on the page. They are mostly employed to format and design the chosen object.

When you click on it, the ribbon for each tab will appear below.

- **Groups:** Related commands or OneNote features are grouped in the ribbon. For instance, the Home tab ribbon comprises the Clipboard group, Basic Text group, Styles group, etc.

- **Commands:** These are buttons on OneNote features that carry out particular functions.

Customizing the Ribbon

You can delete or add any ribbon tabs, groups, and instructions to suit your needs and work.

To customize the ribbon:

1. Simply right-click the ribbon. A menu box shows up.

2. Choose customize the ribbon

The **OneNote Options** dialog box appears.

3. Decide on a choice from Commands can be selected using the drop-down button.

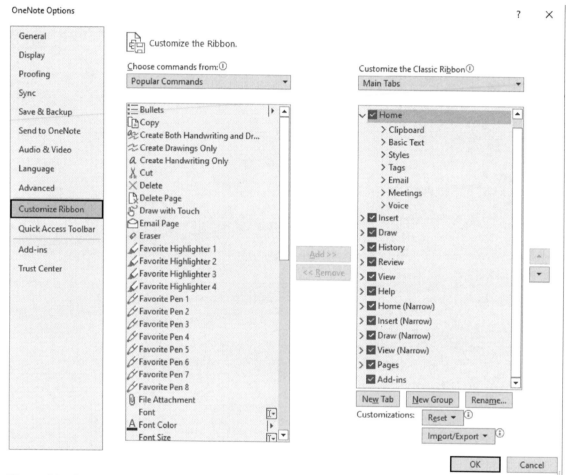

Figure 267: Customize the ribbon

4. Select the New Tab option to open a new tab.

Select the tab in the right-side pane and click the New Group button to add a new group to an existing tab. Then, rename your custom group or tabs using the Rename buttons.
You cannot add commands to OneNote's default groups; you can only add commands to new groups.

5. Use the left-side pane to search for and choose the desired commands.

6. Double-click the command or click the Add button.

7. Click OK.

Select the custom tab, group, or command in the right-side pane and press the Remove button to remove it. You can use the Reset button to remove all personalization whenever you want.

Hiding/unhiding the Ribbon System

You can hide the ribbon and even the ribbon tabs to give yourself more room to view the information on your website.

To hide/unhide the ribbon:

1. The ribbon hides when you click the button for ribbon collapse on the far right of the ribbon. When you click on a tab, the ribbon appears, and when you click away from the ribbon, it disappears. The pin icon replaces the ribbon-collapse icon.

2. To move the ribbon momentarily, click any tab. To put the ribbon in place permanently, click the pin symbol.

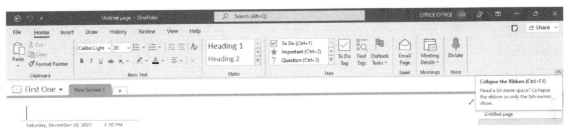

Figure 268: Option for hiding ribbon

As an alternative, you can choose the desired choice by clicking the ribbon ⊡ display options icon.

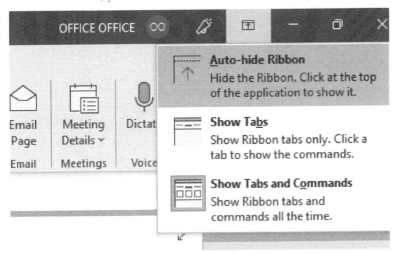

Figure 269: Ribbon display options

5. Backstage View

All OneNote notebooks are managed in one location, called Backstage View. Click on the File tab in the Ribbon Tabs bar to enter OneNote's backstage area.

From backstage, use the left bar tabs to create, open, print, or share your notepad. Tab:

Figure 270: Backstage view

- **New**: You can start a fresh notepad by selecting New.
- **Open** enables you to access the earlier-created notebook from several locations.
- **Info** provides details about the notebook, enabling you to safeguard, check out, and manage your notebook.
- **Print**: Printing your notebook in the format you want is possible.
- **Share** enables online or emails collaboration by allowing you to share your notes.
- **Export:** Exporting your notebook, notebook section, or notebook page to PDF, XPS, word, or other formats is possible.
- **Send** allows you to send your notebook as a pdf file, email attachment, or email body. You can also send your notebook directly to your blog after converting it into a word document.
- **Account** has all the information on the notebook owner. Additionally, you can modify the appearance of your MS Office programs and make additional adjustments from here.
- **Options** launch the OneNote Options window

OneNote Options

All OneNote customizations and default settings can be made in the OneNote Options dialog box. This dialog box named OneNote Options appears when you click the majority of customizable commands in the OneNote user interface.

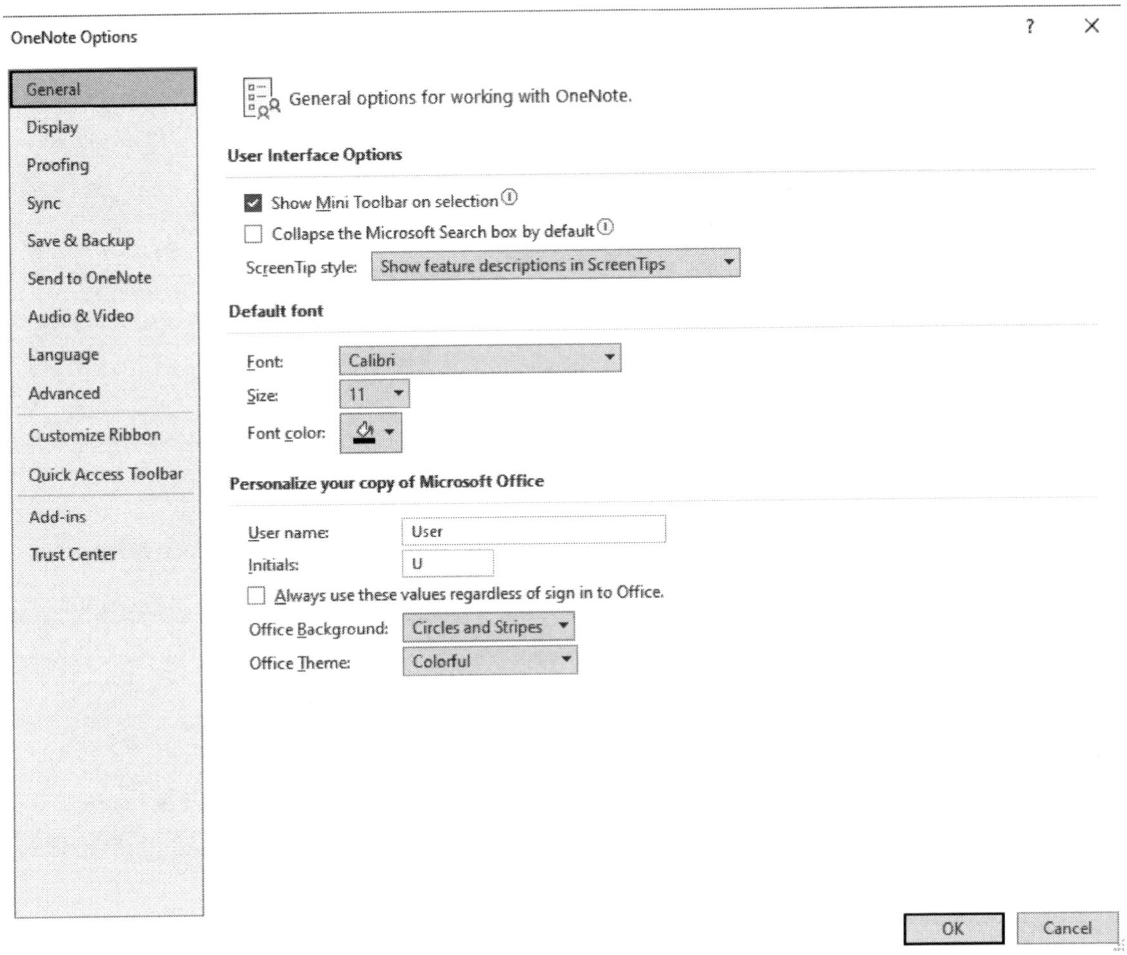

Figure 271: OneNote Options

If you want to customize or change the default settings in OneNote, go to this box. First, choose any option in the left-side pane that corresponds to your preferences, then make your selections in the right-side window. When you are through with the settings, click Ok.

6. Notebook Area

You will insert your note in the notepad section. Depending on the OneNote version, the Notebook area has a distinct layout. Nevertheless, depending on the OneNote version or your notebook view, the common structure of the notebook area displays the name of the open notebook, the sections of the notebook organized at the top of the notebook area or by the left side of the notebook area, and the pages of the current section of the notebook organized at the right side of the notebook area or next to the sections list at the right side.

The OneNote desktop application displays the name of the currently active notebook on the left side of the notebook area, a list of the notebook's sections at the top, a list of the section's pages on the right side, and the page's content in the middle.

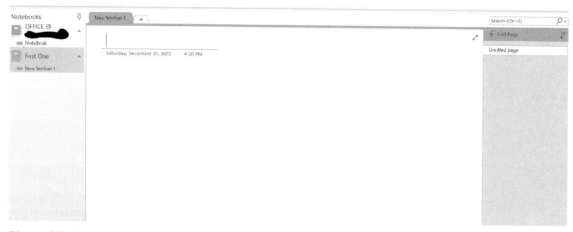

Figure 272: Notebook Area

By pinning the open notebooks list to the left pane of the notebook area, you can personalize the notebook area. To achieve this, select the left-facing pin icon from the box that displays by clicking on the notebook name drop-down icon.

7. OneNote Context Help Feature

Users of OneNote can learn about its functionality by using the context help feature, which provides pertinent information about OneNote commands. For example, to learn more about a specific command:

- Wait a moment after placing your cursor over the command, or hover over it.
- As illustrated below, a context help window detailing the command will pop up.
- On the Office website, click the Tell me more link (which displays some commands) to read more about the command.

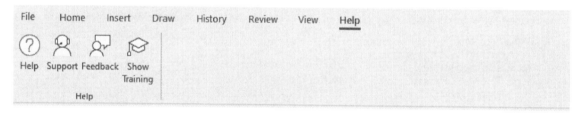

Figure 273: Help option

With the help of this function, you can understand what each OneNote command does.

Understanding the Basic Terms of Microsoft OneNote

Microsoft OneNote is a powerful note-taking application that allows users to capture, organize and share their notes and ideas. It enables users to create notes, to-do lists, drawings, and more. As with any other software, Microsoft OneNote also has its own set of basic terms that are important to understand. This section will provide an overview of the basic terms used in Microsoft OneNote and how they can be used.

Notebooks:

A notebook is the main container for all your notes in OneNote. It is where you store, organize and share your notes, ideas, drawings, and other information. You can create multiple notebooks in OneNote and rename, move, delete or share them. You can also password-protect a notebook to protect its contents from unauthorized access.

Sections:

A section is a collection of pages within a notebook. It allows you to organize your notes into groups and helps you easily find the information you need. You can create multiple sections in a notebook and rename, move, delete or share them.

Pages:

A page is an individual page within a section. It is where you can write, draw and store your notes, ideas, and other information. You can create multiple pages in a section and rename, move, delete or share them.

Tags:

Tags are labels you can use to categorize your notes. They help you quickly find the information you need. You can create your tags or use OneNote's existing ones.

Clipping:

Clipping is copying text, an image, or a web page and pasting it into OneNote. It allows you to capture and store information from different sources quickly.

Search:

Search is a powerful feature in OneNote that allows you to find the notes or information you need quickly. You can search for your notes in OneNote using keywords, tags, or other information.

Comparison between the different versions of Microsoft OneNote

Over the years, Microsoft has released several versions of the software, all of which offer a range of features and capabilities. This section overviews the various versions of Microsoft OneNote and compares their features, benefits, and drawbacks.

Microsoft OneNote for Windows

Microsoft OneNote for Windows is the traditional desktop version of the software. It offers users a range of features, including custom notebooks, online synchronization, and support for multiple languages. It allows users to capture and organize their ideas, store information, and collaborate. OneNote for Windows is available as a part of the Microsoft Office suite or as a standalone application.

OneNote for Windows includes several features that make it an ideal note-taking and organizational tool. It allows users to create custom notebooks, which can be used to store information and collaborate with others. It also offers a range of formatting options, such as bold, italic, and underline, and support for multiple languages. Additionally, OneNote for Windows can be synced with other devices, such as mobile phones and tablets, so users can access their notes wherever they are.

Microsoft OneNote for Mac

Microsoft OneNote for Mac is a version of the software that is designed specifically for Mac users. It offers the same features as OneNote for Windows but with a few additional capabilities. For example, OneNote for Mac provides support for iCloud so that users can sync their notes across multiple devices. It also supports Apple Pencil, so users can draw and annotate their notes.

OneNote for Mac also offers many of the same features as OneNote for Windows. It allows users to create custom notebooks, store information, and collaborate with others. Additionally, it supports multiple languages and allows users to format their notes with bold, italic, and underlined text. OneNote for Mac allows users to sync their notes with other devices, such as iPhones and iPads.

Microsoft OneNote Online

Microsoft OneNote Online is a cloud-based version of the software. It offers the same features as OneNote for Windows and Mac but with a few additional capabilities. For example, OneNote Online allows users to access their notes from anywhere with an internet connection. It also offers support for third-party add-ins so that users can extend the software's functionality. Additionally, OneNote Online allows users to share their notes with others and collaborate in real-time.

OneNote Online offers many of the same features as the other software versions. It allows users to create custom notebooks, store information, and collaborate with others. It also supports multiple languages and allows users to format their notes with bold, italic, and underline text. Additionally, OneNote Online will enable users to sync their notes with other devices, such as mobile phones and tablets

Microsoft OneNote for Mobile

Microsoft OneNote for Mobile is a version of the software that is designed specifically for mobile devices. It offers the same features as OneNote for Windows, Mac, and Online, but with a few additional capabilities. For example, OneNote for Mobile allows users to capture ideas and notes on the go. It also offers support for voice dictation, so users can easily add notes to their notebooks. Additionally, OneNote for Mobile allows users to sync their notes with other devices, such as laptops and tablets.

OneNote for Mobile also offers the same features as the other software versions. For example, it allows users to create custom notebooks, store information, and collaborate with others. It also supports multiple languages and allows users to format their notes with bold, italic, and underline text. OneNote for Mobile will also enable users to sync their notes with other devices, such as iPhones and iPads.

Comparison of Microsoft OneNote Versions

All versions of Microsoft OneNote offer a range of features and capabilities, but each has its advantages and drawbacks. OneNote for Windows is the traditional desktop version of the software and offers many of the same features as the other versions. For example, it allows users to create custom notebooks, store information, and collaborate with others. However, it does not offer support for iCloud or Apple Pencil.

OneNote for Mac is designed specifically for Mac users and offers iCloud and Apple Pencil support. It also allows users to create custom notebooks, store information, and collaborate with others. However, OneNote for Mac does not offer support for third-party add-ins.

OneNote Online is a cloud-based software that allows users to access their notes from anywhere with an internet connection. It also supports third-party add-ins and enables users to share their notes with others and collaborate in real-time. However, OneNote Online does not provide support for Apple Pencil.

OneNote for Mobile is designed specifically for mobile devices and allows users to capture ideas and notes. It also supports voice dictation and enables users to sync their notes with other devices. However, OneNote for Mobile does not support iCloud or third-party add-ins.

Features	Desktop Version	Windows Version	Web Version	Smartphone Version
Recent notes or History	✓	✓		✓
Add Tags	✓	✓	✓	Only To-Do
Find Tags	✓	✓		
Get meeting details from Outlook	✓	✓	✓	
Integrating with Outlook Tasks	✓			
Save as pdf	✓		✓	✓
Wide views	✓	✓	✓	
Views pages of notebooks	✓			

Features	Desktop Version	Windows Version	Web Version	Smartphone Version
you are not working on				
Ink to text	✓	✓		
Ink to shape	✓	✓		
Ink to Maths	✓			
Solve Maths Equations		✓		
Draw Graph		✓		
Translate	✓	✓		
Dictate Note		✓	✓	✓
Copy text from the image	✓			Image with typed text.

93 CREATING AND MANAGING ONENOTE STRUCTURE

OneNote is structured into three main levels:

- **Notebook**

- **Section**

- **Page**

- **Subpage**(optional)

The OneNote structuring features are amazing for you to super-organize your idea, project, or work. To start using OneNote, you need to create a notebook. The new notebook you create will have one section by default, and the section will have a page. You will be adding your note content to pages. Your OneNote can have as many **Notebooks** as you desire. A Notebook can have as many **sections** as you need, and a section can have as many **pages** as required for your work. You can as well add **subpages** to your notebook if needed.

In this chapter, you will learn how to create and manage a notebook, sections, and pages of your notebook using the OneNote desktop version.

Creating and Managing Notebooks

Create and save a new notebook from scratch.

To create a notebook:

1. Open your OneNote app.

2. Click the **File** tab or click on the blank page if you do not have any open notebooks. The app backstage opens.

3. Ensure that the **New** tab at the menu bar is selected.

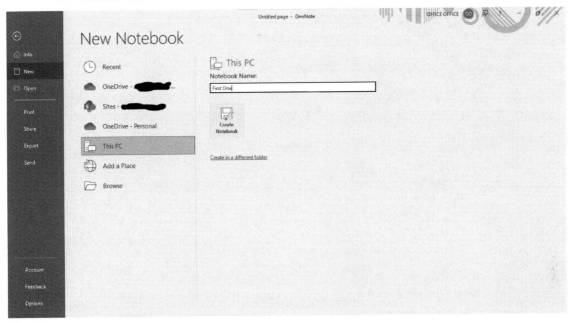

Figure 274: Creating a new Notebook

The **New** tab has two ribbons; the left side for locations and the right-side ribbon for the actual places in the location.

4. Select where you want to save your new notebook from the left ribbon. Select:

- **Recent -** to save your notebook in the folder you recently saved a notebook.

- **OneDrive-Personal-** to save your notebook in your currently signed-in OneDrive account.

- **This PC-** to save your notebook locally in your **PC > local disk (C:) > user > admin > documents > OneNote Notebook** folder (default). You can quickly locate your notebooks by clicking the left pane **Document > OneNote Notebook** folder.

- **Add a Place-** to save your notebook on a different online platform other than the signed-in OneDrive.

- **Browse-** save your notebook locally on your PC in a location other than the default location.

5. Follow the prompts to open the actual folder online or locally, depending on your chosen location.

6. Type in your desired Notebook name.

7. Click on Create Notebook button. Give OneNote a few seconds to create and open your notebook.

The notebook you created will be opened with the name at the top of your notebook area.

Note: OneNote prompts you to save your notebook first to create it and automatically saves your notebook locally or online as you work on it.

If you save your notebook online, OneNote automatically synchronizes your work anytime your PC is connected to the internet by default. A synchronization icon will appear on a notebook name as it is synchronizing, and the icon will disappear when your notebook is up to date.

If, for any reason, you wish to synchronize your notebook anytime you want manually, you can change the default automatic synchronization settings following the steps below:

- Click on the File tab to go to the backstage of OneNote.

- Select info in the left vertical bar.

- Click **View Sync Status**

Figure 275: View sync status

- Check the **Sync Manually** button in the window that pops up.

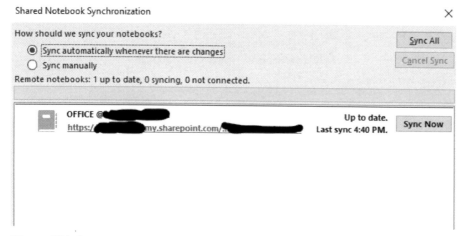

Figure 276: Sync manually

- Anytime you want to synchronize your notebook, click **Sync Now** in front of the notebook or **Sync All** to update all the opened notebooks.
- You can click on the notebook name anytime to open this box to synchronize it.

Anytime your notebook cannot synchronize due to being offline or when you have changed the synchronization setting to manual, a red circle with a white x on it will appear on the notebook name. You can go back online anytime to synchronize your notebook or click on the notebook name to synchronize it manually.

Tips: Save your notebook on OneDrive or any online location to access your notebook anywhere on any device. You can also share your notebook with others for real-life collaboration only if you save your notebook online.

How to open a notebook.

You can open as many notebooks as you want to work on. The list of all your notebooks will be available for you to click and access as desired.

To open an existing notebook:

1. Click on the drop-down arrow beside the active notebook name. Alternatively, Click on **File** to go to the backstage.
2. Click on **Open** Other Notebooks from the list.
3. Select the notebook you want to open from the backstage.

Modifying your notebook properties.

You can change your notebook display name, color, and location after you have created it.

To change your notebook properties:

1. Click on the drop-down button of the active notebook to see the lists of all the opened notebooks.
2. Right-click on the notebook whose property you want to change.

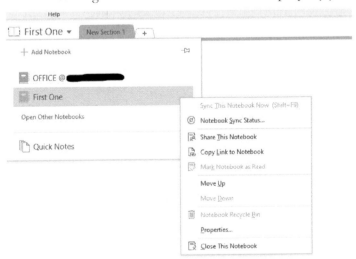

Figure 277: Change your notebook properties

3. Select **Properties** from the drop-down list

4. Choose the property you want to change and make the desired changes.

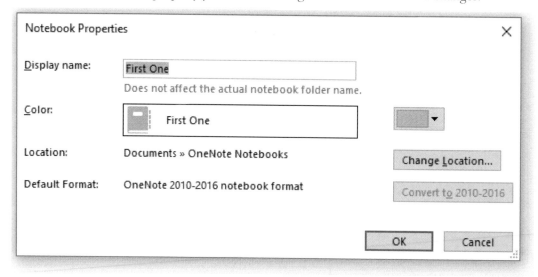

Figure 278: Notebook properties

How to close a notebook.

All the notebooks you open on the OneNote app will remain open even when you close the OneNote app. Anytime you open your OneNote, all the previously opened notebooks will be available. You can decide to close any notebook you will not be working on.

To close a notebook:

1. Click on the drop-down arrow beside the active notebook name.

2. Right-click on the notebook you want to close.

3. Select the close option from the list.

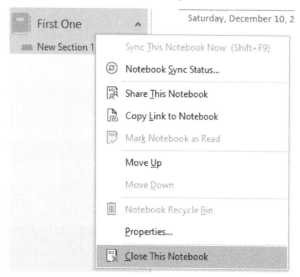

Figure 279: Closing a notebook

How to delete a notebook.

You cannot right-click and choose **delete** (no delete option) to delete a notebook in OneNote, like the usual way of deleting files.

To delete a notebook:

1. Go to the location where you save your notebook (often in your Microsoft account OneDrive if you save it online and your default directory if you save it locally).

2. Right-click on the notebook you want to delete.

3. Select the **delete** option.

Note:

- If you save your notebook online, you must sign in to your Microsoft account, go to OneDrive and locate your notebook.

- To know where your notebook has been saved, hover on the notebook on OneNote and check the information box that appears.

Creating and Managing Sections

OneNote notebook comes with one section, **New Section 1**, by default. You will, at some point, have to work with many sections in your notebook. You want to rename your section, change the section color, and organize or delete your sections. How you can manage your notebook sections is explained below.

Naming your section

To rename your notebook section:

1. Right-click on the section you want to change its name.

2. Select **Rename** in the drop-down menu.

3. Type in your desired name.

4. Press **Enter**.

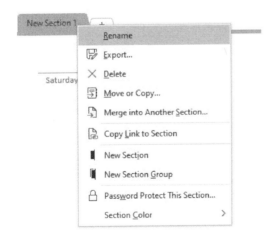

Figure 280: Rename your notebook section

Alternatively,

1. double-click on the section name

2. type in the new name and

3. Press the **Enter** key.

Adding a new section

To add a new section to your notebook:

1. Right-click on the name of any of the sections.

2. Select **New Section** in the drop-down menu.

Alternatively, click on the plus sign beside the last section name.

Changing your section color

To change the color of any of your notebook's sections:

1. Right-click on the section.

2. Click on Section Color.

3. Select your desired color.

Figure 281: Changing section color

Rearranging the sections

To rearrange your notebook's sections:

1. Click, hold, and drag the section you want to relocate.

An arrow will appear on top to indicate where the section will be moved.

2. Locate your desired position and release the mouse to drop the section.

Alternatively,

1. Right-click on the section.

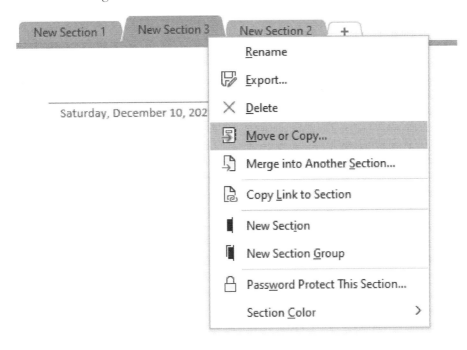

Figure 282: Rearranging sections

2. Select **Move or Copy...** in the contextual menu that appears.

A dialog box appears with the list of all your notebooks and their sections.

3. Select the section whose right the section you want to move will be. i.e., the section you want to move will be at the right of the section you will select in the box.

4. Click on Move.

Duplicating a section

To duplicate your notebook's sections:

1. Click, hold, and drag the section you want to duplicate.

An arrow will appear on top to indicate where the section will be copied.

2. Press and hold down the **Ctrl** key.

3. Locate your desired position and release the mouse to duplicate the section.

4. Release the **Ctrl** key.

Alternatively,

1. Right-click on the section.

2. Select **Move or Copy...** in the contextual menu that appears.

A dialog box appears with the list of all your notebooks and their sections.

3. Select the section whose right the section you want to duplicate will be.

4. Click on Copy.

Deleting a section

To delete a section:

1. Right-click on the section you want to delete.

2. Select Delete from the contextual menu.

Warning: All the pages and contents in the section will be deleted.

Creating and Managing Pages and Subpages

Your new section will have a page named, **Untitled page** by default. As given below, learn how to rename, add, rearrange, delete, and add subpages to your page.

Naming your page

To rename your page:

1. Position your cursor at the top of the line on your page.

2. Type your desired page title.

Your page title will automatically reflect on the OneNote title page and the right-side navigation pane.

Figure 283: Naming your pages

You can alternatively right-click on the page title on the right-side pane and select rename.

Note: The first text you input on your page will be taken as the page title, whether it is on the default line or not. It is always advisable to put the page title on the line.

Adding new pages and subpages

To add a new page to your section:

1. Click on the plus sign at the top of the page pane.

or

Right-click on any of the page names.

2. Select **New Page** from the menu,

3. The two methods above insert a new page at the bottom of your pages.

To insert a new page in the middle of two pages:

- Hover your cursor in the middle of the two pages. A plus sign with a straight line appears.

- Click on the plus sign.

You can also turn a page into a subpage.

To turn a page into a subpage:

- Select the page.

- Click, hold, and drag the page to the right to indent it.
- You can also have a sub-subpage by dragging a subpage further to the right.

Alternatively,

1. right-click on the page and
2. select **Make Subpage** in the menu.

Rearrange your pages

To rearrange your pages:

1. Select the page(s) you want to rearrange in the page pane.
2. Click, hold down and drag the page(s) to the desired position. A thick horizontal line shows you where the page will be moved.
3. Drop the page(s) by releasing the mouse in the desired position.

Alternatively,

1. Right-click on the title page
2. Select **cut**
3. Select a page below which you want to put the page.
4. Right-click and click **paste**.

You can select multiple pages: To do this:

1. Click on the first page
2. Hold down the **Ctrl** key and
3. Click the other pages one after the other.

For selecting pages that are close together:

1. Press down the Shift key
2. Select only the first and the last page of the range.

Delete pages

To delete a page:

1. Select the page(s) you want to delete.
2. Right-click on the page name.
3. Select Delete in the menu that appears.

Create and Manage Quick Notes

A Quick note is like an electronic equivalent of the yellow (small paper) sticky note we use in the office or at home. When you create a quick note, it will instantly save it to your OneNote notebook so that you can search and organize them anytime.

With a quick note, you can catch a raw idea that drops into your mind or put what you want to remember or memorize as you work on your window system.

You can make a quick note on your Windows PC whether your OneNote app is open or closed.

To create a new quick note while the OneNote app is opened:

- Go to the **View** ribbon.

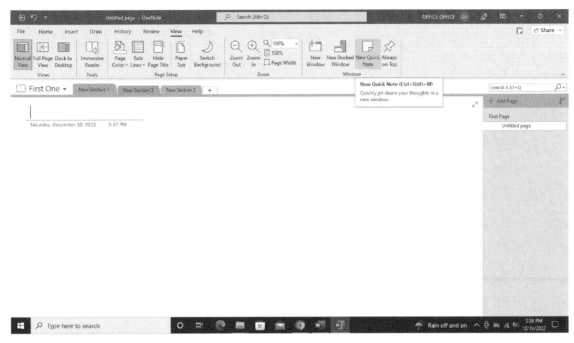

Figure 284: New quick note

- Click on the **New Quick Note** command in the **Windows** group.

- A small window with the OneNote app's full features pops up.

To create a new quick note when OneNote is not running:

- Press the **Windows icon + Alt + N** keys on your keyboard.

- A quick note window pops up.

Work on Quick Note and Pin it to your PC Window

In the quick note window:

- Click on the top three dots to reveal the quick note window toolbar, and click on the page to hide it. With this, you can use any of the features for your quick note.

- To pin an important quick note to your screen, click the top three dots, go to the **View** tab, and click the **Always on Top** command in the **Windows** group.

- Click and drag the quick note anywhere on your screen.

- You can click on the full-screen icon to view the quick note page in full mode.

- Click the X button at the top-right corner to close the quick note when you are done. This will not delete your quick note.

- Your quick note is automatically saved in the unfiled Notes section in your default notebook.

- To review all your quick notes, click on your active notebook name, and select Quick Notes at the bottom of the notebook list that appears. You will see the list of all your quick notes on the right-side page pane. Select the one you want to work on.

Tips

You can move or copy a section from one notebook to the other.

1. Right-click on the section name.
2. Select Move or Copy…
3. Select the notebook you want to move your section to in the dialog box that appears.

You can move or copy a page from one section to another and from one notebook to the other.

1. Right-click on the page name.
2. Select Move or Copy…
3. Double-click on the notebook section you want to move your page to in the dialog box that appears.

You can recover your deleted sections and pages in the Notebook Recycle Bin

Any section or pages you deleted in OneNote will be temporarily stored for 60 days in OneNote recycle bin. You can retrieve your deleted section or page at any time.

To restore a deleted page or section:

1. Right-click on any of your opened notebook's names.
2. Select **Notebook Recycle Bin** from the menu that appears.
3. Right-click on the page or section you want to restore.
4. Select any of the options.

The list of all the opened notebooks sections and pages appears in a dialog box.

5. Double-click where you want to move, copy or merge your section or page.
6. Click on the undo icon to close the **Notebook Recycle Bin**.

OneNote automatically puts the current day and time you open a new page under the title line You can change the time or date by clicking on it and selecting your desired time or date from the calendar or clock that pops up.

Misplaced sections

You can work offline if you have opened your notebook on OneNote for windows or OneNote desktop versions. Your note will synchronize anytime you get back online. If you forget and close your notebook when it has not synchronized, then OneNote will put the section in a shared notebook as a misplaced section until it synchronizes. If OneNote cannot synchronize the section with its file for one reason or another, you can move the section to another notebook or delete it if you don't need it again.

To move the section,

1. Click Misplaced Sections below the notebooks list, and right-click the tab of the misplaced section you want to move.

2. Select **Move or Copy…**

3. Select where you want to move the section in the box that comes up.

4. Press Move.

To delete the section, click Misplaced Sections in the notebook lists, right-click the name of the section you want to delete, and select Delete in the box that comes up.

94 LET'S START

Creating Notes in Microsoft OneNote

Microsoft OneNote is a powerful digital note-taking tool that can help you organize, store, and share notes and other media. It is available for various platforms, including Windows, Mac, iOS, and Android. With its customizable interface and efficient organization system, OneNote can be invaluable for individuals and teams. This guide will demonstrate how to create notes in OneNote and explore some features that will make your experience more efficient and productive.

Getting Started with OneNote

You will need to download the software and create an account to get started. Once you have done this, you can access your notes from any device.

OneNote is an excellent tool for organizing and storing your notes. It allows you to create notebooks, which can be organized into sections, pages, and subpages. You can also customize the appearance of your notes by using different fonts, colors, and backgrounds.

OneNote also has several powerful features that can make your experience more efficient. For example, you can search for keywords or phrases in your notes, add tags and reminders, and take notes on your device's camera.

Adding Content to Notes

Once you have set up your OneNote account, you can add content to your notes. For example, you can type directly into your notes or copy and paste text from other sources. In addition, you can add images, audio recordings, and other media to your notes.

OneNote also has several tools that can help you create more detailed notes. For example, you can use drawing tools to create diagrams and drawings or math tools to add equations to your notes. You can also add hyperlinks to websites or other notes in OneNote.

Using Tables in Notes

OneNote allows you to create tables in your notes. Tables, such as lists, schedules, and project plans, can organize information. Tables can also be used to compare and contrast different ideas or concepts. Creating a table in OneNote is simple. All you need to do is click on the "Table" tab in the ribbon and select the type of table you want to create. You can then type your content into the table or copy and paste it from another source.

You can also customize the appearance of your table. For example, you can change the table's font, size, color, and contents. In addition, you can add borders and shading to make your table look more professional.

Inserting Images and Media into Notes

OneNote makes it easy to insert images and other media into your notes. You can take pictures using your device's camera or upload images from your computer or the web. You can also insert audio recordings, videos, and other files.

Once you have inserted an image or other media, you can customize it by adding captions, notes, and tags. You can also use the drawing tools to add arrows, shapes, and other annotations to your images.

Sharing Notes

OneNote makes it easy to share your notes with others. You can share an entire notebook or just a single page. You can also share notes with specific individuals or groups.

When you share a note, you can control who can access it and what type of access they have. You can also set expiration dates and passwords to ensure that your notes remain secure.

Once you have shared a note, you can collaborate with others in real time. For example, you can add comments, assign tasks, and edit the note. You can also use the chat feature to communicate with other collaborators.

Creating a Daily Journal

Keeping a journal is a great way to document your thoughts and experiences. Microsoft OneNote is a powerful and versatile tool that can help you easily create and organize your journal entries. Here, we will explore the different features of OneNote that can help you create and organize your daily journal. We will also discuss some best practices for using OneNote to keep a journal.

Overview of Microsoft OneNote

Microsoft OneNote is a note-taking application part of the Microsoft Office suite of products. It allows users to create and organize notes, lists, and other types of content. OneNote can be used for various purposes, from taking notes in meetings and classes, tracking tasks and projects, and creating a daily journal.

OneNote provides several features and tools that make it ideal for keeping a daily journal. It offers a variety of formatting options, such as fonts, colors, and styles, that can help you customize your journal entries. It also allows you to create sections and pages to organize your entries and tag entries with keywords for easy searching.

Setting Up Your Journal

Before creating your daily journal in OneNote, you must set up your notebook. To do this, open OneNote and create a new notebook. Give the notebook a name and choose a location to save it. You can also choose password-protect the notebook to keep your entries secure.

Once you have created the notebook, you can begin to set up your journal. Start by creating sections for each day. Then, within each section, create pages for each entry. You can also create sub-pages for each topic if you wish.

Creating a Daily Journal Entry

Once you have set up your journal, you can begin creating daily entries. To create an entry, open the appropriate section and page, and start typing. You can use the formatting options to customize the look of your entry. You can also insert images and other media if you wish.

When writing your entry, try focusing on the day's details. Write down your thoughts and feelings and any events or experiences that stood out. You can also use the entry to reflect on the day and explore any insights or lessons you may have learned.

Organizing and Searching Your Journal

Once you have created your journal entries, you can use OneNote's organizational tools to keep them organized. For example, you can create tags for each entry to help you easily search and find them later. You can also add links to related entries and pages to make it easier to navigate your journal.

OneNote also allows you to password-protect specific sections or pages. This can help you keep certain entries private or secure. You can also share your notebook with others to collaborate on entries or allow them to view your journal.

Best Practices for Keeping a Daily Journal

A daily journal can be a great way to document your thoughts and experiences over time. However, it can also be easy to get overwhelmed or discouraged if you don't have a plan or best practices. Here are some tips to help you get the most out of your daily journal in OneNote:

• Write regularly: Make sure to write in your journal regularly. Set aside sometime each day to write down your thoughts and experiences.

• Be honest: Don't be afraid to write about the difficult moments or things you are struggling with. This can help you gain valuable insights and perspective.

• Be creative: Don't be afraid to try something new or explore different writing styles. This can help you discover new ways to express yourself.

• Track your progress: Use OneNote's organizational tools to track the progress of your journal entries over time. This can help you see how far you have come and motivate you to keep going.

• Share with others: Share your journal with trusted friends or family members to get their feedback and support.

By following these tips, you can make the most of your daily journal in Microsoft OneNote and use it to document your thoughts and experiences in a meaningful and organized way.

Creating a Bullet Journal in Microsoft OneNote

Organizing your daily life, tracking your goals, and getting more done can be made easier with a bullet journal, and Microsoft OneNote is an excellent tool for creating one. With OneNote, you can create a bullet journal that can be easily edited and accessed from various devices, allowing you to stay organized.

What is a Bullet Journal?

A bullet journal is a popular and efficient way to track tasks, goals, and ideas. It uses a simple yet powerful system of symbols and abbreviations to categorize and prioritize tasks. In addition, the bullet journal system is flexible and can be customized to fit the user's needs. As a result, it is an excellent tool for organizing, planning, and tracking tasks and goals.

Benefits of a Bullet Journal in Microsoft OneNote

Using Microsoft OneNote to create a bullet journal can be beneficial in several ways. First, it allows users to easily access their bullet journal from any device with an internet connection, making it easier to stay organized. It also provides users with a wide range of formatting options, making it easier to customize their bullet journal look. Additionally, OneNote can store other types of information, such as images and audio files, making it an excellent tool for tracking and organizing multiple data types.

How to Set Up a Bullet Journal in Microsoft OneNote

Setting up a bullet journal in Microsoft OneNote is easy. First, create a OneNote notebook. This notebook will act as your bullet journal. Next, create sections and pages in your notebook. These sections and pages will organize your tasks, goals, and ideas. Finally, add symbols and abbreviations to categorize and prioritize your tasks.

Tips for Using Your Bullet Journal in Microsoft OneNote

Using your bullet journal in Microsoft OneNote is easy and efficient. Here are some tips to help you get the most out of your bullet journal:

1. Add symbols and abbreviations to help you categorize and prioritize tasks.
2. Use the formatting options to customize the look of your bullet journal.
3. Use the search feature to find tasks and goals quickly.
4. Use the note-taking features to add notes to tasks and goals.
5. Use images, audio, and video to add more information to tasks and goals.
6. Use the sharing feature to collaborate on tasks and goals.

95 ADDING PICTURES AND VIDEOS

We will go through how you can add pictures, videos, and different types of content to your notebooks. We will need to be on the insert tab and focus on the images group.

Figure 285: Insert Tab

The first thing in images is the screen clipping utility. You might be thinking, well, why on earth would you need that after learning to use the OneNote clipper? The OneNote clipper is an installation for your browser. Essentially, it only allows you to clip content from the web.

The screen clipping utility within OneNote allows you to clip anything open on your PC. You can clip a file from a pdf document, an excel spreadsheet, a PowerPoint presentation, and pretty much anything you can open on your pc. You can clip using the screen clipping utility within OneNote, and as you hover over it, you get the screen tip that tells you what it will do. It allows you to take a snapshot of parts of your screen and add it to the page. It says OneNote will hide while you capture web pages, documents, or anything else.

One interesting point we'll get onto a little later when we cover searching is that OneNote can search for text in screen clippings. That is a cool little feature. If you clip a paragraph of text, you can make it searchable. We will emphasize more on that specific aspect a bit later on. First, let's concentrate on utilizing the screen clipping utility.

Still, in the office section, you can click on the London page and add a text note that gives the London office address. You can also add a map that shows where the office is located. Finally, you can open up a google map in your web browser, navigate to the office's address, and maybe take a screen clipping of a certain section of the map.

Because it is in a web browser, you definitely could utilize your clip to OneNote utility, but we will do that slightly differently. First, however, we will utilize the screen clipping option. One thing you must be careful of is that whatever you want to clip needs to be opened directly behind OneNote because as soon as you click on screen clipping, it minimizes OneNote and allows you to clip whatever it finds behind it.

If you want to clip a section from a word document, you must ensure it is directly behind OneNote. To clip the map, you need to have it as the last thing open and open up OneNote before it. When you click on screen clipping, it minimizes and shows what's directly behind it. Your screen faded away and had your cursor as a cross sign. You will clip a specific section of the particular map and pull it through to OneNote. Just drag a significant region with your mouse and let go. It pulls the clipped image (map) directly into your page.

When you take a screen clipping that way, underneath it, you will have the date and time that the screen clipping was taken. You can delete the screen clipping information if you don't want it. An easy way of doing that is as you hover over the text below the image, you'll get a little tab or arrow at the side, and if you click on that, it's going to highlight that text, and you can press the delete key to get rid of it.

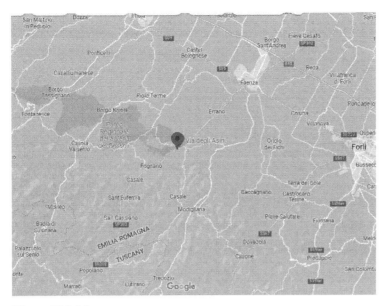

Figure 286: Map

You can then click on the image edge and resize it if it's too big. If you right-click on the image, you can make the text in the image searchable. You will not do that right now but hold that piece of information.

Inserting pictures and online Pictures

This section will go through how you can insert pictures into your pages. We will work predominantly on the insert ribbon, sticking within the images group. You have two options on your image groups: pictures and online pictures. So if you have a particular image that you want to add to your notebook and have that image already stored locally, maybe into your pictures folder, you would use the picture option.

However, if you want to browse online for a picture to use, you could do that through the online pictures option, and we will go through an example of both of them. So let's start with pictures that you have already saved.

Figure 287: Europe page

Currently, we are clicking on the Europe page within the office section, and we have on the page just suggested activities for free time in both of the European office locations, London and Paris. So if we are working on a rollout project, we may send trainers to these different offices worldwide, and those trainers might have to stay there for a couple of weeks. So they'll have some free time and ideas for things they can do there.

To illustrate that point and make it a bit more interesting, we will add some pictures. So that's why we have free time suggested activities and Heading 1 style to that particular piece of text. We then have London underneath and have a heading 2 style applied to that. So now you can add a couple of pictures of some of the main sites in London.

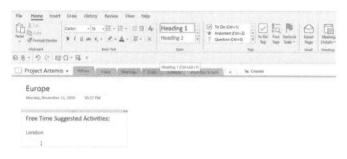

Go to the Insert tab, click on pictures, and it's going to open up file explorer. Navigate to whichever folder you have those pictures stored in. You can see a selection of your pictures and add in whichever one you want, then click on insert, and it will pull the pictures through.

Figure 288: Inserting images

When you insert multiple images, note that they will become part of the same Placeholder. So maybe if you want the image below to be side by side with each other, you can drag them out of that particular Placeholder.

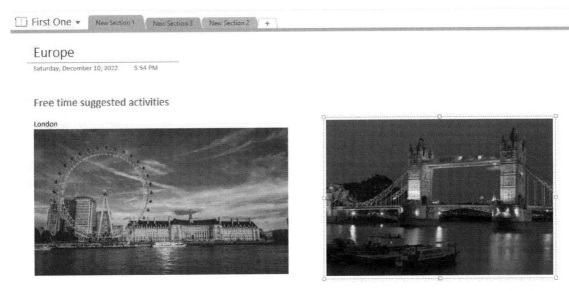

Figure 289: Inserting images and rearranging

Now you might think why that is a problem. If we want to add more text and hit enter a couple of times, it will move down one image, but the other image beside it will stay where it is. So be aware that if you drag an image out of its original Placeholder, you may have to reorganize its placement on your page. Alternatively, you can use control z a couple of times to rearrange your image the way it originally was, just like in words.

96 COLLABORATION FUNCTION

Microsoft OneNote is invaluable for staying connected and collaborating with friends, family, and teammates in real time. From creating a shared to-do list to taking notes during a meeting, OneNote provides various features to help you stay organized and productive. This section will discuss how OneNote can help you work together with others in real-time and how to get the most out of the application.

Benefits of Using OneNote for Collaboration

One of the main benefits of using Microsoft OneNote for collaboration is that it allows multiple people to work together in real time. Any changes or additions made to a document will be visible to everyone who can access the file. This makes it easy to collaborate on projects without constantly emailing back and forth. OneNote also allows multiple users to edit and comment on documents simultaneously, which helps brainstorm and get feedback from others.

Another benefit of using OneNote for collaboration is its secure platform. All documents are stored in the cloud, meaning they can't be lost or stolen. This ensures that your work remains safe and secure, no matter where you are. Additionally, the platform is designed to be easy to use, so you don't have to worry about learning how to use complicated software.

Creating a Shared To-Do List

OneNote is an excellent tool for creating and managing a shared to-do list. You can create a new page and add tasks, which can then be assigned to different people. Once the task is complete, the user can check it off the list. This makes it easy to track who is responsible for what and when tasks need to be completed. Additionally, you can add notes to each task so everyone knows exactly what needs to be done.

Taking Notes During a Meeting

OneNote also makes it easy to take notes during a meeting. You can create a new page for each meeting, and everyone can add their notes in real time. This makes it easy to review the meeting afterward, as all the notes will be in one place. Additionally, you can add images and other documents to the page, making it a great way to store all your meeting materials in one place.

Collaborative Writing Projects

If you're working on a writing project with multiple people, OneNote can be an excellent tool for collaboration. For example, you can create a page for each project section and assign tasks to different people. Then, everyone can add their contributions in real time and comment on each other's work. This makes it easy to ensure that everyone's ideas are heard and that the project progresses quickly.

Working on Presentations Together

OneNote can also be used to create presentations with multiple people. For example, you can create a page for each slide and assign tasks to different people. This makes it easy to ensure that all slides look professional and that the presentation flows well. Additionally, you can add images and other visuals to the page, making it easy to create a visually appealing presentation.

From creating a shared to-do list to taking notes during a meeting, OneNote provides various features to help you stay organized and productive. So whether you're working on a writing project, creating a presentation, or just taking notes, OneNote is the perfect tool for staying connected and getting the most out of your collaborations.

How to Add a OneNote Notebook in Microsoft Teams

Microsoft Teams is a powerful communication and collaboration platform that allows users to interact with each other, share files, and work together from any location. OneNote is a note-taking application that can be used within Microsoft Teams to track tasks, organize content, and take notes. This section will explain how to add a OneNote notebook to Microsoft Teams.

Overview of Microsoft Teams and OneNote

Microsoft Teams is a communication and collaboration platform that helps users stay connected regardless of location. It allows users to chat, share files, and work together in a virtual workspace. OneNote is a note-taking application that can be used within Microsoft Teams to help users organize and keep track of tasks. OneNote notebooks can take notes, write ideas, and store important information.

Steps to Add a OneNote Notebook to Teams

Adding a OneNote notebook to Microsoft Teams is straightforward. Here are the steps to follow:

1. Log into Microsoft Teams and select the team to which you want to add the notebook.

2. Click on the "Files" tab.

3. Select "OneNote" from the menu.

4. Enter a name for the notebook and click "Create."

5. Select the "Share" button to share the notebook with the team.

Benefits of Using a OneNote Notebook with Teams

Using a OneNote notebook with Microsoft Teams provides many benefits, including:

• It allows users to take notes, store important information, and keep track of tasks.

• It provides an easy way to collaborate with colleagues on projects.

• It helps users stay organized and stay on top of their tasks.

• It allows users to access their notes from any device, anytime, or location.

Adding a OneNote notebook to Microsoft Teams is an easy and effective way to stay organized and collaborate with colleagues. It provides users with a powerful tool to take notes, store important information, and keep track of tasks. By leveraging the features of OneNote and Microsoft Teams, users can work together more efficiently and stay connected no matter where they are located.

97 SAVING, SYNCING, AND SHARING

After working on your notebook, several actions can be taken to ensure you keep track of your note. This section covers those actions which you can take to keep your notebooks secure. For instance, you can share your notebook, a page, or a section with others, export, or save them.

To know more about how you can achieve these, let's go.

Sharing

OneNote gives one the option to share notebooks and note pages by giving permissions, links and via emails. You have the ability to control what recipients can access and whether they can view or edit. You can share OneNote notes in a few different ways, so let's look at them. One important point to know when it comes to sharing OneNote notebooks is that sharing only happens for notebooks stored in your OneDrive. That means you should move your locally stored notebook to OneDrive before you share out. However, if you have different notebooks for business and personal, you can store your business notebook in OneDrive, and your "Personal" Notebook can be stored locally in your downloads folder.

If you want to share your "Personal" Notebook with anybody, you need to move it to OneDrive. To do this, open your "Personal" Notebook, navigate to **"File,"** and then go down to your share option what you'll see in there is it says to share this notebook, so you'll need to put it in OneDrive or SharePoint. You're going to put that in OneDrive by selecting it. You could also browse for it if you don't have it listed here; you can name your notebook and choose **"Move notebook."** You will receive a message saying the notebook is syncing to your new location; click "OK." Now that you've done that, you'll see that you now have all of your share options because you've now put it in a location where sharing is available.

Let's go through each of these sharing options one by one.

Sharing With Others

The first option you have here is to share with people. What you can do here is you can invite others via email to share your notebook with them. Enter the email addresses for the people you intend to share with, and of course, if you have any contacts stored in your address book, you can also select them from there.

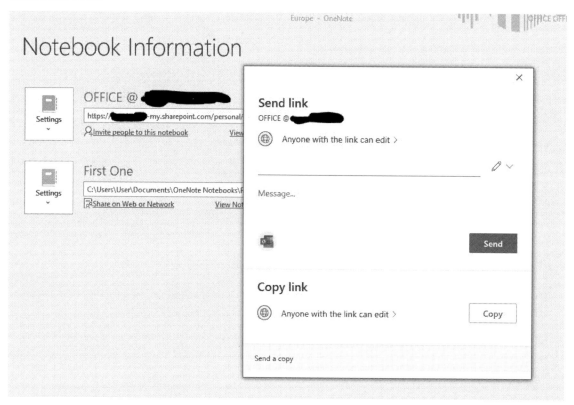

Figure 290: Sharing notebook

You can then choose what level of access I want to give them to this particular notebook. So, do you want them to be able to edit or view this notebook? Type in your message and then click on **"Share."** As soon as you do that, you can see underneath where it says "shared with" it's showing you all of the people you've shared the notebook with.

At some point, if you decide you don't want to share this notebook with a contact, you can also revoke access. All you need to do here is right-click the contact's name, and you have two options: either to **"Remove user"** or **"Change permission."**

If you want to remove the user entirely, select **"Remove user,"** and the user's access has now been revoked.

Sharing With Links

The second option you have is creating a sharing link then forwarding to the desired list of individuals via emails. But, again, you can decide an edit or view permission for the link. So, if you create a link to this notebook that only people can view, you would click **"Create a view link."**

You would then take this little link that it's created, **copy** (CTRL +C) and then **paste** (CTRL + V) into an outlook email and send it out. You'd do the same for an edit link and send it to an outlook distribution list.

Sharing With Meetings

The third option you have in here is to share your notebook with a meeting. Share notebooks during online meetings; essentially, you're all collaborating on the same notebook and adding notes to it. Click **"Share with Meeting,"** and if you have any online meetings in progress, they will be listed in a window, and you can choose which meeting you want to share your notebook in.

Sharing with OneDrive

Finally, you have the move notebook option, which you saw how to use before when you moved your notebook into OneDrive.

You may only share a single page within your notebook. So, if you want to share a page from your notebook, click on the desired page that you want to share, go up to Home tab, and you'll see you have an option here to "Email page," keyboard shortcut Ctrl + Shift + E. What it does is it will open up an outlook email. It's going to attach the contents of that page. You can select who you want to share this with and send that email. The user receives an email with the notebook's name and an open button. If they hit that, it'll open up the notebook in the browser, and if that user makes a change, it will sync that change, and, in your notebook, you'll see the change, with a little marker indicating that the user added it.

Syncing And Saving

One important thing to remember when sharing notebooks is that multiple people can access and edit a notebook anytime. Synchronization is always on as a critical feature, but one can alter this to manually sync.

To do this, go to the **File** tab and ensure you are in the **"Info"** area. What you'll see over on the right-hand side is you have a button here to view sync status, which will show all of the notebooks you have and whether they're synchronized, and the last time they were updated.

The option automatically selected is to sync automatically whenever there are changes. So, if you've shared this notebook with five other people and they're all in this notebook making changes, any changes they make are automatically synchronized so that you can see them.

However, if you prefer to **sync manually,** you have the option as well, and as soon as you do that, it puts a cross over each of these notebooks just to let you know that they're not currently synchronizing, and you can choose which one you want to sync.

So, if you click "**Sync Now**," the icon will change and any updates made since the last sync will be updated. If you have a lot of notebooks in here, to make this easier, you have a single button at the top to "**Sync All**."

Password Protection

Another thing you might want to do when sharing your notebooks is **password-protect sections of the notebook**. This prevents unauthorized access to certain sections of the notebook that you don't want people to see. All you need to do here is select which sections you want to protect. For example, if you want people to see everything in one section but not in another, you must right-click and select "Password protect This section" and click "**Set Password.**" Now, if you share this notebook, people can't see what's in that particular section.

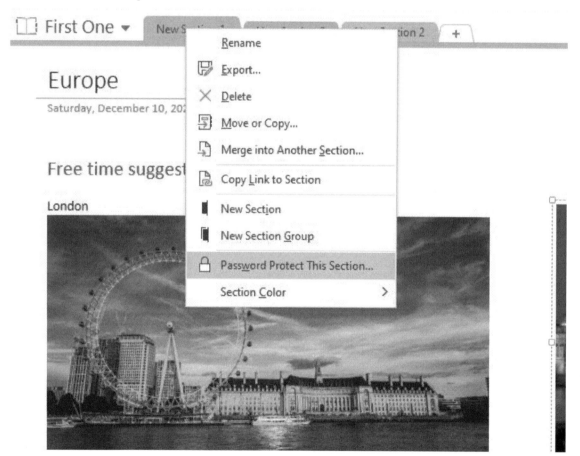

Figure 291: Password Protection

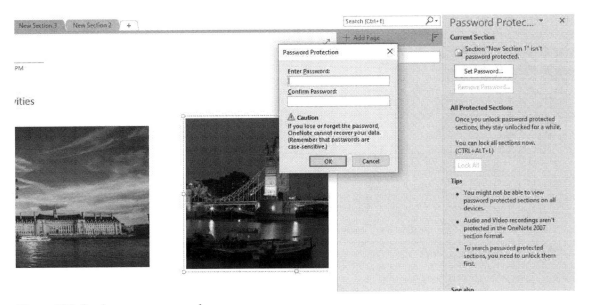

Figure 292: Setting your password

To unprotect, right-click, go back into **"Password protect This Section,"** select **"Remove password,"** and type it in to remove that protection.

Exporting Notebooks

Many of us use OneNote notebooks to organize our lives. It is essential to **know how to back up your OneNote** because technology can fail and when it does, you want to make sure your materials are safe and secure, so it is necessary to back up your work. It is highly recommended that you do this at some point, especially as you get to the end of the school year and leave for the summer or work with other team members. Backing up your notebook in OneNote is a great idea.

There are cases where you may not have access to OneDrive. For example, let's say you're getting a new job or moving to a different district. For some unforeseeable reason, your server goes down, or you need access when you're not online. First, you need to export your OneNote. To do this, go to your **"Files"** tab, and instead of choosing **"Save,"** you're going to choose **"Export."** You'll get several options. First, you can export a page. That's handy if you want to share a page with somebody; you can share a section, or for your use, you can export your entire OneNote notebook, and you will have file types to choose from. You can export them as PDFs but can't edit them in the future. To export your OneNote as a package so you can upload it into OneNote in the future as its full functioning self, you'll need to select **"OneNote Package"** before clicking the export button.

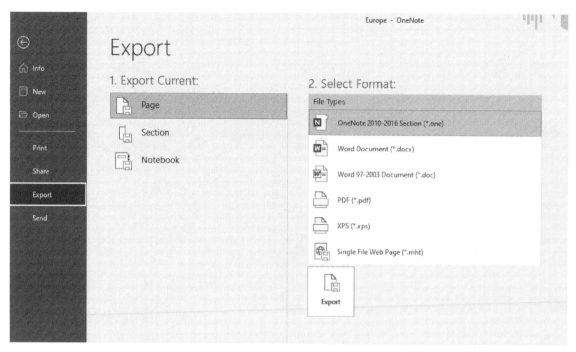

Figure 293: Exporting Notebooks

You're going to tell it where to save on your device, and you have your OneNote notebook saved on your hard drive for loading whatever you want, wherever you want, whether you are online or not. This can also be done for group notebooks, so if you're in charge of your group's notebook, this is a good idea to do every once in a while, but it's also handy for individual notebooks.

98 PROTECTION AND RESTORATION

The Benefits of End-to-End Encryption in Microsoft OneNote

Microsoft OneNote is an incredibly useful tool that allows users to organize their thoughts, collaborate with others, and store data in the cloud. However, as more users take advantage of the platform, they need to understand the security features that Microsoft OneNote provides. One such feature is end-to-end encryption, which ensures that data stored in Microsoft OneNote is secure and private. This section will discuss the benefits of end-to-end encryption in Microsoft OneNote.

What is End-to-End Encryption?

End-to-end encryption is a security protocol that protects data transmitted over a network. It encrypts data at the source so only the sender and recipient can read it. This means that even if a third party intercepts the data, it cannot be read or used. End-to-end encryption is used in many applications, including Microsoft OneNote.

Why is End-to-End Encryption Important in Microsoft OneNote?

Microsoft OneNote stores sensitive data, such as notes and documents, in the cloud. This means that the data is vulnerable to interception and misuse by third parties. End-to-end encryption ensures that the data is secure so only the sender and recipient can access it. This ensures that data stored in Microsoft OneNote is kept private and secure.

How Does End-to-End Encryption Work in Microsoft OneNote?

Microsoft OneNote uses a combination of public and private keys to encrypt data. The public key is shared with the recipient, while the sender keeps the private key secret. When data is sent, it is encrypted with the public key. The recipient then uses their private key to decrypt the data. This ensures that only the sender and recipient can read the data, making it secure from outside interference.

What are the Benefits of End-to-End Encryption in Microsoft OneNote?

The primary benefit of end-to-end encryption in Microsoft OneNote is that it keeps data secure and private. Encrypting data at the source ensures that only the sender and recipient can access it. This prevents third parties from intercepting and misusing the data. Additionally, end-to-end encryption ensures that data is not corrupted or tampered with during transmission. This helps to ensure the integrity of data stored in Microsoft OneNote.

End-to-end encryption is a valuable security feature in Microsoft OneNote. It ensures that data is kept secure and private and not corrupted or tampered with during transmission. By taking advantage of this feature, users can protect their data and ensure that the intended recipient only accesses it.

Security

I wanted to start with what I believe is the essential tool, Security via the **Password** option. If you are like me, you will soon keep a massive amount of data in your OneNote notebooks, and quite a bit should be considered private and classified. You never know if/when you will be hacked, and you certainly do not want to collect your private information in one place for a hacker to steal. The best way to protect your data is to password-protect it. I would suggest you segregate your private information into one Section, a separate page for each type of information, and password-protect the section.

Password protects a Section

Once you have a section you want to protect, click on **Review** -> **Password** (Or right-click the Section tab and select **Password Protect This Section**), and the Password pane will open.

Note: The first Tip on the pane reminds us that you may not be able to access this Section from every device. I have found that I cannot open a password-protected section with OneNote Android. Remember if you need to access the data from a mobile device.

Password protection options

In the **Password Protection** pane are several options and reminders. You can set **Password** (and **Remove Password** if already set). At the bottom of the pane is **Password Options…** Clicking this will open the Options dialog box. In the Passwords section, you have a few options you can select.

Considerations for passwords

Remember

- You can only password-protect sections, not pages or entire notebooks.

- Once you password-protect a section OneNote uses encryption to store that section. So if you forget your password, no one can unlock the protected section.

- If you password-protect a section, it will not be included in any searches. If you need to search a section, unlock it first.

- Tags used in a password-protected section are not included in your tag summary unless you unlock the section.

- Passwords are case-sensitive. Make sure the **Caps Lock** is not on before you enter a password.

Locking a password-protected section

When you are in a password-protected section, the easiest way to lock it is to press CTRL+ALT+L or click the **Lock All** button on the Password Protection pane. Remember, you can set how quickly OneNote locks a section when you leave in the **Password Options** under **File -> Options -> Advanced -> Passwords**.

Doing away with password protection in a section

Click on section tab. Next, click the section or hit enter, enter the password and open the Password Protection pane (**Review -> Password** or right-click section tab and choose **Password Protect This Section**).

Click **Remove Password** button, enter existing password and press **OK**. This will remove password protection from the section.

Some crucial password reminders

- Passwords may only be applied to portions of notebooks, not whole notebooks.

- Case matters in passwords. Before you add or input a password, make sure the Caps Lock key is turned off.

- Password-protected parts in OneNote are secured via encryption. As a result, no one can access your notes if you forget your section passwords (not even Microsoft Technical Support). So when adding and updating passwords to your notebook sections, be cautious.

- Notebook searches do not include password-protected areas. Therefore, you must first unlock that section to include notes from a protected part in a search.

How to Save Passwords in Microsoft OneNote

Saving passwords in Microsoft OneNote is easy and takes only a few steps. Here's how to get started:

A. Creating a Password Notebook

The first step is to create a password notebook in OneNote. This notebook will be used to store all of your passwords, so it should be kept secure. To create a password notebook, open OneNote and click the "New Notebook" button. Next, name the notebook something descriptive (e.g., "Passwords") and select a secure location to store it.

B. Securing Passwords

Once you create a password notebook, you'll need to secure it with a password. To do this, open your notebook and choose the "Protect Notebook" option. Next, enter a strong password, select a password hint, and click "Save." This will ensure that only you can access your passwords.

C. Accessing Saved Passwords

Once you've secured your password notebook, you can begin saving passwords. To do this, open your notebook and choose the "Add Password" option. Next, enter the website's name, the username, and password, before clicking "Save." Finally, you can access the saved passwords when you open the notebook and select the "View Password" option.

Tips and Best Practices

Saving passwords in Microsoft OneNote is a secure and efficient way to store and manage your passwords, but there are a few best practices to keep in mind. Here are some tips for staying secure and organized:

A. Using Strong Passwords

When creating a password for your OneNote notebook, use a unique password. This will help ensure that your passwords are secure and prevent unauthorized access.

B. Storing Passwords in Multiple Locations

It's a good idea to store your passwords in multiple locations, such as a physical notebook or a password manager. This will help ensure you have access to your passwords even if OneNote is unavailable.

C. Regularly Updating Passwords

To stay secure, it's essential to update your passwords regularly. This will help protect your accounts from hackers and other malicious actors.

99 TIPS, FAQS WITH COMMON PROBLEMS AND SOLUTIONS

I. What is Microsoft OneNote?

Microsoft OneNote is a digital note-taking application that helps users capture, organize, and share their notes and ideas. It is available on Windows, macOS, iOS, and Android devices. It offers many features that make note-taking more efficient, including voice dictation, the ability to record audio, and the ability to store photos and screenshots. It also offers collaboration features that allow users to share their notes with others and work on them together in real time.

II. Can I access my Microsoft OneNote files on multiple devices?

Yes, you can access your Microsoft OneNote files on multiple devices. This is because Microsoft OneNote stores all the notes in cloud, allowing one to access them on any device with an internet connection. You can also sync the notes across multiple devices, ensuring that you always have the latest version of your notes wherever you go.

III. How can one share Microsoft OneNote files with others?

You can share entire notebooks or individual pages with others by simply entering their email address. You can also share notes with specific groups of people by creating a shared notebook. This will allow multiple people to view and edit the shared notebook in real time.

IV. What best way to back up my Microsoft OneNote files?

The best way to back up your Microsoft OneNote files is to use Microsoft's OneDrive. OneDrive is a cloud storage service from Microsoft that allows you to store and access your files from anywhere. In addition, your OneNote notes will be automatically backed up to your OneDrive account, ensuring that your notes are safe and secure.

V. How do I troubleshoot Microsoft OneNote errors?

If you are experiencing errors while using Microsoft OneNote, there are a few things you can do to try and troubleshoot the issue. The first step is to make sure that your device has the latest version of OneNote installed. Then, if the issue persists, you can try resetting the application or reinstalling it. Finally, if that doesn't work, you can contact Microsoft support for further assistance.

Is it possible to import notes from 2016 to the 365 version?

Transferring notes from Microsoft OneNote 2016 to Microsoft 365 OneNote is relatively straightforward. The first step is to open the Microsoft OneNote 2016 application and select the notes that need to be transferred. Once the notes have been selected, they can be exported as a zip file. This zip file can then be uploaded to the Microsoft 365 OneNote application. Once the file is uploaded, the notes will be available in the new application.

How do you reset the defaults on the 365 version?

Understanding the Default Settings

The default settings of Microsoft 365 OneNote are the settings that will be applied when you open the application for the first time. These settings include the font size and style, the page size and orientation, and the color scheme. Therefore, it is essential to understand what the default settings are so that you can make the necessary adjustments when you reset the defaults.

Resetting the Default Settings

To reset the defaults on Microsoft 365 OneNote, you must first open the application. Once the application is open, you must navigate to the Options menu. This menu can generally be found under the "Home" tab at the top of the page. Once in the Options menu, you must select the "Reset Defaults" option. This will reset all of the settings to their default values.

Microsoft OneNote Plugins

Whether you're looking to keep track of your ideas or share them with others, Microsoft OneNote can be an excellent tool for staying organized. Not only does it allow you to save and share notes, but it also allows you to organize your notebooks in a variety of ways. The program features an easy-to-use interface, allowing you to stay productive and organized. You can also protect sensitive information with password protection and share your notes with others using email or online services.

You can make your OneNote even more versatile with a wide variety of add-ins. These add-ins are available for desktop and mobile versions of the program, and some are free. You can also download data from other applications and services and upload them to your OneNote.

The OneMore add-in is a good choice if you're looking for a basic image editing solution. This tool lets you resize, crop, and edit images in your OneNote notebooks. The app also allows you to define custom styles, with nine pre-configured styles to start with.

With the OneNote book add-in, you can quickly access your favorite pages or organize course material with customized styles. You can also create desktop shortcuts for your pages.

Another add-in is the Office Lens browser extension, which lets you capture webpages from your browser and send them straight to your OneNote notebook. This plugin works with all versions of OneNote, and it's easier to use as a standalone app.

Types of Microsoft OneNote Plugins

There are a variety of plugins available for Microsoft OneNote. Some of the most popular types of plugins include text formatting, template, search, sharing, and collaboration plugins. Text formatting plugins allow users to quickly and easily format their text, while template plugins provide pre-made templates to help them organize their notes. Search plugins make it easier to find information in OneNote while sharing plugins enable users to quickly and easily share notes with others. Lastly, collaboration plugins allow users to create collaborative workspaces and work on projects together.

How to Install Microsoft OneNote Plugins

Installing Microsoft OneNote plugins is a simple process. To install a plugin, users need to open OneNote, click on the "Extensions" tab, and select the plugin they wish to install. Then, they can follow the instructions to install the plugin. Additionally, users can download plugins from third-party websites as long as the plugins are compatible with OneNote.

100 THE STRATEGIC SHORTCUTS

Keyboard Shortcut Commands

Using keyboard shortcuts will help you work seamlessly and faster. There are a lot of shortcuts in OneNote, but here are the important ones:

- **CTRL + T**: This creates a new section.

- **CTRL + TAB**: This helps you navigate down the sections.
- **CTRL + SHIFT + TAB**: This enables you to navigate up the sections.
- **CTRL + N**: This creates a new page.
- **CTRL + ALT + N**: This creates a new subpage under the current page.
- **CTRL + PAGE DOWN(PGDN)**: This switches pages down the list.
- **CTRL + PAGE UP(PGUP)**: This switches pages up the list.
- **ALT + END**: This takes you to the bottom of the page list, i.e., the last page in your section.
- **ALT + HOME**: This takes you to the top of the page list, i.e., the first page in your section.
- **CTRL + A**: When using it once, this selects a single text line. Use it twice, and it will pick all the lines in your text box. Use it three times, and it will select everything on your page.
- **ALT + SHIFT + UP ARROW/DOWN ARROW**: After highlighting a line of text with your mouse, this will help you move the line up/down quickly. Using this shortcut, you can highlight multiple lines and easily move them up/down. In addition, it helps in rearranging lines of text.
- **CTRL + E**: This takes you straight to the search box.

F11: This switches between full screen and standard screen.

- **CTRL + M**: This opens a new OneNote window. With this, you can do multiple projects side-by-side on a screen

101 CONCLUSION

Microsoft OneNote is a powerful and versatile note-taking application that offers several features and benefits. It is user-friendly, intuitive, highly customizable, and free with a Microsoft account. It is also an excellent tool for collaboration, allowing users to share their notebooks with others and comment and edit notes. Finally, it is available for both Windows and Mac users and mobile devices, making it accessible to a wide range of users. For these reasons, Microsoft OneNote is an invaluable tool for anyone looking to organize their thoughts, ideas, and tasks more efficiently and productively.

MICROSOFT PUBLISHER

INTRODUCTION

Microsoft Publisher is a powerful tool that can help businesses create professional-looking brochures, newsletters, and other marketing materials. With its easy-to-use interface, Publisher makes it easy to design and produce engaging, attractive pieces quickly and efficiently. This guide will provide an overview of the features and benefits of Microsoft Publisher, as well as tips for getting the most out of the program.

Microsoft Publisher is a desktop publishing and layout application part of the Microsoft Office suite. It creates and designs professional-looking marketing and communication materials/documents such as brochures, posters, flyers, business cards, catalogs, and newsletters with a WYSIWYG (what you see is what you get) interface. It is an excellent tool for businesses, organizations, and individuals who need to produce documents quickly and efficiently. Publisher includes various tools and features that make creating and customizing high-quality documents easy. It also integrates with other Microsoft Office applications, so you can easily include data from Excel or Word in your Publisher documents.

What is the Purpose of Microsoft Publisher?

The purpose of Microsoft Publisher is to provide users with a tool for creating professional-quality marketing and communication materials, such as brochures, business cards, newsletters, and websites. It offers a range of features and templates that make it easy to create and design high-quality, professional-looking documents and other materials without requiring specialized design skills. With Microsoft Publisher, users can create various materials for personal or business use, including advertisements, newsletters, calendars, and more.

What are the Benefits of Microsoft Publisher?

Some of the benefits of using Microsoft Publisher include the ability to create professional-looking documents with a variety of pre-designed templates and tools, the ability to customize and personalize documents with your images and text easily, and the ability to integrate with other Microsoft Office applications to include data from other programs in your Publisher documents. Additionally, Publisher includes collaboration features that make it easy to work with others on a document and the ability to save and share your documents in various formats. Overall, Publisher can help you create high-quality documents quickly and easily.

How to Purchase Microsoft Publisher

A. Purchasing Through the Microsoft Store

The easiest way to purchase Microsoft Publisher is through the Microsoft Store. Users can browse the available versions of Microsoft Publisher on the Microsoft Store website and select the best option for their needs. Once a version is selected, users can proceed to checkout and purchase the program. After the purchase, users will receive a download link to install the program.

The Microsoft Store is the official source for purchasing Microsoft products, including Microsoft Publisher. The Microsoft Store offers physical and digital versions of Microsoft Publisher, allowing customers to choose the best version for their needs. Customers who purchase physical versions will receive the product in the mail, while customers who purchase digital versions will receive a download link. Customers can also purchase Microsoft 365, which includes Microsoft Publisher as part of the suite.

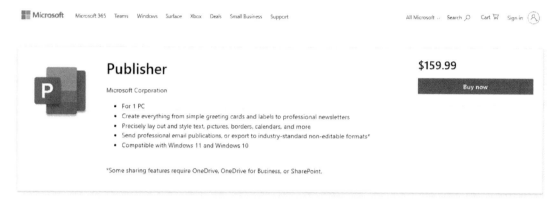

Figure 294: Microsoft Publisher price

Advantages of Buying from Microsoft Store:

The Microsoft Store is the most reliable source for purchasing Microsoft products. All products purchased from the Microsoft Store are genuine and will include the most up-to-date features available. In addition, the Microsoft Store offers support services for their products, so customers can get assistance if they experience any issues.

B. Purchasing Through a Third-Party Retailer

Users can also purchase Microsoft Publisher through a third-party retailer. Third parties include online retailers, such as Amazon and eBay, and physical stores, such as Best Buy and Walmart. These third parties offer a wide range of Microsoft products, including Microsoft Publisher. In addition, many retailers offer physical copies of Microsoft Publisher, which can be purchased in-store or online. In addition, some retailers may offer discounts or deals on the software, so it is worth shopping around to find the best deal.

Advantages of Buying from Third Parties:

The primary advantage of buying from third parties is the cost. Third parties often offer lower prices than the Microsoft Store, making it a more cost-effective option. In addition, third parties may provide more payment options than the Microsoft Store, allowing customers to select the most suitable payment method for their needs.

Disadvantages of Buying from Third Parties:

The primary disadvantage of buying from third parties is the lack of assurance that the product is genuine. Customers may purchase counterfeit versions of Microsoft products, which will not include the most up-to-date features and could cause issues. Additionally, customers may not be able to receive support services from the Microsoft Store if they experience any issues with the product.

What are the elements of Microsoft Publisher?

Some of the main elements of Publisher include:

Templates: Publisher includes a wide range of pre-designed templates that you can use to start your documents. These templates are organized by document type and include brochures, business cards, newsletters, and more options.

Text and image editing tools: Publisher includes various tools you use to add and edit text and images in your documents. These tools include options for changing font, color, size, and alignment of your text and tools for cropping and resizing images.

Design elements: Publisher includes various design elements that you can use to add visual interest to your documents. These elements include shapes, lines, and clip art images you can utilize to create professional-looking layouts.

Collaboration features: Publisher includes collaboration features that make it easy to work with others on a document. These features include tracking changes and adding comments, and the option to co-author a document in real-time.

Export and sharing options: Once you have finished creating your document, Publisher includes various options for saving and sharing it. You can export your document as a PDF, print it, or share it online through Email or social media.

102 INSTALLING PUBLISHER

Difference Between Publisher and Word

Microsoft Publisher and Microsoft Word are part of the Microsoft Office suite of productivity software, but they serve different purposes. Word is a processing program primarily used for creating and editing text-based documents like reports, letters, and resumes. On the other hand, Publisher is a desktop publishing and layout program designed for creating and designing marketing and communication materials, such as brochures, business cards, and newsletters.

While both programs overlap in features and capabilities, some key differences exist. For example, Publisher has a wider range of design and layout tools, including pre-made templates and design elements, that make it easier to create professional-looking materials. On the other hand, Word is better suited for working with text and has more advanced features for editing and formatting text.

The main difference between Publisher and Word is the type of materials they are best suited for creating. Word is a better choice for text-based documents, while Publisher is a better choice for creating materials that require a professional design and layout.

System Requirements

Before installing Microsoft Publisher, you must ensure that your computer meets the system requirements. Microsoft Publisher requires a Windows 8, 10, or 11 operating system, a 1.6 GHz or faster processor, 2 GB RAM, and 4 GB available hard-disk space. You will also need an active internet connection for installation and product activation.

Publisher

	Overview	Requirements
Processor	1.6 GHz, 2-core processor	
Operating system	Windows 11 or Windows 10	
Memory	4 GB (64bit), 2 GB (32bit) RAM	
Hard disk space	4 GB available disk space	
Display	1024 x 768 resolution	
Graphics	DirectX 10 graphics card for graphics hardware acceleration for PC	
Additional system requirements	• Internet access • Microsoft account • See aka.ms/systemrequirements for the full list of system requirements	

Figure 295: System Requirements

How to Install Microsoft Publisher

Installing Microsoft Publisher is a simple process. First, make sure that your computer meets the system requirements outlined above. Once you have confirmed that your computer is compatible, you can begin the installation process.

The easiest way to install Microsoft Publisher is to purchase it online from the Microsoft Store. Once you have purchased the program, you will receive an email with a link to download the software. Click the link and follow the on-screen instructions to install the program.

Alternatively, you can purchase a physical copy of Microsoft Publisher. To install the program, insert the disc into the computer and follow the on-screen instructions. You may be asked to enter a product key during the installation process. Once the installation is complete, you will be ready to use Microsoft Publisher.

103 INTERFACE AND USE

How To Start Publisher

Microsoft Publisher is a desktop app that must be downloaded before using it. There is no online way of accessing Publisher like Word, Excel, PowerPoint, etc.

So, after the installation process is completed, locate the search field on your PC (The search field depends on the version of Windows you are using). *For Windows 10, the search field is located on the taskbar.* Then, type **Publisher,** click on it to open, and you will be taken to the Microsoft Publisher start page.

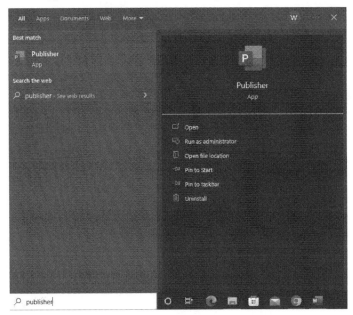

Figure 296: Accessing and searching publisher

Suppose this is an application you would often use, right-click on Publisher in the taskbar and select **Pin to Taskbar**. This will add Publisher to the taskbar, and you can easily open it by clicking on its icon.

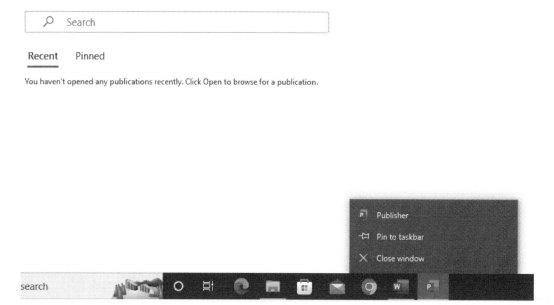

Figure 297: Pin to taskbar

The Backstage View

After launching Microsoft Publisher, you will arrive at the start page, which is also the backstage view. This is where you will carry out some of your Publisher functions, including creating a new design, opening an existing one, and editing an unfinished one.

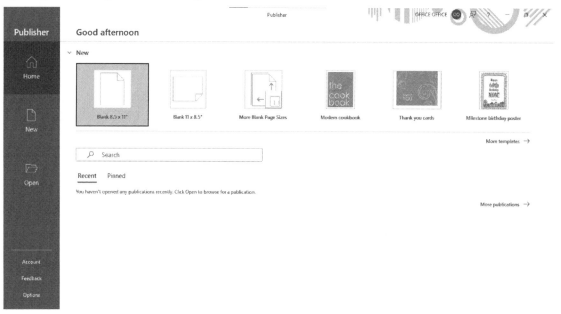

Figure 298: The Backstage View

On the left-hand corner of the start page, you will find options including **Home**, **New**, and **Open**. Also, you can open a **blank page** or a blank Publisher file on the start page. And at the right-hand corner is the option for getting templates, which says **More templates**.

Below the blank pages option, we have **Recent** and **Pinned**. The Recent tab allows you to view your past or recently worked design, while the Pinned tab allows you to pin documents you have formerly worked on.

If there are numerous designs you have done before, you can use the search field to locate a particular design work. This saves you from searching multiple design files to locate work you completed weeks or months back.

When you select the **New** option on the left-hand corner of your screen, you will be presented with numerous templates. You can also search online for new templates if unsatisfied with the ones Office presents.

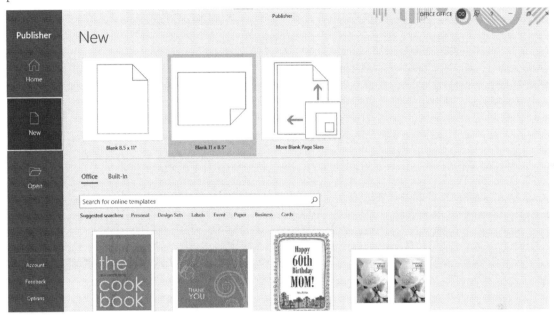

Figure 299: The New option

The provided templates are beautiful and useful depending on the type of design you want to make. For instance, if there is an available birthday template, you can easily edit the birthday template to fit the exact birthday celebration design you want to create. As mentioned earlier, this saves you from the stress of having to create a new birthday template from the beginning. These templates also apply to other works, such as creating a book cover and so much more.

Also, on the left-hand corner of your screen is the **Open** function. Clicking the Open function will show you a list of your recently opened Publisher files. Furthermore, it will also allow you to navigate through OneDrive and your local PC to locate Publisher files you have recently opened.

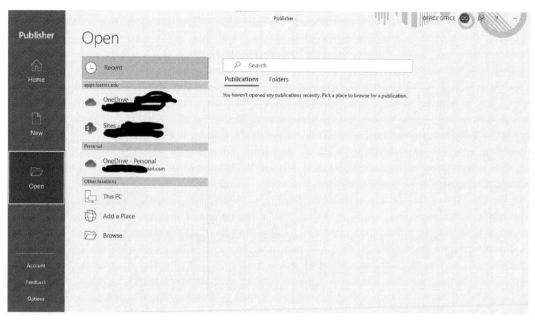

Figure 300: The Open feature

However, you should be able to do almost everything you need from the **Home** function.

THE INTERFACE

The interface contains the tools you need to work with, and all these tools will be discussed as we proceed. In addition, the interface contains the **Tabs/Menus**, **Ribbons**, **Groups**, **Title bar**, **Navigation Pane**, **Quick Access Toolbar**, **Status Bar**, and **Canvas**.

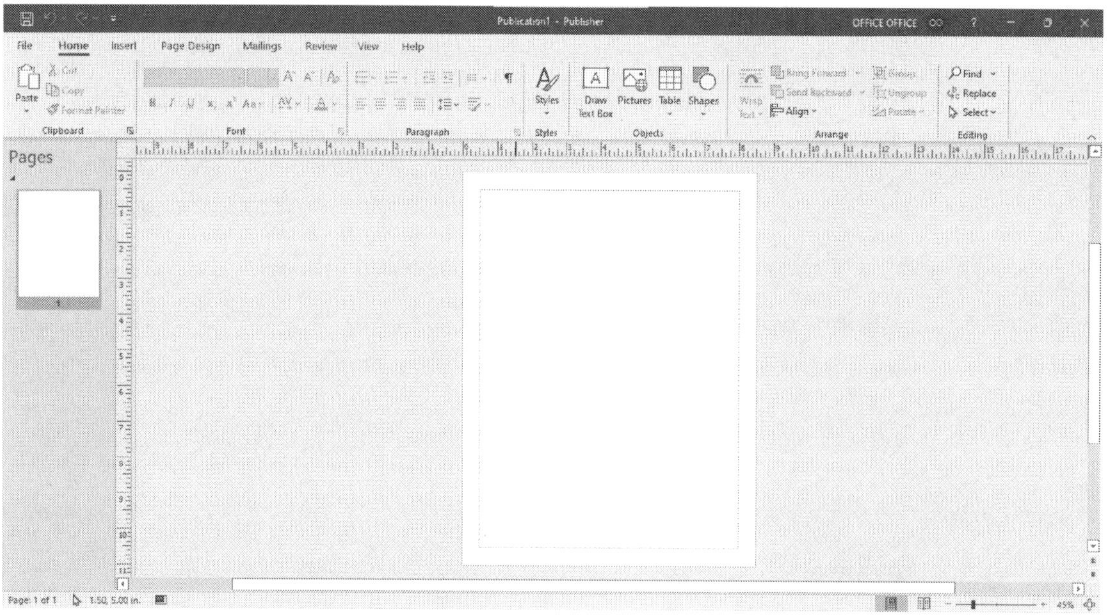

Figure 301: The interface

Tabs

· **Tabs** give you the privilege to switch between separate menus of Publisher. Furthermore, these menus allow you to perform specific tasks like opening a new design, saving a design, inserting pictures, drawing, and many more. The tabs are located at the top of the interface, and you can have additional tabs when you do specific tasks like creating a table, for instance.

Figure 302: The tabs

Ribbon

-   The **ribbon** is described as the toolbar that runs across the top of Publisher below the tabs. The ribbon comprises tabs that keep related tools organized to make them uniquely accessible irrespective of the project you are working on or the device you are using. Furthermore, the ribbon combines the tabs' options in a single floating pane, making it easy to use and accessible. Each tab has its ribbon content.

Figure 303: The Ribbon

Figure 304: The Insert Ribbon

-   The above image depicts the **Home** and **Insert** tabs' ribbon. Hence, it is described as the computer interface design designed as a graphical control element and fitted in a set of toolbars embedded on several tabs.
-   However, if you would like to hide your ribbon, click the small arrow icon on the right corner of the ribbon.

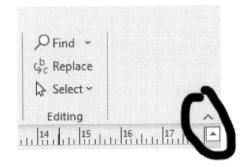

Figure 305: The hide feature

-   You can also display your ribbon permanently by clicking any tab and then clicking the pin icon at the right corner of the ribbon.

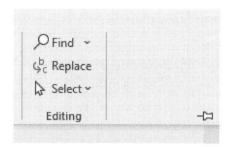

Figure 306: The pin icon

Using The Ribbon

For Publisher, the command center is the ribbon. It offers several commands grouped into groups and displayed on pertinent tabs. To view the command groups, click on a tab's name to activate it. Likewise, commands are activated when you click a tool, gallery option, or button. This ribbon has a place for anything you want to accomplish in Publisher.

Put this to the Test: Make sure Publisher is running, and you have a blank publication open before beginning this activity. Then;

- Examine command groups on the **Home tab.** The majority of people utilize these commands.

- To add applications and media to your publication, select **the Insert tab** and use the commands to construct pages, tables, drawings, building blocks, headers, and footers.

- To view the Shapes gallery, select **Shapes** from the **Illustrations group**. A wide variety of shapes are featured in this collection.

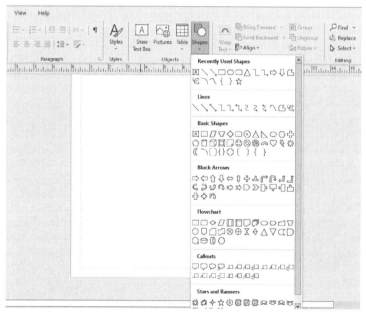

Figure 307: Shapes in the Illustrations group

- Check out the commands by clicking on each tab. Several of these are visible "dialog boxes." For example, to open the Change Template dialog box, click the **Page Design tab**, then click **Change Template in the Template group.**

Figure 308: Changing template

- Click [Cancel], then click on [Home tab]

To use the ribbon:

1. Click on a tab to display the commands

2. Click on a button to activate a command, display a gallery or display a dialog box

   Contextual tabs are additional ones that appear on the ribbon in particular situations. For instance, the Picture Tools: Format tab will show up if you insert a picture. All the tools needed to edit and work with an image are now easily accessible.

With the ribbon, you may edit a publication's content in various ways, including adding new text, formatting it, including images, copying it, and more. In addition, you can interact with the file you generate by going to the Backstage view accessible from the File tab. You can email it, print it off, and save it for later use, among other options.

Backstage Tabs

Figure 309: Backstage tabs

More possibilities for interacting with a publication can be found in the Backstage tabs:

- **Information;** Allows you to control versions and permissions and provides status information about the current publishing.

- **New;** enables one to build a new magazine and offers fast access to various online templates and a gallery of built-in templates.

- **Open;** Gives you the choice of searching your computer, the OneDrive storage, or another location to locate what you need, as well as a list of recent publications.

- **Save;** asks you to save to a location or save your current publication (if it hasn't previously been saved to one).

- You may give your publication a name and location using the Save As function.

- **Print;** enables you to print and see the most recent publication. Also, you can send your publication to others as a PDF or XPS file via Email.

- **Export;** Provides options for saving and printing, as well as the ability to publish as a PDF, XPS, or online publication.

- **Close;** ends the publication you're reading.

- **Account:** Contains user and product data. Offers you a variety of alternatives that will help with the production and editing of your publication.

You can work on your publications and access essential details about the Publisher status from the Backstage view.

Make sure Publisher is running, and you have a blank publication open before beginning this activity.

- To view the Backstage, select the **File tab**. To access details about your publication, such as the Properties, make sure Info is selected in the left green window.

- To view your printing options, **click Print**. An illustration showing how the article will look when printed.

- To view the account choices and product license details, click on **Account**. To close Backstage and return to the publication, click the Back arrow at the top of the green pane.

Group

A **group** is a collective word for a set of tools in Publisher. For instance, the **Font** group in the Home tab is used in formatting text, while the **Illustrations** group in the Insert tab is for adding images to your design.

Title Bar

This is at the top of the interface and tells us our design's name. Presently, the default name Publisher has giving this design is **Pulication1**.

Navigation Pane

You can find this on the left-hand side of the interface. It allows you to manage pages in Publisher; here, you can **add a new page**, **delete a page**, **rename a page**, **add a page number**, and more. To do this, right-click a page in the navigation pane.

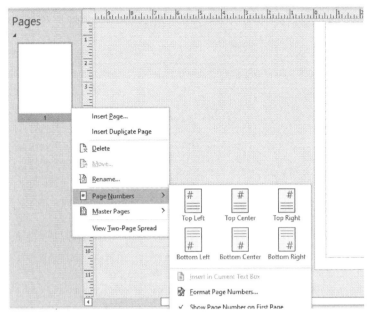

Figure 310: Navigation pane

Quick Access Toolbar

- This is at the right-top corner of the interface. Here, you can find and add shortcuts; presently, the Quick Access Toolbar includes the Save, Undo, and Redo icons. To add more icons, click the small dropdown arrow on the Quick Access Toolbar and choose what you want to include.

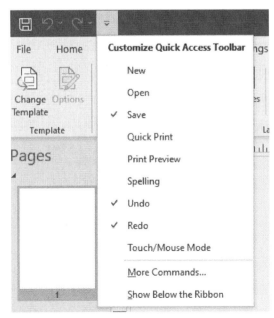

Figure 311: Quick Access Toolbar

Status Bar

This helps you to view the number of pages in your publication, increase and decrease the size of your canvas, and adjust its view. It is the long bar at the bottom of the interface.

Figure 312: Status bar

Also, you can customize the status bar by right-clicking on any part of the bar and choosing what you want or do not want to see on the bar.

Canvas

In addition, we have the canvas, which is the white rectangular part in the middle of the screen. It is on the canvas you design your work.

Figure 313: Canvas

Understanding the Menu Bar

The menu bar is the main navigation system in Microsoft Publisher. It is located at the top of the window and contains a list of commands that can be used to create and edit documents. The most commonly used commands are located in the File and Home menus, allowing users access to publishing tools, settings, formatting options, and more. Additionally, users can use the menu bar to access the help system and search for topics related to Publisher.

Working with the Toolbar

The toolbar below the menu bar provides quick access to commonly used commands. It includes buttons for text formatting, image manipulation, object placement, and more. Users can quickly and easily access the tools they need to create and edit their documents using the toolbar. Additionally, users can customize the toolbar to include only the tools they use most often, making it easier to find the commands they need.

Exploring the Task Pane

The task pane is located on the right side of the Microsoft Publisher window. It is divided into several categories: Create, Design, Layout, and Publish. Each category contains a list of commands that can be used to create and edit documents. Additionally, the task pane can access help topics and search for topics related to Publisher.

Customizing Your Workspace

Microsoft Publisher allows users to customize their workspace to suit their individual needs. Users can move and resize the various elements of the interface, such as the menu bar and toolbar, to create a workspace that is comfortable and efficient. Additionally, users can customize the color scheme and background of the workspace to create a unique look and feel.

104 WORKING WITH DOCUMENTS

Using Microsoft Publisher is simple. After launching the software, users can create a new document or open an existing one. Once the document is opened, users can begin to design and edit it. Various tools and features are available to help users create the perfect document. These tools allow users to add text, images, shapes, and other elements to the document.

Getting started with a blank document

Publisher makes creating different types of publications easy—presentations, brochures, and web pages. However, before we start benefiting from the Sophisticated, easy-to-use Publisher tools to create significant publications, you will need to open the Publisher applications window.

To start the Publisher program, follow these steps:

1. From the Windows Desktop, click Start, and then select Programs. The menu will appear.

2. Select Microsoft Publisher. The Publisher program window will appear on the Desktop. In truth, the Publisher window looks the same as other Office applications, such as Microsoft Word or Excel. However, while these applications typically offer a blank workspace, like a new document or a new spreadsheet to start working on, Publisher opens the Publisher Catalog, which offers three different ways to create new posts: posts by Wizard, posts by design, and blank publications. You will finally find yourself in the Publisher application, whichever way you create the new publication. For the time being, you may wish to close the Catalog by clicking the Close button, located in the upper right corner of the Catalog window, and observe the window's composition. You'll notice the publication appearing clearly while you're still in this window. Note that the widest area of the window is dedicated to publishing. The other areas, such as the menu bar, toolbar, Quick Post Wizard, and status

bar, give a quick way of accessing various commands and functions you use in Publisher or offer information about the publication, such as which page you are currently on and where it is located the mouse pointer on the page of the publication.

Before proceeding, let's discuss some

- The Title bar has the application names and the active document.

- The standard toolbar Includes icons that work as a shortcut to select commands like Save, Print, and Spelling.

- Menu Button - The menu bar has command menus for performing tasks in the program.

- Minimize and Maximize – The Minimize button reduces the Publisher window to a button on the taskbar. You click the button to restore your window. The Maximize button Increases Publisher window to cover the Windows desktop. When the window is maximized, the maximize button becomes the button - restore, clickable to return the window to its previous size.

- The Close button exits the Publisher program.

- Publisher Toolbar Contains tool icons that can be used to draw objects and incorporate images and text frames into the publication.

- The status bar Displays information about the current page number and the mouse pointer's position on the horizontal and vertical rules. It also provides information about an object's height and width that you draw on the publication page.

- The Post window Provides a place to create and enhance the post.

- Scroll bars Allow scrolling to view the current document: left and right with the horizontal scroll bar and up and down with the scroll.

- Publications Wizard facilitates the modification of the main properties of the current publication, such as design, color scheme, page size, and layout.

Wizard Publishing: The Publishing Wizard teaches the step-by-step process for creating a new publication. The assistant will ask questions, and a new publication will be generated from their answers. There are a large number of wizard-based publications available in certain types of publications. For example, when you click Invitations in the Wizard pane of the Catalog window, the view will be offered. Thumbnail preview of several different types of invitations. Select the type of invitation you want to create, then click the Start Wizard button to start the publication creation process.

Publications by design: Design sets allow you to create a family of publications with the same appearance. Each master design set uses a specific set of design elements and colors maintained in all the set publications. For example, you may want to create letterhead, business cards, presentations, and invoices for a small company that shares the same design. You can create these posts by choosing a design set in the Design Sets panel and selecting a specific publication (such as a business card) in the Master Sets window. Then start the publication creation process by clicking the Start Wizard button.

Blank publications:

Another possibility to create a new publication is starting from scratch. However, Publisher will not completely abandon you when you choose this option. The Blank Publications tab offers several blank templates to help you with the new publication's orientation and initial page layout. For example, if you want to create a folded card vertically, you can select the vertically folded card template on the Blank Publications tab. After choosing a template, press the Create button.

If you close the Catalog without realizing it, select the File menu and then New to reopen it. The choice of how to create the new publication will depend on the experience with Publisher and the aspects relating to the publication's design. The Publish Wizard and Layout Sets offer extensive help when laying out your publication; in both cases, such help is provided by an assistant. The wizard-based publication creation option not only helps determine aspects related to the color and layout of the post but also creates placeholder objects in the new publication that your images or design elements can later replace. Attendees offer the new user a quick and easy way to create a new publication. Now, if you want to create a publication where you are going to choose all aspects of your design, maybe it will be easier to create it from scratch than resort to an assistant.

Creating A Publication From A Template

Publisher provides various templates to make creating effective publications quick and simple. All you need to do is select the best template that suits your needs. Once you have chosen a template, you can modify aspects of the publication, such as the color and font schemes.

1. Click **File tab**, press New, then click **BUILT-IN** to view the categories of locally stored templates

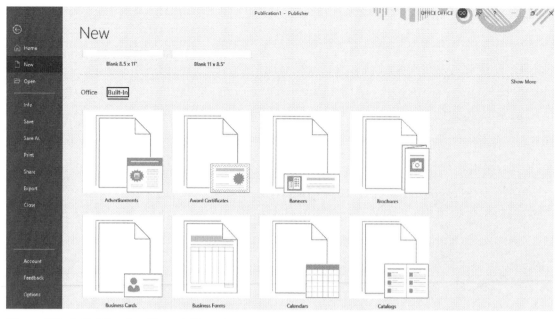

Figure 314: A Publication From A Template

2. **Click on [Brochures]** to display thumbnail previews of built-in brochure templates

3. Click on [Bars] under More Installed Templates to select this template

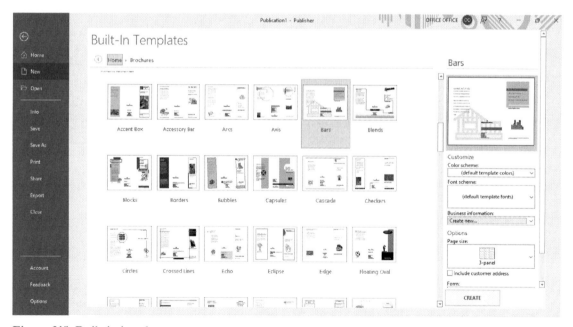

Figure 315: Built-in brochures

4. In the right pane, click on the drop arrow for the **Color scheme**

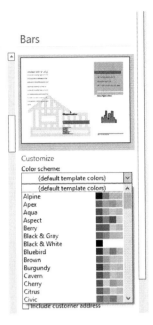

Figure 316: Color scheme

5. Scroll down to and **click on [Moss] to apply** this color scheme

Notice that all the thumbnails are updated to demonstrate the selected color scheme...

6. Click on [CREATE] to come up with a new brochure based on the Bars template

To create a publication:

1. Click on the [File tab], then click on [New]

2. Select a **category**

Figure 317: Template Categories for creating a new publication

3. Select a publication design, if available

4. Adjust the other settings using the right pane, then click on [Create]

In addition to the templates built into Publisher, you can download more templates free from Office.com.

Inserting Pictures

Microsoft Publisher also enables users to add images to their documents. The software includes various features and tools for manipulating images, such as resizing, cropping, and adjusting brightness and contrast. In addition, users can easily add captions and other text to their images.

Knowing how to insert pictures is an essential aspect of working with Publisher. Pictures help to draw attention to a publication and to illustrate your points. The picture must be stored somewhere on your computer and in a suitable file format (such as .jpg or .bmp) to insert a picture from your computer.

To insert a picture:

1. Click on the Insert tab, press Pictures in the Illustrations group

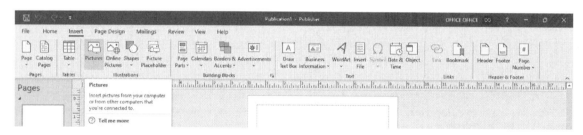

Figure 318: Inserting pictures

2. Select the Pictures icon.

3. Navigate to the desired picture file, then click on [Insert]

• You can accurately resize a picture by selecting it, then clicking on the Picture Tools: Format tab. Specify the exact Height and Width in the Size group on this tab.

105 FORMATTING IN PUBLISHER

Page layout is a key concept to understand when creating documents in Microsoft Publisher. The page layout refers to the arrangement of objects on a page, such as text and graphics. Page layout features in Publisher include the ability to add margin and column guides, as well as the ability to create and manipulate text boxes. Margin guides allow users to easily set the page margins, while column guides allow users to create multiple columns of text on a page. Text boxes allow users to control the size and placement of text on a page.

Working with Page Sizes in Microsoft Publisher

Another important aspect of formatting in Publisher is understanding page sizes. Publisher offers a variety of predefined page sizes, such as standard letter size, legal size, and A4. Publisher also allows users to create custom page sizes. To create a custom page size, users must specify the width and height of the page, as well as the orientation of the page. After a custom page size is created, it can create documents in Publisher.

Changing Page Orientation in Microsoft Publisher

In addition to creating custom page sizes, users can also change the orientation of pages in Publisher. Page orientation refers to page being in portrait or landscape mode. To alter the orientation of a page, users must select the orientation from the Page Setup menu. Once the orientation is set, Publisher will automatically adjust the document accordingly.

Working with Layout Guides

Layout guides help to arrange your publication elements accurately. If you refuse to set up your publication layout, you might encounter improper arrangement or layout of graphics, text, and objects on your publication pages. For example, an object may overlay or rest on another object. A text frame may stumble over the margin, text in one column may spill to the next, and various wrong alignments. Microsoft Publisher provides four apparatuses for setting an accurate and systematic layout for publication pages. They are **margin guides, ruler guides, grid guides, and Baseline**. Using these four layout guides effectively results in a tidy and nice publication.

Margin Guides

These blue border lines indicate the Start and end of the margin. It is an excellent tool for keeping objects within limits by restricting them from going beyond the margin.

Figure 319: The margin guides

If you can't find margin lines or indicators on the pages of your publication, you should call it back by clicking on the **View** tab and placing a checkmark on the Guide check box.

Figure 320: View tab guides

You can change the measurement of your margin, as I have said earlier in this chapter (click on the **Margin**s menu and select the margins option for your publication or select the **Custom Margin** to specify the margin measurement inside Layout Guides).

The Ruler Guides

These are the green lines you can draw horizontally or vertically on the page of your publication to make aligning graphics, text, and other objects convenient. You can draw ruler guides on your publication when required and remove them immediately after you are done if it is a distraction to the next action you want to carry out.

Let me quickly show you two ways of placing ruler guides on your publication page:

☐ **Built-in Ruler Guides**: Press the **Page Design** tab and tap the **Guides** menu, then select any **ruler guides** format you want from the dropdown menu.

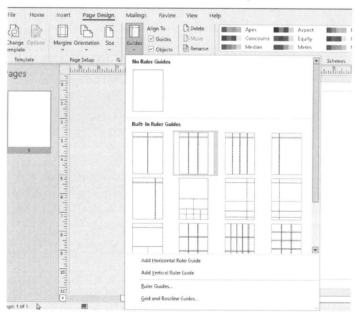

Figure 321: Built-in ruler guides

☐ **Drawing ruler guides**: click the **Page Design** tab and tap the **Guides** menu, then select **Add Horizontal Ruler Guides** or **Add Vertical Ruler Guides**. The horizontal or vertical ruler guide will be placed on your page. **Click and drag it to the desired spot** within the publication page.

Note: when you are done using the ruler guides, you can remove the guides by selecting **No Ruler Guides** from the **Guides** dropdown menu.

Shift or copy the ruler guide by holding the **Ctrl key** and hovering the mouse over the ruler guide until you see a two-headed arrow with a plus icon, then double-click and drag the **ruler** to another position to shift a ruler guide to another location or double-click and drag to another position by left-clicking to copy a ruler guide to another location.

To remove Ruler guides, click the **View** tab and remove the **checkmark** on the **"Guides."**

Grid Guides

These are the grid of blue lines appearing over the publication page. Grid guides are ideal for aligning frames and objects squarely across the page.

To specify grid guides for your publication, click **Page Design** tab and tap **Guides** menu, then select **"Grid and Baseline Guides"** from the dropdown menu to access **"Layout Guides"** dialog box with Grid Guides being selected at default, then adjust **the Grid guides** settings as described below:

1. Specify the number of **rows and columns** of the grid you desire.

2. Specify the **Spacing interval** to control the nearness of the object to the grid. It is always **0.2** by default. You must not set the Spacing below 0.2 unless you want frames and objects to brush each other.

3. (Optional) place a checkmark on the **"Add Center Guide between Columns and Rows"** check box to draw a line between the row and column of the grid you created.

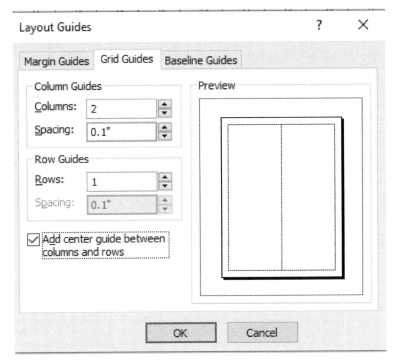

Figure 322: Layout guides

Note: you can remove the grid guides by finding your way to the **layout Guides** dialog box with the Grid Guide tab selected, entering 1 into the column and row text boxes, and click Ok.

To remove Ruler guides, click the **View** tab and remove the **checkmark** on the **"Guides."**

Baselines

Baselines are the horizontal dotted brown line on your publication page to make it easier to align objects, frames, and text lines.

You can specify the interval of the Baseline on **Page Design** tab, then click **Guides** menu and select **"Grid and Baseline Guides"** from the dropdown menu, then click on **Baseline Guides** tab and enter the **Spacing** measurement to decide the space interval of the baselines and the **offset** values into the offset textbox to decide the offset margin settings lines.

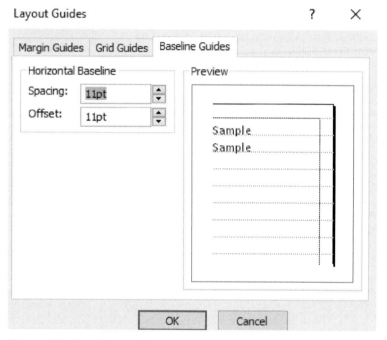

Figure 323: Baseline guides

To make the Baseline visible on your page, click the View tab and place a checkmark on the "Baseline" check box.

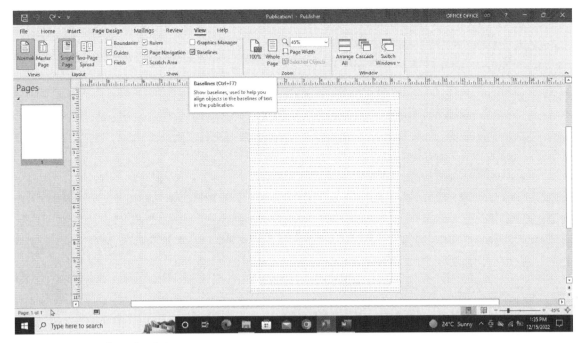

Figure 324: Baseline check box

Aligning Objects To Snap To Guide And Other Objects

Aligning object to ruler or grid guides make frames and object queue up accurately on the page. To make this alignment work, kindly click the **Page Design** tab and place a **checkmark** on the **"Guide"** check box to enable the objects to align to the ruler or grid guides. Likewise, you can place a **checkmark** on the **"Objects"** check box to allow the object to align with other objects on the publication page.

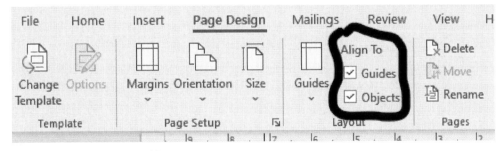

Figure 325: Guides and objects

106 MASTER PAGES

Master pages are a useful tool for creating and working with large publications, where maintaining consistency over multiple pages is essential. A master page can be used to apply design and layout elements to multiple pages at once, saving you the time and effort of applying these elements individually to every page.

Understanding Master Pages

You can access the Master Page view by clicking on the View tab, then clicking on Master Page in the Views group. Using the Master Page view, you can quickly and easily make changes to your whole publication by simultaneously applying elements to some or all of the pages.

Master Pages

A master page is attached to a publication but doesn't appear within the publication itself. By default, all publications (including blank publications) contain a master page. To view the master page for your publication, you must access the Master Page view.

Any changes you make to a master page are applied to all pages within that publication to which that master page is applied. You can use master pages to apply design elements such as headers, footers, page numbers, headings, text, and pictures to multiple pages within a publication. These elements then become part of the background of the pages in the publication and can only be edited using the master page. Keep in mind that when working with a master page, if you want elements to appear on some pages. Still, not others, you will need to choose to apply no master page to some pages, create a second master page, or apply the elements to each page individually. If you decide that you would prefer to add content and design elements to each page individually, then you don't have to use a master page at all; you can leave the master page blank.

Activating Master Page View

Click View Tab

Click **Master Page**.

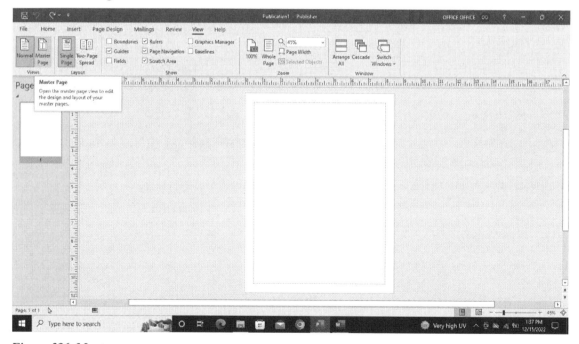

Figure 326: Master page

You can also access Master Page by clicking on the **Page Design tab**

Clicking on Master Pages in the Page Background group

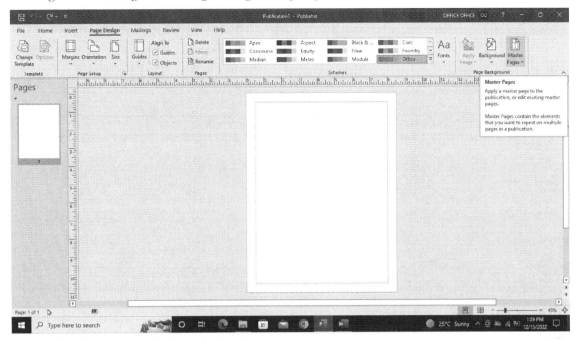

Figure 327: Master Pages in Page Design Tab

Then select **Edit Master Pages,** or by clicking on the Insert tab, then pressing Header or Footer in Header & Footer group.

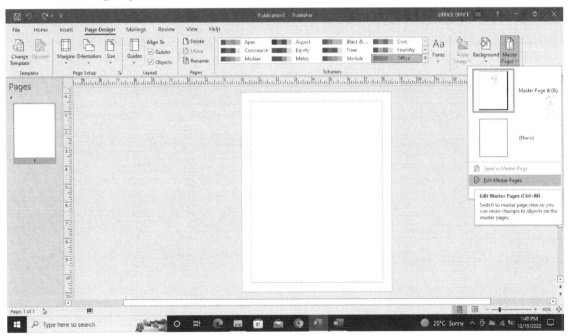

Figure 328: Edit Master Pages

When a publication is in Master Page view, the normal pages of the publication are not displayed. Rather, the master page will appear in the publication window, and the Pages navigation pane will display thumbnail previews of each master page in the publication. In addition, the area surrounding the page in the publication window will change color from grey to yellow, and the Master Page tab will appear on the ribbon, as shown below. This tab is only accessible in the Master Page view and provides a range of commands for working with master pages.

Using Master Pages

You can use master pages to ensure your publication is consistently based on the same layout and design elements. This can save you time and effort and ensure that your final publication looks professional and serves its purpose effectively.

As helpful as master pages are, there will be times when you will find that it is inappropriate to use them in a publication; for example, when using some templates. Because master page elements become part of the background of the pages in a publication, all other content applied to the pages is inserted over the top. Therefore, when using a template, you may find that elements that you placed on the master page are obscured in the publication by objects from the template. As you cannot set content to be placed behind the background, you would be better off applying the elements from the master page to each publication page individually to ensure they are visible.

Using A Master Page

Suppose you have one master page in a publication. In that case, anything you insert on that master page will appear in the background of every normal page in that publication unless you specify otherwise.

You can also send an item from a normal page to a master page so that an element that initially only appeared on one page can appear in the same place on every page (such as a logo).

To use a master page:

1. Click the View tab, then press Master Page in the Views group

2. Insert or apply the desired elements to the master page

3. Click the Master Page tab, then click Close Master Page in the Close group

When your publication is in Master Page view, the Pages navigation pane displays thumbnail previews of each of your master pages. Instead of numbers 1, 2, 3, and so on, the master pages are labeled A, B, C, etc.

Inserting Headers

Traditionally, a header is an object appearing at the top of every page. In Publisher, headers are created on the master page. They appear on every page but can only be modified when the master page is displayed. Headers can include text, page numbers, date and time stamps, and graphics.

To insert a header:

1. Click the Insert tab, then click Header in Header & Footer group

2. Type or insert the desired information

3. Click the Master Page tab before clicking on Close Master Page in the Close group

You can format the text of headers and footers just as you can format ordinary text by changing font, size, style, and alignment.

Inserting Footers

A footer is situated at the bottom of the page. Footers often include information such as page numbers, company names, and taglines. Like headers, footers are inserted on the master page and will appear on every page that the master page is applied.

To insert a footer:

1. Click the Insert tab, then click Footer in Header & Footer group

2. Type or insert the desired information

3. Click the Master Page tab, then click on Close Master Page in the Close group

• Page numbers can be inserted into headers and footers. They can be aligned to the left, right, or center.

Inserting Page Numbers

Page numbers are common in print publications and are especially useful in a publication with many pages. For example, in Publisher, page numbers can be inserted into the header or footer of a master page, where they appear as a hash symbol (#).

When the publication is returned to Normal view, the symbol will become a number corresponding to the page's position in the publication.

To insert page numbers:

1. Click the View tab, then click Master Page in the Views group

2. Click in the header or footer

3. On the Master Page tab, click on Insert Page Number in the Header & Footer group

You can insert page numbers without going into the Master Page view. Instead, click on the Insert tab, click on Page Number in the Header & Footer group, then select the position on the page to insert the numbers. Be aware that this method will affect any headers or footers already applied.

107 SAVING, SHARING, AND EXPORTING YOUR PUBLICATION

Alongside what you can do in the **File** tab is Print, Share, and Export.

Figure 329: Print Share Export

To **print**, click **Print**, which will open a Print dialogue box to adjust your print settings. In addition, a print preview of your publication is displayed on the right.

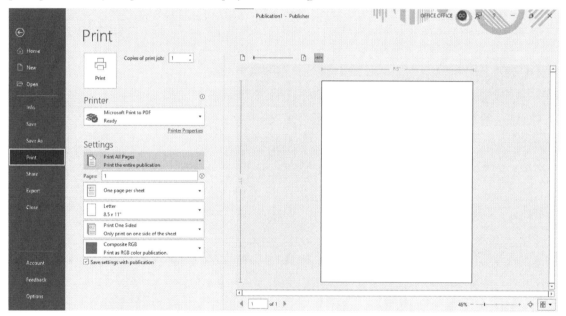

Figure 330: Print dialog box

You can then set the number of copies you want, choose a printer, and the like. Finally, click **Print** to print when you are done with the settings.

To **share your publication**, click the **File** tab and click **Share**. The Share option allows you to share your completed Publisher file via **Email**. Then, you can choose the format you want your file sent.

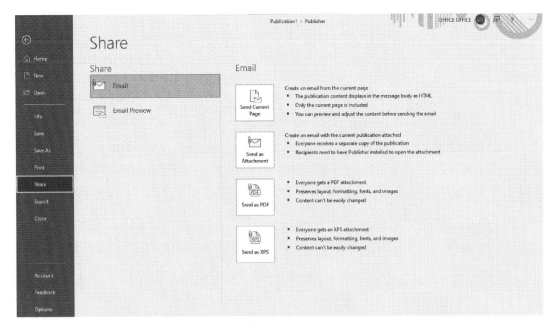

Figure 331: To share a publication

Finally, to **export your publication**, click the **File** tab and click **Export**. You can easily convert your publication (.pub) into other file formats. You can **Create PDF/XPS documents, Publish HTML, change the file type, and other options, including Save for Photo Printing**, **Save for a Commercial Printer**, and **Save for Another Computer**.

Figure 332: Exporting a publication

Create PDF/XPS Document

You can send your publication as a PDF and XPS. Save it to places such as your local computer, network drive, flash drive, and so on.

Publish HTML

If you are thinking of adding one of your pages to your website, you can export it to either a web page (HTML) file with its associated images in a separate folder or a single web page file MHTML that keeps everything within one file. These types of files can also be opened with a web browser.

Change File Type

The *Change File Type* option is very similar to the Save As option. In addition, a Save As button at the bottom of the Change File Type interface makes it easy to choose additional file types to save your publication.

Save for Photo Printing

If your pages contain photos you want printed on a high-resolution printer, you can use this option to have each publication page saved as a high-quality image file. Each page will be a separate JPEG or TIFF image file, depending on the type you specify during the save process. Then you will need to tell Publisher where to save this image set so you can then find a way to get the image files to your printer.

Save for a Commercial Printer

If you plan on having your publication professionally printed, you might want to use this option to have your files packaged together into a printer package that you can then give to the print shop so they will have the best quality files to work with. There are several choices when creating this type of package.

- **Minimum size** – This creates a small file suitable for on-screen display and is not recommended for high-quality print jobs.

- **Standard** – Creates a moderately compressed file suitable for online distribution since the file sizes will be smaller.

- **High-quality printing** – Creates a large file optimized for at-home or copy-shop printing.

- **Commercial Press** – Creates the largest file for the highest quality suited for commercial printers.

- **Custom** – here, you can select the exact options for your package based on your needs.

 After you choose your options, you can click on the *Pack and Go Wizard* buttons to go through the process of creating the printing package. Before doing so, you should decide if you want a Publisher file, a PDF file, or just one. Many printers prefer high-quality PDF files to print from.

You will then be prompted as to where you want to create the files. For example, you can burn them to a CD\DVD, copy them to a flash drive or copy them to your local hard drive.

How To Save Your Publication

- To conserve your work, go up to the left-hand of the mesh and select the **File tab.**

- This opens up what is called **backstage.**

- Within that screen, click on **save as.**

This opens up the **save as** menu; you can choose any location you prefer to insert it.

- After selecting a location, type in a record title and choose to **save**

Your file has been saved.

Save for Another Computer

If you want to transfer your publication to a different computer and ensure that everything you need will be there when you open the file, then you can use the Save for Another Computer option. Usually, you can copy your Publisher file over and be ok, but if the computer you are copying it to doesn't have the same fonts or access to your images, then it might not look the same when you open it on the other computer.

The Wizard for the Save for Another Computer option looks similar to the one for the Save for a Commercial Printer procedure, but you will have the choice of whether or not you want to embed your fonts into your file as well as include linked graphics (figure 40). If you use this option, you might as well check all the boxes to ensure everything you need gets included, even though it will increase your exported file size.

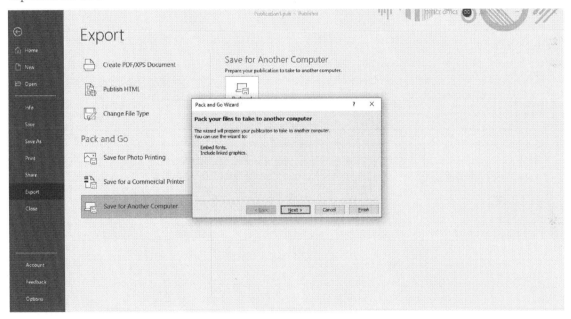

Figure 333: Pack and Go Wizard

108   THE STRATEGIC SHORTCUTS

Familiarize yourself with these shortcut keys to increase the pace and the speed at which you work on Publisher. You must commit them to memory to maximize the Publisher application and gain the most out of it.

SHORTCUT KEYS	FUNCTIONS
Alt + F11	Access the Visual Basic Editor
Alt + F6	take the object to the front
Alt + F8	Access the Macros dialog box
Alt + Shift + D	To insert the recent date
Alt + Shift + F6	Take the object to the back
Alt + Shift + P	To insert the current page number
Alt + Shift + T	To insert the recent time
Ctrl + [	Decrease the font size by 1 point
Ctrl +]	Increase the font size by 1 point
Ctrl + =	Attach or detach Subscript formatting
Ctrl + A	Select all the items on a page or all the text in a text frame.
Ctrl + B	Bold the selected text
Ctrl + E	Center align the text on a paragraph
Ctrl + F	Find specific information
Ctrl + F4	Close currently open publication
Ctrl + H	Find a specific item and replace it with another item.
Ctrl + I	Italicize the selected text
Ctrl + J	Justify the text alignment in a paragraph
Ctrl + K	To insert Hyperlink
Ctrl + L	Align text to the left on the paragraph
Ctrl + M	Switch between the Master page and the current page
Ctrl + N	Open new publication
Ctrl + O	Access the Open Publication dialog box
Ctrl + P	Access the Print dialog box

SHORTCUT KEYS	FUNCTIONS
Ctrl + Page down	Go to the next page
Ctrl + Page up	Go to the previous page
Ctrl + R	Align the text to the right of the paragraph
Ctrl + S	Access the Save dialog box to save your publication
Ctrl + Shift + [	Decrease the space between letters
Ctrl + Shift +]	Increase the space between the selected letters
Ctrl + Shift + <	Decrease the font size of the selected text
Ctrl + Shift + =	Attach or detach Superscript formatting
Ctrl + Shift + >	Increase the font size of the selected text
Ctrl + Shift + D	Share a paragraph consistently horizontally
Ctrl + Shift + F	Access the Font dialog box
Ctrl + Shift + G	Group selected object/ungroup selected object
Ctrl + Shift + H	Access the Hyphenation dialog box
Ctrl + Shift + J	Specify newspaper alignment
Ctrl + Shift + K	Change the Upper case to lower case
Ctrl + Shift + O	Switch boundaries On and Off
Ctrl + Shift + V	Paste the text formatting
Ctrl + Shift + Y	Switch On or Off the Special Character

SHORTCUT KEYS	FUNCTIONS
Ctrl + Shift+ C	Copy the formation on the text
Ctrl + Spacebar	Change the character formatting to the style currently in use
Ctrl + U	Underline the selected text
Ctrl + Y	Redo the last action that you have undone
Ctrl + Z	Undo the last action
F7	Spelling checker

SHORTCUT KEYS	FUNCTIONS
Shift + F7	Thesaurus task pane
Shift + R, F10	switch the snap to guides On and Off

109 CONCLUSION

Microsoft Publisher is a powerful, user-friendly application for creating a wide range of professional-looking documents. It is an ideal choice for businesses and individuals, offering a range of features and customization options to make it easy to create visually appealing documents. With its intuitive design and wide range of features, Microsoft Publisher is an excellent choice for a comprehensive, user-friendly publishing program.

MICROSOFT SHAREPOINT
INTRODUCTION

Microsoft SharePoint is an invaluable platform for businesses and organizations of any size. SharePoint enables users to collaborate on various documents, share data securely, and even access documents remotely. Its technological capabilities meet the needs of businesses, allowing them to be more efficient and cost-effective.

Enhanced Security:

Microsoft SharePoint provides businesses with enhanced security controls, ensuring that only authorized users can access confidential documents. With secure storage and access, businesses can protect their data from unauthorized users and outside threats. In addition, its advanced security features provide businesses with peace of mind, knowing that their data is safe and secure.

In addition, SharePoint's secure environment makes it easier to manage user permissions and access rights. This ensures that only users with the proper permissions can access sensitive data, preventing unauthorized access and protecting confidential information. Businesses can also set up additional security measures, such as two-factor and multi-factor authentication, to protect their confidential data.

Improved Collaboration:

Microsoft SharePoint enables users to collaborate in a secure environment. With SharePoint, businesses can easily manage document sharing and editing, allowing users to work together on a variety of projects. SharePoint also allows users to create and manage team sites, where users can share documents, set deadlines, and discuss tasks with other team members.

SharePoint also offers a variety of collaboration tools, such as shared document libraries, calendars, and discussions. This allows users to coordinate their work better, resulting in improved team collaboration and productivity. SharePoint also makes it easier to manage projects, with project planning and task management features, which help teams stay organized and on track.

Flexible Access:

Microsoft SharePoint allows users to access their documents and data from any location. With its cloud-based platform, users can access documents remotely and securely. This enables businesses to be more flexible and productive, allowing users to access documents and data on the go. SharePoint also makes managing user permissions and access rights easy, ensuring that only users with the proper permissions can access sensitive data.

In addition, SharePoint is compatible with various devices, including PCs, Macs, tablets, and smartphones. This allows users to access their data from any device with an internet connection, making it easier for businesses to remain productive and efficient.

Microsoft SharePoint is an invaluable platform for businesses and organizations of any size. Its enhanced security, improved collaboration, and flexible access make it an ideal solution for businesses looking to improve their productivity and efficiency. With its secure environment, team collaboration tools, and cloud-based platform, SharePoint enables businesses to be more efficient and cost-effective.

Exploring Differences between OneDrive and SharePoint

Microsoft SharePoint is a cloud-based platform built to help businesses and organizations easily collaborate and share information. Though many organizations use SharePoint for collaboration, it is not the only option available. For example, OneDrive is another popular cloud storage platform offered by Microsoft, and there are several key differences between the two.

Comparing OneDrive and SharePoint

OneDrive and SharePoint are both popular cloud-based platforms offered by Microsoft, and it can be helpful to understand the key differences between them.

A. Accessibility

One of the main differences between OneDrive and SharePoint is the accessibility of the platforms. OneDrive is available to any individual with a Microsoft account and is used to store personal files and documents. SharePoint is designed for business and organizational use and requires an Office 365 subscription.

B. Storage Capacity

Another key difference between OneDrive and SharePoint is the storage capacity of the platforms. OneDrive offers up to 1TB of storage for individuals, while SharePoint offers up to 5TB for businesses and organizations.

C. File Organization

Finally, OneDrive and SharePoint differ in how files and documents are organized. OneDrive is designed to store individual files and documents, while SharePoint enables users to organize files into folders and libraries.

Where to Buy Microsoft SharePoint

Microsoft SharePoint is available for purchase through Microsoft or a Microsoft partner. Organizations can purchase SharePoint as a standalone product or as part of an Office 365 subscription. Purchasing SharePoint as part of an Office 365 subscription will provide access to additional features and capabilities, such as collaboration and communication tools and Office applications.

When purchasing SharePoint, organizations should consider the size of the organization and the scope of the project to determine which version of the software is best suited for their needs. Microsoft partners can help organizations assess their requirements and determine the best version of SharePoint.

In addition to purchasing SharePoint through Microsoft or a Microsoft partner, organizations can also purchase SharePoint from a third-party vendor. Third-party vendors may offer different versions of the software with different features and additional support and customization services.

Organizations should research the different versions of SharePoint available to find the best option for their organization's needs. Knowing the differences between OneDrive and SharePoint and where to buy Microsoft SharePoint can help organizations make an informed decision and ensure they purchase the most suitable version of the software for their needs.

110 EXPLORING THE DIFFERENT TYPES OF MICROSOFT SHAREPOINT

Microsoft SharePoint is a potent tool that businesses of all sizes use to increase productivity and teamwork. Users can access organizational data, store and share documents, work together on projects, and do so on a secure platform. Each kind of SharePoint, including SharePoint Foundation, SharePoint Server, and Microsoft Office 365, offers unique features and functionalities.

Overview of Microsoft SharePoint

Microsoft SharePoint is a web-based collaboration platform used by organizations of all sizes to store and share documents, collaborate on projects, and access organizational data. It provides a wide range of tools and features to help facilitate collaboration, communication, and knowledge management. SharePoint allows users to create and manage websites, upload and share documents, host discussion forums, access data and reports, and more. It is a powerful tool that has revolutionized how organizations collaborate and work together.

SharePoint Foundation

SharePoint Foundation is the most basic version of SharePoint. It allows users to create and manage basic websites, document libraries, and lists. In addition, it enables users to collaborate on projects, share documents, and search for content. SharePoint Foundation also provides basic security features such as user authentication and authorization.

SharePoint Server

SharePoint Server is the next step up from SharePoint Foundation. It provides users with many features and tools, including collaboration, search, workflow, and content management. SharePoint Server is a hybrid version of SharePoint that combines the features of the on-premises and online versions. It is typically used by organizations that need the flexibility of the cloud but still want to maintain control over their data and systems. It also includes features such as document libraries, web parts, and web applications. SharePoint Server also provides enhanced security features, such as audit and compliance.

It allows organizations to host their SharePoint environment while taking advantage of the scalability and flexibility of the cloud.

Microsoft 365

Microsoft 365 is a cloud-based suite of productivity tools that includes SharePoint and other Microsoft applications, such as Word, Excel, and PowerPoint. It provides organizations with a comprehensive collaboration, communication, and file-sharing platform. Microsoft 365 also offers a range of advanced features, such as data protection, compliance, and analytics, that are not available with the on-premises or online versions of SharePoint. In addition, office 365 offers enhanced security features, such as advanced authentication and encryption.

SharePoint On-Premises

SharePoint On-Premises is the traditional version of SharePoint installed on an organization's servers. This type of SharePoint requires a physical server and dedicated IT staff to manage and maintain the system. It is typically used by large organizations that need a high degree of control over their data and systems. This type of SharePoint is highly customizable and can be tailored to an organization's specific needs.

SharePoint Online

SharePoint Online is a cloud-based version of SharePoint that Microsoft hosts. It is available as a subscription service and is ideal for organizations that don't have the resources to maintain an on-premises server. This type of SharePoint provides access to the same features as the on-premises version but with the added benefit of being accessible from anywhere with an internet connection.

111UPLOADING DOCUMENTS TO A SHAREPOINT DOCUMENT LIBRARY

With the contemporary interface, you can drag files and folders from your PC to your OneDrive library or SharePoint team site. You may also use the old version to browse and upload your files. See the Differences between the new and old experiences for lists and libraries for more details.

Notes: Microsoft Edge, Google Chrome, and Mozilla Firefox can upload folders to SharePoint. Meanwhile, uploading folders is not possible with Internet Explorer.

- Upload files to your OneDrive or SharePoint site library by dragging them there.

Notes: The new Microsoft Edge or Google Chrome are the most acceptable browsers for dragging and dropping. As an alternative, you may use the Upload command in other browsers.

- If you don't see the option to drag and drop files, you may need to upgrade to the latest version of Office.

1. **Open the site library in OneDrive or SharePoint**

1. Select the Start Windows Start button on your computer and then type File Explorer.

2. Drag and drop files into the SharePoint library

3. Go to the folder containing the documents you wish to upload.

4. Drag the files to the area in the SharePoint library labeled **"drag files here."** Then, when you hover the file over it in the library, it should say, **"Drop here."**

5. Your files should now show in the Document Library

NB: You may get problems due to the file size restriction in SharePoint or timeout errors in your version of Internet Explorer if you upload big files or numerous files that add up to a large total size to a library.

2. **Copying files from one folder to another folder**

SharePoint is a fantastic document management system, but dealing with documents in SharePoint isn't always straightforward. Finally, it has a distinct interface from the standard Windows Explorer view.

The following are some of the most common copy-move jobs addressed:

- Copying files from one folder to another

- Copying files from one document library to another

- Copying files from one site to another

- Making a copy of an existing file

- Transferring files from one folder to another

- Transferring files from one document library to another

- Transferring files across locations

- Reorganizing structure and content after migrating/relocating a large number of files

Step 1: View in Explorer Mode

Using the explorer view, you may open the document library like a normal Windows Explorer folder. In addition, you may add files to this library by dragging and dropping them, making folders, moving and copying, and deleting several files.

The disadvantage:

- This program is only compatible with Windows operating systems: This implies that users who use a Mac will not utilize this feature.

- Only works with Internet Explorer: This option will be grayed out if the user chooses a different browser.

- Only works with Internet Explorer 32-bit: This option will be grayed out if the user does not have Internet Explorer 32-bit installed.

- It only works if the computer has Office components installed.

Go to the library, choose the library tab, and click the **Open in Explorer icon** to view Explorer mode.

Step 2: Dragging and Dropping

You can drag and drop files into SharePoint and Office 365 SharePoint Online folders. This is a significant improvement in browser usability. *NB: You may even drag several files at the same time.*
Limitations:

- It isn't compatible with directories. For example, a folder cannot be dragged and dropped.

- Files cannot be copied across libraries.

- A copy of a file in the same place cannot be cloned.

Step 3: Use the File Sending Option

You may copy a file from one place to another using the **'Send File'** option. Pick a file, click transmit, **"other Location,"** and you'll be presented with a form to fill out, which will ask for the destination location and file name.

This works well if you need to copy one file, but it is not user-friendly since it requires the user to provide a full URL with no browsing option. Users must be capable of opening a new browser, navigating to the desired location, right-clicking, and copying the URL's precise path without any additional parameters. It's a little unintuitive, but it works.

Limitations

1. It can only handle one file at a time. This means that multiple files cannot be copied

2. Only files, not directories, may be copied.

3. It is not user-friendly since the user must input the whole destination URL.

To transfer a SharePoint file to a different library or folder, choose **Other Location**.

Step 4: Make use of the Tru Copy Add-In

The Tru Copy & Paste add-on for SharePoint is a great way to copy, transfer, and deal with files. It enables any end-user to copy a file to the clipboard the same way as a normal Windows copy file capability and then paste it into a target folder or library.

Multiple files and folders may be copied between libraries, sites, and site collections. You may also copy several times to get all of the data you need. In addition, it has features like converting files to PDF, zipping and unzipping zipped folders, batch editing, copying information with files, and a file template gallery, to name a few.

The steps for transferring files include the following:

1. Choose the files you wish to move.

2. Select **Move** from the drop-down menu.

3. Decide on a destination.

4. *Click to Move, and you'll get an email when the copy process begins.* **NB: You may monitor the process at any moment without relying on your computer**

How to request a SharePoint site

You should be a site administrator to create a new SharePoint site. Instead, you need to put in a request in this circumstance. Most businesses have a process in place for finding a team site. For instance, you may fill out a form or email the SharePoint administrator.

To get a team site, you must give the following details to your SharePoint administrator:

- **Site name**.

- **Site template defines the type of site SharePoint generates for you:** There are countless pre-built site templates in SharePoint. Your company may also create its custom website themes.

- **The web address or URL:** This is the one-of-a-kind address where your team's website is housed. All team sites in most companies are linked to the same root web address. Your company may also want to know who has access to the site.

Three different user types, known as SharePoint groups, are pre-installed on all SharePoint team sites:

- Read-Only access is granted to visitors. They may look around your site without contributing anything.

- Team members can add tasks, documents, and other content to the website by uploading and editing them.

- The customization of the site is entirely under the authority of the owners. The SharePoint administrator is likely to assume you are the proud owner of the team site unless you specifically tell them.

NB: You must determine which users belong in these three SharePoint groups.

112 HOW TO CREATE AND SET UP A SITE

One of the most exciting things about SharePoint is allowing users to create and set up sites. You can also add more users and give specified permissions to some (or all). This chapter makes a better explanation and detailed information on managing a site.

How to create a site

Every site is based on templates. The content and basic layout of your site are determined by the template you choose; you can choose from four categories: Duet Enterprise, Collaboration, Custom, and Enterprise. Each of these template categories has various designs created for various uses, such as blogs, team websites, community websites, and project websites. Use the following instructions if you wish to build a new website:

Step 1. Go to the parent site and choose a location for your site.

Step 2. Click the Settings button

Step 3. Once it opens, select Site settings

Step 4. Click on Sites and workspaces

Step 5. Subsequently, the Sites and Workspaces screen opens. Select Create

Step 6. The New SharePoint Site window is then displayed. Enter the site's title directly in the Title box.

Step 7. Also, in the Description box, enter a site description

Step 8. Enter any name you want to be the site's last portion of the URL name in the URL name box, but keep in mind that spaces should not be used in the Web site address.

Step 9. With the diverse options available on the category tab, select the desired template you intend to create for your site. Once that is done, you should add some libraries, lists, pages, and apps based on your preferences.

Step 10. Indicate whether or not you want your new site to appear in the parent site's Quick Launch and Top Link Bar. Do this through the Navigation/Navigation Inheritance section.

Step 11. Click Create

Setting up groups for the site

You can only utilize the Setup Groups for Your Site page when creating individual permissions that do not inherit from the parent site. For example, under user permissions, if you had chosen to utilize the same rights as the parent site, you would have skipped over this box. If not, the following steps describe setting up your special permission groups.

Choose your permissions for any of these three groups:

i. Visitors: This group is only permitted to read the website's content; they are not permitted to add to or edit it.

ii. Members: This group is only permitted to modify their contributions and upload content to the website.

iii. Owners: This group is in absolute control over the Web site.

The group you choose determines the permissions you give.

How to set up permissions for Visitors

Step 1. Allow people to view the site through the Visitors to this Site section by using an existing group or creating a new group.

Step 2. After that, a Select People and Groups window will open, enter a group or person's name in the Find field and click search to search the global directory.

Step 3. Select the name you want to add from the result list that pops up and Click Add. You can also search and add as many names then click OK once completed.

How to set up permissions for Members

In the section outlined for Members of this Site, use the same steps mentioned above to give users permission to contribute to the site. In addition, users in the Members category can view, edit, add, and delete site content.

How to set up permissions for Owners

Similarly, the same step for the Visitors and Members groups applies to the Owners of this Site section. Again, do this to give users total control of the site.

Once that is done, Click OK.

How to modify site permissions

Always remember the security measures you want to implement for your website when granting authorization to groups. One of the many features that let you customize the types of content that can be added, viewed, updated, and removed from your website is permissions (and by who). You must first comprehend the actions users will take on your site to decide on permissions. The permission levels you can grant to individuals and groups are compiled in the list below.

Full Control: This includes full control and all permissions.

Design: Here, the permissions are to view, add, approve, update, customize, and delete.

Edit: Users can create, edit, and remove lists with this privilege. Users can also browse, add, remove, and update lists and documents.

Contribute: Viewing, adding, deleting, and updating documents and list items is the only permission granted to users in this category.

Read: Users are capable of viewing list items and pages and download documents here.

View Only: There is access to list items, pages, and documents. Specific server-side file handlers prevent downloading documents that can only be seen in the browser.

To view site permissions, click the People and Groups option in the Site Settings page. Make more adjustments to your website using the instructions below:

How to add a Group or User to a Site

Step 1. Go to the Site and Select the Settings button

Step 2. If you want to access the Site Settings window, click Site Settings

Step 3. Selecting Site Permissions in the Site Settings window causes the Site Permissions window to open.

Step 4. On the Permissions tab of the ribbon, click Grant Permissions.

Step 5. The Share site window is then displayed. Next, create an email invitation message and add the members you want to let users know they can access the site.

Step 6. Fill out the Users/Groups box with the name (or names) of the groups or users you want to add to the website. The names you type will be searched for by SharePoint using Active Directory.

Step 7. Add an optional personal message alongside the invitation

Step 8. Select SHOW OPTIONS if you wish to change the default permission level or add users without sending any email invitations.

Step 9. Additionally, you can deactivate the email invitation by clicking the button next to "Send an email invitation" and unchecking it.

Step 11. Click Share after completing the steps.

Step 12. By using the Share option from the toolbar, you may also share with others.

How to modify Permissions on a Site

Step 1. Visit the site, then select SHARE from the toolbar. By doing so, the sharing site is opened, giving you access to both views and inviting visitors to your site.

Step 2. To send an email to all those having access to your site, click Shared with.

Step 3. Click Email Everyone to generate and send an email to everyone with whom you have shared site permissions.

Step 4. To access and change site permissions, click Advanced. This opens the Site Permissions window, where you can create a new group, grant permissions to individuals, and edit membership and permission levels for the entire group.

Step 5. Press the checkbox near the user or group you want to edit, then click Edit User Permissions button.

Step 6. Confirm the appropriate boxes in the Edit Permissions window, then click OK.

How to Delete a User from a Group

Step 1. Navigate to the relevant website and click the Settings option.

Step 2. Once the Settings will, Click Site Settings.

Step 3. Under Users and Permissions (while on Site Settings page), press People and Groups.

Step 4. Continue by clicking the group name you wish to edit.

Step 5. Click the checkbox next to the name of the person you wish to delete, then click the drop-down arrow for more Actions.

Step 6. Once the Actions pop up, click Remove Users from Group, then click OK to complete the action.

113 SHAREPOINT TIPS AND TRICKS

To get started smoothly on SharePoint, you should understand specific tips and tricks. Getting familiar with those tips will aid you in customizing the site conveniently and give you the capabilities to meet the company's needs. So I will start by introducing you to the tips one after the other.

CREATING SHAREPOINT ALERTS

Alerts setup is one of the essential things you should do on your site. If you create alerts on your team, you will be notified anytime a change is made to your documents and files stored in your library. It is the best choice for tracking your documents for any changes you or your team members may make.

Install an alert for the contents inside the Document app with the following steps:

1) Open your team site and choose the **Document** on the Left Navigation pane.

2) Click the **(…) Ellipsis** on the top of the Document and choose **Alert me** from the drop-down menu to access the Alert Me When Items change dialog box.

3) Set a **Name** for your Alert within the title text box, such as Document modification notification.

4) Supply the **name of other people** that should receive an alert whenever a change is made on any document using the **"Send Alerts to the text box."**

5) Move to the Delivery Method section and indicate the method you want for receiving alerts, such as via **Email Message Or Text Message**.

6) Go to Change Type Section and choose the one that best describes the notification you wish to receive, such as New Items are added, All changes, etc.

7) Enter the time you want to be notified when the changes are made in the Send Alerts for the changes section.

8) Move to When to Send Alerts section and specify how often you want the alerts delivered.

9) Click Ok to confirm the alert setup. Henceforth, you will be notified of any changes that are being made to the contents of your document app.

STAY UPDATED WITH NEWS

This SharePoint feature enables you to create and share news content on the Team site, Microsoft Teams, communication site, and others. First, you must open the medium you want to share the news. For the sake of this lesson, I will share the news with the Team site. Study the following steps to create and share news on SharePoint:

1) Open your Team site, click the Add menu, and select News post from the drop-down list.

2) Create your new post, such as adding the post's title and the information you want to share, then click plus icon to add content to the team site.

3) Click Create button at the top right side of the screen to create the News post for everyone to follow.

FINDING A DOCUMENT ON SHAREPOINT

The central means of searching for items on Microsoft 365 is using the Search box. It's the same principle on SharePoint. Though you can use "Find a file" at the top of the folder/document. Check how to search for a document using the two boxes separately:

- **Search Box:** this is the box at the SharePoint site's top right corner. It is designed for searching the SharePoint site as a whole. Enter the keyword(s) you want to search and strike the Search icon. SharePoint will search through your file names, readable PDF files, metadata, and office document and present the result.

- **Find a File** placed at the top of the folder/document. It can be used to search for file names, readable PDF files, metadata, and the selected document library office document.

MOVING AND COPYING FILES AND DOCUMENTS

To move or copy files/documents, study the recommended steps below:

1. Select the items you want to move or copy.

2. Click over the **(…) Ellipses** at the top next to the Delete button, and select Move to/Copy to.

3. Choose the folder where you are moving or copying the file under the **"Choose a destination"** section. You can also click the **Browse** sites to see the full list of folders in your site where you can move or copy.

4. Click **Move Or Copy Here** to confirm the process.

114 DETECTING SHAREPOINT IN MICROSOFT TEAMS

Microsoft Teams is part of the application with a Microsoft 365 subscription, depending on your subscription package. Microsoft Teams is gaining popularity very fast. It is a team collaboration competitor to Zoom, Slack, and others.

This section will show you the relationship between SharePoint and Microsoft Teams and how to access some functionality of SharePoint from Microsoft Teams.

REASON FOR SHAREPOINT AND MICROSOFT TEAMS PARTNERSHIP

Each Microsoft Team directly has a replica of the Sharepoint Team site that is attached to it. You will notice that "team" is used almost in each section of this book. The reason is that Microsoft perceives teams as a significant commodity for grouping multiple members of people who are working together for a common purpose.

GAIN ACCESS TO SHAREPOINT FILES ON TEAMS

Microsoft Teams involves various channels. Although the channel deals with specific chats for introducing the topic being discussed, each channel includes a file tab for uploading files to the channel, which other people can view and access by clicking the file tab.

The Files tab in each channel is attached and stored in a document folder on the SharePoint site.

To view the SharePoint site in Microsoft Teams, use the following steps:

1. Click the **Ellipsis (…)** and choose **Open** in SharePoint from the drop-down list.

2. SharePoint will be opened with the team you created on Microsoft Teams.

Note: you landed on the document app of the SharePoint site because you opened the SharePoint site on the Files tab of Microsoft Teams.

The SharePoint site will open with the team you create on the Microsoft Team. If you create a new team and select Open in SharePoint, SharePoint will be opened with the new team you've just created.

ADD THE PAGES AND LISTS OF SHAREPOINT TO THE TEAMS

There is always a default file tab and wiki tab for each channel in a Team team. However, you can add tabs to the channel. For instance, you can add a specific page or tab to the SharePoint site. The following are the steps for adding a new SharePoint tab or page to a Team channel:

1. Move to the Left Navigation menu and click on **Teams**.
2. Extend the **channel** and choose the **channel** you want to add to a SharePoint tab.
3. Click **(+) plus** sign at the right side of the existing tab to open the Add a Tab dialog box.
4. Click the **SharePoint** icon to add SharePoint functionality.
5. Choose the **List Or Page** you wish to add and click **Save** button. The page or list you have just created in SharePoint will be added as a tab on the Teams channel for anyone in the Teams to view or access.

Adding a SharePoint page to a Team tab provides you a shortcut to view SharePoint content without leaving the comfort of your team application.

Note: you can add saved content on SharePoint and display the content in a tab such as Microsoft Word, PowerPoint, or Excel.

- **How to add, edit, and delete library and list columns**

To organize and display things that are most essential to you (such as specific columns), to add filtering or sorting, or to have a more engaging design, you may build custom views of libraries and lists. As long as you have the requisite privileges, you can build a private view (that only you can see) or a public view (that anybody using the list may see).

- **Make a new view based on the previous one**

Organize SharePoint lists by creating new views and hiding or showing columns. The default view is the first one. The View choices menu allows you to add other views. Creating a view may store various sort, filter, and grouping choices from the column headers or filter pane. In addition, the view will store the columns you've displayed or hidden and the column widths.

1. **Select View options from your list's command bar**

If the View options button isn't visible, check sure you're not changing the list or selecting one or more items. It's also possible that you don't have authorization. In such a situation, contact the Office 365 administrator, site proprietors, or list.

2. Select Save View As from the drop-down menu
3. Click **OK** after entering the new name.

How to use the OneDrive for Business library

If your company has used SharePoint 2010 or SharePoint 2013, the Library bar in OneDrive will seem quite similar. A variety of settings and features may enhance the OneDrive Business experience.

Using Custom Views in the OneDrive Library

"View Format" and **"Manage Views"** are on the left side of the OneDrive ribbon bar. Custom ... be built and applied to your OneDrive document collection or list from here. A custom view enables ... to organize your data to best fit your organization's and team's needs.

To make that custom view, click the **"Create View"** button in this area of the ribbon bar. The OneDrive for Business ribbon bar has to View Format and Manage Views tabs.

- **Standard View:** Created for personal or public usage, the standard view is a fantastic choice for document libraries or listings. Data columns may be rearranged and sorted alphabetically, by date, and in other ways. Even information that isn't required to be shown may be excluded from your custom display.

- **Calendar View:** This is great for changing the view of a team calendar, and it may also be personal or public. You may see information for specific periods, such as weekly, and arrange it chronologically or in any manner you choose.

- **Access View:** This view is only compatible with Microsoft Access and may build forms based on data from lists and tables in the database.

- **Datasheet View:** This view works well with Microsoft Excel data and is accessible both publicly and privately. Because this view allows for mass editing and fast modification, it enables you to modify and arrange spreadsheet column orders to meet your organizational requirements.

- **Grant View:** With public and private settings, this is a fantastic way to organize data linked to Microsoft Project. This view may visually represent a team's progress over time.

- **SharePoint Designer Custom View:** This is a fantastic choice for administrators who want to build a custom view. This would only be done if the out-of-the-box product failed to satisfy the user's requirements.

115 SECURING SHAREPOINT

Every Site Owner's concern is generally focused on security, which is understandable. As a Site or Content Owner, you want to ensure that your site is not only visually beautiful and contains the appropriate content but is also secure in terms of accidental deletions and data loss. This chapter offers a list of 15 settings/features that will enable you to safeguard your SharePoint site and get sufficient sleep.

In The Sharepoint Admin Center, Change External Sharing

Thee External Sharing is allowed by default on all Team Sites (sites linked to Microsoft 365 Groups). However, why not disable external sharing entirely on a specific site if your content is purely for internal usage? This will restrict users from sharing the site and its files and folders outside of the company, minimizing data loss by accident.

The following are ways to go about this:

1. **External Sharing Default Settings (Tenant-level)**

Once you've decided whether or not to enable external sharing, you can configure it in the SharePoint Admin Center for the entire tenant. This is how you do it:

- Go to Office 365 Admin Panel.

- Press SharePoint Admin Center

- Choose Sharing once you're in the SharePoint Admin Center.

- The external sharing options section is the first setup.

- It's essential to remember that the settings you make here are tenant-wide, which means they'll apply to all your environment's sites. You'll also be able to control sharing at the site level.

- Furthermore, you will see that OneDrive is not as limited as SharePoint. In other words, you won't be able to configure OneDrive to Anyone (anonymous) sharing if you make SharePoint accessible to new and existing guests. It must be accessible in the same way that SharePoint is flexible.

- It is suggested that SharePoint and OneDrive be configured for anyone. If you're worried about the safety of your SharePoint sites, you'll be able to change the settings at a site level.

2. Default File And Folder Sharing Links

The **file and folder links** settings area is the next important section to configure (or leave alone, which is also a good approach). The default sort of Link you get when you Share or Copy Link for a file or folder is basically what you manage here.

- Scroll to the bottom of the **File and folder links** area of the **SharePoint Admin Center's Sharing** page.

- What you may change in this section is the default link users will see when they copy or share a document or folder from SharePoint. Unfortunately, only persons in your organization are the default setting. Still, you can edit it for anyone with the Link (Anonymous) or Specific people (the Link will only work for the names/emails the user selects).

- Changing the default to anyone with the Link is not suggested; otherwise, you'll end up with many anonymous links and have no way of knowing who clicked on them. As a result, you can leave the settings in this area alone.

3. External Sharing Default Settings (Site-Level)

Recall how you earlier set up the external sharing settings at the tenant level. You can also define options at the site level! This way, you can declare that external sharing is enabled for the entire tenant but is disabled at the site level. At this time, the sites, of course, honor the default tenant configuration. They can't be any more liberal than the tenant-level options. This is how you do it.

- Select **Active Sites** from the **SharePoint Admin Center.**

- Then, in the upper-right-hand corner, click the small "I" in a circle beside the site. You'll see an area at the bottom right where you can change **this site's external sharing settings.**

- Beside the external sharing area, select **edit** in the bottom-right corner.

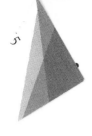

This site's external sharing options will now be displayed to you. Tenant-level settings are respected. They cannot, in other words, be more liberal than tenant-level settings. For example, you won't be able to select anyone (anonymous sharing) as an option at the site level if you deactivate it at the tenant level.

- To understand the options in the **Admin Center,** a prepared side-by-side picture below compares the site-level external sharing option in the Admin Center to the **end-user options for sharing files and folders from within SharePoint.**

Restrict Sharing By Domain

If external sharing is required, you can enable it for designated/trusted domains (for example, from your clients or vendors) while prohibiting it from others. You can, for example, block sharing to the gmail.com and yahoo.com domains for a specific site. A system like this could assist limit data sharing that isn't necessary. Likewise, you can block specific domains at the global (tenant) or site level.

1. Blocking Domain At Tenant Level

- Go to Office 365 Admin Center.
- Choose **SharePoint Admin Center** below **Admin Centers.**
- Below **Policies,** select **Sharing.**
- To open a drop-down menu, click **"More external sharing settings"** in the middle of the screen.
- **Limit external sharing by domain** is checked, click **Add domains,** select **Block specific domains** radio option on the pop-up screen on the right, **enter the domain you want to block,** and hit **Save.**
- To save your changes, go to the bottom of the screen and hit **Save.**

2. Blocking Domain At Site Level

You can also block external sharing by domain in SharePoint Online for a specific site rather than the entire tenant.

- Go to **Active Sites** in the **SharePoint Admin Center,** check the box beside a site, hit **Sharing,** then under **Advanced settings for External sharing,** select **Limit sharing by domain.**
- A similar pop-up will display at this stage, allowing you to specify domains to block.

Administration Settings Sharing Settings, And Link Permission By Default

You may also change the default sharing URLs from the SharePoint Admin Center. You can restrict this at the site level, just like external sharing. For example, if you alter the Link from "People in your organization" to **"People with existing access,"** you won't be able to generate links to files and folders that could grant access to people who don't currently have access to the site. Furthermore, you can set the created link **"view only"** by default, avoiding accidental modifications.

In The Admin Center, Specify The Network Location/Ip Address.

Another way of making your SharePoint site more secure is to identify allowed IP addresses from which the site can be viewed. Considering the prevailing work-from-home trend, this may no longer be feasible, but if you have specific locations/offices where the site should be available, it's worth exploring.

116   GENERAL SHORTCUTS

Shortcut Keys	Functions
Alt + N	Create a new document
Tab	Navigating through a document
Alt + S	Introducing the Search box
Alt + U	Upload your Document
Shift + F10	Open the context menu for the selected item
Alt + Y	Syncing the Library
Ctrl + X	Cut the text
Ctrl + C	Copy the text
Ctrl + V	Paste the text
Shift + Enter	Expand the site menus and list or ribbon
Esc	Contrast/close the ribbon
Alt + B	Publish the opened page
Alt + S	Share the selected Document or folder
Alt + U	Upload a document inside Add a document dialog box
Shift + F10	Open the context menu for the selected item

Shortcut Keys	Functions
I	Open/close the information/Details pane
Alt + Y	Sync the library to your PC
Alt + M	Open the More menu for the selected item.
Ctrl + E	Center align the paragraph
Ctrl + L	Left align the paragraph
Ctrl + R	Right align the paragraph
Ctrl + Spacebar	Clear the formatting
Ctrl + B	Apply/remove bold formatting
Ctrl + U	Apply/remove Underline formatting
Ctrl + I	Apply/remove Italic formatting
Ctrl + M	Indent the paragraph
Ctrl + K	Insert a hyperlink
Ctrl + Shift + M	Move the paragraph to the left/remove the paragraph indent

117   CONCLUSION

Microsoft SharePoint is an invaluable platform for businesses and organizations of any size. Its enhanced security, improved collaboration, and flexible access make it an ideal solution for businesses looking to improve their productivity and efficiency. With its secure environment, team collaboration tools, and cloud-based platform, SharePoint enables businesses to be more efficient and cost-effective.

Manufactured by Amazon.ca
Bolton, ON